History of Early Human Migrations

Compiled by

Silvia Herbert

Scribbles

Year of Publication 2018

ISBN : 9789352979288

Book Published by

Scribbles

(An Imprint of Alpha Editions)

email - alphaedis@gmail.com

Produced by: PediaPress GmbH
Limburg an der Lahn
Germany
http://pediapress.com/

Contents

Articles   **1**

Early humans   **1**

  Early expansions of hominins out of Africa   1

  Homo erectus 12

  Clactonian 30

  Micoquien 35

Dispersal throughout Africa   **39**

  Sub-Saharan Africa 39

Early northern Africa dispersal   **101**

  Recent African origin of modern humans 101

Coastal migration   **117**

  Southern Dispersal 117

Dispersal throughout Eurasia   **119**

  Upper Paleolithic 119

  Mammoth steppe 133

  Interbreeding between archaic and modern humans 143

  Mousterian 157

Europe   **163**

  European early modern humans 163

  Art of the Upper Paleolithic 175

  Hominid dispersals in Europe 182

Last Glacial Maximum   **187**

  Solutrean 187

  Magdalenian 193

  Settlement of the Americas 199

  Genetic history of indigenous peoples of the Americas 218

  Pre-modern human migration 233

  Neolithic Revolution 244

  Indo-European migrations 260

  Proto-Uralic homeland hypotheses 334

  Nilo-Saharan languages 337

  Niger–Congo languages 350

  Circumpolar peoples 368

Appendix   **371**

  References 371

  Article Sources and Contributors 401

  Image Sources, Licenses and Contributors 404

Article Licenses   **411**

Index   **413**

Early humans

Early expansions of hominins out of Africa

Hominin timeline

Axis scale: million years

🖑

Also see: *Life timeline* and *Nature timeline*

Several **early expansions of hominins out of Africa** and into Eurasia took place between 2.12 and 0.20 million years ago (mya). Known in the literature as **Out of Africa I**, these early hominin expansions contrast the later expansions of anatomically modern humans into Eurasia (*Out of Africa II*)[1] that may have started about 0.194 million years ago.

The earliest claimed evidence for hominins out of Africa, as of July 2018, are stone tools from Shangchen, central China (2.12 mya). It is not known which species of hominin produced them, but the date, if it is correct, is roughly contemporary with the earliest known *Homo habilis* in Africa, and therefore the very earliest uncontroversial representative of the *Homo* genus. The earliest hominin skeletons in Eurasia are from the site of Dmanisi in Georgia, all representatives of *Homo erectus*. Before the discovery of the Shangcheng tools, these skeletons were also the earliest evidence for hominins out of Africa. After these initial waves out of Africa, additional waves seem to have taken place around 1.4 mya (early Acheulean industries) and 0.8 mya (cleaver-producing Acheulean groups).

Until the early 1980s, early humans were thought to have been restricted to the African continent in the Early Pleistocene, or until about 0.8 mya; Hominin migrations outside East Africa were apparently rare in the Early Pleistocene, leaving a record of events broken in space and time.

Evolution in Africa

Australopithecina emerge about 5.6 million years ago, in East Africa (Afar Depression). Gracile australopithecines (*Australopithecus afarensis*) emerge in the same region, around 4 million years ago. The earliest known retouched tools were found in Lomekwi, Kenya, and date back to 3.3 Ma, in the late Pliocene. They might be the product of *Australopithecus garhi* or *Paranthropus aethiopicus*, the two known hominins contemporary with the tools.

Homo is assumed to have emerged by around 2 million years ago, *Homo habilis* being found at about 2.1 million years ago at Lake Turkana, Kenya.

The delineation of the "human" genus, *Homo*, from Australopithecus is somewhat contentious, for which reason the superordinate term "hominin" is often used to include both. "Hominin" technically includes pre-human species as old as 10 million years ago (the separation of Homininae into Hominini and

Gorillini). Possibly pre-human hominin expansion out of Africa has been associated with *Graecopithecus* and *Ouranopithecus*, found in Greece and Anatolia and dated to c. 8 million years ago, but these are probably Homininae but not Hominini. Possibly related are the Trachilos footprints found in Crete, dated to close to 6 million years ago.

Homo erectus

"Early hominin expansion out of Africa" is closely related to the emergence of *Homo erectus* just after 2 million years ago. The two species would have lived face to face in East Africa for nearly half a million years.

The oldest *Homo erectus* fossils appear almost contemporaneously, at around 1.9 to 1.8 million years ago, both in Africa and in the Caucasus. The ancestors of Indonesian *Homo floresiensis* may have left Africa even earlier.[2]

The earliest well-dated Eurasian *H. erectus* site is Dmanisi in Georgia, securely dated to 1.8 Ma.[3] A skull found at Dmanisi is evidence for caring for the old. The skull shows that this *Homo erectus* was advanced in age and had lost all but one tooth years before death, and it is perhaps unlikely that this hominid would have survived alone. It is not certain, however, that this is sufficient proof for caring – a partially paralysed chimpanzee at the Gombe reserve survived for years without help.

The earliest known evidence for African *H. erectus*, dubbed *Homo ergaster*, is a single occipital bone (KNM-ER 2598), described as "H. erectus-like", and dated to about 1.9 Mya (contemporary with *Homo rudolfensis*). This is followed by a fossil gap, the next available fossil being KNM-ER 3733, a skull dated to 1.6 Mya.[4] Early Pleistocene sites in North Africa, the geographical intermediate of East Africa and Georgia, are in poor stratigraphic context. The earliest of the dated is Ain Hanech in northern Algeria (c. 1.8 – 1.2 Ma), an Oldowan grade layer. These sites attest that early *Homo erectus* have crossed the North African tracts, which are usually hot and dry.:[2]

There is little time between *Homo erectus*' apparent arrival in South Caucasus around 1.8 Ma, and its probable arrival in East and Southeast Asia. There is evidence of *H. erectus* in Yuanmou, China, dating to 1.7 Ma and in Sangiran, on Java, Indonesia, from 1.66 Ma.

It appears *H. erectus* took longer to move into Europe, the earliest site being Barranco León in southeastern Spain dated to 1.4 Ma and a controversial Pirro Nord in Southern Italy, allegedly from 1.7 – 1.3 Ma.

In any case, by 1 Ma, *Homo erectus* had settled in most of the Old World. It is hard to say, however, whether settlement was continuous in Western Europe, or if successive waves repopulated the territory in glacial interludes. Early

Acheulean tools at Ubeidiya from 1.4 Ma is some evidence for a continuous settlement in the West, as successive waves out of Africa after then would likely have brought Acheulean technology to Western Europe.Wikipedia:Citation needed

Routes out of Africa

Sinai Peninsula

The Sinai Peninsula is the simplest African exit route, being since the Pliocene the only land bridge between the two continents of the Old World. Unless one arguesWikipedia:Citation needed for boats on behalf of *Homo erectus*, it is surely the only way out. However, it was hard to access until the Middle Pleistocene. The Nile was a much smaller river and followed a different course.

There are two Eurasian entryways that take advantage of the Sinai. First, the Levantine corridor, which moves north along the Eastern Mediterranean. Second, down the eastern bank of the Red Sea. Archaeological efforts in Arabia are limited, and attention is usually given to the Levantine corridor.

Bab-el-Mandeb

The Bab-el-Mandeb is a 30 km strait between East Africa and the Arabian Peninsula, with a small island, Perim, 3 km off the Arabian bank. The strait has a major appeal in the study of Eurasian expansion in that it brings East Africa in direct proximity with Eurasia. It does not require hopping from one water body to the next across the North African desert.Wikipedia:Citation needed

The land connection with Arabia disappeared in the Pliocene, and though it may have briefly reformed, the evaporation of the Red Sea and associated increase in salinity would have left traces in the fossil record after just 200 years and evaporite deposits after 600 years. Neither have been detected. A strong current flows from the Red Sea into the Indian Ocean and crossing would have been difficult without a land connection.

Oldowan grade tools are reported from Perim Island,[5] implying that the strait could have been crossed in the Early Pleistocene, but these finds have yet to be confirmed.

Strait of Gibraltar

The Strait of Gibraltar is the Atlantic entryway to the Mediterranean, where Spanish and Moroccan banks are only 14 km apart. A decrease in sea levels in the Pleistocene due to glaciation would not have brought this down to less than 10 km. Deep currents push westwards, and surface water flows strongly back into the Mediterranean.

Entrance into Eurasia across the strait of Gibraltar could explain the hominin remains at Barranco León in southeastern Spain (1.4 Ma) and Sima del Elefante in northern Spain (1.2 Ma). But the site of Pirro Nord in southern Italy,

allegedly from 1.3 – 1.7 Ma, suggests a possible arrival from the East. Resolution is insufficient to settle the matter.

Strait of Sicily

The modern Strait of Sicily separates Tunisia and Sicily by 145 km, but is
shallow and would have been much narrower in glacial maxima. We have a
poor understanding of plate tectonics of this area for the greater part of the
Pleistocene. But while plate tectonics could have made the strait narrower
than predicted by the lowering of sea levels alone, contrast of Pleistocene fauna
strongly argues against an actual land bridge.[3] Since the strait is only 400 km
away from the North African hominin site of Ain Hanech in Algeria (1.8 Ma
or 1.2 Ma) it remains a plausible route for Early Pleistocene expansion into
Eurasia. But there is close to no evidence for a hominin passage. Alimen based
most of her argument[6] in favour of such a migration on Bianchini's discovery[7]
of Sicilian Oldowan grade tools. Radiometric dates, however, have not been
produced, and the artefacts might as well be from the Middle Pleistocene.

Crossing straits

Presence of hominin remains in Indonesian islands is good evidence for seafaring by *Homo erectus* late in the Early Pleistocene. Bednarik suggests that
navigation had appeared by 1 Ma, possibly to exploit offshore fishing grounds.

He has reproduced a primitive dirigible raft to demonstrate the feasibility of faring across the Lombok Strait on such a device, which he believes to have been done before 850 ka. The strait has maintained a width of at least 20 km for the whole of the Pleistocene. Such an achievement by *Homo erectus* in the Early Pleistocene offers some strength to the suggested water routes out of Africa, as the Gibraltar, Sicilian, and Bab-el-Mandeb exit routes are harder to consider if boats are deemed beyond the capacities of *Homo erectus*.

It is unlikely that hominins populated Eurasia after a one-off event getting a few hominins across a strait (such as a *Homo erectus* family drifting on flood debris and landing on a Eurasian bank). There are biological constraints to the minimum size a population must maintain to avoid extinction. That is to say, if less than 50 hominins at once made it into Eurasia and lost contact with African hominins, the population would likely undergo an extinction vortex, in part due to inbreeding.[8]

Causes for hominin dispersals

Climate change and hominin flexibility

For a given species in a given environment, available resources will limit the number of individuals that can survive indefinitely. This is the carrying capacity. Upon reaching this threshold, individuals may find it easier to gather resources in the poorer yet less exploited peripheral environment than in the preferred habitat. *Homo habilis* could have developed some baseline behavioural flexibility prior to its expansion into the peripheries (such as encroaching into the predatory guild[9]). This flexibility could then have been positively selected and amplified, leading to *Homo erectus'* adaptation to the peripheral open habitats. A new and environmentally flexible hominin population could have come back to the old niche and replace the ancestral population. Moreover, some step-wise shrinking of the woodland and the associated reduction of hominin carrying capacity in the woods around 1.8 Ma, 1.2 Ma, and 0.6 Ma would have stressed the carrying capacity's pressure for adapting to the open grounds.

With *Homo erectus'* new environmental flexibility, favourable climate fluxes likely opened it the way to the Levantine corridor, perhaps sporadically, in the Early Pleistocene.

Chasing fauna

Lithic analysis implies that Oldowan hominins were not predators.[10] However, *Homo erectus* appears to have followed animal migrations to the north during wetter periods, likely as a source of scavenged food. The sabre-tooth cat

Megantereon was an apex predator of the Early and Middle Pleistocene (before MIS 12). It became extinct in Africa c. 1.5 Ma, but had already moved out through the Sinai, and is among the faunal remains of the Levantine hominin site of Ubeidiya, c. 1.4 Ma. It could not break bone marrow and its kills were likely an important food source for hominins,[11] especially in glacial periods.

In colder Eurasian times, the hominin diet would have to be principally meat-based and Acheulean hunters must have competed with cats.Wikipedia:Citation needed

Coevolved zoonotic diseases

Bar-Yosef and Belfer-Cohen suggest that the success of hominins within Eurasia once out of Africa is in part due to the absence of zoonotic diseases outside their original habitat. Zoonotic diseases are those that are transmitted from animals to humans. While a disease specific to hominins must keep its human host alive long enough to transmit itself, zoonotic diseases will not necessarily do so as they can complete their life cycle without humans. Still, these infections are well accustomed to human presence, having evolved alongside them. The higher an African ape's population density, the better a disease fares. 55% of chimps at the Gombe reserve die of disease, most of them zoonotic.[12] The majority of these diseases are still restricted to hot and damp African environments. Once hominins had moved out into drier and colder habitats of higher latitudes, one major limiting factor in population growth was out of the equation.

Physiological traits

While *Homo habilis* was certainly bipedal, its long arms are indicative of an arboreal adaptation. *Homo erectus* had longer legs and shorter arms, revealing a transition to obligate terrestriality, though it remains unclear how this change in relative leg length might have been an advantage. Sheer body size, on the other hand, seems to have allowed for better walking energy efficiency and endurance. A larger *Homo erectus* would also dehydrate more slowly and could thus cover greater distances before facing thermoregulatory limitations. The ability for prolonged walking at a normal pace would have been a decisive factor for effective colonisation of Eurasia.[14]

Figure 1: *Forensic interpretation of Homo habilis*[13]

Brain thermoregulation

Thermoregulation and dehydration are major problems that need to be dealt with to move into the open grasslands. In particular, vascularisation of the brain is crucial in maintaining it in the narrow frame of tolerable temperatures.

Bones of the higher cranium grow in response to expansion of cerebral mass, in such a way that brain tissue and blood vessels mold the inner brain case. Endocranial casts of fossil skulls allow approximating brain vascularisation.[16] Dean Falk noticed that a single large vessel, the occipital marginal sinus, was responsible for irrigating most of the brain in early australopiths (*Australopithecus afarensis*, *Paranthropus robustus* and *boisei*). The vessel grew smaller with time to be progressively replaced by a network of small veins in later hominins, starting with *Homo habilis* and continuing well into Eurasia. She interprets the change as an adaptation to cool the brain,[17] which she uses to advance her "radiator theory" for accelerated encephalisation from *Homo habilis* onwards. To Falk, bipedalism, which predates large brains, favoured a rewiring of cerebral blood vessels into a gravity-assisted irrigation network, itself allowing the cool down needed for encephalisation.

Endocranial casts of *Homo habilis* and *Homo erectus* differ in the organisation of the frontal lobe, in particular in the prefrontal cortex where higher mental

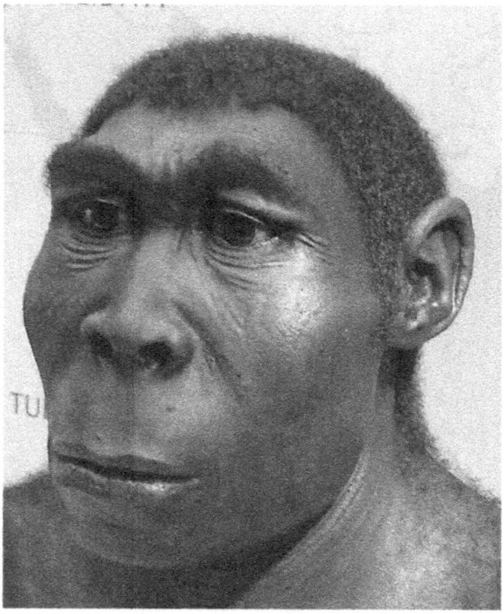

Figure 2: *Forensic interpretation of an adult male Homo erectus.*[15]

functions of consciousness and abstraction occur.[18] By themselves, mental capacities have likely played a role in the success of Eurasian colonisation. They
would have allowed for greater social complexity, predation and sharing prey,
and an overall higher quality diet.[19] If we are to believe Bednarik and his
seafaring Indonesian *Homo erectus*, then the brain must have played a role in
crossing channels.

According to Wheeler, loss of functional body hair would have helped prevent
hyperthermia, since hair will obstruct air flow over the skin and restrict cooling by evaporation. He further suggests that body cooling due to hair loss has
relieved a thermal constraint on brain size (but in a response to Falk's radiator
hypothesis, Ralph Holloway maintains that there is no evidence for a temperature constraint on brain size). However, differences in body hair between
Homo habilis and *Homo erectus* are impossible to test, and it will remain unclear whether hair loss was part of the hominin adaptation or preadaptation to
Eurasia.

Further reading

- Antón, Susan C.; Swisher, Carl C., III (2004), "Early Dispersals of *Homo* from Africa", *Annual Review of Anthropology*, **33**: 271–96, doi: 10.1146/annurev.anthro.33.070203.144024[20].

- Eudald Carbonell; Marina Mosquera; Xosé Pedro Rodríguez; José María Bermúdez de Castro; Francesc Burjachs; Jordi Rosell; Robert Sala; Josep Vallverdú (2008), (subscription required), "Eurasian Gates: The Earliest Human Dispersals", *Journal of Anthropological Research*, **64** (2): 195–228, doi: 10.3998/jar.0521004.0064.202[21], JSTOR 20371223[22].

- Ciochon, Russell L. (2010), "Divorcing Hominins from the *Stegodon–Ailuropoda* Fauna: New Views on the Antiquity of Hominins in Asia", in John G. Fleagle et al. (eds), *Out of Africa I: The First Hominin Colonization of Eurasia*, Vertebrate Paleobiology and Paleoanthropology Series, Dordrecht: Springer, pp. 111–26, doi: 10.1007/978-90-481-9036-2_8[23], ISBN 978-90-481-9035-5. ISBN 978-90-481-9036-2 (online).

- Dennell, Robin (2009), *The Palaeolithic Settlement of Asia*, Cambridge World Archaeology, Cambridge: Cambridge University Press, ISBN 978-0-521-84866-4. ISBN 978-0-521-61310-1 (paperback).

- Dennell, Robin (2010), "'Out of Africa I': Current Problems and Future Prospects", in John G. Fleagle et al. (eds), *Out of Africa I: The First Hominin Colonization of Eurasia*, Vertebrate Paleobiology and Paleoanthropology Series, Dordrecht: Springer, pp. 247–74, doi: 10.1007/978-90-481-9036-2_15[24], ISBN 978-90-481-9035-5. ISBN 978-90-481-9036-2 (online).

- Rabett, Ryan J. (2012), *Human Adaptation in the Asian Palaeolithic: Hominin Dispersal and Behaviour during the Late Quaternary*[25], Cambridge: Cambridge University Press, ISBN 978-1-107-01829-7.

- Zaim, Yahdi (2010), "Geological Evidence for the Earliest Appearance of Hominins in Indonesia", in John G. Fleagle et al. (eds), *Out of Africa I: The First Hominin Colonization of Eurasia*, Vertebrate Paleobiology and Paleoanthropology Series, Dordrecht: Springer, pp. 97–110, doi: 10.1007/978-90-481-9036-2_7[26], ISBN 978-90-481-9035-5. ISBN 978-90-481-9036-2 (online).

Homo erectus

Homo erectus	
Temporal range: 1.9–0.5 Ma	
Pre꞉Є OSD C P T J K PgN	
Early Pleistocene – Late Pleistocene	

Reconstructed skeleton of
Tautavel Man[27]

Scientific classification 🖉	
Kingdom:	Animalia
Phylum:	Chordata
Class:	Mammalia
Order:	Primates
Suborder:	Haplorhini
Infraorder:	Simiiformes
Family:	Hominidae
Subfamily:	Homininae
Tribe:	Hominini
Genus:	_Homo_
Species:	†_H. erectus_

Binomial name
Homo erectus
(Mayr 1950)

Synonyms

- † _Anthropopithecus erectus_ (Dubois 1892)
- † _Pithecanthropus erectus_ (Dubois 1894)
- † _Sinanthropus pekinensis_
- † _Javanthropus soloensis_
- † _Meganthropus paleojavanicus_

- † *Telanthropus capensis*
- † *Homo georgicus*
- † *Homo ergaster*?

Homo erectus (meaning "upright human") is an extinct species of archaic humans that lived throughout most of the Pleistocene geological epoch. Its earliest fossil evidence dates to 1.8 million years ago (discovered 1991 in Dmanisi, Georgia).[30]

A debate regarding the classification, ancestry, and progeny of *H. erectus*, especially in relation to *Homo ergaster*, is ongoing, with two major positions:

1) *H. erectus* is the same species as *H. ergaster*, and thereby *H. erectus* is a direct ancestor of the later hominins including *Homo heidelbergensis*, *Homo antecessor*, *Homo neanderthalensis*, *Homo Denisova*, and *Homo sapiens*; or,

2) it is in fact an Asian species or subspecies distinct from African *H. ergaster*.[31]

Some paleoanthropologists consider *H. ergaster* to be a variety, that is, the "African" variety, of *H. erectus*; the labels "*Homo erectus sensu stricto*" (strict sense) for the Asian species and "*Homo erectus sensu lato*" (broad sense) have been offered for the greater species comprising both Asian and African populations.

Known varieties of *H. erectus* in the narrow sense (the Asian species) were likely extinct by 500,000 years ago (certainly by 140,000 years ago).[32]

The discovery of Dmanisi skull 5 in 2013 re-opened the taxonomical debate.[33] Considering the large morphological variation among all Dmanisi skulls, researchers now suggest that several early human ancestors variously classified, for example, as *Homo ergaster*, or *Homo rudolfensis*, and perhaps even *Homo habilis*, should instead be designated as subspecies of *Homo erectus*.

Discovery and type specimen

The Dutch anatomist Eugène Dubois, inspired by Darwin's theory of evolution as it applied to humanity, set out in 1886 for Asia (despite Darwin's theory of African origin) to find a human ancestor. In 1891, his team discovered a human fossil on the island of Java, Dutch East Indies (now Indonesia). Excavated from the bank of the Solo River at Trinil, in East Java, he named the species *Pithecanthropus erectus*—from the Greek πίθηκος, *píthēkos* "ape", and ἄνθρωπος *ánthrōpos* "human"—based on a skullcap (calotte) and a femur like that of *Homo sapiens*.

Figure 3: *Forensic reconstruction of an adult female Homo erectus.*[28]

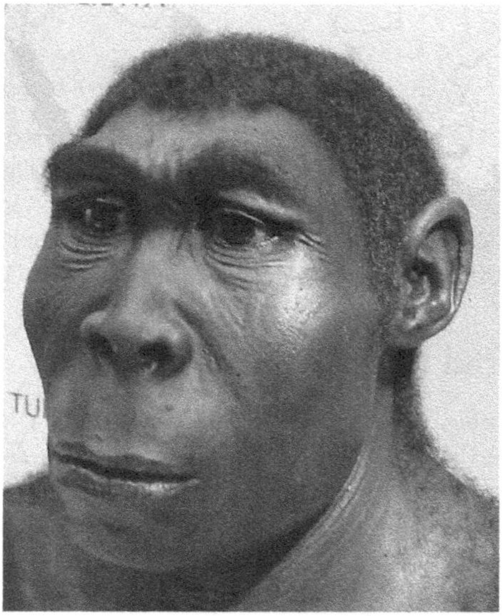

Figure 4: *Forensic reconstruction of an adult male Homo erectus.*[29]

Dubois' 1891 find was the first fossil of a *Homo*-species (or any hominin species) found as result of a directed expedition and search (the first recognized human fossil had been the circumstantial discovery of *Homo neanderthalensis* in 1856; see List of human evolution fossils). The Java fossil from Indonesia aroused much public interest. It was dubbed by the popular press as *Java Man*; but few scientists accepted Dubois' argument that his fossil was the transitional form—the so-called "missing link"—between humans and nonhuman apes.[34]

Most of the spectacular discoveries of *H. erectus* next took place at the Zhoukoudian Project, now known as the *Peking Man* site, in Zhoukoudian, China. This site was first discovered by Johan Gunnar Andersson in 1921 and was first excavated in 1921, and produced two human teeth. Davidson Black's initial description (1921) of a lower molar as belonging to a previously unknown species (which he named *Sinanthropus pekinensis*)[35] prompted widely publicized interest. Extensive excavations followed, which altogether uncovered 200 human fossils from more than 40 individuals including five nearly complete skullcaps. Franz Weidenreich provided much of the detailed description of this material in several monographs published in the journal *Palaeontologica Sinica* (Series D).

Nearly all of the original specimens were lost during World War II; however, authentic casts were made by Weidenreich, which exist at the American Museum of Natural History in New York City and at the Institute of Vertebrate Paleontology and Paleoanthropology in Beijing, and are considered to be reliable evidence.

Similarities between *Java Man* and *Peking Man* led Ernst Mayr to rename both *Homo erectus* in 1950.

Throughout much of the 20th century, anthropologists debated the role of *H. erectus* in human evolution. Early in the century, due in part to the discoveries at Java and Zhoukoudian, that modern humans first evolved in Asia was widely accepted. A few naturalists—Charles Darwin most prominent among them—theorized that humans' earliest ancestors were African: Darwin pointed out that chimpanzees and gorillas, humans' closest relatives, evolved and exist only in Africa.

Origin and dispersal

The derivation of the genus *Homo* from *Australopithecina* took place in East Africa after 3 million years ago. The inclusion of species dated to just before 2 million years ago, *Homo habilis* and *Homo rudolfensis*, into *Homo* is somewhat contentious. Especially as *H. habilis* appears to have coexisted with *H. ergaster/erectus* for a substantial period after 2 Mya, it has been proposed that *ergaster* may not be directly derived from *habilis*.[36]

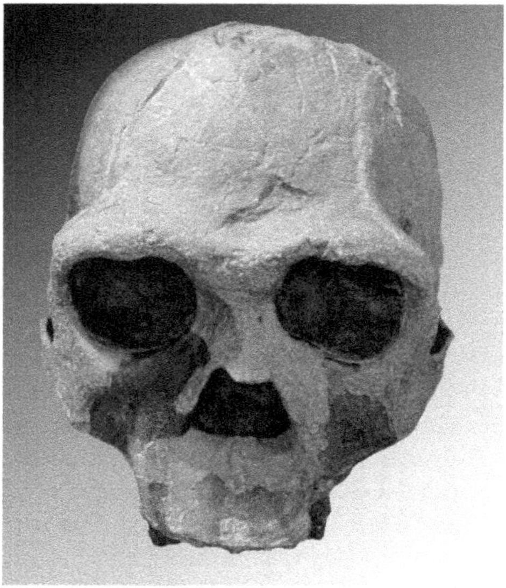

Figure 5: *KNM-ER 3733 (1.6 Mya, discovered 1975 at Koobi Fora, Kenya)*

In any case, *H. ergaster/erectus* was present in Africa and Western Asia by 1.8 Mya, and widely dispersed throughout Eurasia (including Europe, Indonesia, China) by 0.5 Mya.

Africa

In the 1950s, archaeologists John T. Robinson and Robert Broom named *Telanthropus capensis*; Robinson had discovered a jaw fragment in 1949 in Swartkrans, South Africa. Later,Wikipedia:Manual of Style/Dates and numbers#Chronological items SimonettaWikipedia:Manual of Style/Words to watch#Unsupported attributions proposed to re-designate it to *Homo erectus*, and Robinson agreed.

From the 1950s forward, numerous finds in East Africa suggested sympatric coexistence for *H. ergaster* and *H. habilis* for several hundred millenia, which tends to confirm the hypothesis that they represent separate lineages from a common ancestor; that is, the ancestral relationship between them was not anagenetic, but was cladogenetic, which here suggests that a subgroup population of *H. habilis*—or of a common ancestor of *H. habilis* and *H. ergaster/erectus*—became reproductively isolated from the main-group population, eventually evolving into the new species *Homo ergaster* (*Homo erectus sensu lato*).[37]

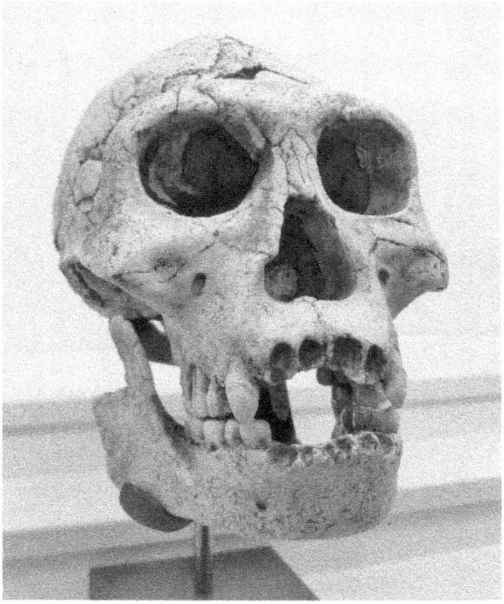

Figure 6: *Dmanisi skull 3 (fossils skull D2700 and jaw D2735,*
two of several found in Dmanisi in the Georgian Transcaucasus)

In 1961, Yves Coppens discovered a skull in northern Chad. He coined the name *Tchadanthropus uxoris* for what he considered the earliest fossil human discovered in north Africa. Although once considered to be a specimen of *H. habilis*, *T. uxoris* has been subsumed into *H. erectus* but it is no longer considered a valid taxon. It was reported that the fossil "had been so eroded by wind-blown sand that it mimicked the appearance of an australopith, a primitive type of *hominid*". It is probably only 10,000 years old according to stratigraphy, paleontology and C14 dating presented in Michel Servant's PhD as early as 1973[38].

Asia

Homo erectus georgicus is the subspecies name assigned to fossil skulls and jaws found in Dmanisi, Georgia. First proposed as a separate species, it is now classified within *H. erectus*. The site was discovered in 1991 by Georgian scientist David Lordkipanidze. Five skulls were excavated from 1991 forward, including a "very complete" skull in 2005. Excavations at Dmanisi have yielded 73 stone tools for cutting and chopping and 34 bone fragments from unidentified fauna.

Figure 7: *Location of Dmanisi discovery, Georgia*

After their initial assessment, some scientists were persuaded to name the
Dmanisi find as a new species, *Homo georgicus*, which they posited as a descendant of African *Homo habilis* and an ancestor to Asian *Homo erectus*.
This classification, however, was not supported, and the fossil was instead
designated a divergent subgroup of *Homo erectus*.

The fossil skeletons present a species primitive in its skull and upper body but
with relatively advanced spine and lower limbs, implying greater mobility than
the previous morphology. It is now thought *not* to be a separate species, but
to represent a stage soon after the transition between *H. habilis* to *H. erectus*; it has been dated at 1.8 Mya. The assemblage includes one of the largest
Pleistocene *Homo* mandibles (D2600), one of the smallest Lower Pleistocene
mandibles (D211), a nearly complete sub-adult (D2735), and a toothless specimen D3444/D3900.

Two of the skulls—D2700, with a brain volume of 600 cubic centimetres
(37 cu in), and D4500 or Dmanisi Skull 5, with a brain volume of about 546
centimetres—present the two smallest and most primitive Hominina skulls
from the Pleistocene period. The variation in these skulls were compared
to variations in modern humans and within a sample group of chimpanzees.
The researchers found that, despite appearances, the variations in the Dmanisi
skulls were no greater than those seen among modern people and among chimpanzees. These findings suggest that previous fossil finds that were classified
as different species on the basis of the large morphological variation among

them—including *Homo rudolfensis*, *Homo gautengensis*, *H. ergaster*, and potentially even *H. habilis*—should perhaps be re-classified to the same lineage as *Homo erectus*.

Taxonomy

Paleoanthropologists continue to debate the classification of *Homo erectus* and *Homo ergaster* as separate species. One school of thought suggests dropping the taxon *Homo erectus* and equating *H. erectus* with the archaic *H. sapiens*. Another calls *H. ergaster* the direct African ancestor of *H. erectus*, proposing that *erectus* emigrated out of Africa to Asia while branching into a distinct species. Some scholars dispense with the species name *ergaster*, making no distinction between such fossils as the Turkana Boy and Peking Man.Wikipedia:Citation needed Still, *"Homo ergaster"* has gained some acceptance as a valid taxon, and the two species are still usually defined as distinct African and Asian populations of the greater species *H. erectus*, that is, *"Homo erectus sensu lato"*.

Some have insisted that Ernst Mayr's biological species definition cannot be used to test the above hypotheses—that is, that the two species might be considered the same. Alternatively, the amount of variation of cranial morphology between known specimens of *H. erectus* and *H. ergaster* can be compared to the same variation within an appropriate population of living primates (that is, one of similar geographical distribution or close evolutionary relationship), such that: if the amount of variation between *H. erectus* and *H. ergaster* is greater than that within an appropriately selected population, for example, say, macaques, then *H. erectus* and *H. ergaster* may be considered as two different species.

Finding an extant (i.e., living) model suitable for field study, analysis, and comparison is very important; and selecting a living sample population of an appropriate species can be difficult. (For example, the morphological variation among the global population of *H. sapiens* is small, so our own species diversity may not be a trustworthy comparison. Fossils found in Dmanisi, Georgia were originally designated as a separate (but closely related) species; but subsequent specimens showed their variation to be within the range of *Homo erectus*. and they are now classified as *Homo erectus georgicus*.) New foot tracks found in 2009 in Kenya and reported in Science by Matthew Bennett of Bournemouth University in Britain and his colleagues, confirmed that the gait of Homo erectus was heel-to-toe, walking as a modern human does, rather than with the australopithecine-like method of its own ancestors.

H. erectus fossils show a cranial capacity greater than that of *Homo habilis* (although the Dmanisi specimens have distinctively small crania): the earliest

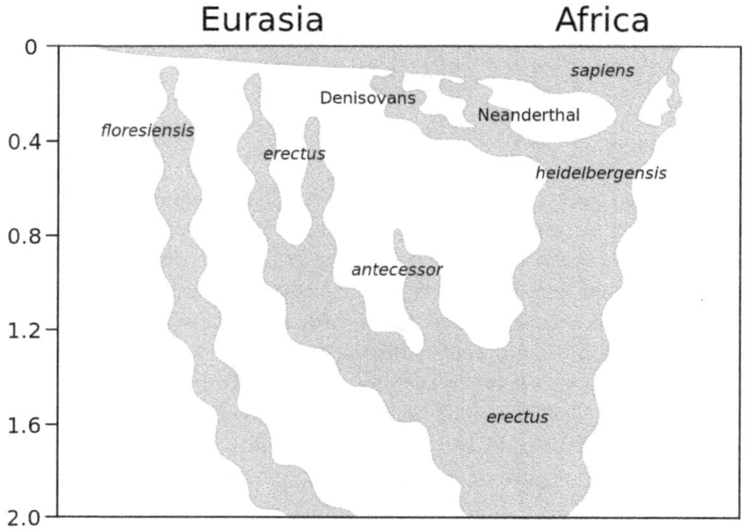

Figure 8: *One proposed model of the evolution of several species of genus Homo over the last 2 million years (vertical axis) based on Stringer (2012).*

fossils show a cranial capacity of 850 cm³, while later Javan specimens measure up to 1100 cm³,[39] overlapping that of *H. sapiens.*; the frontal bone is less sloped and the dental arcade smaller than that of the australopithecines; the face is more orthognatic (less protrusive) than either the australopithecines or *H. habilis*, with large brow-ridges and less prominent zygomata (cheekbones). The early hominins stood about 1.79 m (5 ft 10 in)—only 17 percent of modern male humans are taller—and were extraordinarily slender, with long arms and legs.

Sexual dimorphism in *H. erectus*—males are about 25% larger than females—is slightly greater than seen in the later *H. sapiens*, but less than that of the earlier genus *Australopithecus*. Regarding evolution of human physiology, the discovery of the skeleton of "Turkana boy" (*Homo ergaster*) near Lake Turkana, Kenya, by Richard Leakey and Kamoya Kimeu in 1984—one of the most complete hominin skeletons ever discovered—has contributed greatly to the interpretation.

Stringer (2003, 2012) and Reed, et al. (2004) and others have produced schematic graph-models for interpreting the evolution of *Homo sapiens* from earlier species of *Homo*, including *Homo erectus* and/or *Homo ergaster, see* graphs at right. Blue areas denote the existence of one or more hominin species at a given time and place (that is, region). These and other interpretations differ mainly in the taxonomy and geographical distribution of species.

Stringer (*see* upper graph-model) depicts the presence of *H. erectus* as dominating the temporal and geographic development of human evolution; and as persisting broadly throughout Africa and Eurasia for nearly 2 million years, eventually evolving into *H. heidelbergensis / H. rhodesiensis*, which in turn evolved into *H. sapiens*. Reed, et al. shows *Homo ergaster* as the ancestor of *Homo erectus*; then it is *ergaster*, or a variety of *ergaster*, or perhaps a hybrid of *ergaster* and *erectus*, which develops into species that evolve into archaic and then modern humans and then out of Africa.

Both models show the Asian variety of *Homo erectus* going extinct recently. And both models indicate species admixture: early modern humans spread from Africa across different regions of the globe and interbred with earlier descendants of *H. heidelbergensis / H. rhodesiensis*, namely the Neanderthals, Denisovans, as well as unknown archaic African hominins. *See* admixture; and *see* Neanderthal admixture theory.

Behaviour

Tool use

The Paleolithic Age (Old Stone Age) of prehistoric human history and industry is dated from 2.6 million years ago to about 10,000 years ago;[41] thus it closely coincides with the Pleistocene epoch of geologic time, which is 2.58 million to 11,700 years ago. The beginning of early human evolution reaches back to the earliest innovations of primitive technology and tool culture. H. erectus were the first to use fire to cook and to make hand axes out of stone.Wikipedia:Citation needed

Homo ergaster used more diverse and sophisticated stone tools than its predecessors, where early *Homo erectus* used comparatively primitive tools. This is probably because *H. ergaster* inherited, used, and created tools first of Oldowan technology and later advanced the technology to the Acheulean. Because the use of Acheulean tools began ca. 1.8 million years ago,[42] and the line of *H. erectus* diverged some 200,000 years before the general innovation of Acheulean industry in Africa, then it is plausible that the Asian migratory descendants of *H. erectus* made no use of Acheulean technology. It has been suggested that the Asian *H. erectus* may have been the first humans to use rafts to travel over bodies of water, including oceans. And the oldest stone tool found in Turkey reveals that hominins passed through the Anatolian gateway from western Asia to Europe approximately 1.2 million years ago—much earlier than previously thought.[43]

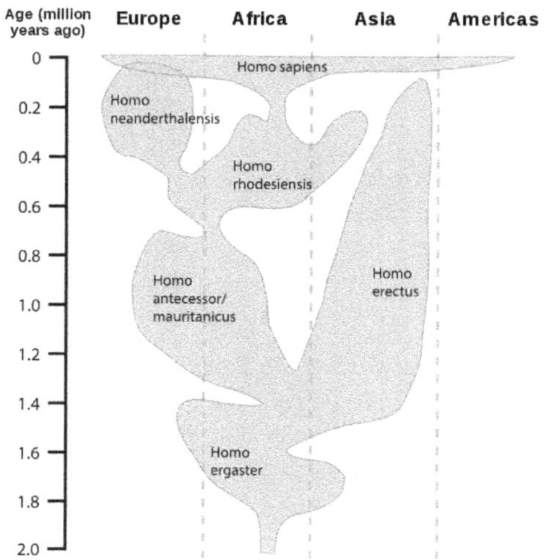

Figure 9: *An alternate graph-model of the temporal and geographical distribution of several Homo species, evolving over the last two million years ; proposed by Reed, et al., redrawn from Stringer.*[40] *Note the depiction of Homo ergaster as an ancestor of Homo erectus.*

Use of fire

East African sites, such as Chesowanja near Lake Baringo, Koobi Fora, and Olorgesailie in Kenya, show potential evidence that fire was utilized by early humans. At Chesowanja, archaeologists found fire-hardened clay fragments, dated to 1.42 M.Y.A. Analysis showed that, in order to harden it, the clay must have been heated to about 400 °C (752 °F). At Koobi Fora, two sites show evidence of control of fire by *Homo erectus* at about 1.5 M.Y.A., with reddening of sediment associated with heating the material to 200–400 degrees Celsius (392–752 degrees Fahrenheit). At a "hearth-like depression" at a site in Olorgesailie, Kenya, some microscopic charcoal was found—but that could have resulted from natural brush fires.

In Gadeb, Ethiopia, fragments of welded tuff that appeared to have been burned, or scorched, were found alongside *H. erectus*–created Acheulean artifacts; but such re-firing of the rocks may have been caused by local volcanic activity. In the Middle Awash River Valley, cone-shaped depressions of reddish clay were found that could have been created only by temperatures of 200 °C (392 °F) or greater. These features are thought to be burnt tree stumps such that the fire was likely away from a habitation site. Burnt stones are found in the Awash Valley, but naturally burnt (volcanic) welded tuff is also found in the area.

A site at Bnot Ya'akov Bridge, Israel is reported to show evidence that *H. erectus* or *H. ergaster* controlled fire there between 790,000 and 690,000 years ago.; to date this claim has been widely accepted. Some evidence is found that *H. erectus* was controlling fire less than 250,000 years ago. Evidence also exists that *H. erectus* were cooking their food as early as 500,000 years ago. Re-analysis of burnt bone fragments and plant ashes from the Wonderwerk Cave, South Africa, has been dubbed evidence supporting human control of fire there by 1 M.Y.A.

There is archaeological evidence that *Homo erectus* cooked their food.

Sociality

Homo erectus was probably the first hominin to live in a hunter-gatherer society, and anthropologists such as Richard Leakey believe that *erectus* was socially more like modern humans than the more *Australopithecus*-like species before it. Likewise, increased cranial capacity generally coincides with the more sophisticated tools occasionally found with fossils.

The discovery of Turkana boy (*H. ergaster*) in 1984 evidenced that, despite its *Homo sapiens*-like anatomy, *ergaster* may not have been capable of producing sounds comparable to modern human speech. It likely communicated in a proto-language lacking the fully developed structure of modern human language but more developed than the non-verbal communication used by chimpanzees. This inference is challenged by the find in Dmanisi, Georgia, of an *H. ergaster* / *erectus* vertebrae (at least 150,000 years earlier than the Turkana Boy) that reflects vocal capabilities within the range of *H. sapiens*. Both brain size and the presence of the Broca's area also support the use of articulate language.

Linguist Daniel Everett has argued that *H. erectus* may have been the first hominin to evolve the capability of language because their level of social organization and technical sophistication must have required a complex communication system.[44]

H. erectus was probably the first hominin to live in small, familiar band-societies similar to modern hunter-gatherer band-societies, and is thought to be the first hominin species to hunt in coordinated groups, to use complex tools, and to care for infirm or weak companions.

Descendants and subspecies

Hominin timeline

```
0 —
  —
1 —
  —
  —
  —
  —
  —
  —
  —
  —
10 —
```

Axis scale: million years

Also see: *Life timeline* and *Nature timeline*

Homo erectus is the most, or one of the most, long-lived species of *Homo*, having existed well over one million years and perhaps over two million years;

by contrast, *Homo sapiens* emerged about a quarter million years ago. If considering *Homo erectus* in its strict sense (that is, as referring to only the Asian variety) no consensus has been reached as to whether it is ancestral to *H. sapiens* or any later human species.

Homo erectus

- *Homo erectus erectus* (Java Man)
- *Homo erectus yuanmouensis* (Yuanmou Man)
- *Homo erectus lantianensis* (Lantian Man)
- *Homo erectus nankinensis* (Nanjing Man)
- *Homo erectus pekinensis* (Peking Man)
- *Homo erectus palaeojavanicus* (Meganthropus)
- *Homo erectus soloensis* (Solo Man)[45]
- *Homo erectus tautavelensis* (Tautavel Man)
- *Homo erectus georgicus*
- *Homo erectus bilzingslebenensis*

"Wushan Man" is suggested to be *Homo erectus wushanensis*, but some supect that it's a stem-orangutan.

Related species

On many archaic humans there is no definite consensus as to whether they should be classified as subspecies of either *H. erectus* or *H. sapiens*, or as separate species

- African *H. erectus* candidates
  - *Homo ergaster* ("African *H. erectus*)
  - *Homo naledi* (or *H. e. naledi*)
- Eurasian *H. erectus* candidates:
  - *Homo antecessor* (or *H. e. antecessor*)
  - *Homo heidelbergensis* (or *H. e. heidelbergensis*)
  - *Homo cepranensis* (or *H. e. cepranensis*)
  - *Homo floresiensis* (or *H. e. florsiensis*)[46]
- *Homo sapiens* candidates
  - *Homo neanderthalensis* (or *H. s. neanderthalensis*)
  - *Homo denisova* (or *H. s. denisova* or *Homo* sp. *Altai*, and *Homo sapiens* subsp. *Denisova*)
  - *Homo rhodesiensis* (or *H. s. rhodensis*)
  - *Homo heidelbergensis* (or *H. s. heidelbergensis*)
  - *Homo sapiens idaltu*
  - the Narmada fossil, discovered in 1982 in Madhya Pradesh, India, was at first suggested as *H. erectus* (*Homo erectus narmadensis*) but later recognized as *H. sapiens*.[47]

Individual fossils

Some of the major *Homo erectus* fossils:

- Indonesia (island of Java): Trinil 2 (holotype), Sangiran collection, Sambungmachan collection, Ngandong collection
- China ("Peking Man"): Lantian (Gongwangling and Chenjiawo), Yunxian, Zhoukoudian, Nanjing, Hexian
- Kenya: KNM ER 3883, KNM ER 3733
- Vértesszőlős, Hungary "Samu"
- Vietnam: Northern, Tham Khuyen, Hoa BinhWikipedia:Citation needed
- Republic of Georgia: Dmanisi collection ("Homo erectus georgicus")
- Ethiopia: Daka calvaria
- Eritrea: Buia cranium (possibly H. ergaster)
- Denizli Province, Turkey: Kocabas fossil

Gallery

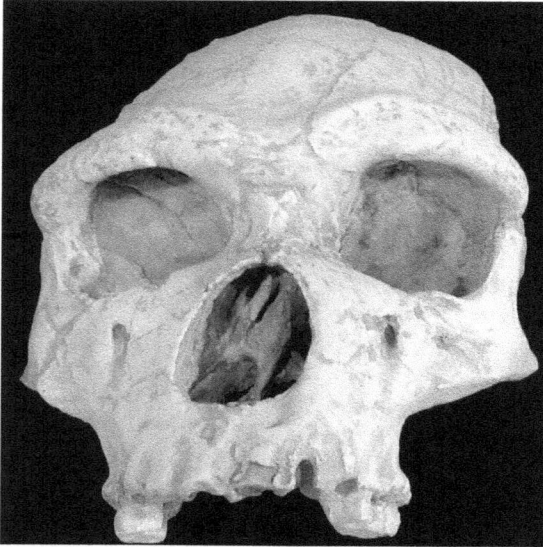

Figure 10: *Homo erectus tautavelensis skull.*

Figure 11: *Replica of lower jaws of Homo erectus from Tautavel, France.*

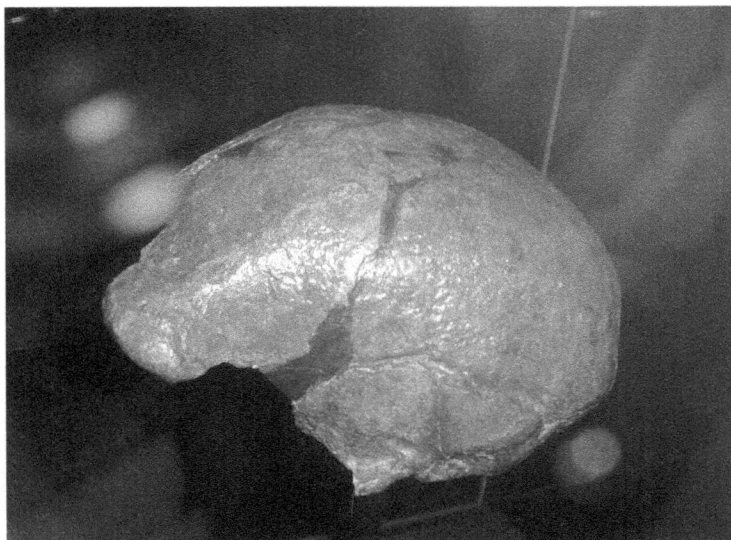

Figure 12: *Calvaria "Sangiran II" original, collection Koenigswald, Senckenberg Museum.*

Figure 13: *A reconstruction based on evidence from the Daka Member, Ethiopia*

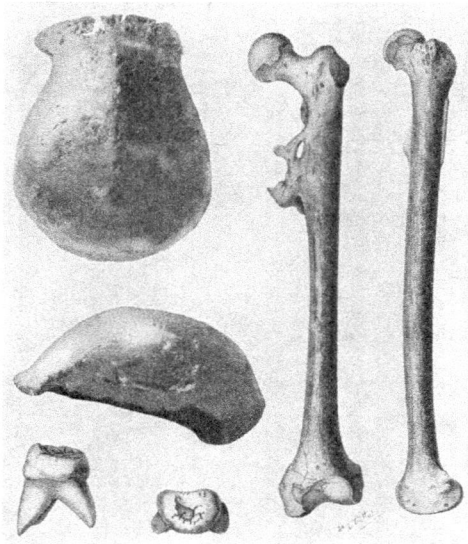

Figure 14: *Original fossils of Pithecanthropus erectus (now Homo erectus) found in Java in 1891.*

Further reading

- Leakey, Richard; Walker, Alan (November 1985). "Homo Erectus Unearthed". *National Geographic*. Vol. 168 no. 5. pp. 624–629. ISSN 0027-9358[48]. OCLC 643483454[49].

External links

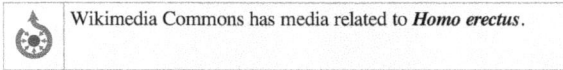

> Wikimedia Commons has media related to *Homo erectus*.

- Homo erectus[50] Origins - Exploring the Fossil Record - Bradshaw Foundation
- Archaeology Info[51]
- Homo erectus[52] – The Smithsonian Institution's Human Origins Program
- Possible co-existence with Homo Habilis[53] – BBC News
- John Hawks's discussion of the Kocabas fossil[54]
- Peter Brown's Australian and Asian Palaeoanthropology[55]
- The Age of Homo erectus[56] – Interactive Map of the Journey of Homo erectus out of Africa
- Human Timeline (Interactive)[57] – Smithsonian, National Museum of Natural History (August 2016).

Clactonian

Clactonian

Geographical range	Afro-Eurasia
Period	Lower Paleolithic
Dates	c. 424,000 – c. 400,000 BP
Type site	Clacton-on-Sea
Major sites	Barnham, Nile, Swanscombe Heritage Park
Characteristics	Clactonian Hand-axe from Rickson's Farm pit, Clacton, Essex.
Preceded by	Acheulean
Followed by	Mousterian

The **Clactonian** is the name given by archaeologists to an industry of European flint tool manufacture that dates to the early part of the interglacial period known as the Hoxnian, the Mindel-Riss or the Holstein stages (c. 400,000 years ago). Clactonian tools were made by *Homo heidelbergensis*.

It is named after 400,000-year-old finds made by Hazzledine Warren in a palaeochannel at Clacton-on-Sea in the English county of Essex in 1911. The artefacts found there included flint chopping tools, flint flakes and the tip of a worked wooden shaft along with the remains of a giant elephant and hippopotamus. Further examples of the tools have been found at sites including Barnfield Pit and Rickson's Pit, near Swanscombe in Kent and Barnham in Suffolk; similar industries have been identified across Northern Europe. The Clactonian industry involved striking thick, irregular flakes from a core of flint, which was then employed as a chopper. The flakes would have been used as crude knives or scrapers. Unlike the Oldowan tools from which Clactonian ones derived, some were notched implying that they were attached to a handle or shaft. Retouch is uncommon and the prominent bulb of percussion on the flakes indicates use of a hammerstone.

Within the banks of the Nile River, at the 100 foot terrace, excavations located Egyptian version of Clactonian.

The Clactonian controversy

The Clactonian industry may have co-existed with the Acheulean industry, which used identical basic techniques but which also had handaxe technology; tools made by bifacially working a flint core. In the 1990s it was argued that the difference between Clactonian and Acheulean may be a false distinction. The Clactonian industry may in fact be the same thing as the Acheulean and only assessed as being different due to its tools being Acheulean ones made by individuals who had no need for handaxes on the occasion that they made them. Differences in environment and the availability and quality of local raw materials may account for the differences between the two industries, which, at one point it was inferred, were only perceived by modern archaeologists.

However, the 2004 excavation of a butchered Pleistocene elephant at the Southfleet Road site of High Speed 1 in Kent recovered numerous Clactonian flint tools but no handaxes. As a handaxe would have been more useful than a chopper in dismembering an elephant carcass it is considered strong evidence of the Clactonian being a separate industry. Flint of sufficient quality was available in the area and it is likely that the people who carved up the elephant did not possess the knowledge to make the more advanced bifacial handaxe. Proponents of the Clactonian as an independent industry point to the lack of concrete evidence in favour of it being an anomalous Acheulean industry. The precise provenance of the few attributed bifacial Clactonian tools (which point to Acheulean influence) is in dispute.

The traditional chronology of Clactonian being followed by Acheulean is also being increasingly challenged since finds of Acheulean tools were made at Box-grove in Sussex and High Lodge in Suffolk. These finds came from deposits connected with the Anglian Stage, the glaciation that preceded the Hoxnian Stage and therefore would have preceded the Clactonian. Whether or not they are separate industries it would seem that the 'Clactonian' and 'Acheulean' stone tool makers would have had cultural contact with each other.

File:England location map.svg

Map of England showing important sites of the Clactonian industry (clickable map).

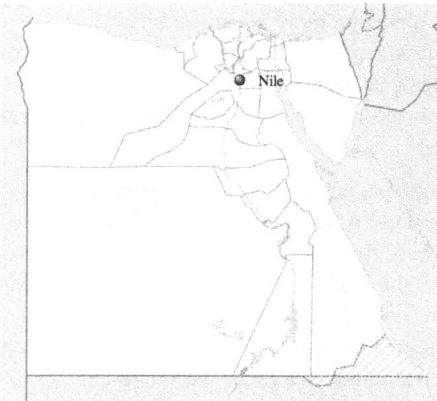

File:Egypt adm location map.svg

Map of Egypt showing claimed Clactonian sites (clickable map).

References

Butler, C, *Prehistoric Flintwork*, Tempus : Strood, 2005

External links

- Drawings of Clactonian tools[58]
- "Stone Age elephant remains found"[59]

The Paleolithic ↑ Pliocene (before *Homo*)

Lower Paleolithic
(c. 3.3 Ma – 300 ka)

- Oldowan (2.6–1.7 Ma)
- Madrasian Culture (1.5 Ma)
- Soanian (0.5–0.13 Ma)
- Acheulean (1.76–0.1 Ma)
- Clactonian (0.3–0.2 Ma)

- Acheulo-Yabrudian complex (400-200 bp)

Middle Paleolithic
(300–45 ka)

- Mousterian (160–35-30 ka)
- Aterian (c. 145,000–c. 20,000 bp)
- Micoquien (130–70 ka)

- Sangoan (130-10 bp)

Upper Paleolithic
(50–10 ka)

- Emiran (50,000–40,000 bp)
- Bohunician (∼48,000 bp)
- Ahmarian (46,000-42,000 bp)
- Châtelperronian (∼44,500 – 36,000 bp)
- Lincombian-Ranisian-Jerzmanowician (43-32 ka)
- Aurignacian (46-43,000 – c. 26,000 bp)
- Khormusan (42,000-18,000 bp)
- Baradostian (36-18 ka)
- Périgordian (35–20 ka)
- Gravettian (33–24 ka)
- Antelian (32–20 bp)
- Mal'ta–Buret' culture (24,000 - 15,00 bp)
- Solutrean (22–17 ka)
- Halfan culture (22,000-14,000)

- Afontova Gora (21,000-12,000}
- Epigravettian (20-10 ka)
- Zarzian culture (20,000-10,000 bp)
- Iberomaurusian (~25/23,000-11,000 cal bp)
- Kebaran (18,000 – 12,500 bp)
- Magdalenian (17–12 ka)
- Trialetian (16,000-8,000 bp)
- Hamburg (15,500-13,100 bp)
- Eburran industry (15,000-5,000 bp)
- Qadan culture (15,000 BP — 11,000 bp)
- Sebilian (15,00 -11,00 bp)
- Natufian culture (14,500–11,500 bp)
- Federmesser (14–13 ka)
- Ahrensburg (13–12 ka)
- Khiamian (12,200 and 10,800 bp)
- Swiderian (11–8 ka)

↓ Mesolithic
↓ Stone Age

- $\underline{v}$
- $\underline{t}$
- $\underline{e}^{60}$

Micoquien

Micoquien

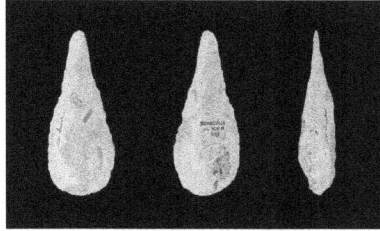

Geographical range	Europe
Period	Middle Paleolithic
Dates	c. 130,000 – c. 60,000 BCE
Type site	La Micoque
Major sites	Balve Cave, Eem, Les Eyzies-de-Tayac-Sireuil
Preceded by	Acheulean, Mousterian
Followed by	Mousterian

File:Europe blank laea location map.svg

Map of Europe showing important sites of the Micoquien (clickable map).

The Paleolithic ↑ Pliocene (before *Homo*)

Lower Paleolithic
(c. 3.3 Ma – 300 ka)

- Oldowan (2.6–1.7 Ma)
- Madrasian Culture (1.5 Ma)
- Soanian (0.5–0.13 Ma)

- Acheulean (1.76–0.1 Ma)
- Clactonian (0.3–0.2 Ma)

- Acheulo-Yabrudian complex (400-200 bp)

Middle Paleolithic
(300–45 ka)

- Mousterian (160–35-30 ka)
- Aterian (c. 145,000–c. 20,000 bp)
- Micoquien (130–70 ka)

- Sangoan (130-10 bp)

Upper Paleolithic
(50–10 ka)

- Emiran (50,000–40,000 bp)
- Bohunician (~48,000 bp)
- Ahmarian (46,000-42,000 bp)
- Châtelperronian (~44,500 – 36,000 bp)
- Lincombian-Ranisian-Jerzmanowician (43-32 ka)
- Aurignacian (46-43,000 – c. 26,000 bp)
- Khormusan (42,000-18,000 bp)
- Baradostian (36-18 ka)
- Périgordian (35–20 ka)
- Gravettian (33–24 ka)
- Antelian (32–20 bp)
- Mal'ta–Buret' culture (24,000 - 15,00 bp)
- Solutrean (22–17 ka)
- Halfan culture (22,000-14,000)
- Afontova Gora (21,000-12,000}
- Epigravettian (20-10 ka)
- Zarzian culture (20,000-10,000 bp)
- Iberomaurusian (~25/23,000-11,000 cal bp)
- Kebaran (18,000 – 12,500 bp)
- Magdalenian (17–12 ka)
- Trialetian (16,000-8,000 bp)
- Hamburg (15,500-13,100 bp)
- Eburran industry (15,000-5,000 bp)
- Qadan culture (15,000 BP — 11,000 bp)
- Sebilian (15,00 -11,00 bp)
- Natufian culture (14,500–11,500 bp)
- Federmesser (14–13 ka)
- Ahrensburg (13–12 ka)
- Khiamian (12,200 and 10,800 bp)

- Swiderian (11–8 ka)

↓ Mesolithic
↓ Stone Age

- <u>v</u>
- <u>t</u>
- <u>e</u>[61]

The **Micoquien** is an early middle paleolithic industry, that is found in the Eemian and in an early episode of the Würm glaciation (about 130,000 to 60,000 BCE). The Micoquien is distinguished technologically by the appearance of distinctly asymmetrical bifaces. Its discoverer and namer was the archeologist and art trader Otto Hauser.[62,63,64] Hauser then sold a great number of so-called Micoque-wedges that he found in excavations in La Micoque (in Les Eyzies-de-Tayac-Sireuil, Dordogne, France) to museums and collectors.

The specially formed handaxes from La Micoque exhibited an often a rounded base. The problem with the term Micoquien is that later excavations have revealed an older time placement for the La Micoque axes, which are now dated in the Riss glaciation.[65,66]

A wider artifact from the Micoquien is the Keilmesser (bifacially worked knife), which has a clearer chronology in Central Europe. From this some archeologists have proposed substituting the term Keilmesser group for Micoquien.[67]

Micoquien artifacts are distributed across all of Eastern Europe and Central Europe. In Germany they can be found at Balver Höhle and Lonetal.

References

- Debénath, A.; Rigaud, J.-Ph. (1986), Le gisement de La Micoque.- in: Rigaud, J.-Ph. (dir.): Informa-tions archéologiques: circonscription d'Aquitaine; Gallia Préhist. 29; CNRS; Paris; 236-237.
- Debénath, A.; Rigaud, J.-Ph. (1991), La Micoque.- Gallia Informations Préhistoire et Histoire; 1991-1; CNRS; Paris; 21-25.
- Hauser, O. (1916), La Micoque, die Kultur einer neuen Diluvialrasse. Leipzig.
- Peyrony, D. (1933), La Micoque et ses diverses industries.- XVe Congrès International d'Anthropolo-gie et d'Archéologie Préhistorique (suite), Ve Session de l'Institut International d'Anthropologie; Paris 20-27 Septembre 1931; Librairie E. Nourry; Paris; Extrait; 1-6.
- Peyrony, D. (1938), La Micoque. Les fouilles récentes. Leur signification.- Bulletin de la Société Pré-historique Française 35; Paris; 121; 257-288.

- Rosendahl, G. (1999), La Micoque und das Micoquien in den altsteinzeitlichen Sammlungen des Reiss-Museums Mannheim.- Mannh.
  Geschichtsblätter N. F. 6; Ubstadt-Weiher; 315-351.

External links

- ⚗ Media related to Micoquien at Wikimedia Commons
- (in German) Geröllgeräte-Industrien[68]
- (in German) Rosendahl, G. (2004), Die oberen Schichten von La Micoque.[69]

Dispersal throughout Africa

Sub-Saharan Africa

Sub-Saharan Africa is, geographically, the area of the continent of Africa that lies south of the Sahara. According to the United Nations, it consists of all African countries that are fully or partially located south of the Sahara. It contrasts with North Africa, whose territories are part of the League of Arab states within the Arab world. Somalia, Djibouti, Comoros and Mauritania are geographically in Sub-Saharan Africa, but are likewise Arab-speaking states and part of the Arab world.[71]

The Sahel is the transitional zone in between the Sahara and the tropical savanna of the Sudan region and farther south the forest-savanna mosaic of tropical Africa.

Since probably 3500 BCE,[72] the Saharan and Sub-Saharan regions of Africa have been separated by the extremely harsh climate of the sparsely populated Sahara, forming an effective barrier interrupted by only the Nile in Sudan, though the Nile was blocked by the river's cataracts. The Sahara pump theory explains how flora and fauna (including *Homo sapiens*) left Africa to penetrate the Middle East and beyond. African pluvial periods are associated with a Wet Sahara phase, during which larger lakes and more rivers existed.

The use of the term has been criticized because it refers to the South only by cartography conventions and projects a connotation of inferiority; a vestige of colonialism, which some say, divided Africa into European terms of homogeneity.

Figure 15: ***Dark and lighter green:*** *Definition of "Sub-Saharan Africa" as used in the statistics of the United Nations institutions.* ***Lighter green:*** *However, Sudan is classified as North Africa by the United Nations Statistics Division.*[70]

Etymology

Geographers historically divided the region into several distinct ethnographic sections based on each area's respective inhabitants.

Commentators in Arabic in the medieval period used the general term *bilâd as-sûdân* ("Land of the Blacks") for the vast Sudan region (an expression denoting West and Central Africa), or sometimes extending from the coast of West Africa to Western Sudan.[73] Its equivalent in Southeast Africa was *Zanj* ("Country of the Blacks"), which was situated in the vicinity of the Great Lakes region.

The geographers drew an explicit ethnographic distinction between the Sudan region and its analogue Zanj, from the area to their extreme east on the Red Sea coast in the Horn of Africa. In modern-day Ethiopia and Eritrea was *Al-Habash* or Abyssinia,[74] which was inhabited by the *Habash* or Abyssinians, who were the forebears of the Habesha.[75] In northern Somalia was *Barbara* or the *Bilad al-Barbar* ("Land of the Berbers"), which was inhabited by the Eastern *Baribah* or *Barbaroi*, as the ancestors of the Somalis were referred to by medieval Arab and ancient Greek geographers, respectively.[76,77,78]

Figure 16: *Red: Arab states in Africa (Arab League and UNESCO).*

In the 19th and 20th centuries, the populations south of the Sahara were divided into three broad ancestral groups: Hamites and Semites in the Horn of Africa and Sahel related to those in North Africa, who spoke languages belonging to the Afroasiatic family; Negroes in most of the rest of the subcontinent (hence, the former toponym *Black Africa* for Tropical Africa), who spoke languages belonging to the Niger-Congo and Nilo-Saharan families; and Khoisan in Southern Africa, who spoke languages belonging to the Khoisan family.

Climate zones and ecoregions

Sub-Saharan Africa has a wide variety of climate zones or biomes. South Africa and the Democratic Republic of the Congo in particular are considered Megadiverse countries. It has a dry winter season and a wet summer season.

- The Sahel shoots across all of Africa at a latitude of about 10° to 15° N. Countries that include parts of the Sahara Desert proper in their northern territories and parts of the Sahel in their southern region include Mauritania, Mali, Niger, Chad and Sudan. The Sahel has a hot semi-arid climate.
- South of the Sahel, there is a belt of savanna (Guinean forest-savanna mosaic, Northern Congolian forest-savanna mosaic), widening to include most of South Sudan and Ethiopia in the east (East Sudanese savanna).

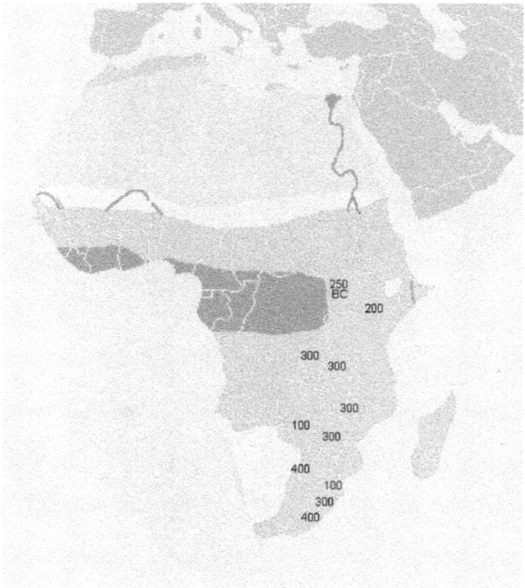

Figure 17: *Simplified climatic map of Africa: Sub-Saharan Africa consists of the Sahel and the Horn of Africa in the north (yellow), the tropical savannas (light green) and the tropical rainforests (dark green) of Equatorial Africa, and the arid Kalahari Basin (yellow) and the "Mediterranean" south coast (olive) of Southern Africa. The numbers shown correspond to the dates of all Iron Age artifacts associated with the Bantu expansion.*

- The Horn of Africa globally includes hot desert climate along the coast but hot semi-arid climate can be found much more in the interior, contrasting with savannah and moist broadleaf forests in the interior of Ethiopia.
- Tropical Africa encompasses tropical rainforest stretching along the southern coast of West Africa and across most of Central Africa (the Congo) west of the African Great Lakes
- The Eastern miombo woodlands are an ecoregion of Tanzania, Malawi, and Mozambique.
- The Serengeti ecosystem is located in northwestern Tanzania and extends to southwestern Kenya.
- The Kalahari Basin includes the Kalahari Desert, which is surrounded by a belt of semi-desert.
- The Bushveld is a tropical savanna ecoregion of Southern Africa.
- The Karoo is a semi-desert in western South Africa.

Figure 18: *Ethnographic map of Africa, from Meyers Blitz-Lexikon (1932).*

History

Prehistory

According to paleontology, early hominid skull anatomy was similar to that of their close cousins, the great African forest apes, gorilla and chimpanzee. However, they had adopted a bipedal locomotion and freed hands, giving them a crucial advantage enabling them to live in both forested areas and on the open savanna at a time when Africa was drying up, with savanna encroaching on forested areas. This occurred 10 million to 5 million years ago.[79]

By 3 million years ago several australopithecine hominid species had developed throughout southern, eastern and central Africa. They were tool users rather than tool manufacturers. The next major evolutionary step occurred around 2.3 million BCE, when primitive stone tools were used to scavenge the carcasses of animals killed by other predators, both for their meat and their marrow. In hunting, *H. habilis* was most likely not capable of competing with large predators and was more prey than hunter, although *H. habilis* probably did steal eggs from nests and may have been able to catch small game and weakened larger prey such as cubs and older animals. The tools were classed as Oldowan.[80]

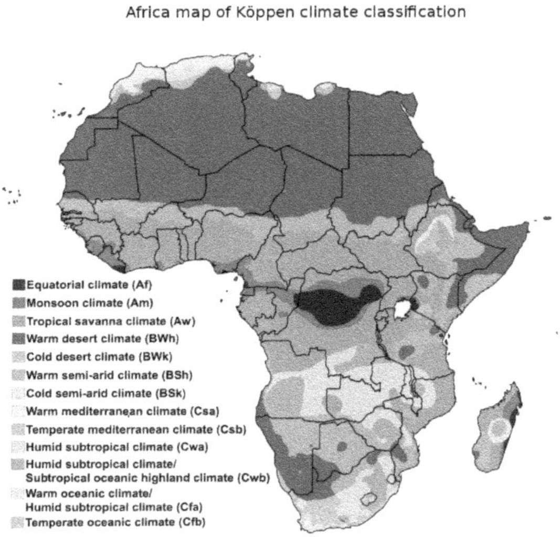

Africa map of Köppen climate classification

- ■ Equatorial climate (Af)
- ■ Monsoon climate (Am)
- ■ Tropical savanna climate (Aw)
- ■ Warm desert climate (BWh)
- ■ Cold desert climate (BWk)
- ■ Warm semi-arid climate (BSh)
- ■ Cold semi-arid climate (BSk)
- ■ Warm mediterranean climate (Csa)
- ■ Temperate mediterranean climate (Csb)
- ■ Humid subtropical climate (Cwa)
- ■ Humid subtropical climate/
  Subtropical oceanic highland climate (Cwb)
- ■ Warm oceanic climate/
  Humid subtropical climate (Cfa)
- ■ Temperate oceanic climate (Cfb)

Figure 19: *Climate zones of Africa, showing the ecological break between the hot desert climate of North Africa and the Horn of Africa (red), the hot semi-arid climate of the Sahel and areas surrounding deserts (orange) and the tropical climate of Central and Western Africa (blue). Southern Africa has a transition to semi-tropical or temperate climates (green), and more desert or semi-arid regions, centered on Namibia and Botswana.*

Roughly 1.8 million years ago, *Homo ergaster* first appeared in the fossil record in Africa. From *Homo ergaster*, *Homo erectus* (upright man) evolved 1.5 million years ago. Some of the earlier representatives of this species were small-brained and used primitive stone tools, much like *H. habilis*. The brain later grew in size, and *H. erectus* eventually developed a more complex stone tool technology called the Acheulean. Potentially the first hominid to engage in hunting, *H. erectus* mastered the art of making fire. They were the first hominids to leave Africa, going on to colonize the entire Old World, and perhaps later on giving rise to *Homo floresiensis*. Although some recent writers suggest that *H. georgicus*, a *H. habilis* descendant, was the first and most primitive hominid to ever live outside Africa, many scientists consider *H. georgicus* to be an early and primitive member of the *H. erectus* species.[81]

The fossil record shows *Homo sapiens* lived in southern and eastern Africa anywhere from 100,000 to 150,000 years ago. Between 50,000 and 60,000 years ago, their expansion out of Africa launched the colonization of the planet by modern humans. By 10,000 BCE, *Homo sapiens* had spread to all corners

Figure 20: *Stone chopping tool from Olduvai Gorge*

of the world. This dispersal of the human species is suggested by linguistic, cultural and genetic evidence.[82]

After the Sahara became a desert, it did not present a totally impenetrable barrier for travelers between north and south because of the application of animal husbandry towards carrying water, food, and supplies across the desert. Prior to the introduction of the camel,[83] the use of oxen, mule, and horses for desert crossing was common, and trade routes followed chains of oases that were strung across the desert. The trans-saharan trade was in full motion by 500 BCE with Carthage being a major economic force for its establishment.[84,85,86] It is thought that the camel was first brought to Egypt after the Persian Empire conquered Egypt in 525 BCE, although large herds did not become common enough in North Africa for camels to be the pack animal of choice for the trans-saharan trade.[87]

Central Africa

Archaeological finds in Central Africa provide evidence of human settlement that may date back over 10 000 years. According to Zangato and Holl, there is evidence of iron-smelting in the Central African Republic and Cameroon that may date back to 3000 to 2500 BCE. Extensive walled sites and settlements have recently been found in Zilum, Chad. The area is located approximately

Figure 21: *Nzinga Mbande, queen of the Bantu Ndongo and Matamba kingdoms*

60 km (37 mi) southwest of Lake Chad, and has been radiocarbon dated to the first millennium BCE.[88,89]

Trade and improved agricultural techniques supported more sophisticated societies, leading to the early civilizations of Sao, Kanem, Bornu, Shilluk, Baguirmi, and Wadai.[90]

Following the Bantu Migration into Central Africa, during the 14th century, the Luba Kingdom in southeast Congo came about under a king whose political authority derived from religious, spiritual legitimacy. The kingdom controlled agriculture and regional trade of salt and iron from the north and copper from the Zambian/Congo copper belt.[91]

Rival kingship factions which split from the Luba Kingdom later moved among the Lunda people, marrying into its elite and laying the foundation of the Lunda Empire in the 16th century. The ruling dynasty centralised authority among the Lunda under the Mwata Yamyo or Mwaant Yaav. The Mwata Yamyo's legitimacy, like that of the Luba king, came from being viewed as a spiritual religious guardian. This imperial cult or system of divine kings was spread to most of central Africa by rivals in kingship migrating and forming new states. Many new states received legitimacy by claiming descent from the Lunda dynasties.

Figure 22: *Stone city of Gondershe, Somalia*

The Kingdom of Kongo existed from the Atlantic west to the Kwango river to the east. During the 15th century, the Bakongo farming community was united with its capital at M'banza-Kongo, under the king title, Manikongo. Other significant states and peoples included the Kuba Kingdom, producers of the famous raffia cloth, the Eastern Lunda, Bemba, Burundi, Rwanda, and the Kingdom of Ndongo.

Horn of Africa

The Axumite Empire spanned the southern Sahara, south Arabia and the Sahel along the western shore of the Red Sea. Located in northern Ethiopia and Eritrea, Aksum was deeply involved in the trade network between India and the Mediterranean. Growing from the proto-Aksumite Iron Age period circa the 4th century BCE, it rose to prominence by the 1st century CE. The Aksumites constructed monolithic stelae to cover the graves of their kings, such as King Ezana's Stele. The later Zagwe dynasty, established in the 12th century, built churches out of solid rock. These rock-hewn structures include the Church of St. George at Lalibela.

In ancient Somalia, city-states flourished such as Opone, Mosyllon and Malao that competed with the Sabaeans, Parthians and Axumites for the wealthy Indo–Greco–Roman trade.[92]

In the Middle Ages, several powerful Somali empires dominated the regional trade including the Ajuran Sultanate, which excelled in hydraulic engineering

Figure 23: *Fasilides Castle, Ethiopia*

and fortress building,[93] the Sultanate of Adal, whose General Ahmed Gurey was the first African commander in history to use cannon warfare on the continent during Adal's conquest of the Ethiopian Empire,[94] and the Geledi Sultanate, whose military dominance forced governors of the Omani empire north of the city of Lamu to pay tribute to the Somali Sultan Ahmed Yusuf.[95] In the late 19th century after the Berlin conference had ended, European empires sailed with their armies to the Horn of Africa. The imperial armies in Somalia alarmed the Dervish leader Mohammed Abdullah Hassan, who gathered Somali soldiers from across the Horn of Africa and began one of the longest anti-colonial wars known as the Somaliland Campaign.

Southern Africa

Settlements of Bantu-speaking peoples, who were iron-using agriculturists and herdsmen, were already present south of the Limpopo River by the 4th or 5th century displacing and absorbing the original Khoisan speakers. They slowly moved south, and the earliest ironworks in modern-day KwaZulu-Natal Province are believed to date from around 1050. The southernmost group was the Xhosa people, whose language incorporates certain linguistic traits from the earlier Khoisan inhabitants. They reached the Fish River in today's Eastern Cape Province.

Figure 24: *Great Zimbabwe: Tower in the Great Enclosure*

Monomotapa was a medieval kingdom (c. 1250–1629), which existed between the Zambezi and Limpopo rivers of Southern Africa in the territory of modern-day Zimbabwe and Mozambique. Its old capital was located at Great Zimbabwe.

In 1487, Bartolomeu Dias became the first European to reach the southernmost tip of Africa. In 1652, a victualling station was established at the Cape of Good Hope by Jan van Riebeeck on behalf of the Dutch East India Company. For most of the 17th and 18th centuries, the slowly expanding settlement was a Dutch possession.

Great Britain seized the Cape of Good Hope area in 1795, ostensibly to prevent it from falling into the hands of the French but also to use Cape Town in particular as a stop on the route to Australia and India. It was later returned to the Dutch in 1803, but soon afterwards the Dutch East India Company declared bankruptcy, and the British annexed the Cape Colony in 1806.

The Zulu Kingdom was a Southern African tribal state in what is now KwaZulu-Natal in southeastern South Africa. The small kingdom gained world fame during and after the Anglo-Zulu War.

During the 1950s and early 1960s, most Sub-Saharan African nations achieved independence from colonial rule.[96]

Figure 25: *The Tongoni Ruins south of Tanga in Tanzania*

Southeast Africa

According to the theory of recent African origin of modern humans, the main-stream position held within the scientific community, all humans originate from either Southeast Africa or the Horn of Africa.[97] During the first mil-lennium CE, Nilotic and Bantu-speaking peoples moved into the region, and the latter now account for three-quarters of Kenya's population.

On the coastal section of Southeast Africa, a mixed Bantu community devel-oped through contact with Muslim Arab and Persian traders, leading to the development of the mixed Arab, Persian and African Swahili City States. The Swahili culture that emerged from these exchanges evinces many Arab and Islamic influences not seen in traditional Bantu culture, as do the many Afro-Arab members of the Bantu Swahili people. With its original speech com-munity centered on the coastal parts of Tanzania (particularly Zanzibar) and Kenya – a seaboard referred to as the Swahili Coast – the Bantu Swahili lan-guage contains many Arabic loan-words as a consequence of these interac-tions.[98]

The earliest Bantu inhabitants of the Southeast coast of Kenya and Tanzania encountered by these later Arab and Persian settlers have been variously identi-fied with the trading settlements of Rhapta, Azania and Menouthias referenced in early Greek and Chinese writings from 50 CE to 500 CE,[99,100,101,102,103,104]

Figure 26: *Sphinx of the Nubian Emperor Taharqa*

ultimately giving rise to the name for Tanzania. These early writings perhaps document the first wave of Bantu settlers to reach Southeast Africa during their migration.

Between the 14th and 15th centuries, large medieval Southeast African kingdoms and states emerged, such as the Buganda[105] and Karagwe kingdoms of Uganda and Tanzania.

During the early 1960s, the Southeast African nations achieved independence from colonial rule.

Sudan

Nubia in present-day Northern Sudan and southernmost of Egypt, was referred to as "Aethiopia" ("land of the burnt face") by the Greeks.

Nubia at her greatest phase is considered Sub-Saharan Africa's oldest urban civilisation. Nubia was a major source of gold for the ancient world. Nubians built famous structures and numerous pyramids. Sudan, the site of ancient Nubia, has more pyramids than anywhere in the world.[106]

Figure 27: *Nok sculpture, terracotta, Louvre*

Western Africa

The Bantu expansion is a major migration movement originating in West Africa around 2500 BCE, reaching East and Central Africa by 1000 BCE and Southern Africa by the early centuries CE.

The Djenné-Djenno city-state flourished from 250 BCE to 900 CE and was influential to the development of the Ghana Empire.

The Nok culture is known from a type of terracotta figure found in Nigeria, dating to between 500 BCE and 200 CE.

There were a number of medieval empires of the southern Sahara and the Sahel, based on trans-Saharan trade, including the Ghana Empire and the Mali Empire, Songhai Empire, the Kanem Empire and the subsequent Bornu Empire.[107] They built stone structures like in Tichit, but mainly constructed in adobe. The Great Mosque of Djenne is most reflective of Sahelian architecture and is the largest adobe building in the world.

In the forest zone, several states and empires emerged. The Ashanti Empire arose in the 16th century in modern-day Ghana and Ivory Coast. The Kingdom of Nri, was established by the Igbo in the 11th century. Nri was famous for having a priest-king who wielded no military power. Nri was a rare African state which was a haven for freed slaves and outcasts who sought refuge in their territory. Other major states included the kingdoms of Ifẹ and Oyo in the western block of Nigeria which became prominent about 700–900 and 1400 respectively, and center of Yoruba culture. The Yoruba's built massive mud walls around their cities, the most famous being Sungbo's Eredo. Another prominent kingdom in southwestern Nigeria was the Kingdom of Benin 9th–11th century whose power lasted between the 15th and 19th century and was one of the greatest Empires of African history documented all over the world. Their dominance reached as far as the well-known city of Eko which was named Lagos by the Portuguese traders and other early European settlers. The Edo speaking people of Benin are known for their famous bronze casting and rich coral, wealth, ancient science and technology and the Walls of Benin, which is the largest man-made structure in the world.

In the 18th century, the Oyo and the Aro confederacy were responsible for most of the slaves exported from Nigeria, with Great Britain, France and Portugal shipping the majority of the slaves. Following the Napoleonic Wars, the British expanded trade with the Nigerian interior. In 1885, British claims to a West African sphere of influence received international recognition, and in the following year the Royal Niger Company was chartered under the leadership of Sir George Taubman Goldie. In 1900, the company's territory came under the control of the British Government, which moved to consolidate its hold over the area of modern Nigeria. On 1 January 1901, Nigeria became a British protectorate, part of the British Empire, the foremost world power at the time.

By 1960, most of the region achieved independence from colonial rule.

Demographics

Population

According to the 2017 revision of the World Population Prospects, the population of sub-Saharan Africa was 995,694,907 in 2016. The current growth rate is 2.3%. The UN predicts for the region a population between 1.5 and 2 billion by 2050 with a population density of 80 per km^2 compared to 170 for Western Europe, 140 for Asia and 30 for the Americas.

Sub-Saharan African countries top the list of countries and territories by fertility rate with 40 of the highest 50, all with TFR greater than 4 in 2008. All are above the world average except South Africa and Seychelles. More than 40% of the population in sub-Saharan countries is younger than 15 years old, as well as in Sudan, with the exception of South Africa.[108]

Figure 28: *Population density in Africa, 2006*

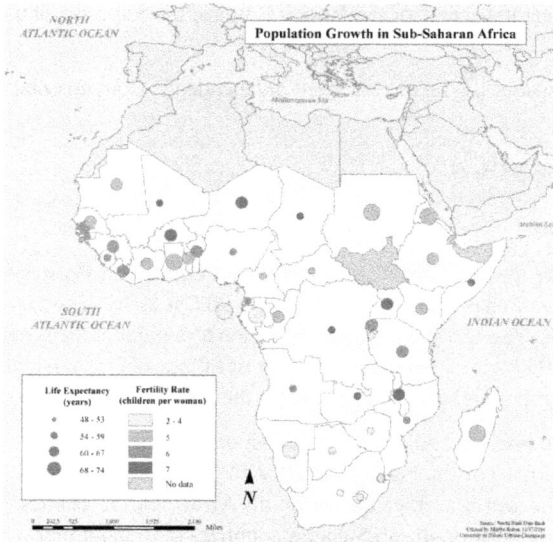

Figure 29: *Fertility rates and life expectancy in Sub-Saharan Africa*

Country	Population	Area (km²)	Literacy (M/-F)[109]	GDP per Capita	Trans[110] (Rank/-Score)	Life (Exp.)	HDI	EODBR/-SAB[111][112]	PFI[113] (RANK/-MARK)
Angola	18,498,000	1,246,700	82.9%/54.2%	6000	168/2	42.4	0.486	172/171	132/58,43
Burundi	8,988,091	27,830	67.3%/52.2%	101	168/1.8	49	0.316	176/130	103/29,00
Democratic Republic of the Congo	68,692,542	2,345,410	80.9%/54.1%	91	162/11.9	46.1	0.286	182/152	146/53,50
Cameroon	18,879,301	475,440	77%/59.8%	687	146/2.2	50.3	0.482	171/174	109/30,50
Central African Republic	4,511,488	622,984	64.8%/33.5%	22	158/2.8	44.4	0.343	183/159	80/17,75
Chad	10,329,208	1,284,000	40.8%/12.8%	266	175/1.6	50.6	0.328	178/182	132/44,50
Republic of the Congo	3,700,000	342,000	90.5%/79.0%	1,145	162/1.9	54.8	0.533	N/A	116/34,25
Equatorial Guinea	633,441	28,051	93.4%/80.3%	7,470	168/1.8	51.1	0.537	170/178	158/65,50
Gabon	1,514,993	267,667	88.5%/79.7%	4,263	106/2.9	56.7	0.674	158/152	129/43,50
Kenya	39,002,772	582,650	77.7%/70.2	976	146/2.2	57.8	0.519	95/124	96/25,00
Nigeria	174,507,539	923,768	84.4%/72.7%	6,204	136/27	57	0.504	131/120	112/34.24
Rwanda	10,473,282	26,338	71.4%/59.8%	263	89/3.3	46.8	0.429	67/11	157/64,67
São Tomé and Príncipe	212,679	1,001	92.2%/77.9%	N/A	111/2.8	65.2	0.509	180/140	NA
Tanzania	44,928,923	945,087	77.5%/62.2%	339	126/2.6	51.9	0.466	131/120	NA/15,50
Uganda	32,369,558	236,040	76.8%/57.7	274	130/2.5	50.7	0.446	112/129	86/21,50
Sudan	31,894,000	1,886,068	79.6%/60.8%	2,500	176/1.5	62.57	0.408	154/118	148/54,00

Country								
South Sudan	8,260,490	619,745	N/A					
Djibouti	516,055	23,000	N/A	817	111/2.8	54.5	0.430 163/177	110/31,00
Eritrea	5,647,168	121,320	N/A	160	126/2.6	57.3	0.349 175/181	175/115,50
Ethiopia	85,237,338	1,127,127	50%/28.8%	161	120/2.7	52.5	0.363 107/93	140/49,00
Somalia	9,832,017	637,657	N/A	N/A	180/1.1	47.7	N/A N/A	164/77,50
Botswana	1,990,876	600,370	80.4%/81.8%	8,532	37/5.6	49.8	0.633 45/83	62/15,50
Comoros	752,438	2,170	N/A	382	143/2.3	63.2	0.433 162/168	82/19,00
Lesotho	2,130,819	30,355	73.7%/90.3%	528	89/3.3	42.9	0.450 130/131	99/27,50
Madagascar	19,625,000	587,041	76.5%/65.3%	238	99/3.0	59	0.480 134/12	134/45,83
Malawi	14,268,711	118,480	N/A	145	89/3.3	47.6	0.400 132/128	62/15,50
Mauritius	1,284,264	2,040	88.2%/80.5%	4,522	42/5.4	73.2	0.728 17/10	51/14,00
Mozambique	21,669,278	801,590	N/A	330	130/2.5	42.5	0.322 135/96	82/19,00
Namibia	2,108,665	825,418	86.8%/83.6%	2166	56/4.5	52.5	0.625 66/123	35/9,00
Seychelles	87,476	455	91.4%/92.3%	7,005	54/4.8	72.2	0.773 111/81	72/16,00
South Africa	52,981,991	1,219,912	N/A	3,562	55/4.7	50.7	0.619 34/67	33/8,50
Swaziland	1,123,913	17,363	80.9%/78.3%	1,297	79/3.6	40.8	0.522 115/158	144/52,50
Zambia	11,862,740	752,614	N/A	371	99/3.0	41.7	0.430 90/94	97/26,75
Zimbabwe	11,392,629	390,580	92.7%/86.2%	N/A	146/2.2	42.7	0.376 159/155	136/46,50
Benin	8,791,832	112,620	47.9%/42.3%	323	106/2.9	56.2	0.427 172/155	97/26,75
Mali	12,666,987	1,240,000	32.7%/15.9%	290	111/2.8	53.8	0.359 156/139	38/8,00

			25.3%	1,360	79/3.6	51	0.331 150/116	N/A
Burkina Faso	15,730,977	274,200	25.3%	1,360	79/3.6	51	0.331 150/116	N/A
Cape Verde	499,000	322,462						
Ivory Coast	20,617,068	322,463						
Gambia	1,782,893	11,295						
Ghana	24,200,000	238,535						
Guinea	10,057,975	245,857						
Guinea-Bissau	1,647,000	36,125						
Liberia	4,128,572	111,369						
Mauritania	3,359,185	1,030,700						
Niger	17,129,076	1,267,000						
Senegal	12,855,153	196,712						
Sierra Leone	6,190,280	71,740						
Togo	7,154,237	56,785						

GDP per Capita *(2006 in dollars (US$))*, **Life (Exp.)** *(Life Expectancy 2006)*, **Literacy (Male/Female 2006)**, **Trans** *(Transparency 2009)*, **HDI** *(Human Development Index)*, **EODBR** *(Ease of Doing Business Rank June 2008 through May 2009)*, **SAB** *(Starting a Business June 2008 through May 2009)*, **PFI** *(Press Freedom Index 2009)*

Languages and ethnic groups

Sub-Saharan Africa contains over 1,000 languages, which is around 1/6 of the world's total.[114]

Afroasiatic

With the exception of the extinct Sumerian (a language isolate) of Mesopotamia, Afro-Asiatic has the oldest documented history of any language family in the world. Egyptian was recorded as early as 3200 BCE. The Semitic branch was recorded as early as 2900 BCE in the form of the Akkadian language of Mesopotamia (Assyria and Babylonia) and circa 2500 BCE in the form of the Eblaite language of north eastern Syria.[115]

The distribution of the Afroasiatic languages within Africa is principally concentrated in North Africa and the Horn of Africa. Languages belonging to the family's Berber branch are mainly spoken in the north, with its speech area extending into the Sahel (northern Mauritania, northern Mali, northern Niger).[116] The Cushitic branch of Afroasiatic is centered in the Horn, and is also spoken in the Nile Valley and parts of the African Great Lakes region. Additionally, the Semitic branch of the family, in the form of Arabic, is widely spoken in the parts of Africa that are within the Arab world. South Semitic languages are also spoken in parts of the Horn of Africa (Ethiopia, Eritrea). The Chadic branch is distributed in Central and West Africa.[117] Hausa, its most widely spoken language, serves as a lingua franca in West Africa (Niger, Ghana, Togo, Benin, Cameroon, and Chad).[118]

Khoisan

The several families lumped under the term Khoi-San include languages indigenous to Southern Africa and Tanzania, though some, such as the Khoi languages, appear to have moved to their current locations not long before the Bantu expansion.[119] In Southern Africa, their speakers are the Khoikhoi and San (Bushmen), in Southeast Africa, the Sandawe and Hadza.

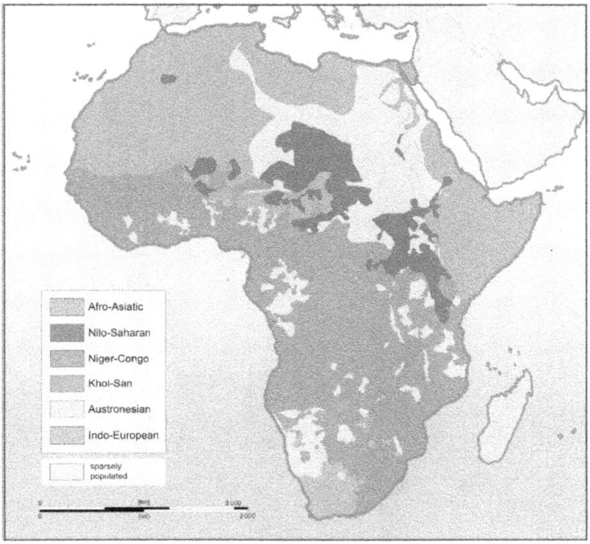

Figure 30:
Map showing the traditional language families spoken in Africa:
Afroasiatic
Austronesian
Indo-European
Khoisan
Niger-Congo
Nilo-Saharan

Niger–Congo

The Niger–Congo family is the largest in the world in terms of the number of languages (1,436) it contains.[120] The vast majority of languages of this family are tonal such as Yoruba, and Igbo, However, others such as Fulani and Wolof are not. A major branch of the Niger–Congo languages is Bantu, which covers a greater geographic area than the rest of the family. Bantu speakers represent the majority of inhabitants in southern, central and southeastern Africa, though San, Pygmy, and Nilotic groups, respectively, can also be found in those regions. Bantu-speakers can also be found in parts of Central Africa such as the Gabon, Equatorial Guinea and southern Cameroon. Swahili, a Bantu language with many Arabic, Persian and other Middle Eastern and South Asian loan words, developed as a *lingua franca* for trade between the different peoples in southeastern Africa. In the Kalahari Desert of Southern Africa, the distinct people known as Bushmen (also "San", closely related to, but distinct from

Figure 31: *A San man (Khoisan)*

Figure 32: *An Afrikaner family (Indo-European)*

"Hottentots") have long been present. The San evince unique physical traits, and are the indigenous people of southern Africa. Pygmies are the pre-Bantu indigenous peoples of Central Africa.

Nilo-Saharan

The Nilo-Saharan languages are concentrated in the upper parts of the Chari and Nile rivers of Central Africa and Southeast Africa. They are principally spoken by Nilotic peoples and are also spoken in Sudan among the Fur, Masalit, Nubian and Zaghawa peoples and in West and Central Africa among

Figure 33: *Saho women (Afroasiatic)*

Figure 34: *Maasai women and children (Nilo-Saharan)*

the Songhai, Zarma and Kanuri. The Old Nubian language is also a member of this family.

Major languages of Africa by region, family and number of primary language speakers in millions:

Figure 35: *Yoruba drummers (Niger-Congo)*

Central Africa	Horn of Africa	Southeast Africa	Southern Africa	West Africa

• Niger–Congo, Bantu
  • Lingala[121]
  • Kinyarwanda: 12[122]
  • Kongo: 5+[123,124]
  • Tshiluba
  • Kirundi[125]
• Nilo-Saharan
  • Nubian: 5+
  • Fur: 5+[126]
  • Zaghawa[127]
  • Masalit
• Niger–Congo
  • Kordofanian languages
    • Nuba[128]
	• Afro-Asiatic
	  • Semitic
	    • Amharic: 20+
	    • Tigrinya: 5
	  • Cushitic
	    • Somali: 10–15
	    • Oromo: 30–35
	• Nilo-Saharan: <1[129]
	  • Gumuz
	  • Anuak
	  • Kunama
	  • Nara
	• Niger–Congo: <1[130]
	  • Zigula
		• Niger–Congo, Bantu:
		  • Swahili: 5–10
		  • Gikuyu: 9
		  • Ganda: 6
		  • Luhya: 6
		• Austronesian
		  • Malagasy: 20+[131]
		• Niger–Congo, Ubangian
		  • Gbaya: 2[132]
		  • Banda: 1–2
		  • Zande[133]
		• Nilo-Saharan
		  • Kanuri: 10[134,135,136]
		  • Luo: 5[137,138]
		  • Sara: 3–4
		  • Kalenjin: 5
		  • Dinka
		  • Nuer
		  • Shilluk
		  • Maasai: 1–2
			• Niger–Congo, Bantu
			  • Zulu: 10[139]
			  • Xhosa: 8
			  • Shona: 7
			  • Sotho: 5
			  • Tswana: 4[140]
			  • Umbundu: 4
			  • Northern Sotho: 4
			  • Chichewa: 8[141,142]
			  • Makua: 8[143]
			• Indo-European
			  • Germanic
			    • Afrikaans: 7–10
			  • Romance
			    • Portuguese: 14	

- Niger–Congo
  - Benue–Congo
    - Ibibio (Nigeria): 7
  - Volta–Niger
    - Igbo (Nigeria): 30–35
    - Yoruba: 40
  - Kwa:
    - Akan (Ghana, Ivory Coast): 20–25
  - Gur
    - More: 5
  - Senegambian
    - Fula (West Africa): 40[144,145,146]
    - Wolof: 8
- Afro-Asiatic
  - Chadic
    - Hausa: 50
- Nilo-Saharan
  - Saharan
    - Kanuri: 10
    - Songhai: 5[147]
    - Zarma: 5

Genetic history

A 2017 archaeogenetic study of prehistoric fossils in Sub-Saharan Africa observed a wide-ranging early presence of Khoisan populations in the region. Khoisan-related ancestry was inferred to have contributed to two thirds of the ancestry of hunter-gatherer populations inhabiting Malawi between 8,100 and 2,500 years ago and to one third of the ancestry of hunter gatherers inhabiting Tanzania as late as 1,400 years ago. Also in Tanzania, a pastoralist individual was found to carry ancestry related to the pre-pottery Levant. These diverse early ancestries are believed to have been largely replaced after the Bantu expansion into central, eastern and southern Africa.[148]

A 2009 genetic clustering study, which genotyped 1327 polymorphic markers in various African populations, identified six ancestral clusters through Bayesian analysis and fourteen ancestral clusters through STRUCTURE analysis within the continent. The clustering corresponded closely with ethnicity, culture and language.

In addition, whole genome sequencing analysis of modern populations inhabiting Sub-Saharan Africa has observed several primary inferred ancestry components: a Pygmy-related component carried by the Mbuti and Biaka Pygmies in Central Africa, a Khoisan-related component carried by Khoisan-speaking populations in Southern Africa, a Niger-Congo-related component carried by Niger-Congo-speaking populations throughout Sub-Saharan Africa, a Nilo-Saharan-related component carried by Nilo-Saharan-speaking populations in the Nile Valley and African Great Lakes, and a West Eurasian-related component carried by Afroasiatic-speaking populations in the Horn of Africa and Nile Valley.

Major cities

Sub-Saharan Africa has several large cities. Lagos is a city in the Nigerian state of Lagos. The city, with its adjoining conurbation, is the most populous in Nigeria, and the second most populous on the African continent after Cairo, Egypt. It is one of the fastest growing cities in the world, and also one of the most populous urban agglomerations. Lagos is a major financial centre in Africa; the megacity has the highest GDP, and also houses one of the largest and busiest ports on the continent.

Dar es Salaam is the former capital as well as the most populous city in Tanzania and a regionally important economic centre. It is located on the Swahili coast.

Johannesburg is the largest city in South Africa. It is the provincial capital and largest city in Gauteng, which is the wealthiest province in South Africa. While

Figure 36: *Lagos*

Figure 37: *Nairobi*

Figure 38: *Johannesburg*

Johannesburg is not one of South Africa's three capital cities, it is the seat of the Constitutional Court. The city is located in the mineral-rich Witwatersrand range of hills and is the centre of large-scale gold and diamond trade

Nairobi is the capital and the largest city of Kenya. The name comes from the Maasai phrase *Enkare Nyrobi*, which translates to "cool water", a reference to the Nairobi River which flows through the city. The city is popularly referred to as the Green City in the Sun.

Other major cities in Sub-Saharan Africa include Abidjan, Cape Town, Kinshasa, Luanda, Mogadishu, Addis Ababa.

Economy

In the mid-2010s, private capital flows to Sub-Saharan Africa – primarily from the BRICs, private-sector investment portfolios, and remittances – began to exceed official development assistance.

As of 2011, Africa is one of the fastest developing regions in the world. Six of the world's ten fastest-growing economies over the previous decade were situated below the Sahara, with the remaining four in East and Central Asia. Between 2011 and 2015, the economic growth rate of the average nation in Africa is expected to surpass that of the average nation in Asia. Sub-Saharan

Figure 39: *The Athlone Power Station in Cape Town, South Africa*

Africa is by then projected to contribute seven out of the ten fastest growing economies in the world. According to the World Bank, the economic growth rate in the region had risen to 4.7% in 2013, with a rate of 5.2% forecasted for 2014. This continued rise was attributed to increasing investment in infrastructure and resources as well as steady expenditure per household.

Energy and power

Oil production by country

(with other key actors of African or oil economy)

Rank	Area	bb/day	Year	Like...
–	W: World	85540000	2007 est.	
01	E: Russia	9980000	2007 est.	
02	Ar: Saudi Arb	9200000	2008 est.	
04	As: Libya	4725000	2008 est.	Iran

10	Af: Nigeria/Africa	2352000	2011 est.	Norway
15	Af: Algeria	2173000	2007 est.	
16	Af: Angola	1910000	2008 est.	
17	Af: Egypt	1845000	2007 est.	
27	Af: Tunisia	664000	2007 est.	Australia
31	Af: Sudan	466100	2007 est.	Ecuador
33	Af: Eq.Guinea	368500	2007 est.	Vietnam
38	Af: DR Congo	261000	2008 est.	
39	Af: Gabon	243900	2007 est.	
40	Af: Sth Africa	199100	2007 est.	
45	Af: Chad	156000	2008 est.	Germany
53	Af: Cameroon	87400	2008 est.	France
56	E: France	71400	2007	
60	Af: Ivory Coast	54400	2008 est.	
–	**Af: Africa**	**10780400**	**2011**	**Russia**

Source: CIA.gov[149], World
Facts Book > Oil exporters.

As of 2009[150], fifty percent of Africa is rural with no access to electricity. Africa generates 47 GW of electricity, less than 0.6% of the global market share. Many countries are affected by power shortages.

Because of rising prices in commodities such as coal and oil, thermal sources of energy are proving to be too expensive for power generation. Sub-Saharan Africa is expected to build additional hydropower generation capacity of at least 20,165 MW by 2014. The region has the potential to generate 1,750 TWh of energy, of which only 7% has been explored. The failure to exploit its full energy potential is largely due to significant underinvestment, as at least four times as much (approximately $23 billion a year) and what is currently spent is invested in operating high cost power systems and not on expanding the infrastructure.

African governments are taking advantage of the readily available water resources to broaden their energy mix. Hydro Turbine Markets in Sub-Saharan Africa generated revenues of $120.0 million in 2007 and is estimated to reach $425.0 million.Wikipedia:Manual of Style/Dates and numbers#Chronological items Asian countries, notably China, India, and Japan, are playing an active role in power projects across the African continent. The majority of these power projects are hydro-based because of China's vast experience in the construction of hydro-power projects and part of the Energy & Power Growth Partnership Services programme.

With electrification numbers, Sub-Saharan Africa with access to the Sahara and being in the tropical zones has massive potential for solar photovoltaic electrical potential.[151] Six hundred million people could be served with electricity based on its photovoltaic potential.[152] China is promising to train 10,000 technicians from Africa and other developing countries in the use of solar energy technologies over the next five years. Training African technicians to use solar power is part of the China-Africa science and technology cooperation agreement signed by Chinese science minister Xu Guanhua and African counterparts during premier Wen Jiabao's visit to Ethiopia in December 2003.

The New Partnership for Africa's Development (NEPAD) is developing an integrated, continent-wide energy strategy. This has been funded by, amongst others, the African Development Bank (AfDB) and the EU-Africa Infrastructure Trust Fund. These projects must be sustainable, involve a cross-border dimension and/or have a regional impact, involve public and private capital, contribute to poverty alleviation and economic development, involve at least one country in Sub-Saharan Africa.

Media

Radio is the major source of information in Sub-Saharan Africa.[153] Average coverage stands at more than a third of the population. Countries such as Gabon, Seychelles, and South Africa boast almost 100% penetration. Only five countries – Burundi, Djibouti, Eritrea, Ethiopia, and Somalia – still have a penetration of less than 10%. Broadband penetration outside of South Africa has been limited where it is exorbitantly expensive.[154,155] Access to the internet via cell phones is on the rise.

Television is the second major source of information. Because of power shortages, the spread of television viewing has been limited. Eight percent have television, a total of 62 million. But those in the television industry view the region as an untapped green market. Digital television and pay for service are on the rise.[156]

Figure 40: *Skyline of Libreville, Gabon*

Infrastructure

According to researchers at the Overseas Development Institute, the lack of infrastructure in many developing countries represents one of the most significant limitations to economic growth and achievement of the Millennium Development Goals (MDGs).[157,158,158] Less than 40% of rural Africans live within two kilometers of an all-season road, the lowest level of rural accessibility in the developing world. Spending on roads averages just below 2% of GDP with varying degree among countries. This compares with 1% of GDP that is typical in industrialised countries, and 2–3% of GDP found in fast-growing emerging economies. Although the level of effort is high relative to the size of Africa's economies, it remains little in absolute terms, with low-income countries spending an average of about US$7 per capita per year.[159] Infrastructure investments and maintenance can be very expensive, especially in such as areas as landlocked, rural and sparsely populated countries in Africa.

Infrastructure investments contributed to Africa's growth, and increased investment is necessary to maintain growth and tackle poverty. The returns to investment in infrastructure are very significant, with on average 30–40% returns for telecommunications (ICT) investments, over 40% for electricity generation and 80% for roads.

In Africa, it is argued that in order to meet the MDGs by 2015 infrastructure investments would need to reach about 15% of GDP (around $93 billion a

Figure 41: *Downtown Luanda, Angola*

year). Currently, the source of financing varies significantly across sectors. Some sectors are dominated by state spending, others by overseas development aid (ODA) and yet others by private investors. In Sub-Saharan Africa, the state spends around $9.4 billion out of a total of $24.9 billion. In irrigation, SSA states represent almost all spending; in transport and energy a majority of investment is state spending; in ICT and water supply and sanitation, the private sector represents the majority of capital expenditure. Overall, aid, the private sector and non-OECD financiers between them exceed state spending. The private sector spending alone equals state capital expenditure, though the majority is focused on ICT infrastructure investments. External financing increased from $7 billion (2002) to $27 billion (2009). China, in particular, has emerged as an important investor.

Oil and minerals

The region is a major exporter to the world of gold, uranium, chromium, vanadium, antimony, coltan, bauxite, iron ore, copper and manganese. South Africa is a major exporter of manganese as well as chromium. A 2001 estimate is that 42% of the world's reserves of chromium may be found in South Africa. South Africa is the largest producer of platinum, with 80% of the total world's annual mine production and 88% of the world's platinum reserve. Sub-Saharan Africa produces 33% of the world's bauxite, with Guinea as the major supplier. Zambia is a major producer of copper. Democratic Republic

Figure 42: *Phenakite from the Jos Plateau, Plateau State, Nigeria*

of Congo is a major source of coltan. Production from Congo is very small but has 80% of proven reserves. Sub-saharan Africa is a major producer of gold, producing up to 30% of global production. Major suppliers are South Africa, Ghana, Zimbabwe, Tanzania, Guinea, and Mali. South Africa had been first in the world in terms of gold production since 1905, but in 2007 it moved to second place, according to GFMS, the precious metals consultancy. Uranium is major commodity from the region. Significant suppliers are Niger, Namibia, and South Africa. Namibia was the number one supplier from Sub-Saharan Africa in 2008. The region produces 49% of the world's diamonds.

By 2015, it is estimated that 25% of North American oil will be from Sub-Saharan Africa, ahead of the Middle East. Sub-Saharan Africa has been the focus of an intense race for oil by the West, China, India, and other emerging economies, even though it holds only 10% of proven oil reserves, less than the Middle East. This race has been referred to as the second Scramble for Africa. All reasons for this global scramble come from the reserves' economic benefits. Transportation cost is low and no pipelines have to be laid as in Central Asia. Almost all reserves are offshore, so political turmoil within the host country will not directly interfere with operations. Sub-Saharan oil is viscous, with a very low sulfur content. This quickens the refining process and effectively reduces costs. New sources of oil are being located in Sub-Saharan Africa

Figure 43: *Agricultural fields in Rwanda's Eastern Province*

more frequently than anywhere else. Of all new sources of oil, ⅓ are in Sub-Saharan Africa.[160]

Agriculture

Sub-Saharan Africa has more variety of grains than anywhere in the world. Between 13,000 and 11,000 BCE wild grains began to be collected as a source of food in the cataract region of the Nile, south of Egypt. The collecting of wild grains as source of food spread to Syria, parts of Turkey, and Iran by the eleventh millennium BCE. By the tenth and ninth millennia southwest Asians domesticated their wild grains, wheat, and barley after the notion of collecting wild grains spread from the Nile.[161]

Numerous crops have been domesticated in the region and spread to other parts of the world. These crops included sorghum, castor beans, coffee, cotton[162] okra, black-eyed peas, watermelon, gourd, and pearl millet. Other domesticated crops included teff, enset, African rice, yams, kola nuts, oil palm, and raffia palm.[163]

Domesticated animals include the guinea fowl and the donkey.

Agriculture represents 20% to 30% of GDP and 50% of exports. In some cases, 60% to 90% of the labor force are employed in agriculture. Most agricultural activity is subsistence farming. This has made agricultural activity vulnerable to climate change and global warming. Biotechnology has been

Figure 44: *The Naute Fruit Farm at the Naute*
Dam outside of Keetmanshoop, Namibia

advocated to create high yield, pest and environmentally resistant crops in the hands of small farmers. The Bill and Melinda Gates foundation is a strong advocate and donor to this cause. Biotechnology and GM crops have met resistance both by natives and environmental groups.[164]

Cash crops include cotton, coffee, tea, cocoa, sugar, and tobacco.

The OECD says Africa has the potential to become an agricultural superbloc if it can unlock the wealth of the savannahs by allowing farmers to use their land as collateral for credit. There is such international interest in Sub-Saharan agriculture, that the World Bank increased its financing of African agricultural programs to $1.3 billion in the 2011 fiscal year. Recently, there has been a trend to purchase large tracts of land in Sub-Sahara for agricultural use by developing countries. Early in 2009, George Soros highlighted a new farmland buying frenzy caused by growing population, scarce water supplies and climate change. Chinese interests bought up large swathes of Senegal to supply it with sesame. Aggressive moves by China, South Korea and Gulf states to buy vast tracts of agricultural land in Sub-Saharan Africa could soon be limited by a new global international protocol.

Figure 45: *The University of Botswana's Earth*
Science building in Gaborone, Botswana

Education

Forty percent of African scientists live in OECD countries, predominantly in Europe, the United States and Canada. This has been described as an African brain drain.Wikipedia:Citation needed According to Naledi Pandor, the South African Minister of Science and Technology, even with the drain enrollments in Sub-Saharan African universities tripled between 1991 and 2005, expanding at an annual rate of 8.7%, which is one of the highest regional growth rates in the world.Wikipedia:Citation needed In the last 10 to 15 years interest in pursuing university level degrees abroad has increased. In some OECD countries, like the United States, Sub-Saharan Africans are the most educated immigrant group.

According to the CIA, low global literacy rates are concentrated in Sub-Saharan Africa, West Asia and South Asia. However, the literacy rates in Sub-Saharan Africa vary significantly between countries. The highest registered literacy rate in the region is in Zimbabwe (90.7%; 2003 est.), while the lowest literacy rate is in South Sudan (27%).

Sub-Saharan African countries spent an average of 0.3% of their GDP on science and technology on in 2007. This represents an increase from US$1.8 billion in 2002 to US$2.8 billion in 2007, a 50% increase in spending.

Figure 46: *The University of Antananarivo in Antananarivo, Madagascar*

Major progress in access to education

At the World Conference held in Jomtien, Thailand in 1990, delegates from 155 countries and representatives of some 150 organizations gathered with the goal to promote universal primary education and the radical reduction of illiteracy before the end of the decade. The World Education Forum, held ten years later in Dakar, Senegal, provided the opportunity to reiterate and reinforce these goals. This initiative contributed to having education made a priority of the Millennium Development Goals in 2000, with the aim of achieving universal schooling (MDG2) and eliminating gender disparities, especially in primary and secondary education (MDG3).[165] Since the World Education Forum in Dakar, considerable efforts have been made to respond to these demographic challenges in terms of education. The amount of funds raised has been decisive. Between 1999 and 2010, public spending on education as a percentage of gross national product (GNP) increased by 5% per year in sub-Saharan Africa, with major variations between countries, with percentages varying from 1.8% in Cameroon to over 6% in Burundi.[166] As of 2015, governments in sub-Saharan Africa spend on average 18% of their total budget on education, against 15% in the rest of the world.

In the years immediately after the Dakar Forum, the efforts made by African States towards achieving EFA produced multiple results in sub-Saharan Africa.

The greatest advance was in access to primary education, which governments had made their absolute priority. The number of children in primary school in sub-Saharan Africa thus rose from 82 million in 1999 to 136.4 million in 2011. In Niger for example, the number of children entering school increased more than three and a half times between 1999 and 2011. In Ethiopia, over the same period, over 8.5 million more children were admitted to primary school. The net rate of first year access in sub-Saharan Africa has thus risen by 19 points in 12 years, from 58% in 1999 to 77% in 2011. Despite the considerable efforts, the latest available data from the UNESCO Institute for Statistics estimates that, for 2012, there were still 57.8 million children who were not in school. Of these, 29.6 million were in sub-Saharan Africa alone, a figure which has not changed for several years. Many sub-Saharan countries have notably included the first year of secondary school in basic education. In Rwanda, the first year of secondary school was attached to primary education in 2009, which significantly increased the number of pupils enrolled at this level of education.[167,168] In 2012 the primary completion rate (PCR) – which measures the proportion of children reaching the final year of primary school – was 70%, meaning that more than three out of ten children entering primary school do not reach the final primary year.

Health

In 1987, the Bamako Initiative conference organized by the World Health Organization was held in Bamako, the capital of Mali, and helped reshape the health policy of Sub-Saharan Africa. The new strategy dramatically increased accessibility through community-based healthcare reform, resulting in more efficient and equitable provision of services. A comprehensive approach strategy was extended to all areas of health care, with subsequent improvement in the health care indicators and improvement in health care efficiency and cost.

In 2011, Sub-Saharan Africa was home to 69% of all people living with HIV/AIDS worldwide. In response, a number of initiatives have been launched to educate the public on HIV/AIDS. Among these are combination prevention programmes, considered to be the most effective initiative, the abstinence, be faithful, use a condom campaign, and the Desmond Tutu HIV Foundation's outreach programs. According to a 2013 special report issued by the Joint United Nations Programme on HIV/AIDS (UNAIDS), the number of HIV positive people in Africa receiving anti-retroviral treatment in 2012 was over seven times the number receiving treatment in 2005, with an almost 1 million added in the last year alone.[15] The number of AIDS-related deaths in Sub-Saharan Africa in 2011 was 33 percent less than the number in 2005. The number of new HIV infections in Sub-Saharan Africa in 2011 was 25 percent less than the number in 2001.

Figure 47: *The Komfo Anokye Hospital in Kumasi, Ghana*

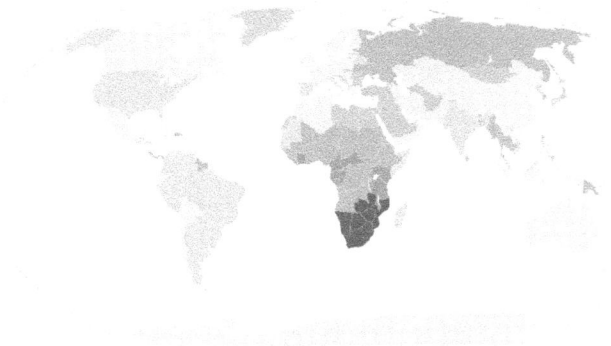

Figure 48: *Estimated prevalence in % of HIV among young adults (15–49) per country as of 2011.*

Malaria is an endemic illness in Sub-Saharan Africa, where the majority of malaria cases and deaths worldwide occur. Routine immunization has been introduced in order to prevent measles. Onchocerciasis ("river blindness"), a common cause of blindness, is also endemic to parts of the region. More than 99% of people affected by the illness worldwide live in 31 countries therein. In response, the African Programme for Onchocerciasis Control (APOC) was launched in 1995 with the aim of controlling the disease. Maternal mortality is another challenge, with more than half of maternal deaths in the world occurring in Sub-Saharan Africa. However, there has generally been progress here as well, as a number of countries in the region have halved their levels of maternal mortality since 1990. Additionally, the African Union in July 2003 ratified the Maputo Protocol, which pledges to prohibit female genital mutilation (FGM).[169]

National health systems vary between countries. In Ghana, most health care is provided by the government and largely administered by the Ministry of Health and Ghana Health Services. The healthcare system has five levels of providers: health posts which are first level primary care for rural areas, health centers and clinics, district hospitals, regional hospitals and tertiary hospitals. These programs are funded by the government of Ghana, financial credits, Internally Generated Fund (IGF), and Donors-pooled Health Fund.

Religion

African countries below the Sahara are largely Christian, while those above the Sahara, in North Africa, are predominantly Islamic. There are also Muslim majorities in parts of the Horn of Africa (Djibouti and Somalia) and in the Sahel and Sudan regions (the Gambia, Sierra Leone, Guinea, Mali, Niger and Senegal), as well as significant Muslim communities in Ethiopia and Eritrea, and on the Swahili Coast (Tanzania and Kenya).[170] Mauritius is the only country in Africa to have a Hindu majority.

Traditional African religions can be broken down into linguistic cultural groups, with common themes. Among Niger–Congo-speakers is a belief in a creator God; ancestor spirits; territorial spirits; evil caused by human ill will and neglecting ancestor spirits; priest of territorial spirits. New world religions such as Santería, Vodun, and Candomblé, would be derived from this world view. Among Nilo-Saharan speakers is the belief in Divinity; evil is caused by divine judgement and retribution; prophets as middlemen between Divinity and man. Among Afro-Asiatic-speakers is henotheism, the belief in one's own gods but accepting the existence of other gods; evil here is caused by malevolent spirits. The Semitic Abrahamic religion of Judaism is comparable to

Figure 49: *The Bujumbura Cathedral in Bujumbura, Burundi*

Figure 50: *Mosque in Nouakchott, Mauritania*

Sixteen Principal Odu

Name	1	2	3	4
Ogbe	I	I	I	I
Oyeku	II	II	II	II
Iwori	II	I	I	II
Odi	I	II	II	I
Irosun	I	I	II	II
Iwonrin	II	II	I	I
Obara	I	II	II	II
Okanran	II	II	II	I
Ogunda	II	I	I	II
Osa	II	I	I	I
Ika	II	I	II	II
Oturupon	II	II	I	II
Otura	I	II	I	I
Irete	I	I	II	I
Ose	I	II	I	II
Ofun	II	I	II	I

Figure 51: *Ifá divination and its four digit binary code*

the latter world view.[171] San religion is non-theistic but a belief in a Spirit or Power of existence which can be tapped in a trance-dance; trance-healers.[172]

Traditional religions in Sub-Saharan Africa often display complex ontology, cosmology and metaphysics. Mythologies, for example, demonstrated the difficulty fathers of creation had in bringing about order from chaos. Order is what is right and natural and any deviation is chaos. Cosmology and ontology is also neither simple or linear. It defines duality, the material and immaterial, male and female, heaven and earth. Common principles of being and becoming are widespread: Among the Dogon, the principle of *Amma* (being) and *Nummo* (becoming), and among the Bambara, *Pemba* (being) and *Faro* (becoming).[173]

West Africa

- Akan mythology
- Ashanti mythology (Ghana)
- Dahomey (Fon) mythology
- Efik mythology (Nigeria, Cameroon)
- Igbo mythology (Nigeria, Cameroon)
- Serer religion and Serer creation myth (Senegal, Gambia and Mauritania)
- Yoruba mythology (Nigeria, Benin)

Central Africa

- Dinka mythology (South Sudan)
- Lotuko mythology (South Sudan)
- Bushongo mythology (Congo)
- Bambuti (Pygmy) mythology (Congo)
- Lugbara mythology (Congo)

Southeast Africa

- Akamba mythology (eastern Kenya)
- Masai mythology (Kenya, Tanzania)

Southern Africa

- Khoisan religion
- Lozi mythology (Zambia)
- Tumbuka mythology (Malawi)
- Zulu mythology (South Africa)

Sub-Saharan traditional divination systems display great sophistication. For example, the bamana sand divination uses well established symbolic codes that can be reproduced using four bits or marks. A binary system of one or two marks are combined. Random outcomes are generated using a fractal recursive process. It is analogous to a digital circuit but can be reproduced on any surface with one or two marks. This system is widespread in Sub-Saharan Africa.[174]Wikipedia:Citing sources

Culture

Sub-Saharan Africa is diverse, with many communities, villages and cities, each with their own beliefs and traditions. Traditional African Societies are communal, they believe that the needs of the many far out weigh an individual needs and achievements. Basically, an individual's keep must be shared with other extended family members. Extended families are made up of various individuals and families who have shared responsibilities within the community. This extended family is one of the core aspects of every African community. "An African will refer to an older person as auntie or uncle. Siblings of parents will be called father or mother rather than uncle and aunt. Cousins will be called brother or sister". This system can be very difficult for outsiders to understand; however, it is no less important. "Also reflecting their communal ethic, Africans are reluctant to stand out in a crowd or to appear different from their neighbors or colleagues, a result of social pressure to avoid offense to group standards and traditions." Women also have a very important role in African culture because they take care of the house and children. Traditionally "men do the heavy work of clearing and plowing the land, women sow

Figure 52: *A traditional polyrhythmic kalimba*

the seeds, tend the fields, harvest the crops, haul the water, and bear the major burden for growing the family's food". Despite their work in the fields women are expected to be subservient to men in some African cultures. "When young women migrate to cities, this imbalance between the sexes, as well as financial need, often causes young women of lower economic status, who lack education and job training, to have sexual relationships with older men who are established in their work or profession and can afford to support a girlfriend or two".

Music

Traditional Sub-Saharan African music is as diverse as the region's various populations. The common perception of Sub-Saharan African music is that it is rhythmic music centered around the drums. It is partially true. A large part of Sub-Saharan music, mainly among speakers of Niger–Congo and Nilo-Saharan languages, is rhythmic and centered around the drum. Sub-Saharan music is polyrhythmic, usually consisting of multiple rhythms in one composition. Dance involves moving multiple body parts. These aspect of Sub-Saharan music has been transferred to the new world by enslaved Sub-Saharan Africans and can be seen in its influence on music forms as Samba, Jazz, Rhythm and Blues, Rock & Roll, Salsa, Reggae and Rap music.[175]

Figure 53: *Two Bambara Chiwara c. late 19th early 20th centuries. Female (left) and male Vertical styles.*

But Sub-Saharan music involves a lot of music with strings, horns, and very little poly-rhythms. Music from the eastern sahel and along the nile, among the Nilo-Saharan, made extensive use of strings and horns in ancient times. Among the Afro-Asiatics, we see extensive use of string instruments. Dancing involve swaying body movements and footwork. Among the San is extensive use of string instruments with emphasis on footwork.[176]

Modern Sub-Saharan African music has been influence by music from the New World (Jazz, Salsa, Rhythm and Blues etc.) vice versa being influenced by enslaved Sub-Saharan Africans. Popular styles are Mbalax in Senegal and Gambia, Highlife in Ghana, Zoblazo in Ivory Coast, Makossa in Cameroon, Soukous in the Democratic Republic of Congo, Kizomba in Angola, and Mbaqanga in South Africa. New World styles like Salsa, R&B/Rap, Reggae, and Zouk also have widespread popularity.

Art

The oldest abstract art in the world is a shell necklace, dated to 82,000 years in the Cave of Pigeons in Taforalt, eastern Morocco. The second oldest abstract form of art and the oldest rock art is found in the Blombos Cave at the Cape in

South Africa, dated 77,000 years. Sub-Saharan Africa has some of the oldest and most varied style of rock art in the world.

Although Sub-Saharan African art is very diverse there are some common themes. One is the use of the human figure. Second, there is a preference for sculpture. Sub-Saharan African art is meant to be experienced in three dimensions, not two. A house is meant to be experienced from all angles. Third, art is meant to be performed. Sub-Saharan Africans have specific name for masks. The name incorporates the sculpture, the dance, and the spirit that incorporates the mask. The name denotes all three elements. Fourth, art that serves a practical function, utilitarian. The artist and craftsman are not separate. A sculpture shaped like a hand can be used as a stool. Fifth, the use of fractals or non-linear scaling. The shape of the whole is the shape of the parts at different scales. Before the discovery of fractal geometry], Leopold Sedar Senghor, Senegal's first president, referred to this as "dynamic symmetry." William Fagg, the British art historian, compared it to the logarithmic mapping of natural growth by biologist D'Arcy Thompson. Lastly, Sub-Saharan African art is visually abstract, instead of naturalistic. Sub-Saharan African art represents spiritual notions, social norms, ideas, values, etc. An artist might exaggerated the head of a sculpture in relations to the body not because he does not know anatomy but because he wants to illustrate that the head is the seat of knowledge and wisdom. The visual abstraction of African art was very influential in the works of modernist[177] artist like Pablo Picasso, Henri Matisse, and Jacques Lipchitz.[178]

Cuisine

Sub-Saharan African cuisine like everything about Africa is very diverse. A lot of regional overlapping occurs, but there are dominant elements region by region.

West African cuisine can be described as starchy, flavorfully spicey. Dishes include fufu, kenkey, couscous, garri, foutou, and banku. Ingredients are of native starchy tubers, yams, cocoyams, and cassava. Grains include millet, sorghum, and rice, usually in the sahel, are incorporated. Oils include palm oil and shea butter(sahel). One finds recipes that mixes fish and meat. Beverages are palm wine(sweet or sour) and millet beer. Roasting, baking, boiling, frying, mashing, and spicing are all cooking techniques.

Southeast African cuisine especially those of the Swahilis reflects its Islamic, geographical Indian Ocean cultural links. Dishes include ugali, sukuma wiki, and halva. Spices such as curry, saffron, cloves, cinnamon, pomegranate juice, cardamon, ghee, and sage are used, especially among Muslims. Meat includes

Figure 54: *A plate of fufu accompanied with peanut soup*

Figure 55: *Ugali and cabbage*

Figure 56: *This meal, consisting of injera and several kinds of wat (stew), is typical of Ethiopian and Eritrean cuisine.*

cattle, sheep, and goats, but is rarely eaten since its viewed as currency and wealth.

In the Horn of Africa, pork and non-fish seafood is avoided by Christians and Muslims. Dairy products and all meats are avoided during lent by Ethiopians. Maize (corn) is a major staple. Cornmeal is used to make ugali, a popular dish with different names. Teff is used to make injera or canjeero (Somali) bread. Other important foods include enset, noog, lentils, rice, banana, leafy greens, chiles, peppers, coconut milk and tomatoes. Beverages are coffee (domesticated in Ethiopia), chai tea, fermented beer from banana or millet. Cooking techniques include roasting and marinating.

Central African cuisine connects with all major regions of Sub-Saharan Africa: Its cuisine reflects that. Ugali and fufu are eaten in the region. Central African cuisine is very starchy and spicy hot. Dominant crops include plantains, cassava, peanuts, chillis, and okra. Meats include beef, chicken, and sometimes exotic meats called bush meat (antelope, warthog, crocodile). Widespread spicy hot fish cuisine is one of the differentiating aspects. Mushroom is sometimes used as a meat substitute.

Traditional Southern African cuisine surrounds meat. Traditional society typically focused on raising, sheep, goats, and especially cattle. Dishes include

Figure 57: *The Ashanti Kente cloth patterns*

braai (barbecue meat), sadza, bogobe, pap (fermented cornmeal), milk products (buttermilk, yoghurt). Crops utilised are sorghum, maize (corn), pumpkin beans, leafy greens, and cabbage. Beverages include ting (fermented sorghum or maize), milk, chibuku (milky beer). Influences from the Indian and Malay community can be seen its use of curries, sambals, pickled fish, fish stews, chutney, and samosa. European influences can be seen in cuisines like biltong (dried beef strips), potjies (stews of maize, onions, tomatoes), French wines, and crueler or koeksister (sugar syrup cookie).

Clothing

Like most of the world, Sub-Saharan Africans have adopted Western-style clothing. In some country like Zambia, used Western clothing has flooded markets, causing great angst in the retail community. Sub-Saharan Africa boasts its own traditional clothing style[179]. Cotton seems to be the dominant material.

In East Africa, one finds extensive use of cotton clothing. Shemma, shama, and kuta are types of Ethiopian clothing. Kanga are Swahili cloth that comes in rectangular shapes, made of pure cotton, and put together to make clothing. Kitenges are similar to kangas and kikoy, but are of a thicker cloth, and have an edging only on a long side. Kenya, Uganda, Tanzania, and South Sudan are

Figure 58: *Kangas*

some of the African countries where kitenge is worn. In Malawi, Namibia and Zambia, kitenge is known as Chitenge. One of the unique materials, which is not a fiber and is used to make clothing is barkcloth, an innovation of the Baganda people of Uganda. It came from the Mutuba tree (Ficus natalensis).[180] On Madagascar a type of draped cloth called lamba is worn.

In West Africa, again cotton is the material of choice. In the Sahel and other parts of West Africa the boubou and kaftan style of clothing are featured. Kente cloth is created by the Akan people of Ghana and Ivory Coast, from silk of the various moth species in West Africa. Kente comes from the Ashanti twi word *kenten* which means basket. It is sometimes used to make dashiki and kufi. Adire is a type of Yoruba cloth that is starch resistant. Raffia cloth[181] and barkcloth are also utilised in the region.

In Central Africa, the Kuba people developed raffia cloth from the raffia plant fibers. It was widely used in the region. Barkcloth was also extensively used.

In Southern Africa one finds numerous uses of animal hide and skins for clothing. The Ndau in central Mozambique and the Shona mix hide with barkcloth and cotton cloth. Cotton cloth is referred to as machira. Xhosa, Tswana, Sotho, and Swazi also made extensive use of hides. Hides come from cattle, sheep, goat, and elephant. Leopard skins were coveted and were a symbol of kingship

Figure 59: *The Stade Félix Houphouët-Boigny in Abidjan, Ivory Coast*

in Zulu society. Skins were tanned to form leather, dyed, and embedded with beads.

Sports

Football (soccer) is the most popular sport in Sub-Saharan Africa. Sub-Saharan men are its main patrons. Major competitions include the African Champions League, a competition for the best clubs on the continent and the Confederation Cup, a competition primarily for the national cup winner of each African country. The Africa Cup of Nations is a competition of 16 national teams from various African countries held every two years. South Africa hosted the 2010 FIFA World Cup, a first for a Sub-Saharan country. In 2010, Cameroon played in the World Cup for the sixth time, which is the current record for a Sub-Saharan team. In 1996 Nigeria won the Olympic gold for football. In 2000 Cameroon maintained the continent's supremacy by winning the title too. Momentous achievements for Sub-Saharan African football. Famous Sub-Saharan football stars include Abedi Pele, Emmanuel Adebayor, George Weah, Michael Essien, Didier Drogba, Roger Milla, Nwankwo Kanu, Jay-Jay Okocha, Bruce Grobbelaar, Samuel Eto'o, Kolo Touré, Yaya Touré, Sadio Mané and Pierre-Emerick Aubameyang. The most talented Sub-Saharan African football players find themselves courted and sought after by

Figure 60: *The Namibia rugby team*

European leagues. There are currently more than 1000 Africans playing for European clubs. Sub-Saharan Africans have found themselves the target of racism by European fans. FIFA has been trying hard to crack down on racist outburst during games.

Rugby is also popular in Sub-Saharan Africa. The Confederation of African Rugby governs rugby games in the region. South Africa is a major force in the game and won the Rugby World Cup in 1995 and in 2007. Africa is also allotted one guaranteed qualifying place in the Rugby World Cup.

Boxing is also a popular sport. Battling Siki the first world champion to come out of Sub-Saharan Africa. Countries such as Nigeria, Ghana and South Africa have produced numerous professional world champions such as Dick Tiger, Hogan Bassey, Gerrie Coetzee, Samuel Peter, Azumah Nelson and Jake Matlala.

Cricket has a following. The African Cricket Association is an international body which oversees cricket in African countries. South Africa and Zimbabwe have their own governing bodies. In 2003 the Cricket World Cup was held in South Africa, first time it was held in Sub-Saharan Africa.

Over the years, Ethiopia and Kenya have produced many notable long-distance athletes. Each country has federations that identify and cultivate top talent. Athletes from Ethiopia and Kenya hold, save for two exceptions, all the men's

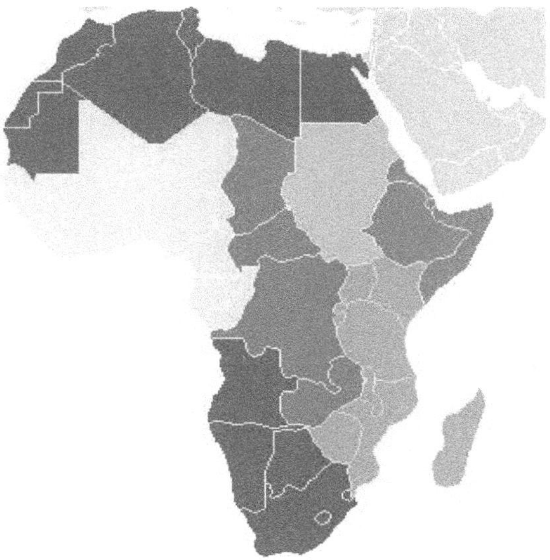

Figure 61: *Geo-political map of Africa divided for eth-nomusicological purposes, after Alan P. Merriam, 1959.*

outdoor records for Olympic distance events from 800m to the marathon.[182] Famous runners include Haile Gebrselassie, Kenenisa Bekele, Paul Tergat, and John Cheruiyot Korir.[183]

Tourism

The development of tourism in this region has been identified as having the ability to create jobs and improve the economy. South Africa, Namibia, Mauritius, Botswana, Ghana, Cape Verde, Tanzania, and Kenya have been identified as having well developed tourism industries. Cape Town and the surrounding area is very popular with tourists.

List of countries and regional organization

Only seven African countries are not geopolitically a part of Sub-Saharan Africa: Algeria, Egypt, Libya, Morocco, Tunisia, Western Sahara (claimed by Morocco) and Sudan; they form the UN subregion of Northern Africa, which also makes up the largest bloc of the Arab World. Nevertheless, some international organisations include Sudan as part of Sub-Saharan Africa. Although a long-standing member of the Arab League, Sudan has around 30%

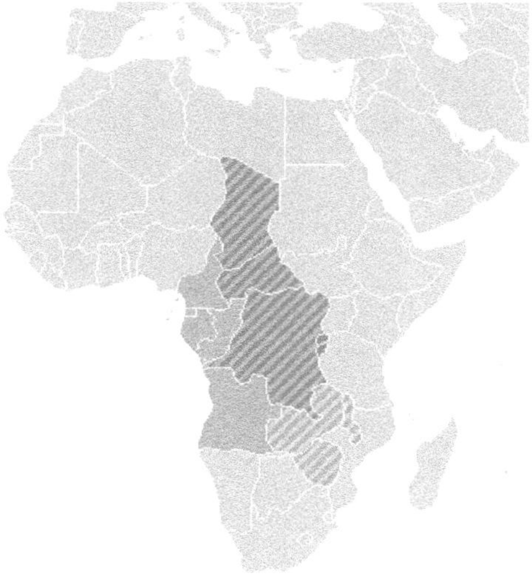

Figure 62:
Central Africa
Middle Africa (UN subregion)
Central African Federation (defunct)

non-Arab populations in the west (Darfur, Masalit, Zaghawa), far north (Nubian) and south (Kordofan, Nuba).[184,185] Mauritania and Niger only include a band of the Sahel along their southern borders. All other African countries have at least significant portions of their territory within Sub-Saharan Africa.

Central Africa

*   South Sudan *cap.* Juba *cur.* Sudanese pound (SDG) *lang.* English

ECCAS (Economic Community of Central African States)

*   Angola (also in SADC) *cap.* Luanda *cur.* Angolan kwanza (Kz) *lang.* Portuguese
*   Burundi (also in EAC) *cap.* Bujumbura *cur.* Burundian franc (FBu) *lang.* French
*   Democratic Republic of the Congo (also in SADC) *cap.* Kinshasa *cur.* Congolese franc (FC) *lang.* French
*   Rwanda (also in EAC) *cap.* Kigali *cur.* Rwandan franc (RF) *lang.* Kinyarwanda, French, English
*   São Tomé and Príncipe *cap.* São Tomé *cur.* São Tomé and Príncipe dobra (Db) *lang.* Portuguese

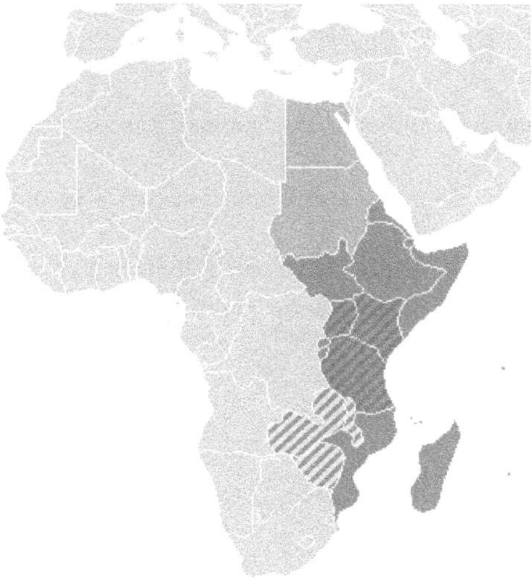

Figure 63:
Eastern Africa (UN subregion)
East African Community
Central African Federation (defunct)
Geographic East Africa, including the UN subregion and East African Community

CEMAC (Economic and Monetary Community of Central Africa)

- Cameroon *cap.* Yaoundé *cur.* Central African CFA franc (FCFA) *lang.* English, French
- Central African Republic *cap.* Bangui *cur.* Central African CFA franc (FCFA) *lang.* Sango, French
- Chad *cap.* N'Djamena *cur.* Central African CFA franc (FCFA) *lang.* French, Arabic
- Republic of the Congo *cap.* Brazzaville *cur.* Central African CFA franc (FCFA) *lang.* French
- Equatorial Guinea *cap.* Malabo *cur.* Central African CFA franc (FCFA) *lang.* Spanish, French
- Gabon *cap.* Libreville *cur.* Central African CFA franc (FCFA) *lang.* French

East Africa

Horn of Africa

- ▨ Djibouti *cap.* Djibouti *cur.* Djiboutian franc (Fdj) *lang.* Arabic, French
- ▨ Eritrea *cap.* Asmara *cur.* Eritrean nakfa (Nfk) *lang.*' Tigrinya, Arabic, Italian, English
- ▨ Ethiopia *cap.* Addis Ababa *cur.* Ethiopian birr (Br) *lang.* Amharic
- ▨ Somalia *cap.* Mogadishu *cur.* Somali shilling (So.Sh) *lang.* Somali, Arabic

Southeast Africa

EAC

- ▨ Burundi (also in ECCAS) *cap.* Bujumbura *cur.* Burundian franc (FBu) *lang.* Kirundi, French
- ▨ Kenya *cap.* Nairobi *cur.* Kenyan shilling (KSh) *lang.* Swahili, English
- ▨ Rwanda (also in ECCAS) *cap.* Kigali *cur.* Rwandan franc (RF) *lang.* Kinyarwanda, French, English
- ▨ Tanzania (also in SADC) *cap.* Dodoma *cur.* Tanzanian shilling (TSh) *lang.* Swahili, English
- ▨ Uganda *cap.* Kampala *cur.* Ugandan shilling (USh) *lang.* Swahili, English

Southern Africa

SADC (Southern African Development Community)

- ▨ Angola (also in ECCAS) *cap.* Luanda *cur.* Angolan kwanza (Kz) *lang.* Portuguese
- ▨ Botswana *cap.* Gaborone *cur.* Botswana pula (P) *lang.* Tswana, English
- ▨ Comoros *cap.* Moroni *cur.* Comorian franc (CF) *lang.* Comorian, Arabic, French
- ▨ Lesotho *cap.* Maseru *cur.* Lesotho loti (L)(M) *lang.* Sesotho, English
- Madagascar *cap.* Antananarivo *cur.* Malagasy ariary (MGA) *lang.* Malagasy, French
- ▨ Malawi *cap.* Lilongwe *cur.* Malawian kwacha (MK) *lang.* English
- ▨ Mauritius *cap.* Port Louis *cur.* Mauritian rupee (R) *lang.* English
- ▨ Mozambique *cap.* Maputo *cur.* Mozambican metical (MTn) *lang.* Portuguese
- ▨ Namibia *cap.* Windhoek *cur.* Namibian dollar (N$) *lang.* English
- ▨ Seychelles *cap.* Victoria *cur.* Seychellois rupee (SR)(SRe) *lang.* Seychellois Creole, English, French

Figure 64:
Southern Africa (UN subregion)
geographic, including above
Southern African Development Community (SADC)

- ▶ South Africa *cap.* Bloemfontein, Cape Town, Pretoria *cur.* South African rand (R) *lang.* 11 official languages
- ▶ Swaziland *cap.* Mbabane *cur.* Swazi lilangeni (L)(E) *lang.* SiSwati, English
- ▶ Zambia *cap.* Lusaka *cur.* Zambian kwacha (ZK) *lang.* English
- ▶ Zimbabwe *cap.* Harare *cur.* Zimbabwean dollar ($) *lang.* English

Sudan

Depending on classification Sudan is often not considered part of Sub-Saharan Africa, as it is considered part of North Africa.

- ▶ Sudan *cap.* Khartoum *cur.* Sudanese pound (SDG) *lang.* Arabic and English

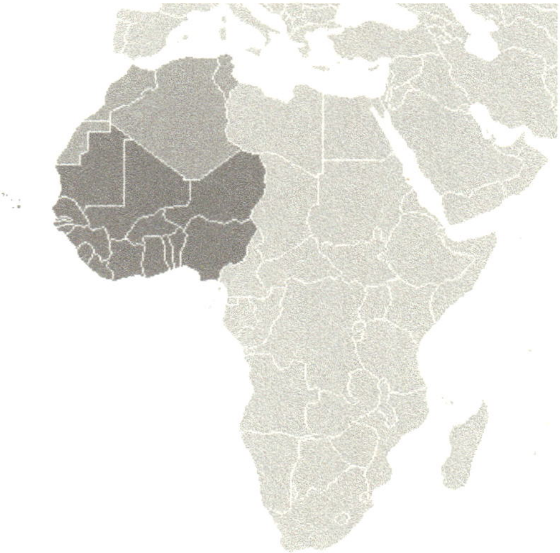

Figure 65:
Western Africa (UN subregion)
Maghreb

West Africa

- 🏳️ Mauritania *cap.* Nouakchott *cur.* Mauritanian ouguiya (UM)(sometimes, like Sudan, considered part of North Africa)

ECOWAS (Economic Community of West African States)

- 🏳️ Ivory Coast *cap.* Abidjan, Yamoussoukro *cur.* West African CFA franc (CFA)
- 🏳️ The Gambia *cap.* Banjul *cur.* Gambian dalasi (D)
- 🏳️ Ghana *cap.* Accra *cur.* Ghanaian cedi (GH₵)
- 🏳️ Guinea *cap.* Conakry *cur.* Guinean franc (FG)
- 🏳️ Liberia *cap.* Monrovia *cur.* Liberian dollar (L$)
- 🏳️ Nigeria *cap.* Abuja *cur.* Nigerian naira (N)
- 🏳️ Sierra Leone *cap.* Freetown *cur.* Sierra Leonean leone (Le)

UEMOA (West African Economic and Monetary Union)

- 🏳️ Benin *cap.* Porto-Novo *cur.* West African CFA franc (CFA)
- 🏳️ Burkina Faso *cap.* Ouagadougou *cur.* West African CFA franc (CFA)
- 🏳️ Ivory Coast *cap.* Abidjan, Yamoussoukro *cur.* West African CFA franc (CFA)

- ▬ Guinea-Bissau *cap.* Bissau *cur.* West African CFA franc (CFA)
- ▨ Mali *cap.* Bamako *cur.* West African CFA franc (CFA)
- ▭ Niger *cap.* Niamey *cur.* West African CFA franc (CFA)
- ▊·▊ Senegal *cap.* Dakar *cur.* West African CFA franc (CFA)
- ▤ Togo *cap.* Lomé *cur.* West African CFA franc (CFA)

Sources

☉ This article incorporates text from a free content work. Licensed under CC-BY-SA License statement[186]: *Digital Services for Education in Africa*[187], Agence Française de Développement, Agence universitaire de la Francophonie, Orange & UNESCO, Agence Française de Développement & UNESCO. To learn how to add open license text to Wikipedia articles, please see Wikipedia:Adding open license text to Wikipedia. For information on reusing text from Wikipedia, please see the terms of use.

References

- *Taking Action to Reduce Poverty in Sub-Saharan Africa*, World Bank Publications (1997), ISBN 0-8213-3698-3.

Further reading

- Chido, Diane E. From Chaos to Cohesion: A Regional Approach to Security, Stability, and Development in Sub-Saharan Africa.[188] Carlisle, Pa.: Strategic Studies Institute and U.S. Army War College Press, 2013.
- Petringa, Maria: *Brazza, A Life for Africa*. Bloomington, Indiana: AuthorHouse, 2006. ISBN 978-1-4259-1198-0
- Wm. Roger Louis and Jean Stengers: *E.D. Morel's History of the Congo Reform Movement*, Clarendon Press Oxford, 1968.

External links

- African People Website[189]
- 50 Factoids about Sub-Saharan Africa[190]
- The Story of Africa – BBC World Service[191]

Early northern Africa dispersal

Recent African origin of modern humans

In paleoanthropology, the **recent African origin of modern humans**, also called the "**Out of Africa**" **theory** (**OOA**), **recent single-origin hypothesis** (**RSOH**), **replacement hypothesis**, or **recent African origin model** (**RAO**), is the dominant model of the geographic origin and early migration of anatomically modern humans (*Homo sapiens*).

The model proposes a "single origin" of *Homo sapiens* in the taxonomic sense, precluding parallel evolution of traits considered anatomically modern in other regions, but not precluding limited admixture between *H. sapiens* and archaic humans in Europe and Asia.[192] *H. sapiens* most likely developed in the Horn of Africa between 300,000 and 200,000 years ago. The "recent African origin" model proposes that all modern non-African populations are substantially descended from populations of *H. sapiens* that left Africa after that time.

There were at least several "out-of-Africa" dispersals of modern humans, possibly beginning as early as 270,000 years ago, and certainly during 130,000 to 115,000 ago via northern Africa. These early waves appear to have mostly died out or retreated by 80,000 years ago.[193]

The most significant "recent" wave took place about 70,000 years ago, via the so-called "Southern Route", spreading rapidly along the coast of Asia and reaching Australia by around 65,000–50,000 years ago.[194] while Europe was populated by an early offshoot which settled the Near East and Europe less than 55,000 years ago.[195,196]

■	170 - 130
■	70 - 60
▦	50 - 40
▨	35 - 25
▦	15 - 12
▦	9 - 7

Figure 66: *Map of the migration of modern humans out of Africa, based on mitochondrial DNA. Colored rings indicate thousand years before present.*

In the 2010s, studies in population genetics have uncovered evidence of interbreeding of *H. sapiens* with archaic humans both in Africa and in Eurasia, which means that all modern population groups, both African and non-African, while mostly derived from early *H. sapiens*, to a lesser extent are also descended from regional variants of archaic humans.

Proposed waves

> *See Early hominin expansions out of Africa for archaic humans (*H. erectus, H. heidelbergensis, Neanderthals, Denisovans).

"Recent African origin," or *Out of Africa II*, refers to the migration of anatomically modern humans (*Homo sapiens*) out of Africa after their emergence at c. 300,000 to 200,000 years ago, in contrast to "Out of Africa I", the migration of archaic humans from Africa to Eurasia between roughly 1.8 to 0.5 million years ago.

Since the early 21st century, the picture of "recent single-origin" migrations has become significantly more complex, not just due to the discovery of modern-archaic admixture but also due to the increasing evidence that the "recent out-of-Africa" migration took place in a number of waves spread over a long time period. As of 2010, there were two main accepted dispersal routes for the out-of-Africa migration of early anatomically modern humans: via the "Northern Route" (via Nile Valley and Sinai) and the "Southern Route" via the Bab al Mandab strait.[197]

- Posth et al. (2017) suggest that early *Homo sapiens*, or "another species in Africa closely related to us," might have first migrated out of Africa around 270,000 years ago.[198]
- Finds at Misliya cave, which include a partial jawbone with eight teeth have been dated to around 185,000 years ago. Layers dating from between 250,000 and 140,000 years ago in the same cave contained tools of the Levallois type which could put the date of the first migration even earlier if the tools can be associated with the modern human jawbone finds.
- An Eastward Dispersal from Northeast Africa to Arabia during 150–130 kya based on the finds at Jebel Faya dated to 127 kya (discovered in 2011). Possibly related to this wave are the finds from Zhirendong cave, Southern China, dated to more than 100 kya.[197] Other evidence of modern human presence in China has been dated to 80,000 years ago.
- The most significant dispersal took place around 70,000 years ago via the so-called Southern Route, either before[199] or after the Toba event, which happened between 69,000 and 77,000 years ago.[199] This dispersal followed the southern coastline of Asia, and reached Australia around 65,000-50,000 years ago. Western Asia was "re-occupied" by a different derivation from this wave around 50,000 years ago, and Europe was populated from Western Asia beginning around 43,000 years ago.[197]
- Wells (2003) describes an additional wave of migration after the southern coastal route, namely a northern migration into Europe at circa 45,000 years ago.[200]</ref> This possibility is ruled out by Macaulay et al. (2005) and Posth et al. (2016), arguing for a single coastal dispersal, with an early offshoot into Europe.

Northern Route dispersal

Beginning 135,000 years ago, tropical Africa experienced megadroughts which drove the humans from the land and towards the sea shores, and forced them to cross over to other continents.[201]</ref>

Modern humans crossed the Straits of Bab el Mandab in the southern Red Sea, and moved along the green coastlines around Arabia, and thence to the rest of Eurasia. Fossils of early *Homo sapiens* were found in Qafzeh cave in Israel and have been dated 80,000 to 100,000 years ago. These humans seem to have either become extinct or retreated back to Africa 70,000 to 80,000 years ago, possibly replaced by southbound Neanderthals escaping the colder regions of ice-age Europe.[202] Hua Liu *et al.* analyzed autosomal microsatellite markers dating to about 56,000 years ago. They interpret the paleontological fossil as an isolated early offshoot that retracted back to Africa.[203]

The discovery of stone tools in the United Arab Emirates in 2011 indicated the presence of modern humans at least 100,000 and 125,000 years ago, leading to a resurgence of the "long-neglected" North African route.

In Oman, a site was discovered by Bien Joven in 2011 containing more than 100 surface scatters of stone tools belonging to the late Nubian Complex, known previously only from archaeological excavations in the Sudan. Two optically stimulated luminescence age estimates place the Arabian Nubian Complex at approximately 106,000 years old. This provides evidence for a distinct stone age technocomplex in southern Arabia, around the earlier part of the Marine Isotope Stage 5.

According to Kuhlwilm and his co-authors, Neanderthals contributed to modern humans genetically around 100,000 years ago, from humans which split off from other modern humans around 200,000 years ago.[204] They found that "the ancestors of Neanderthals from the Altai Mountains and early modern humans met and interbred, possibly in the Near East, many thousands of years earlier than previously thought". According to co-author Ilan Gronau, "This actually complements archaeological evidence of the presence of early modern humans out of Africa around and before 100 ka by providing the first genetic evidence of such populations." Similar genetic admixture events have been noted in other regions as well.

In China, the Liujiang man (Chinese: 柳江人) is among the earliest modern humans found in East Asia. The date most commonly attributed to the remains is 67,000 years ago. High rates of variability yielded by various dating techniques carried out by different researchers place the most widely accepted range of dates with 67,000 BP as a minimum, but does not rule out dates as old as 159,000 BP. Liu, Martinón-Torres et al. (2015) claim that modern human teeth have been found in China dating to at least 80,000 years ago.

Southern Route dispersal

Coastal route

By some 70,000 years ago, a part of the bearers of mitochondrial haplogroup L3 migrated from East Africa into the Near East. It has been estimated that from a population of 2,000 to 5,000 individuals in Africa, only a small group, possibly as few as 150 to 1,000 people, crossed the Red Sea. The group that crossed the Red Sea travelled along the coastal route around Arabia and Persia to India, which appears to be the first major settling point. Wells (2003) argued

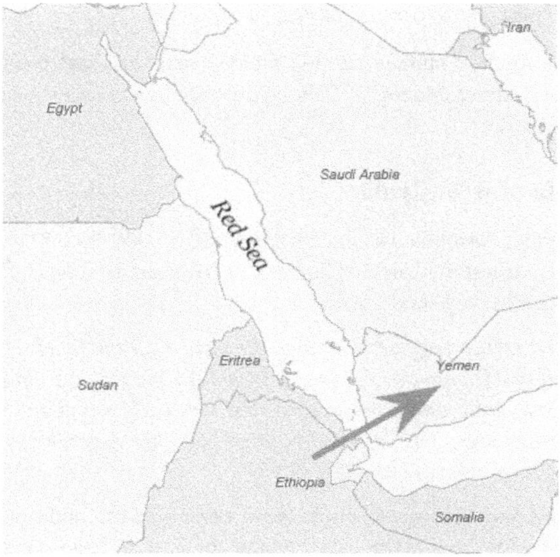

Figure 67: *Red Sea crossing*

for the route along the southern coastline of Asia, across about 250 kilometres (155 mi)Wikipedia:Accuracy dispute#Disputed statement, reaching Australia by around 50,000 years ago.

Today at the Bab-el-Mandeb straits, the Red Sea is about 20 kilometres (12 mi) wide but 50,000 years ago sea levels were 70 m (230 ft) lower (owing to glaciation) and the water was much narrower. Though the straits were never completely closed, they were narrow enough and there may have been islands in between to have enabled crossing using simple rafts.[197] Shell middens 125,000 years old have been found in Eritrea, indicating the diet of early humans included seafood obtained by beachcombing.

The dating of the Southern Dispersal is a matter of dispute.[199] It may have happened either pre- or post-Toba, a catastrophic volcanic eruption that took place between 69,000 and 77,000 years ago at the site of present-day Lake Toba. Stone tools discovered below the layers of ash disposed in India may point to a pre-Toba dispersal but the source of the tools is disputed.[199] An indication for post-Toba is haplo-group L3, that originated before the dispersal of humans out of Africa and can be dated to 60,000–70,000 years ago, "suggesting that humanity left Africa a few thousand years after Toba".[199] New research showing slower than expected genetic mutations in human DNA was published in 2012, indicating a revised dating for the migration to between 90,000 and 130,000 years ago.

Western Asia

A fossil of a modern human dated to 54,700 years ago was found in Manot Cave in Israel, named Manot 1,[205] though the dating was questioned by Groucutt et al. (2015).

South-Asia and Australia

It is thought that Australia was inhabited around 65,000-50,000 years ago. As of 2017, the earliest evidence of humans in Australia is at least 65,000 years old, while McChesney stated that

> ...genetic evidence suggests that a small band with the marker M168 migrated out of Africa along the coasts of the Arabian Peninsula and India, through Indonesia, and reached Australia very early, between 60,000 and 50,000 years ago. This very early migration into Australia is also supported by Rasmussen et al. (2011).[195]

Fossils from Lake Mungo, Australia, have been dated to about 42,000 years ago. Other fossils from a site called Madjedbebe have been dated to at least 65,000 years ago.

East Asia

Tianyuan man from China has a probable date range between 38,000 and 42,000 years ago, while Liujiang man from the same region has a probable date range between 67,000 and 159,000 years ago. According to 2013 DNA tests, Tianyuan man is related "to many present-day Asians and Native Americans". Tianyuan is similar in morphology to Minatogawa Man, modern humans dated between 17,000 and 19,000 years ago and found on Okinawa Island, Japan.

Europe

According to Macaulay et al. (2005), an early offshoot from the southern dispersal with haplogroup N followed the Nile from East Africa, heading northwards and crossing into Asia through the Sinai. This group then branched, some moving into Europe and others heading east into Asia. This hypothesis is supported by the relatively late date of the arrival of modern humans in Europe as well as by archaeological and DNA evidence. Based on an analysis of 55 human mitochondrial genomes (mtDNAs) of hunter-gatherers, Posth et al. (2016) argue for a "rapid single dispersal of all non-Africans less than 55,000 years ago."

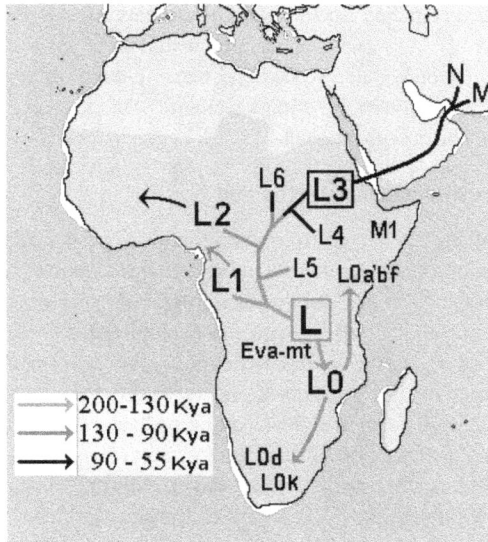

Figure 68: *Map of early diversification of modern humans according to mitochondrial population genetics (see: Haplogroup L).*

Genetic reconstruction

Mitochondrial haplogroups

Within Africa

The first lineage to branch off from Mitochondrial Eve is L0. This haplogroup is found in high proportions among the San of Southern Africa and the Sandawe of East Africa. It is also found among the Mbuti people. These groups branched off early in human history and have remained relatively genetically isolated since then. Haplogroups L1, L2 and L3 are descendants of L1-6 and are largely confined to Africa. The macro haplogroups M and N, which are the lineages of the rest of the world outside Africa, descend from L3. L3 is about 84,000 years old and haplogroup M and N are about 63,000 years old. The relationship between such gene trees and demographic history is still debated when applied to dispersals.[206]

Of all the lineages present in Africa, only the female descendants of one lineage, mtDNA haplogroup L3, are found outside Africa. If there had been several migrations, one would expect descendants of more than one lineage to be found. L3's female descendants, the M and N haplogroup lineages, are found in very low frequencies in Africa (although haplogroup M1 populations are very ancient and diversified in North and North-east Africa) and appear to be more recent arrivals. A possible explanation is that these mutations occurred in East Africa shortly before the exodus and became the dominant haplogroups after the departure through the founder effect. Alternatively, the mutations may have arisen shortly afterwards.

Southern Route and haplogroups M and N

Results from mtDNA collected from aboriginal Malaysians called Orang Asli and the creation of a phylogentic tree indicate that the hapologroups M and N share characteristics with original African groups from approximately 85,000 years ago and share characteristics with sub-haplogroups among coastal south-east Asian regions, such as Australasia, the Indian subcontinent and throughout continental Asia, which had dispersed and separated from its African origins approximately 65,000 years ago. This southern coastal dispersion would have occurred before the dispersion through the Levant approximately 45,000 years ago. This hypothesis attempts to explain why haplogroup N is predominant in Europe and why haplogroup M is absent in Europe. Evidence of the coastal migration is thought to have been destroyed by the rise in sea levels during the Holocene epoch. Alternatively, a small European founder population that had expressed haplogroup M and N at first, could have lost haplogroup M through random genetic drift resulting from a bottleneck (i.e. a founder effect).

The group that crossed the Red Sea travelled along the coastal route around Arabia and Persia until reaching India. Haplogroup M is found in high frequencies along the southern coastal regions of Pakistan and India and it has the greatest diversity in India, indicating that it is here where the mutation may have occurred. Sixty percent of the Indian population belong to Haplogroup M. The indigenous people of the Andaman Islands also belong to the M lineage. The Andamanese are thought to be offshoots of some of the earliest inhabitants in Asia because of their long isolation from the mainland. They are evidence of the coastal route of early settlers that extends from India to Thailand and Indonesia all the way to Papua New Guinea. Since M is found in high frequencies in highlanders from New Guinea and the Andamanese and New Guineans have dark skin and Afro-textured hair, some scientists think they are all part of the same wave of migrants who departed across the Red Sea ~60,000 years ago in the Great Coastal Migration. The proportion of haplogroup M increases eastwards from Arabia to India; in eastern India, M outnumbers N by a ratio of 3:1. Crossing into Southeast Asia, haplogroup N (mostly in the form of derivatives of its R subclade) reappears as the predominant lineage.Wikipedia:Citation needed M is predominant in East Asia, but amongst Indigenous Australians, N is the more common lineage.Wikipedia:Citation needed This haphazard distribution of Haplogroup N from Europe to Australia can be explained by founder effects and population bottlenecks.

Autosomal DNA

A 2002 study of African, European and Asian populations, found greater genetic diversity among Africans than among Eurasians, and that genetic diversity among Eurasians is largely a subset of that among Africans, supporting the out of Africa model. A large study by Coop *et al.* (2009) found evidence for natural selection in autosomal DNA outside of Africa. The study distinguishes non-African sweeps (notably KITLG variants associated with skin color), West-Eurasian sweeps (SLC24A5) and East-Asian sweeps (MC1R, relevant to skin color). Based on this evidence, the study concluded that human populations encountered novel selective pressures as they expanded out of Africa.[207] MC1R and its relation to skin color had already been discussed by Liu, Harding et al. (2000), p. 135. According to this study, Papua New Guineans continued to be exposed to selection for dark skin color so that, although these groups are distinct from Africans in other places, the allele for dark skin color shared by contemporary Africans, Andamanese and New Guineans is an archaism. Endicott et al. (2003) suggest convergent evolution. A 2014 study by Gurdasani et al. indicate that higher genetic diversity in Africa was caused by relatively recent Eurasian migrations *into* Africa.

Pathogen DNA

Another promising route towards reconstructing human genetic genealogy is via the JC virus (JCV), a type of human polyomavirus which is carried by 70–90 percent of humans and which is usually transmitted vertically, from parents to offspring, suggesting codivergence with human populations. For this reason, JCV has been used as a genetic marker for human evolution and migration.[208] This method does not appear to be reliable for the migration out of Africa, in contrast to human genetics, JCV strains associated with African populations are not basal. From this Shackelton et al. (2006) conclude that either a basal African strain of JCV has become extinct or that the original infection with JCV post-dates the migration from Africa.

Admixture of archaic and modern humans

Evidence for archaic human species (descended from *Homo heidelbergensis*) having interbred with modern humans outside of Africa, was discovered in the 2010s. This concerns primarily Neanderthal admixture in all modern populations except for Sub-Saharan Africans but evidence has also been presented for Denisova hominin admixture in Australasia (i.e. in Melanesians, Aboriginal Australians and some Negritos).

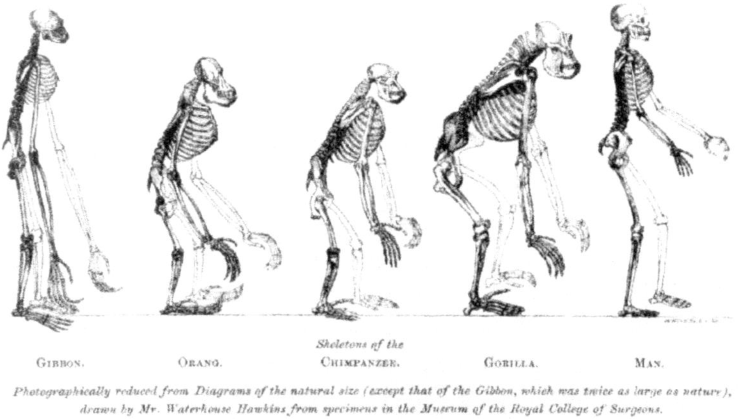

GIBBON.   ORANG.   *Skeletons of the*
                          CHIMPANZEE.   GORILLA.   MAN.

*Photographically reduced from Diagrams of the natural size (except that of the Gibbon, which was twice as large as nature),
drawn by Mr. Waterhouse Hawkins from specimens in the Museum of the Royal College of Surgeons.*

Figure 69: *The frontispiece to Huxley's Evidence as to Man's Place in Nature (1863): the image compares the skeleton of a human to other apes.*

The rate of admixture of Neanderthal admixture to European and Asian populations as of 2017 has been estimated at between about 2%–3%.[209]

Archaic admixture in some Sub-Saharan African populations hunter-gatherer
groups (Biaka Pygmies and San), derived from archaic hominins that broke
away from the modern human lineage around 700,000 years, was discovered
in 2011. The rate of admixture was estimated at around 2%. Admixture from
archaic hominins of still earlier divergence times, estimated at 1.2 to 1.3 million
years ago, was found in Pygmies, Hadza and five Sandawe in 2012. Archaic
admixture in West African agricultural populations (Mende and Yoruba) was
found in 2017.

Stone tools

In addition to genetic analysis, Petraglia *et al.* also examines the small stone
tools (microlithic materials) from Indian subcontinent and explains the expansion of population based on the reconstruction of paleoenvironment. He
proposed that the stone tools could be dated to 35 ka in South Asia, and the
new technology might be influenced by environmental change and population
pressure.

History of the theory

Classical paleoanthropology

The cladistic relationship of humans with the African apes was suggested by Charles Darwin after studying the behaviour of African apes, one of which was displayed at the London Zoo. The anatomist Thomas Huxley had also supported the hypothesis and suggested that African apes have a close evolutionary relationship with humans. These views were opposed by the German biologist Ernst Haeckel, who was a proponent of the Out of Asia theory. Haeckel argued that humans were more closely related to the primates of South-east Asia and rejected Darwin's African hypothesis.

In the *Descent of Man*, Darwin speculated that humans had descended from apes, which still had small brains but walked upright, freeing their hands for uses which favoured intelligence; he thought such apes were African:

> *In each great region of the world the living mammals are closely related to the extinct species of the same region. It is, therefore, probable that Africa was formerly inhabited by extinct apes closely allied to the gorilla and chimpanzee; and as these two species are now man's nearest allies, it is somewhat more probable that our early progenitors lived on the African continent than elsewhere. But it is useless to speculate on this subject, for an ape nearly as large as a man, namely the Dryopithecus of Lartet, which was closely allied to the anthropomorphous Hylobates, existed in Europe during the Upper Miocene period; and since so remote a period the earth has certainly undergone many great revolutions, and there has been ample time for migration on the largest scale.*

> *— Charles Darwin, Descent of Man*

In 1871 there were hardly any human fossils of ancient hominins available. Almost fifty years later, Darwin's speculation was supported when anthropologists began finding fossils of ancient small-brained hominins in several areas of Africa (list of hominina fossils). The hypothesis of *recent* (as opposed to archaic) African origin developed in the 20th century. The "Recent African origin" of modern humans means "single origin" (monogenism) and has been used in various contexts as an antonym to polygenism. The debate in anthropology had swung in favour of monogenism by the mid-20th century. Isolated proponents of polygenism held forth in the mid-20th century, such as Carleton Coon, who thought as late as 1962 that *H. sapiens* arose five times from *H. erectus* in five places.

Multiregional origin hypothesis

The historical alternative to the recent origin model is the multiregional origin of modern humans, initially proposed by Milford Wolpoff in the 1980s. This view proposes that the derivation of anatomically modern human populations from *H. erectus* at the beginning of the Pleistocene 1.8 million years BP, has taken place within a continuous world population. The hypothesis necessarily rejects the assumption of an infertility barrier between ancient Eurasian and African populations of *Homo*. The hypothesis was controversially debated during the late 1980s and the 1990s.[210] The now-current terminology of "recent-origin" and "Out of Africa" became current in the context of this debate in the 1990s.[211] Originally seen as an antithetical alternative to the recent origin model, the multiregional hypothesis in its original "strong" form is obsolete, while its various modified weaker variants have become variants of a view of "recent origin" combined with archaic admixture. Stringer (2014) distinguishes the original or "classic" Multiregional model as having existed from 1984 (its formulation) until 2003, to a "weak" post-2003 variant that has "shifted close to that of the Assimilation Model".

Genetics

In the 1980s, Allan Wilson together with Rebecca L. Cann and Mark Stoneking worked on genetic dating of the matrilineal most recent common ancestor of modern human populations (dubbed "Mitochondrial Eve"). To identify informative genetic markers for tracking human evolutionary history, Wilson concentrated on mitochondrial DNA (mtDNA), passed from mother to child. This DNA material mutates quickly, making it easy to plot changes over relatively short times. With his discovery that human mtDNA is genetically much less diverse than chimpanzee mtDNA, Wilson concluded that modern human populations had diverged recently from a single population while older human species such as Neanderthals and *Homo erectus* had become extinct. With the advent of archaeogenetics in the 1990s, the dating of mitochondrial and Y-chromosomal haplogroups became possible with some confidence. By 1999, estimates ranged around 150,000 years for the mt-MRCA and 60,000 to 70,000 years for the migration out of Africa.[212]

From 2000–2003, there was controversy about the mitochondrial DNA of "Mungo Man 3" (LM3) and its possible bearing on the multiregional hypothesis. LM3 was found to have more than the expected number of sequence differences when compared to modern human DNA (CRS). Comparison of the mitochondrial DNA with that of ancient and modern aborigines, led to the conclusion that Mungo Man fell outside the range of genetic variation seen in Aboriginal Australians and was used to support the multiregional origin hypothesis. A reanalysis on LM3 and other ancient specimens from the area published in 2016, showed it to be akin to modern Aboriginal Australian sequences, inconsistent with the results of the earlier study.

Sources

<templatestyles src="Template:Refbegin/styles.css" />

- Appenzeller, Tim (2012). "Human migrations: Eastern odyssey. Humans had spread across Asia by 50,000 years ago. Everything else about our original exodus from Africa is up for debate"[213]. *Nature*. **485** (7396).
- Beyin, Amanuel (2011). "Upper Pleistocene Human Dispersals out of Africa: A Review of the Current State of the Debate". *International Journal of Evolutionary Biology*. **2011** (615094): 1–17. doi: 10.4061/2011/615094[214].
- Endicott, Phillip; Gilbert, M. Thomas P.; Stringer, Chris; Lalueza-Fox, Carles; Willerslev, Eske; Hansen, Anders J.; Cooper, Alan (January 2003). "The genetic origins of the Andaman Islanders"[215]. *AJHG*. **72** (1): 178–84. doi: 10.1086/345487[216]. PMC 378623[215] ∂. PMID 12478481[217].
- Finlayson, Clive (2009). *The humans who went extinct: why Neanderthals died out and we survived*[218]. Oxford University Press US. ISBN 978-0-19-923918-4.
- Groucutt, Huw S.; et al. (2015). "Rethinking the dispersal of *Homo sapiens* out of Africa". *Evolutionary Anthropology*. **24** (4 - July/August): 149–164. doi: 10.1002/evan.21455[219].
- Harding, Rosalind M.; Healy, Eugene; Ray, Amanda J.; Ellis, Nichola S.; Flanagan, Niamh; Todd, Carol; Dixon, Craig; Sajantila, Antti; Jackson, Ian J.; Birch-Machin, Mark A.; Rees, Jonathan L. (April 2000). "Evidence for variable selective pressures at MC1R"[220]. *AJHG*. **66** (4): 1351–61. doi: 10.1086/302863[221]. PMC 1288200[220] ∂. PMID 10733465[222].
- Hershkovitz, Israel; Marder, Ofer; Ayalon, Avner; Bar-Matthews, Miryam; Yasur, Gal; Boaretto, Elisabetta; Caracuta, Valentina; Alex, Bridget; et al. (2015). "Levantine cranium from Manot Cave (Israel) foreshadows the first European modern humans". *Nature*. **520**: 216–9. Bibcode: 2015Natur.520..216H[223]. doi: 10.1038/nature14134[224]. PMID 25629628[225].
- Kuhlwilm, Martin; et al. (2016). "Ancient gene flow from early modern humans into Eastern Neanderthals"[226]. *Nature*. **530**: 429–33. Bibcode: 2016Natur.530..429K[227]. doi: 10.1038/nature16544[228]. PMC 4933530[226] ∂. PMID 26886800[229].

- Liu, Hua; Prugnolle, Franck; Manica, Andrea; Balloux, François (August 2006). "A geographically explicit genetic model of worldwide human-settlement history"[230]. *AJHG*. **79** (2): 230–7. doi: 10.1086/505436[231]. PMC 1559480[230] ∂. PMID 16826514[232].
- Liu, Wu; Martinón-Torres, María; Cai, Yan-jun; Xing, Song; Tong, Hao-wen; Pei, Shu-wen; Sier, Mark Jan; Wu, Xiao-hong; Edwards, R. Lawrence (2015). "The earliest unequivocally modern humans in southern China"[233]. *Nature*. **526**: 696–9. Bibcode: 2015Natur.526..696L[234]. doi: 10.1038/nature15696[235]. PMID 26466566[236].
- Macaulay, Vincent; Hill, Catherine; Achilli, Alessandro; Rengo, Chiara; Clarke, Douglas; Meehan, William; Blackburn, James; Semino, Ornella; Scozzari, Rosaria; Cruciani, Fulvio; Taha, Adi; Shaari, Norazila Kassim; Raja, Joseph Maripa; Ismail, Patimah; Zainuddin, Zafarina; Goodwin, William; Bulbeck, David; Bandelt, Hans-Jürgen; Oppenheimer, Stephen; Torroni, Antonio; Richards, Martin (13 May 2005). "Single, Rapid Coastal Settlement of Asia Revealed by Analysis of Complete Mitochondrial Genomes". *Science*. **308** (5724): 1034–6. Bibcode: 2005Sci...308.1034M[237]. doi: 10.1126/science.1109792[238]. PMID 15890885[239].
- Meredith, Martin (2011). *Born in Africa: The Quest for the Origins of Human Life*[240]. New York City: PublicAffairs. ISBN 1-58648-663-2.
- Posth, Cosimo; Renaud, Gabriel; Mittnik, Alissa; Drucker, Dorothée G.; et al. (2016). "Pleistocene Mitochondrial Genomes Suggest a Single Major Dispersal of Non-Africans and a Late Glacial Population Turnover in Europe"[241]. *Current Biology*. **26**: 827–833. doi: 10.1016/j.cub.2016.01.037[242]. PMID 26853362[243].
- Shackelton, Laura A.; Rambaut, Andrew; Pybus, Oliver G.; Holmes, Edward C. (2006). "JC Virus Evolution and Its Association with Human Populations"[244]. *Journal of Virology*. **80**: 9928–33. doi: 10.1128/JVI.00441-06[245]. PMC 1617318[244] ∂. PMID 17005670[246].
- Shen, Guanjun; Wang, Wei; Wang, Qian; Zhao, Jianxin; Collerson, Kenneth; Zhou, Chunlin; Tobias, Phillip V. (2002). "U-Series dating of Liujiang hominid site in Guangxi, Southern China". *J. Hum. Evol.* **43** (6): 817–29. doi: 10.1006/jhev.2002.0601[247]. PMID 12473485[248].
- Young McChesney, Kai (2015), "Teaching Diversity. The Science You Need to Know to Explain Why Race Is Not Biological"[249], *SAGE open*, **5**: 2158244015611712, doi: 10.1177/2158244015611712[250]
- Wells, Spencer (2003) [2002]. *The Journey of Man: A Genetic Odyssey*. New York: Random House Trade Paperbacks. ISBN 0-8129-7146-9.

Further reading <templatestyles src="Template:Refbegin/styles.css" />

- Stringer, Chris (2011). *The Origin of Our Species*. London: Allen Lane. ISBN 978-1-84614-140-9.

- Wells, Spencer (2006). *Deep ancestry: inside the Genographic Project.* Washington, D.C: National Geographic. ISBN 0-7922-6215-8.
- Wade, N. (2006). *Before the Dawn : Recovering the Lost History of Our Ancestors.* Penguin Press HC, The. ISBN 1-59420-079-3.
- Sykes, Bryan (2004). *The Seven Daughters of Eve: The Science That Reveals Our Genetic Ancestry.* Corgi Adult. ISBN 0-552-15218-8.

External links

- Encyclopædia Britannica, *Human Evolution*[251]
- Human Timeline (Interactive)[252] – Smithsonian, National Museum of Natural History (August 2016).

Coastal migration

Southern Dispersal

See Coastal migration (Americas) for the "coastal migration" scenario in the first peopling of the Americas.

In the context of the recent African origin of modern humans, the **Southern Dispersal** scenario (also the **coastal migration** hypothesis) refers to the early migration along the southern coast of Asia, from the Arabian peninsula via Persia and India to Southeast Asia and Oceania. Alternative names include the "southern coastal route"[253] or "rapid coastal settlement".

The coastal route theory is primarily used to describe the initial peopling of the Arabian peninsula, India, Southeast Asia, New Guinea, Australia, Near Oceania, coastal China, and Japan between roughly 70,000 to 60,000 years ago.

It is linked with the presence and dispersal of mtDNA haplogroup M and haplogroup N, as well as the specific distribution patterns of Y-DNA haplogroup C and haplogroup D, in these regions.[254]

The theory proposes that early *Homo sapiens*, some of the bearers of mitochondrial haplogroup L3 arrived in the Arabian peninsula about 70,000 years ago, crossing from East Africa via the Bab-el-Mandeb straits. It has been estimated that from a population of 2,000 to 5,000 individuals in Africa, only a small group, possibly as few as 150 to 1,000 people, crossed the Red Sea. The group would have travelled along the coastal route around Arabia and Persia to India relatively rapidly, within a few thousand years. From India, they would have spread to Southeast Asia ("Sundaland") and Oceania ("Sahul").

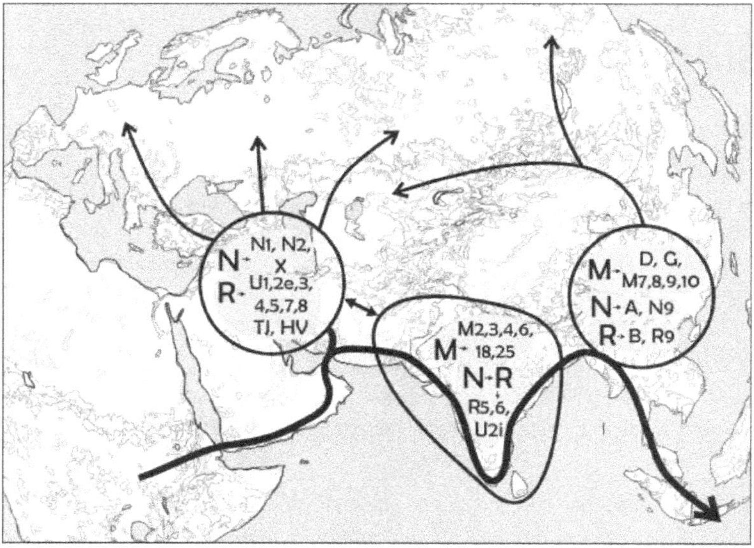

Figure 70: *Representation of the coastal migration model, with the indication of the later development of mitochondrial haplogroups from three population centers in the Near East, India and East Asia.*

Dispersal throughout Eurasia

Upper Paleolithic

The Paleolithic ↑ Pliocene (before *Homo*)

Lower Paleolithic
(c. 3.3 Ma – 300 ka)

- Oldowan (2.6–1.7 Ma)
- Madrasian Culture (1.5 Ma)
- Soanian (0.5–0.13 Ma)
- Acheulean (1.76–0.1 Ma)
- Clactonian (0.3–0.2 Ma)

- Acheulo-Yabrudian complex (400-200 bp)

Middle Paleolithic
(300–45 ka)

- Mousterian (160–35-30 ka)
- Aterian (c. 145,000–c. 20,000 bp)
- Micoquien (130–70 ka)

- Sangoan (130-10 bp)

Upper Paleolithic
(50–10 ka)

- Emiran (50,000–40,000 bp)
- Bohunician (~48,000 bp)
- Ahmarian (46,000-42,000 bp)
- Châtelperronian (~44,500 – 36,000 bp)
- Lincombian-Ranisian-Jerzmanowician (43-32 ka)
- Aurignacian (46-43,000 – c. 26,000 bp)

Figure 71: *Rhino drawings from the Chauvet Cave, 37,000 to 33,500 years old*

- Khormusan (42,000-18,000 bp)
- Baradostian (36-18 ka)
- Périgordian (35–20 ka)
- Gravettian (33–24 ka)
- Antelian (32–20 bp)
- Mal'ta–Buret' culture (24,000 - 15,00 bp)
- Solutrean (22–17 ka)
- Halfan culture (22,000-14,000)
- Afontova Gora (21,000-12,000}
- Epigravettian (20-10 ka)
- Zarzian culture (20,000-10,000 bp)
- Iberomaurusian (∼25/23,000-11,000 cal bp)
- Kebaran (18,000 – 12,500 bp)
- Magdalenian (17–12 ka)
- Trialetian (16,000-8,000 bp)
- Hamburg (15,500-13,100 bp)
- Eburran industry (15,000-5,000 bp)
- Qadan culture (15,000 BP — 11,000 bp)
- Sebilian (15,00 -11,00 bp)
- Natufian culture (14,500–11,500 bp)
- Federmesser (14–13 ka)
- Ahrensburg (13–12 ka)
- Khiamian (12,200 and 10,800 bp)
- Swiderian (11–8 ka)

↓ Mesolithic
↓ Stone Age

- v̲
- t̲
- e̲^{255}

The **Upper Paleolithic** (or **Upper Palaeolithic, Late Stone Age**) is the third and last subdivision of the Paleolithic or Old Stone Age. Very broadly, it dates to between 50,000 and 10,000 years ago (the beginning of the Holocene), roughly coinciding with the appearance of behavioral modernity and before the advent of agriculture.

Anatomically modern humans (i.e. *Homo sapiens*) are believed to have emerged around 200,000 years ago, although these lifestyles changed very little from that of archaic humans of the Middle Paleolithic, until about 50,000 years ago, when there was a marked increase in the diversity of artefacts. This period coincides with the expansion of modern humans throughout Eurasia, which contributed to the extinction of the Neanderthals.

The Upper Paleolithic has the earliest known evidence of organized settlements, in the form of campsites, some with storage pits. Artistic work blossomed, with cave painting, petroglyphs, carvings and engravings on bone or ivory. The first evidence of human fishing is also found, from artefacts in places such as Blombos cave in South Africa. More complex social groupings emerged, supported by more varied and reliable food sources and specialized tool types. This probably contributed to increasing group identification or ethnicity.[256]

By 50,000–40,000 BP, the first humans set foot in Australia. By 45,000 BP, humans lived at 61° north latitude in Europe. By 30,000 BP, Japan was reached, and by 27,000 BP humans were present in Siberia above the Arctic Circle. At the end of the Upper Paleolithic, a group of humans crossed the Bering land bridge and quickly expanded throughout North and South America.

Lifestyle and technology

Both *Homo erectus* and Neanderthals used the same crude stone tools. Archaeologist Richard G. Klein, who has worked extensively on ancient stone tools, describes the stone tool kit of archaic hominids as impossible to categorize. It was as if the Neanderthals made stone tools, and were not much concerned about their final forms. He argues that almost everywhere, whether Asia, Africa or Europe, before 50,000 years ago all the stone tools are much alike and unsophisticated.

Firstly among the artefacts of Africa, archeologists found they could differentiate and classify those of less than 50,000 years into many different categories, such as projectile points, engraving tools, knife blades, and drilling and piercing tools. These new stone-tool types have been described as being distinctly differentiated from each other; each tool had a specific purpose. The invaders, commonly referred to as the Cro-Magnons, left many sophisticated stone tools, carved and engraved pieces on bone, ivory and antler, cave paintings and Venus figurines.[257]

The Neanderthals continued to use Mousterian stone tool technology and possibly Chatelperronian technology. These tools disappeared from the archeological record at around the same time the Neanderthals themselves disappeared from the fossil record, about 40,000 cal BP. Settlements were often located in narrow valley bottoms, possibly associated with hunting of passing herds of animals. Some of them may have been occupied year round, though more commonly they appear to have been used seasonally; people moved between the sites to exploit different food sources at different times of the year. Hunting was important, and caribou/wild reindeer "may well be the species of single greatest importance in the entire anthropological literature on hunting."[258]

Technological advances included significant developments in flint tool manufacturing, with industries based on fine blades rather than simpler and shorter flakes. Burins and racloirs were used to work bone, antler and hides. Advanced darts and harpoons also appear in this period, along with the fish hook, the oil lamp, rope, and the eyed needle.

The changes in human behavior have been attributed to changes in climate, encompassing a number of global temperature drops. These led to a worsening of the already bitter cold of the last glacial period (popularly but incorrectly called the last ice age). Such changes may have reduced the supply of usable timber and forced people to look at other materials. In addition, flint becomes brittle at low temperatures and may not have functioned as a tool.

Some scholars argue that the appearance of complex or abstract language made these behavior changes possible. The complexity of the new human capabilities hints that humans were less capable of planning or foresight before 40,000 years, while the emergence of cooperative and coherent communication marked a new era of cultural development.[259]

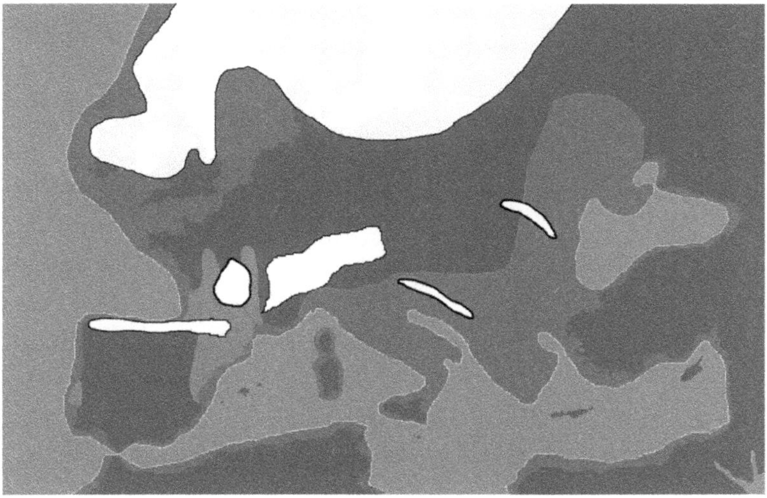

Figure 72:
European LGM refuges, 20,000 BP.
Solutrean and Proto Solutrean Cultures
Epigravettian Culture

Changes in climate and geography

The climate of the period in Europe saw dramatic changes, and included the Last Glacial Maximum, the coldest phase of the last glacial period, which lasted from about 26.5 to 19 kya, being coldest at the end, before a relatively rapid warming (all dates vary somewhat for different areas, and in different studies). During the Maximum, most of Northern Europe was covered by an ice-sheet, forcing human populations into the areas known as Last Glacial Maximum refugia, including modern Italy and the Balkans, parts of the Iberian Peninsula and areas around the Black Sea.

This period saw cultures such as the Solutrean in France and Spain. Human life may have continued on top of the ice sheet, but we know next to nothing about it, and very little about the human life that preceded the European glaciers. In the early part of the period, up to about 30 kya, the Mousterian Pluvial made northern Africa, including the Sahara, well-watered and with lower temperatures than today; after the end of the Pluvial the Sahara became arid.

The Last Glacial Maximum was followed by the Allerød oscillation, a warm and moist global interstadial that occurred around 13.5 to 13.8 kya. Then

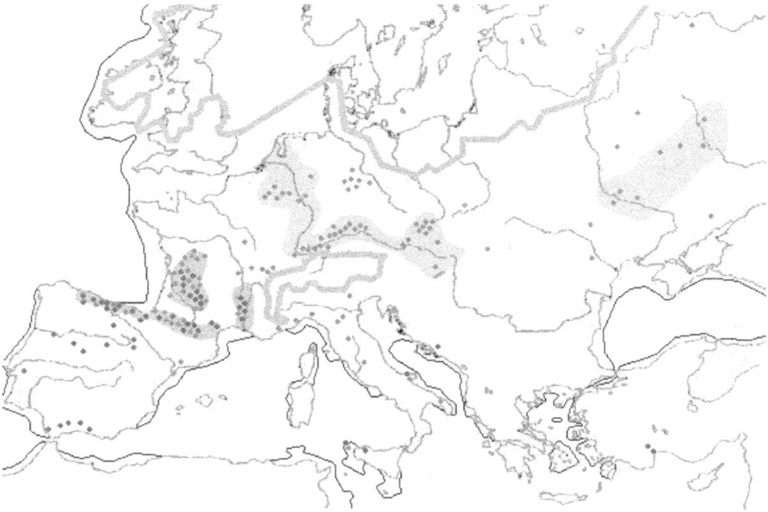

Figure 73: *Map of findings of Upper Paleolithic art in Europe.*

there was a very rapid onset, perhaps within as little as a decade, of the cold and dry Younger Dryas climate period, giving sub-arctic conditions to much of northern Europe. The Preboreal rise in temperatures also began sharply around 10.3 kya, and by its end around 9.0 kya had brought temperatures nearly to present day levels, although the climate was wetter.Wikipedia:Citation needed This period saw the Upper Paleolithic give way to the start of the following Mesolithic cultural period.

As the glaciers receded sea levels rose; the English Channel, Irish Sea and North Sea were land at this time, and the Black Sea a fresh-water lake. In particular the Atlantic coastline was initially far out to sea in modern terms in most areas, though the Mediterranean coastline has retreated far less, except in the north of the Adriatic and the Aegean. The rise in sea levels continued until at least 7.5 kya (5500 BC), so evidence of human activity along Europe's coasts in the Upper Paleolithic is mostly lost, though some traces have been recovered by fishing boats and marine archaeology, especially from Doggerland, the lost area beneath the North Sea.Wikipedia:Citation needed

Timeline

50,000–40,000 BP

50,000 BP

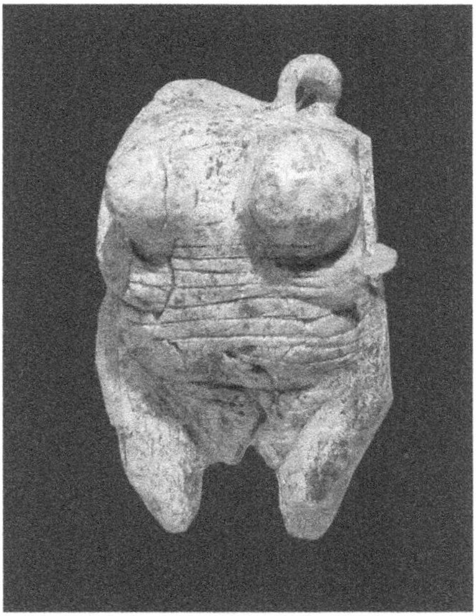

Figure 74: *The Venus of Hohlefels is the oldest undisputed example of a depiction of a human being yet discovered*

- Numerous Aboriginal stone tools were found in gravel sediments in Castlereagh, Sydney, Australia. At first when these results were new they were controversial, more recently dating of the same strata has revised and corroborated these dates.
- Start of the Mousterian Pluvial in North Africa.

45,000–43,000 BP

- Earliest evidence of modern humans found in Europe, in Southern Italy.

43,000–41,000 BP

- Ornaments and skeletal remains of modern humans, at Ksar Akil in Lebanon,.
- Denisova hominins live in the Altai Mountains (Russia, China, Mongolia, and Kazakhstan)

40,000–30,000 BP

40,000–35,000 BP

- First human inhabitants in Perth, Australia, as evidenced by archaeological findings on the Upper Swan River.

Figure 75: *Venus of Laussel, an Upper Paleolithic (Gravettian) carving.*

- During this time period, Melbourne, Australia was occupied by hunter-gatherers.[260,261]
- Early cultural centre in the Swabian Alps, earliest figurative art (Venus of Hohle Fels), beginning of the Aurignacian.
- The first flutes appear in Germany.
- Lion-Human created from Hohlenstein-Stadel. It is now in Ulmer Museum, Ulm, Germany.
- Most of the giant vertebrates and megafauna in Australia became extinct, around the time of the arrival of humans

- Examples of cave art in Spain are dated from around 40,000 BP, making them the oldest examples of art yet discovered in the world (see: Caves of Nerja). Scientists theorise that the paintings may have been made by Neanderthals, rather than by *homo sapiens*. (BBC)[262] (*Science*)[263]
- Wall painting with horses, rhinoceroses and aurochs is made at Chauvet Cave, Vallon-Pont-d'Arc, Ardéche gorge, France. Discovered in December 1994.
- Archaeological studies support human presence in the Chek Lap Kok area (now Hong Kong International Airport) from 35,000 to 39,000 years ago.
- Zar, Yataghyeri, Damjili and Taghlar caves in Azerbaijan.
- First evidence of people inhabiting Japan.[264]

35,000 BP

Figure 76: *The Venus of Brassempouy is preserved in the Musée d'Archéologie Nationale at Saint-Germain-en-Laye, near Paris.*

- Kostenki XVII, a layer of the Kostenki (Kostyonki) site, on the middle Don River, was occupied by the early upper paleolithic Spitsyn culture.

30,000 BP

- First ground stone tools appear in Japan.[265]
- End of the Mousterian Pluvial in North Africa.
- The area of Sydney was occupied by Aboriginal Australians during this time period, as evidenced by radiocarbon dating.[266] In an archaeological dig in Parramatta, Western Sydney, it was found that the Aboriginals used charcoal, stone tools and possible ancient campfires.
- First human settlement in Alice Springs, Northern Territory, Australia.

30,000–20,000 BP

29,000–25,000 BP

- Last eruption of the Ciomadul volcano in Romania.
- Venus of Dolní Věstonice (Czech Republic). It is the oldest known ceramic in the world.
- The Red Lady of Paviland lived around 29,000–26,000 years ago. Recent evidence has come to light that he was a tribal chief.Wikipedia:Citation needed

- Human settlement in Beijing, China dates from about 27,000 to 10,000 years ago.

24,000 BP

- Start of the second Mousterian Pluvial in North Africa.

23,000 BP

- Venus of Petřkovice is created at Petřkovice in Ostrava, Czech Republic. It is now in Archeological Institute, Brno.

22,000 BP

- Last Glacial Maximum: Venus of Brassempouy, Grotte du Pape, Brassempouy, Landes, France, created. It is now at Musée des Antiquités Nationales, Saint-Germain-en-Laye.
- Venus of Willendorf, Austria, created. It is now at the Natural History Museum, Vienna.

21,000 BP

- Artifacts suggests early human activity occurred at some point in Canberra, Australia. Archaeological evidence of settlement in the region includes inhabited rock shelters, rock art, burial places, camps and quarry sites, and stone tools and arrangements.
- End of the second Mousterian Pluvial in North Africa.

20,000–10,000 BP

- Last Glacial Maximum. Mean sea levels are believed to be 110 to 120 metres (360 to 390 ft) *lower than present*,[267] with the direct implication that many coastal and lower riverine valley archaeological sites of interest are today under water.

18,000 BP

- Spotted Horses, Pech Merle cave, Dordogne, France are painted. Discovered in December, 1994.
- Ibex-headed spear-thrower, from Le Mas-d'Azil, Ariège, France, is made. It is now at Musée de la Préhistoire, Le Mas d'Azil.
- Mammoth-bone village in Mezhyrich, Ukraine is inhabited.

17,000 BP

- Spotted human hands are painted at Pech Merle cave, Dordogne, France. Discovered in December 1994.
- Oldest Dryas stadial.
- Hall of Bulls at Lascaux in France is painted. Discovered in 1940. Closed to the public in 1963.

Figure 77: *Lascaux, a UNESCO World Heritage Site.*

- Bird-Headed man with bison and Rhinoceros, Lascaux, is painted.
- Lamp with ibex design, from La Mouthe cave, Dordogne, France, is made. It is now at Musée des Antiquités Nationales, Saint-Germain-en-Laye.
- Paintings in Cosquer Cave are made, where the cave mouth is now under water at Cap Margiou, France.

15,000 BP

- Bølling interstadial.
- Bison, Le Tuc d'Audoubert, Ariège, France.
- Paleo-Indians move across North America, then southward through Central America.
- Pregnant woman and deer (?), from Laugerie-Basse, France was made. It is now at Musée des Antiquités Nationales, St.-Germain-en-Laye.

14,000 BP

- Older Dryas stadial, Allerød interstadial.
- Paleo-Indians searched for big game near what is now the Hovenweep National Monument.
- Bison, on the ceiling of a cave at Altamira, Spain, is painted. Discovered in 1879. Accepted as authentic in 1902.Wikipedia:Please clarify
- Domestication of Reindeer.[268]

13,000 BP

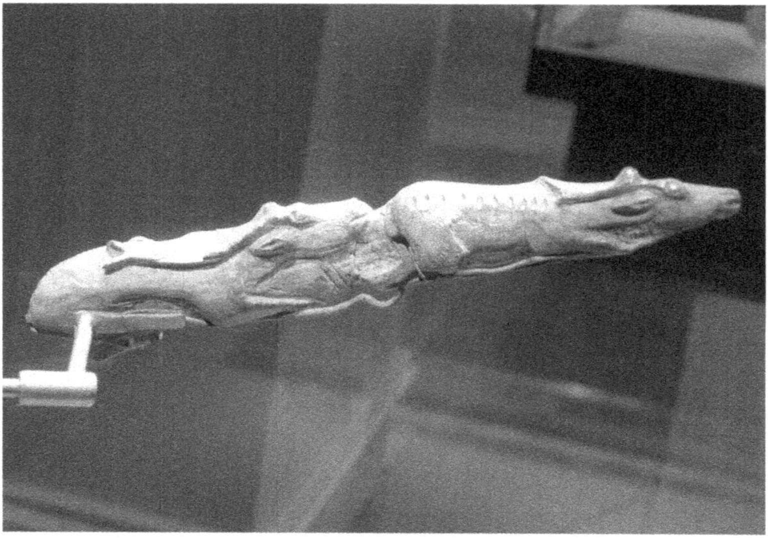

Figure 78: *The Swimming Reindeer, created 13,000 years ago.*

* Younger Dryas stadial.
* Beginning of the Holocene extinction.

12,000 BP

* Wooden buildings in South America (Chile).
* First pottery vessels (Japan).

11,000 BP

* First evidence of human settlement in Argentina.
* The Arlington Springs Man dies on the island of Santa Rosa, off the coast of California, United States.
* Human remains deposited in caves which are now located off the coast of Yucatán, Mexico.
* Creswellian culture settlement on Hengistbury Head, England, dates from around this year.

10,000 BP

* Evidence of a massacre near Lake Turkana, Kenya indicates upper paleolithic warfare.[269]

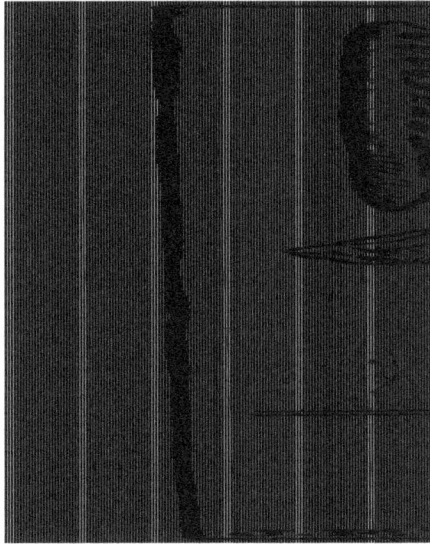

Figure 79: *Reindeer Age articles*

Cultures

The Upper Paleolithic in the Franco-Cantabrian region:

- The Châtelperronian culture was located around central and south western France, and northern Spain. It appears to be derived from the Mousterian culture, and represents the period of overlap between Neanderthals and *Homo sapiens*. This culture lasted from approximately 45,000 BP to 40,000 BP.
- The Aurignacian culture was located in Europe and south west Asia, and flourished between 43,000 and 36,000 BP. It may have been contemporary with the Périgordian (a contested grouping of the earlier Châtelperronian and later Gravettian cultures).
- The Gravettian culture was located across Europe. Gravettian sites generally date between 33,000 and 20,000 BP.
- The Solutrean culture was located in eastern France, Spain, and England. Solutrean artifacts have been dated c. 22,000 to 17,000 BP.
- The Magdalenian culture left evidence from Portugal to Poland during the period from 17,000 to 12,000 BP.

- Central and east Europe:
  - 33,000 BP, Gravettian culture in southern Ukraine.
  - 30,000 BP, Szeletian culture

- 22,000 BP, Pavlovian, Aurignacian cultures
- 13,000 BP, Ahrensburg culture (Western Germany, Netherlands, England)
- 12,000 BP, Epigravettian
- North and west Africa, and Sahara:
  - 32,000 BP, Aterian culture (Algeria, Libya)
  - 12,000 BP, Ibero-Maurusian (a.k.a. Oranian, Ouchtatian), and Sebilian cultures
  - 10,000 BP, Capsian culture (Tunisia, Algeria)
- Central, south, and east Africa:
  - 50,000 BP, Fauresmith culture
  - 30,000 BP, Stillbayan culture
  - 12,000 BP, Lupembian culture
  - 11,000 BP, Magosian culture (Zambia, Tanzania)
  - 9,000 BP, Wiltonian culture
- West Asia (including Middle East):
  - 50,000 BP, Jabroudian culture (Levant)
  - 40,000 BP, Amoudian culture
  - 30,000 BP, Emireh culture
  - 20,000 BP, Aurignacian culture
  - 12,000 BP, Kebarian, Athlitian cultures
- South, central and northern Asia:
  - 30,000 BP, Angara culture
  - 11,000 BP, Khandivili culture
- East and southeast Asia:
  - 50,000 BP, Ngandong culture
  - 30,000 BP, Sen-Doki culture
  - 16,000 BP, Jōmon period starts in Ancient Japan
  - 12,000 BP, pre-Jōmon ceramic culture (Japan)
  - 10,000 BP, Hoabinhian culture (Northern Vietnam)
  - 9,000 BP, Jōmon culture (Japan)
- Oceania
  - 40,000 BP, Whadjuk and Noongar culture (Perth, Australia)[270]
  - 35,000 BP, Wurundjeri, Boonwurrung and Wathaurong culture (Melbourne, Australia)[271]
  - 30,000 BP, Eora and Darug culture (Sydney, Australia)
  - 30,000 BP, Arrernte culture (Alice Springs, Central Australia)

References

- Gilman, Antonio (1996). "Explaining the Upper Palaeolithic Revolution". Pp. 220–239 (Chap. 8) in *Contemporary Archaeology in Theory: A Reader*. Cambridge, MA: Blackwell.

External links

- The Upper Paleolithic Revolution[272]
- Picture Gallery of the Paleolithic (reconstructional palaeoethnology)[273], Libor Balák at the Czech Academy of Sciences, the Institute of Archaeology in Brno, The Center for Paleolithic and Paleoethnological Research

Mammoth steppe

During the Last Glacial Maximum, the **mammoth steppe** was the Earth's most extensive biome. It spanned from Spain eastwards across Eurasia to Canada and from the arctic islands southwards to China. It had a cold, dry climate, the vegetation was dominated by palatable high-productivity grasses, herbs and willow shrubs, and the animal biomass was dominated by the bison, horse, and the woolly mammoth. This ecosystem covered wide areas of the northern part of the globe, thrived for approximately 100,000 years without major changes, and then suddenly became all but extinct about 12,000 years ago.

Naming

At the end of the 19th century, Alfred Nehring (1890) and Jan Czerski (Iwan Dementjewitsch Chersky, 1891) proposed that during the last glacial period a major part of northern Europe had been populated by large herbivores and that a steppe climate had prevailed there. In 1982, the scientist R. Dale Guthrie coined the term "mammoth steppe" for this paleoregion.

Origin of the mammoth steppe

The last glacial period, commonly referred to as the 'Ice Age', spanned from 126,000 YBP–11,700 YBP and was the most recent glacial period within the current ice age which occurred during the last years of the Pleistocene era. It reached its peak during the last glacial maximum, when ice sheets commenced advancing from 33,000 years BP and reached their maximum positions 26,500 years BP. Deglaciation commenced in the Northern Hemisphere approximately 19,000 years BP, and in Antarctica approximately 14,500 years BP, which is

Figure 80: *Ukok Plateau, one of the last remnants of the mammoth steppe*

consistent with evidence that it was the primary source for an abrupt rise in the sea level at that time.

During the peak of the last glacial maximum, a vast mammoth steppe stretched from Spain across Eurasia and over the Bering land bridge into Alaska and the Yukon where it was stopped by the Wisconsin glaciation. This land bridge existed because more of the planet's water was locked up in ice than now and therefore the sea levels were lower. When the sea levels began to rise this bridge was inundated around 11,000 years BP.

During glacial periods, there is clear evidence for intense aridity due to water being held in glaciers and their associated effects on climate. The mammoth steppe was like a huge 'inner court' that was surrounded on all sides by moisture-blocking features: massive continental glaciers, high mountains, and frozen seas. These kept rainfall low and created more days with clear skies than are seen today, which increased evaporation in the summer leading to aridity, and radiation of warmth from the ground into the black night sky in the winter leading to cold. This is thought to have been caused by seven factors:

1. The driving force for the core Asian steppe was an enormous and stable high-pressure system north of the Tibetan Plateau.
2. Deflection of the larger portion of the Gulf Stream southward, past southern Spain onto the coast of Africa, reduced temperatures (hence moisture

and cloud cover) that the North Atlantic Current brings to Western Europe.

3. Growth of the Scandinavian ice sheet created a barrier to North Atlantic moisture.

4. Icing over of the North Atlantic sea surface with reduced flow of moisture from the east.

5. The winter (January) storm track seems to have swept across Eurasia on this axis.

6. Lowered sea levels exposed a large continental shelf to the north and east producing a vast northern plain which increased the size of the continent to the north.

7. North American glaciers shielded interior Alaska and the Yukon Territory from moisture flow. These physical barriers to moisture flow created a vast arid basin or protected 'inner court' spanning parts of three continents.

Biota

Animal biomass and plant productivity of the mammoth steppe were similar to today's African savannah. There is no comparison to it today.

Plants

The paleo-environment changed across time, a proposal that is supported from mammoth dung samples found in northern Yakutia. During Pleniglacial interstadials, alder, birch, and pine trees survived in northern Siberia, however during the Last Glacial Maximum only a treeless steppe vegetation existed. At the onset of the Late Glacial Interstadial (15,000–11,000 BP), global warming resulted in shrub and dwarf birch in northeastern Siberia, which was then colonized by open woodland with birch and spruce during the Younger Dryas (12,900–11,700 YBP). By the Holocene (10,000 YBP), patches of closed larch and pine forests developed. Past researchers had once assumed that the mammoth steppe was very unproductive because they had assumed that its soils had a very low carbon content; however, these soils (yedoma) were preserved in the permafrost of Siberia and Alaska and are the largest reservoir of organic carbon known. It was a highly productive environment. The vegetation was dominated by palatable high-productivity grasses, herbs and willow shrubs.

See further:Gallery of mammoth steppe plants

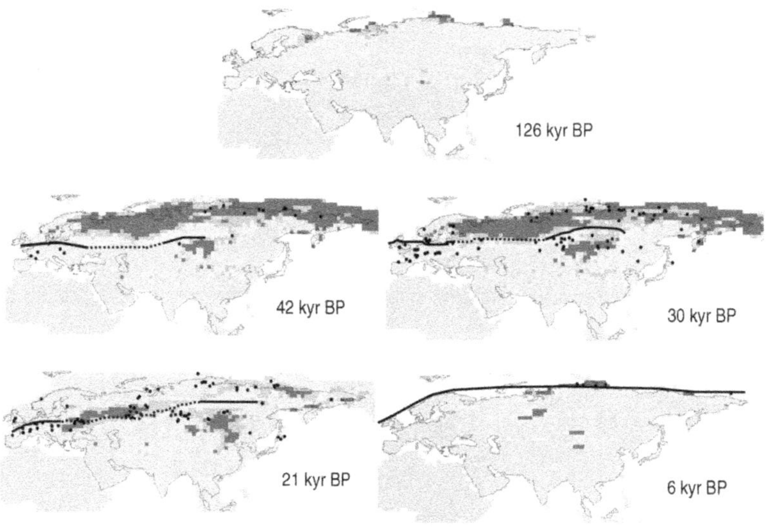

Figure 81: *Climatic suitability for the woolly mammoths in the Late Pleistocene and Holocene. Increasing intensities of red represent increasing suitability of the climate and increasing intensities of green represent decreasing suitability. Black points are the records of mammoth presence for each of the periods. Black lines represent the northern limit of modern humans and black dotted lines indicate uncertainty in the limit of modern humans (D. Nogués-Bravo et al. 2008).*

Animals

The mammoth steppe was dominated in biomass by bison, horse, and the woolly mammoth, and was the center for the evolution of the Pleistocene woolly fauna. On Wrangel Island, the remains of woolly mammoth, woolly rhinoceros, horse, bison and musk ox have been found. Reindeer and small animal remains do not preserve, but reindeer excrement has been found in sediment. In the most arid regions of the mammoth steppe that were to the south of Central Siberia and Mongolia, woolly rhinoceros were common but woolly mammoths were rare. Reindeer live in the far north of Mongolia today and historically their southern boundary passed through Germany and along the steppes of eastern Europe, indicating they once covered much of the mammoth steppe. Mammoths survived on the Taimyr Peninsula until the Holocene. A small population of mammoth survived on St. Paul Island, Alaska, up until 3750 BC, and the small mammoths of Wrangel Island survived until 1650 BC. Bison in Alaska and the Yukon, and horses and muskox in northern Siberia, have survived the loss of the mammoth steppe. One study has proposed that a change of suitable climate caused a significant drop in the mammoth population size, which made them vulnerable to hunting from expanding human populations. The coincidence of both of these impacts in the Holocene most likely set the place and time for the extinction of the woolly mammoth.

Decline of the mammoth steppe

The mammoth steppe had a cold, dry climate. During the past interglacial warmings, forests of trees and shrubs expanded northwards into the mammoth steppe, when northern Siberia, Alaska and the Yukon (Beringia) would have formed a mammoth steppe refugium. When the planet grew colder again, the mammoth steppe expanded. This ecosystem covered wide areas of the northern part of the globe, thrived for approximately 100,000 years without major changes, and then suddenly became extinct about 12,000 years ago.

There are two theories about the decline of the mammoth steppe.

Climate change

The Climatic Hypothesis assumes that the vast mammoth ecosystem could have only existed within a certain range of climatic parameters. At the beginning of the Holocene 10,000 years ago, mossy forests, tundra, lakes and wetlands displaced mammoth steppe. It has been assumed that in contrast to other previous interglacials the cold dry climate switched to a warmer wetter climate that, in turn, caused the disappearance of the grasslands and their dependent megafauna.

The extinct steppe bison (*Bison priscus*) survived across the northern region of central eastern Siberia until 8000 years ago. A study of the frozen mummy of a steppe bison found in northern Yakutia, Russia indicated that it was a pasture grazer in a habitat that was becoming dominated by shrub and tundra vegetation. Higher temperature and rainfall led to a decrease in its previous habitat during the early Holocene, and this led to population fragmentation followed by extinction.

In 2017 a study looked at the environmental conditions across Europe, Siberia and the Americas from 25,000–10,000 YBP. The study found that prolonged warming events leading to deglaciation and maximum rainfall occurred just prior to the transformation of the rangelands that supported megaherbivores into widespread wetlands that supported herbivore-resistant plants. The study proposes that moisture-driven environmental change led to the megafaunal extinctions, and that Africa's trans-equatorial position allowed rangeland to continue to exist between the deserts and the central forests; therefore fewer megafauna species became extinct there.

Human predation

The Ecosystem Hypothesis assumes that the vast mammoth ecosystem extended over a range of many regional climates and was not affected by climate fluctuations. Its highly productive grasslands were maintained by animals trampling any mosses and shrubs, and actively transpiring grasses and herbs dominated. At the beginning of the Holocene the rise in precipitation was accompanied by increased temperature, and so its climatic aridity did not change substantially. As a result of human hunting, the decreasing density of the animals was not enough to maintain the grasslands, leading to an increase in forests, shrubs and mosses with further animal reduction due to loss of feed. The mammoth continued to exist on isolated Wrangel Island until a few thousand years ago, and some of the other megafauna from that time still exist today, which indicates that something other than climate change was responsible for megafaunal extinctions.

Remains of mammoth that had been hunted by humans 45,000 YBP have been found at Yenisei Bay in the central Siberian Arctic. Two other sites in the Maksunuokha River valley to the south of the Shirokostan Peninsula, northeast Siberia, dated between 14,900 and 13,600 years ago showed the remains of mammoth hunting and the production of micro-blades similar to those found in northwest North America, suggesting a cultural connection.

Last remnants

During the Holocene, the arid-adapted species became extinct or were reduced to minor habitats. Cold and dry conditions similar to the last glacial period are found today in the eastern Altai-Sayan mountains of Central Eurasia, with no significant changes occurring between the cold phase of the Pleistocene and the Holocene. Recent paleo-biome reconstruction and pollen analysis suggest that some present-day Altai-Sayan areas could be considered the closest analogy to the mammoth steppe environment. The environment of this region is considered to have been stable for the past 40,000 years. The Eastern part of the Altai-Sayan region forms a Last Glacial refugium. In both the Last Glacial and modern times, the eastern Altai-Sayan region has supported large herbivore and predator species adapted to the steppe, desert and alpine biomes where these biomes have not been separated by forest belts. None of the surviving Pleistocene mammals live in temperate forest, taiga, or tundra biomes. The areas of Ukok-Sailiugem in the southern Altai Republic, and Khar Us Nuur and Uvs Nuur (Ubsunur Hollow) in western Mongolia, have supported reindeer and saiga antelope since the glacial period.

Figure 82: *Ubsunur Hollow Biosphere Reserve located on the border of Mongolia and the Republic of Tuva is one of the last remnants of the mammoth steppe*

Image gallery

The paleo-environment changed across time. Below is a gallery of mammoth steppe plants, the location where they have been identified as widespread, the time period and supporting citations.

Figure 83: *Artemisia, Taymyr lowlands 24,000–10,300 YBP, Yakutia 22,500 YBP, Alaska and the Yukon 15,000-11,500 YBP*

Figure 84: *Cyperaceae (sedges), Yakutia 22,500
YBP, Alaska and the Yukon 15,000-11,500 YBP*

Figure 85: *Gramineae (grasses), Taymyr lowlands 24,000–10,300
YBP, Yakutia 22,500 YBP, Alaska and the Yukon 15,000-11,500 YBP*

Figure 86: *Salix (willow), Taymyr lowlands 24,000–10,300 YBP, Yakutia 22,500 YBP, Alaska and the Yukon 15,000-11,500 YBP*

Figure 87: *Rubus chamaemorus (cloudberry) Yakutia 22,500 YBP*

Figure 88: *Potentilla (cinquefoil) Yakutia 22,500 YBP*

Figure 89: *Larch Taymyr lowlands*
48,000–25,000 YBP, then later 9,400-2,900 YBP

Figure 90: *Betula nana (dwarf birch) Taymyr lowlands 48,000–25,000 YBP*

References

Interbreeding between archaic and modern humans

There is evidence for **interbreeding between archaic and modern humans** during the Middle Paleolithic and early Upper Paleolithic. The interbreeding happened in several independent events that included Neanderthals, Denisovans, as well as several unidentified hominins respectively.

In Eurasia, interbreeding between Neanderthals and Denisovans (both assumed to be derived from Eurasian *Homo heidelbergensis*) with modern humans took place several times between about 100,000 and 40,000 years ago, both before and after the recent out-of-Africa migration 70,000 years ago. Neanderthal-derived DNA was found in the genome of contemporary populations in Europe and Asia, estimated as accounting for between 1% and 6% of modern genomes. The highest rates of archaic admixture overall have been found in indigenous Oceanian and Southeast Asian populations, with an estimated 4–6% of the genome of modern Melanesians being derived from Denisovans.

Neanderthal-derived and Denisovan-derived ancestry is significantly absent from most modern populations in Sub-Saharan Africa. However, archaic alleles consistent with several independent admixture events in the subcontinent have been found.

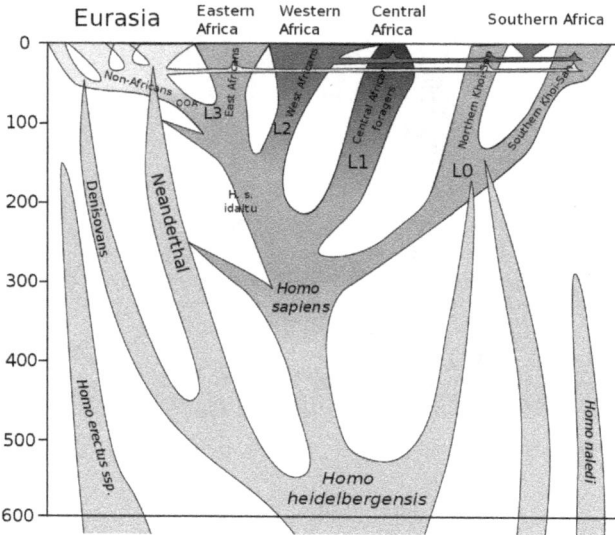

Figure 91: *A model of the phylogeny of H. sapiens over the last 600,000 years (vertical axis). The horizontal axis represents geographic location; the vertical axis represents time in thousands of years ago.*[274] *Homo heidelbergensis is shown as diverging into Neanderthals, Denisovans and H. sapiens. With the expansion of H. sapiens after 200 kya, Neanderthals, Denisovans and unspecified archaic African hominins are displayed as again subsumed into the H. sapiens lineage. Possible admixture events involving certain modern populations in Africa are also shown.*

Neanderthals

Genetics

Proportion of admixture

Through whole-genome sequencing of three Vindija Neanderthals, a draft sequence of the Neanderthal genome was published by a team of researchers led by Richard Green on 7 May 2010 in the journal *Science* and revealed that Neanderthals shared more alleles with Eurasian populations (e.g. French, Han Chinese, and Papua New Guinean) than with Sub-Saharan African populations (e.g. Yoruba and San). According to their paper, the observed excess of genetic similarity is best explained by recent gene flow from Neanderthals to modern humans after the migration out of Africa. Green et al. (2010) estimated the proportion of Neanderthal-derived ancestry to be 1–4% of the Eurasian genome. The proportion was estimated to be 1.5–2.1% in Prüfer et al. (2013), but it was later revised to a higher 1.8–2.6% by Prüfer et al. (2017). The same study noted that East Asians carry more Neandertal DNA (2.3–2.6%) than Western Eurasians (1.8–2.4%) Lohse and Frantz (2014) infer an even higher rate of 3.4–7.3%.

Distance to lineages

Presenting a high-quality genome sequence of a female Altai Neanderthal, it has been found that the Neanderthal component in non-African modern humans is more related to the Mezmaiskaya Neanderthal (Caucasus) than to the Altai Neanderthal (Siberia) or the Vindija Neanderthals (Croatia). By high-coverage sequencing the genome of a 50,000-year-old female Vindija Neanderthal fragment, it was later found that the Vindija and Mezmaiskaya Neanderthals did not seem to differ in the extent of their allele-sharing with modern humans. In this case, it was also found that the Neanderthal component in non-African modern humans is more closely related to the Vindija and Mezmaiskaya Neanderthals than to the Altai Neandertal. These results suggest that a majority of the admixture into modern humans came from Neanderthal populations that had diverged (about 80–100kya) from the Vindija and Mezmaiskaya Neanderthal lineages before the latter two diverged from each other.

Analyzing chromosome 21 of the Altai (Siberia), El Sidrón (Spain), and Vindija (Croatia) Neanderthals, it is determined that—of these three lineages—only the El Sidrón and Vindija Neanderthals display significant rates of gene flow (0.3–2.6%) into modern humans, suggesting that the El Sidrón and Vindija Neanderthals are more closely related than the Altai Neanderthal to the Neanderthals that interbred with modern humans about 47,000–65,000 years ago. Conversely, it is also determined that significant rates of modern human gene flow into Neanderthals occurred—of the three examined lineages—for only the Altai Neanderthal (0.1–2.1%), suggesting that modern human gene flow into Neanderthals mainly took place after the separation of the Altai Neanderthals from the El Sidrón and Vindija Neanderthals that occurred roughly 110,000 years ago. The findings show that the source of modern human gene flow into Neanderthals originated from a population of early modern humans from about 100,000 years ago, predating the out-of-Africa migration of the modern human ancestors of present-day non-Africans.

Introgressed genome

About 20% of the Neanderthal genome has been found introgressed in the modern human population (by analyzing East Asians and Europeans), but the figure has also been estimated at one-third.

In Papuans, introgressed Neanderthal alleles are found in highest frequency in genes expressed in the brain, whereas Denisovan alleles have the highest frequency in genes expressed in bones and other tissues.

Subpopulation admixture rate

A higher Neanderthal admixture was found in East Asians than in Europeans, which is estimated to be about 20% more introgression into East Asians. This could possibly be explained by the occurrence of further admixture events in the early ancestors of East Asians after the separation of Europeans and East Asians, dilution of Neanderthal ancestry in Europeans by populations with low Neanderthal ancestry from later migrations, or natural selection that may have been relatively lower in East Asians than in Europeans. Studies indicate that a reduced efficacy of purifying selection against Neanderthal alleles in East Asians could not account for the greater proportion of Neanderthal ancestry of East Asians, thus favoring more-complex models involving additional pulses of Neanderthal introgression into East Asians. It has also been observed that there's a small but significant variation of Neanderthal admixture rates within European populations, but no significant variation within East Asian populations.

Genomic analysis suggests that there is a global division in Neanderthal introgression between Sub-Saharan African populations and other modern human groups (including North Africans) rather than between African and non-African populations. North African groups share a similar excess of derived alleles with Neanderthals as do non-African populations, whereas Sub-Saharan African groups are the only modern human populations that generally did not experience Neanderthal admixture. The Neanderthal genetic signal among North African populations was found to vary depending on the relative quantity of autochthonous North African, European, Near Eastern and Sub-Saharan ancestry. Using f4 ancestry ratio statistical analysis, the Neanderthal inferred admixture was observed to be: highest among the North African populations with maximal autochthonous North African ancestry such as Tunisian Berbers, where it was at the same level or even higher than that of Eurasian populations (100–138%); high among North African populations carrying greater European or Near Eastern admixture, such as groups in North Morocco and Egypt (~60–70%); and lowest among North African populations with greater Sub-Saharan admixture, such as in South Morocco (20%). Quinto et al. (2012) therefore postulate that the presence of this Neanderthal genetic signal in Africa is not due to recent gene flow from Near Eastern or European populations since it is higher among populations bearing indigenous pre-Neolithic North African ancestry. The Neanderthal-linked haplotype B006 of the dystrophin gene has also been found among nomad pastoralist groups in the Sahel and Horn of Africa, who are associated with northern populations. Consequently, the presence of this B006 haplotype on the northern and northeastern perimeter of Sub-Saharan Africa is attributed to gene flow from a non-African point of origin. Low but significant rates of Neanderthal admixture has also been observed for the Maasai of East Africa. After identifying African and non-African ancestry among the Maasai, it can be concluded that recent non-African modern human (post-Neanderthal) gene flow was the source of the contribution since around an estimated 30% of the Maasai genome can be traced to non-African introgression from about 100 generations ago.

Mitochondrial DNA

No evidence of Neanderthal mitochondrial DNA has been found in modern humans. This would suggest that successful admixture with Neanderthals happened paternally rather than maternally on the side of Neanderthals. Possible hypotheses are that Neanderthal mitochondrial DNA had detrimental mutations that led to the extinction of carriers, that the hybrid offspring of Neanderthal mothers were raised in Neanderthal groups and became extinct with them, or that female Neanderthals and male Sapiens did not produce fertile offspring.

As shown in an interbreeding model produced by Neves and Serva (2012), the Neanderthal admixture in modern humans may have been caused by a very low rate of interbreeding between modern humans and Neanderthals, with the exchange of one pair of individuals between the two populations in about every 77 generations. This low rate of interbreeding would account for the absence of Neanderthal mitochondrial DNA from the modern human gene pool as found in earlier studies, as the model estimates a probability of only 7% for a Neanderthal origin of both mitochondrial DNA and Y chromosome in modern humans.

Cabrera et al. (2017) suggest that the Neanderthal genes observed in certain modern populations in Africa may have been brought from Eurasia around 70 kya by males bearing the paternal haplogroup E and females carrying the maternal haplogroup L3.

Reduced contribution

It has been found that there is a presence of large genomic regions with strongly reduced Neanderthal contribution in modern humans due to negative selection, partly caused by hybrid male infertility. These large regions of low Neanderthal contribution were most-pronounced on the X chromosome—with fivefold lower Neanderthal ancestry compared to autosomes—and contained relatively high numbers of genes specific to testes. This means that modern humans have relatively few Neanderthal genes that are located on the X chromosome or expressed in the testes, consistent with the fact that male infertility is affected by a disproportionately large amount of genes on X chromosomes. It has also been shown that Neanderthal ancestry has been selected against in conserved biological pathways, such as RNA processing.

Consistent with the hypothesis that purifying selection has reduced Neanderthal contribution in present-day modern human genomes, Upper Paleolithic Eurasian modern humans (such as the Tianyuan modern human) carry more Neanderthal DNA (about 4–5%) than present-day Eurasians modern humans (about 1–2%).

Changes in modern humans

Genes affecting keratin were found to have been introgressed from Neanderthals into modern humans (shown in East Asians and Europeans), suggesting that these genes gave a morphological adaptation in skin and hair to modern humans to cope with non-African environments. This is likewise for several genes involved in medical-relevant phenotypes, such as those affecting systemic lupus erythematosus, primary biliary cirrhosis, Crohn's disease, optic disk size, smoking behavior, interleukin 18 levels, and diabetes mellitus type 2.

Researchers found Neanderthal introgression of 18 genes—several of which are related to UV-light adaptation—within the chromosome 3p21.31 region (HYAL region) of East Asians. The introgressive haplotypes were positively selected in only East Asian populations, rising steadily from 45,000 years BP until a sudden increase of growth rate around 5,000 to 3,500 years BP. They occur at very high frequencies among East Asian populations in contrast to other Eurasian populations (e.g. European and South Asian populations). The findings also suggests that this Neanderthal introgression occurred within the ancestral population shared by East Asians and Native Americans.

Evans et al. (2006) had previously suggested that a group of alleles collectively known as haplogroup D of microcephalin, a critical regulatory gene for brain volume, originated from an archaic human population. The results show that haplogroup D introgressed 37,000 years ago (based on the coalescence age of derived D alleles) into modern humans from an archaic human population that separated 1.1 million years ago (based on the separation time between D and non-D alleles), consistent with the period when Neanderthals and modern humans co-existed and diverged respectively. The high frequency of the D haplogroup (70%) suggest that it was positively selected for in modern humans. The distribution of the D allele of microcephalin is high outside Africa but low in sub-Saharan Africa, which further suggest that the admixture event happened in archaic Eurasian populations. This distribution difference between Africa and Eurasia suggests that the D allele originated from Neanderthals according to Lari et al. (2010), but they found that a Neanderthal individual from the Mezzena Rockshelter (Monti Lessini, Italy) was homozygous for an ancestral allele of microcephalin, thus providing no support that Neanderthals contributed the D allele to modern humans and also not excluding the possibility of a Neanderthal origin of the D allele. Green et al. (2010), having analyzed the Vindija Neanderthals, also could not confirm a Neanderthal origin of haplogroup D of the microcephalin gene.

It has been found that HLA-A*02, A*26/*66, B*07, B*51, C*07:02, and C*16:02 of the immune system were contributed from Neanderthals to modern humans. After migrating out of Africa, modern humans encountered and interbred with archaic humans, which was advantageous for modern humans in rapidly restoring HLA diversity and acquiring new HLA variants that are better adapted to local pathogens.

It has been found that introgressed Neanderthal genes exhibit cis-regulatory effects in modern humans, contributing to the genomic complexity and phenotype variation of modern humans. Looking at heterozygous individuals (carrying both Neanderthal and modern human versions of a gene), the allele-specific expression of introgressed Neanderthal alleles was found to be significantly lower in the brain and testes relative to other tissues. In the brain, this was most pronounced at the cerebellum and basal ganglia. This downregulation suggests that modern humans and Neanderthals possibly experienced a relative higher rate of divergence in these specific tissues.

Studying the high-coverage female Vindija Neanderthal genome, Prüfer et al. (2017) identified several Neanderthal-derived gene variants, including those that affect levels of LDL cholesterol and vitamin D, and has influence on eating disorders, visceral fat accumulation, rheumatoid arthritis, schizophrenia, as well as the response to antipsychotic drugs.

Examining European modern humans in regards to the Altai Neanderthal genome in high-coverage, results show that Neanderthal admixture is associated with several changes in cranium and underlying brain morphology, suggesting changes in neurological function through Neanderthal-derived genetic variation. Neanderthal admixture is associated with an expansion of the posterolateral area of the modern human skull, extending from the occipital and inferior parietal bones to bilateral temporal locales. In regards to modern human brain morphology, Neanderthal admixture is positively correlated with an increase in sulcal depth for the right intraparietal sulcus and an increase in cortical complexity for the early visual cortex of the left hemisphere. Neanderthal admixture is also positively correlated with an increase in white and gray matter volume localized to the right parietal region adjacent to the right intraparietal sulcus. In the area overlapping the primary visual cortex gyrification in the left hemisphere, Neanderthal admixture is positively correlated with gray matter volume. The results also show evidence for a negative correlation between Neanderthal admixture and white matter volume in the orbitofrontal cortex.

Population substructure theory

Although less parsimonious than recent gene flow, the observation may have been due to ancient population sub-structure in Africa, causing incomplete genetic homogenization within modern humans when Neanderthals diverged while early ancestors of Eurasians were still more closely related to Neanderthals than those of Africans to Neanderthals. On the basis of allele frequency spectrum, it was shown that the recent admixture model had the best fit to the results while the ancient population sub-structure model had no fit—demonstrating that the best model was a recent admixture event that was preceded by a bottleneck event among modern humans—thus confirming recent admixture as the most parsimonious and plausible explanation for the observed excess of genetic similarities between modern non-African humans and Neanderthals. On the basis of linkage disequilibrium patterns, a recent admixture event is likewise confirmed by the data. From the extent of linkage disequilibrium, it was estimated that the last Neanderthal gene flow into early ancestors of Europeans occurred 47,000–65,000 years BP. In conjunction with archaeological and fossil evidence, the gene flow is thought likely to have occurred somewhere in Western Eurasia, possibly the Middle East. Through another approach—using one genome each of a Neanderthal, Eurasian, African, and chimpanzee (outgroup), and dividing it into non-recombining short sequence blocks—to estimate genome-wide maximum-likelihood under different models, an ancient population sub-structure in Africa was ruled out and a Neanderthal admixture event was confirmed.

Morphology

The early Upper Paleolithic burial remains of a modern human child from Abrigo do Lagar Velho (Portugal) features traits that indicates Neanderthal interbreeding with modern humans dispersing into Iberia. Considering the dating of the burial remains (24,500 years BP) and the persistence of Neanderthal traits long after the transitional period from a Neanderthal to a modern human population in Iberia (28,000–30,000 years BP), the child may have been a descendant of an already heavily-admixed population.

The remains of an early Upper Paleolithic modern human from Peştera Muierilor (Romania) of 35,000 years BP shows a morphological pattern of European early modern humans, but possesses archaic or Neanderthal features, suggesting European early modern humans interbreeding with Neanderthals. These features include a large interorbital breadth, a relatively flat superciliary arches, a prominent occipital bun, an asymmetrical and shallow mandibular notch shape, a high mandibular coronoid processus, the relative perpendicular mandibular condyle to notch crest position, and a narrow scapular glenoid fossa.

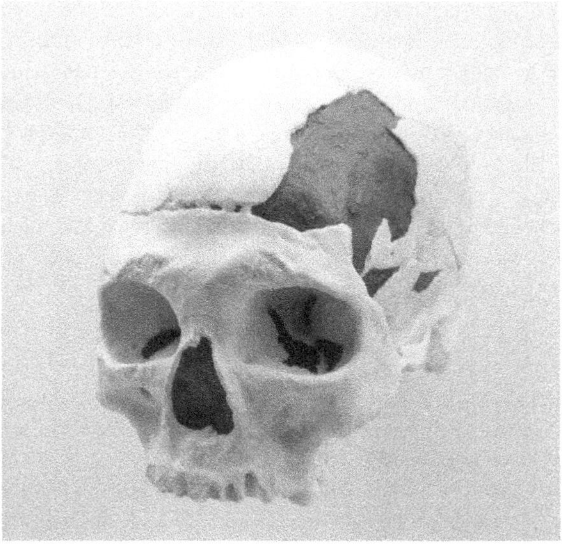

Figure 92: *The modern human Oase 2 skull (cast depicted), found in Peştera cu Oase, displays archaic traits due to possible hybridization with Neanderthals.*

The early modern human Oase 1 mandible from Peştera cu Oase (Romania) of 34,000–36,000 ^{14}C years BP presents a mosaic of modern, archaic, and possible Neanderthal features. It displays a lingual bridging of the mandibular foramen, not present in earlier humans except Neanderthals of the late Middle and Late Pleistocene, thus suggesting affinity with Neanderthals. Concluding from the Oase 1 mandible, there was apparently a significant craniofacial change of early modern humans from at least Europe, possibly due to some degree of admixture with Neanderthals.

The earliest (before about 33 ka BP) European modern humans and the subsequent (Middle Upper Paleolithic) Gravettians, falling anatomically largely inline with the earliest (Middle Paleolithic) African modern humans, also show traits that are distinctively Neanderthal, suggesting that a solely Middle Paleolithic modern human ancestry was unlikely for European early modern humans.

A late-Neanderthal jaw (more specifically, a corpus mandibulae remnant) from the Mezzena rockshelter (Monti Lessini, Italy) shows indications of a possible interbreeding in late Italian Neanderthals. The jaw falls within the morphological range of modern humans, but also displayed strong similarities with some of the other Neanderthal specimens, indicating a change in late Neanderthal morphology due to possible interbreeding with modern humans.

The Manot 1, a partial calvaria of a modern human that was recently discovered at the Manot Cave (Western Galilee, Israel) and dated to 54.7±5.5 kyr BP, represents the first fossil evidence from the period when modern humans successfully migrated out of Africa and colonized Eurasia. It also provides the first fossil evidence that modern humans inhabited the southern Levant during the Middle to Upper Palaeolithic interface, contemporaneously with the Neanderthals and close to the probable interbreeding event. The morphological features suggest that the Manot population may be closely related or given rise to the first modern humans who later successfully colonized Europe to establish early Upper Palaeolithic populations.

History

The hypothesis, variously under the names of interbreeding, hybridization, admixture or hybrid-origin theory, has been discussed ever since the discovery of Neanderthal remains in the 19th century, though earlier writers believed that Neanderthals were a direct ancestor of modern humans. Thomas Huxley suggested that many Europeans bore traces of Neanderthal ancestry, but associated Neanderthal characteristics with primitivism, writing that since they "belong to a stage in the development of the human species, antecedent to the differentiation of any of the existing races, we may expect to find them in the lowest of these races, all over the world, and in the early stages of all races".

Hans Peder Steensby in the 1907 article *Racestudier i Danmark* ("Race studies in Denmark") rejected that Neanderthals were ape-like or inferior, and, while emphasizing that all modern humans are of mixed origins, suggested interbreeding as the best available explanation of a significant number of observations which by then were available.

In the early twentieth century, Carleton Coon argued that the Caucasoid race is of dual origin consisting of Upper Paleolithic (mixture of *H. sapiens* and *H. neanderthalensis*) types and Mediterranean (purely *H. sapiens*) types. He repeated his theory in his 1962 book *The Origin of Races*.

Denisovans

Denisovan DNA has been found in modern humans, and it has been estimated that 90% of the Denisovan genome is still present. It has been shown that Melanesians (e.g. Papua New Guinean and Bougainville Islander) share relatively more alleles with Denisovans when compared to other Eurasians and Africans. It estimated that 4% to 6% of the genome in Melanesians derives from Denisovans, while no other Eurasians or Africans displayed contributions of the Denisovan genes. It has been observed that Denisovans contributed

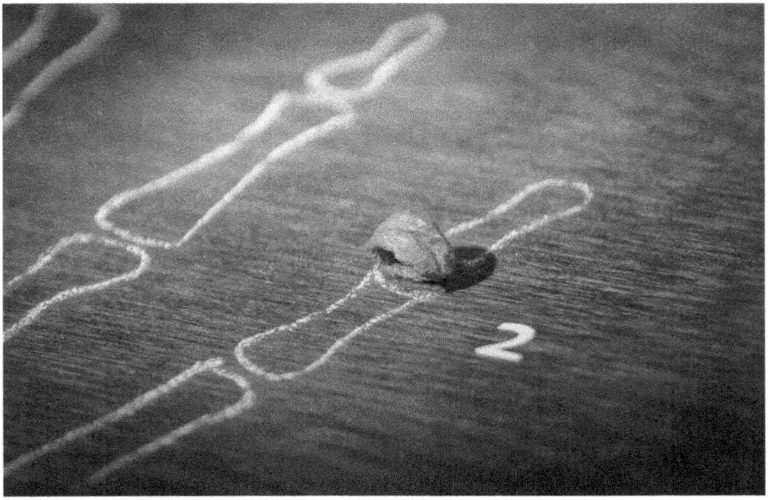

Figure 93: *The Denisovan genome was sequenced from the distal manual phalanx fragment (replica depicted) found in the Denisova cave.*

genes to Melanesians but not to East Asians, indicating that there was interaction between the early ancestors of Melanesians with Denisovans but that this interaction did not take place in the regions near southern Siberia, where as-of-yet the only Denisovan remains have been found. In addition, Aboriginal Australians also show a relative increased allele sharing with Denisovans, compared to other Eurasians and African populations, consistent with the hypothesis of increased admixture between Denisovans and Melanesians.

Reich et al. (2011) produced evidence that the highest presence of Denisovan admixture is in Oceanian populations, followed by many Southeast Asian populations, and none in East Asian populations. There is significant Denisovan genetic material in eastern Southeast Asian and Oceanian populations (e.g. Aboriginal Australians, Near Oceanians, Polynesians, Fijians, eastern Indonesians, Philippine Mamanwa and Manobo), but not in certain western and continental Southeast Asian populations (e.g. western Indonesians, Malaysian Jehai, Andaman Onge, and mainland Asians), indicating that the Denisovan admixture event happened in Southeast Asia itself rather than mainland Eurasia. The observation of high Denisovan admixture in Oceania and the lack thereof in mainland Asia suggests that early modern humans and Denisovans had interbred east of the Wallace Line that divides Southeast Asia according to Cooper and Stringer (2013).

Skoglund and Jakobsson (2011) observed that particularly Oceanians, followed by Southeast Asians populations, have a high Denisovans admixture relative to other populations. Furthermore, they found possible low traces of Denisovan admixture in East Asians and no Denisovan admixture in Native Americans. In contrast, Prüfer et al. (2013) found that mainland Asian and Native American populations may have a 0.2% Denisovan contribution, which is about twenty-five times lower than Oceanian populations. The manner of gene flow to these populations remains unknown. However, Wall et al. (2013) stated that they found no evidence for Denisovan admixture in East Asians.

Findings indicate that the Denisovan gene flow event happened to the common ancestors of Aboriginal Filipinos, Aboriginal Australians, and New Guineans. New Guineans and Australians have similar rates of Denisovan admixture, indicating that interbreeding took place prior to their common ancestors' entry into Sahul (Pleistocene New Guinea and Australia), at least 44,000 years ago. It has also been observed that the fraction of Near Oceanian ancestry in Southeast Asians is proportional to the Denisovan admixture, except in the Philippines where there is a higher proportional Denisovan admixture to Near Oceanian ancestry. Reich et al. (2011) suggested a possible model of an early eastward migration wave of modern humans, some who were Philippine/New Guinean/Australian common ancestors that interbred with Denisovans, respectively followed by divergence of the Philippine early ancestors, interbreeding between the New Guinean and Australian early ancestors with a part of the same early-migration population that did not experience Denisovan gene flow, and interbreeding between the Philippine early ancestors with a part of the population from a much-later eastward migration wave (the other part of the migrating population would become East Asians).

It has been shown that Eurasians have some but significant lesser archaic-derived genetic material that overlaps with Denisovans, stemming from the fact that Denisovans are related to Neanderthals—who contributed to the Eurasian gene pool—rather than from interbreeding of Denisovans with the early ancestors of those Eurasians.

The skeletal remains of an early modern human from the Tianyuan cave (near Zhoukoudian, China) of 40,000 years BP showed a Neanderthal contribution within the range of today's Eurasian modern humans, but it had no discernible Denisovan contribution. It is a distant relative to the ancestors of many Asian and Native American populations, but post-dated the divergence between Asians and Europeans. The lack of a Denisovan component in the Tianyuan individual suggests that the genetic contribution had been always scarce in the mainland.

Exploring the immune system's HLA alleles, it has been suggested that HLA-B*73 introgressed from Denisovans into modern humans in western Asia due to the distribution pattern and divergence of HLA-B*73 from other HLA alleles. In modern humans, HLA-B*73 is concentrated in western Asia, but it is rare or absent elsewhere. Even though HLA-B*73 is not present in the sequenced Denisovan genome, the study noted that it was associated to the Denisovan-derived HLA-C*15:05 from the linkage disequilibrium, consistent with the estimated 98% of those modern humans who carried B*73 also carried C*15:05.

The Denisovan's two HLA-A (A*02 and A*11) and two HLA-C (C*15 and C*12:02) allotypes correspond to common alleles in modern humans, whereas one of the Denisovan's HLA-B allotype corresponds to a rare recombinant allele and the other is absent in modern humans. It is thought that these must have been contributed from Denisovans to modern humans, because it is unlikely to have been preserved independently in both for so long due to HLA alleles' high mutation rate.

It has been found that a EPAS1 gene variant was introduced from Denisovans to modern humans. The ancestral variant upregulates hemoglobin levels to compensate for low oxygen levels—such as at high altitudes—but this also has the maladaption of increasing blood viscosity. The Denisovan-derived variant on the other hand limits this increase of hemoglobin levels, thus resulting in a better altitude adaption. The Denisovan-derived EPAS1 gene variant is common in Tibetans and was positively selected in their ancestors after they colonized the Tibetan plateau.

Archaic African hominins

Rapid decay of fossils in Sub-Saharan African environments makes it currently unfeasible to compare modern human admixture with reference samples of archaic Sub-Saharan African hominins.

From three candidate regions with introgression found by searching for unusual patterns of variations (showing deep haplotype divergence, unusual patterns of linkage disequilibrium, and small basal clade size) in 61 non-coding regions from two hunter-gatherer groups (Biaka Pygmies and San who have significant admixture) and one West African agricultural group (Mandinka who don't have significant admixture), it is concluded that roughly 2% of the genetic material found in these Sub-Saharan African populations was inserted into the human genome approximately 35,000 years ago from archaic hominins that broke away from the modern human lineage around 700,000 years ago. A survey for the introgressive haplotypes across many Sub-Saharan populations suggest that this admixture event happened with archaic hominins who once inhabited Central Africa.

Researching high-coverage whole-genome sequences of fifteen Sub-Saharan hunter-gatherer males from three groups—five Pygmies (three Baka, a Bedzan, and a Bakola) from Cameroon, five Hadza from Tanzania, and five Sandawe from Tanzania—there are signs that the ancestors of the hunter-gatherers interbred with one or more archaic human populations, probably over 40,000 years ago. Analysis of putative introgressive haplotypes in the fifteen hunter-gatherer samples suggests that the archaic African population and modern humans diverged around 1.2 to 1.3 million years ago.

Xu et al. (2017) analysed the evolution of the Mucin 7 protein in the saliva of certain African populations (Yoruba) and found evidence that a species of archaic humans may have contributed DNA into their gene pool. This species was unidentified and was referred to as a ghost population of humans. Skoglund et al. (2017) examined the genomes of various ancient and recent populations in Africa and likewise identified evidence pointing to an extinct group of archaic humans, a "basal western African population lineage", which appears to have contributed DNA into the gene pool of modern populations in West Africa (Mende and Yoruba).

Indirect evidence

Human papillomavirus type 58 causes cervical cancer in 10–20% of cases in East Asia. It is rarely found elsewhere. An estimate of the date of evolution of the most recent common ancestor places it at 478,600 years ago (95% HPD 391,000–569,600). As this date is before the generally accepted date of the evolution of modern humans, this suggests that this virus was transmitted to humans from a now extinct hominin. As this virus is usually transmitted sexually this furthermore suggests that mating occurred in this area between modern humans and a now extinct hominin species.

Mousterian

Mousterian

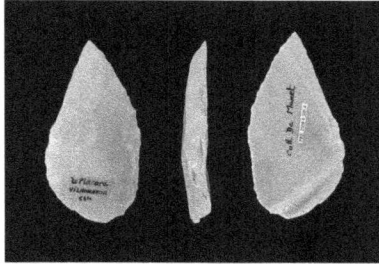

Geographical range	Africa and Eurasia
Period	Middle Paleolithic
Dates	160,000 – 35,000-30,000 BP[275,276]
Type site	Le Moustier
Major sites	Creswell Crags, Lynford Quarry, Arcy-sur-Cure, Vindija Cave, Atapuerca Mountains, Zafarraya, Gorham's Cave, Devil's Tower, Haua Fteah
Preceded by	Acheulean, Micoquien, Clactonian
Followed by	Châtelperronian, Emiran, Aterian

The Paleolithic ↑ Pliocene (before *Homo*)

Lower Paleolithic
(c. 3.3 Ma – 300 ka)

- Oldowan (2.6–1.7 Ma)
- Madrasian Culture (1.5 Ma)
- Soanian (0.5–0.13 Ma)
- Acheulean (1.76–0.1 Ma)
- Clactonian (0.3–0.2 Ma)

- Acheulo-Yabrudian complex (400-200 bp)

Middle Paleolithic
(300–45 ka)

- Mousterian (160–35-30 ka)
- Aterian (c. 145,000–c. 20,000 bp)
- Micoquien (130–70 ka)

- Sangoan (130-10 bp)

Upper Paleolithic
(50–10 ka)

- Emiran (50,000–40,000 bp)
- Bohunician (~48,000 bp)
- Ahmarian (46,000-42,000 bp)
- Châtelperronian (~44,500 – 36,000 bp)
- Lincombian-Ranisian-Jerzmanowician (43-32 ka)
- Aurignacian (46-43,000 – c. 26,000 bp)
- Khormusan (42,000-18,000 bp)
- Baradostian (36-18 ka)
- Périgordian (35–20 ka)
- Gravettian (33–24 ka)
- Antelian (32–20 bp)
- Mal'ta–Buret' culture (24,000 - 15,00 bp)
- Solutrean (22–17 ka)
- Halfan culture (22,000-14,000)
- Afontova Gora (21,000-12,000}
- Epigravettian (20-10 ka)
- Zarzian culture (20,000-10,000 bp)
- Iberomaurusian (~25/23,000-11,000 cal bp)
- Kebaran (18,000 – 12,500 bp)
- Magdalenian (17–12 ka)
- Trialetian (16,000-8,000 bp)
- Hamburg (15,500-13,100 bp)
- Eburran industry (15,000-5,000 bp)
- Qadan culture (15,000 BP — 11,000 bp)
- Sebilian (15,00 -11,00 bp)
- Natufian culture (14,500–11,500 bp)
- Federmesser (14–13 ka)
- Ahrensburg (13–12 ka)
- Khiamian (12,200 and 10,800 bp)
- Swiderian (11–8 ka)

↓ Mesolithic
↓ Stone Age

- v
- t
- e[277]

The **Mousterian** (or **Mode III**) is a techno-complex (archaeological industry) of flint lithic tools associated primarily with Neanderthals, as well as with the

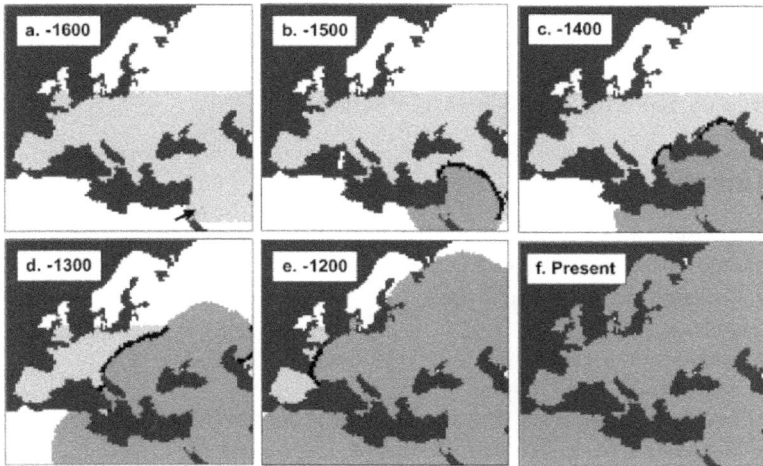

Figure 94: *mtDNA-based simulation of the species Homo sapiens in Europe starting 1600 generations ago. Homo neanderthalensis range in light grey.*

earliest anatomically modern humans in Eurasia. The Mousterian largely defines the latter part of the Middle Paleolithic, the middle of the West Eurasian Old Stone Age. It lasted roughly from 160,000 BP to 35,000-30,000 BP.

Naming

The culture was named after the type site of Le Moustier, a rock shelter in the Dordogne region of France. Similar flintwork has been found all over unglaciated Europe and also the Near East and North Africa. Handaxes, racloirs and points constitute the industry; sometimes a Levallois technique or another prepared-core technique was employed in making the flint flakes.

Characteristics

The European Mousterian is the product of Neanderthals. It existed roughly from 160,000 BP to 35,000-30,000 BP.[278] Some assemblages, namely those from Pech de l'Aze, include exceptionally small points prepared using the Levallois technique among other prepared core types, causing some researchers to suggest that these flakes take advantage of greater grip strength possessed by Neanderthals. In North Africa and the Near East, Mousterian tools were also produced by anatomically modern humans. In the Levant, for example, assemblages produced by Neanderthals are indistinguishable from those made by Qafzeh type modern humans.[279]

Possible variants are Denticulate, Charentian (Ferrassie & Quina) named after the Charente region,[280] Typical and the Acheulean Tradition (MTA) - Type-A and Type-B.[281] The industry continued alongside the new Châtelperronian industry during the 45,000-40,000 BP period.[282]

Locations

- Mousterian artifacts have been found in Haua Fteah in Cyrenaica and other sites in Northwest Africa.
- Contained within a cave in the Syria region, along with a Neanderthaloid skeleton.
- Located in the Haibak valley of Afghanistan.
- Zagros and Central Iran
- The archaeological site of Atapuerca, Spain, contains Mousterian objects.
- Gorham's Cave in Gibraltar contains Mousterian objects.
- Uzbekistan has sites of Mousterian culture, including Teshik-Tash.
- Turkmenistan also has Mousterian relics.
- Siberia has many sites with Mousterian style implements, eg Denisova Cave.
- Israel is one of the places where remains of both Neandertals and Homo sapiens sapiens have been found in association with Mousterian artifacts.[283]
- Lynford Quarry near near Mundford, Norfolk, England has yielded Mousterian tools

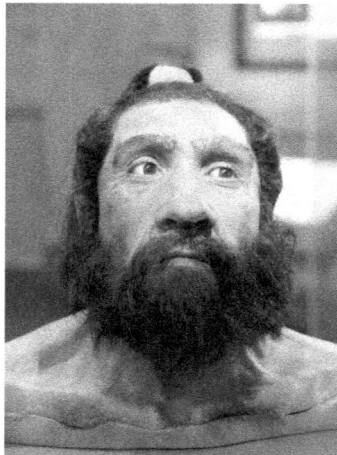

Figure 95: *Artistic impression of the head of the Shanidar 1 fossil, a Homo neanderthalensis male who lived circa 70000 BCE discovered in the mid-20th century at the Mousterian archaeological site Shanidar Cave*

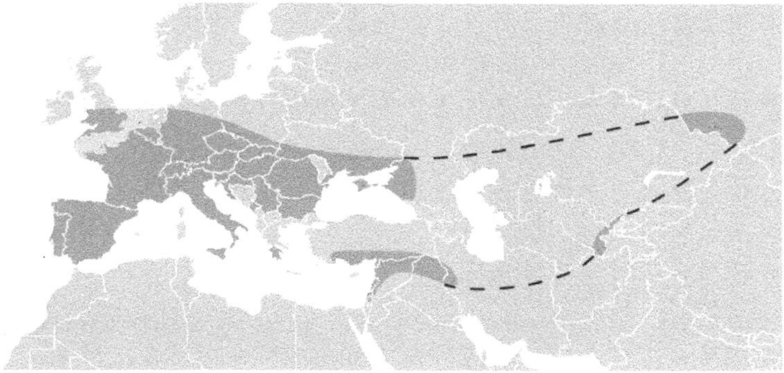

Figure 96: *Range of Homo neanderthalensis. Mousterian industries have been found outside this range (e.g., Jordan, Saudi Arabia).*

Figure 97: *Restoration of Le Moustier Homo neanderthalensis by Charles R. Knight*

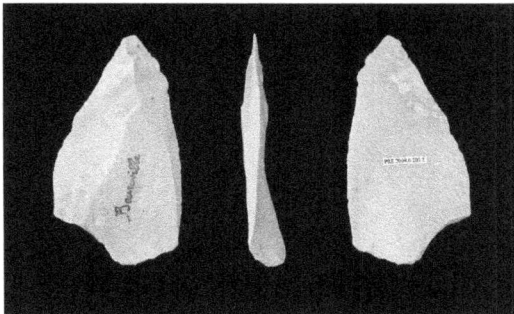

Figure 98: *Levallois points*

External links

Wikimedia Commons has media related to *Mousterian*.

- Neanderthals' Last Stand Is Traced[284] — New York Times article (Published: September 13, 2006)

Preceded by **Micoquien**	**Mousterian** 600,000 years before present — 40,000 years before present	Succeeded by **Châtelperronian**

Europe

European early modern humans

European early modern humans (EEMH) in the context of the Upper Paleolithic in Europe refers to the early presence of anatomically modern humans in Europe. The term "early modern" is usually taken to include fossils of the Aurignacian, Gravettian, Solutrean and Magdalenian, extending throughout the Last Glacial Maximum (LGM), covering the period of roughly 45,000 to 15,000 years ago.[285] The description as "modern" is used as contrasting with the "archaic" Neanderthals which lived in Europe during 300,000 to 40,000 years ago.

The term EEMH is equivalent to **Cro-Magnon Man**, or **Cro-Magnons**, a term derived from the Cro-Magnon rock shelter in southwestern France, where the first EEMH were found in 1868. Louis Lartet (1869) proposed *Homo sapiens fossilis* as the systematic name for "Cro-Magnon Man". W. K. Gregory (1921) proposed the subspecies name *Homo sapiens cro-magnonensis*. In literature published since the late 1990s, the term EEMH is generally preferred over the common name Cro-Magnon, which has no formal taxonomic status, as it refers neither to a species or subspecies nor to an archaeological phase or culture.

The earliest known remains of EEMH can be dated to before 40,000 years ago (40 ka) with some certainty: those from Grotta del Cavallo in Italy, and from Kents Cavern in England, radiocarbon dated to 45–41 ka. A number of other early fossils are dated close to or just after 40ka, including fossils found in Romania (Peştera cu Oase, 42–37 ka) and Russia (Kostenki-14, 40–35 ka). The Siberian Ust'-Ishim man, dated to 45 ka, was not geographically found in Europe, and indeed is not part of the "Western Eurasian" genetic lineage, but intermediate between the Western Eurasian and East Asian lineages.[286]

The EEMH lineage in the European Mesolithic is also known as "West European Hunter-Gatherer" (WHG). These mesolithic hunter-gatherers emerge after the end of the LGM ca. 15 ka and are described as more gracile than the

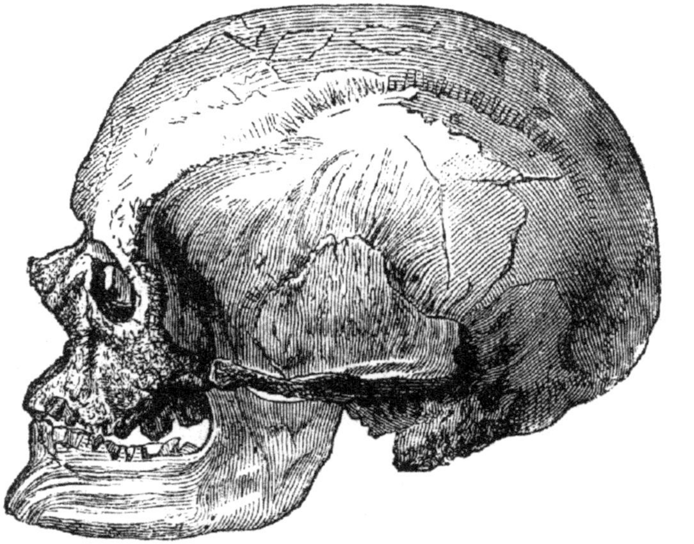

Figure 99: *Cro-Magnon 1 skull (1884 drawing)*

Figure 100: *Tool from Cro-Magnon – Louis Lartet Collection*

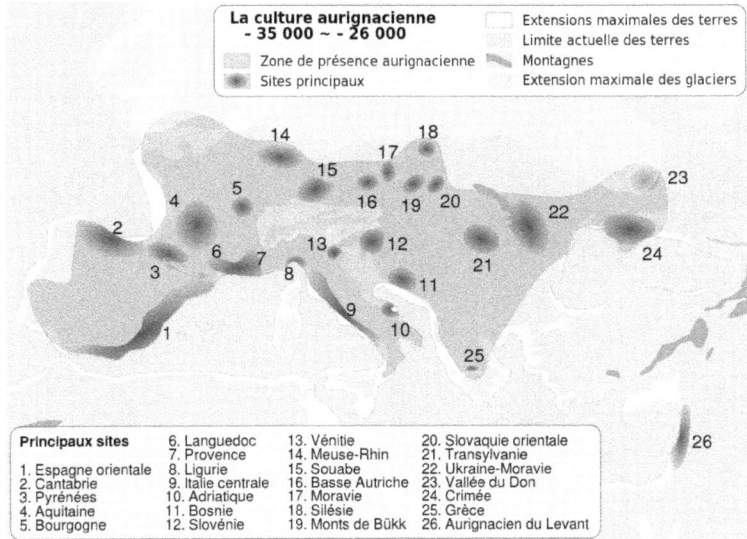

Figure 101: *Map of the distribution of the main pre-LGM Aurignacian sites.*

Upper Paleolithic Cro-Magnons.[287] The WHG lineage survives in contemporary Europeans, albeit only as a minor contribution overwhelmed by the later Neolithic and Bronze Age migrations.

Chronology

While anatomically modern humans (AMH) may have been present in West Asia since before 250 ka,[288] modern non-Africans mainly descend from the main successful out of Africa expansion at around 65 ka. This movement was an offshoot of the rapid expansion within East Africa associated with mtDNA haplogroup L3.[289] EEMH are associated with mtDNA haplogroup N, also widespread in Central Asia, and with Y-chromosomal haplogroup IJK.

AMH are estimated to have interbred with Neanderthals during about 65 to 47 ka, most likely in West Asia.[290] It is this basal West Eurasian lineage that began to move into Europe beginning about 45 ka. Neanderthals are extinct shortly after this time, presumably being outcompeted or actively killed by the advancing EEMH. Admixture with Neanderthals appears to cease almost entirely after 45 ka, in spite of several millennia of continued co-existence of AMH and Neanderthals in Europe.

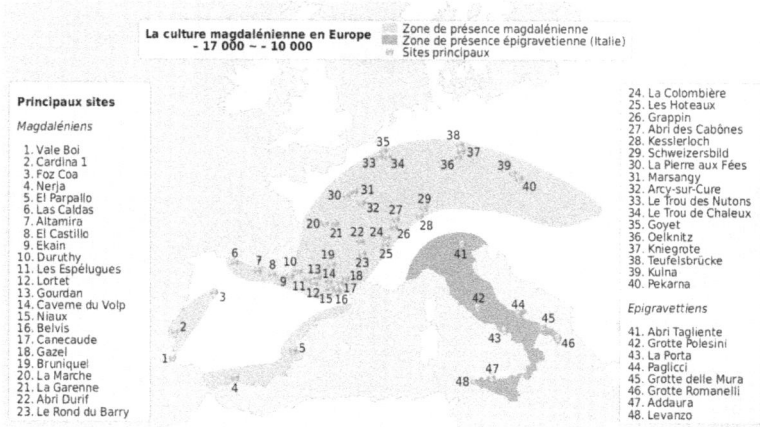

Figure 102: *Map of Magdalenian sites at the transition between the Upper Paleolithic and the Mesolithic.*

There are two main hypothesis as to the route taken by the earliest AMH entering Europe, following the Danubian corridor or the Mediterranean coast along the Balkans. Support for either hypothesis relies on accurate dating of the earliest known fossils in the region. High-precision dating of the earliest Proto-Aurignacian sites in Europe, Riparo Mochi (Italy), Geissenklösterle (Germany), and Isturitz (France), have yielded dates of close to 42 ka, indicating that EEMH spread throughout Western Europe very rapidly.[291]

EEMH sites in Europe earlier than 37 ka are also termed Proto-Aurignacian. The Aurignacian proper, the stage associated with the original Cro-Magnon find, appears to have developed within Europe. It lasts from 37 ka until about 28 ka.

The Gravettian is the European culture immediately preceding the LGM, about 28 to 22 ka, but the early Gravettian overlaps with the later Aurignacian, from as early as 33 ka.[292] During the LGM proper, beginning about 22 ka, there are two main refugia, the Solutrean in Southwestern Europe, and the Epi-Gravettian in Italy and Southeastern Europe.

With advancing deglaciation, after about 17 ka, finds associated with the Magdalenian, are transitional to the mesolithic hunter-gatherer (WHG) populations. The European Mesolithic is taken to begin after about 14 ka (Azilian).

Physical attributes

Cro-Magnons were anatomically modern, straight limbed and tall compared to the contemporaneous Neanderthals. They are thought to have stood on average 1.66 to 1.71 m (5 ft 5 in to 5 ft 7 in) tall. They differ from modern-day humans in having a more robust physique and a slightly larger cranial capacity. The Cro-Magnons had fairly low skulls, with wide faces, robust mandibles, blunted chins, narrow noses, and moderate to no prognathism. A distinctive trait was the rectangular eye orbits, similar to those of modern Ainu people. Their vocal apparatus was like that of present-day humans and they could speak. Their brain capacity was about 1,600 cc (98 cu in), larger than the average for modern Europeans.

Mitochondrial DNA analysis places the early European population as sister group to the East Asian groups of the Upper Paleolithic, dating the divergence to some 50,000 years ago.

Analysis of ancient DNA of EEMH and Mesolithic fossils suggests that alleles related to the light skin characteristic of modern Europeans (TYRP1 SLC24A5 and SLC45A2) were not yet present. They are thought to have arisen during the LGM, most likely in the Caucasus, and were spread to Europe in a "selective sweep" during the late Upper Paleolithic to early Mesolithic, between ca. 19 to 11 ka.[293] The HERC2 variation for blue eyes first appears around 14 ka in Italy and the Caucasus.

Behavior and culture

The flint tools found in association with the remains at Cro-Magnon have associations with the Aurignacian culture that Lartet had identified a few years before he found the first skeletons. The Aurignacian differ from the earlier cultures by their finely worked bone or antler points and flint points made for hafting, the production of Venus figurines and cave painting.[294] They pierced bones, shells and teeth to make body ornaments. The figurines, cave-paintings, ornaments and the mysterious Venus figurines are a hallmark of Cro-Magnon culture, contrasting with the utilitarian culture of the Neanderthals.

Like most early humans, the Cro-Magnons were primarily big-game hunters, killing mammoth, cave bears, horses, and reindeer. They hunted with spears, javelins, and spear-throwers. Archery had not yet been invented. They would have been nomadic or semi-nomadic, following the annual migration of their prey, and would also have eaten plant materials. In Mezhirich village in Ukraine, several huts built from mammoth bones possibly representing semi-permanent hunting camps have been unearthed.

Figure 103: *Aurignacian painting of cave lions from Chauvet Cave, Ardèche (museum replica)*

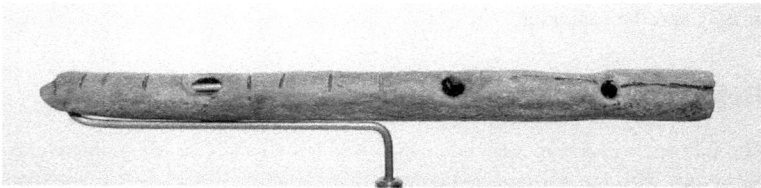

Figure 104: *Aurignacian bone flute from Geissenklösterle (Swabia)*

Finds of spun, dyed, and knotted flax fibers among Cro-Magnon artifacts in Dzudzuana shows they made cords for hafting stone tools, weaving baskets, or sewing garments.[295] Apart from the mammoth bone huts mentioned, they constructed shelters of rocks, clay, branches, and animal hide/fur. Manganese and iron oxides were used in rock paintings.

Assemblages and fossils

Site	Region (country)	Industry	Age (ka)	Description
Grotta del Cavallo	Italy	Proto-Aurignacian	44	In November 2011, tests conducted at the Oxford Radiocarbon Accelerator Unit in England on what were previously thought to be Neanderthal baby teeth, which had been unearthed in 1964 from the Grotta del Cavallo in Italy. These were identified as the oldest anatomically modern remains ever discovered in Europe, dating from between 43,000 and 45,000 years ago. No tools were associated with the find.
Geis-senklösterle	Central Europe (Germany)	Proto-Aurignacian	42	The bone flute of Geissenklösterle (Swabia) has been radiocarbon dated to 43-42 ka. The so-called adorant from the Geißenklösterle cave is somewhat younger (40-35 ka). Other paleolithic art of the early Aurignacian was found in the Swabian Alb area, including Venus of Hohle Fels and the Lion-man figurine (see Caves and Ice Age Art in the Swabian Jura)[296] No dated human remains are associated with these finds.
Kent's Cavern	Western Europe (UK)	Proto-Aurignacian	41	The Kent's Cavern find is a prehistoric maxilla (upper jaw-bone) fragment was uncovered in the cavern during a 1927 excavation in Kents Cavern by the Torquay Natural History Society, and named *Kent's Cavern 4*. In 2011 the fossil was tested and redated to at least 41,500 years old and confirmed to be Cro-Magnon, making it the earliest anatomically modern human (AMH) fossil yet discovered in Western Europe. Though the find is too fragmentary to compare the anatomy to the Cro-Magnon find, the associated tools are Aurignacian.Wikipedia:Please clarify
Kostenki-14	Eastern Europe (Russia)	Proto-Aurignacian	38	A male from Kostenki-14 (Markina Gora), dated 35–40 ka, was found to have a close relationship to both "Mal'ta boy" (24 ka) of central Siberia (Ancient North Eurasian) and to the later Mesolithic hunter-gatherers of Europe and western Siberia, as well as with a basal population ancestral to Early European Farmers.[297]

Peştera cu Oase	South-eastern Europe (Ro-mania)	Proto-Aurignacian	38	**Figure 105:** *Forensic reconstruction of Oase 2 (2017 photograph)* *Peştera cu Oase* ("Bones Cave") near the Iron Gates in Romania appears to be a cave bear den; the human remains may have been prey or carrion. No tools are associated with the finds. Oase 1 holotype is a robust mandible which combines a variety of archaic, derived early modern, and possibly Neanderthal features. The modern attributes place it close to EEMH among Late Pleistocene samples. The fossil is one of the few finds in Europe which could be directly dated and is at least 37,800 years old. Oase 2 (and fragments Oase 3), discovered in 2005, is the skull of a young male, again with mosaic features, some of which are paralleled in the Oase 1 mandible.
Kostenki-12	Eastern Europe (Russia)	Aurignacian	33	Dated at 32,600 ± 1,100 radio-carbon years, the find from Kostenki consists of a tibia and a fibula in a rich culture layer. The occupation layers contain bone and ivory artifacts, including possible figurative art, and fossil shells imported more than 500 kilometers.
Gower	Western Europe (UK)	Aurignacian	33	Despite its name, the Red Lady of Paviland is a partial skele-ton of a young male, lacking a skull. It was discovered in 1823 in a cave burial in Gower, South Wales, United King-dom. The bones were stained with ochre, and it was the first human fossil to have been found anywhere in the world. At 33,000 years old, it is still the oldest ceremonial burial of a modern human ever discovered anywhere in Western Europe. Associated finds were red ochre anointing, a mam-moth skull, and personal decorations suggesting shamanism or other religious practice. Grave goods are considered late Aurignacian or Early Gravettian in appearance. Genetic anal-ysis of mtDNA yielded the Haplogroup H, the most common group in Europe.
La Quina Aval	Western Europe (France)	Aurignacian	33	Consisting of a partial juvenile mandible, the find is also associated with early Aurignacian tools. The jaw has some archaic features, though it is mainly modern. The find is dated to max 33,000 - 32,000 radiocarbon years.
Les Roisà Mouthiers	Western Europe (France)	Aurignacian	32	There are diagnostic modern human remains associated with a later Aurignacian assemblage at Les Roisà Mouthiers, France. The date is likely not older than 32,000 radiocarbon years.

Mladeč caves	Central Europe (Czech Republic)	Aurignacian	31	The Mladeč caves in Moravia have yielded the remains of several individuals, but few artifacts. The artifacts found have tentatively been classified as Aurignacian. The finds have been radiocarbon dated to around 31,000 radiocarbon years (somewhat older in calendar years), *Mladeč 2* is dated to 31,320 +410, -390, *Mladeč 9a* to 31,500 +420, -400 and *Mladeč 8* to 30,680 +380, -360 ^{14}C years.
Peştera Muierilor	South-eastern Europe (Romania)	Aurignacian	31	The Peştera Muierilor ("Women's Cave") find is a single, fairly complete cranium of a woman with rugged facial traits and otherwise modern skull features, found in a lower gallery of the cave, among numerous cave bear remains. Radiocarbon dating yielded an age of 30,150 ± 800 years. No associated tools were found.
Muierii and Cioclovina Caves	South-eastern Europe (Romania)	Aurignacian	30	Cioclovina 1 is a complete neurocranium from a robust individual lacking all facial bones. The find is from a cave bear den, Cioclovina Cave, Romania. It is dated at 29,000 ± 700 radiocarbon years.
Cro-Magnon	Western Europe (France)	Aurignacian	29	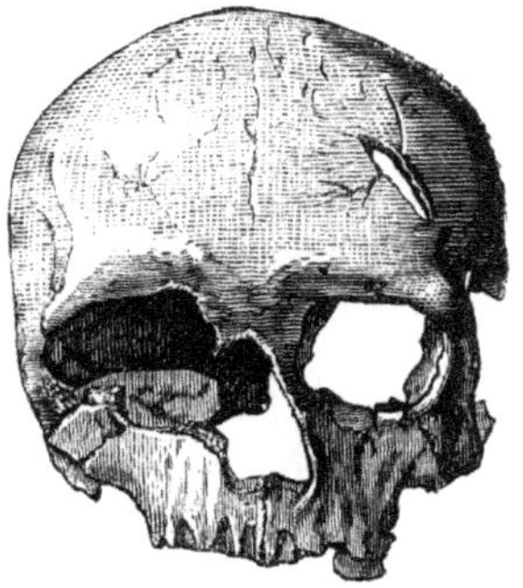 \n\n**Figure 106:** *Cro-Magnon 2, the female skull found at Cro-Magnon (1884 drawing)*

				The original Cro-Magnon find was discovered in a rock shelter at Les Eyzies, Dordogne, France. The type specimen from the site is Cro-Magnon 1, a male, carbon dated to about 28,000 ^{14}C years old. (27,680 ± 270 BP). Compared to Neanderthals, the skeletons showed the same high forehead, upright posture and slender (*gracile*) skeleton as modern humans. The other specimens from the site are a female, Cro-Magnon 2, and another male, Cro-Magnon 3. The condition and placement of the remains of Cro-Magnon 1, along with pieces of shell and animal teeth in what appear to have been pendants or necklaces, raises the question of whether they were buried intentionally. If Cro-Magnons buried their dead intentionally, it suggests they had a knowledge of ritual, by burying their dead with necklaces and tools, or an idea of disease and that the bodies needed to be contained.[298] Analysis of the pathology of the skeletons shows that the humans of this period led a physically difficult life. In addition to infection, several of the individuals found at the shelter had fused vertebrae in their necks, indicating traumatic injury; the adult female found at the shelter had survived for some time with a skull fracture. As these injuries would be life-threatening even today, this suggests that Cro-Magnons relied on community support and took care of each other's injuries. The Abri of Cro-Magnon is part of the UNESCO World Heritage of the "Prehistoric Sites and Decorated Caves of the Vézère Valley".
Předmostí	Central Europe (Czech Republic)	Aurignacian-Gravettian	26	The Předmostí site, near Přerov, Moravia was discovered in the late 19th century. Excavations were conducted between 1884 and 1930. As the original material was lost during World War II, in the 1990s, new excavations were conducted. The Předmostí site appears to have been a living area with associated burial ground with some 20 burials, including 15 complete human interments, and portions of five others, representing either disturbed or secondary burials. Cannibalism has been suggested to explain the apparent subsequent disturbance, though it is not widely accepted. The non-human fossils are mostly mammoth. Many of the bones are heavily charred, indicating they were cooked. Other remains include fox, reindeer, ice-age horse, wolf, bear, wolverine, and hare. Remains of three dogs were also found, one of which had a mammoth bone in its mouth. The Předmostí site is dated to between 24,000 and 27,000 years old. The people were essentially similar to the French Cro-Magnon finds. Though undoubtedly modern, they had robust features indicative of a big-game hunter lifestyle. They also share square eye socket openings found in the French material.
Balzi Rossi	Italy	Aurignacian-Gravettian	25	Grimaldi Man is a find from the Ligurian Coast in Italy. The caves yielded several finds, among them two fairly complete skeletons in the lower Aurignacian layer. Though the age and accompanying tools suggests Cro-Magnon, the skeletons differ physically from the large and robust Cro-Magnons, being slender and rather short.[299] The remains from one of the caves, the "Barma Grande", have in recent time been radiocarbon dated to 25 ka.[300] The Venus figurines of Balzi Rossi have been dated to the later Gravettian or Epi-Gravettian, 24 to 19 ka.[301]

Abrigo do Lagar Velho	Western Europe (Portugal)	Gravettian	24	The Lapedo child from Abrigo do Lagar Velho, Portugal, about 24,000 years old, a fairly complete and quite robust skeleton, possibly showing some Neanderthal traits.
Abri Pataud	Western Europe (France)	Solutrean	21	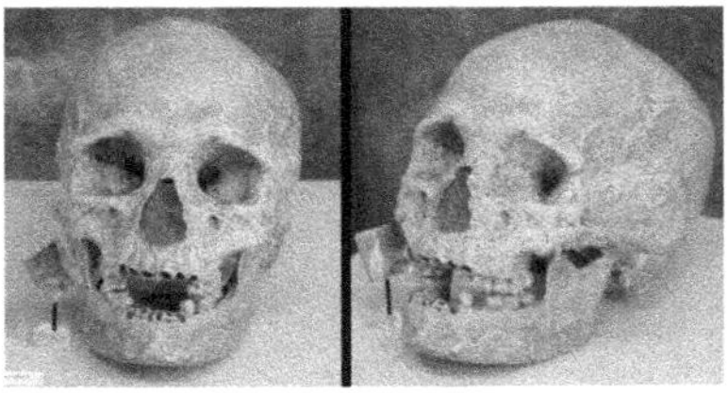 **Figure 107:** *Skull of the Pataud woman* The Abri Pataud shelter shows human habitation throughout the Aurignacian to Solutrean, but was abandoned in the early Magdalenian, about 17 ka. The "Pataud woman" is the name given to the remains of a young woman, about 20 years old, deposited with the body of a newborn child, and is about 21,000 years old. The woman's skull was buried separately, about four meters from the body, lying protected between stones.
Chancelade	Western Europe (France)	Magdalenian	15	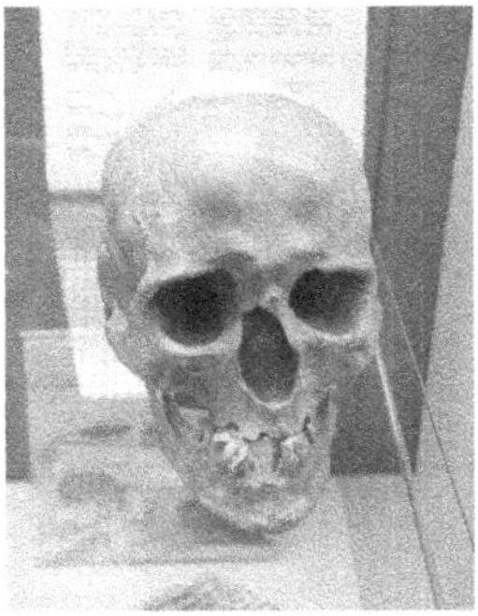 **Figure 108:** *The Chancalade skull* Chancelade man, a short and stocky older man buried in Chancelade, France, was found with Magdalenian tools. Several other more fragmentary finds, like the skeleton from Laugerie-Basse and the Duruthy cave near Sorde-l'Abbaye has traditionally been linked to the Chancelade man. The morphological difference in the Chancelade skull compared to the "stockier" Cro-Magnon type has been taken as evidence for a Gravettian or Magdalenian-era influx of a different population unrelated to the Aurignacian EEMH.
Cap Blanc rock shelter	Western Europe (France)	Magdalenian-Azilian	14	Magdalenian Girl is a female skeleton, discovered in Dordogne in 1911. Dating to the later Magdalenian, transitional to the beginning Mesolithic.

Grotte du Bichon	Western Europe (Switzerland)	Magdalenian-Azilian	14	Bichon man is the skeleton of a young male of the mesolithic hunter-gatherer (WHG) lineage.
Ripari Villabruna	Italy	Magdalenian-Azilian	14	Villabruna 1 is a skeleton, dated 14.1-13.8 ka, buried in a shallow pit, the head turned to the left with arms stretched touching the body, with grave goods typical of hunter-gatherer equipment. Villabruna 1 is the oldest bearer of Y-haplogroup R1b found in Europe, and has been taken as a representative of the beginning post-LGM (Mesolithic) migration movement from the Near East.

Genetics

The lineage of EEMH contributes substantially to the modern populations indigenous to Europe. EEMH populations during the Last Glacial Maximum were probably confined to refugia, associated with the Solutrean and Gravettian cultures. From there, Europe was re-peopled during the Holocene climatic optimum. The genetic contribution of these populations to modern Europeans is dubbed "West European Hunter-Gatherer" (WHG). The identification of the WHG component in modern populations is based on the analysis of the genome of a Mesolithic hunter-gatherer buried c. 8000 years ago in the Loschbour rock shelter in Müllerthal, near Heffingen, Luxembourg.[302]

According to Fu et al. (2016), the mesolithic WHG lineage (dubbed the "Villabruna Cluster") already contains post-LGM admixture from the Near East and Caucasus, ending the period of isolation in EEMH of c. 37 to 14 ka.[303]

The WHG populations mixed extensively with the expanding Early European Farmers (EEF) populations during the European Neolithic.[304]

In terms of unipaternal lineages, EEMH were descended from the patrilineal Y-DNA haplogroups Haplogroup IJ and C1,[305,306] and maternal mt-DNA haplogroup N (and descendant haplogroups R and U).[307] Y-haplogroup IJ likely arose still in Southwest Asia. haplogroup I emerged about 35 to 30 ka, either in Europe or West Asia. Y-haplogroup K2a* (K-M2308) is associated with Central Asia, found in Siberian Ust'-Ishim man, but also in the Proto-Aurignacian Oase 1 fossil (Romania). Mt-haplogroup U5 arose in Europe just prior to the LGM, between 35 and 25 ka.

"Bichon man", an Azilian (early Mesolithic) skeleton found in the Swiss Jura, was found to be associated with the WGH lineage He was a bearer of Y-DNA haplogroup I2a and mtDNA haplogroup U5b1h.[308]

Art of the Upper Paleolithic

The **art of the Upper Paleolithic** is amongst the oldest art known (sometimes called prehistoric art). Older possible examples include the incised ochre from Blombos Cave. Upper Paleolithic art is found in Aurignacian Europe and the Levant some 40,000 years ago, and on the island of Sulawesi in Indonesia at a similar date, suggesting a much older origin perhaps in Africa. Cave art in Europe continued to the Mesolithic (at the beginnings of the Holocene) about 12,000 years ago. As this corresponds to the final phase of the last glacial period, Upper Paleolithic art is also known as "**Ice Age art**".

As a notable aspect of what some call the "Upper Paleolithic Revolution", and evidence for behavioral modernity, the appearance of art in part helps us define the Upper Paleolithic itself. Art helps define what makes us human – it is part of what we are or can be (e.g. Steven Mithen, and *The Mind in the Cave* by David Lewis-Williams). Paleolithic art includes rock and cave painting, jewelry, drawing, carving, engraving and sculpture in: clay, bone, antler, stone and ivory, such as the Venus figurines, and musical instruments such as flutes.

Decoration was also made on functional tools, such as spear throwers, perforated batons and lamps.

Common subject matters include the animals that were hunted (e.g. reindeer, horses, bison, birds and mammoth) and predators and other animals that were not (e.g. lions, other big cats, bears and the woolly rhinoceros); the human form was often expressed – especially female shapes (they often look either: young, old, or pregnant). Men are also depicted, such as the 'Pin Hole man'.

Europe and the Levant (Ice Age art)

Hominin timeline

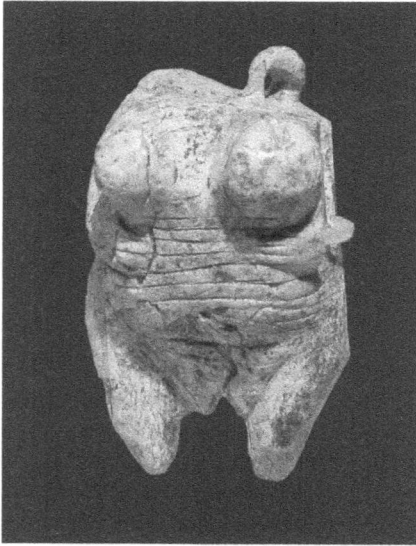

Figure 109: *Venus of Hohle Fels, an Upper Paleolithic fig-urine, the earliest known, undisputed example of a depiction of a human being in prehistoric art (ivory, height 6 cm (2.4 in))*

Figure 110: *Venus of Laussel, an Upper Paleolithic (Aurignacian) carving*

Figure 111: *Venus of Willendorf*

Axis scale: million years

Also see: *Life timeline* and *Nature timeline*

The vast majority of Ice Age art will not have survived; apart from work in wood, leather and other very perishable materials, the antler and bone which are very commonly used would normally decay if not buried in dry caves and shelters. There is evidence for some craft specialization, and the transport over considerable distances of materials such as stone and, above all marine shells, much used for jewellery and probably decorating clothes. Shells from Mediterranean species have been found at Gönnersdorf, over 1,000 kilometres from the Mediterranean coast. The higher sea levels today mean that the level and nature of coastal settlements in the Upper Paleolithic are unable to be explored and remain largely mysterious.[309]

Engravings on flat pieces of stones are found in considerable numbers (up to 5,000 at one Spanish site) at sites with the appropriate geology, with the marks sometimes so shallow and faint that the technique involved is closer to drawing – many of these were not spotted by the earliest excavators, and found by later teams in spoil heaps. Painted plaques are less common. It is possible that they were used in rituals, or alternatively heated on a fire and wrapped as personal warmers. Either type of use may account for the many broken examples, often with the fragments dispersed over some distance (up to 30 metres apart at Gönnersdorf). Many sites have large quantities of flat stones apparently used as flooring, with only a minority decorated.[310]

Ice Age art can be naturalistic and figurative; it can also be geometric and non-representational. Some of the oldest works of art were found in the Schwäbische Alb, Baden-Württemberg, Germany. The Venus figurine known as the Venus of Hohle Fels, dates to some 40,000 years ago. Other fine examples of art from the Upper Palaeolithic (broadly 40,000 to 10,000 years ago) includes: cave painting (such as at Chauvet, Lascaux, Altamira, Cosquer, and Pech Merle), incised / engraved cave art such as at Creswell Crags, portable art (such as animal carvings and sculptures like the Venus of Willendorf), and open-air art (such as the rock art of the Côa Valley and Mazouco in Portugal; Domingo García and Siega Verde in Spain; and Fornols-Haut in France). There are numerous carved or engraved pieces of bone and ivory, such as the Swimming Reindeer found in France from the Magdalenian period. These include spear throwers, including one shaped like a mammoth, and many of the type of objects called a bâton de commandement. One of the most famous pieces of portable art from Britain is the Robin Hood Cave Horse from Derbyshire. Other examples include the Kendrick's Cave Decorated Horse Jaw.

Many of the finest examples were featured in the *Ice Age Art: Arrival of the Modern Mind* exhibition at the British Museum in 7 February – 26 May 2013.

East Asia

Cave paintings from the Indonesian island of Sulawesi were in 2014 found to be 40,000 years old, a similar date to the oldest European cave art, which suggests a much older origin for this type of art, perhaps in Africa.

A cave at Turobong in South Korea containing human remains has been found to contain carved deer bones and depictions of deer that may be as much as 40,000 years old.[311] Petroglyphs of deer or reindeer found at Sokchang-ri may also date to the Upper Paleolithic. Potsherds in a style reminiscent of early Japanese work have been found at Kosan-ri on Jeju island, which, due to lower sea levels at the time, would have been accessible from Japan.[312]

Africa

The oldest African petroglyphs are dated to approximately the Mesolithic and late Upper Paleolithic boundary, about 10,000 to 12,000 years ago. Zimbabwe's oldest art finds date to at least 10,000 years (dated to sediment layers containing painted rock fragments). The earliest undisputed African rock art

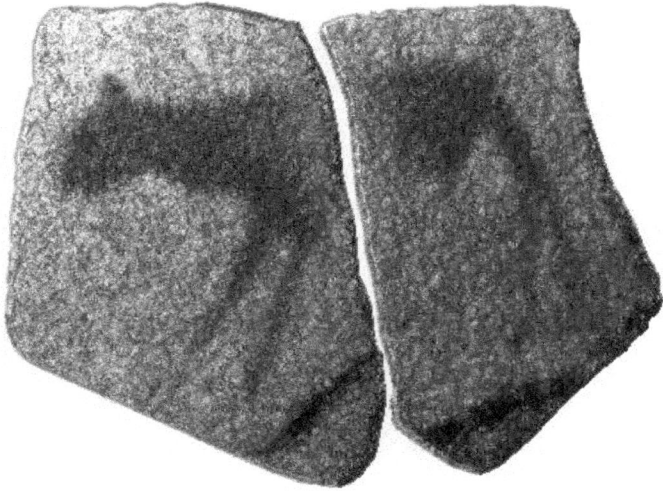

Figure 112: *Zoomorphic pictogram on stone slab from the MSA of Apollo 11 Cave*

dates back about 10,000 years, apparently originating in the Nile Valley and spread as far west as Mali.

From the Apollo 11 Cave complex in Namibia, seven stone plaquettes painted with figures of animals have been recovered from a horizon dated to between 22,500 and 27,500 years ago.[313]

The Blombos cave in South Africa yielded hatched patterns incised on pieces of ochre dated to as early as 70,000 years ago, which has been classified as "art" in some publications.

Australia

The Bradshaws are a unique form of rock art found in Western Australia. They are predominantly human figures drawn in fine detail with accurate anatomical proportioning. They have been dated at over 17,000 years old.Wikipedia:Citation needed

Gabarnmung, or Nawarla Gabarnmung, is an Aboriginal archaeological and rock art site in south-western Arnhem Land, in the Top End of Australia's Northern Territory. The rock shelter features prehistoric paintings of fish, including the barramundi, wallabies, crocodiles, people and spiritual figures. Most of the paintings are located on the shelter's ceiling, but many are found

Figure 113: *Bradshaw rock paintings found in the*
north-west Kimberley region of Western Australia

on the walls and pillars of the site. A slab of painted rock which fell to the floor
had ash adhering which was radiocarbon dated at 27,631 ±717 years Cal BP
which indicates that the ceiling must have been painted before 28,000 years
ago.

Radiocarbon dating of charcoal excavated from the base of the lowest stratigraphic layer of the floor returned a mean age of 45,189 ±1089 years Cal BP
suggesting the oldest date for the earliest human habitation. Faceted and use-
striated hematite crayons have been recovered from nearby locations (Malakunanja II and Nauwalabila 1) in strata dated from 45,000 to 60,000 years old
which suggests that the Gabarnmung shelter may have been decorated from its
inception.

Americas

Peru, including an area of the central Andes stretching from Ecuador to northern Chile, shows evidence of human habitation dating to roughly 10,000
BCE.[314] Early art from the area includes rock paintings in the Toquepala Caves
that date to 9500 BCE .[315] Burial sites in Peru, such as the one at Telarmachay,
as old as 8600-7200 BCE, contained evidence of ritual burial, with deposits of
red ocher and bead necklaces marking the site.[316]

References

<templatestyles src="Template:Refbegin/styles.css" />

- Bahn, Paul G; Vertut, Jean (1997). *Journey Through the Ice Age*[317]. University of California Press. ISBN 978-0-520-21306-7.
- Chase, Philip G (2005). *The Emergence of Culture: The Evolution of a Uniquely Human Way of Life*. Birkhäuser. ISBN 978-0-387-30512-7.
- Coulson, David; Campbell, Alec (2001). *African Rock Art*. Harry N. Abrams, Inc. ISBN 0-8109-4363-8.
- Lavallée, Danièle (1995). *The First South Americans*. Bahn, Paul G (trans.). University of Utah Press. ISBN 0-87480-665-8.
- Portal, Jane (2000). *Korea: Art and Archaeology*. Thames & Hudson. ISBN 0-7141-1487-1.
- Thackeray, Anne I.; Thackeray, JF; Beaumont, PB; Vogel, JC; et al. (2 October 1981). "Dated Rock Engravings from Wonderwerk Cave, South Africa". *Science*. **214** (4516): 64–67. doi: 10.1126/science. 214.4516.64[318]. PMID 17802575[319].

Further reading

- Cook, Jill (2013). *Ice Age art: the arrival of the modern mind*. The British Museum Press. ISBN 978 0 7141 2333 2.

External links

- EuroPreArt Database of European Prehistoric Art[320]
- Human Timeline (Interactive)[321] – Smithsonian, National Museum of Natural History (August 2016).
- Image Database Paleolithic art in Northern Spain[322]

Hominid dispersals in Europe

Hominid dispersals in Europe refers to the colonisation of the European continent by various species of hominid, including hominins and archaic and modern humans.

Short and repetitive migrations of archaic humans before 1 million years ago suggest that their residence in Europe was not permanent at the time. Colonisation of Europe in prehistory was not achieved in one immigrating wave, but instead through multiple dispersal events. Most of these instances in Eurasia were limited to 40th parallel north. Besides the findings from East Anglia, the first constant presence of humans in Europe begins 500,000-600,000 years ago. However, this presence was limited to western Europe, not reaching places like the Russian plains, until 200,000-300,000 years ago. The exception to this was discovered in East Anglia, England, where hominids briefly inhabited 700,000 years ago. Prior to arriving in Europe, the source of hominids appeared to be East Africa, where stone tools and hominid fossils are the most abundant and recorded. Arising in Europe at least 400,000 years ago, the Neanderthals would become more stable residents of the continent, until they were displaced by a more recent migration of African hominids, in their new home are referred to as European early modern humans (historically called Cro-Magnon Man), leading to the extinction of Neanderthals about 40,000 years ago.

Pre-human hominids

In the early Miocene, Europe had a subtropical climate and was intermittently connected to Africa by land bridges. At the same time, Africa was becoming more arid, prompting the dispersal of its tropical fauna—including primates—north into Europe. Apes first appear in the European fossil record 17 million years ago with *Griphopithecus*. The closely related *Kenyapithecus* is also known from fossils in Germany, Slovakia and Turkey. Both *Griphopithecus* and *Kenyapithecus* are considered likely to be ancestral to the great apes. From 13 million to 9 million years ago, hominids flourished in Europe and underwent an adaptive radiation as they diversified in response to a gradually cooling climate. Middle Miocene European hominids include *Pierolapithecus*, *Anoiapithecus*, *Dryopithecus*, *Hispanopithecus*, and *Rudapithecus*. The diversity and early appearance of great apes in Europe has led some scientists to theorise that hominids in fact evolved there, before dispersing "back to Africa" in the Middle Miocene.

Around 9 million years ago most of Europe's hominid species fell victim to the Vallesian crisis, an extinction event caused by the disappearance of the

Figure 114: *A fragment of skull belonging to Ouranopithecus macedoniensis, a hominid found in Europe in the Late Miocene*

continent's forests. Some hominid species survived the event: *Orepithecus*, which became isolated in forest refugia; and *Ouranopithecus*, which adapted to the open environments of the late Miocene. However, both were extinct by 7 million years ago.

In 2017, a reanalysis of *Graecopithecus* fossils from Greece and Bulgaria, previously associated with *Ouranopithecus*, concluded that the species was in fact a hominin dating to just after the last common ancestor of humans and chimpanzees (about 7.2 million years ago). The authors suggested that the origins of the human lineage were therefore in the Mediterranean, not Africa. Others are sceptical of their claims.

Although subtropical conditions returned to Europe in the Pliocene (5.33–2.58 million years ago), there are no known fossil hominids from this period.

Archaic humans

Homo erectus populations lived in southeastern Europe by 1.8 million years ago.

The most archaic human fossils from the Middle Pleistocene (780,000-125,000 years ago) have been found in Europe. Remains of *Homo heidelbergensis* have been found as far north as the Atapuerca Mountains in Gran

Dolina, Spain, and the oldest specimens can be dated from 850,000 to 200,000 years ago.

Neanderthals evolved from a branch of *Homo heidelbergensis* that migrated to Europe during the Middle Pleistocene. Neanderthal populations date back at least as far as 400,000 years ago in the Atapuerca Mountains, Spain. While lacking the robustness attributed to west European Neanderthal morphology, other populations did inhabit parts of eastern Europe and western Asia. Between 45,000 - 35,000 years ago, modern humans (*Homo sapiens*) replaced all Neanderthal populations in Europe anatomically and genetically. This is evident in the transfer and combination of technology and culture.

Anatomically modern humans

The recent expansion of anatomically modern humans reached Europe around 40,000 years ago, from Central Asia and the Middle East, as a result of cultural adaption to big game hunting of sub-glacial steppe fauna.[323] Neanderthals were present both in the Middle East and in Europe, and the arriving populations of anatomically modern humans (also known as "Cro-Magnon" or European early modern humans) have interbred with Neanderthal populations to a limited degree.

Modern human remains dating to 43-45,000 years ago have been discovered in Italy and Britain, with the remains found of those that reached the European Russian Arctic 40,000 years ago.

The composition of European populations was later altered by further migrations, notably the Neolithic expansion from the Middle East, and still later the Chalcolithic population movements associated with Indo-European expansion.

The modern indigenous population of Europe is composed of three major foundational populations, dubbed "Western Hunter-Gatherers" (WHG), "Early European Farmers" (EEF) and "Ancient North Eurasian" (ANE). WHG represents the remnant of the original Cro-Magnon population after they re-peopled Europe after the Last Glacial Maximum. EEF represents the introgression of Near Eastern populations during the Neolithic Revolution, and ANE is associated both with the Mesolithic Uralic expansion to Northern Europe and the Indo-European expansion to Europe in the Chalcolithic.[324]

Pressures favoring migration

Homo ergaster specimens indicate a change toward a diet more reliant on animal products, evident by greater encephalization with higher energy requirements. This transition to becoming more carnivorous affected the way of life
unlike primates before. Archaeological evidence of cut bones from large mammals and broken stone tools increasing in frequency support this increasing
trend. To meet increasing demand of calories, the range of hominids would
have expanded, making the necessary hunting versus prior scavenging possible. It is believed that the adjustments required to meet these new demands
would expand the home range size eight to ten times. Range could also increase
or decrease in size due to environmental changes. A more recent example is
absence of humans in Britain during the last glacial maximum which ended
in the Late Pleistocene, 10,000 years ago. At this time, Russia had an influx
of people following the major prey species shifting to this region. It has been
argued that Neanderthals', and previous hominids', expansion northward were
limited by lacking proper thermoregulation. Behavioural adaptations such as
clothes-making to overcome the cold is evident in archaeological finds. The
potential to expand also grew with the Neanderthal reaching the status of top
carnivores. These humans could fear less during expansion, without the worry
of other predators. The desire to push into these northern areas was influenced
by this requirement to eat a lot of meat to satisfy the human brain which uses
20% of the body's energy. Larger game for hunting is available the closer you
are to the poles.

External links

• The Settlement and Colonization of Europe[325]

Last Glacial Maximum

Solutrean

Solutrean

The Solutrean culture in Europe
- 20 000 ~ - 15 000
- Area of Solutrean presence
- Principal sites

Principal sites

1. Vale Comprido
2. Casa da Moura
3. La Pileta
4. El Parpalló
5. Chufín Cave
6. Isturitz
7. Roc de Sers
8. Le Placard
9. Devil's Furnace
10. Combe-Saunière
11. The Masters
12. Solutré
13. Oulon
14. Salpêtrière

Geograph-ical range	Western Europe
Period	Upper Paleolithic
Dates	c. 22,000 – c. 17,000 BP
Type site	Parc archéologique et botanique de Solutré
Preceded by	Gravettian
Followed by	Magdalenian in France, Spain and Portugal, but in the latter after a transition through the Badegoulien

File:Europe blank laea location map.svg

Map of Europe showing important sites of the Solutrean (clickable map).

The Paleolithic ↑ Pliocene (before *Homo*)

Lower Paleolithic
(c. 3.3 Ma – 300 ka)

- Oldowan (2.6–1.7 Ma)
- Madrasian Culture (1.5 Ma)
- Soanian (0.5–0.13 Ma)
- Acheulean (1.76–0.1 Ma)
- Clactonian (0.3–0.2 Ma)

- Acheulo-Yabrudian complex (400-200 bp)

Middle Paleolithic
(300–45 ka)

- Mousterian (160–35-30 ka)
- Aterian (c. 145,000–c. 20,000 bp)
- Micoquien (130–70 ka)

- Sangoan (130-10 bp)

Upper Paleolithic
(50–10 ka)

- Emiran (50,000–40,000 bp)
- Bohunician (~48,000 bp)
- Ahmarian (46,000-42,000 bp)
- Châtelperronian (~44,500 – 36,000 bp)
- Lincombian-Ranisian-Jerzmanowician (43-32 ka)
- Aurignacian (46-43,000 – c. 26,000 bp)
- Khormusan (42,000-18,000 bp)
- Baradostian (36-18 ka)
- Périgordian (35–20 ka)

- Gravettian (33–24 ka)
- Antelian (32–20 bp)
- Mal'ta–Buret' culture (24,000 - 15,00 bp)
- Solutrean (22–17 ka)
- Halfan culture (22,000-14,000)
- Afontova Gora (21,000-12,000}
- Epigravettian (20-10 ka)
- Zarzian culture (20,000-10,000 bp)
- Iberomaurusian (~25/23,000-11,000 cal bp)
- Kebaran (18,000 – 12,500 bp)
- Magdalenian (17–12 ka)
- Trialetian (16,000-8,000 bp)
- Hamburg (15,500-13,100 bp)
- Eburran industry (15,000-5,000 bp)
- Qadan culture (15,000 BP — 11,000 bp)
- Sebilian (15,00 -11,00 bp)
- Natufian culture (14,500–11,500 bp)
- Federmesser (14–13 ka)
- Ahrensburg (13–12 ka)
- Khiamian (12,200 and 10,800 bp)
- Swiderian (11–8 ka)

↓ Mesolithic
↓ Stone Age

- $\underline{v}$
- $\underline{t}$
- $\underline{e}^{326}$

The **Solutrean** industry is a relatively advanced flint tool-making style of the Upper Palaeolithic of the Final Gravettian, from around 22,000 to 17,000 BP. Solutrean sites have been found in modern-day France, Spain and Portugal.

Details

The term *Solutrean* comes from the type-site of "Cros du Charnier", dating to around 21,000 years ago and located at Solutré, in east-central France near Mâcon. The Rock of Solutré site was discovered in 1866 by the French geologist and paleontologist Henry Testot-Ferry. It is now preserved as the Parc archéologique et botanique de Solutré.

The industry was named by Gabriel de Mortillet to describe the second stage of his system of cave chronology, following the Mousterian, and he considered it synchronous with the third division of the Quaternary period. The era's finds include tools, ornamental beads, and bone pins as well as prehistoric art.

Solutrean tool-making employed techniques not seen before and not rediscovered for millennia. The Solutrean has relatively finely worked, bifacial points made with lithic reduction percussion and pressure flaking rather than cruder flintknapping. Knapping was done using antler batons, hardwood batons and soft stone hammers. This method permitted the working of delicate slivers of flint to make light projectiles and even elaborate barbed and tanged arrowheads. Large thin spearheads; scrapers with edge not on the side but on the end; flint knives and saws, but all still chipped, not ground or polished; long spear-points, with tang and shoulder on one side only, are also characteristic implements of this industry. Bone and antler were used as well.

The Solutrean may be seen as a transitory stage between the flint implements of the Mousterian and the bone implements of the Magdalenian epochs. Faunal finds include horse, reindeer, mammoth, cave lion, rhinoceros, bear and aurochs. Solutrean finds have also been made in the caves of Les Eyzies and Laugerie Haute, and in the Lower Beds of Creswell Crags in Derbyshire, England (Proto-Solutrean). The industry first appeared in what is now SpainWikipedia:Citation needed, and disappears from the archaeological record around 17,000 BP.

Solutrean hypothesis in North American archaeology

The "Solutrean hypothesis" argues that people from Europe may have been among the earliest settlers of the Americas. Its notable recent proponents include Dennis Stanford of the Smithsonian Institution and Bruce Bradley of the University of Exeter. This hypothesis contrasts with the mainstream archaeological orthodoxy that the North American continent was first populated by people from Asia, either by the Bering land bridge (i.e. Beringia) at least 13,500 years ago,[327] or by maritime travel along the Pacific coast, or by both. The idea of a Clovis-Solutrean link remains controversial and does not enjoy wide acceptance. The hypothesis is challenged by large gaps in time between the Clovis and Solutrean eras, a lack of evidence of Solutrean seafaring, lack of specific Solutrean features and tools in Clovis technology, the difficulties of the route, and other issues.

In 2014, the autosomal DNA of a male infant from a 12,500-year-old deposit in Montana was sequenced. The skeleton was found in close association with several Clovis artifacts. Comparisons showed strong affinities with DNA from Siberian sites, and virtually ruled out any close affinity of Anzick-1 with European sources. The DNA of the Anzick-1 sample showed strong affinities with sampled Native American populations, which indicated that the samples derive from an ancient population that lived in or near Siberia, the Upper Palaeolithic Mal'ta population.

Gallery

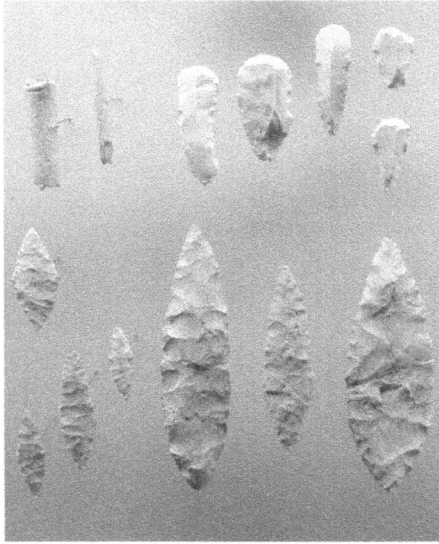

Figure 115: *Solutrean tools, 22,000–17,000 BP, Crot du Charnier, Solutré-Pouilly, Saône-et-Loire, France*

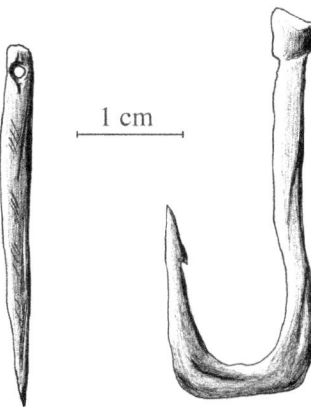

Figure 116: *The Solutrean toolkit includes the world's earliest identifiable sewing needles.*

External links

Wikimedia Commons has media related to *Solutrean*.

- Clovis and Solutrean: Is There a Common Thread?[328] by James M. Chandler
- Stone Age Columbus[329] BBC TV programme summary
- "America's Stone Age Explorers"[330] transcript of 2004 NOVA program on PBS
- Images of Solutrean artifacts[331]
- Radical theory of first Americans places Stone Age Europeans in Delmarva 20,000 years ago[332] Washington Post article from 28 February 2012
- Picture gallery of the Paleolithic (reconstructional palaeoethnology)[333], Libor Balák at the Czech Academy of Sciences, the Institute of Archaeology in Brno, The Center for Paleolithic and Paleoethnological Research

Magdalenian

Magdalenian

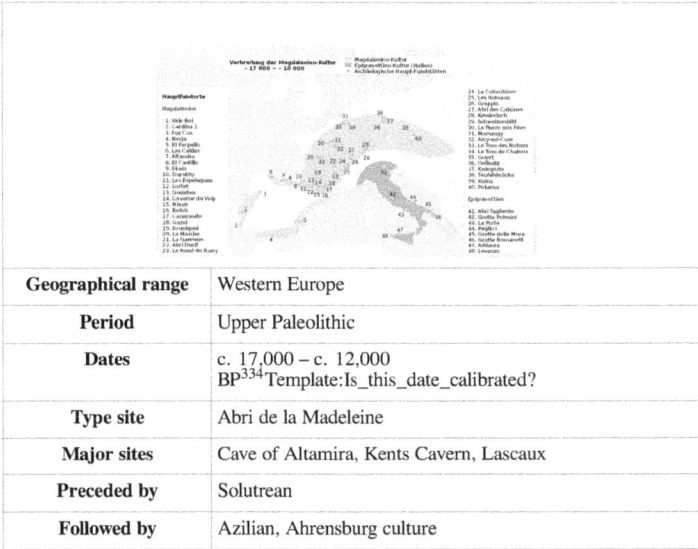

Geographical range	Western Europe
Period	Upper Paleolithic
Dates	c. 17,000 – c. 12,000 BP[334]Template:Is_this_date_calibrated?
Type site	Abri de la Madeleine
Major sites	Cave of Altamira, Kents Cavern, Lascaux
Preceded by	Solutrean
Followed by	Azilian, Ahrensburg culture

The Paleolithic ↑ Pliocene (before *Homo*)

Lower Paleolithic
(c. 3.3 Ma – 300 ka)

- Oldowan (2.6–1.7 Ma)
- Madrasian Culture (1.5 Ma)
- Soanian (0.5–0.13 Ma)
- Acheulean (1.76–0.1 Ma)
- Clactonian (0.3–0.2 Ma)

- Acheulo-Yabrudian complex (400-200 bp)

Middle Paleolithic
(300–45 ka)

- Mousterian (160–35-30 ka)
- Aterian (c. 145,000–c. 20,000 bp)
- Micoquien (130–70 ka)

- Sangoan (130-10 bp)

Upper Paleolithic
(50–10 ka)

- Emiran (50,000–40,000 bp)
- Bohunician (∼48,000 bp)
- Ahmarian (46,000-42,000 bp)
- Châtelperronian (∼44,500 – 36,000 bp)
- Lincombian-Ranisian-Jerzmanowician (43-32 ka)
- Aurignacian (46-43,000 – c. 26,000 bp)
- Khormusan (42,000-18,000 bp)
- Baradostian (36-18 ka)
- Périgordian (35–20 ka)
- Gravettian (33–24 ka)
- Antelian (32–20 bp)
- Mal'ta–Buret' culture (24,000 - 15,00 bp)
- Solutrean (22–17 ka)
- Halfan culture (22,000-14,000)
- Afontova Gora (21,000-12,000}
- Epigravettian (20-10 ka)
- Zarzian culture (20,000-10,000 bp)
- Iberomaurusian (∼25/23,000-11,000 cal bp)
- Kebaran (18,000 – 12,500 bp)
- Magdalenian (17–12 ka)
- Trialetian (16,000-8,000 bp)
- Hamburg (15,500-13,100 bp)
- Eburran industry (15,000-5,000 bp)
- Qadan culture (15,000 BP — 11,000 bp)
- Sebilian (15,00 -11,00 bp)
- Natufian culture (14,500–11,500 bp)
- Federmesser (14–13 ka)
- Ahrensburg (13–12 ka)
- Khiamian (12,200 and 10,800 bp)
- Swiderian (11–8 ka)

↓ Mesolithic
↓ Stone Age

- v̲
- t̲
- e̲[335]

The **Magdalenian** (also **Madelenian**; French: *Magdalénien*) refers to one of the later cultures of the Upper Paleolithic in western Europe, dating from around 17,000 to 12,000 years ago.Template:Is_this_date_calibrated? It is named after the type site of La Madeleine, a rock shelter located in the Vézère valley, commune of Tursac, in the Dordogne department of France.

Originally termed *L'âge du renne* (the Age of the Reindeer) by Édouard Lartet and Henry Christy, the first systematic excavators of the type site, in their publication of 1875, the Magdalenian is synonymous in many people's minds with reindeer hunters, although Magdalenian sites also contain extensive evidence for the hunting of red deer, horses, and other large mammals present in Europe toward the end of the last ice age. The culture was geographically widespread, and later Magdalenian sites have been found from Portugal in the west to Poland in the east. It is the third epoch of Gabriel de Mortillet's cave chronology system, corresponding roughly to the Late Pleistocene.

Period biology

The Magdalenian epoch was a long one, represented by numerous stations, whose contents show progress in the arts and general culture. It was characterized by a cold and dry climate, the existence of humans in association with the reindeer, and the extinction of the mammoth. The use of bone and ivory for various implements, already begun in the preceding Solutrian epoch, was much increased, and the period is essentially a bone period. The bone instruments are quite varied: spear-points, harpoon-heads, borers, hooks, and needles.

Most remarkable is the evidence La Madeleine affords of prehistoric art. Numbers of bones, reindeer antlers, and animal teeth were found, with crude pictures carved or etched on them of seals, fishes, reindeer, mammoths, and other creatures. The best of these are a mammoth engraved on a fragment of its own ivory;Wikipedia:Accuracy dispute#Disputed statement a dagger of reindeer antler, with a handle in form of a reindeer; a cave-bear cut on a flat piece of schist; a seal on a bear's tooth; a fish drawn on a reindeer antler; and a complete picture, also on reindeer antler, showing horses, an aurochs, trees, and a snake biting a man's leg. The man is naked, which, together with the snake, suggests a warm climate in spite of the presence of the reindeer.

The fauna of the Magdelenian epoch seems, indeed, to have included tigers and other tropical species side by side with reindeer, blue foxes, Arctic hares, and other polar creatures. Magdelenian humans appear to have been of low stature, dolichocephalic, with a low retreating forehead and prominent brow ridges.

Duration

The culture spans from approximately 17,000 to 12,000 BP,Template:Is_this_date_calibrated?   toward the end of the last ice age. The Magdalenian tool culture is characterised by regular blade industries

Figure 117: *Magdalenian tools and weapons, 17,000–9,000 BCE, Abri de la Madeleine, Tursac, Dordogne, France*

Figure 118: *Magdalenian people dwelt not just in caves, but also in tents such as this one of Pincevent (France) that dates to 12,000 years ago.Template:Is_this_date_calibrated?*

struck from carinated cores. Typologically, the Magdalenian is divided into six phases which are generally agreed to have chronological significance. The earliest phases are recognised by the varying proportion of blades and specific varieties of scrapers, the middle phases marked by the emergence of a microlithic component (particularly the distinctive denticulated microliths), and the later phases by the presence of uniserial (phase 5) and biserial 'harpoons' (phase 6) made of bone, antler, and ivory.[336]

There is extensive debate about the precise nature of the earliest Magdalenian assemblages, and it remains questionable whether the Badegoulian culture is, in fact, the earliest phase of the Magdalenian. Similarly, finds from the forest of Beauregard near Paris often have been suggested as belonging to the earliest Magdalenian.[337] The earliest Magdalenian sites are all found in France. The Epigravettian is a similar culture appearing at the same time. Its known range extends from southeast France to the western shores of the Volga River, Russia, with a large number of sites in Italy.

The later phases of the Magdalenian are also synonymous with the human re-settlement of north-western Europe after the Last Glacial Maximum during the Late Glacial Maximum. Research in Switzerland, southern Germany,[338] and Belgium[339] has provided AMS radiocarbon dating to support this. Being hunter gatherers, Magdalenians did not simply re-settle permanently in north-west Europe, however, as they often followed herds and moved depending on seasons.

By the end of the Magdalenian, the lithic technology shows a pronounced trend toward increased microlithisation. The bone harpoons and points have the most distinctive chronological markers within the typological sequence. As well as flint tools, the Magdalenians are best known for their elaborate worked bone, antler, and ivory that served both functional and aesthetic purposes, including perforated batons. Examples of Magdalenian portable art include batons, figurines, and intricately engraved projectile points, as well as items of personal adornment including sea shells, perforated carnivore teeth (presumably necklaces), and fossils.

The sea shells and fossils found in Magdalenian sites may be sourced to relatively precise areas of origin, and so have been used to support hypothesis of Magdalenian hunter-gatherer seasonal ranges, and perhaps trade routes. Cave sites such as the world famous Lascaux contain the best known examples of Magdalenian cave art. The site of Altamira in Spain, with its extensive and varied forms of Magdalenian mobiliary art has been suggested to be an agglomeration site where many small groups of Magdalenian hunter-gatherers congregated.[340]

In northern Spain and south-west France this tool culture was superseded by the Azilian culture. In northern Europe it was followed by different variants of the Tjongerian techno-complex. It has been suggested that key Late-glacial sites in south-western Britain also may be attributed to the Magdalenian, including the famous site of Kent's Cavern, although this remains open to debate.

Besides La Madeleine, the chief stations of the epoch are Les Eyzies, Laugerie-Basse, and Gorges d'Enfer in the Dordogne; Grotte du Placard in Charente and others in south-west France.

References

Bibliography

- ⓦ This article incorporates text from a publication now in the public domain: Chisholm, Hugh, ed. (1911). "Madelenian". *Encyclopædia Britannica*. **17** (11th ed.). Cambridge University Press. pp. 283–284.
- Charles, R. (1996): Back into the North: the Radiocarbon evidence for the Human Recolonisation of the North Western Ardennes after the Last Glacial Maximum. Proceedings of the Prehistoric Society 62: 1-17.
- Conkey, M.J. (1980): The identification of prehistoric hunter-gatherer aggregation sites: the case of Altimira. Current Anthropology 21: 609-630.
- Hemingway, M.F. (1980): The Initial Magdalenian in France. British Archaeological Reports International Series 90. 2 Vols.
- Housley, R.A, Gamble, C.S., Street, M. & Pettit, P. (1997): Radiocarbon Evidence for the Lateglacial Human Recolonisation of Northern Europe. Proceedings of the Prehistoric Society 63.
- Lartet, E & Christy, H. (1875): Reliquae Aquitanicae: being contributions to the archaeology of Périgord and adjoining provinces of Southern France. Williams & Norgate. London.
- Sonneville-Bordes, D. de & Perrot J. (1954–1956): Lexique typologique du Paléolithique supérieur. Bulletin de la Société Préhistorique Française 51: 327-335, 52: 76-79, 53: 408-412, 53: 547-549.
- Straus, Lawrence Guy (1992) : Iberia Before the Iberians. University of New Mexico Press.

External links

Wikimedia Commons has media related to *Magdalenian*.

- Encyclopedia of Prehistory article as PDF[341]
- pictures and description of the La Madeleine site[342]
- Picture Gallery of the Paleolithic (reconstructional palaeoethnology)[343],
  Libor Balák at the Czech Academy of Sciences, the Institute of Archaeology in Brno, The Center for Paleolithic and Paleoethnological Research

Settlement of the Americas

The first **settlement of the Americas** began when Paleolithic hunter-gatherers first entered North America from the North Asian Mammoth steppe via the Beringia land bridge, which had formed between northeastern Siberia and western Alaska due to the lowering of sea level during the Last Glacial Maximum. These populations expanded south of the Laurentide Ice Sheet and rapidly throughout both North and South America, by 14,000 years ago. The earliest populations in the Americas, before roughly 10,000 years ago, are known as Paleo-Indians.

The peopling of the Americas was a long-standing open question, and while advances in archaeology, Pleistocene geology, physical anthropology, and DNA analysis have shed progressively more light on the subject, significant questions remain unresolved. While there is general agreement that the Americas were first settled from Asia, the pattern of migration, its timing, and the place(s) of origin in Eurasia of the peoples who migrated to the Americas remain unclear.

The prevalent migration models outline different time frames for the Asian migration from the Bering Straits and subsequent dispersal of the founding population throughout the continent. Indigenous peoples of the Americas have been linked to Siberian populations by linguistic factors, the distribution of blood types, and in genetic composition as reflected by molecular data, such as DNA.

The "Clovis first theory" refers to the 1950s hypothesis that the Clovis culture represents the earliest human presence in the Americas, beginning about 13,000 years ago; evidence of pre-Clovis cultures has accumulated since 2000, pushing back the posible date of the first peopling of the Americas to about 13,200–15,500 years ago.

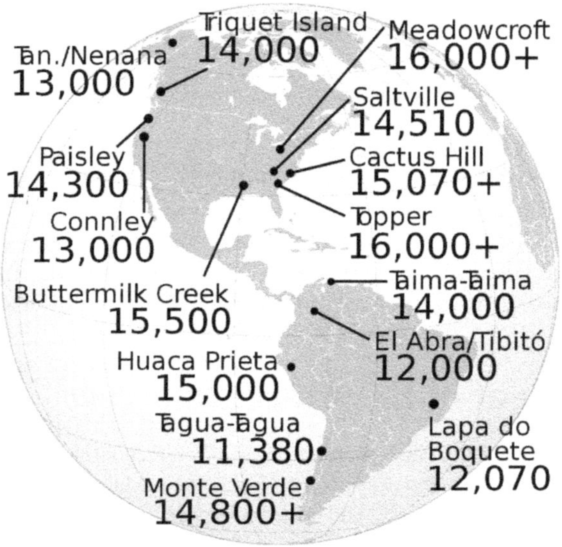

Triquet Island
Tan./Nenana 14,000   Meadowcroft
13,000   16,000+
                      Saltville
                      14,510
Paisley   Cactus Hill
14,300   15,070+
Connley   Topper
13,000   16,000+
Buttermilk Creek   Taima-Taima
   15,500   14,000
                      El Abra/Tibitó
Huaca Prieta   12,000
   15,000
Tagua-Tagua   Lapa do
   11,380   Boquete
Monte Verde   12,070
   14,800+

Figure 119: *Map of the earliest securely dated sites showing human presence in the Americas, 16–13 ka for North America and 15–11 ka for South America.*

The environment during the latest Pleistocene

For an introduction to the radiocarbon dating techniques used by archaeologists and geologists, see radiocarbon dating.

Emergence and submergence of Beringia

During the Wisconsin Glaciation, varying portions of the Earth's water were stored as glacier ice. As water accumulated in glaciers, the volume of water in the oceans correspondingly decreased, resulting in lowering of global sea level. The variation of sea level over time has been reconstructed using oxygen isotope analysis of deep sea cores, the dating of marine terraces, and high resolution oxygen isotope sampling from ocean basins and modern ice caps. A drop of eustatic sea level by about 60 m to 120 m lower than present-day levels, commencing around 30,000 years BP, created Beringia, a durable and extensive geographic feature connecting Siberia with Alaska. With the rise of sea level after the Last Glacial Maximum (LGM), the Beringian land bridge was again submerged. Estimates of the final re-submergence of the Beringian land bridge based purely on present bathymetry of the Bering Strait and eustatic sea level curve place the event around 11,000 years BP (Figure 1). Ongoing research reconstructing Beringian paleogeography during deglaciation could

PALE Paleoenvironmental Atlas of Beringia
Coastline 21,000 Cal years BP

Figure 120: *Figure1. Submergence of the Beringian land bridge with post-Last Glacial Maximum (LGM) rise in eustatic sea level*

change that estimate and possible earlier submergence could further constrain models of human migration into North America.

Glaciers

The onset of the Last Glacial Maximum after 30,000 years BP saw the expansion of alpine glaciers and continental ice sheets that blocked migration routes out of Beringia. By 21,000 years BP, and possibly thousands of years earlier, the Cordilleran and Laurentide ice sheets coalesced east of the Rocky Mountains, closing off a potential migration route into the center of North America. Alpine glaciers in the coastal ranges and the Alaskan Peninsula isolated the interior of Beringia from the Pacific coast. Coastal alpine glaciers and lobes of Cordilleran ice coalesced into piedmont glaciers that covered large stretches of the coastline as far south as Vancouver Island and formed an ice lobe across the Straits of Juan de Fuca by 15,000 ^{14}C years BP (18,000 cal years BP). Coastal alpine glaciers started to retreat around 19,000 cal years BP while Cordilleran ice continued advancing in the Puget lowlands up to 14,000 ^{14}C years BP (16,800 cal years BP) Even during the maximum extent of coastal ice, unglaciated refugia persisted on present-day islands, that supported terrestrial and marine mammals. As deglaciation occurred, refugia expanded until the coast became ice-free by 15,000 cal years BP. The retreat of glaciers on the Alaskan Peninsula provided access from Beringia to the Pacific coast by around 17,000 cal years BP. The ice barrier between interior Alaska and the Pacific coast broke up starting around 13,500 ^{14}C years (16,200 cal years) BP. The ice-free corridor to the interior of North America opened between 13,000 and 12,000 cal years BP. Glaciation in eastern Siberia during the LGM was limited to alpine and valley glaciers in mountain ranges and did not block access between Siberia and Beringia.

Climate and biological environments

The paleoclimates and vegetation of eastern Siberia and Alaska during the Wisconsin glaciation have been deduced from high resolution oxygen isotope data and pollen stratigraphy. Prior to the Last Glacial Maximum, climates in eastern Siberia fluctuated between conditions approximating present day conditions and colder periods. The pre-LGM warm cycles in Arctic Siberia saw flourishes of megafaunas. The oxygen isotope record from the Greenland Ice Cap suggests that these cycles after about 45k years BP lasted anywhere from hundreds to between one and two thousand years, with greater duration of cold periods starting around 32k cal years BP. The pollen record from Elikchan Lake, north of the Sea of Okhotsk, shows a marked shift from tree and shrub pollen to herb pollen prior to 26k ^{14}C years BP, as herb tundra replaced boreal forest and shrub steppe going into the LGM. A similar record of tree/shrub pollen being replaced with herb pollen as the LGM approached was recovered near the Kolyma River in Arctic Siberia. The abandonment of the northern regions of Siberia due to rapid cooling or the retreat of game species with the onset of the LGM has been proposed to explain the lack of archaeosites in that region dating to the LGM. The pollen record from the Alaskan side shows shifts between herb/shrub and shrub tundra prior to the LGM, suggesting less dramatic warming episodes than those that allowed forest colonization on the Siberian side. Diverse, though not necessarily plentiful, megafaunas were present in those environments. Herb tundra dominated during the LGM, due to cold and dry conditions.

Coastal environments during the Last Glacial Maximum were complex. The lowered sea level, and an isostatic bulge equilibrated with the depression beneath the Cordilleran Ice Sheet, exposed the continental shelf to form a coastal plain. While much of the coastal plain was covered with piedmont glaciers, unglaciated refugia supporting terrestrial mammals have been identified on Haida Gwaii, Prince of Wales Island, and outer islands of the Alexander Archipelago. The now-submerged coastal plain has potential for more refugia. Pollen data indicate mostly herb/shrub tundra vegetation in unglaciated areas, with some boreal forest towards the southern end of the range of Cordilleran ice. The coastal marine environment remained productive, as indicated by fossils of pinnipeds. The highly productive kelp forests over rocky marine shallows may have been a lure for coastal migration. Reconstruction of the southern Beringian coastline also suggests potential for a highly productive coastal marine environment.

Environmental changes during deglaciation

Pollen data indicate a warm period culminating between 14k and 11k ^{14}C years BP (17k-13k cal years BP) followed by cooling between 11k-10k ^{14}C years BP (13k-11.5k cal years BP). Coastal areas deglaciated rapidly as coastal alpine glaciers, then lobes of Cordilleran ice, retreated. The retreat was accelerated as sea levels rose and floated glacial termini. Estimates of a fully ice-free coast range between 16k and 15k cal years BP. Littoral marine organisms colonized shorelines as ocean water replaced glacial meltwater. Replacement of herb/ shrub tundra by coniferous forests was underway by 12.4k ^{14}C years BP (15k cal years BP) north of Haida Gwaii. Eustatic sea level rise caused flooding, which accelerated as the rate grew more rapid.

The inland Cordilleran and Laurentide ice sheets retreated more slowly than did the coastal glaciers. Opening of an ice-free corridor did not occur until after 13k to 12k cal years BP. The early environment of the ice-free corridor was dominated by glacial outwash and meltwater, with ice-dammed lakes and periodic flooding from the release of ice-dammed meltwater. Biological productivity of the deglaciated landscape was gained slowly. The earliest possible viability of the ice-free corridor as a human migration route has been estimated at 11.5k cal years BP.

Birch forests were advancing across former herb tundra in Beringia by 14.3ka ^{14}C years BP (17k cal years BP) in response to climatic amelioration, indicating increased productivity of the landscape.

Chronology and sources of migration

The archaeological community is in general agreement that the ancestors of the Indigenous peoples of the Americas of historical record entered the Americas at the end of the Last Glacial Maximum (LGM), shortly after 20,000 years ago, with ascertained archaeological presence shortly after 16,000 years ago.

There remain uncertainties regarding the precise dating of individual sites and regarding conclusions drawn from population genetics studies of contemporary Native Americans. It is also an open question whether this post-LGM migration represented the first peopling of the Americas, or whether there had been an earlier, pre-LGM migration which had reached South America as early as 40,000 years ago.

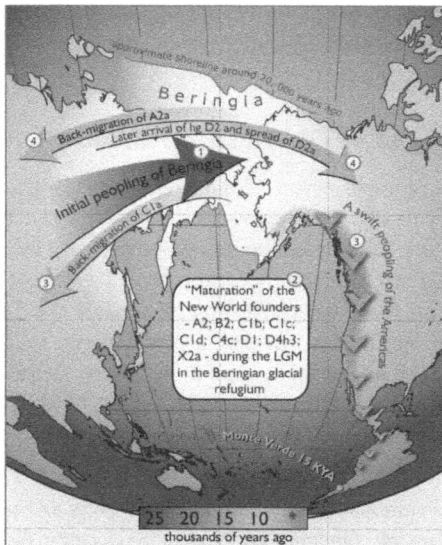

Figure 121: *Figure 2. Schematic illustration of maternal (mtDNA) gene-flow in and out of Beringia (long chronology, single source model).*

Chronology

In the early 21st century, the models of the chronology of migration are divided into two general approaches.

The first is the *short chronology theory*, that the first migration occurred after the Last Glacial Maximum, which went into decline after about 19,000 years ago, and was then followed by successive waves of immigrants.

The second theory is the *long chronology theory,* which proposes that the first group of people entered the Americas at a much earlier date, possibly before 40,000 years ago, followed by a much later second wave of immigrants.

The Clovis First theory, which dominated thinking on New World anthropology for much of the 20th century, was challenged by the secure dating of archaeosites in the Americas to before 13kya in the 2000s. The "short chronology" scenario, in the light of this, refers to a peopling of the Americas shortly after 19,000 years ago, while the "long chronology" scenario permits pre-LGM presence, by around 40 kya.

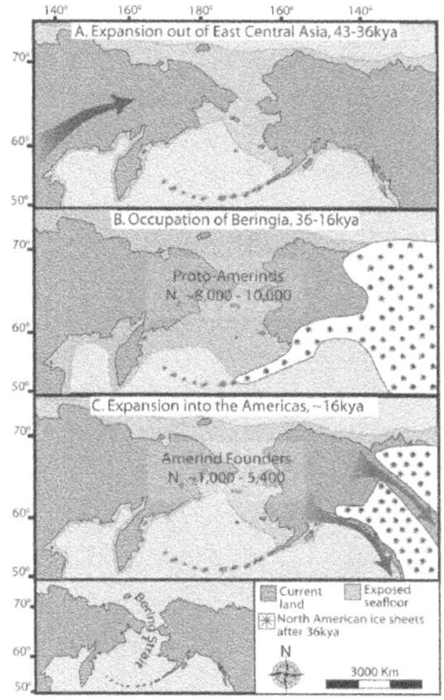

Figure 122: *Map of Beringia showing the exposed seafloor and glaciation at 40 kya and 16 kya. The green arrow indicates the "interior migration" model along an ice-free corridor separating the major continental ice sheets, the red arrow indicates the "coastal migration" model, both leading to a "rapid colonization" of the Americas after c. 16 kya.*[344]

Evidence for pre-LGM human presence

Pre-Last Glacial Maximum migration across Beringia into the Americas has been proposed to explain purported pre-LGM ages of archaeosites in the Americas such as Bluefish Caves and Old Crow Flats in the Yukon Territory, and Meadowcroft Rock Shelter in Pennsylvania. The earlier ^{14}C date from a bone artifact at the Old Crow Flats site has been supplanted by an Accelerator Mass Spectrometry ^{14}C date that indicates a Holocene age.

Pre-LGM human presence in South America rests partly on the chronology of the controversial Pedra Furada rock shelter in Piauí, Brazil. A 2003 study dated evidence for the controlled use of fire to before 40 kya.[345] Additional evidence has been adduced from the morphology of Luzia Woman fossil, which was described as Australoid. This interpretation was challenged in a 2003 review which concluded the features in question could also have arisen by genetic drift.

The interpretations of butcher marks and the geologic association of bones at the Bluefish Cave and Old Crow Flats sites have been called into question.[346] The ages of the earliest positively identified artifacts at the Meadowcroft site are constrained by a compiled age estimate from ^{14}C in the range of 12k-15k ^{14}C years BP (13.8k-18.5k cal years BP). The Meadowcroft Rockshelter site and the Monte Verde site in southern Chile, with a date of 14.8k cal years BP, are the archaeosites in the Americas with the oldest dates that have gained broad acceptance.

Stones described as probable tools, hammerstones and anvils, have been found in southern California, at the Cerutti Mastodon site, that are associated with a mastodon skeleton which appeared to have been processed by humans. The mastodon skeleton was dated by thorium-230/uranium radiometric analysis, using diffusion–adsorption–decay dating models, to 130.7 ± 9.4 thousand years ago. No human bones were found, and the claims of tools and bone processing have been described as "not plausible".[347]

The Yana River Rhino Horn site (RHS) has dated human occupation of eastern Arctic Siberia to 27k ^{14}C years BP (31.3k cal years BP). That date has been interpreted by some as evidence that migration into Beringia was imminent, lending credence to occupation of Beringia during the LGM. However, the Yana RHS date is from the beginning of the cooling period that led into the LGM. But, a compilation of archaeosite dates throughout eastern Siberia suggest that the cooling period caused a retreat of humans southwards. Pre-LGM lithic evidence in Siberia indicate a settled lifestyle that was based on local resources, while post-LGM lithic evidence indicate a more migratory lifestyle.

The oldest archaeosite on the Alaskan side of Beringia date to 12k ^{14}C years BP (14k cal years BP). It is possible that a small founder population had entered Beringia before that time. However, archaeosites that date closer to the Last Glacial Maximum on either the Siberian or the Alaskan side of Beringia are lacking.

Genomic age estimates

Studies of Amerindian genetics have used high resolution analytical techniques applied to DNA samples from modern Native Americans and Asian populations regarded as their source populations to reconstruct the development of human Y-chromosome DNA haplogroups (yDNA haplogroups) and human mitochondrial DNA haplogroups (mtDNA haplogroups) characteristic of Native American populations. Models of molecular evolution rates were used to estimate the ages at which Native American DNA lineages branched off from their parent lineages in Asia and to deduce the ages of demographic events. One model (Tammetal 2007) based on Native American mtDNA Haplotypes (Figure 2) proposes that migration into Beringia occurred between 30k and 25k cal years BP, with migration into the Americas occurring around 10k to 15k years after isolation of the small founding population. Another model

(Kitchen et al. 2008) proposes that migration into Beringia occurred approximately 36k cal years BP, followed by 20k years of isolation in Beringia. A third model (Nomatto et al. 2009) proposes that migration into Beringia occurred between 40k and 30k cal years BP, with a pre-LGM migration into the Americas followed by isolation of the northern population following closure of the ice-free corridor. Evidence of Australo-Melanesians admixture in Amazonian populations was found by Skoglund and Reich (2016).[348]

A study of the diversification of mtDNA Haplogroups C and D from southern Siberia and eastern Asia, respectively, suggests that the parent lineage (Subhaplogroup D4h) of Subhaplogroup D4h3, a lineage found among Native Americans and Han Chinese, emerged around 20k cal years BP, constraining the emergence of D4h3 to post-LGM. Age estimates based on Y-chromosome micro-satellite diversity place origin of the American Haplogroup Q1a3a (Y-DNA) at around 10k to 15k cal years BP. Greater consistency of DNA molecular evolution rate models with each other and with archaeological data may be gained by the use of dated fossil DNA to calibrate molecular evolution rates.

Source populations

There is general agreement among anthropologists that the source populations for the migration into the Americas originated from an area somewhere east of the Yenisei River. The common occurrence of the mtDNA Haplogroups A, B, C, and D among eastern Asian and Native American populations has long been recognized, along with the presence of Haplogroup X. As a whole, the greatest frequency of the four Native American associated haplogroups occurs in the Altai-Baikal region of southern Siberia. Some subclades of C and D closer to the Native American subclades occur among Mongolian, Amur, Japanese, Korean, and Ainu populations.

Human genomic models

The development of high-resolution genomic analysis has provided opportunities to further define Native American subclades and narrow the range of Asian subclades that may be parent or sister subclades. For example, the broad geographic range of Haplogroup X has been interpreted as allowing the possibility of a western Eurasian, or even a European source population for Native Americans, as in the Solutrean hypothesis, or suggesting a pre-Last Glacial Maximum migration into the Americas. The analysis of an ancient variant of Haplogroup X among aboriginals of the Altai region indicates common ancestry with the European strain rather than descent from the European strain. Further division of X subclades has allowed identification of Subhaplogroup X2a, which is regarded as specific to Native Americans. With further definition of subclades related to Native American populations, the requirements for sampling Asian populations to find the most closely related subclades grow more specific. Subhaplogroups D1 and D4h3 have been regarded as Native American specific based on their absence among a large sampling of populations regarded as potential descendants of source populations, over a wide area of Asia. Among the 3764 samples, the Sakhalin - lower Amur region was represented by 61 Oroks. In another study, Subhaplogroup D1a has been identified among the Ulchis of the lower Amur River region(4 among 87 sampled, or 4.6%), along with Subhaplogroup C1a (1 among 87, or 1.1%). Subhaplogroup C1a is regarded as a close sister clade of the Native American Subhaplogroup C1b. Subhaplogroup D1a has also been found among ancient Jōmon skeletons from Hokkaido The modern Ainu are regarded as descendants of the Jōmon. The occurrence of the Subhaplogroups D1a and C1a in the lower Amur region suggests a source population from that region distinct from the Altai-Baikal source populations, where sampling did not reveal those two particular subclades. The conclusions regarding Subhaplogroup D1 indicating potential source populations in the lower Amur and Hokkaido areas stand in contrast to the single-source migration model.

Subhaplogroup D4h3 has been identified among Han Chinese. Subhaplogroup D4h3 from China does not have the same geographic implication as Subhaplotype D1a from Amur-Hokkaido, so its implications for source models are more speculative. Its parent lineage, Subhaplotype D4h, is believed to have emerged in east Asia, rather than Siberia, around 20k cal years BP. Subhaplogroup D4h2, a sister clade of D4h3, has also been found among Jōmon skeletons from Hokkaido. D4h3 has a coastal trace in the Americas.

The contrast between the genetic profiles of the Hokkaido Jōmon skeletons and the modern Ainu illustrates another uncertainty in source models derived from modern DNA samples:

> However, probably due to the small sample size or close consanguinity among the members of the site, the frequencies of the haplogroups in Funadomari skeletons were quite different from any modern populations, including Hokkaido Ainu, who have been regarded as the direct descendant of the Hokkaido Jomon people.

The descendants of source populations with the closest relationship to the genetic profile from the time when differentiation occurred are not obvious. Source population models can be expected to become more robust as more results are compiled, the heritage of modern proxy candidates becomes better understood, and fossil DNA in the regions of interest is found and considered.

HTLV-1 genomics

The Human T cell Lymphotrophic Virus 1 (HTLV-1) is a virus transmitted through exchange of bodily fluids and from mother to child through breast milk. The mother-to-child transmission mimics a hereditary trait, although such transmission from maternal carriers is less than 100%. The HTLV virus genome has been mapped, allowing identification of four major strains and analysis of their antiquity through mutations. The highest geographic concentrations of the strain HLTV-1 are in sub-Saharan Africa and Japan. In Japan, it occurs in its highest concentration on Kyushu. It is also present among African descendants and native populations in the Caribbean region and South America. It is rare in Central America and North America. Its distribution in the Americas has been regarded as due to importation with the slave trade.

The Ainu have developed antibodies to HTLV-1, indicating its endemicity to the Ainu and its antiquity in Japan. A subtype "A" has been defined and identified among the Japanese (including Ainu), and among Caribbean and South American isolates. A subtype "B" has been identified in Japan and India. In 1995, Native Americans in coastal British Columbia were found to have both subtypes A and B. Bone marrow specimens from an Andean mummy about 1500 years old were reported to have shown the presence of the A subtype. The finding ignited controversy, with contention that the sample DNA was insufficiently complete for the conclusion and that the result reflected modern contamination. However, a re-analysis indicated that the DNA sequences were consistent with, but not definitely from, the "cosmopolitan clade" (subtype A). The presence of subtypes A and B in the Americas is suggestive of a Native American source population related to the Ainu ancestors, the Jōmon.

Physical anthropology

Paleoamerican skeletons in the Americas such as Kennewick Man (Washington State), Hoya Negro skeleton (Yucatán), Luzia Woman and other skulls from the Lagoa Santa site (Brazil), Buhl Woman (Idaho), Peñon Woman III, two skulls from the Tlapacoya site (Mexico City), and 33 skulls from Baja California have exhibited craniofacial traits distinct from most modern Native Americans, leading physical anthropologists to the opinion that some Paleoamericans were of an Australoid rather than Siberian origin. The most basic measured distinguishing trait is the dolichocephaly of the skull. Some modern isolates such as the Pericúes of Baja California and the Fuegians of Tierra del Fuego exhibit that same morphological trait. Other anthropologists advocate an alternative hypothesis that evolution of an original Beringian phenotype gave rise to a distinct morphology that was similar in all known Paleoamerican skulls, followed by later convergence towards the modern Native American phenotype. Resolution of the issue awaits the identification of a Beringian phenotype among paleoamerican skulls or evidence of a genetic clustering among examples of the Australoid phenotype.

A report published in the *American Journal of Physical Anthropology* in January 2015 reviewed craniofacial variation focussing on differences between early and late Native Americans and explanations for these based on either skull morphology or molecular genetics. Arguments based on molecular genetics have in the main, according to the authors, accepted a single migration from Asia with a probable pause in Berengia, plus later bi-directional gene flow. Studies focussing on craniofacial morphology have argued that Paleoamerican remains have "been described as much closer to African and Australo-Melanesians populations than to the modern series of Native Americans", suggesting two entries into the Americas, an early one occurring before a distinctive East Asian morphology developed (referred to in the paper as the "Two Components Model". A third model, the "Recurrent Gene Flow" [RGF] model, attempts to reconcile the two, arguing that circumarctic gene flow after the initial migration could account for morphological changes. It specifically re-evaluates the original report on the Hoya Negro skeleton which supported the RGF model, the authors disagreed with the original conclusion which suggested that the skull shape did not match those of modern Native Americans, arguing that the "skull falls into a subregion of the morphospace occupied by both Paleoamericans and some modern Native Americans."

Stemmed points

Stemmed points are a lithic technology distinct from Beringian and Clovis types. They have a distribution ranging from coastal east Asia to the Pacific coast of South America. The emergence of stemmed points has been traced to Korea during the upper Paleolithic. The origin and distribution of stemmed points have been interpreted as a cultural marker related to a source population from coastal east Asia.

Migration routes

Interior route

Historically, theories about migration into the Americas have centered on migration from Beringia through the interior of North America. The discovery of artifacts in association with Pleistocene faunal remains near Clovis, New Mexico in the early 1930s required extension of the timeframe for the settlement of North America to the period during which glaciers were still extensive. That led to the hypothesis of a migration route between the Laurentide and Cordilleran ice sheets to explain the early settlement. The Clovis site was

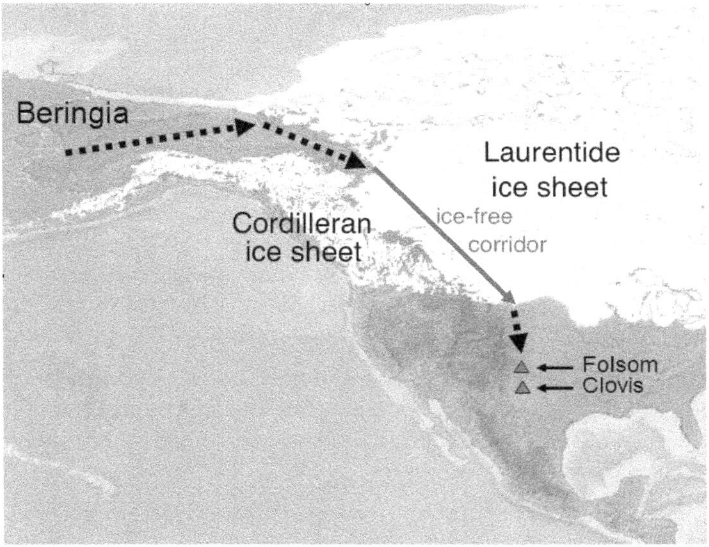

Figure 123: *Map showing the approximate location of the ice-free corridor along the Continental Divide, separating the Cordilleran and Laurentide ice sheets. Also indicated are the locations of the Clovis and Folsom Paleo-Indian sites.*

host to a lithic technology characterized by spear points with an indentation, or flute, where the point was attached to the shaft. A lithic complex characterized by the *Clovis Point* technology was subsequently identified over much of North America and in South America. The association of Clovis complex technology with late Pleistocene faunal remains led to the theory that it marked the arrival of big game hunters that migrated out of Beringia then dispersed throughout the Americas, otherwise known as the Clovis First theory.

Recent radiocarbon dating of Clovis sites has yielded ages of 11.1k to 10.7k ^{14}C years BP (13k to 12.6k cal years BP), somewhat later than dates derived from older techniques. The re-evaluation of earlier radiocarbon dates led to the conclusion that no fewer than 11 of the 22 Clovis sites with radiocarbon dates are "problematic" and should be disregarded, including the type site in Clovis, New Mexico. Numerical dating of Clovis sites has allowed comparison of Clovis dates with dates of other archaeosites throughout the Americas, and of the opening of the ice-free corridor. Both lead to significant challenges to the Clovis First theory. The Monte Verde site of Southern Chile has been dated at 14.8k cal years BP. The Paisley Cave site in eastern Oregon yielded a ^{14}C date of 12.4k years (14.5k cal years) BP, on a coprolite with human DNA and ^{14}C dates of 11.3k-11k (13.2k-12.9k cal years) BP on horizons containing western stemmed points. Artifact horizons with non-Clovis lithic assemblages and pre-Clovis ages occur in eastern North America, although the maximum ages tend to be poorly constrained.

Geological findings on the timing of the ice-free corridor also challenge the notion that Clovis and pre-Clovis human occupation of the Americas was a result of migration through that route following the Last Glacial Maximum. Pre-LGM closing of the corridor may approach 30k cal years BP and estimates of ice retreat from the corridor are in the range of 12 to 13k cal years BP. Viability of the corridor as a human migration route has been estimated at 11.5k cal years BP, later than the ages of the Clovis and pre-Clovis sites. Dated Clovis archaeosites suggest a south-to-north spread of the Clovis culture.

Pre-Last Glacial Maximum migration into the interior has been proposed to explain pre-Clovis ages for archaeosites in the Americas, although pre-Clovis sites such as Meadowcroft Rock Shelter, Monte Verde, and Paisley Cave have not yielded confirmed pre-LGM ages.

The interior route is consistent with the spread of the Na Dene language group and Subhaplogroup X2a into the Americas after the earliest paleoamerican migration.

Pacific coastal route

Pacific models propose that people first reached the Americas via water travel, following coastlines from northeast Asia into the Americas. Coastlines are unusually productive environments because they provide humans with access to a diverse array of plants and animals from both terrestrial and marine ecosystems. While not exclusive of land-based migrations, the Pacific 'coastal migration theory' helps explain how early colonists reached areas extremely distant from the Bering Strait region, including sites such as Monte Verde in southern Chile and Taima-Taima in western Venezuela. Two cultural components were discovered at Monte Verde near the Pacific coast of Chile. The youngest layer is radiocarbon dated at 12,500 radiocarbon years (~14,000 cal BP) Wikipedia:Citation needed and has produced the remains of several types of seaweeds collected from coastal habitats. The older and more controversial component may date back as far as 33,000 years, but few scholars currently accept this very early component.Wikipedia:Citation needed

As the chronology of deglaciation in the interior and coastal regions of North America became better understood, the coastal migration hypothesis was advanced by Knute Fladmark as an alternative to the ice-free corridor hypothesis. Debate on coastal versus interior migration for initial settlement has centered on evidence for chronology of initial settlement of Beringia, interior North America, the Pacific coast of the Americas, and timing of the opening

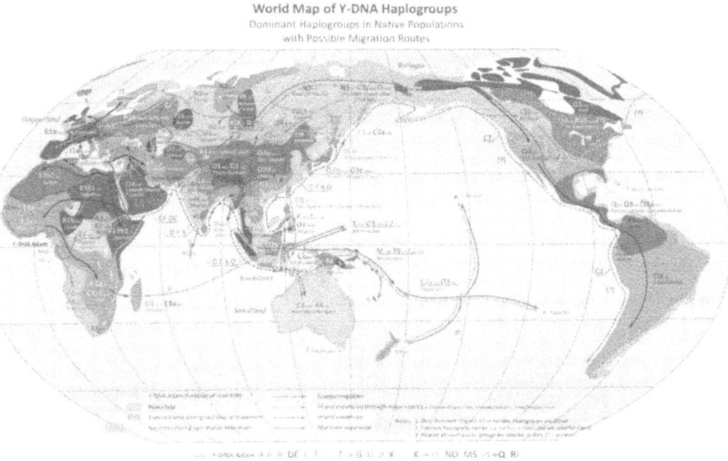

Figure 124: *Possible migration routes to the Americas as predicted by the distribution of Y-DNA haplogroups:Wikipedia:Accuracy dispute#Disputed statement A Pacific coastal route is suggested by the representation of the spread of haplogroup C2 in this map (brown dashed line).*

of coastal versus interior migration routes indicated by geological evidence. Complicating the debate has been the absence of archaeological data from the coastal and interior migration routes from the periods when the initial migration is proposed to have occurred. A recent variation of the coastal migration hypothesis is the marine migration hypothesis, which proposes that migrants with boats settled in coastal refugia during deglaciation of the coast. The proposed use of boats adds a measure of flexibility to the chronology of coastal migration, as a continuous ice-free coast (16k-15k cal years BP) would no longer be required. A coastal east Asian source population is integral to the marine migration hypothesis.

In 2014, the autosomal DNA of a toddler from Montana, dated at 10.7k ^{14}C years (12.5-12.7 cal years) BP was sequenced. The DNA was taken from a skeleton referred to as Anzick-1, found in close association with several Clovis artifacts. The analysis yielded identification of the mtDNA as belonging to Subhaplogroup D4h3a, a rare subclade of D4h3 occurring along the west coast of the Americas, as well as geneflow related to the Siberian Mal'ta population. The data indicate that Anzick-1 is from a population directly ancestral to present South American and Central American Native American populations. Anzick-1 is less closely related to present North American Native American populations. D4h3a has been identified as a clade associated with coastal migration.

The problems associated with finding archaeological evidence for migration during a period of lowered sea level are well known. Sites related to the first migration are usually submerged, so the location of such sites is obscured. Certain types of evidence dependent on organic material, such as radiocarbon dating, may be destroyed by submergence. Wave action can destroy site structures and scatter artifacts along a prograding shoreline. Additionally, Pacific coastal conditions tend to be unstable due to steep unstable terrain, earthquakes, tsunamis, and volcanoes. Strategies for finding earliest migration sites include identifying potential sites on submerged paleoshorelines, seeking sites in areas uplifted either by tectonics or isostatic rebound, and looking for riverine sites in areas that may have attracted coastal migrants. Otherwise, coastal archaeology is dependent on secondary evidence related to lifestyles and technologies of maritime peoples from sites similar to those that would be associated with the original migration.

Other coastal models, dealing specifically with the peopling of the Pacific Northwest and California coasts, have been advocated by archaeologists Knut Fladmark, Roy Carlson, James Dixon, Jon Erlandson, Ruth Gruhn, and Daryl Fedje. In a 2007 article in the *Journal of Island and Coastal Archaeology*, Erlandson and his colleagues proposed a corollary to the coastal migration theory—the "kelp highway hypothesis"—arguing that productive kelp forests supporting similar suites of plants and animals would have existed near the end of the Pleistocene around much of the Pacific Rim from Japan to Beringia, the Pacific Northwest, and California, as well as the Andean Coast of South America. Once the coastlines of Alaska and British Columbia had deglaciated about 16,000 years ago, these kelp forest (along with estuarine, mangrove, and coral reef) habitats would have provided an ecologically similar migration corridor, entirely at sea level, and essentially unobstructed.

A 2016 DNA analysis of plants and animals suggest a coastal route was feasible.[349]

East Asians: Paleoindians of the coast

The boat-builders from Southeast Asia (Austronesian peoples) may have been one of the earliest groups to reach the shores of North America.[350,351] One theory suggests people in boats followed the coastline from the Kurile Islands to Alaska down the coasts of North and South America as far as Chile. 62 54, 57. The Haida nation on the Queen Charlotte Islands off the coast of British Columbia may have originated from these early Asian mariners between 25,000 and 12,000 years ago. Early watercraft migration would also explain the habitation of coastal sites in South America such as Pikimachay Cave in

Peru by 20,000 years ago (disputed) and Monte Verde in Chile by 13,000 years ago [6 30; 8 383].

'There was boat use in Japan 20,000 years ago,' says Jon Erlandson, a University of Oregon anthropologist. 'The Kurile Islands (north of Japan) are like stepping stones to Beringia,' the then continuous land bridging the Bering Strait. Migrants, he said, could have then skirted the tidewater glaciers in Canada right on down the coast. [7 64]'

Problems with evaluating coastal migration models

The coastal migration models provide a different perspective on migration to the New World, but they are not without their own problems. One such problem is that global sea levels have risen over 120 metres (390 ft) since the end of the last glacial period, and this has submerged the ancient coastlines that maritime people would have followed into the Americas. Finding sites associated with early coastal migrations is extremely difficult—and systematic excavation of any sites found in deeper waters is challenging and expensive. On the other hand, there is evidence of marine technologies found in the hills of the Channel Islands of California, circa 10,000 BCE.[352] If there was an early pre-Clovis coastal migration, there is always the possibility of a "failed colonization". Another problem that arises is the lack of hard evidence found for a "long chronology" theory. No sites have yet produced a consistent chronology older than about 12,500 radiocarbon years (~14,500 calendar years) Wikipedia:Citation needed, but research has been limited in South America related to the possibility of early coastal migrations.

Y-DNA among South American and Alaskan natives

The micro-satellite diversity and distribution of a Y lineage specific to South America suggest that certain Amerindian populations became isolated after the initial colonization of their regions. The Na-Dené, Inuit and Indigenous Alaskan populations exhibit haplogroup Q (Y-DNA) mutations, but are distinct from other indigenous Amerindians with various mtDNA and autosomal DNA (atDNA) mutations. This suggests that the earliest migrants into the northern extremes of North America and Greenland derived from later migrant populations.

Other hypotheses

There exists a number of theories for pre-Columbian trans-oceanic migrations
into the Americas.

Bibliography

<templatestyles src="Template:Refbegin/styles.css" />

• Adovasio, J. M., with Jake Page. *The First Americans: In Pursuit of
  Archaeology's Greatest Mystery.* New York: Random House, 2002.
• Bradley, B.; Stanford, D. (2004). "The North Atlantic ice-edge corridor:
  a possible Palaeolithic route to the New World". *World Archaeology.* **36**
  (4): 459–478. doi: 10.1080/0043824042000303656[353].
• Bradley, B.; Stanford, D. (2006). "The Solutrean-Clovis connection: re-
  ply to Straus, Meltzer and Goebel". *World Archaeology.* **38** (4): 704–714.
  doi: 10.1080/00438240601022001[354]. JSTOR 40024066[355].
• Dennis J. Stanford, Bruce Bradely, *Pre-Clovis First Americans: The
  Origin of America's Clovis Culture* (University of California Press, 2012).
  ISBN 978-0-520-22783-5
• Dennis J. Stanford, Bruce A. Bradley, *Across Atlantic Ice: The Ori-
  gin of America's Clovis Culture* (University of California Press (2012).
  ISBN 978-0-520-22783-5
• Diamond, Jared, *Guns, germs and steel. A short history of everybody for
  the last 13,000 years,* 1997.
• Dixon, E. James. *Quest for the Origins of the First Americans.* University
  of New Mexico Press. 1993.
• Dixon, E. James. *Bones, Boats, and Bison: the Early Archeology of
  Western North America.* University of New Mexico Press. 1993, 1999??
• Erlandson, Jon M. *Early Hunter-Gatherers of the California Coast.*
  Plenum Press. 1994.
• Erlandson, Jon M (2001). "The Archaeology of Aquatic Adaptations:
  Paradigms for a New Millennium". *Journal of Archaeological Research.*
  9 (4): 287–350. doi: 10.1023/a:1013062712695[356].
• Erlandson, Jon M. Anatomically Modern Humans, Maritime Migrations,
  and the Peopling of the New World. In *The First Americans: The Pleis-
  tocene Colonization of the New World*, edited by N. Jablonski, 2002.
  pp. 59–92. Memoirs of the California Academy of Sciences. San Fran-
  cisco.
• Erlandson, Jon. M.; Graham, M. H.; Bourque, Bruce J.; Corbett, Debra;
  Estes, James A.; Steneck, R. S. (2007). "The Kelp Highway Hypothesis:
  Marine Ecology, The Coastal Migration Theory, and the Peopling of the

Americas". *Journal of Island and Coastal Archaeology*. **2** (2): 161–174. doi: 10.1080/15564890701628612[357].

- Eshleman, Jason A.; Malhi, Ripan S.; Glenn Smith, David (2003). "Mitochondrial DNA Studies of Native Americans: Conceptions and Misconceptions of the Population Prehistory of the Americas". *Evolutionary Anthropology*. **12**: 7–18. doi: 10.1002/evan.10048[358].

- Fedje; Christensen (1999). "Modeling Paleoshorelines and Locating Early Holocene Coastal Sites in Haida Gwaii". *American Antiquity*. **64** (4): 635–652. doi: 10.2307/2694209[359].

- Greenman, E. F. (1963). "The Upper Palaeolithic and the New World". *Current Anthropology*. **4**: 41–66. doi: 10.1086/200337[360].

- Hey, Jody (2005). "On the Number of New World Founders: A Population Genetic Portrait of the Peopling of the Americas"[361]. *PLOS Biology*. **3** (6): e193. doi: 10.1371/journal.pbio.0030193[362]. PMC 1131883[361] ⊚ . PMID 15898833[363].

- Nina G. Jablonski (2002). *The First Americans: The Pleistocene Colonization of the New World*[364]. California Academy of Sciences. ISBN 978-0-940228-50-4.

- Jones, Peter N. *Respect for the Ancestors: American Indian Cultural Affiliation in the American West*. Boulder, Colorado: Bauu Press. 2004, 2005.

- Lauber, Patricia. *Who Came First? New Clues to Prehistoric Americans*. Washington, D.C.: National Geographic Society, 2003.

- Matson and Coupland. *The Prehistory of the Northwest Coast*. Academic Press. New York. 1995.

- David J. Meltzer (2009). *First Peoples in a New World: Colonizing Ice Age America*[365]. University of California Press. ISBN 978-0-520-94315-5.

- Snow, Dean R. "The First Americans and the Differentiation of Hunter-Gatherer Cultures." In Bruce G. Trigger and Wilcomb *E. Washburn, eds., *The Cambridge History of the Native Peoples of the Americas, Volume I: North America* (Cambridge: Cambridge University Press, 1996), 125-199.

- Spencer Wells (2002). *The Journey of Man: A Genetic Odyssey*[366]. Princeton University Press. ISBN 0-691-11532-X.

- Evidence Supports Earlier Date for People in North America, April 4, 2008[367]

External links

- "The first Americans: How and when were the Americas populated?"[368], *Earth*, January 2016
- "When Did Humans Come to the Americas?" - *Smithsonian Magazine* February 2013[369]
- Ordering information and news items for *The Dene–Yeniseian Connection*; the 2011 2nd printing has corriagenda for 14 articles in the 2010 ist printing[370]
- Journey of Man: A Genetic Odyssey (movie)[371] on YouTube - by Spencer Wells - PBS and National Geographic Channel, 2003 - 120 Minutes, UPC/EAN: 841887001267
- Atlas of the Human Journey[372], Genographic Project, National Geographic
- Journey of Mankind - Genetic Map[373] – Bradshaw Foundation
- The Paleoindian Period[374] – United States Department of the Interior, National Park Service
- Alabama Archaeology: Prehistoric Alabama[375] – The University of Alabama, Department of Archaeology
- The Paleoindian Database[376] – The University of Tennessee, Department of Anthropology.
- Paleoindians and the Great Pleistocene Die-Off[377] – American Academy of Arts and Sciences, National Humanities Center

Genetic history of indigenous peoples of the Americas

The genetic history of Indigenous peoples of the Americas (also named **Amerindians** or **Amerinds** in physical anthropology) is divided into two sharply distinct episodes: the in initial peopling of the Americas during about 20,000 to 14,000 years ago (20–14 kya), and European contact, after about 500 years ago. The former is the determinant factor for the number of genetic lineages, zygosity mutations and founding haplotypes present in today's Indigenous Amerindian populations.

Most Amerindians groups are derived from a basal **Ancestral lineage**, which formed in Siberia prior to the Last Glacial Maximum, between about 36,000 and 25,000 years ago, from a combination of early East Asian and Ancient

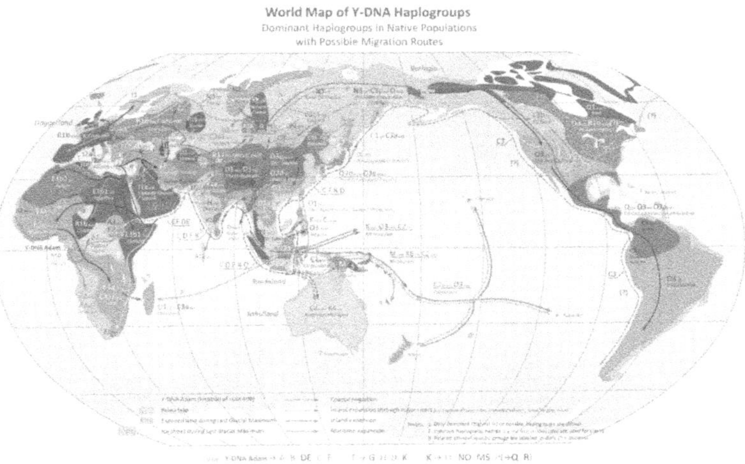

Figure 125: *Possible migration routes to the Americas as predicted by the distribution of Y-DNA haplogroups: inland route (purple lines), Pacific coastal route (brown dashed line), and possible trans-Atlantic route (light blue double line).*

North Eurasian ancestry and which dispersed throughout the Americas after about 16,000 years ago (an exception are the Na Dene and Eskimo–Aleut speaking groups, which are partially derived from Siberian populations which entered the Americas at a later time).[378]

In the early 2000s, archaeogenetics was primarily based on Human Y-chromosome DNA haplogroups and Human mitochondrial DNA haplogroups.[379] Autosomal "atDNA" markers are also used, but differ from mtDNA or Y-DNA in that they overlap significantly.

Analyses of genetics among Amerindian and Siberian populations have been used to argue for early isolation of founding populations on Beringia and for later, more rapid migration from Siberia through Beringia into the New World. The microsatellite diversity and distributions of the Y lineage specific to South America indicates that certain Amerindian populations have been isolated since the initial colonization of the region. The Na-Dené, Inuit and Indigenous Alaskan populations exhibit Haplogroup Q-M242; however, they are distinct from other indigenous Amerindians with various mtDNA and atDNA mutations. This suggests that the peoples who first settled the northern extremes of North America and Greenland derived from later migrant populations than those who penetrated farther south in the Americas. Linguists and biologists have reached a similar conclusion based on analysis of Amerindian language groups and ABO blood group system distributions.

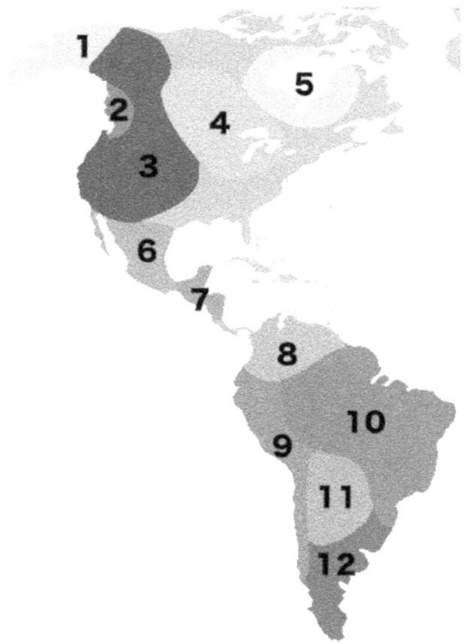

Figure 126:
Genetic groups according to Tribal DNA
<templatestyles src= 'Template:Refbegin/styles.css " />
1. Arctic
2. Salishan
3. Athabaskan
4. North Amerindian
5. Ojibwa
6. Mexica
7. Maya
8. Chibcha
9. Andean
10. Amazonian
11. Gran Chaco
12. Patagonian

Autosomal DNA

Genetic diversity and population structure in the American landmass is also done using autosomal (atDNA) micro-satellite markers genotyped; sampled from North, Central, and South America and analyzed against similar data available from other indigenous populations worldwide. The Amerindian populations show a lower genetic diversity than populations from other continental regions. Observed is a decreasing genetic diversity as geographic distance from the Bering Strait occurs, as well as a decreasing genetic similarity to

Siberian populations from Alaska (the genetic entry point). Also observed is evidence of a higher level of diversity and lower level of population structure in western South America compared to eastern South America. There is a relative lack of differentiation between Mesoamerican and Andean populations, a scenario that implies that coastal routes were easier for migrating peoples (more genetic contributors) to traverse in comparison with inland routes.

The over-all pattern that is emerging suggests that the Americas were colonized by a small number of individuals (effective size of about 70), which grew by a factor of 10 over 800 – 1000 years. The data also shows that there have been genetic exchanges between Asia, the Arctic, and Greenland since the initial peopling of the Americas.

Moreno-Mayar et al. (2018) have identified a basal **Ancestral Native American** (ANA) lineage. This lineage formed by admixture of early East Asian and Ancient North Eurasian lineages prior to the Last Glacial Maximum, ca. 36–25 kya. Basal ANA diverged into an "Ancient Beringian" (AB) lineage at ca. 20 kya. The non-AB lineage further diverged into "Northern Native American" (NNA) and "Southern Native American" (SNA) lineages between about 17.5 and 14.6 kya. Most pre-Columbian lineages are derived from NNA and SNA, except for the American Arctic, where there is evidence of later (after 10kya) admixture from Paleo-Siberian lineages.[378]

In 2014, the autosomal DNA of a 12,500+-year-old infant from Montana was sequenced. The DNA was taken from a skeleton referred to as Anzick-1, found in close association with several Clovis artifacts. Comparisons showed strong affinities with DNA from Siberian sites, and virtually ruled out that particular individual had any close affinity with European sources (the "Solutrean hypothesis"). The DNA also showed strong affinities with all existing Amerindian populations, which indicated that all of them derive from an ancient population that lived in or near Siberia, the Upper Palaeolithic Mal'ta population.

According to an autosomal genetic study from 2012, Native Americans descend of at least three main migrant waves from East Asia. Most of it is traced back to a single ancestral population, called 'First Americans'. However, those who speak Inuit languages from the Arctic inherited almost half of their ancestry from a second East Asian migrant wave. And those who speak Na-dene, on the other hand, inherited a tenth of their ancestry from a third migrant wave. The initial settling of the Americas was followed by a rapid expansion southwards, by the coast, with little gene flow later, especially in South America. One exception to this are the Chibcha speakers, whose ancestry comes from both North and South America.

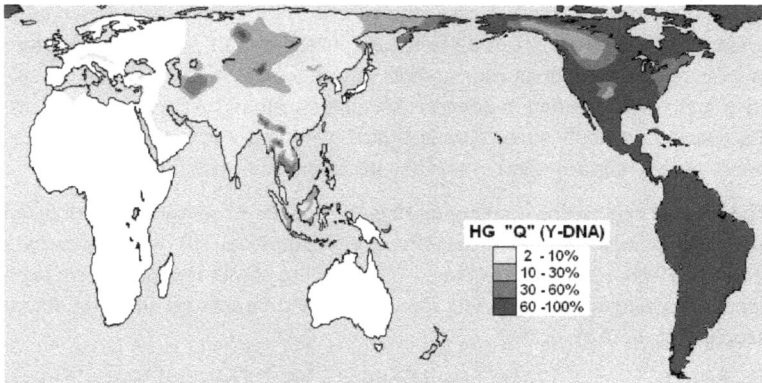

Figure 127: *Spread of Haplogroup Q in indigenous populations.*

Linguistic studies have backed up genetic studies, with ancient patterns having been found between the languages spoken in Siberia and those spoken in the Americas.Wikipedia:Please clarify

Two 2015 autosomal DNA genetic studies confirmed the Siberian origins of the Natives of the Americas. However an ancient signal of shared ancestry with Australasians (Natives of Australia, Melanesia and the Andaman Islands) was detected among the Natives of the Amazon region. The migration coming out of Siberia would have happened 23,000 years ago.

Paternal lineages

A "Central Siberian" origin has been postulated for the paternal lineage of the source populations of the original migration into the Americas.

Membership in haplogroups Q and C3b implies indigenous American patrilineal descent.

Haplogroup Q

Q-M242 (mutational name) is the defining (SNP) of Haplogroup Q (Y-DNA) (phylogenetic name). Within the Q clade, there are 14 haplogroups marked by 17 SNPs.[2009] In Eurasia, haplogroup Q is found among indigenous Siberian populations, such as the modern Chukchi and Koryak peoples. In particular, two groups exhibit large concentrations of the Q-M242 mutation, the Ket (93.8%) and the Selkup (66.4%) peoples. The Ket are thought to be the only survivors of ancient wanderers living in Siberia. Their population size is very

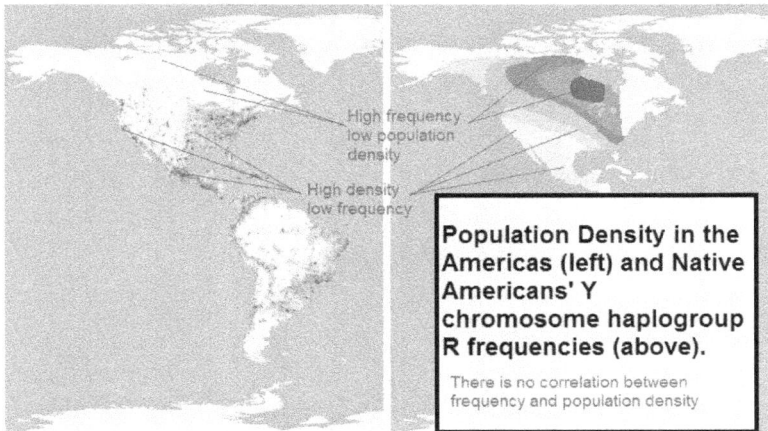

Figure 128: *Y chromosome R haplogroup among Native Americans (right; Malhi et al., 2008), and population density mapping (left) indicate a non-correlation between haplogroup R frequency and population density. The study of Malhi et al. 2008 suggest European admixture has resulted in a decreasing gradient of haplogroup R in Native Americans.*

small; there are fewer than 1,500 Ket in Russia.[2002] The Selkup have a slightly larger population size than the Ket, with approximately 4,250 individuals.

Starting the Paleo-Indians period, a migration to the Americas across the Bering Strait (Beringia) by a small population carrying the Q-M242 mutation took place. A member of this initial population underwent a mutation, which defines its descendant population, known by the Q-M3 (SNP) mutation. These descendants migrated all over the Americas.

Haplogroup Q-M3 is defined by the presence of the rs3894 (M3) (SNP). The Q-M3 mutation is roughly 15,000 years old as that is when the initial migration of Paleo-Indians into the Americas occurred. Q-M3 is the predominant haplotype in the Americas, at a rate of 83% in South American populations, 50% in the Na-Dené populations, and in North American Eskimo-Aleut populations at about 46%. With minimal back-migration of Q-M3 in Eurasia, the mutation likely evolved in east-Beringia, or more specifically the Seward Peninsula or western Alaskan interior. The Beringia land mass began submerging, cutting off land routes.[380]

Since the discovery of Q-M3, several subclades of M3-bearing populations have been discovered. An example is in South America, where some populations have a high prevalence of (SNP) M19 which defines subclade **Q-M19**. M19 has been detected in (59%) of Amazonian Ticuna men and in (10%) of

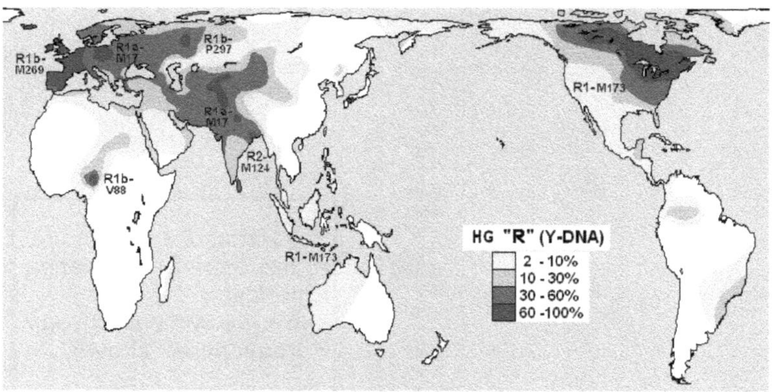

Figure 129: *Spread of Haplogroup R in Indigenous populations.*

Wayuu men. Subclade M19 appears to be unique to South American Indigenous peoples, arising 5,000 to 10,000 years ago. This suggests that population
isolation and perhaps even the establishment of tribal groups began soon after
migration into the South American areas. Other American subclades include
Q-L54, Q-Z780, Q-MEH2, Q-SA01, and Q-M346 lineages. In Canada, two
other lineages have been found. These are Q-P89.1 and Q-NWT01.

The principal-component analysis suggests a close genetic relatedness between
some North American Amerindians (the Chipewyan and the Cheyenne) and
certain populations of central/southern Siberia (particularly the Kets, Yakuts,
Selkups, and Altays), at the resolution of major Y-chromosome haplogroups.
This pattern agrees with the distribution of mtDNA haplogroup X, which is
found in North America, is absent from eastern Siberia, but is present in the
Altais of southern central Siberia. Similarly, the Asian populations closest to
Native Americans are characterized by a predominance of lineage P-M45* and
low frequencies of C-RPS4Y.

Haplogroup R1

Haplogroup R1 (Y-DNA) (specifically R1b) is the second most predominant
Y haplotype found among indigenous Amerindians after Q (Y-DNA). The
distribution of R1 is believed by some to be associated with the re-settlement
of Eurasia following the last glacial maximum. One theory put forth is that
R1 entered the Americas with the initial founding population, suggesting prehistoric Amerindian immigration from Asia through Beringia and correlating
mostly with the frequency of haplogroups Q-M3 and P-M45*. A second theory is that it was introduced during European colonization. R1 is very common

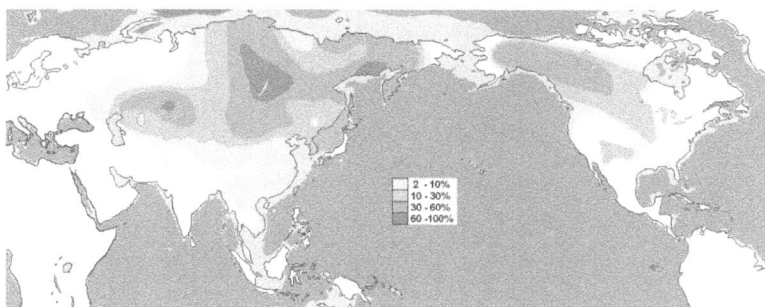

Figure 130: *Spread of Haplogroup C-M217 in Indigenous populations.*

throughout all of Eurasia except East Asia and Southeast Asia. **R1 (M173)** is found predominantly in North American groups like the Ojibwe (50-79%), Seminole (50%), Sioux (50%), Cherokee (47%), Dogrib (40%) and Tohono O'odham (Papago) (38%).

A study of Raghavan et al. 2013 found that autosomal evidence indicates that skeletal remain of a south-central Siberian child carrying R* y-dna (Mal'ta boy-1) "is basal to modern-day western Eurasians and genetically closely related to modern-day Amerindians, with no close affinity to east Asians. This suggests that populations related to contemporary western Eurasians had a more north-easterly distribution 24,000 years ago than commonly thought." Sequencing of another south-central Siberian (Afontova Gora-2) revealed that "western Eurasian genetic signatures in modern-day Amerindians derive not only from post-Columbian admixture, as commonly thought, but also from a mixed ancestry of the First Americans." It is further theorized if "Mal'ta might be a missing link, a representative of the Asian population that admixed both into Europeans and Native Americans."

Haplogroup C-P39

Haplogroup C-M217 is mainly found in indigenous Siberians, Mongolians and Kazakhs. Haplogroup C-M217 is the most widespread and frequently occurring branch of the greater (Y-DNA) haplogroup C-M130. Haplogroup C-M217 descendant **C-P39** is commonly found in today's Na-Dené speakers, with the highest frequency found among the Athabaskans at 42%. This distinct and isolated branch **C-P39** includes almost all the Haplogroup C-M217 Y-chromosomes found among all indigenous peoples of the Americas. The Na-Dené groups are also unusual among indigenous peoples of the Americas in having a relatively high frequency of Q-M242 (25%).

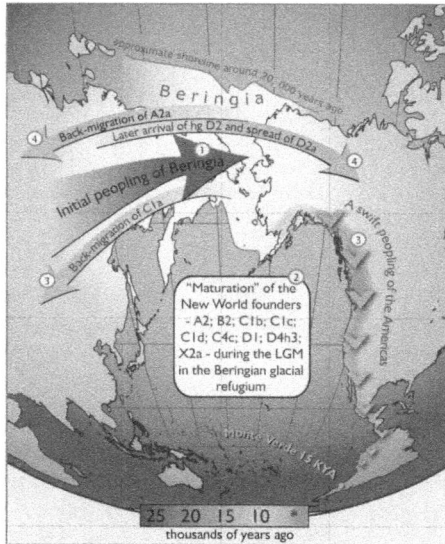

Figure 131: *Schematic illustration of maternal (mtDNA) gene-flow in and out of Beringia, from 25,000 years ago to present.*

Some researchers feel that this may indicate that the Na-Dené migration occurred from the Russian Far East after the initial Paleo-Indian colonization, but prior to modern Inuit, Inupiat and Yupik expansions.

Maternal lineages

The common occurrence of the mtDNA Haplogroups A, B, C, and D among eastern Asian and Amerindian populations has long been recognized, along with the presence of Haplogroup X. As a whole, the greatest frequency of the four Amerindian associated haplogroups occurs in the Altai-Baikal region of southern Siberia. Some subclades of C and D closer to the Amerindian subclades occur among Mongolian, Amur, Japanese, Korean, and Ainu populations.

When studying human mitochondrial DNA (mtDNA) haplogroups, the results indicated until recentlyWikipedia:Manual of Style/Dates and numbers that Indigenous Amerindian haplogroups, including haplogroup X, are part of a single founding East Asian population. It also indicates that the distribution of mtDNA haplogroups and the levels of sequence divergence among linguistically similar groups were the result of multiple preceding migrations from Bering Straits populations. All indigenous Amerindian mtDNA can be traced back to five haplogroups, A, B, C, D and X. More specifically, indigenous Amerindian mtDNA belongs to sub-haplogroups A2, B2, C1, D1, and X2a (with minor groups C4c, D2, D3, and D4h3). This suggests that 95% of Indigenous Amerindian mtDNA is descended from a minimal genetic founding female population, comprising sub-haplogroups A2, B2, C1b, C1c, C1d, and D1. The remaining 5% is composed of the X2a, D2, D3, C4, and D4h3 sub-haplogroups.

X is one of the five mtDNA haplogroups found in Indigenous Amerindian peoples. Unlike the four main American mtDNA haplogroups (A, B, C and D), X is not at all strongly associated with east Asia. Haplogroup X genetic sequences diverged about 20,000 to 30,000 years ago to give two sub-groups, X1 and X2. X2's subclade X2a occurs only at a frequency of about 3% for the total current indigenous population of the Americas. However, X2a is a major mtDNA subclade in North America; among the Algonquian peoples, it comprises up to 25% of mtDNA types. It is also present in lower percentages to the west and south of this area — among the Sioux (15%), the Nuu-chah-nulth (11%–13%), the Navajo (7%), and the Yakama (5%). Haplogroup X is more strongly present in the Near East, the Caucasus, and Mediterranean Europe. The predominant theory for sub-haplogroup X2a's appearance in North America is migration along with A, B, C, and D mtDNA groups, from a source in the Altai Mountains of central Asia.

Sequencing of the mitochondrial genome from Paleo-Eskimo remains (3,500 years old) are distinct from modern Amerindians, falling within sub-haplogroup D2a1, a group observed among today's Aleutian Islanders, the Aleut and Siberian Yupik populations. This suggests that the colonizers of the far north, and subsequently Greenland, originated from later coastal populations. Then a genetic exchange in the northern extremes introduced by the Thule people (proto-Inuit) approximately 800–1,000 years ago began. These final Pre-Columbian migrants introduced haplogroups A2a and A2b to the existing Paleo-Eskimo populations of Canada and Greenland, culminating in the modern Inuit.

A 2013 study in *Nature* reported that DNA found in the 24,000-year-old remains of a young boy from the archaeological Mal'ta-Buret' culture suggest that up to one-third of indigenous Americans' ancestry can be traced back to western Eurasians, who may have "had a more north-easterly distribution 24,000 years ago than commonly thought" "We estimate that 14 to 38 percent of Amerindian ancestry may originate through gene flow from this ancient population," the authors wrote. Professor Kelly Graf said,

> *"Our findings are significant at two levels. First, it shows that Upper Paleolithic Siberians came from a cosmopolitan population of early modern humans that spread out of Africa to Europe and Central and South*

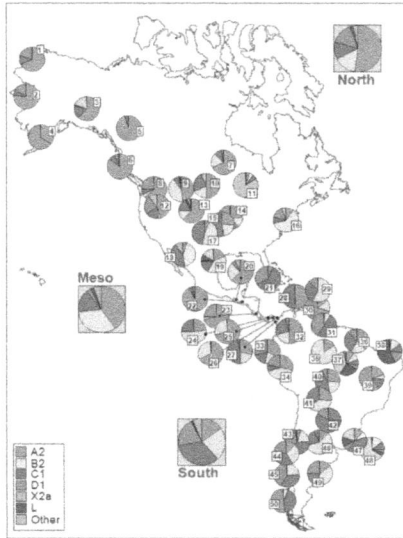

Figure 132: *Frequency distribution of the main mtDNA American haplogroups in Native American populations.*

Asia. Second, Paleoindian skeletons like Buhl Woman with phenotypic traits atypical of modern-day indigenous Americans can be explained as having a direct historical connection to Upper Paleolithic Siberia."

A route through Beringia is seen as more likely than the Solutrean hypothesis. An abstract in a 2012 issue of the "American Journal of Physical Anthropology" states that "The similarities in ages and geographical distributions for C4c and the previously analyzed X2a lineage provide support to the scenario of a dual origin for Paleo-Indians. Taking into account that C4c is deeply rooted in the Asian portion of the mtDNA phylogeny and is indubitably of Asian origin, the finding that C4c and X2a are characterized by parallel genetic histories definitively dismisses the controversial hypothesis of an Atlantic glacial entry route into North America."

Another study, also focused on the mtDNA (that which is inherited through only the maternal line), revealed that the indigenous people of the Americas have their maternal ancestry traced back to a few founding lineages from East Asia, which would have arrived via the Bering strait. According to this study, it is probable that the ancestors of the Native Americans would have remained for a time in the region of the Bering Strait, after which there would have been a rapid movement of settling of the Americas, taking the founding lineages to South America.

According to a 2016 study, focused on mtDNA lineages, "a small population entered the Americas via a coastal route around 16.0 ka, following previous isolation in eastern Beringia for ~2.4 to 9 thousand years after separation from eastern Siberian populations. Following a rapid movement throughout the Americas, limited gene flow in South America resulted in a marked phylogeographic structure of populations, which persisted through time. All of the ancient mitochondrial lineages detected in this study were absent from modern data sets, suggesting a high extinction rate. To investigate this further, we applied a novel principal components multiple logistic regression test to Bayesian serial coalescent simulations. The analysis supported a scenario in which European colonization caused a substantial loss of pre-Columbian lineages".

Paleoamericans

There is genetic evidence for an early wave of migration to the Americas. It is uncertain whether this "Paleoamerican" (also "Paleoamerind", not to confused with the term Paleo-Indian used of the early phase of Amerinds proper) migration took place in the early Holocene, thus only shortly predating the main Amerind peopling of the Americas, or whether it may have reached the Americas substantially earlier, before the Last Glacial Maximum.[381] Genetic evidence for "Paleoamerinds" consists of the presence of apparent admixture of archaic Sundadont lineages to the remote populations in the South American rainforest and in, and in the genetics and cranial morphology of Patagonians-Fuegians.[382] Nomatto et al. (2009) proposed into Beringia occurred between 40k and 30k cal years BP, with a pre-LGM migration into the Americas followed by isolation of the northern population following closure of the ice-free corridor. Evidence of people from Australia and Melanesia admixture in Amazonian populations was found by Skoglund and Reich (2016).[383]

Archaeological evidence for pre-LGM human presence in the Americas was first presented in the 1970s. notably the "Luzia Woman" skull found in Brazil and the Monte Verde site in Chile, both discovered in 1975.[384]

Old World genetic admixture

Substantial racial admixture has taken place during and since the European colonization of the Americas.

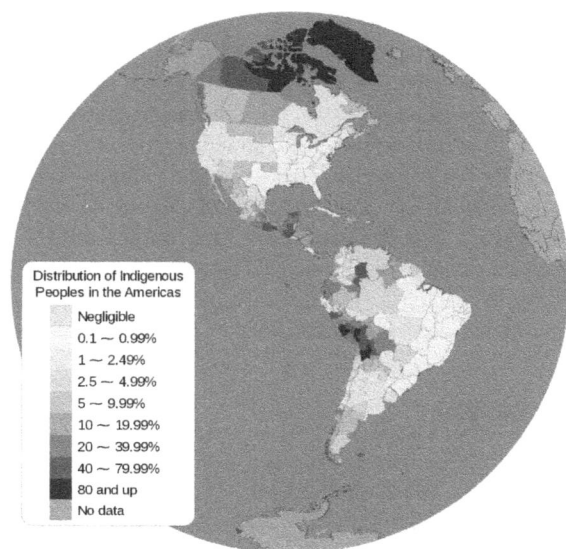

Figure 133: *The current distribution of indigenous peoples (based on self-identification, not genetic data).*

South and Central America

In Latin America in particular, significant racial admixture took place between the indigenous Amerind population, the European-descended colonial population, and the Sub-Saharan African populations imported as slaves. From about 1700, a Latin American terminology developed to refer to the various combinations of mixed racial descent produced by this.[385]

Many individuals who self-identify as one race exhibit genetic evidence of a multiracial ancestry. The European conquest of South and Central America, beginning in the late 15th century, was initially executed by male soldiers and sailors from the Iberian Peninsula (Spain and Portugal).Wikipedia:Identifying reliable sources The new soldier-settlers fathered children with Amerindian women and later with African slaves.Wikipedia:Identifying reliable sources These mixed-race children were generally identified by the Spanish colonist and Portuguese colonist as *"Castas"*.

North America

The North American fur trade during the 16th century brought many more European men, from France, Ireland, and Great Britain, who took North Amerindian women as wives. Their children became known as *"Métis"* or *"Bois-Brûlés"* by the French colonists and *"mixed-bloods"*, *"half-breeds"* or *"country-born"* by the English colonists and Scottish colonists.

Native Americans in the United States are more likely than any other racial group to practice racial exogamy, resulting in an ever-declining proportion of indigenous ancestry among those who claim a Native American identity. In the United States 2010 census, nearly 3 million people indicated that their race was Native American (including Alaska Native). This is based on self-identification, and there are no formal defining criteria for this designation. Especially numerous was the self-identification of Cherokee ethnic origin, a phenomenon dubbed the "Cherokee Syndrome". The context is the cultivation of an opportunistic ethnic identity related to the preceived prestige associated with Native American ancestry. Native American identity in the Eastern United States is mostly detached from genetic descent, and embraced by people of predominantly European ancestry.[386] Some tribes have adopted criteria of racial purity, usually through a Certificate of Degree of Indian Blood, and practice disenrollment of tribal members unable to provide proof of Native American ancestry. This topic has become a contentious issue in Native American reservation politics,

Blood groups

Prior to the 1952 confirmation of DNA as the hereditary material by Alfred Hershey and Martha Chase, scientists used blood proteins to study human genetic variation. The ABO blood group system is widely credited to have been discovered by the Austrian Karl Landsteiner, who found three different blood types in 1900. Blood groups are inherited from both parents. The ABO blood type is controlled by a single gene (the ABO gene) with three alleles: i, I^A, and I^B.

Research by Ludwik and Hanka Herschfeld during World War I found that the frequencies of blood groups A, B and O differed greatly from region to region. The "O" blood type (usually resulting from the absence of both A and B alleles) is very common around the world, with a rate of 63% in all human populations. Type "O" is the primary blood type among the indigenous populations of the Americas, in-particular within Central and South America populations, with a frequency of nearly 100%. In indigenous North American populations the frequency of type "A" ranges from 16% to 82%. This suggests again that the initial Amerindians evolved from an isolated population with a minimal number of individuals.

Figure 134: *Frequency of O group in indigenous populations.*
Note the predominance of this group in Indigenous Americans.

Distribution of ABO blood types

in various modern Indigenous Amerindian populations

Test results as of 2008[387]

PEOPLE GROUP	O (%)	A (%)	B (%)	AB (%)
Blackfoot Confederacy (N. American Indian)	17	82	0	1
Bororo (Brazil)	100	0	0	0
Eskimos (Alaska)	38	44	13	5
Inuit (Eastern Canada & Greenland)	54	36	23	8
Hawaiians (Polynesians, non-Amerindian)	37	61	2	1
Indigenous North Americans (as a whole Native Nations/First Nations)	79	16	4	1
Maya (modern)	98	1	1	1
Navajo	73	27	0	0
Peru	100	0	0	0

Further reading

<templatestyles src="Template:Refbegin/styles.css" />

- Peter N. Jones (October 2002). *American Indian mtDNA, Y chromosome genetic data, and the peopling of North America*[388]. Bauu Institute. ISBN 978-0-9721349-1-0.
- Joseph Frederick Powell (2005). *The first Americans: race, evolution, and the origin of Native Americans*[389]. Cambridge University Press. ISBN 978-0-521-82350-0.
- Francisco M. Salzano; Maria Cátira Bortolini (2002). *The evolution and genetics of Latin American populations*[390]. Cambridge University Press. ISBN 978-0-521-65275-9.
- "The peopling of the Americas: Genetic ancestry influences health"[391]. *scientific journal American Journal of Physical Anthropology*. University of Oklahoma. 2009. Retrieved 2009-11-21.

Pre-modern human migration

This article focusses on prehistorical migration since the Neolithic period until AD 1800. See Early human migrations for migration prior to the Neolithic, History of human migration for modern history, and human migration for contemporary migration.

Paleolithic migration prior to end of the Last Glacial Maximum spread anatomically modern humans throughout Afro-Eurasia and to the Americas. During the Holocene climatic optimum, formerly isolated populations began to move and merge, giving rise to the pre-modern distribution of the world's major language families.

In the wake of the population movements of the Mesolithic came the Neolithic revolution, followed by the Indo-European expansion in Eurasia and the Bantu expansion in Africa.

Population movements of the proto-historical or early historical period include the Migration period, followed by (or connected to) the Slavic, Magyar Norse, Turkic and Mongol expansions of the medieval period.

The last world regions to be permanently settled were the Pacific Islands and the Arctic, reached during the 1st millennium AD.

Since the beginning of the Age of Exploration and the beginning of the Early Modern period and its emerging colonial empires, an accelerated pace of migration on the intercontinental scale became possible.

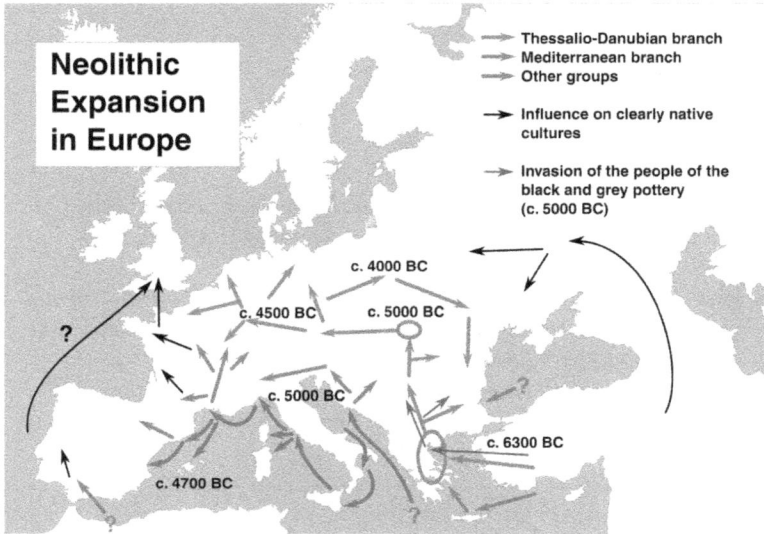

Figure 135: *Neolithic expansions from the 7th to the 5th millennium BC*

Prehistory

Neolithic to Chalcolithic

Agriculture is believed to have first been practised around 10,000 BC in the Fertile Crescent (see Jericho). From there, it propagated as a "wave" across Europe, a view supported by Archaeogenetics, reaching northern Europe some 5 millennia ago.

Bronze Age

The proposed Indo-European migration has variously been dated to the end of the Neolithic (Marija Gimbutas: Corded Ware culture, Yamna culture, Kurgan culture), the early Neolithic (Colin Renfrew: Starčevo-Körös, Linearband-keramic) and the late Palaeolithic (Marcel Otte, Paleolithic Continuity Theory).

The speakers of the Proto-Indo-European language are usually believed to have originated to the North of the Black Sea (today Eastern Ukraine and Southern Russia), and from there they gradually migrated into, and spread their language by cultural diffusion to, Anatolia, Europe, and Central Asia Iran and South Asia starting from around the end of the Neolithic period (see Kurgan hypothesis). Other theories, such as that of Colin Renfrew, posit their development much

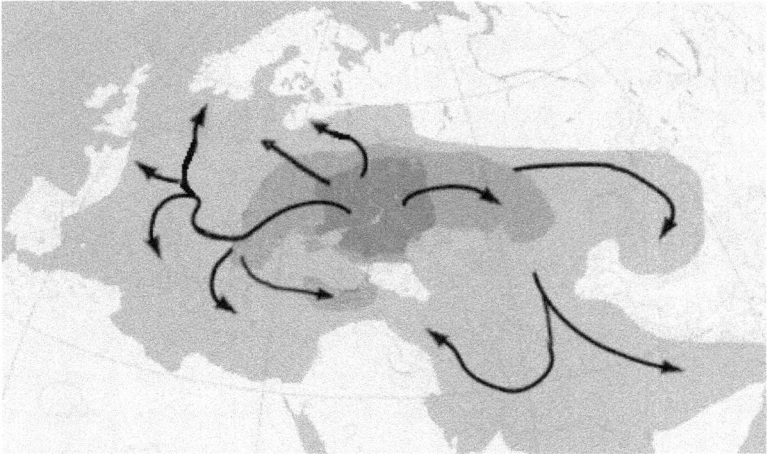

Figure 136: *Scheme of Indo-European migrations from c. 4000 to 1000 BC according to the Kurgan hypothesis. The purple area corresponds to the assumed Urheimat (Samara culture, Sredny Stog culture). The red area corresponds to the area which may have been settled by Indo-European-speaking peoples up to c. 2500 BC; the orange area to 1000 BC.*

earlier, in Anatolia, and claim that Indo-European languages and culture spread as a result of the agricultural revolution in the early Neolithic.

Relatively little is known about the inhabitants of pre-Indo-European "Old Europe". The Basque language remains from that era, as do the indigenous languages of the Caucasus. The Sami are genetically distinct among the peoples of Europe,Wikipedia:Citation needed but the Sami languages, as part of the Uralic languages, spread into Europe about the same time as the Indo-European languages. However, since that period speakers of other Uralic languages such as the Finns and the Estonians have had more contact with other Europeans, thus today sharing more genes with them than the Sami.

The earliest migrations we can reconstruct from historical sources are those of the 2nd millennium BC. The Proto-Indo-Iranians began their expansion from c. 2000 BC, the Rigveda documenting the presence of early Indo-Aryans in the Punjab from the late 2nd millennium BC, and Iranian tribes being attested in Assyrian sources as in the Iranian plateau from the 9th century BC. In the Late Bronze Age, the Aegean and Anatolia were overrun by moving populations, summarized as the "Sea Peoples", leading to the collapse of the Hittite Empire and ushering in the Iron Age.

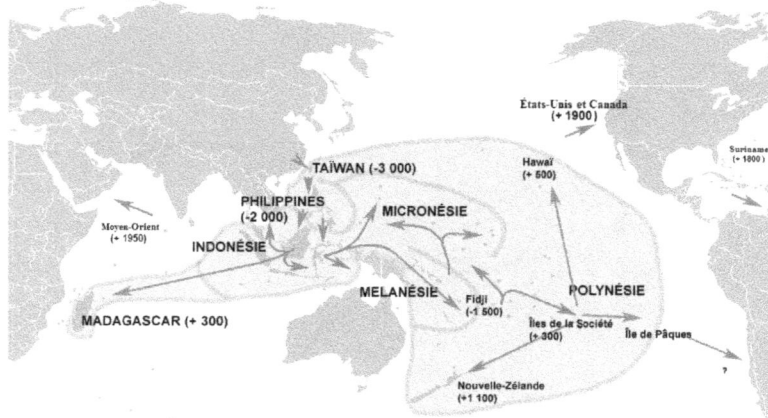

Figure 137: *Austronesians expansion map*

Austronesian expansion

The islands of the Pacific were populated during c. 1600 BC and AD 1000. The Lapita people, who got their name from the archaeological site in Lapita, New Caledonia, where their characteristic pottery was first discovered, came from Austronesia, probably New Guinea, reaching the Solomon Islands, around 1600 BC, and later to Fiji, Samoa and Tonga. By the beginning of the 1st millennium BC, most of Polynesia was a loose web of thriving cultures who settled on the islands' coasts and lived off the sea. By 500 BC Micronesia was completely colonized; the last region of Polynesia to be reached was New Zealand in around 1000.

Bantu expansion

The Bantu expansion is the major prehistoric migratory pattern that shaped the ethno-linguistic composition of Sub-Saharan Africa.[392]

The Bantu, a branch of the Niger-Congo phylum, originated in West Africa around the Benue-Cross rivers area in southeastern Nigeria. Beginning in the 2nd millennium BC, they spread to Central Africa, and later, during the 1st millennium BC onward southeastern, spreading pastoralism and agriculture. During the 1st millennium AD, they populated Southern African. In the process, the Bantu languages displaced the Khoisan languages indigenous to Central and Southern Africa.

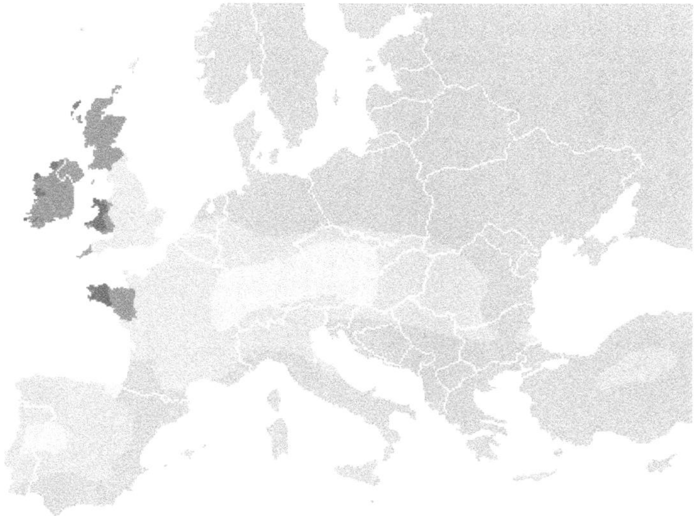

Figure 138: *Celtic expansion in Europe, 6th–3rd century BC*

Arctic peoples

The final region to be permanently settled by humans was the Arctic, reached by the Dorset culture during about 500 BC to AD 1500. The Inuit are the descendants of the Thule culture, which emerged from western Alaska around AD 1000 and gradually displaced the Dorset culture.

Proto-historical and early historical migration

The German term *Landnahme* ("land-taking") is sometimes used in historiography for a migration event associated with a founding legend, e.g. of the conquest of Canaan in the Hebrew Bible, the Indo-Aryan migration and expansion within India alluded to in the Rigveda, the invasion traditions in the Irish Mythological Cycle, accounting for how the Gaels came to Ireland the arrival of the Franks Austrasia during the Migration period, the Anglo-Saxon invasion of Britain, the settlement of Iceland in the Viking Age, the Slavic migrations, the Hungarian conquest , etc.

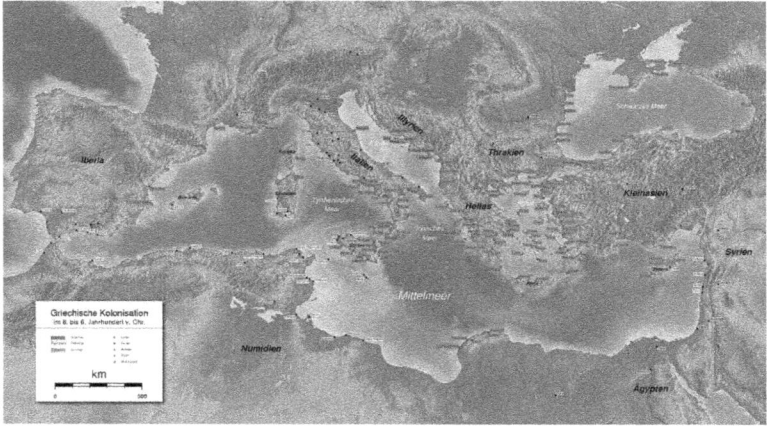

Figure 139: *Map of Phoenician (in yellow) and
Greek colonies (in red) around 8th to 6th century BC*

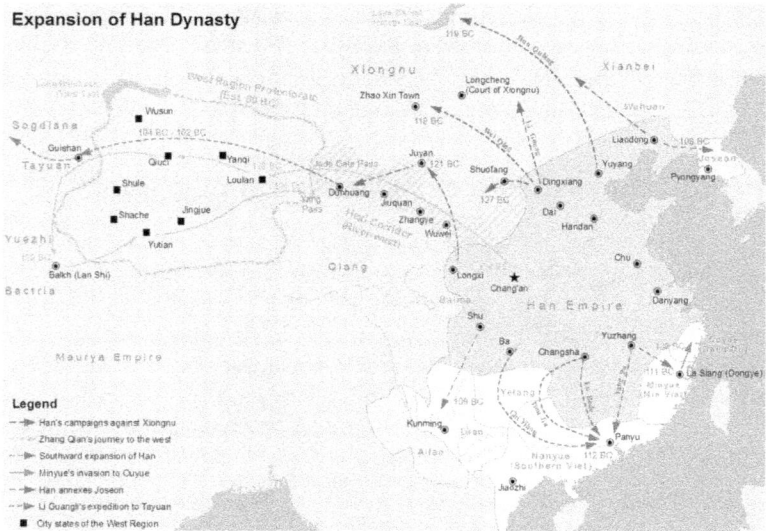

Figure 140: *Map showing the southward migration of the Han Chinese (in yellow)*

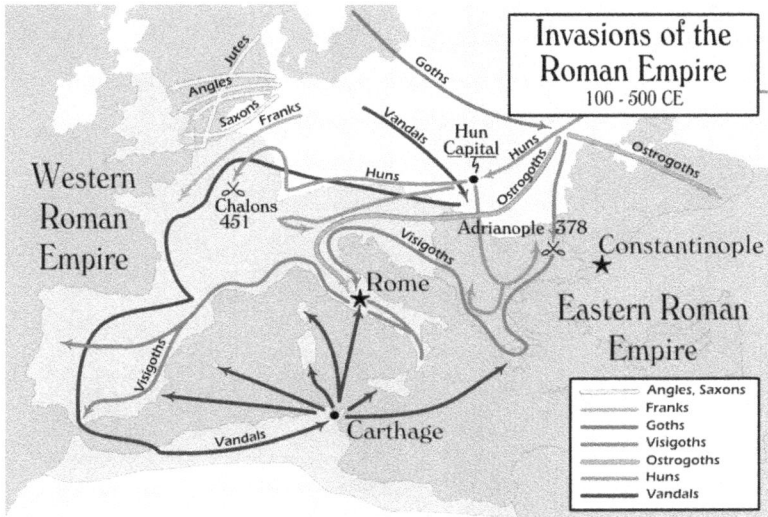

Figure 141: *2nd to 5th century migrations. See also map of the world in 820.*

Iron Age

The Dorian invasion of Greece led to the Greek Dark Ages. The Urartians were displaced by Armenians, and the Cimmerians and the Mushki migrated from the Caucasus into Anatolia. A Thraco-Cimmerian connection links these movements to the Proto-Celtic world of central Europe, leading to the introduction of Iron to Europe and the Celtic expansion to western Europe and the British Isles around 500 BC.

Migration period

Western historians refer to the period of migrations that separated Antiquity from the Middle Ages in Europe as the *Great Migrations* or as the Migrations Period. This period is further divided into two phases.

The first phase, from 300 to 500, saw the movement of Germanic, Sarmatian and Hunnic tribes and ended with the settlement of these peoples in the areas of the former Western Roman Empire. (See also: Ostrogoths, Visigoths, Burgundians, Suebi, Alamanni, Marcomanni).

The second phase, between 500 and 900, saw Slavic, Turkic and other tribes on the move, re-settling in Eastern Europe and gradually making it predominantly Slavic. Moreover, more Germanic tribes migrated within Europe during this period, including the Lombards (to Italy), and the Angles, Saxons, and

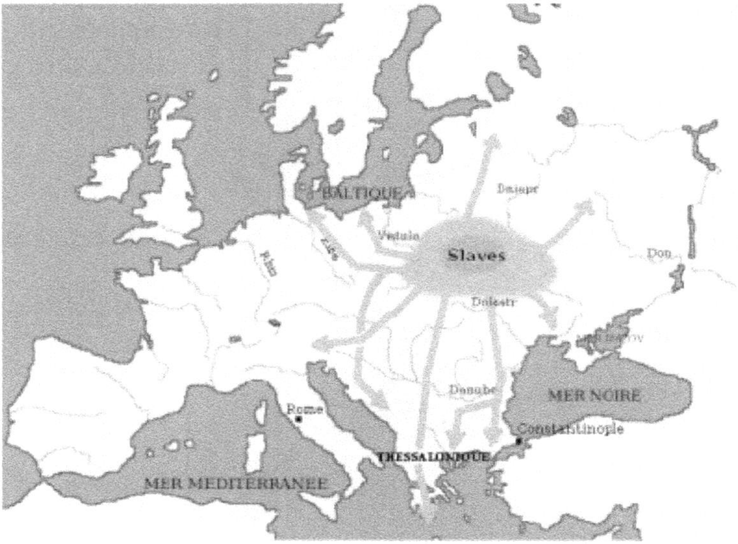

Figure 142: *Migration of Slavic peoples in the 5th to 10th centuries.*

Jutes (to the British Isles). See also: Avars, Bulgars, Huns, Arabs, Vikings, Varangians. The last phase of the migrations saw the coming of the Hungarians to the Pannonian plain.

German historians of the 19th century referred to these Germanic migrations as the *Völkerwanderung*, the migrations of the peoples.

The European migration period is connected with the simultaneous Turkic expansion which at first displaced other peoples towards the west, and by High Medieval times, the Seljuk Turks themselves reached the Mediterranean.

Early medieval period

The medieval period, although often presented as a time of limited human mobility and slow social change in the history of Europe, in fact saw widespread movement of peoples. The Vikings from Scandinavia raided all over Europe from the 8th century and settled in many places, including Normandy, the north of England, Scotland and Ireland (most of whose urban centres were founded by the Vikings). The Normans later conquered the Saxon Kingdom of England, most of Ireland, southern Italy and Sicily.

Iberia was invaded by Muslim Arabs, Berbers and Moors in the 8th century, founding new Kingdoms such as al Andalus and bringing with them a wave of

Figure 143:
Map of Vietnam showing the conquest of the south (the Nam tiến), 1069–1757
900 AD
1760 AD

settlers from North Africa. The invasion of North Africa by the Banu Hilal, a warlike Arab Bedouin tribe, was a major factor in the linguistic, cultural Arabization of the Maghreb.

Late Middle Ages

Massive migrations of Germans took place into East Central and Eastern Europe, reaching its peak in the 12th to 14th centuries. These Ostsiedlung settlements in part followed territorial gains of the Holy Roman Empire, but areas beyond were settled, too.

At the end of the Middle Ages, the Romani (gypsies) arrived in Europe from the Middle East. They originate in India, probably an offshoot of the Domba people of Northern India who had left for Sassanid Persia around the 5th century.

Early Modern period

Early Modern Europe

Internal European migration stepped up in the Early Modern Period. In this period, major migration within Europe included the recruiting by monarchs of landless laborers to settle depopulated or uncultivated regions and a series of forced migration caused by religious persecution. Notable examples of this phenomenon include the expulsion of the Jews from Spain in 1492, mass migration of Protestants from the Spanish Netherlands to the Dutch Republic after the 1580s, the expulsion of the Moriscos (descendants of former Muslims) from Spain in 1609, and the expulsion of the Huguenots from France in the 1680s. Since the 14th century, the Serbs started leaving the areas of their medieval Kingdom and Empire that was overrun by the Ottoman Turks and migrated to the north, to the lands of today's Vojvodina (northern Serbia), which was ruled by the Kingdom of Hungary at that time. The Habsburg monarchs of Austria encouraged them to settle on their frontier with the Turks and provide military service by granting them free land and religious toleration. The two greatest migrations took place in 1690 and 1737. Other instances of labour recruitments include the Plantations of Ireland - the settling of Ireland with Protestant colonists from England, Scotland and Wales in the period 1560–1690 and the recruitment of Germans by Catherine the Great of Russia to settle the Volga region in the 18th century.

Colonial empires

European Colonialism from the 16th to the early 20th centuries led to an imposition of a European colonies in many regions of the world, particularly in the Americas, South Asia, Sub-Saharan Africa and Australia, where European languages remain either prevalent or in frequent use as administrative languages. Major human migration before the 18th century was largely state directed. For instance, Spanish emigration to the New World was limited to settlers from Castile who were intended to act as soldiers or administrators. Mass immigration was not encouraged due to a labour shortage in Europe (of which Spain was the worst affected by a depopulation of its core territories in the 17th century).

Europeans also tended to die of tropical diseases in the New World in this period and for this reason England, France and Spain preferred using slaves as free labor in their American possessions. Many historians attribute a change in this pattern in the 18th century to population increases in Europe.

However, in the less tropical regions of North America's east coast, large numbers of religious dissidents, mostly English Puritans, settled during the early

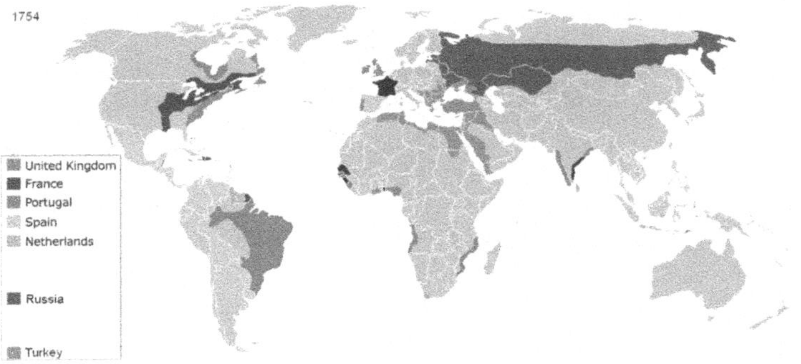

Figure 144: *Map of colonial empires throughout the world in 1754, prior to the Seven Years' War*

17th century. Spanish restrictions on emigration to Latin America were re-
voked and the English colonies in North America also saw a major influx of
settlers attracted by cheap or free land, economic opportunity and the continued lure of religious toleration.

A period in which various early English colonies had a significant amount of
self-rule prevailed from the time of the Plymouth colony's founding in 1620
through 1676, as the mother country was wracked by revolution and general
instability. However, King William III decisively intervened in colonial affairs after 1688 and the English colonies gradually came more directly under
royal governance, with a marked effect on the type of emigration. During the
early 18th century, significant numbers of non-English seekers of greater religious and political freedom were allowed to settle within the British colonies,
including Protestant Palatine Germans displaced by French conquest, French
Huguenots disenfranchised by an end of religious tolerance, Scotch-Irish Pres-
byterians, Quakers who were often Welsh, as well as Presbyterian and Catholic
Scottish Highlanders seeking a new start after a series of unsuccessful revolts.

The English colonists who came during this period were increasingly moved
by economic necessity. Some colonies, including Georgia, were settled heavily
by petty criminals and indentured servants who hoped to pay off their debts.
By 1800, European emigration had transformed the demographic character of
the American continent. This was also due in part to the devastating effect of
European diseases and warfare on Native American populations.

The European settlers' influence elsewhere was less pronounced as in South
Asia and Africa, European settlement in this period was limited to a thin layer
of administrators, traders and soldiers.

Further reading

- Reich, David (2018). *Who We Are And How We Got Here - Ancient DNA and the New Science of the Human Past*. Pantheon Books. ISBN 978-1101870327.

Neolithic Revolution

The **Neolithic Revolution, Neolithic Demographic Transition, Agricultural Revolution**, or **First Agricultural Revolution**, was the wide-scale transition of many human cultures during the Neolithic period from a lifestyle of hunting and gathering to one of agriculture and settlement, making an increasingly larger population possible. These settled communities permitted humans to observe and experiment with plants to learn how they grew and developed. This new knowledge led to the domestication of plants.[393]

Archaeological data indicates that the domestication of various types of plants and animals happened in separate locations worldwide, starting in the geological epoch of the Holocene around 12,500 years ago. It was the world's first historically verifiable revolution in agriculture. The Neolithic Revolution greatly narrowed the diversity of foods available, resulting in a downturn in human nutrition.

The Neolithic Revolution involved far more than the adoption of a limited set of food-producing techniques. During the next millennia it would transform the small and mobile groups of hunter-gatherers that had hitherto dominated human pre-history into sedentary (non-nomadic) societies based in built-up villages and towns. These societies radically modified their natural environment by means of specialized food-crop cultivation, with activities such as irrigation and deforestation which allowed the production of surplus food. Other developments found very widely are the domestication of animals, pottery, polished stone tools, and rectangular houses.

These developments, sometimes called the **Neolithic package**, provided the basis for densely populated settlements, specialization and division of labour, more trade, the development of non-portable art and architecture, centralized administrations and political structures, hierarchical ideologies, depersonalized systems of knowledge (e.g. writing), and property ownership. The earliest known civilization developed in Sumer in southern Mesopotamia (c. 5,500 BP); its emergence also heralded the beginning of the Bronze Age.

The relationship of the above-mentioned Neolithic characteristics to the onset of agriculture, their sequence of emergence, and empirical relation to each other at various Neolithic sites remains the subject of academic debate, and

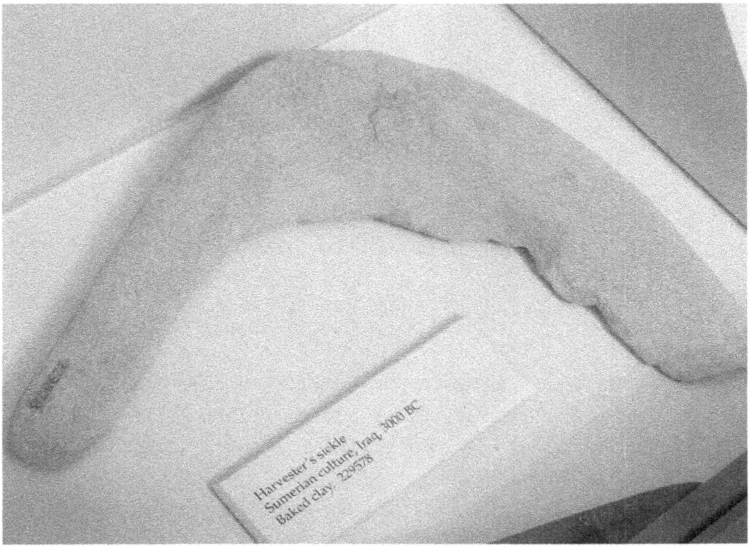

Figure 145: *A Sumerian harvester's sickle, dated to 3,000 BC*

varies from place to place, rather than being the outcome of universal laws of social evolution.[394] The Levant saw the earliest developments of the Neolithic Revolution from around 10,000 BC, followed by sites in the wider Fertile Crescent.

Agricultural transition

The term *Neolithic Revolution* was coined in 1923 by V. Gordon Childe to describe the first in a series of agricultural revolutions in Middle Eastern history. The period is described as a "revolution" to denote its importance, and the great significance and degree of change affecting the communities in which new agricultural practices were gradually adopted and refined.

The beginning of this process in different regions has been dated from 10,000 to 8,000 BC in the Fertile Crescent[395] and perhaps 8000 BC in the Kuk Early Agricultural Site of Melanesia.[396] This transition everywhere seems associated with a change from a largely nomadic hunter-gatherer way of life to a more settled, agrarian-based one, with the inception of the domestication of various plant and animal species—depending on the species locally available, and probably also influenced by local culture. Recent archaeological research suggests that in some regions such as the Southeast Asian peninsula, the transition from hunter-gatherer to agriculturalist was not linear, but region-specific.

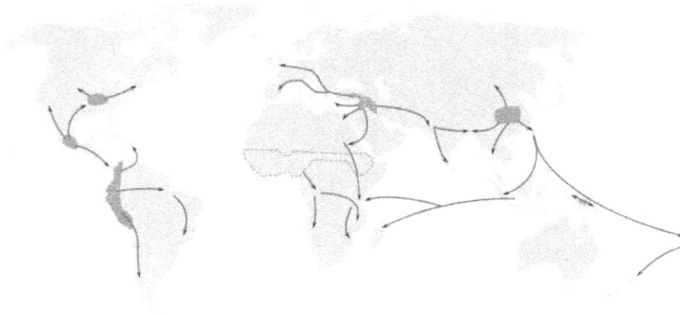

Figure 146: *Map of the world showing approximate centers of origin of agriculture and its spread in prehistory: the Fertile Crescent (11,000 BP), the Yangtze and Yellow River basins (9,000 BP) and the New Guinea Highlands (9,000–6,000 BP), Central Mexico (5,000–4,000 BP), Northern South America (5,000–4,000 BP), sub-Saharan Africa (5,000–4,000 BP, exact location unknown), eastern North America (4,000–3,000 BP).*

Figure 147: *Knap of Howar farmstead on a site occupied from 3,700 BC to 2,800 BC*

There are several competing (but not mutually exclusive) theories as to the factors that drove populations to take up agriculture. The most prominent of these are:

- The Oasis Theory, originally proposed by Raphael Pumpelly in 1908, popularized by V. Gordon Childe in 1928 and summarised in Childe's book *Man Makes Himself*. This theory maintains that as the climate got drier due to the Atlantic depressions shifting northward, communities contracted to oases where they were forced into close association with animals, which were then domesticated together with planting of seeds. However, today this theory has little support amongst archaeologists because subsequent climate data suggests that the region was getting wetter rather than drier.[397]
- The Hilly Flanks hypothesis, proposed by Robert Braidwood in 1948, suggests that agriculture began in the hilly flanks of the Taurus and Zagros mountains, where the climate was not drier as Childe had believed, and fertile land supported a variety of plants and animals amenable to domestication.
- The Feasting model by Brian Hayden suggests that agriculture was driven by ostentatious displays of power, such as giving feasts, to exert dominance. This required assembling large quantities of food, which drove agricultural technology.
- The Demographic theories proposed by Carl Sauer and adapted by Lewis Binford and Kent Flannery posit an increasingly sedentary population that expanded up to the carrying capacity of the local environment and required more food than could be gathered. Various social and economic factors helped drive the need for food.
- The evolutionary/intentionality theory, developed by David Rindos and others, views agriculture as an evolutionary adaptation of plants and humans. Starting with domestication by protection of wild plants, it led to specialization of location and then full-fledged domestication.
- Peter Richerson, Robert Boyd, and Robert Bettinger make a case for the development of agriculture coinciding with an increasingly stable climate at the beginning of the Holocene. Ronald Wright's book and Massey Lecture Series *A Short History of Progress* popularized this hypothesis.
- The postulated Younger Dryas impact event, claimed to be in part responsible for megafauna extinction and ending the last glacial period, could have provided circumstances that required the evolution of agricultural societies for humanity to survive. The agrarian revolution itself is a reflection of typical overpopulation by certain species following initial events during extinction eras; this overpopulation itself ultimately propagates the extinction event.

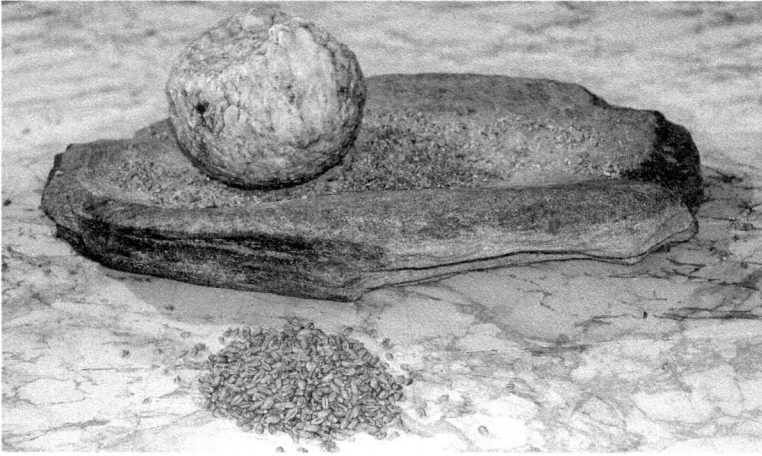

Figure 148: *Neolithic grindstone or quern for processing grain*

- Leonid Grinin argues that whatever plants were cultivated, the independent invention of agriculture always took place in special natural
  environments (e.g., South-East Asia). It is supposed that the cultivation
  of cereals started somewhere in the Near East: in the hills of Palestine or
  Egypt. So Grinin dates the beginning of the agricultural revolution within
  the interval 12,000 to 9,000 BP, though in some cases the first cultivated
  plants or domesticated animals' bones are even of a more ancient age of
  14–15 thousand years ago.[398]
- Andrew Moore suggested that the Neolithic Revolution originated over
  long periods of development in the Levant, possibly beginning during the
  Epipaleolithic. In *"A Reassessment of the Neolithic Revolution"*, Frank
  Hole further expanded the relationship between plant and animal domestication. He suggested the events could have occurred independently over
  different periods of time, in as yet unexplored locations. He noted that no
  transition site had been found documenting the shift from what he termed
  immediate and delayed return social systems. He noted that the full range
  of domesticated animals (goats, sheep, cattle and pigs) were not found
  until the sixth millennium at Tell Ramad. Hole concluded that *"close
  attention should be paid in future investigations to the western margins
  of the Euphrates basin, perhaps as far south as the Arabian Peninsula,
  especially where wadis carrying Pleistocene rainfall runoff flowed."*[399]

Domestication of plants

Once agriculture started gaining momentum, around 9000 BC, human activity resulted in the selective breeding of cereal grasses (beginning with emmer, einkorn and barley), and not simply of those that would favour greater caloric returns through larger seeds. Plants with traits such as small seeds or bitter taste would have been seen as undesirable. Plants that rapidly shed their seeds on maturity tended not to be gathered at harvest, therefore not stored and not seeded the following season; years of harvesting selected for strains that retained their edible seeds longer.

Several plant species, the "pioneer crops" or Neolithic founder crops, were identified by Daniel Zohary, who highlighted the importance of the three cereals, and suggested that domestication of flax, peas, chickpeas, bitter vetch and lentils came a little later. Based on analysis of the genes of domesticated plants, he preferred theories of a single, or at most a very small number of domestication events for each taxon that spread in an arc from the Levantine corridor around the Fertile Crescent and later into Europe.[400,401] Gordon Hillman and Stuart Davies carried out experiments with wild wheat varieties to show that the process of domestication would have occurred over a relatively short period of between 20 and 200 years.[402] Some of these pioneering attempts failed at first and crops were abandoned, sometimes to be taken up again and successfully domesticated thousands of years later: rye, tried and abandoned in Neolithic Anatolia, made its way to Europe as weed seeds and was successfully domesticated in Europe, thousands of years after the earliest agriculture. Wild lentils presented a different problem: most of the wild seeds do not germinate in the first year; the first evidence of lentil domestication, breaking dormancy in their first year, was found in the early Neolithic at Jerf el Ahmar (in modern Syria), and quickly spread south to the Netiv HaGdud site in the Jordan Valley. This process of domestication allowed the founder crops to adapt and eventually become larger, more easily harvested, more dependableWikipedia:Please clarify in storage and more useful to the human population.

Selectively propagated figs, wild barley and wild oats were cultivated at the early Neolithic site of Gilgal I, where in 2006 archaeologists found caches of seeds of each in quantities too large to be accounted for even by intensive gathering, at strata datable to c. 11,000 years ago. Some of the plants tried and then abandoned during the Neolithic period in the Ancient Near East, at sites like Gilgal, were later successfully domesticated in other parts of the world.

Once early farmers perfected their agricultural techniques like irrigation, their crops would yield surpluses that needed storage. Most hunter gatherers could not easily store food for long due to their migratory lifestyle, whereas those with a sedentary dwelling could store their surplus grain. Eventually granaries

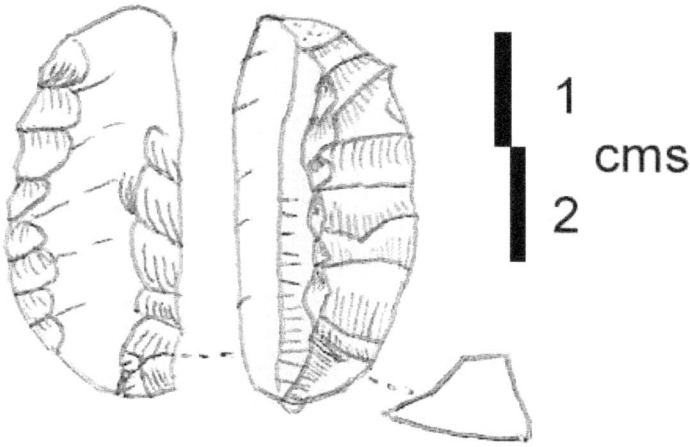

Figure 149: *An "Orange slice" sickle blade element with inverse, discontinuous retouch on each side, not denticulated. Found in large quantities at Qaraoun II and often with Heavy Neolithic tools in the flint workshops of the Beqaa Valley in Lebanon. Suggested by James Mellaart to be older than the Pottery Neolithic of Byblos (around 8,400 cal. BP).*

were developed that allowed villages to store their seeds longer. So with more food, the population expanded and communities developed specialized workers and more advanced tools.

The process was not as linear as was once thought, but a more complicated effort, which was undertaken by different human populations in different regions in many different ways.

In the Fertile Crescent

Early agriculture is believed to have originated and become widespread in Southwest Asia around 10,000–9,000 BP, though earlier individual sites have been identified. The Fertile Crescent region of Southwest Asia is the centre of domestication for three cereals (einkorn wheat, emmer wheat and barley), four legumes (lentil, pea, bitter vetch and chickpea), and flax. Domestication was a slow process involving multiple sites for each crop.

Finds of large quantities of seeds and a grinding stone at the paleolithic site of Ohalo II in the vicinity of the Sea of Galilee, dated to around 19,400 BP, has shown some of the earliest evidence for advanced planning of plant food

Figure 150: *Clay human figurine (Fertility goddess) Tappeh Sarab, Kermanshah, c. 7000–6100 BC*

consumption and suggests that humans at Ohalo II processed the grain before
consumption.[403] Tell Aswad is the oldest site of agriculture, with domesticated
emmer wheat dated to 10,800 BP.[404] Soon after came hulled, two-row barley
found domesticated earliest at Jericho in the Jordan valley and Iraq ed-Dubb
in Jordan.[405] Other sites in the Levantine corridor that show the first evidence
of agriculture include Wadi Faynan 16 and Netiv Hagdud. Jacques Cauvin
noted that the settlers of Aswad did not domesticate on site, but *"arrived, perhaps from the neighbouring Anti-Lebanon, already equipped with the seed for
planting"*. The Heavy Neolithic Qaraoun culture has been identified at around
fifty sites in Lebanon around the source springs of the River Jordan, but never
reliably dated.

In China

Northern China appears to have been the domestication center for foxtail millet
(*Setaria italica*) and broomcorn millet (*Panicum miliaceum*) with evidence of
domestication of these species approximately 8,000 years ago. These species
were subsequently widely cultivated in the Yellow River basin (7,500 years
ago). Rice was domesticated in southern China later on. Soybean was domesticated in northern China 4,500 years ago. Orange and peach also originated
in China. They were cultivated around 2500 BC.[406]

Figure 151: *Nile River Valley, Egypt*

In Africa

On the African continent, three areas have been identified as independently developing agriculture: the Ethiopian highlands, the Sahel and West Africa. By contrast, Agriculture in the Nile River Valley is thought to have developed from the original Neolithic Revolution in the Fertile Crescent. Many grinding stones are found with the early Egyptian Sebilian and Mechian cultures and evidence has been found of a neolithic domesticated crop-based economy dating around 7,000 BP.[407,408] Unlike the Middle East, this evidence appears as a "false dawn" to agriculture, as the sites were later abandoned, and permanent farming then was delayed until 6,500 BP with the Tasian and Badarian cultures and the arrival of crops and animals from the Near East.

Bananas and plantains, which were first domesticated in Southeast Asia, most likely Papua New Guinea, were re-domesticated in Africa possibly as early as 5,000 years ago. Asian yams and taro were also cultivated in Africa.

The most famous crop domesticated in the Ethiopian highlands is coffee. In addition, khat, ensete, noog, teff and finger millet were also domesticated in the Ethiopian highlands. Crops domesticated in the Sahel region include sorghum and pearl millet. The kola nut was first domesticated in West Africa. Other crops domesticated in West Africa include African rice, yams and the oil palm.

Agriculture spread to Central and Southern Africa in the Bantu expansion during the 1st millennium BC to 1st millennium AD.

In the Americas

Maize (corn), beans and squash were among the earliest crops domesticated in Mesoamerica, with maize beginning about 4000 BC, squash as early as 6000 BC, and beans by no later than 4000 BC. Potatoes and manioc were domesticated in South America. In what is now the eastern United States, Native Americans domesticated sunflower, sumpweed and goosefoot around 2500 BC. Sedentary village life based on farming did not develop until the second millennium BC, referred to as the formative period.

In New Guinea

Evidence of drainage ditches at Kuk Swamp on the borders of the Western and Southern Highlands of Papua New Guinea shows evidence of the cultivation of taro and a variety of other crops, dating back to 11,000 BP. Two potentially significant economic species, taro (*Colocasia esculenta*) and yam (*Dioscorea* sp.), have been identified dating at least to 10,200 calibrated years before present (cal BP). Further evidence of bananas and sugarcane dates to 6,950 to 6,440 BP. This was at the altitudinal limits of these crops, and it has been suggested that cultivation in more favourable ranges in the lowlands may have been even earlier. CSIRO has found evidence that taro was introduced into the Solomon Islands for human use, from 28,000 years ago, making taro cultivation the earliest crop in the world.[409,410] It seems to have resulted in the spread of the Trans–New Guinea languages from New Guinea east into the Solomon Islands and west into Timor and adjacent areas of Indonesia. This seems to confirm the theories of Carl Sauer who, in "Agricultural Origins and Dispersals", suggested as early as 1952 that this region was a centre of early agriculture.

Domestication of animals

When hunter-gathering began to be replaced by sedentary food production it became more profitable to keep animals close at hand.Wikipedia:Citation needed Therefore, it became necessary to bring animals permanently to their settlements, although in many cases there was a distinction between relatively sedentary farmers and nomadic herders.Wikipedia:No original research The animals' size, temperament, diet, mating patterns, and life span were factors in the desire and success in domesticating animals. Animals that provided milk, such as cows and goats, offered a source of protein that was renewable and therefore quite valuable. The animal's ability as a worker (for example

Figure 152: *Dromedary caravan in Algeria*

ploughing or towing), as well as a food source, also had to be taken into account. Besides being a direct source of food, certain animals could provide leather, wool, hides, and fertilizer. Some of the earliest domesticated animals included dogs (East Asia, about 15,000 years ago), sheep, goats, cows, and pigs.

Domestication of animals in the Middle East

The Middle East served as the source for many animals that could be domesticated, such as sheep, goats and pigs. This area was also the first region to domesticate the dromedary. Henri Fleisch discovered and termed the Shepherd Neolithic flint industry from the Bekaa Valley in Lebanon and suggested that it could have been used by the earliest nomadic shepherds. He dated this industry to the Epipaleolithic or Pre-Pottery Neolithic as it is evidently not Paleolithic, Mesolithic or even Pottery Neolithic.[411] The presence of these animals gave the region a large advantage in cultural and economic development. As the climate in the Middle East changed and became drier, many of the farmers were forced to leave, taking their domesticated animals with them. It was this massive emigration from the Middle East that would later help distribute these animals to the rest of Afroeurasia. This emigration was mainly on an east-west axis of similar climates, as crops usually have a narrow optimal climatic range outside of which they cannot grow for reasons of light or

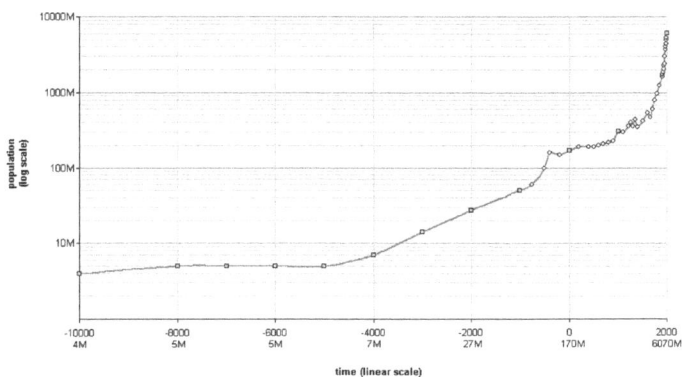

Figure 153: *World population (estimated) did not rise for a few millennia after the Neolithic revolution.*

rain changes. For instance, wheat does not normally grow in tropical climates, just like tropical crops such as bananas do not grow in colder climates. Some authors, like Jared Diamond, have postulated that this East-West axis is the main reason why plant and animal domestication spread so quickly from the Fertile Crescent to the rest of Eurasia and North Africa, while it did not reach through the North-South axis of Africa to reach the Mediterranean climates of South Africa, where temperate crops were successfully imported by ships in the last 500 years.[412] Similarly, the African Zebu of central Africa and the domesticated bovines of the fertile-crescent — separated by the dry sahara desert — were not introduced into each other's region.

Consequences

Social change

Despite the significant technological advance, the Neolithic revolution did not lead immediately to a rapid growth of population. Its benefits appear to have been offset by various adverse effects, mostly diseases and warfare.[413]

The introduction of agriculture has not necessarily led to unequivocal progress. The nutritional standards of the growing Neolithic populations were inferior to that of hunter-gatherers. Several ethnological and archaeological studies conclude that the transition to cereal-based diets caused a reduction in life expectancy and stature, an increment in infant mortality and infectious diseases,

Figure 154: *Domesticated cow being milked in Ancient Egypt*

the development of chronic, inflammatory or degenerative diseases (such as obesity, type 2 diabetes and cardiovascular diseases) and multiple nutritional deficiencies, including vitamin deficiencies, iron deficiency anemia and mineral disorders affecting bones (such as osteoporosis and rickets) and teeth. Average height went down from 5'10" (178 cm) for men and 5'6" (168 cm) for women to 5'5" (165 cm) and 5'1" (155 cm), respectively, and it took until the twentieth century for average human height to come back to the pre-Neolithic Revolution levels.

The traditional view is that agricultural food production supported a denser population, which in turn supported larger sedentary communities, the accumulation of goods and tools, and specialization in diverse forms of new labor. The development of larger societies led to the development of different means of decision making and to governmental organization. Food surpluses made possible the development of a social elite who were not otherwise engaged in agriculture, industry or commerce, but dominated their communities by other means and monopolized decision-making. Jared Diamond (in The World Until Yesterday) identifies the availability of milk and cereal grains as permitting mothers to raise both an older (e.g. 3 or 4 year old) and a younger child concurrently. The result is that a population can increase more rapidly. Diamond points out that agriculture brought about deep social divisions and encouraged gender inequality.

Subsequent revolutions

Andrew Sherratt has argued that following upon the Neolithic Revolution was a second phase of discovery that he refers to as the secondary products revolution. Animals, it appears, were first domesticated purely as a source of meat.[414] The Secondary Products Revolution occurred when it was recognised that animals also provided a number of other useful products. These included:

* hides and skins (from undomesticated animals)
* manure for soil conditioning (from all domesticated animals)
* wool (from sheep, llamas, alpacas, and Angora goats)
* milk (from goats, cattle, yaks, sheep, horses and camels)
* traction (from oxen, onagers, donkeys, horses, camels and dogs)
* guarding and herding assistance (dogs)

Sherratt argued that this phase in agricultural development enabled humans to make use of the energy possibilities of their animals in new ways, and permitted permanent intensive subsistence farming and crop production, and the opening up of heavier soils for farming. It also made possible nomadic pastoralism in semi arid areas, along the margins of deserts, and eventually led to the domestication of both the dromedary and Bactrian camel. Overgrazing of these areas, particularly by herds of goats, greatly extended the areal extent of deserts.

Living in one spot would have more easily permitted the accrual of personal possessions and an attachment to certain areas of land. From such a position, it is arguedWikipedia:Manual of Style/Words to watch#Unsupported attributions, prehistoric people were able to stockpile food to survive lean times and trade unwanted surpluses with others. Once trade and a secure food supply were established, populations could grow, and society would have diversified into food producers and artisans, who could afford to develop their trade by virtue of the free time they enjoyed because of a surplus of food. The artisans, in turn, were able to develop technology such as metal weapons. Such relative complexity would have required some form of social organisation to work efficiently, so it is likely that populations that had such organisation, perhaps such as that provided by religion, were better prepared and more successful. In addition, the denser populations could form and support legions of professional soldiers. Also, during this time property ownership became increasingly important to all people. Ultimately, Childe argued that this growing social complexity, all rooted in the original decision to settle, led to a second Urban Revolution in which the first cities were built.Wikipedia:Citation needed

Disease

Throughout the development of sedentary societies, disease spread more rapidly than it had during the time in which hunter-gatherer societies existed. Inadequate sanitary practices and the domestication of animals may explain the rise in deaths and sickness following the Neolithic Revolution, as diseases jumped from the animal to the human population. Some examples of infectious diseases spread from animals to humans are influenza, smallpox, and measles. In concordance with a process of natural selection, the humans who first domesticated the big mammals quickly built up immunities to the diseases as within each generation the individuals with better immunities had better chances of survival. In their approximately 10,000 years of shared proximity with animals, such as cows, Eurasians and Africans became more resistant to those diseases compared with the indigenous populations encountered outside Eurasia and Africa.[415] For instance, the population of most Caribbean and several Pacific Islands have been completely wiped out by diseases. 90% or more of many populations of the Americas were wiped out by European and African diseases before recorded contact with European explorers or colonists. Some cultures like the Inca Empire did have a large domestic mammal, the llama, but llama milk was not drunk, nor did llamas live in a closed space with humans, so the risk of contagion was limited. According to bioarchaeological research, the effects of agriculture on physical and dental health in Southeast Asian rice farming societies from 4000 to 1500 B.P. was not detrimental to the same extent as in other world regions.

Technology

In his book *Guns, Germs, and Steel*, Jared Diamond argues that Europeans and East Asians benefited from an advantageous geographical location that afforded them a head start in the Neolithic Revolution. Both shared the temperate climate ideal for the first agricultural settings, both were near a number of easily domesticable plant and animal species, and both were safer from attacks of other people than civilizations in the middle part of the Eurasian continent. Being among the first to adopt agriculture and sedentary lifestyles, and neighboring other early agricultural societies with whom they could compete and trade, both Europeans and East Asians were also among the first to benefit from technologies such as firearms and steel swords.

Archaeogenetics

The dispersal of Neolithic culture from the Middle East has recently been associated with the distribution of human genetic markers. In Europe, the spread of the Neolithic culture has been associated with distribution of the E1b1b lineages and Haplogroup J that are thought to have arrived in Europe from North Africa and the Near East respectively. In Africa, the spread of farming, and notably the Bantu expansion, is associated with the dispersal of Y-chromosome haplogroup E1b1a from West Africa.

Bibliography

- Bailey, Douglass. (2001). *Balkan Prehistory: Exclusions, Incorporation and Identity.* Routledge Publishers. ISBN 0-415-21598-6.
- Bailey, Douglass. (2005). *Prehistoric Figurines: Representation and Corporeality in the Neolithic.* Routledge Publishers. ISBN 0-415-33152-8.
- Balter, Michael (2005). *The Goddess and the Bull: Catalhoyuk, An Archaeological Journey to the Dawn of Civilization.* New York: Free Press. ISBN 0-7432-4360-9.
- Bellwood, Peter. (2004). *First Farmers: The Origins of Agricultural Societies.* Blackwell Publishers. ISBN 0-631-20566-7
- Bocquet-Appel, Jean-Pierre, editor and Ofer Bar-Yosef, editor, *The Neolithic Demographic Transition and its Consequences*, Springer (October 21, 2008), hardcover, 544 pages, ISBN 978-1402085383, trade paperback and Kindle editions are also available.
- Cohen, Mark Nathan (1977)*The Food Crisis in Prehistory: Overpopulation and the Origins of Agriculture.* New Haven and London: Yale University Press. ISBN 0-300-02016-3.
- Diamond, Jared (1997). *Guns, germs and steel. A short history of everybody for the last 13,000 years.*
- Diamond, Jared (2002). "Evolution, Consequences and Future of Plant and Animal Domestication". *Nature*, Vol 418.
- Harlan, Jack R. (1992). *Crops & Man: Views on Agricultural Origins* ASA, CSA, Madison, WI. https://web.archive.org/web/20060819110723/http://www.hort.purdue.edu/newcrop/history/lecture03/r_3-1.html
- Wright, Gary A. (1971). "Origins of Food Production in Southwestern Asia: A Survey of Ideas" Current Anthropology, Vol. 12, No. 4/5 (Oct.–Dec., 1971), pp. 447–477
- Kuijt, Ian; Finlayson, Bill. (2009). "Evidence for food storage and predomestication granaries 11,000 years ago in the Jordan Valley"[416]. PNAS, Vol. 106, No. 27, pp. 10966 –10970.

External links

- The Agricultural Revolution[417] on YouTube: Crash Course World History #1

Indo-European migrations

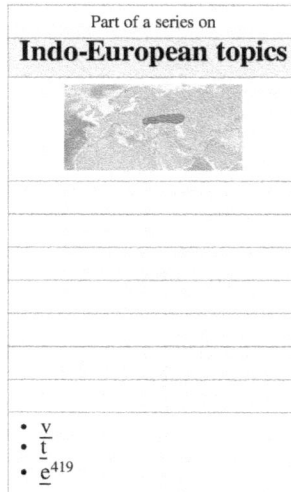

Part of a series on
Indo-European topics
• <u>v</u>
• <u>t</u>
• <u>e</u>[419]

Indo-European migrations were the migrations of pastoral peoples speaking the Proto-Indo-European language (PIE), who departed from the Yamnaya and related cultures in the Pontic–Caspian steppe, starting at <u>c.</u> 4000 BCE. Their descendants spread throughout Europe and parts of Asia, forming new cultures with the people they met on their way, including the Corded Ware culture in Northern Europe and the Vedic culture in the Indian subcontinent. These migrations ultimately seeded the cultures and languages of most of Europe, Greater Iran, and much of the Indian subcontinent (and subsequently resulted in the largest and most broadly spoken language family in the world).

Modern knowledge of these migrations is based on data from linguistics, archaeology, anthropology and genetics. Linguistics describes the similarities between various languages, and the linguistic laws at play in the changes in those languages (see Indo-European studies). Archaeological data describes the spread of the Proto-Indo-European culture and language in several stages: from the Proto-Indo-European homeland (probably situated in the Pontic–Caspian steppe), into Western Europe, Central, South and (very sporadically) Eastern Asia by migrations and by language shift through elite-recruitment as described by anthropological research.[420,421] Recent genetic research has a growing contribution to the understanding of the historical relations between various historical cultures.

The Indo-European languages and cultures spread in various stages. Early migrations from c. 4200–3000 BCE brought archaic proto-Indo-European into the lower Danube valley,[422] Anatolia,[423,424] and the Altai region.[425]

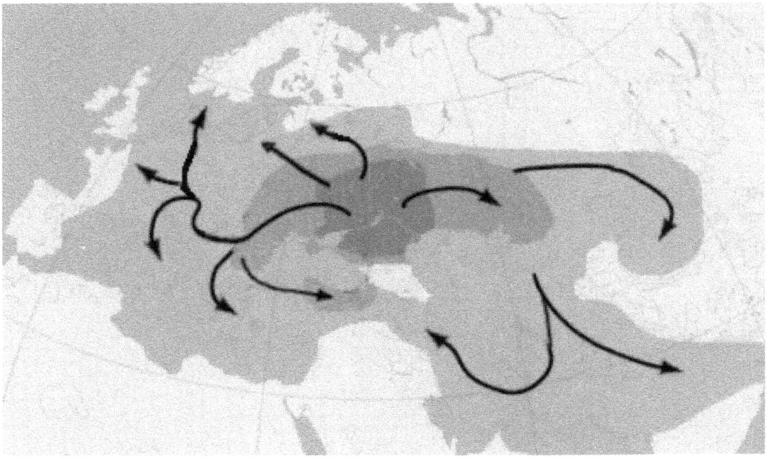

Figure 155:
*Scheme of Indo-European migrations from c. 4000
to 1000 BCE according to the Kurgan hypothesis
The assumed Urheimat (Samara culture, Sredny
Stog culture) and the subsequent Yamna culture.
Area possibly settled up to c. 2500 BCE.
Area settled up to 1000 BCE.*[418]

Proto-Celtic and Proto-Italic probably developed in and spread from Central Europe into western Europe after new Yamnaya migrations into the Danube Valley,[426,427] while Proto-Germanic and Proto-Balto-Slavic may have developed east of the Carpathian mountains, at present-day Ukraine,[428] moving north and spreading with the Corded Ware culture in Middle Europe (third millennium BCE).[429,430,431] Alternatively, a European branch of Indo-European dialects, termed "North-west Indo-European" and associated with the Beaker culture, may have been ancestral to not only Celtic and Italic, but also to Germanic and Balto-Slavic.

The Indo-Iranian language and culture emerged at the Sintashta culture (c. 2100–1800 BCE), at the eastern border of the Yamna horizon and the Corded ware culture, growing into the Andronovo culture (c. 1800–800 BCE). Indo-Aryans moved into the Bactria–Margiana Archaeological Complex (c. 2300–1700 BCE) and spread to the Levant (Mitanni), northern India (Vedic people, c. 1500 BCE), and China (Wusun).[421] The Iranian languages spread throughout the steppes with the Scyths and into Iran with the Medes, Parthians and Persians from ca. 800 BCE.[421]

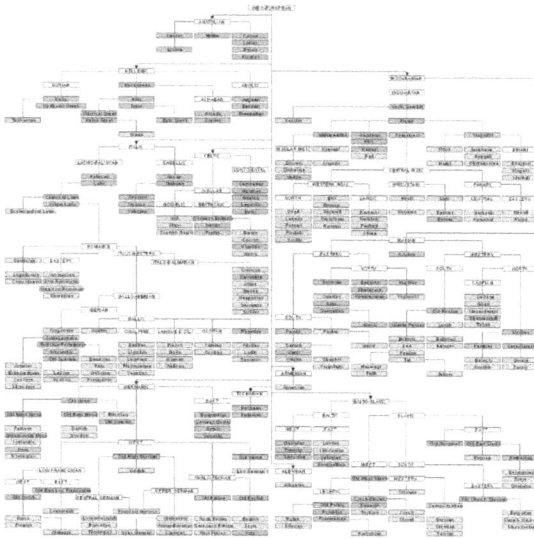

Figure 156: *Classification of Indo-European languages.*
Red: *Extinct languages.* **White:** *Categories or unattested proto-languages.*
Left half: *Centum languages.* **Right half:** *Satem languages.*

Fundaments

Linguistics: relations between languages

Indo-European languages

The Indo-European languages constitute a family of several hundred related languages and dialects. There are about 439 languages and dialects, according to the 2009 *Ethnologue* estimate, about half of these (221) belonging to the Indo-Aryan subbranch originating in South Asia. The Indo-European family includes most of the major current languages of Europe, the Iranian plateau, the northern half of the Indian Subcontinent, Sri Lanka and was also predominant in ancient Anatolia. With written attestations appearing since the Bronze Age in the form of the Anatolian languages and Mycenaean Greek, the Indo-European family is significant to the field of historical linguistics as possessing the second-longest recorded history, after the Afroasiatic family.

Indo-European languages are spoken by almost 3 billion native speakers, the largest number by far for any recognised language family. Of the 20 languages with the largest numbers of native speakers according to *Ethnologue*, twelve are Indo-European: Spanish, English, Hindi, Portuguese, Bengali, Russian,

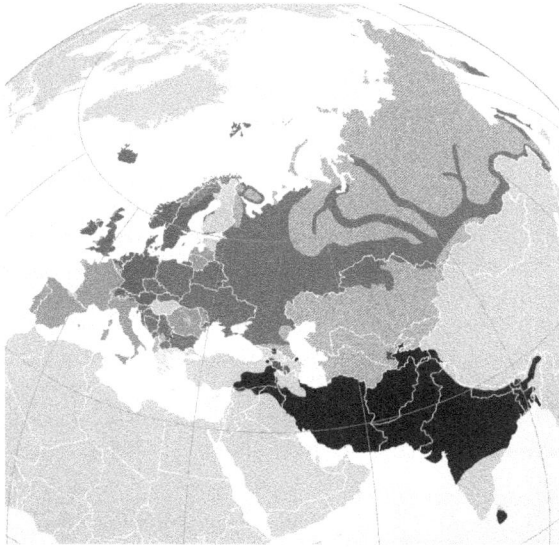

Figure 157:
*A map showing the approximate present-day distribution of
the Indo-European branches within their homelands of Europe
and Asia. The following legend is given in the chronological or-
der of the earliest surviving written attestations of each branch:*
Hellenic (Greek)
Indo-Iranian
Italic (Romance)
Celtic
Germanic
Armenian
Baltic
Slavic
Albanian
Non-Indo-European languages
Dotted and striped areas indicate where multilingualism is
common (more visible upon full enlargement of the map).

German, Punjabi, Marathi, French, Urdu, Italian, accounting for over 1.7 billion native speakers.

The similarities between various European languages, Sanskrit and Persian were noted by Sir William Jones when learning Sanskrit in India, concluding that all these languages originated from the same source.[432,433] Several disputed proposals link Indo-European to other major language families.

Development of the Indo-European languages

Proto-Indo-European language

The Proto-Indo-European language (PIE) is the linguistic reconstruction of a common ancestor of the Indo-European languages spoken by the Proto-Indo-Europeans. PIE was the first proposed proto-language to be widely accepted by linguists. Far more work has gone into reconstructing it than any other proto-language and it is by far the most well-understood of all proto-languages of its age. During the 19th century, the vast majority of linguistic work was devoted to reconstruction of Proto-Indo-European or its daughter proto-languages such as Proto-Germanic, and most of the current techniques of historical linguistics (e. g. the comparative method and the method of internal reconstruction) were developed as a result.

Scholars estimate that PIE may have been spoken as a single language (before divergence began) around 3500 BCE, though estimates by different authorities can vary by more than a millennium. The most popular hypothesis for the origin and spread of the language is the Kurgan hypothesis, which postulates an origin in the Pontic–Caspian steppe of Eastern Europe.

The existence of PIE was first postulated in the 18th century by Sir William Jones, who observed the similarities between Sanskrit, Ancient Greek, and Latin. By the early 20th century, well-defined descriptions of PIE had been developed that are still accepted today (with some refinements). The largest developments of the 20th century have been the discovery of Anatolian and Tocharian languages and the acceptance of the laryngeal theory. The Anatolian languages have also spurred a major re-evaluation of theories concerning the development of various shared Indo-European language features and the extent to which these features were present in PIE itself.

PIE is thought to have had a complex system of morphology that included inflections (suffixing of roots, as in *who, whom, whose*), and ablaut (vowel alterations, as in *sing, sang, sung*). Nouns used a sophisticated system of declension and verbs used a similarly sophisticated system of conjugation.

Relationships to other language families, including the Uralic languages, have been proposed but remain controversial. There is no written evidence of Proto-Indo-European, so all knowledge of the language is derived by reconstruction from later languages using linguistic techniques such as the comparative method and the method of internal reconstruction.

Pre-Proto-Indo-European

The Indo-Hittite hypothesis postulates a common predecessor for both the Anatolian languages and the other Indo-European languages, called Indi-Hittite or Indo-Anatolian.[420] Although it is obvious that PIE had predecessors,[434] the Indo-Hittite hypothesis is not widely accepted, and there is little to suggest that it is possible to reconstruct a proto-Indo-Hittite stage that differs substantially from what is already reconstructed for PIE.

A shared common ancestor of Indo-European and Uralic, Indo-Uralic, has been postulated as a possible pre-PIE.[435] According to Kortlandt, "Indo-European is a branch of Indo-Uralic which was radically transformed under the influence of a North Caucasian substratum when its speakers moved from the area north of the Caspian Sea to the area north of the Black Sea."[435,436,437]

- According to Allan R. Bomhard, "Proto-Indo-European is the result of the imposition of a Eurasiatic language – to use Greenberg's term – on a population speaking one or more primordial Northwest Caucasian languages."[438] See also *The Origins of Proto-Indo-European: The Caucasian Substrate Hypothesis*.[439]
- According to Bernard Sergent, the lithic assemblage of the first Kurgan culture in Ukraine (Sredni Stog II), which originated from the Volga and South Urals, recalls that of the Mesolithic-Neolithic sites to the east of the Caspian sea, Dam Dam Chesme II and the cave of Djebel.[440] He places the roots of Gimbutas' Kurgan cradle of Indo-Europeans in a more southern cradle, and adds that the Djebel material is related to a Paleolithic material of Northwestern Iran, the Zarzian culture, dated 10,000–8,500 BCE, and in the more ancient Kebarian of the Near East. He concludes that more than 10,000 years ago the Indo-Europeans were a small people grammatically, phonetically and lexically close to Semitic-Hamitic populations of the Near East.[441]</ref>

Anthony notes that the validity of such deep relationships cannot be reliably demonstrated due to the time-depth involved, and also notes that the similarities may be explained by borrowings from PIE into proto-Uralic.[434] Yet, Anthony also notes that the North Caucasian communities "were southern participants in the steppe world".[420]

Spread of IE-languages II

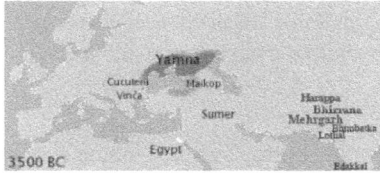
Figure 158: *3500 BCE*

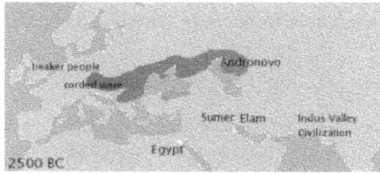
Figure 159: *2500 BCE*

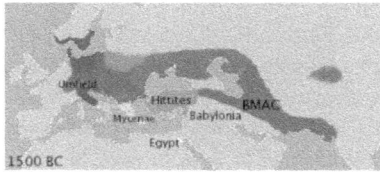
Figure 160: *1500 BCE*

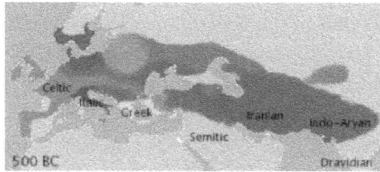
Figure 161: *500 BCE*

Figure 162: *500 CE*

Spread of IE-languages I

Figure 163: *4000 BCE*

Figure 164: *3000 BCE*

Figure 165: *2000 BCE*

Figure 166: *500 BCE*

Genesis of Indo-European languages

Using a mathematical analysis borrowed from evolutionary biology, Don Ringe and Tandy Warnow propose the following evolutionary tree of Indo-European branches:[442]

- Pre-Anatolian (before 3500 BCE)
- Pre-Tocharian
- Pre-Celtic and Pre-Italic (before 2500 BCE)
- [Pre-Germanic?][443] Proto-Germanic dates from c. 500 BCE.[444]</ref>
- Pre-Armenian and Pre-Greek (after 2500 BCE)
- [Pre-Germanic?]
- Pre-Balto-Slavic[442]
- Proto-Indo-Iranian (2000 BCE)

David Anthony, following the methodology of Ringe and Warnow, proposes the following sequence:[445]

- Pre-Anatolian (4200 BCE)
- Pre-Tocharian (3700 BCE)
- Pre-Germanic (3300 BCE)
- Pre-Celtic and Pre-Italic (3000 BCE)
- Pre-Armenian (2800 BCE)
- Pre-Balto-Slavic (2800 BCE)
- Pre-Greek (2500 BCE)
- Proto-Indo-Iranian (2200 BCE); split between Iranian and Old Indic 1800 BCE

Ringe and Warnow's methodology may be outdated, and not accurately reflect the development of the IE languages.Wikipedia:Citation needed

Archaeology: migrations from the steppe Urheimat

Archaeological research has unearthed a broad range of historical cultures which can be related to the spread of the Indo-European languages. Various steppe-cultures show strong similarities with the Yamna-horizon at the Pontic steppe, while the time-range of several Asian cultures also coincides with the proposed trajectory and time-range of the Indo-European migrations.[446,420]

According to the widely accepted Kurgan hypothesis or *Steppe theory*, the Indo-European language and culture spread in several stages from the Proto-Indo-European Urheimat in the Eurasian Pontic steppes into Western Europe, Central and South Asia, through folk migrations and so-called elite recruitment.[420,421] This process started with the introduction of cattle at the Eurasian steppes around 5200 BCE, and the mobilisation of the steppe herder cultures with the introduction of wheeled wagons and horse-back riding, which led to

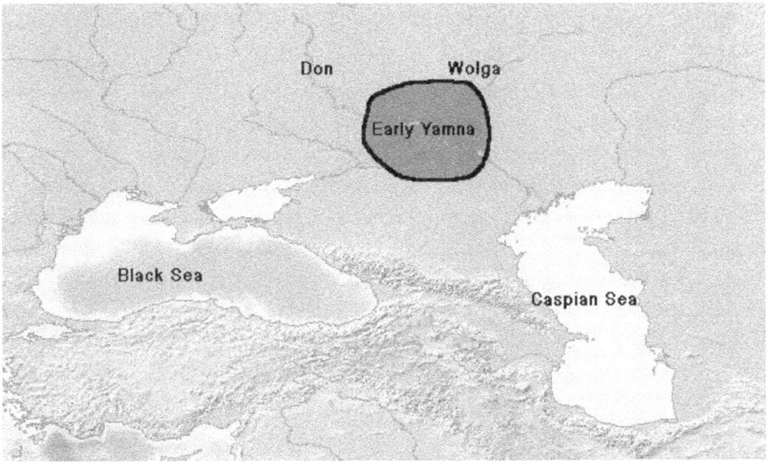

Figure 167: *Location of early Yamna culture*

a new kind of culture. Between 4,500 and 2,500 BCE, this "horizon", which includes several distinctive cultures, spread out over the Pontic steppes, and outside into Europe and Asia.[420]

Early migrations at ca. 4200 BCE brought steppe herders into the lower Danube valley, either causing or taking advantage of the collapse of Old Europe.[422] According to Anthony, the Anatolian branch,[447] to which the Hittites belong,[448] probably arrived in Anatolia from the Danube valley.[423,449] According to Mathieson & Reich et al. (2017), it is unlikely that the Anatolian branch arrived in Anatolia via the Balkans.[450]

Migrations eastward from the Yamna culture founded the Afanasevo culture[425] which developed into the Tocharians.[451] The Tarim mummies may represent a migration of Tocharian speakers from the Afanasevo culture into the Tarim Basin.[452] Migrations southward may have founded the Maykop culture,[453] but the Maykop origins could also have been in the Caucasus.[454]

The western Indo-European languages (Germanic, Celtic, Italic) probably spread into Europe from the Balkan-Danubian complex, a set of cultures in Southeastern Europe.[426] At ca. 3000 BCE a migration of Proto-Indo-European speakers from the Yamna-culture took place toward the west, along the Danube river,[427] Slavic and Baltic developed a little later at the middle Dniepr (present-day Ukraine),[428] moving north toward the Baltic coast.[455] The Corded Ware culture in Middle Europe (third millennium BCE), which materialized with a massive migration from the Eurasian steppes to Central

Europe,[431] probably played a central role in the spread of the pre-Germanic and pre-Balto-Slavic dialects.[429,430]

The eastern part of the Yamna horizon and the Corded ware culture contributed to the Sintashta culture (c. 2100–1800 BCE), where the Indo-Iranian language and culture emerged, and where the chariot was invented.[420] The Indo-Iranian language and culture was further developed in the Andronovo culture (c. 1800–800 BCE), and influenced by the Bactria–Margiana Archaeological Complex (c. 2300–1700 BCE). The Indo-Aryans split off around 1800–1600 BCE from the Iranians,[456] whereafter Indo-Aryan groups moved to the Levant (Mitanni), northern India (Vedic people, c. 1500 BCE), and China (Wusun).[421] The Iranian languages spread throughout the steppes with the Scyths and into Iran with the Medes, Parthians and Persians from ca. 800 BCE.[421]

Anthropology: Elite recruitment and language shift

According to Marija Gimbutas, the process of *"Indo-Europeanization"* of Europe was essentially a cultural, not a physical transformation.[457] It is understood as a migration of Yamnaya people to Europe, as military victors, successfully imposing a new administrative system, language and religion upon the indigenous groups, referred to by Gimbutas as *Old Europeans*.[458,459] The Yamnaya people's social organization, especially a patrilinear and patriarchal structure, greatly facilitated their effectiveness in war.[460] According to Gimbutas, the social structure of *Old Europe* "contrasted with the Indo-European Kurgans who were mobile and non-egalitarian" with a hierarchically organised tripartite social structure; the IE were warlike, lived in smaller villages at times, and had an ideology that centered on the virile male, reflected also in their pantheon. In contrast, the indigenous groups of *Old Europe* had neither a warrior class nor horses.[461,462]

Indo-European languages probably spread through language shifts.[463,464] Small groups can change a larger cultural area,[465,420] and elite male dominance by small groups may have led to a language shift in northern India.[466,467,468]

According to Guus Kroonen, Indo-Europeans encountered existing populations that spoke dissimilar, unrelated languages when they migrated to Europe from Yamnaya steppes.[469] Relatively little is known about the Pre-Indo-European linguistic landscape of Europe, except for Basque, as the *Indo-Europeanization* of Europe caused a largely unrecorded, massive linguistic extinction event, most likely through language-shift.[469] Guus Kroonen's study reveals that PIE speech contains a clear Neolithic signature emanating from the Aegean language family and thus patterns with the prehistoric migration of Europe's first farming populations.

According to Edgar Polomé, 30 % of non-Indo-European substratum found in modern German derives from non-Indo-European-speakers of Funnelbeaker Culture indigenous to southern Scandinavia.[470] When Yamnaya Indo-European speakers came into contact with the indigenous peoples during the third millennium BCE, they came to dominate the local populations yet parts of the indigenous lexicon persisted in the formation of Proto-Germanic, thus lending to the Germanic languages the status of *Indo-Europeanized* languages. According again to Marija Gimbutas, Corded Ware cultures migration to Scandinavia "synthesized" with the Funnelbeaker culture, giving birth to the Proto-Germanic language.[457]

David Anthony, in his "revised Steppe hypothesis"[471] notes that the spread of the Indo-European languages probably did not happen through "chain-type folk migrations", but by the introduction of these languages by ritual and political elites, which were emulated by large groups of people,[472,473]</ref> a process which he calls "elite recruitment".[474]

According to Parpola, local elites joined "small but powerful groups" of Indo-European speaking migrants.[463] These migrants had an attractive social system and good weapons, and luxury goods which marked their status and power. Joining these groups was attractive for local leaders, since it strengthened their position, and gave them additional advantages.[475] These new members were further incorporated by matrimonial alliances.[476,464]

According to Joseph Salmons, language shift is facilitated by "dislocation" of language communities, in which the elite is taken over.[477] According to Salmons, this change is facilitated by "systematic changes in community structure", in which a local community becomes incorporated in a larger social structure.[477,478] Note also that the "Ancestral North Indians" and "Ancestral South Indians" mixed between 4,200 to 1,900 years ago (2200 BCE – 100 CE), where after a shift to endogamy took place.</ref>

Genetic relations between historical populations

Since the 2000s genetical studies are assuming a prominent role in the research on Indo-European migrations. Whole-genome studies reveal relations between various cultures and the time-range in which those relations were established. Research by Haak et al. (2015) showed that ∼75% of the Corded Ware ancestry came from Yamna-related populations,[431] while Allentoft et al. (2015) shows that the Sintashta culture is genetically related to the Corded Ware culture.[479] Quiles (2017) has proposed a relation between the "expansion of peoples belonging to haplogroup R1b in Eurasia" and the diffusion of Indo-European languages.[480]

Ecological studies: widespread drought, urban collapse, and pastoral migrations

Climate change and drought may have triggered both the initial dispersal of Indo-European speakers, and the migration of Indo-Europeans from the steppes in south central Asia and India.

Around 4200–4100 BCE a climate change occurred, manifesting in colder winters in Europe.[481] Steppe herders, archaic Proto-Indo-European speakers, spread into the lower Danube valley about 4200–4000 BCE, either causing or taking advantage of the collapse of Old Europe.[422]

The Yamna horizon was an adaptation to a climate change which occurred between 3500 and 3000 BCE, in which the steppes became drier and cooler. Herds needed to be moved frequently to feed them sufficiently, and the use of wagons and horse-back riding made this possible, leading to "a new, more mobile form of pastoralism".[482]

In the second millennium BCE widespread aridization lead to water shortages and ecological changes in both the Eurasian steppes and south Asia.[483,484] At the steppes, humidization lead a change of vegetation, triggering "higher mobility and transition to the nomadic cattle breeding".[484,485]</ref>[486] Water shortage also had a strong impact in south Asia, "causing the collapse of sedentary urban cultures in south central Asia, Afghanistan, Iran, and India, and triggering large-scale migrations".

Origins of the Indo-Europeans

Urheimat

Urheimat hypotheses

The Proto-Indo-European Urheimat hypotheses are tentative identifications of the *Urheimat*, or primary homeland, of the hypothetical Proto-Indo-European language. Such identifications attempt to be consistent with the glottochronology of the language tree and with the archaeology of those places and times. Identifications are made on the basis of how well, if at all, the projected migration routes and times of migration fit the distribution of Indo-European languages, and how closely the sociological model of the original society reconstructed from Proto-Indo-European lexical items fits the archaeological profile.

Since the early 1980s[487] the mainstream consensus among Indo-Europeanists favors Marija Gimbutas' "Kurgan hypothesis",[488,489,490,491] c.q. David Anthony's "Revised Steppe theory", derived from Gimbutas' pioneering work,[420] placing the Indo-European homeland in the Pontic steppe, more specifically, between the Dniepr (Ukraine) and the Ural river (Russia), of the Chalcolithic

Figure 168: *The Proto-Indo-European homeland according to the Kurgan hypothesis (dark green) and the present-day distribution of Indo-European languages in Eurasia (light green)*

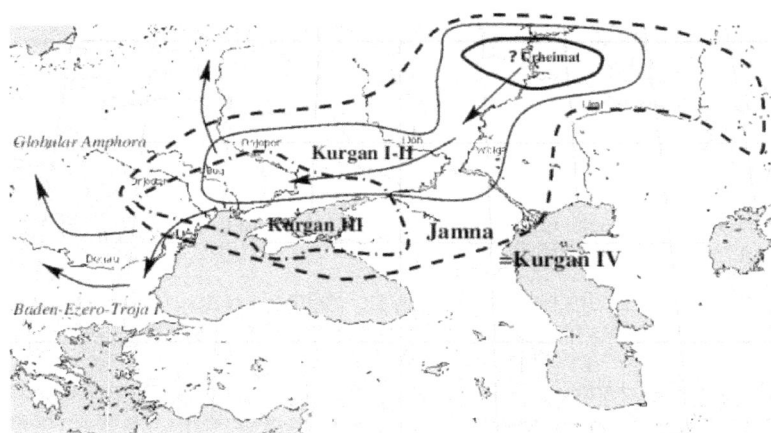

Figure 169: *The development of the Kurgan culture according to Marija Gimbutas' Kurgan hypothesis*

period (4th to 5th millennia BCE),[488] where various related cultures developed.[488,420] The Pontic steppe is a large area of grasslands in far Eastern Europe, located north of the Black Sea, Caucasus Mountains and Caspian Sea and including parts of eastern Ukraine, southern Russia and northwest Kazakhstan. This is the time and place of the earliest domestication of the horse, which according to this hypothesis was the work of early Indo-Europeans, allowing them to expand outwards and assimilate or conquer many other cultures.[420] The Yamna culture (3300–2500 BCE),[420] located on the middle Don and Volga, is the specific culture from where this expansion in its major form started.[420]

The primary competitor is the Anatolian hypothesis advanced by Colin Renfrew,[489,491] which states that the Indo-European languages began to spread peacefully into Europe from Asia Minor (modern Turkey) from around 7000 BCE with the Neolithic advance of farming (*wave of advance*).[488] Another theory which has drawn considerable attention is the Armenian plateau hypothesis of Gamkrelidze and Ivanov, who have argued that the urheimat was south of the Caucasus, specifically, "within eastern Anatolia, the southern Caucasus and northern Mesopotamia" in the fifth to fourth millennia BCE.[492,488,489,491]

All hypotheses assume a significant period (at least 1500–2000 years) between the time of the Proto-Indo-European language and the earliest attested texts, at Kültepe, c. 19th century BCE.

The Kurgan hypothesis and the "revised steppe theory"

The Kurgan hypothesis (also theory or model) argues that the people of an archaeological "Kurgan culture" (a term grouping the Yamna or Pit Grave culture and its predecessors) in the Pontic steppe were the most likely speakers of the Proto-Indo-European language. The term is derived from *kurgan* (курган), a Turkic loanword in Russian for a tumulus or burial mound. An origin at the Pontic-Caspian steppes is the most widely accepted scenario of Indo-European origins.[493,494,490,491,495]
Strazny: "The single most popular proposal is the Pontic steppes (see the Kurgan hypothesis) [...]"[494]</ref>

Marija Gimbutas formulated her Kurgan hypothesis in the 1950s, grouping together a number of related cultures at the Pontic steppes. She defined the "Kurgan culture" as composed of four successive periods, with the earliest (Kurgan I) including the Samara and Seroglazovo cultures of the Dnieper/ Volga region in the Copper Age (early 4th millennium BCE). The bearers of these cultures were nomadic pastoralists, who, according to the model, by the early 3rd millennium expanded throughout the Pontic-Caspian steppe and into Eastern Europe.[496]

Gimbutas' grouping is nowadays considered to have been too broad. According to Anthony, it is better to speak of the Yamna culture or of a "Yamna horizon", which included several related cultures, as the defining Proto-Indo-European culture at the Pontic steppe.[420] David Anthony has incorporated recent developments in his "revised steppe theory", which also supports a steppe origin of the Indo-European languages.[420,497] Anthony emphasizes the Yamnaya culture as the origin of the Indo-European dispersal.[420,497] Recent research by Haak et al. (2015) confirms the migration of Yamnaya-people into western Europe, forming the Corded Ware culture.[431]

Proto-Indo-Europeans

The Proto-Indo-Europeans were the speakers of the Proto-Indo-European language (PIE), a reconstructed prehistoric language of Eurasia. Knowledge of them comes chiefly from the linguistic reconstruction, along with material evidence from archaeology and archaeogenetics.

According to some archaeologists, PIE speakers cannot be assumed to have been a single, identifiable people or tribe, but were a group of loosely related populations ancestral to the later, still partially prehistoric, Bronze Age Indo-Europeans. This view is held especially by those archaeologists who posit an original homeland of vast extent and immense time depth. However, this view is not shared by linguists, as proto-languages generally occupy small geographical areas over a very limited time span, and are generally spoken by close-knit communities such as a single small tribe.

The Proto-Indo-Europeans were likely to have lived during the late Neolithic, or roughly the 4th millennium BCE. Mainstream scholarship places them in the forest-steppe zone immediately to the north of the western end of the Pontic-Caspian steppe in Eastern Europe. Some archaeologists would extend the time depth of PIE to the middle Neolithic (5500 to 4500 BCE) or even the early Neolithic (7500 to 5500 BCE), and suggest alternative Proto-Indo-European Urheimats.

By the late third millennium BCE, offshoots of the Proto-Indo-Europeans had reached Anatolia (Hittites), the Aegean (Mycenaean Greece), Western Europe, and southern Siberia (Afanasevo culture).[498]

Pre-Proto-Indo-Europeans

The proto-Indo-Europeans, i. e. the Yamnaya people and the related cultures, seem to have been a mix from eastern European hunter-gatherers; and people related to the near east,[499] i. e. Caucasus hunter-gatherers[500] i. e. Iran Chalcolithic people with a Caucasian hunter-gatherer component.[501,502]

Eurogenes Blog: "Lazaridis et al. show that Early to Middle Bronze Age

steppe groups, including Yamnaya, tagged by them as Steppe EMBA, are best modeled with formal statistics as a mixture of Eastern European Hunter-Gatherers (EHG) and Chalcolithic farmers from western Iran. The mixture ratios are 56.8/43.2, respectively. However, they add that a model of Steppe EMBA as a three-way mixture between EHG, the Chalcolithic farmers and Caucasus Hunter-Gatherers (CHG) is also a good fit and plausible."[503]
See also:

- Stephanie Dutchen (2014), *New Branch Added to European Family Tree. Genetic analysis reveals Europeans descended from at least three ancient groups*[504];
- Richard Gray (2015), *Modern Europeans descend from FOUR groups of hunter-gatherers: New strand of DNA discovered in the Caucasus is the 'missing piece in the ancestry puzzle'*[505];
- Dieneke's Anthropology Blog, *West Asian in the flesh (hunter-gatherers from Georgia) (Jones et al. 2015)*[506];
- For what they were... we are (2016), *Caucasus and Swiss hunter-gatherer genomes*[507].</ref>

According to Haak et al. (2015), "the Yamnaya steppe herders of this time were descended not only from the preceding eastern European hunter-gatherers, but from a population of Near Eastern ancestry."[499]

According to Jones et al. (2015), Caucasus hunter-gatherers (CHG) "genomes significantly contributed to the Yamnaya steppe herders who migrated into Europe ~3,000 BCE, supporting a formative Caucasus influence on this important Early Bronze age culture. CHG left their imprint on modern populations from the Caucasus and also central and south Asia possibly marking the arrival of Indo-Aryan languages."[500,508]</ref>

According to Lazaridis et al. (2016), "a population related to the people of the Iran Chalcolithic contributed ~ 43 % of the ancestry of early Bronze Age populations of the steppe."[501] These Iranian Chacolithic people were a mixture of "the Neolithic people of western Iran, the Levant, and Caucasus Hunter Gatherers".[501,509]

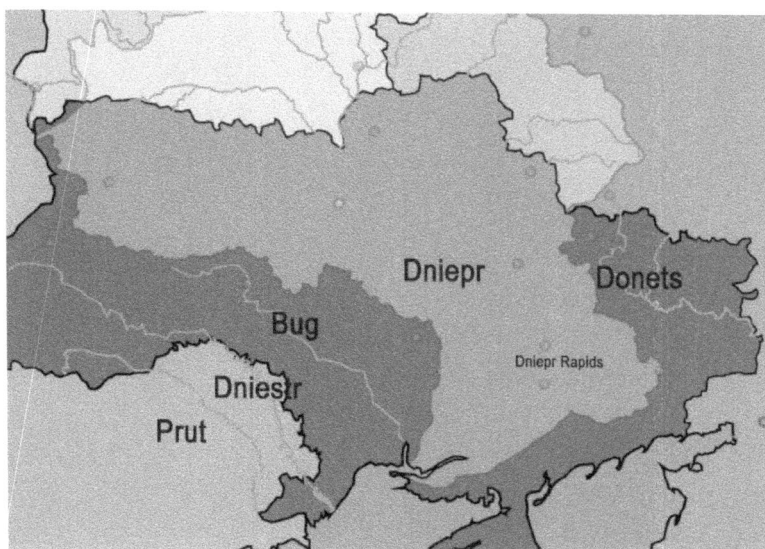

Figure 170: *Ukraine rivers*

Development of the steppe cultures

Pre-Yamnaya

According to Anthony, the development of the Proto-Indo-European cultures started with the introduction of cattle at the Pontic-Caspian steppes.[510] Until ca. 5200–5000 BCE the Pontic-Caspian steppes were populated by hunter-gatherers.[511] According to Anthony, the first cattle herders arrived from the Danube Valley at ca. 5800–5700 BCE, descendants from the first European farmers.[512] They formed the Criş culture (5800–5300 BCE), creating a cultural frontier at the Prut-Dniestr watershed.[513] The adjacent Bug-Dniester culture (6300–5500 BCE) was a local forager culture, from where cattle breeding spread to the steppe peoples.[514] The Dniepr Rapids area was the next part of the Pontic-Caspian steppes to shift to cattle-herding. It was the densely populated area of the Pontic-Caspian steppes at the time, and had been inhabited by various hunter-gatherer populations since the end of the Ice Age. From ca. 5800–5200 it was inhabited by the first phase of the Dnieper-Donets culture, a hunter-gatherer culture contemporaneous with the Bug-Dniestr culture.[515]

At ca. 5200–5000 BCE the non-Indo-European Cucuteni-Tripolye culture (6000–3500 BCE) appears east of the Carpathian mountains,[516] moving the cultural frontier to the Southern Bug valley,[517] while the foragers at the

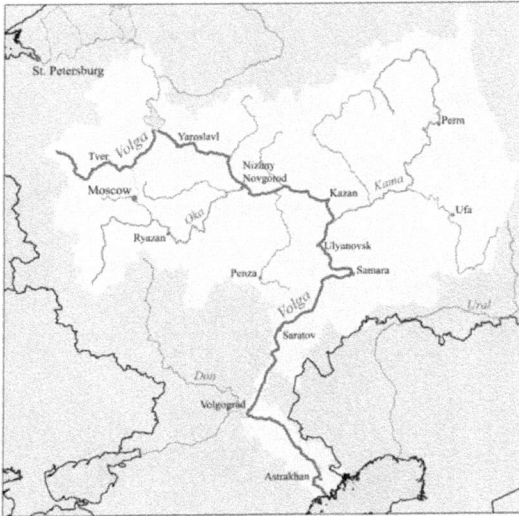

Figure 171: *Volga river*

Dniepr Rapids shifted to cattle herding, marking the shift to Dniepr-Donets II (5200/5000 – 4400/4200 BCE).[518] The Dniepr-Donets culture kept cattle not only for ritual sacrifices, but also for their daily diet.[519] The Khvalynsk culture (4700–3800 BCE),[519] located at the middle Volga, which was connected with the Danube Valley by trade networks,[520] also had cattle and sheep, but they were "more important in ritual sacrifices than in the diet".[521] The Samara culture (early 5th millennium BCE),[522] north of the Khvalynsk culture, interacted with the Khvalynsk culture,[523] while the archaeological findings seem related to those of the Dniepr-Dontes II Culture.[523]

The Sredny Stog culture (4400–3300 BCE)[524] appears at the same location as the Dniepr-Donets culture, but shows influences from people who came from the Volga river region.[525]

Yamnaya

The Khvalynsk culture (4700–3800 BCE)[519] (middle Volga) and the Don-based Repin culture (ca.3950–3300 BCE)[526] preceded the Yamnaya culture (3300–2500 BCE),[527] which originated in the Don-Volga area.[527] Late pottery from these two cultures can barely be distinguished from early Yamna pottery.[528]

The Yamna horizon was an adaptation to a climate change which occurred between 3500 and 3000 BCE, in which the steppes became drier and cooler. Herds needed to be moved frequently to feed them sufficiently, and the use of wagons and horse-back riding made this possible, leading to "a new, more mobile form of pastoralism".[482] It was accompanied by new social rules and institutions, to regulate the local migrations in the steppes, creating a new social awareness of a distinct culture, and of "cultural Others" who did not participate in these new institutions.[527]

The Yamna culture c.q. horizon (a.k.a. Pit Grave culture) spreads quickly across the Pontic-Caspian steppes between ca. 3400 and 3200 BCE.[529] According to Anthony, "the spread of the Yamnaya horizon was the material expression of the spread of late Proto-Indo-European across the Pontic-Caspian steppes."[530] Anthony further notes that "the Yamnaya horizon is the visible archaeological expression of a social adjustment to high mobility – the invention of the political infrastructure to manage larger herds from mobile homes based in the steppes."[531] The Yamnaya horizon represents the classical reconstructed Proto-Indo-European society with stone idols, predominantly practising animal husbandry in permanent settlements protected by hillforts, subsisting on agriculture, and fishing along rivers. According to Gimbutas, contact of the Yamna culture with late Neolithic Europe cultures results in the "kurganized" Globular Amphora and Baden cultures.Wikipedia:Citation needed Anthony excludes the Globular Amphora culture.[420]

The Maykop culture (3700–3000) emerges somewhat earlier in the northern Caucasus. Although considered by Gimbutas as an outgrowth of the steppe cultures, it is related to the development of Mesopotamia, and Anthony does not consider it to be a Proto-Indo-European culture.[420] The Maykop culture shows the earliest evidence of the beginning Bronze Age, and Bronze weapons and artifacts are introduced to the Yamna horizon.

Between 3100–2600 BCE Yamna people into the Danube Valley as far as Hungary.[532] This migration probably gave rise to Proto-Celtic[533] and Pre-Italic.[533] Pre-Germanic dialects may have developed between the Dniestr (west Ukraine) and the Vistula (Poland) at c. 3100–2800 BCE, and spread with the Corded Ware culture.[534] Slavic and Baltic developed at the middle Dniepr (present-day Ukraine)[428] at c. 2800 BCE, also spreading with the Corded Ware horizon.[455]

Post-Yamnaya

In the northern Don-Volga area the Yamnaya culture was followed by the Poltavka culture (2700–2100 BCE), while the Sintashta culture (2100–1800) extended the Indo-European culture zone east of the Ural mountains, giving rise to Proto-Indo-Iranian and the subsequent spread of the Indo-Iranian languages toward India and the Iranian plateau.[420]

Early migrations: Archaic Proto-Indo-European

Europe and Anatolia (5th–4th millennium BCE)

Europe: Migration into the Danube Valley (4200 BCE)

According to Anthony, steppe herders, archaic Proto-Indo-European speakers, spread into the lower Danube valley about 4200–4000 BCE, either causing or taking advantage of the collapse of Old Europe.[422] According to Anthony, their languages "probably included archaic Proto-Indo-European dialects of the kind partly preserved later in Anatolian."[535] According to Anthony their descendants later moved into Anatolia, at an unknown time, but maybe as early as 3,000 BCE.[423] According to Mathieson & Reich et al. (2017), it is unlikely that the Anatolian branch arrived in Anatolia via the Balkans.

According to Parpola, the appearance of Indo-European speakers from Europe into Anatolia, and the appearance of Hittite, is related to later migrations of Proto-Indo-European speakers from the Yamna-culture into the Danube Valley at ca. 2800 BCE,[449,427] which is in line with the "customary" assumption that the Anatolian Indo-European language was introduced into Anatolia somewhere in the third millennium BCE.

Anatolia: Archaic Proto-Indo-European (Hittites; 4500–3500 BCE)

The Anatolians were a group of distinct Indo-European peoples who spoke the Anatolian languages and shared a common culture. The Anatolian languages were a branch of the larger Indo-European language family.

Although the Hittites are placed in the 2nd millennium BCE,[448] the Anatolian branch seems to have separated at a very early stage from Proto-Indo-European, or may have developed from an older Pre-Proto-Indo-European ancestor.[536] If it separated from Proto-Indo-European, it likely did so between 4500–3500 BCE.[537]

The archaeological discovery of the archives of the Hittites and the belonging of the Hittite language to a separate Anatolian branch of the Indo-European languages caused a sensation among historians, forcing a re-evaluation of Near Eastern history and Indo-European linguistics. In accordance with the Kurgan hypothesis, J. P. Mallory notes in Encyclopedia of Indo-European Culture that it is likely that the Anatolians reached the Near East from the north, either via the Balkans or the Caucasus in the 3rd millennium BCE. According to Anthony, descendants of archaic Proto-Indo-European steppe herders, who moved into the lower Danube valley about 4200–4000 BCE, later moved into

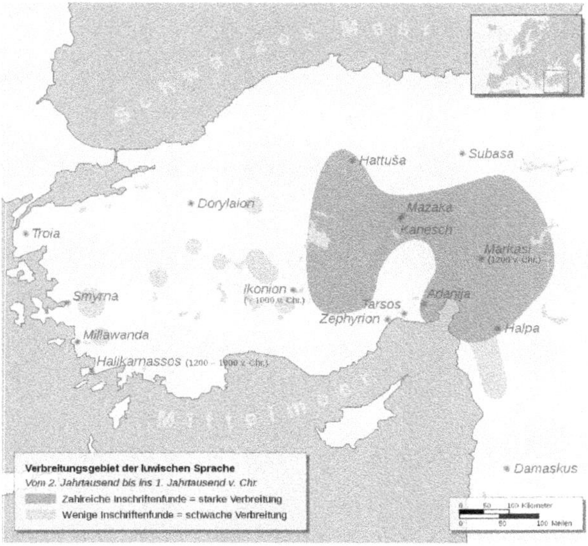

Figure 172: *Area where the second millennium BCE Luwian language was spoken*

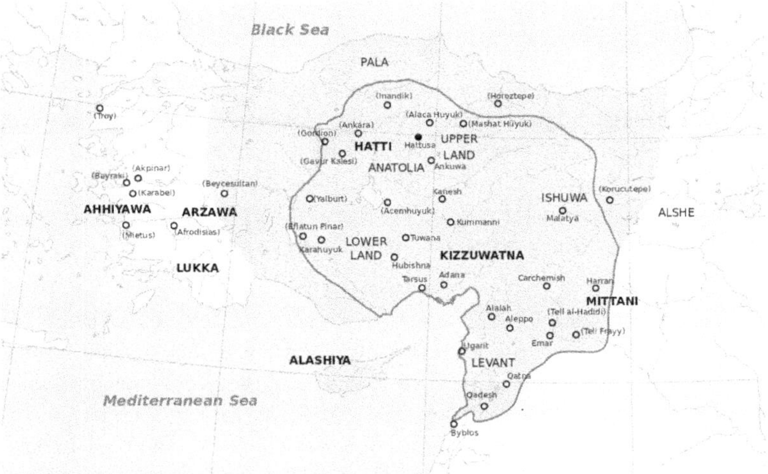

Figure 173: *The Hittite Empire at its greatest extent under Suppiluliuma I (c. 1350–1322 BCE) and Mursili II (c. 1321–1295 BCE)*

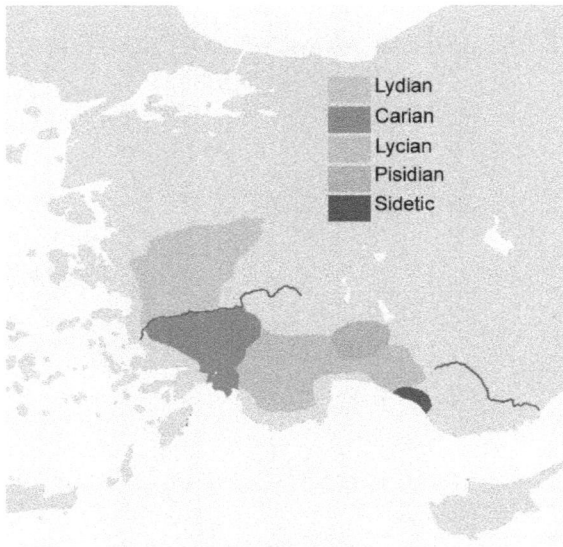

Figure 174: *Anatolian languages attested in the mid-first millennium BCE*

Anatolia, at an unknown time, but maybe as early as 3,000 BCE.[538] According to Parpola the movement into Anatolia took place at a later date.[449] According to Mathieson & Reich et al. (2017), it is unlikely that the Anatolian branch arrived in Anatolia via the Balkans.

Together with the Tocharians, the Anatolians constituted the first known wave of Indo-European emigrants out of the Eurasian steppe. Although they had wagons, they probably emigrated before Indo-Europeans had learned to use chariots for war. It is likely that their arrival was one of gradual settlement and not as an invading army. The Anatolians' earliest linguistic and historical attestation are as names mentioned in Assyrian mercantile texts from 19th-century BCE Kanesh.

The Hittites, who established an extensive empire in the Middle East in the 2nd millennium BCE, are by far the best known members of the Anatolian group. The history of the Hittite civilization is known mostly from cuneiform texts found in the area of their kingdom, and from diplomatic and commercial correspondence found in various archives in Egypt and the Middle East. Despite the use of *Hatti* for their core territory, the Hittites should be distinguished from the Hattians, an earlier people who inhabited the same region (until the beginning of the 2nd millennium). The Hittite military made successful use of chariots. Although belonging to the Bronze Age, they were the forerunners

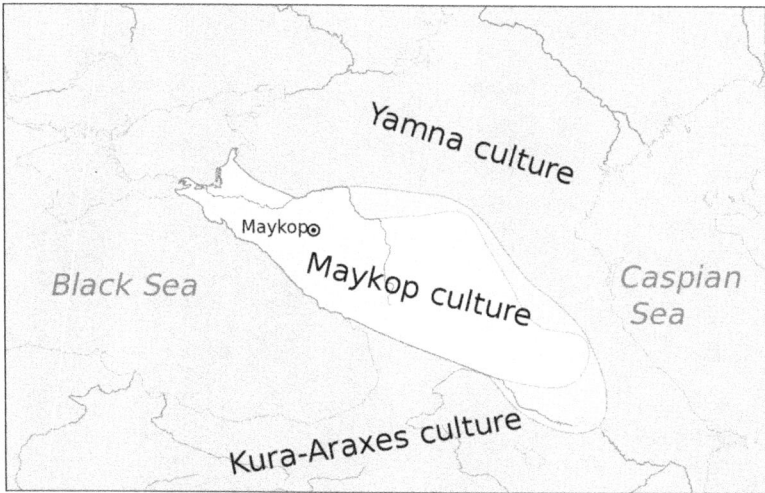

Figure 175: *Geographic extent of the Maykop culture*

of the Iron Age, developing the manufacture of iron artifacts from as early as the 14th century, when letters to foreign rulers reveal the latter's demand for iron goods. The Hittite empire reached its height during the mid-14th century under Suppiluliuma I, when it encompassed an area that included most of Asia Minor as well as parts of the northern Levant and Upper Mesopotamia. After 1180 BCE, amid the Bronze Age Collapse in the Levant associated with the sudden arrival of the Sea Peoples, the kingdom disintegrated into several independent "Neo-Hittite" city-states, some of which survived until as late as the 8th century BCE. The lands of the Anatolian peoples were successively invaded by a number of peoples and empires at high frequency: the Phrygians, Bithynians, the Medes, the Persians, the Greeks, the Galatian Celts, Romans and the Oghuz Turks. Many of these invaders settled in Anatolia, in some cases causing the extinction of the Anatolian languages. By the Middle Ages, all the Anatolian languages (and the cultures accompanying them) were extinct, although there may be lingering influences on the modern inhabitants of Anatolia, most notably Armenians.

Northern Caucasus: The Maykop culture (3700–3000 BCE)

The Maykop culture (also spelled Maikop), c. 3700–3000 BCE, was a major Bronze Age archaeological culture in the Western Caucasus region of Southern Russia. It extends along the area from the Taman Peninsula at the Kerch Strait to near the modern border of Dagestan and southwards to the Kura River. The

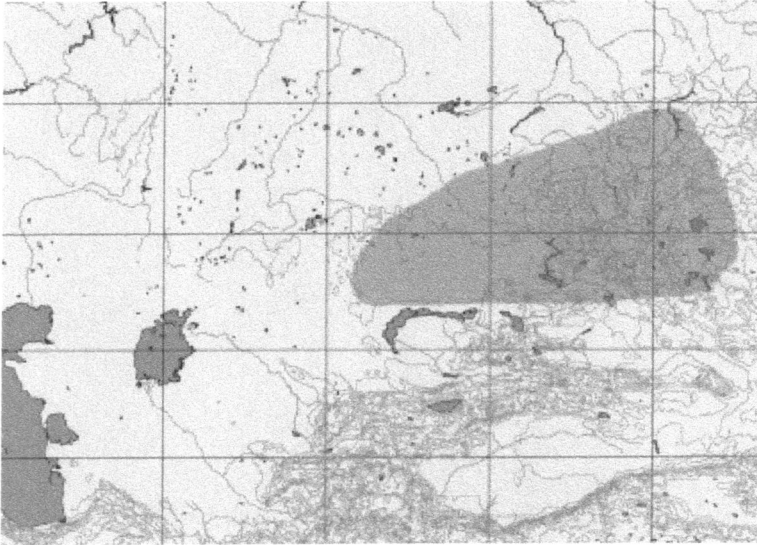

Figure 176: *The geographic extent of the Afanasevo culture*

culture takes its name from a royal burial found in Maykop kurgan in the Kuban River valley.

According to Mallory and Adams, migrations southward founded the Maykop culture (c. 3500–2500 BCE).[453] Yet, according to Mariya Ivanova the Maykop origins were on the Iranian Plateau,[454] while kurgans from the beginning of the 4th millennium at Soyuqbulaq in Azerbaijan, which belong to the Leyla-Tepe culture, show parallels with the Maykop kurgans. According to Museyibli, "the Leylatepe Culture tribes migrated to the north in the mid-fourth millennium and played an important part in the rise of the Maikop Culture of the North Caucasus."

Asia (3500–2500 BCE)

Afanasevo culture

The Afanasievo culture (3300 to 2500 BCE) is the earliest Eneolithic archaeological culture found until now in south Siberia, occupying the Minusinsk Basin, Altay and Eastern Kazakhstan. It originated with a migration of people from the pre-Yamnaya Repin culture, at the Don river,[526] and is related to the Tocharians.[539]

Radiocarbon gives dates as early as 3705 BCE on wooden tools and 2874 BCE on human remains for the Afanasievo culture. The earliest of these dates has now been rejected, giving a date of around 3300 BCE for the start of the culture.[540]

The Tocharians

The Tocharians, or "Tokharians" (/təˈkɛəriənz/ or /təˈkɑːriənz/) were inhabitants of medieval oasis city-states on the northern edge of the Tarim Basin (modern Xinjiang, China). Their Tocharian languages (a branch of the Indo-European family) are known from manuscripts from the 6th to 8th centuries CE, after which they were supplanted by the Turkic languages of the Uyghur tribes. These people were called "Tocharian" by late 19th-century scholars who identified them with the *Tókharoi* described by ancient Greek sources as inhabiting Bactria. Although this identification is now generally considered mistaken, the name has become customary.

The Tocharians are thought to have developed from the Afanasevo culture of eastern Siberia (c. 3500–2500 BCE).[539] It is believed that the Tarim mummies, dated from 1800 BCE, represent a migration of Tocharian speakers from the Afanasevo culture in the Tarim Basin in the early 2nd millennium BCE.[452] By the end of the 2nd millennium BCE, the dominant people as far east as the Altai Mountains southward to the northern outlets of the Tibetan Plateau were anthropologically Caucasian, with the northern part speaking Iranian Scythian languages and the southern parts Tocharian languages, having Mongoloid populations as their northeastern neighbors.[541] These two groups were in competition with each other until the latter overcame the former. The turning point occurred around the 5th to 4th centuries BCE with a gradual Mongolization of Siberia, while Eastern Central Asia (East Turkistan) remained Caucasian and Indo-European-speaking until well into the 1st millennium CE.[542]

The Sinologist Edwin G. Pulleyblank has suggested that the Yuezhi, the Wusun the Dayuan, the Kangju and the people of Yanqi, could have been Tocharian-speaking. Of these the Yuezhi are generally held to have been Tocharians. The Yuezhi were originally settled in the arid grasslands of the eastern Tarim Basin area, in what is today Xinjiang and western Gansu, in China. After the Yuezhi were defeated by the Xiongnu, in the 2nd century BCE, a small group, known as the Little Yuezhi, fled to the south, later spawning the Jie people who dominated the Later Zhao until their complete extermination by Ran Min in the Wei–Jie war. The majority of the Yuezhi however migrated west to the Ili Valley, where they displaced the Sakas (Scythians). Driven from the Ili Valley shortly afterwards by the Wusun, the Yuezhi migrated to Sogdia and then Bactria, where they are often identified with the *Tókharoi* (Τοχάριοι) and *Asioi* of Classical sources. They then expanded into northern South Asia, where one branch of the Yuezhi founded the Kushan Empire. The Kushan empire stretched from Turfan in the Tarim Basin to Pataliputra on the Gangetic plain at its greatest extent, and played an important role in the development of the Silk Road and the transmission of Buddhism to China. Tocharian languages continued to be spoken in the city-states of the Tarim Basin, only becoming extinct in the Middle Ages.

Europe

Origins of the European IE languages

Mallory notes that the Italic, Celtic and Germanic languages are closely related, which accords with their historic distribution. The Germanic languages are also related to the Baltic and Slavic languages, which in turn share similarities with the Indo-Iranic languages.[543] The Greek, Armenian and Indo-Iranian languages are also related, which suggests "a chain of central Indo-European dialects stretching from the Balkans across the Black sea to the east Caspian".[543] And the Celtic, Italic, Anatolian and Tocharian languages preserve archaisms which are preserved only in those languages.[543] According to David Anthony, pre-Germanic split-off earliest (3300 BCE), followed by pre-Italic and pre-Celtic (3000 BCE), pre-Armenian (2800 BCE), pre-Balto-Slavic (2800 BCE) and pre-Greek (2500 BCE).[445]

Three autosomal genetic studies in 2015 gave support to the Kurgan hypothesis of Gimbutas regarding the proto-Indo-European homeland. According to those studies, haplogroups R1b and R1a would have expanded from the West Eurasian Steppe, along with the Indo-European languages; they also detected an autosomal component present in modern Europeans which was not present in Neolithic Europeans, which would have been introduced with paternal lineages R1b and R1a, as well as Indo-European Languages.[544,545]

The Balkan-Danubian complex and the Dniestr and Dniepr rivers

Dniestr,
Vistula, Dniepr

Figure 178: *Dniester river*

Figure 179: *Vistula river*

Figure 180: *Dniepr river*

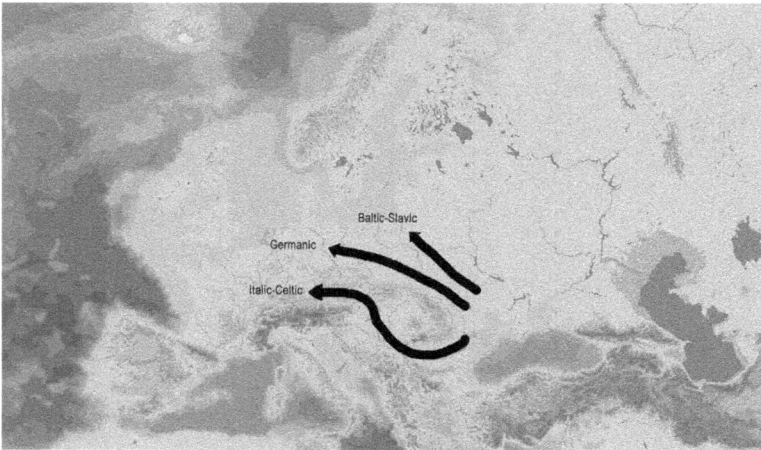

Figure 177: *IE migrations north and south of the Carpa-
tian mountains, and the subsequent development of Celtic,
Germanic, and Balto-Slavic, according to Anthony (2007)*

Figure 181: *Course of the Danube, marked in red*

The Balkan-Danubian complex is a set of cultures in Southeast Europe from which the western Indo-European languages probably spread into western Europe from c. 3500 BCE.[426] According to Anthony, Pre-Italic, Pre-Celtic and Pre-Germanic may have split-off here from Proto-Indo-European.[546]

The Usatovo culture developed in south-eastern Central Europe at around 3300–3200 BCE at the Dniestr river.[547] Although closely related to the Tripolye culture, it is contemporary with the Yamna culture, and resembles it in significant ways.[548] According to Anthony, it may have originated with "steppe clans related to the Yamnaya horizon who were able to impose a patron-client relationship on Tripolye farming villages".[549]

According to Anthony, the Pre-Germanic dialects may have developed in this culture between the Dniestr (west Ukraine) and the Vistula (Poland) at c. 3100–2800 BCE, and spread with the Corded Ware culture.[534]

Between 3100–2800/2600 BCE, when the Yamna horizon spread fast across the Pontic Steppe, a real folk migration of Proto-Indo-European speakers from the Yamna-culture took place into the Danube Valley,[427] moving along Usatovo territory toward specific destinations, reaching as far as Hungary,[550] where as many as 3,000 kurgans may have been raised.[551] Bell Beaker sites at Budapest, dated c. 2800–2600 BCE, may have aided in spreading Yamna dialects into Austria and southern Germany at their west, where Proto-Celtic may have developed.[533] Pre-Italic may have developed in Hungary, and spread toward Italy via the Urnfield culture and Villanovan culture.[533] According to Anthony, Slavic and Baltic developed at the middle Dniepr (present-day Ukraine)[428] at c. 2800 BCE, spreading north from there.[455]

According to Parpola, this migration into the Danube Valley is related to the appearance of Indo-European speakers from Europe into Anatolia, and the appearance of Hittite.[449]

The Balkan languages (Thracian, Dacian, Illyrian) may have developed among of the early Indo-European populations of southeastern Europe. In the early Middle Ages their territory was occupied by migrating Slavic people, and by east Asian steppe peoples.

Corded Ware culture (3000–2400 BCE)

The Corded Ware culture in Middle Europe (c. 3200[552] or 2,900–2450 or 2350 cal.[552] BCE) is hypothesized to have played an essential role in the origin and spread of the Indo-European languages in Europe during the Copper and Bronze Ages.[429,430] David Anthony states that "Childe (1953:133-38) and Gimbutas (1963) speculated that migrants from the steppe Yamnaya culture (3300–2600 BCE) might have been the creators of the Corded Ware culture and carried IE languages into Europe from the steppes."[553] According to

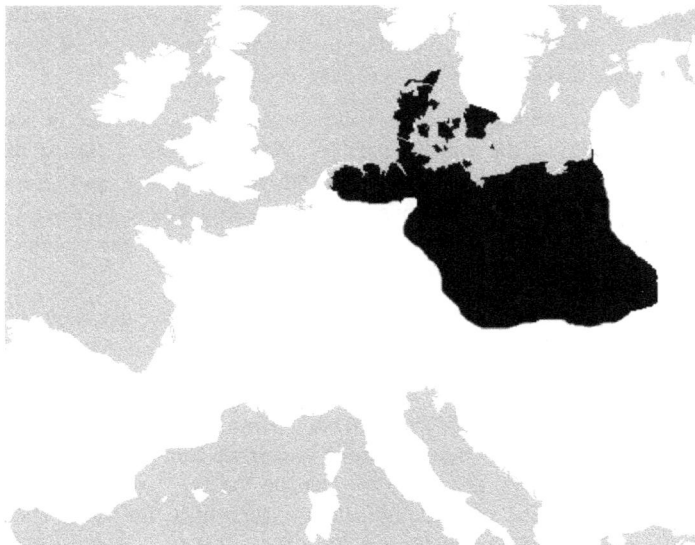

Figure 182: *Extent of the Funnelbeaker culture (Trichterbecherkultur, TRB) c. 4300–2800 BCE*

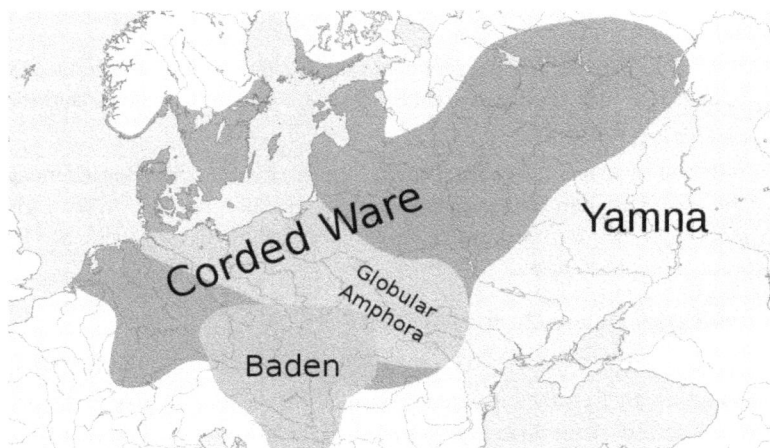

Figure 183: *Approximate extent of the Corded Ware horizon with adjacent third-millennium cultures (Baden culture and Globular Amphora culture; after EIEC)*

Gimbutas, the Corded Ware culture was preceded by the Globular Amphora culture (3400–2800 BCE), which she also regarded to be an Indo-European culture. The Globular Amphora culture stretched from central Europe to the Baltic sea, and emerged from the Funnelbeaker culture.[554]

According to Mallory, the Corded Ware culture may be postulated as "the common prehistoric ancestor of the later Celtic, Germanic, Baltic, Slavic, and possibly some of the Indo-European languages of Italy". Yet, Mallory also notes that the Corded Ware can not account for Greek, Illyrian, Thracian and East Italic, which may be derived from Southeast Europe.[555] According to Anthony, the Corded ware horizon may have introduced Germanic, Baltic and Slavic into northern Europe.[533]

The Corded Ware spread across northern Europe after 3000 BCE, with an "initial rapid spread" between 2900 and 2700 BCE.[533] Around 2400 BCE the people of the Corded Ware replaced their predecessors and expanded to Danubian and Nordic areas of western Germany. A related branch invaded Denmark and southern Sweden. In places a continuity between Funnelbeaker and Corded Ware can be demonstrated, whereas in other areas Corded Ware heralds a new culture and physical type.[556] According to Cunliffe, most of the expansion was clearly intrusive. Yet, according to Furholt, the Corded Ware culture was an indigenous development,[553] connecting local developments into a larger network.[557]

Recent research by Haak et al. found that four late Corded Ware people (2500–2300 BCE) buried at Esperstadt, Germany, were genetically very close to the Yamna-people, stating that a massive migration took place from the Eurasian steppes to Central Europe.[431,558] Haak et al. (2015) note that German Corded ware "trace ∼75% of their ancestry to the Yamna,"[559] envisioning a migration of both males and females from the Yamna culture through western Ukraine and Poland into Germany.[560] Allentoft et al. (2015) envision a migration from the Yamna culture towards northern Europe, both via Central Europe and the territory of present-day Russia, toward the Baltic area and the eastern periphery of the Corded ware culture.[561] In supplementary information to Haak et al. (2015) Anthony, together with Lazaridis, Haak, Patterson, and Reich, notes that the mass migration of Yamna people to northern Europe shows that "the languages could have been introduced simply by strength of numbers: via major migration in which both sexes participated."[562,563]

- "[...] our results level the playing field between the two leading hypotheses [the Steppe hypotheses and the Anatolian hypothesis] of Indo-European origins, as we now know that both the Early Neolithic and the Late Neolithic were associated with major migrations."[562]</ref>

Figure 184: *Extent of the Beaker-culture*

Anthony (2017) relates these close genetical similarities, and the development of the Corded ware culture, to the early third century Yamna-migrations into the Danube-valley, stating that "[t]he migration stream that created these intrusive cemeteries now can be seen to have continued from eastern Hungary across the Carpatians into southern Poland, where the earlies material traits of the Corded ware horizon appeared."[557,564]

Volker Heyd has cautioned to be careful with drawing too strong conclusions from those genetic similarities between Corded Ware and Yamna, noting the small number of samples; the late dates of the Esperstadt graves, which could also have undergone Bell Beaker admixture; the presence of Yamna-ancestry in western Europe before the Danube-expansion; and the risks of extrapolating "the results from a handful of individual burials to whole ethnically interpreted populations."[565] Heyd confirms the close connection between Corded Ware and Yamna, but also states that "neither a one-to-one translation from Yamnaya to CWC, nor even the 75:25 ratio as claimed (Haak *et al.* 2015:211) fits the archaeological record."[565]

Beaker culture (2900–1800 BCE)

The Bell Beaker-culture (*c.* 2900–1800 BCE[567]) may have spread proto-Celtic. More recently Mallory has suggested that the Beaker culture was associated with a European branch of Indo-European dialects, termed "North-west

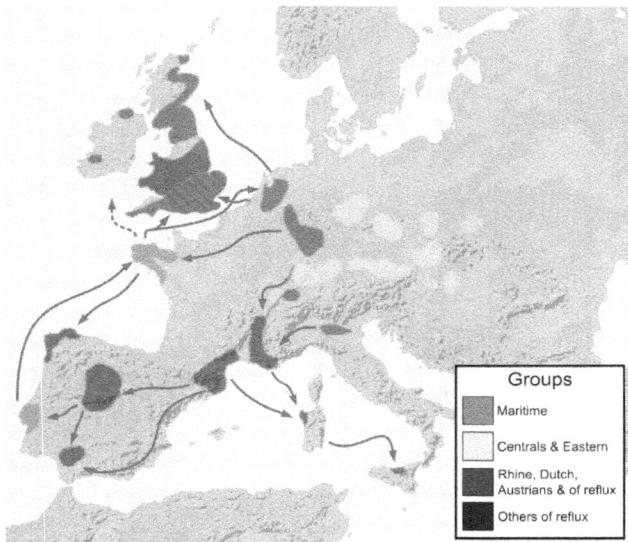

Figure 185: *Generalised distribution and movements of Bell-Beaker cultures*[566]

Indo-European", ancestral to not only Celtic but equally Italic, Germanic and Balto-Slavic.[568]

The initial moves from the Tagus estuary were maritime. A southern move led to the Mediterranean where 'enclaves' were established in south-western Spain and southern France around the Golfe du Lion and into the Po valley in Italy, probably via ancient western Alpine trade routes used to distribute jadeite axes. A northern move incorporated the southern coast of Armorica. The enclave established in southern Brittany was linked closely to the riverine and landward route, via the Loire, and across the Gâtinais valley to the Seine valley, and thence to the lower Rhine. This was a long-established route reflected in early stone axe distributions and it was via this network that Maritime Bell Beakers first reached the Lower Rhine in about 2600 BCE.[569]

Germanic

The Germanic peoples (also called Teutonic, Suebian or Gothic in older literature) are an Indo-European ethno-linguistic group of Northern European origin, identified by their use of the Germanic languages which diversified out of Proto-Germanic starting during the Pre-Roman Iron Age.

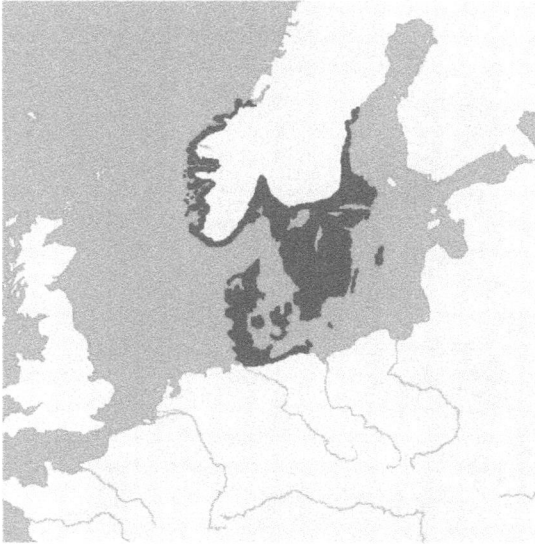

Figure 186: *Map of the Nordic Bronze Age culture, c. 1200 BCE*

The term "Germanic" originated in classical times, when groups of tribes were referred to using this term by Roman authors. For them, the term was not necessarily based upon language, but rather referred to tribal groups and alliances who were considered less civilised than the Celtic Gauls living in the region of modern France. Tribes referred to as Germanic in that period lived generally to the north and east of the Gauls with the Rhine as a approximate border line.

In modern times the term occasionally has been used to refer to ethnic groups who speak a Germanic language and claim ancestral and cultural connections to ancient Germanic peoples. Within this context, modern Germanic peoples include the Norwegians, Swedes, Danes, Icelanders, Germans, Austrians, English, Dutch, Afrikaners, Flemish, Frisians and others.

The Germanic languages are spoken by a sizable population in Western Europe, North America, and Australasia. The common ancestor of all of the languages in this branch is called Proto-Germanic (also known as Common Germanic), which was spoken in approximately the middle of the 1st millennium BCE in Iron Age northern Europe. Proto-Germanic, along with all of its descendants, is characterized by a number of unique linguistic features, most famously the consonant change known as Grimm's law. Early varieties of Germanic enter history with the Germanic tribes moving south from northern Europe in the 2nd century BCE, to settle in north-central Europe.

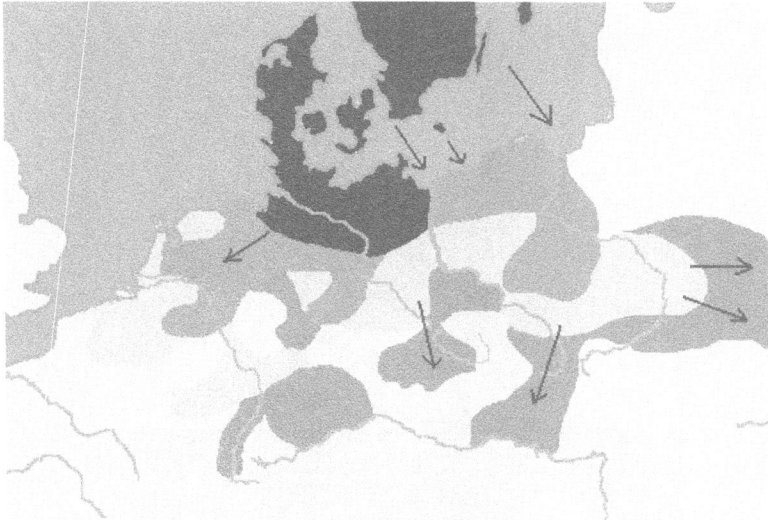

Figure 187:
The expansion of the Germanic tribes 750 BC – AD 1
(after the Penguin Atlas of World History 1988):
Settlements before 750 BC
New settlements by 500 BC
New settlements by 250 BC
New settlements by AD 1

The most widely spoken Germanic languages are English and German, with approximately 300–400 million native English speakers[570] and over 100 million native German speakers.[571] They belong to the West Germanic family. The West Germanic group also includes other major languages, such as Dutch with 23 million,[572] Low Saxon with approximately 5 million speakers in Germany and 1.7 million in the Netherlands, and Afrikaans with over 6 million native speakers. The North Germanic languages include Norwegian, Danish, Swedish, Icelandic, and Faroese, which have a combined total of about 20 million speakers.[573] There is also the East Germanic branch, which includes languages such as Gothic, Burgundian, and Vandalic, but it has been extinct for at least two centuries. The SIL *Ethnologue* lists 48 different living Germanic languages, with the Western branch accounting for 42, and the Northern for 6 languages.[574] The total number of Germanic languages is unknown, as some of them, especially East Germanic languages, disappeared shortly after the Migration Period.

Figure 188: *Romance languages in Europe*

Italic and Celtic

Italic

The Italic languages are a subfamily of the Indo-European language family originally spoken by Italic peoples. They include the Romance languages derived from Latin (Italian, Sardinian, Spanish, Catalan, Portuguese, French, Romanian, Occitan, etc.); a number of extinct languages of the Italian Peninsula, including Umbrian, Oscan, Faliscan, South Picene; and Latin itself. At present, Latin and its daughter Romance languages are the only surviving languages of the Italic language family.

The most widely accepted theory suggests that Latins and other proto-Italic tribes first entered in Italy with the late Bronze Age Proto-Villanovan culture, then part of the central European Urnfield culture system.[575,576] In particular various authors, like Marija Gimbutas, had noted important similarities between Proto-Villanova, the South-German Urnfield culture of Bavaria-Upper Austria[459] and Middle-Danube Urnfield culture.[577,578] According to David W. Anthony, proto-Latins originated in today's eastern Hungary, kurganized around 3100 BCE by the Yamna culture,[579] while Kristian Kristiansen associated the Proto-Villanovans with the Velatice-Baierdorf culture of Moravia and Austria.[580]

Figure 189:
Diachronic distribution of Celtic peoples:
core Hallstatt territory, by the 6th century BCE
maximal Celtic expansion, by 275 BCE
Lusitanian area of Iberia where Celtic presence is uncertain
the six Celtic nations which retained significant num-
bers of Celtic speakers into the Early Modern period
areas where Celtic languages remain widely spoken today

Today the Romance languages, which comprise all languages that descended from Latin, are spoken by more than 800 million native speakers worldwide, mainly in the Americas, Europe, and Africa. Romance languages are either official, co-official, or significantly used in 72 countries around the globe.

Additionally, Latin had a great influence on both the grammar and the lexicon of West Germanic languages. Romance words make respectively 59 %, 20 % and 14 % of English, German and Dutch vocabularies.[581] Those figures can rise dramatically when only non-compound and non-derived words are included. Accordingly, Romance words make roughly 35% of the vocabulary of Dutch.

Celtic

The Celts (/'kɛlts/, occasionally /'sɛlts/, see pronunciation of *Celtic*) or Kelts were an ethnolinguistic group of tribal societies in Iron Age and Medieval Europe who spoke Celtic languages and had a similar culture, although the relationship between the ethnic, linguistic and cultural elements remains uncertain and controversial.

The earliest archaeological culture that may justifiably be considered Proto-Celtic is the Late Bronze Age Urnfield culture of Central Europe, which flourished from around 1200 BCE. Their fully Celtic descendants in central Europe were the people of the Iron Age Hallstatt culture (c. 800–450 BCE) named for the rich grave finds in Hallstatt, Austria. By the later La Tène period (c. 450 BCE up to the Roman conquest), this Celtic culture had expanded by diffusion or migration to the British Isles (Insular Celts), France and The Low Countries (Gauls), Bohemia, Poland and much of Central Europe, the Iberian Peninsula (Celtiberians, Celtici and Gallaeci) and Italy (Golaseccans, Lepontii, Ligures and Cisalpine Gauls)[582] and, following the Gallic invasion of the Balkans in 279 BCE, as far east as central Anatolia (Galatians).[583]

The Celtic languages (usually pronounced /'kɛltɪk/ but sometimes /'sɛltɪk/) are descended from Proto-Celtic, or "Common Celtic"; a branch of the greater Indo-European language family. The term "Celtic" was first used to describe this language group by Edward Lhuyd in 1707.[584]

Modern Celtic languages are mostly spoken on the north-western edge of Europe, notably in Ireland, Scotland, Wales, Brittany, Cornwall, and the Isle of Man, and can be found spoken on Cape Breton Island. There are also a substantial number of Welsh speakers in the Patagonia area of Argentina. Some people speak Celtic languages in the other Celtic diaspora areas of the United States,[585] Canada, Australia,[586] and New Zealand.[587] In all these areas, the Celtic languages are now only spoken by minorities though there are continuing efforts at revitalization. Welsh is the only Celtic language not classified as "endangered" by UNESCO.

During the 1st millennium BCE, they were spoken across much of Europe, in the Iberian Peninsula, from the Atlantic and North Sea coastlines, up to the Rhine valley and down the Danube valley to the Black Sea, the northern Balkan Peninsula and in central Asia Minor. The spread to Cape Breton and Patagonia occurred in modern times. Celtic languages, particularly Irish, were spoken in Australia before federation in 1901 and are still used there to some extent.[588]

Balto-Slavic

The Balto-Slavic language group traditionally comprises the Baltic and Slavic languages, belonging to the Indo-European family of languages. Baltic and Slavic languages share several linguistic traits not found in any other Indo-European branch, which points to a period of common development. Most Indo-Europeanists classify Baltic and Slavic languages into a single branch,

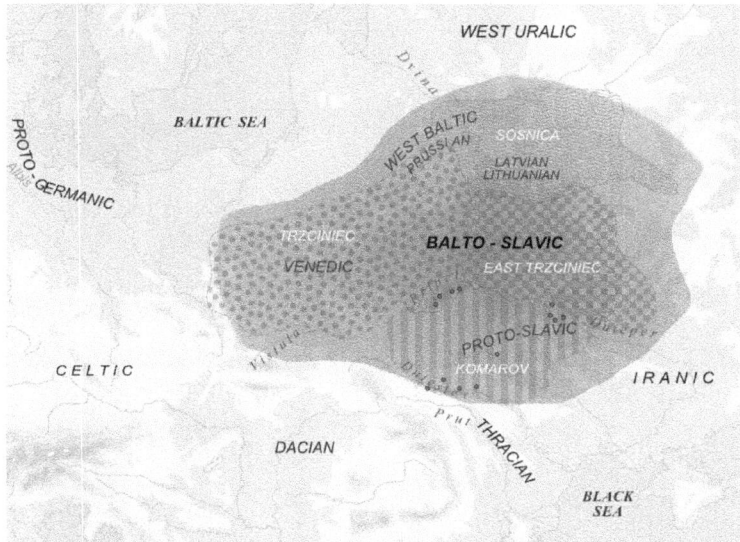

Figure 190: *Area of Balto-Slavic dialectic continuum (purple) with proposed material cultures correlating to speakers Balto-Slavic in Bronze Age (white). Red dots indicate archaic Slavic hydronyms.*

even though some details of the nature of their relationship remain in dispute[589] in some circles, usually due to political controversies. Some linguists, however, have recently suggested that Balto-Slavic should be split into three equidistant nodes: Eastern Baltic, Western Baltic and Slavic.[590,591]

A Proto-Balto-Slavic language is reconstructable by the comparative method, descending from Proto-Indo-European by means of well-defined sound laws, and out of which modern Slavic and Baltic languages descended. One particularly innovative dialect separated from the Balto-Slavic dialect continuum and became ancestral to the Proto-Slavic language, from which all Slavic languages descended.

Balts

The Balts or Baltic peoples (Lithuanian: *baltai*, Latvian: *balti*) are an Indo-European ethno-linguistic group who speak the Baltic languages, a branch of the Indo-European language family, which was originally spoken by tribes living in area east of Jutland peninsula in the west and Moscow, Oka and Volga rivers basins in the east. One of the features of Baltic languages is the number of conservative or archaic features retained.[592] Among the Baltic peoples are

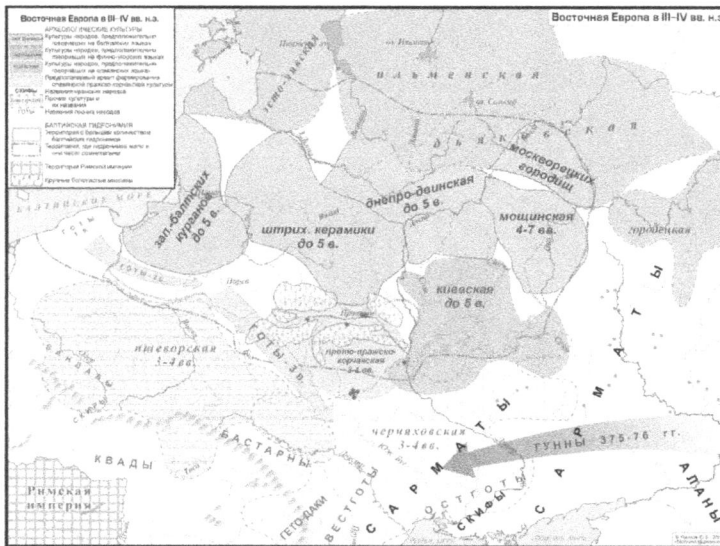

Figure 191: *Eastern Europe in 3rd–4th century CE with archaeological cultures identified as Baltic-speaking in purple. Their area extended from the Baltic Sea to modern Moscow.*

modern Lithuanians, Latvians (including Latgalians) – all Eastern Balts – as well as the Old Prussians, Yotvingians and Galindians – the Western Balts – whose people also survived, but their languages and cultures are now extinct, and are now being assimilated into the Eastern Baltic community.

Slavs

The Slavs are an Indo-European ethno-linguistic group living in Central Europe, Eastern Europe, Southeast Europe, North Asia and Central Asia, who speak the Indo-European Slavic languages, and share, to varying degrees, certain cultural traits and historical backgrounds. From the early 6th century they spread to inhabit most of Central and Eastern Europe and Southeast Europe. Slavic groups also ventured as far as Scandinavia, constituting elements amongst the Vikings;[593,594] whilst at the other geographic extreme, Slavic mercenaries fighting for the Byzantines and Arabs settled Asia Minor and even as far as Syria.[595] Later, East Slavs (specifically, Russians and Ukrainians) colonized Siberia[596] and Central Asia.[597] Every Slavic ethnicity has emigrated to other parts of the world.[598,599] Over half of Europe's territory is inhabited by Slavic-speaking communities.[600]

Figure 192: *Slavic peoples in 6th century*

Figure 193: *Slavic tribes from the 7th to 9th centuries in Europe, surrounding the Avars in south-eastern Europe.*

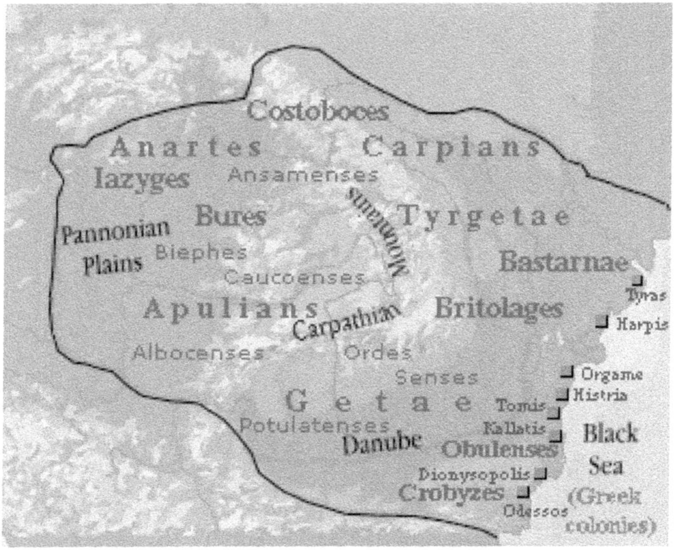

Figure 194: *Dacia during the reign of Burebista*

Modern nations and ethnic groups called by the ethnonym *Slavs* are considerably diverse both genetically and culturally, and relations between them – even within the individual ethnic groups themselves – are varied, ranging from a sense of connection to mutual feelings of hostility.[601]

Present-day Slavic people are classified into East Slavic (chiefly Belarusians, Russians and Ukrainians), West Slavic (chiefly Poles, Czechs, Slovaks, Wends and Sorbs), and South Slavic (chiefly Bosniaks, Bulgarians, Croats, Goranis, Macedonians, Montenegrins, Serbs and Slovenes). For a more comprehensive list, see the ethnocultural subdivisions.

Balkan languages

Thracian and Dacian

Thracian

The Thracian language was the Indo-European language spoken in Southeast Europe by the Thracians, the northern neighbors of the Greeks. Some authors group Thracian and Dacian into a southern Baltic linguistic family. The Thracians inhabited a large area in southeastern Europe, including parts of the ancient provinces of Thrace, Moesia, Macedonia, Dacia, Scythia Minor, Sarmatia, Bithynia, Mysia, Pannonia, and other regions of the Balkans and

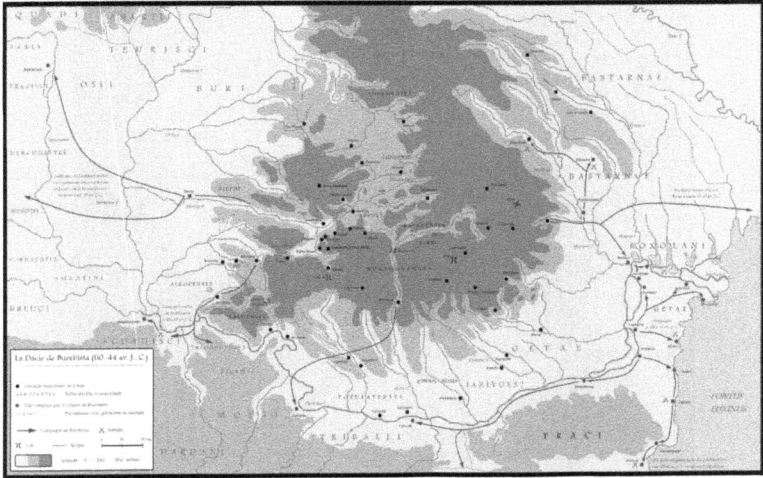

Figure 195: *Map of Dacia, 1st century BCE*

Anatolia. This area extended over most of the Balkans region, and the Getae north of the Danube as far as beyond the Bug and including Panonia in the west.[602]

The origins of the Thracians remain obscure, in the absence of written historical records. Evidence of proto-Thracians in the prehistoric period depends on artifacts of material culture. Leo Klejn identifies proto-Thracians with the multi-cordoned ware culture that was pushed away from Ukraine by the advancing timber grave culture. It is generally proposed that a proto-Thracian people developed from a mixture of indigenous peoples and Indo-Europeans from the time of Proto-Indo-European expansion in the Early Bronze Age[603] when the latter, around 1500 BCE, mixed with indigenous peoples.[604] We speak of proto-Thracians from which during the Iron Age[605] (about 1000 BCE) Dacians and Thracians begin developing.

Dacian

The Dacians (/'deɪʃənz/; Latin: *Daci*, Ancient Greek: Δάκοι,[606] Δάοι,[606] Δάκαι[607]) were an Indo-European people, part of or related to the Thracians. Dacians were the ancient inhabitants of Dacia, located in the area in and around the Carpathian Mountains and west of the Black Sea. This area includes the present-day countries of Romania and Moldova, as well as parts of Ukraine,[608] Eastern Serbia, Northern Bulgaria, Slovakia,[609] Hungary and Southern Poland.[608]

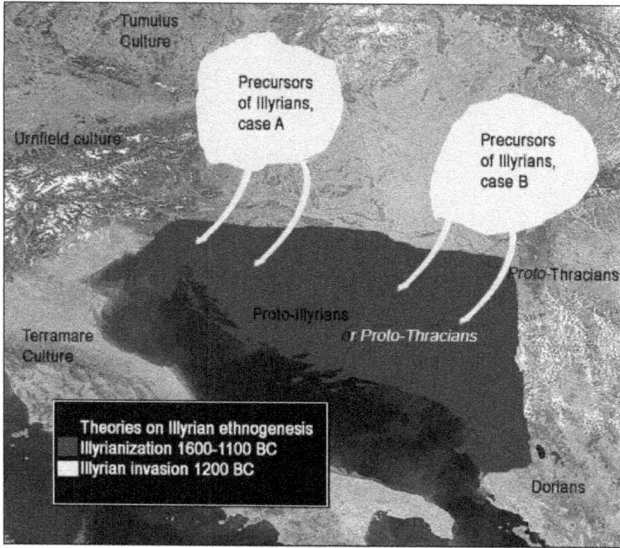

Figure 196: *Ethnogenesis of the Illyrians*

The Dacians spoke the Dacian language, believed to have been closely related to Thracian, but were somewhat culturally influenced by the neighbouring Scythians and by the Celtic invaders of the 4th century BCE. The Dacians and Getae were always considered as Thracians by the ancients (Dio Cassius, Trogus Pompeius, Appian, Strabo and Pliny the Elder), and were both said to speak the same Thracian language.[610,611]

Evidence of proto-Thracians or proto-Dacians in the prehistoric period depends on the remains of material culture. It is generally proposed that a proto-Dacian or proto-Thracian people developed from a mixture of indigenous peoples and Indo-Europeans from the time of Proto-Indo-European expansion in the Early Bronze Age (3,300–3,000 BCE) when the latter, around 1500 BCE, conquered the indigenous peoples. The indigenous people were Danubian farmers, and the invading people of the 3rd millennium BCE were Kurgan warrior-herders from the Ukrainian and Russian steppes.[612]

Indo-Europeanization was complete by the beginning of the Bronze Age. The people of that time are best described as proto-Thracians, which later developed in the Iron Age into Danubian-Carpathian Geto-Dacians as well as Thracians of the eastern Balkan Peninsula.[613]

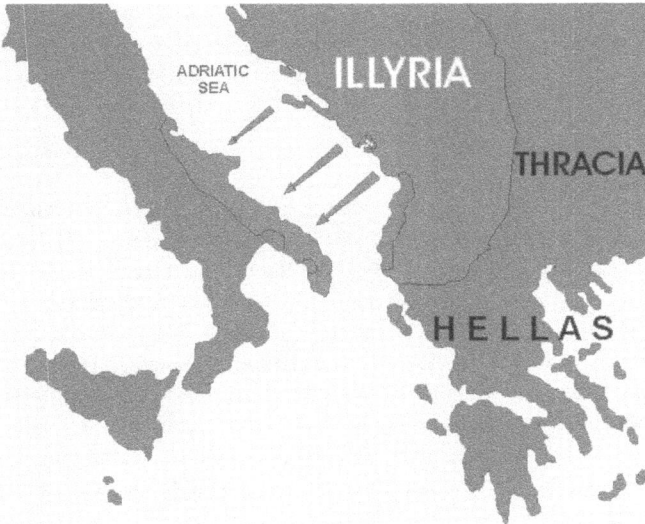

Figure 197: *Illyrian colonisation of Italy, 9th century BCE*[614]

Illyrian

The Illyrians (Ancient Greek: Ἰλλυριοί, *Illyrioi*; Latin: *Illyrii* or *Illyri*) were a group of Indo-European tribes in antiquity, who inhabited part of the western Balkans and the south-eastern coasts of the Italian peninsula (Messapia).[615] The territory the Illyrians inhabited came to be known as Illyria to Greek and Roman authors, who identified a territory that corresponds to the Croatia, Bosnia and Herzegovina, Slovenia, Montenegro, part of Serbia and most of Albania, between the Adriatic Sea in the west, the Drava river in the north, the Morava river in the east and the mouth of the Aoos river in the south. The first account of Illyrian peoples comes from the *Periplus of Pseudo-Scylax*, an ancient Greek text of the middle of the 4th century BCE that describes coastal passages in the Mediterranean.

These tribes, or at least a number of tribes considered "Illyrians proper", of which only small fragments are attested enough to classify as branches of Indo-European;[616] were probably extinct by the 2nd century CE.[617]

The name "Illyrians", as applied by the ancient Greeks to their northern neighbors, may have referred to a broad, ill-defined group of peoples, and it is today unclear to what extent they were linguistically and culturally homogeneous. The Illyrian tribes never collectively regarded themselves as 'Illyrians', and it is unlikely that they used any collective nomenclature for themselves.[618] The name *Illyrians* seems to be the name applied to a specific Illyrian tribe, which was the first to come in contact with the ancient Greeks during the Bronze Age, causing the name *Illyrians* to be applied to all people of similar language and customs.[619]

Albanian

Albanian (*shqip* [ʃcip] or *gjuha shqipe* [ˈɟuha ˈʃcipɛ], meaning *Albanian language*) is an Indo-European language spoken by approximately 7.4 million people, primarily in Albania, Kosovo, the Republic of Macedonia and Greece, but also in other areas of the Balkans in which there is an Albanian population, including Montenegro and Serbia (Presevo Valley). Centuries-old communities speaking Albanian-based dialects can be found scattered in Greece, southern Italy, Sicily, and Ukraine.[620] As a result of a modern diaspora, there are also Albanian speakers elsewhere in those countries and in other parts of the world, including Scandinavia, Switzerland, Germany, Austria and Hungary, United Kingdom, Turkey, Australia, New Zealand, Netherlands, Singapore, Brazil, Canada, and the United States.

The earliest written document that mentions the Albanian language is a late 13th-century crime report from Dubrovnik. The first audio recording of the Albanian language was made by Norbert Jokl on 4 April 1914 in Vienna.

Armenic and Greek

Armenian

The Armenian Highland lies in the highlands surrounding Mount Ararat, the highest peak of the region. In the Bronze Age, several states flourished in the area of Greater Armenia, including the Hittite Empire (at the height of its power), Mitanni (South-Western historical Armenia), and Hayasa-Azzi (1600–1200 BCE). Soon after Hayasa-Azzi were the Nairi (1400–1000 BCE) and the Kingdom of Urartu (1000–600 BCE), who successively established their sovereignty over the Armenian Highland. Each of the aforementioned nations and tribes participated in the ethnogenesis of the Armenian people.[621] Yerevan, the modern capital of Armenia, was founded in 782 BCE by king Argishti I.

A minority view also suggests that the Indo-European homeland may have been located in the Armenian Highland.[622]

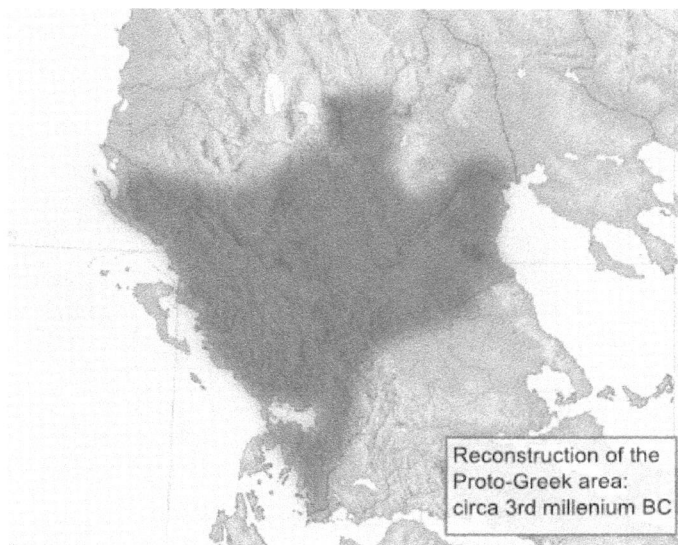

Figure 198: *A reconstruction of the third-millennium BCE "Proto-Greek area", according to Bulgarian linguist Vladimir Georgiev.*

Hellenic Greek

Hellenic is the branch of the Indo-European language family that includes the different varieties of Greek.[623] In traditional classifications, Hellenic consists of Greek alone,[624,625] but some linguists group Greek together with various ancient languages thought to have been closely related or distinguish varieties of Greek that are distinct enough to be considered separate languages.[626,627]

The Proto-Greeks, who spoke the predecessor of the Mycenaean language, are mostly placed in the Early Helladic period in Greece (early 3rd millennium BCE; circa 3200 BCE) towards the end of the Neolithic in Southern Europe.

Sea Peoples and the Bronze Age Collapse

In the 13th century BCE, at the end of the Bronze Age, seafaring invaders from Europe and the Aegean, known as the Sea Peoples, entered the Eastern Mediterranean, invading Anatolia, Syria, Canaan, Cyprus and Egypt. The invasions by the Sea Peoples ushered the Bronze Age Collapse, which resulted in the cultural collapse of Mycenean Greece, the Hittite Empire, the New Kingdom of Egypt and the civilizations of Canaan and Syria. The Sea Peoples are regarded as being composed of various groups of Indo-European[628] and non-Indo-European peoples.

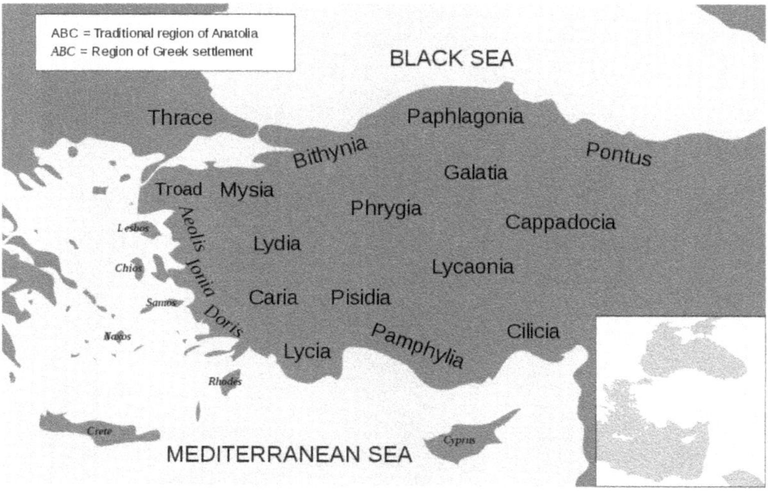

Figure 199: *Location of Phrygia in Anatolia*

Groups of the Sea Peoples mentioned in Egyptian documents are the Ekwesh, a group of Bronze Age Greeks (Achaeans, called *Ahhiyawa* in Hittite texts); Teresh (*Tyrsenoi*), known to later Greeks as sailors and pirates from Anatolia, ancestors of the Etruscans; Luka, an Anatolian coastal people of western Anatolia, also known from Hittite sources (their name survives in classical Lycia on the southwest coast of Anatolia); Sherden, probably Sardinians (the Sherden acted as mercenaries of the Egyptians in the Battle of Kadesh, 1299 BCE); Shekelesh, probably identical with the Italic tribe called Siculi; and Peleset, generally believed to refer to the Philistines, who perhaps came from Crete and were the only major tribe of the Sea Peoples to settle permanently in Palestine.

Phrygian

The Phrygians (gr. Φρύγες, *Phrúges* or *Phrýges*) were an ancient Indo-European people. After the collapse of the Hittite Empire at the beginning of the twelfth century BCE, the political vacuum in central-western Anatolia was filled by a wave of Indo-European migrants and "Sea Peoples", including the Phrygians, who established their kingdom with a capital eventually at Gordium. It is presently unknown whether the Phrygians were actively involved in the collapse of the Hittite capital Hattusa or whether they simply moved into the vacuum left by the collapse of Hittite hegemony.

The Phrygian language /ˈfrɪdʒiən/ was the language spoken by the Phrygians in Asia Minor during Classical Antiquity (ca. 8th century BCE to 5th century

CE). Phrygian is considered by some linguists to have been closely related to Greek.[629,630] The similarity of some Phrygian words to Greek ones was observed by Plato in his *Cratylus* (410a). However, Eric P. Hamp suggests that Phrygian was related to Italo-Celtic in a hypothetical "Northwest Indo-European" group.

According to Herodotus, the Phrygians were initially dwelling in the southern Balkans under the name of Bryges (Briges), changing it to Phruges after their final migration to Anatolia, via the Hellespont. Though the migration theory is still defended by many modern historians, most archaeologists have abandoned the migration hypothesis regarding the origin of the Phrygians due to a lack substantial archaeological evidence, with the migration theory resting only on the accounts of Herodotus and Xanthus.

From tribal and village beginnings, the state of Phrygia arose in the eighth century BCE with its capital at Gordium. During this period, the Phrygians extended eastward and encroached upon the kingdom of Urartu, the descendants of the Hurrians, a former rival of the Hittites. Meanwhile, the Phrygian Kingdom was overwhelmed by Cimmerian invaders around 690 BCE, then briefly conquered by its neighbour Lydia, before it passed successively into the Persian Empire of Cyrus the Great and the empire of Alexander and his successors, was taken by the Attalids of Pergamon, and eventually became part of the Roman Empire. The last mention of the Phrygian language in literature dates to the fifth century CE and it was likely extinct by the seventh century.

Indo-Iranian migrations

Indo-Iranian peoples are a grouping of ethnic groups consisting of the Indo-Aryan, Iranian, Dardic and Nuristani peoples; that is, speakers of Indo-Iranian languages, a major branch of the Indo-European language family.

The Proto-Indo-Iranians are commonly identified with the Sintashta culture and the subsequent Andronovo culture within the broader Andronovo horizon, and their homeland with an area of the Eurasian steppe that borders the Ural River on the west, the Tian Shan on the east.

The Indo-Iranians interacted with the Bactria-Margiana Culture, also called "Bactria–Margiana Archaeological Complex". Proto-Indo-Iranian arose due to this influence.[631] The Indo-Iranians also borrowed their distinctive religious beliefs and practices from this culture.[631]

The Indo-Iranian migrations took place in two waves.[632,633] The first wave consisted of the Indo-Aryan migration into the Levant, founding the Mittani kingdom, and a migration south-eastward of the Vedic people, over the Hindu Kush into northern India.[421] The Indo-Aryans split-off around 1800–1600

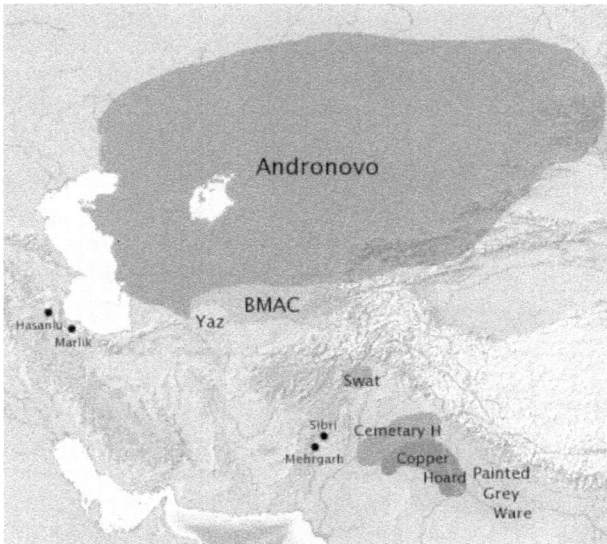

Figure 200: *Archaeological cultures associated with the Indo-Iranian and Indo-Aryan migration: The Andronovo culture is regarded as the origin of the Indo-Iranians, who later interacted with the BMAC, from which they borrowed part of their distinctive religious beliefs. The Yaz culture is also associated with Indo-Iranian migrations. The Gandhara grave, Cemetery H, Copper Hoard and Painted Grey Ware cultures are associated with Indo-Aryan migrations (according to EIEC).*

BCE from the Iranians,[456] where-after they were defeated and split into two groups by the Iranians,[634] who dominated the Central Eurasian steppe zone[635] and "chased [the Indo-Aryans] to the extremities of Central Eurasia".[635] One group were the Indo-Aryans who founded the Mitanni kingdom in northern Syria;[636] (c. 1500–1300 BCE) the other group were the Vedic people.[637] Christopher I. Beckwith suggests that the Wusun, an Indo-European Caucasian people of Inner Asia in antiquity, were also of Indo-Aryan origin.[638]

The second wave is interpreted as the Iranian wave,[639] and took place in the third stage of the Indo-European migrations[421] from 800 BCE onwards.

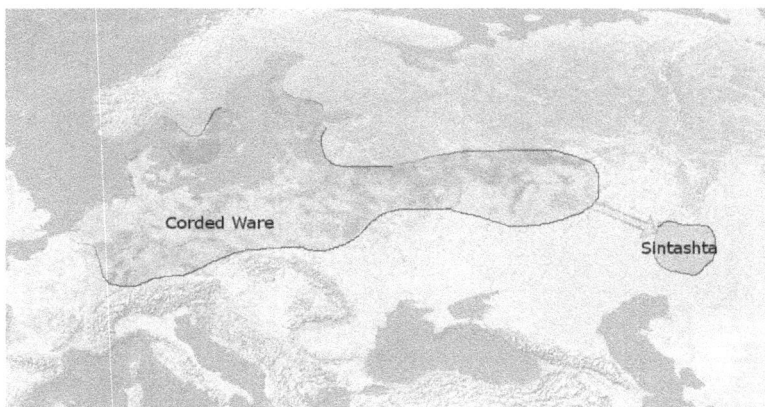

Figure 201: *According to Allentoft (2015), the Sintashta culture probably derived from the Corded Ware Culture.*

Sintashta-Petrovka and Andronovo culture

Sintashta-Petrovka culture

The Sintashta culture, also known as the Sintashta-Petrovka culture or Sintashta-Arkaim culture, is a Bronze Age archaeological culture of the northern Eurasian steppe on the borders of Eastern Europe and Central Asia, dated to the period 2100–1800 BCE. It is probably the archaeological manifestation of the Indo-Iranian language group.[640]

The Sintashta culture emerged from the interaction of two antecedent cultures. Its immediate predecessor in the Ural-Tobol steppe was the Poltavka culture, an offshoot of the cattle-herding Yamnaya horizon that moved east into the region between 2800 and 2600 BCE. Several Sintashta towns were built over older Poltavka settlements or close to Poltavka cemeteries, and Poltavka motifs are common on Sintashta pottery. Sintashta material culture also shows the influence of the late Abashevo culture, a collection of Corded Ware settlements in the forest steppe zone north of the Sintashta region that were also predominantly pastoralist.[641] Allentoft et al. (2015) also found close autosomal genetic relationship between peoples of Corded Ware culture and Sintashta culture.

The earliest known chariots have been found in Sintashta burials, and the culture is considered a strong candidate for the origin of the technology, which spread throughout the Old World and played an important role in ancient warfare. Sintashta settlements are also remarkable for the intensity of copper mining and bronze metallurgy carried out there, which is unusual for a steppe culture.

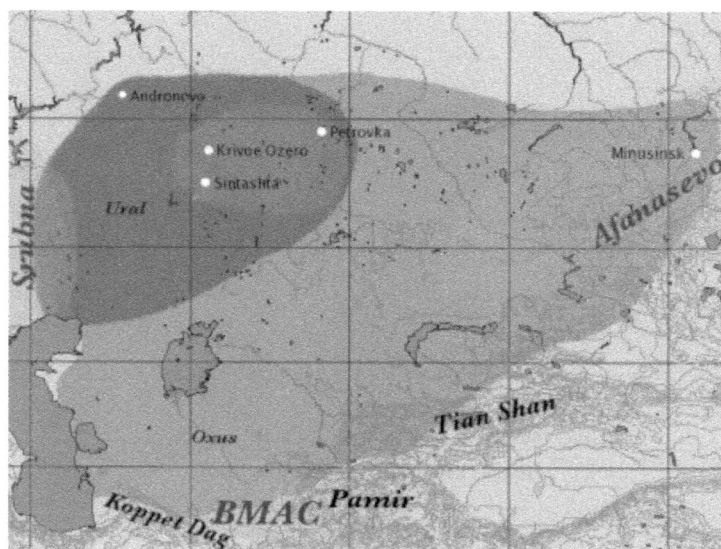

Figure 202: *Map of the approximate maximal extent of the Andronovo culture. The formative Sintashta-Petrovka culture is shown in darker red. The location of the earliest spoke-wheeled chariot finds is indicated in purple. Adjacent and over-lapping cultures (Afanasevo culture, Srubna culture, BMAC) are shown in green.*

Because of the difficulty of identifying the remains of Sintashta sites beneath those of later settlements, the culture was only recently distinguished from the Andronovo culture. It is now recognised as a separate entity forming part of the 'Andronovo horizon'.

Andronovo culture

The Andronovo culture is a collection of similar local Bronze Age Indo-Iranian cultures that flourished c. 1800–900 BCE in western Siberia and the west Asiatic steppe.[642] It is probably better termed an archaeological complex or archaeological horizon. The name derives from the village of Andronovo (55°53′N 55°42′E[643]), where in 1914, several graves were discovered, with skeletons in crouched positions, buried with richly decorated pottery. The older Sintashta culture (2100–1800), formerly included within the Andronovo culture, is now considered separately, but regarded as its predecessor, and accepted as part of the wider Andronovo horizon. At least four sub-cultures of the Andronovo horizon have been distinguished, during which the culture expands towards the south and the east:

- **Sintashta-Petrovka-Arkaim** (Southern Urals, northern Kazakhstan, 2200–1600 BCE)
  - the Sintashta fortification of ca. 1800 BCE in Chelyabinsk Oblast
  - the Petrovka settlement fortified settlement in Kazakhstan
  - the nearby Arkaim settlement dated to the 17th century
- **Alakul** (2100–1400 BCE) between Oxus and Jaxartes, Kyzylkum desert
  - **Alekseyevka** (1300–1100 BCE "final Bronze") in eastern Kazakhstan, contacts with Namazga VI in Turkmenia
  - Ingala Valley in the south of the Tyumen Oblast
- **Fedorovo** (1500–1300 BCE) in southern Siberia (earliest evidence of cremation and fire cult)[644]
  - Beshkent-Vakhsh (1000–800 BCE)

The geographical extent of the culture is vast and difficult to delineate exactly. On its western fringes, it overlaps with the approximately contemporaneous, but distinct, Srubna culture in the Volga-Ural interfluvial. To the east, it reaches into the Minusinsk depression, with some sites as far west as the southern Ural Mountains, overlapping with the area of the earlier Afanasevo culture. Additional sites are scattered as far south as the Koppet Dag (Turkmenistan), the Pamir (Tajikistan) and the Tian Shan (Kyrgyzstan). The northern boundary vaguely corresponds to the beginning of the Taiga. In the Volga basin, interaction with the Srubna culture was the most intense and prolonged, and Federovo style pottery is found as far west as Volgograd.

Most researchers associate the Andronovo horizon with early Indo-Iranian languages, though it may have overlapped the early Uralic-speaking area at its northern fringe.

Bactria-Margiana Culture

The Bactria-Margiana Culture, also called "Bactria-Margiana Archaeological Complex" (BMAC), was a non-Indo-European culture which influenced the Indo-European groups of the second stage of the Indo-European migrations.[631] It was centered in what is nowadays northwestern Afghanistan and southern Turkmenistan,[631] and had an elaborate trade-network reachings as far as the Indus civilisation, the Iranian plateau, and the Persian Gulf.[645] Finds within BMAC sites include an Elamite-type cylinder seal and a Harappan seal stamped with an elephant and Indus script found at Gonur-depe.[646]

Proto-Indo-Iranian arose due to this BMAC-influence.[631] The Indo-Iranians also borrowed their distinctive religious beliefs and practices from this culture.[631] According to Anthony, the Old Indic religion probably emerged among Indo-European immigrants in the contact zone between the Zeravshan River (present-day Uzbekistan) and (present-day) Iran.[647] It was "a syncretic mixture of old Central Asian and new Indo-European elements",[647]

Figure 203: *The extent of the BMAC (after EIEC)*

which borrowed "distinctive religious beliefs and practices"[631] from the Bactria–Margiana Culture.[631] At least 383 non-Indo-European words were borrowed from this culture, including the god Indra and the ritual drink Soma.[648]

Indo-Aryan migrations

Syria: Mitanni

Mitanni (Hittite cuneiform *KUR^{URU}Mi-ta-an-ni*), also *Mittani* (*Mi-it-ta-ni*) or *Hanigalbat* (Assyrian *Hanigalbat, Khanigalbat* cuneiform *Ḫa-ni-gal-bat*) or *Naharin* in ancient Egyptian texts was an Hurrian-speaking state in northern Syria and south-east Anatolia from c. 1500–1300 BCE. Founded by an Indo-Aryan ruling class governing a predominantly Hurrian population, Mitanni came to be a regional power after the Hittite destruction of Amorite Babylon and a series of ineffectual Assyrian kings created a power vacuum in Mesopotamia.

At the beginning of its history, Mitanni's major rival was Egypt under the Thutmosids. However, with the ascent of the Hittite empire, Mitanni and Egypt made an alliance to protect their mutual interests from the threat of Hittite domination. At the height of its power, during the 14th century BCE, Mitanni had outposts centered around its capital, Washukanni, whose location has been determined by archaeologists to be on the headwaters of the Khabur

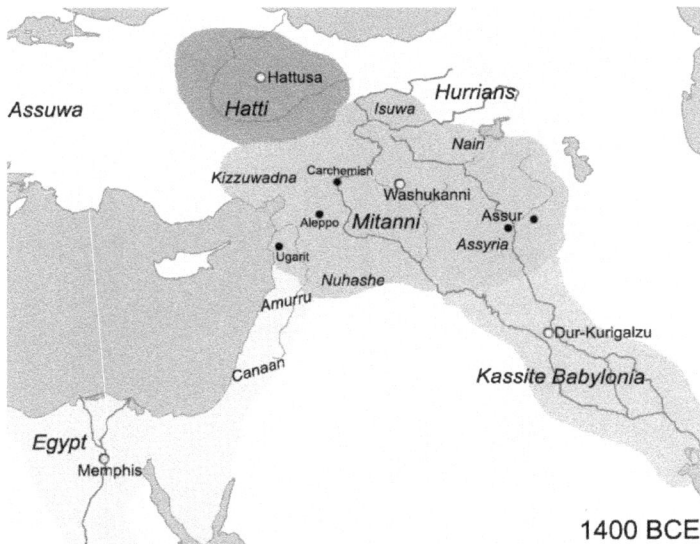

Figure 204: *Map of the Near East, c. 1400 BCE,*
showing the Kingdom of Mitanni at its greatest extent

River. Eventually, Mitanni succumbed to Hittite and later Assyrian attacks, and was reduced to the status of a province of the Middle Assyrian Empire.

Their sphere of influence is shown in Hurrian place names, personal names and the spread through Syria and the Levant of a distinct pottery type.

India: Vedic culture

> **Spread of Vedic culture**

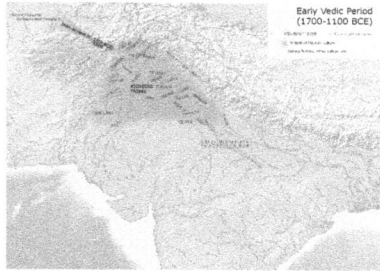

Figure 206: *Early Vedic Period*

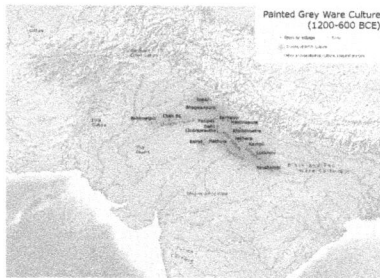

Figure 207: *Painted Grey
Ware culture (1200–600 BCE)*

Figure 208: *Kingdoms, tribes and theo-logical schools of the Late Vedic Period*

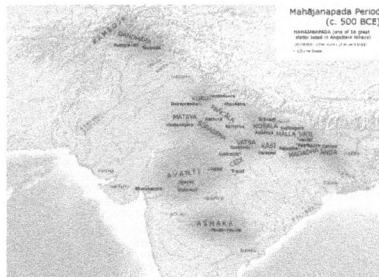

Figure 209: *Mahajanapadas (c. 500 BCE)*

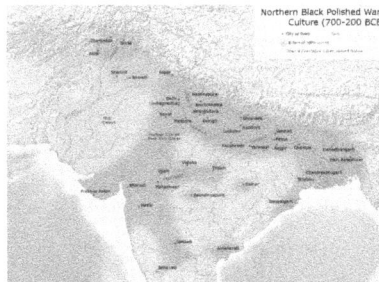

Figure 210: *Northern Black Pol-ished Ware Culture (700–200 BCE)*

The Indo-Aryan peoples started to migrate into north-western India around 1500 BCE, as a slow diffusion during the Late Harappan period, establishing the Vedic religion during the Vedic period (c. 1500–500 BCE).

The research on the Indo-Aryan migrations began with the study of the Rig Veda in the mid-19th century by Max Muller, and gradually evolved from a theory of a large scale invasion of a racially and technologically superior people to being a slow diffusion of small numbers of nomadic people that had

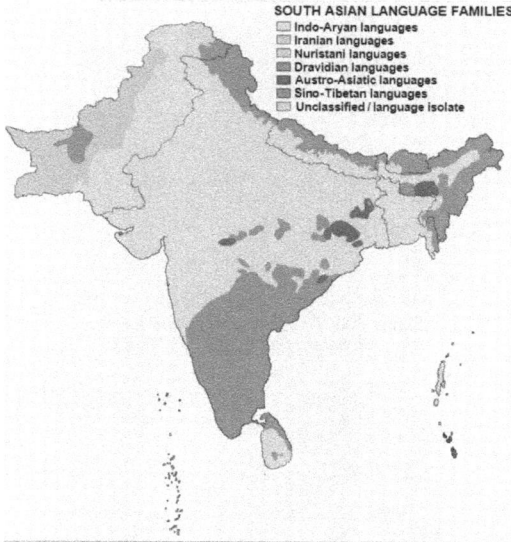

Figure 205: *Language families in the Indian subcontinent*

a disproportionate societal impact on a large urban population. Contemporary claims of Indo-Aryan migrations are drawn from linguistic,[649] archaeological, literary and cultural sources.

During the early part of the Vedic period, the Indo-Aryans settled into northern India, bringing with them their specific religious traditions. The associated culture[650]</ref> was initially a tribal, pastoral society centred in the northwestern parts of the Indian subcontinent; it spread after 1200 BCE to the Ganges Plain, as it was shaped by increasing settled agriculture, a hierarchy of four social classes, and the emergence of monarchical, state-level polities.[651,652]

The end of the Vedic period witnessed the rise of large, urbanized states as well as of shramana movements (including Jainism and Buddhism) which challenged the Vedic orthodoxy.[653] Around the beginning of the Common Era, the Vedic tradition formed one of the main constituents of the so-called "Hindu synthesis"[654]

Inner Asia: Wusun and Yuezhi

According to Christopher I. Beckwith the Wusun, an Indo-European Caucasian people of Inner Asia in antiquity, were also of Indo-Aryan origin.[655] From the Chinese term Wusun, Beckwith reconstructs the Old Chinese *âswin, which he compares to the Old Indic aśvin "the horsemen", the name of the Rigvedic

Figure 211: *The Tarim Basin, 2008*

Figure 212: *Wusun and their neighbours during the late 2nd century BCE, take note that the Yancai did not change their name to Alans until the 1st century.*

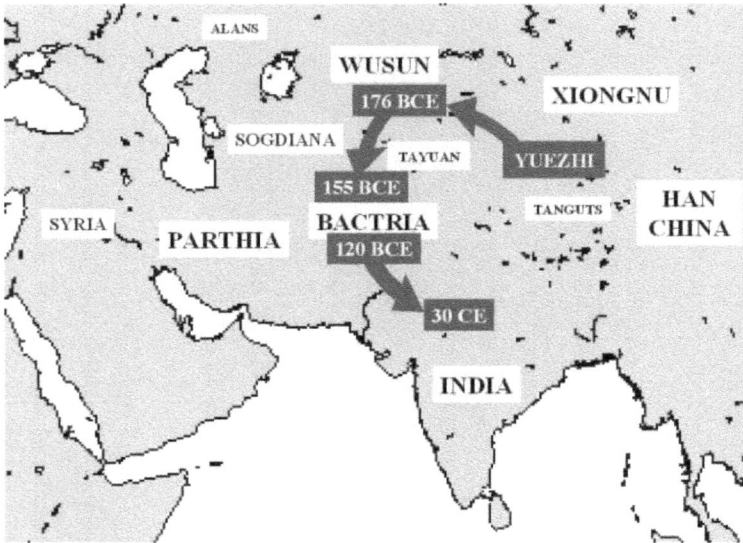

Figure 213: *The migrations of the Yuezhi through*
Central Asia, from around 176 BCE to 30 CE

twin equestrian gods.[655] Beckwith suggests that the Wusun were an eastern remnant of the Indo-Aryans, who had been suddenly pushed to the extremeties of the Eurasian Steppe by the Iranian peoples in the 2nd millennium BCE.[656]

The Wusun are first mentioned by Chinese sources as vassals in the Tarim Basin of the Yuezhi,[657] another Indo-European Caucasian people of possible Tocharian stock.[452]   Around 175 BCE, the Yuezhi were utterly defeated by the Xiongnu, also former vassals of the Yuezhi. The Yuezhi subsequently attacked the Wusun and killed their king (Kunmo Chinese: 昆彌 or Kunmi Chinese: 昆莫) Nandoumi (Chinese: 難兜靡), capturing the Ili Valley from the Saka (Scythians) shortly afterwards. In return the Wusun settled in the former territories of the Yuezhi as vassals of the Xiongnu.

The son of Nandoumi was adopted by the Xiongnu king and made leader of the Wusun. Around 130 BCE he attacked and utterly defeated the Yuezhi, settling the Wusun in the Ili Valley.

After the Yuezhi were defeated by the Xiongnu, in the 2nd century BCE, a small group, known as the Little Yuezhi, fled to the south, while the majority migrated west to the Ili Valley, where they displaced the Sakas (Scythians). Driven from the Ili Valley shortly afterwards by the Wusun, the Yuezhi migrated to Sogdia and then Bactria, where they are often identified with the

Tokhárioi (Τοχάριοι) and *Asioi* of Classical sources. They then expanded into northern South Asia, where one branch of the Yuezhi founded the Kushan Empire. The Kushan empire stretched from Turfan in the Tarim Basin to Pataliputra on the Gangetic plain at its greatest extent, and played an important role in the development of the Silk Road and the transmission of Buddhism to China.

Soon after 130 BCE the Wusun became independent of the Xiongnu, becoming trusted vassals of the Han Dynasty and powerful force in the region for centuries. With the emerging steppe federations of the Rouran, the Wusun migrated into the Pamir Mountains in the 5th century CE. They are last mentioned in 938 when a Wusun chieftain paid tribute to the Liao dynasty.

The Indo-European eastward expansion in the 2nd millennium BCE had a significant influence on Chinese culture, introducing the chariot, horse burials, the domesticated horse,[658] iron technology, and wheeled vehicles,[659,660,661,662] fighting styles, head-and-hoof rituals, art motifs and myths.

Mesopotamia – Kassites

The appearance of the Kassites in Mesopotamia in the 18th century BCE has been connected to the contemporary Indo-European expansion into the region at the time.[663]

The Kassites gained control of Babylonia after the Hittite sack of the city in 1595 BCE (i.e. 1531 BCE per the short chronology), and established a dynasty based in Dur-Kurigalzu. The Kassites were members of a small military aristocracy but were efficient rulers and not locally unpopular. The horse, which the Kassites worshipped, first came into use in Babylonia at this time. The Kassites were polytheistic, and the name of some 30 gods are known.

The Kassite language has not been classified. However, several Kassite leaders bore Indo-European names, and the Kassites worshipped several Indo-Aryan gods, suggesting that the Kassites were under significant Indo-European influence. The reign of the Kassites laid the essential groundwork for the development of subsequent Babylonian culture.

Egypt – Hyksos

The migration of the Hyksos from the Levant to Egypt in the 18th century BCE has been contected to the contemporary Indo-European expansion into the Middle East at the time.[663]

Beginning around 1630 BCE, the Hyksos, possibly related to the Amorites, seized control of Egypt, establishing their Fifteenth Dynasty with its capital at Avaris. Although vilified in later Egyptian texts, the Hyksos became highly

Egyptianized and ruled as pharaohs listed as legitimate kings in the Turin Papyrus. The Hyksos capital was seized around 1521 BCE by the Theban Ahmose, founder of the Eighteenth Dynasty, and the Hyksos were expelled. The Hyksos may have been related to the later Habiru, etymologically connected to the term Hebrew.

The Hyksos practiced horse burials, and their chief deity, their native storm god, became associated with the Egyptian storm and desert god, Seth. Although most Hyksos names seem Semitic, the Hyksos also included Hurrians, who, while speaking an isolated language, were under the rule and influence of Indo-Aryans.

The Hyksos brought several technical improvements to Egypt, as well as cultural infusions such as new musical instruments and foreign loan words. The changes introduced include new techniques of bronze working and pottery, new breeds of animals, and new crops. In warfare, they introduced the horse and chariot, the composite bow, improved battle axes, and advanced fortification techniques. Because of these cultural advances, Hyksos rule brought Egypt out of its technological backwardness and was decisive for Egypt's later empire in the Middle East.

Levant – Maryuannu

In the mid-2nd millennium BCE, control of the Levant was seized by people known as Maryannu in Akkadian texts. Many of these intruders had Indo-Aryan names. The Amarna letters show that in the early 14th century BCE, most of the important cities of Palestine and Syria were controlled by men of either Indo-Aryan or Hurrian (who were under Indo-Aryan rule and influence at the time) names. Among the Indo-Aryan rulers of Palestine mentioned in the Amarna letters we find Induruta as lord of Achshaph, Biridiya as lord of Megiddo, Widia as lord of Ashkelon, Shuwardata as lord of Hebron, Zatatna and Surata as lords of Acre, Biryawaza as lord of Damascus, and other places, while Abdu-Heba, lord of Jerusalem has a Hurrian name.

Iranians

Iranian plateau

The Iranian peoples[664] (also known as Iranic peoples) are an Indo-European ethno-linguistic group that comprise the speakers of Iranian languages. Their historical areas of settlement were on the Iranian plateau (mainly Iran, Azerbaijan and Afghanistan) and certain neighbouring areas of Asia (such as parts of the Caucasus, Eastern Turkey, Northeast Syria, Uzbekistan, Tajikistan, Bahrain, Oman, northern Iraq, Northwestern and Western Pakistan) reflecting changing geopolitical range of the Persian empires and the Iranian history.

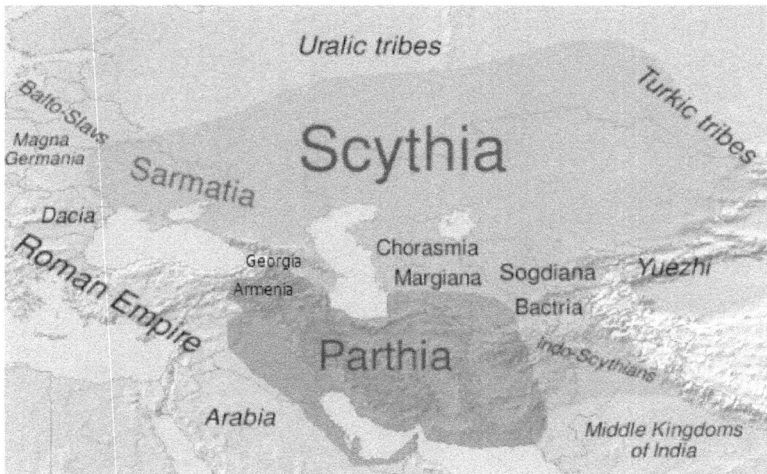

Figure 214: *Distribution of Iranian peoples in 100 BCE:*
shown is Sarmatia, Scythia, Bactria and the Parthian Empire.

The Medes, Parthians and Persians begin to appear on the western Iranian plateau from c. 800 BCE, after which they remained under Assyrian rule for several centuries, as it was with the rest of the peoples in the Near East. The Achaemenids replaced Median rule from 559 BCE. Around the first millennium CE, the Kambojas, the Pashtuns and the Baloch began to settle on the eastern edge of the Iranian plateau, on the mountainous frontier of northwestern and western Pakistan, displacing the earlier Indo-Aryans from the area.

Their current distribution spreads across the Iranian plateau, and stretches from the Caucasus in the north to the Persian Gulf in the south, and from the Indus River in the east to eastern Turkey in the west – a region that is sometimes called the "Iranian cultural continent", or Greater Iran by some scholars, and represents the extent of the Iranian languages and significant influence of the Iranian peoples, through the geopolitical reach of the Iranian empire.[665]

The Iranians comprise the present day Persians, Lurs, Ossetians, Kurds, Pashtuns, Balochs, Tajiks and their sub-groups of the historic Medes, Massagetaes, Sarmatians, Scythians, Parthians, Alans, Bactrians, Soghdians and other people of Central Asia, the Caucasus and the Iranian plateau. Another possible group are the Cimmerians who are mostly supposed to have been related to either Iranian or Thracian speaking groups, or at least to have been ruled by an Iranian elite.

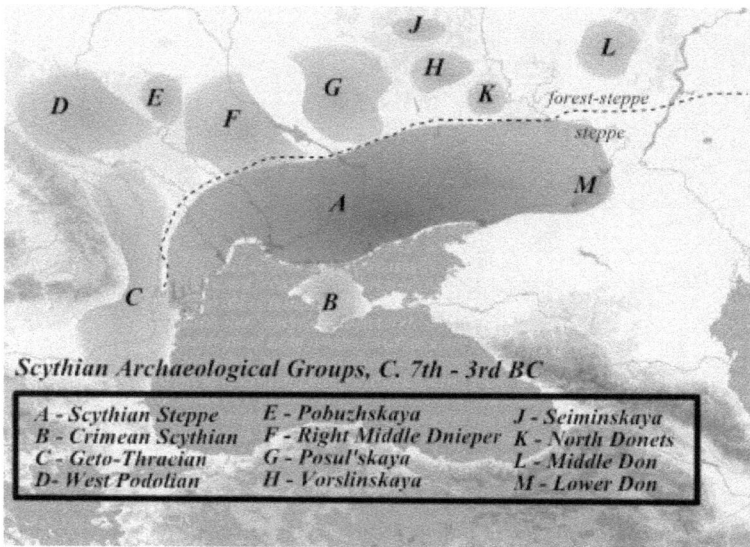

Figure 215: *Scythian and related archaeological groups in circum-Pontic region, c. 7th to 3rd centuries BCE*

Scythians

The first Iranians to reach the Black Sea may have been the Cimmerians in the 8th century BCE, although their linguistic affiliation is uncertain. They were followed by the Scythians, who would dominate the area, at their height, from the Carpathian Mountains in the west, to the eastern-most fringes of Central Asia in the east, including the Indo-Scythian Kingdom in India. For most of their existence, they were based in what is modern-day Ukraine and southern European Russia.

Sarmatian tribes, of whom the best known are the Roxolani (Rhoxolani), Iazyges (Jazyges) and the Alani (Alans), followed the Scythians westwards into Europe in the late centuries BCE and the 1st and 2nd centuries of the Common Era (The Age of Migrations). The populous Sarmatian tribe of the Massagetae, dwelling near the Caspian Sea, were known to the early rulers of Persia in the Achaemenid Period. In the east, the Saka occupied several areas in Xinjiang, from Khotan to Tumshuq.

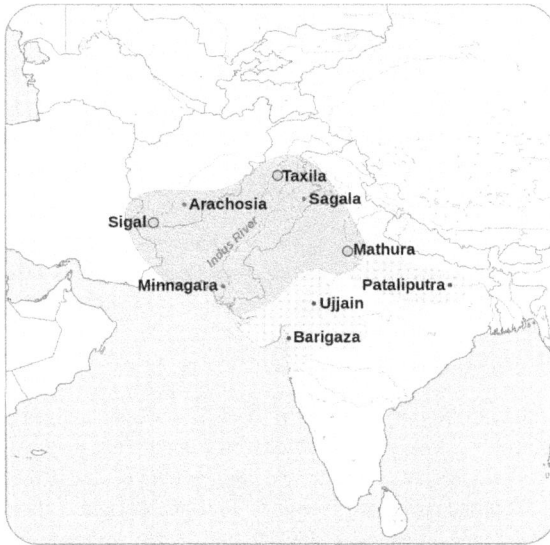

Figure 216: *Territories (full line) and expansion (dotted line) of the Indo-Scythians Kingdom at its greatest extent*

Decline in central Asia

In Central Asia, the Turkic languages have marginalized Iranian languages as a result of the Turkic expansion of the early centuries CE. In Eastern Europe, Slavic and Germanic peoples assimilated and absorbed the native Iranian languages (Scythian and Sarmatian) of the region. Extant major Iranian languages are Persian, Pashto, Kurdish, and Balochi, besides numerous smaller ones.

Alternative hypotheses

Anatolian hypothesis

The Anatolian hypothesis proposes that the dispersal of Proto-Indo-Europeans originated in Neolithic Anatolia. The hypothesis suggests that the speakers of the Proto-Indo-European language (PIE) lived in Anatolia during the Neolithic era, and associates the distribution of historical Indo-European languages with the expansion during the Neolithic revolution during the 7th and 6th millennia BCE. The alternative and more academically favored view is the Kurgan hypothesis.

The main proponent of the Anatolian hypothesis was Colin Renfrew, who in 1987 suggested a peaceful Indo-Europeanization of Europe from Anatolia from around 7000 BCE with the advance of farming by demic diffusion ("wave of advance"). Accordingly, most of the inhabitants of Neolithic Europe would have spoken Indo-European languages, and later migrations would at best have replaced these Indo-European varieties with other Indo-European varieties.

The main strength of the farming hypothesis lies in its linking of the spread of Indo-European languages with an archaeologically known event (the spread of farming) that is often assumed as involving significant population shifts.

Paleolithic Continuity Paradigm

The "Paleolithic Continuity Paradigm" is a hypothesis suggesting that the Proto-Indo-European language (PIE) can be traced back to the Upper Paleolithic, several millennia earlier than the Chalcolithic or at the most Neolithic estimates in other scenarios of Proto-Indo-European origins. Its main proponents are Marcel Otte, Alexander Häusler, and Mario Alinei.

The PCT posits that the advent of Indo-European languages should be linked to the arrival of Homo sapiens in Europe and Asia from Africa in the Upper Paleolithic. Employing "lexical periodization", Alinei arrives at a timeline deeper than even that of Colin Renfrew's Anatolian hypothesis.[666]

Since 2004, an informal workgroup of scholars who support the Paleolithic Continuity hypothesis has been held online. Apart from Alinei himself, its leading members (referred to as "Scientific Committee" in the website) are linguists Xaverio Ballester (University of Valencia) and Francesco Benozzo (University of Bologna). Also included are prehistorian Marcel Otte (Université de Liège) and anthropologist Henry Harpending (University of Utah).

It is not listed by Mallory among the proposals for the origins of the Indo-European languages that are widely discussed and considered credible within academia.

Indian origins

The notion of "indigenous Aryans" posits that speakers of Indo-Aryan languages are "indigenous" to the Indian subcontinent. Scholars like Jim G. Shaffer and B. B. Lal note the absence of archaeological remains of an Aryan "conquest", and the high degree of physical continuity between Harappan and Post-Harappan society. They support the controversial hypothesis that the Indo-Aryan civilization was not introduced by Aryan migrations, but originated in pre-Vedic India.

In recent years, the concept of "indigenous Aryans" has been increasingly conflated with an "Out of India" origin of the Indo-European language family. This contrasts with the model of Indo-Aryan migration which posits that Indo-Aryan tribes migrated to India from Central Asia. Some furthermore claim that all Indo-European languages originated in India.[667]</ref> These claims remain problematic.Wikipedia:Please clarify[668]</ref>

References

Web

Sources

<templatestyles src="Template:Refbegin/styles.css" />

- Allentoft; Sikora; et al. (2015). "Population genomics of Bronze Age Eurasia"[669]. *Nature*. **522**: 167–172. Bibcode: 2015Natur.522..167A[670]. doi: 10.1038/nature14507[671]. PMID 26062507[672].
- Anthony, David W. (2007). *The Horse The Wheel And Language. How Bronze-Age Riders From the Eurasian Steppes Shaped The Modern World*. Princeton University Press.
- Anthony, David; Ringe, Don (2015), "The Indo-European Homeland from Linguistic and Archaeological Perspectives", *Annual Review of Linguistics*, **1**: 199–219, doi: 10.1146/annurev-linguist-030514-124812[673]
- Anthony, David (2017), "Archaeology and Language: Why Archaeologists Care About the Indo-European Problem", in Crabtree, P.J.; Bogucki, P., *European Archaeology as Anthropology: Essays in Memory of Bernard Wailes*[674], University of Pennsylvania Press
- Basu; Namita Mukherjee; Sangita Roy; Sanghamitra Sengupta; Sanat Banerjee; Madan Chakraborty; Badal Dey; Monami Roy; Bidyut Roy; Nitai P. Bhattacharyya; Susanta Roychoudhury; Partha P. Majumder (2003), "Ethnic India: A Genomic View, With Special Reference to Peopling and Structure"[675], *Genome Research*, **13**: 2277–2290, doi: 10.1101/gr.1413403[676], PMC 403703[677] ᵷ, PMID 14525929[678]
- Beckwith, Christopher I. (16 March 2009). *Empires of the Silk Road: A History of Central Eurasia from the Bronze Age to the Present*[679]. Princeton University Press. ISBN 1-4008-2994-1. Retrieved 30 December 2014.
- Boardman, John (1982), *The Cambridge Ancient History, Volume III, Part I: The Prehistory of the Balkans; the Middle East and the Aegean World, Tenth to Eighth Centuries B.C.*[680], Cambridge, United Kingdom: Cambridge University Press, ISBN 0-521-22496-9

- Boardman, John; Hammond, Nicholas Geoffrey Lemprière (1982), *The Cambridge Ancient History: The Expansion of the Greek World, Eighth to Six Centuries B.C*[681], Cambridge, United Kingdom: Cambridge University Press, ISBN 0-521-23447-6
- Bojtar, Endre (1999), *Foreword to the Past: A Cultural History of the Baltic People*, Central European University Press
- Bradley, Richard (2007). *The Prehistory of Britain and Ireland*. Cambridge, UK: Cambridge University Press. ISBN 0-521-84811-3.
- Bryant, Edwin (2001). *The Quest for the Origins of Vedic Culture: The Indo-Aryan Migration Debate*. Oxford University Press. ISBN 0-19-513777-9.
- Coleman, John E. (2000). "An Archaeological Scenario for the 'Coming of the Greeks' ca. 3200 B.C."[682] *The Journal of Indo-European Studies*. **28** (1–2): 101–153.
- Demkina, T.S. (2017), "Paleoecological Crisis in the Steppes of the Lower Volga Region in the Middle of the Bronze Age (III–II centuries BC)", *Eurasian Soil Science*, **50** (7): 791–804, Bibcode: 2017EurSS.. 50..791D[683], doi: 10.1134/S1064229317070018[684]
- Dumitrescu, Vlad; Boardman, John; Hammond, N. G. L; Kollberger, E (1982). *The prehistory of Romania from the earliest times to 1000 BC. The Prehistory of the Balkans, the Middle East and the Aegean World, Tenth to Eighth Centuries BC*. The Cambridge Ancient History. CUP. ISBN 978-0521224963.
- Ellis, Robert (1861). *The Armenian Origin of the Etruscans*. Parker, Son and Bourn.WP:NOTRS
- Flood, Gavin D. (1996). *An Introduction to Hinduism*. Cambridge University Press.
- Fortson, IV, Benjamin W. (2011). *Indo-European Language and Culture: An Introduction*[685]. John Wiley & Sons. ISBN 1-4443-5968-1. Retrieved 30 October 2012.
- Frazee, Charles A. (1997), *World History: Ancient and Medieval Times to A.D. 1500*[686], Barron's Educational Series, ISBN 0-8120-9765-3
- Georgiev, Vladimir Ivanov (1981). *Introduction to the History of the Indo-European Languages*[687]. Sofia: Bulgarian Academy of Sciences.
- Gimbutas, Marija (1997). Dexter, Miriam Robbins; Jones-Bley, Karlene, eds. *The Kurgan Culture and the Indo-Europeanization of Europe: Selected Articles From 1952 to 1993*[688]. Journal of Indo-European Studies Monograph Series. **18**. Institute for the Study of Man. ISBN 978-094169456-8.
- Grigoriev, Stanislav (2002). "Ancient Indo-Europeans"[689]. Chelyabinsk. Rifei.
- Haak, Wolfgang (2015), "Massive migration from the steppe was a source

for Indo-European languages in Europe", *Nature*, **522**: 207–211, arXiv:
1502.02783[690] ∂ , Bibcode: 2015Natur.522..207H[691], doi: 10.1038/
nature14317[692], PMC 5048219[693] ∂ , PMID 25731166[694]

- Harmatta, János (1992). "The Emergence of the Indo-Iranians: The Indo-Iranian Languages". In Dani, A. H.; Masson, V. M. *History of Civilizations of Central Asia: The Dawn of Civilization: Earliest Times to 700 B.C.*[695] (PDF). UNESCO. pp. 346–370. ISBN 978-92-3-102719-2. Retrieved 29 May 2015.
- Heyd, Volker (2017), "Kossinna's smile", *Antiquity*, **91** (356): 348–359, doi: 10.15184/aqy.2017.21[696]
- Hiltebeitel, Alf (2002). "Hinduism". In Joseph Kitagawa. *The Religious Traditions of Asia: Religion, History, and Culture*[697]. Routledge.
- Hock, Hans Heinrich; Joseph, Brian Daniel (1996). *Language History, Language Change, and Language Relationship: An Introduction to Historical and Comparative Linguistics*[698]. Walter de Gruyter. ISBN 3-1101-4784-X. Retrieved 30 October 2012.
- Hollar, Sherman (2011). *Mesopotamia*[699]. Britannica Educational Publishing. ISBN 1-61530-575-0. Retrieved February 15, 2015.
- Husovská, Ludmilá (1998). *Slovakia: walking through centuries of cities and towns*[700]. Príroda. ISBN 978-8007010413.
- Ivanova, M. (2012), "Kaukasus und Orient: Die Entstehung des 'Maikop-Phänomens' im 4. Jahrtausend v. Chr", *Praehistorische Zeitschrift*, **87** (1): 1–28
- Jones, Eppie R. (2016), "Upper Palaeolithic genomes reveal deep roots of modern Eurasians", *Nature Communications*, **6**: 8912, Bibcode: 2015NatCo...6E8912J[701], doi: 10.1038/ncomms9912[702], PMC 4660371[703] ∂ , PMID 26567969[704]
- Kidner, Frank; Bucur, Maria; Mathisen, Ralph; McKee, Sally; Weeks, Theodore (December 27, 2007). *Making Europe: People, Politics, and Culture*[705]. Cengage Learning. ISBN 0-618-00479-3. Retrieved February 14, 2015.
- Kohl, Philip L. (2007). *The Making of Bronze Age Eurasia*. Cambridge Universy Press. ISBN 1139461990.
- Kortlandt, Frederik (2010), *An outline of proto-indo-european (working paper)*[706] (PDF)
- Krech, Volkhard; Steinicke, Marian (2011). *Dynamics in the History of Religions between Asia and Europe: Encounters, Notions, and Comparative Perspectives*[707]. Brill. ISBN 90-04-22535-8. Retrieved 30 December 2014.
- Lazaridis, Iosif; Haak, Wolfgang; Patterson, Nick; Anthony, David; Reich, David (2015), "Supplementary Information 11. Relevance of ancient DNA to the problem of Indo-European language dispersals", *Massive*

migration from the steppe is a source for Indo-European languages in Europe

- Lazaridis, Iosif (2016), "The genetic structure of the world's first farmers", bioRxiv 059311[708] ⓐ
- Loewe, Michael; Shaughnessy, Edward L. (1999). *The Cambridge History of Ancient China: From the Origins of Civilization to 221 BC*[709]. Cambridge University Press. ISBN 0-5214-7030-7. Retrieved November 1, 2013.
- Mallory, J.P. (1989). *In Search of the Indo-Europeans: Language, Archaeology, and Myth*. London: Thames & Hudson. ISBN 0-500-27616-1.
- Mallory, J.P. (1999), *In Search of the Indo-Europeans: Language, Archaeology, and Myth* (reprint ed.), London: Thames & Hudson, ISBN 0-500-27616-1
- Mallory, J.P.; Adams, D.Q. (1997). *Encyclopedia of Indo-European Culture*. Taylor & Francis.
- Mallory, J.P. (2002), "Archaeological models and Asian Indo-Europeans", in Sims-Williams, Nicholas, *Indi-Iranian languages and peoples*, Oxford University Press
- Mallory, J.P. (2013), "Twenty-first century clouds over Indo-European homelands"[710] (PDF), *Journal of Language Relationship*, **9**
- Mountain, Harry (1998). *The Celtic Encyclopedia*. Universal. ISBN 978-1581128901.
- Nandris, John (1976). Friesinger, Herwig; Kerchler, Helga; Pittioni, Richard; Mitscha-Märheim, Herbert, eds. "The Dacian Iron Age – A Comment in a European Context"[711]. *Archaeologia Austriaca* (Festschrift für Richard Pittioni zum siebzigsten Geburtstag ed.). Vienna: Deuticke. **13** (13–14). ISBN 978-3700544203. ISSN 0003-8008[712].
- Nichols, Johanna (1997), "The Epicenter of the Indo-European Linguistic Spread", in Blench, Roger; Spriggs, Matthew, *Archaeology and Language I: Theoretical and Methodological Orientations*, Routledge
- Nichols, Johanna (1999), "The Eurasian Spread Zone and the Indo-European Dispersal", in Blench, Roger; Spriggs, Matthew, *Archaeology and Language II: Correlating archaeological and Linguistic Hypotheses*, Routledge
- Parpola, Asko (1998). "Aryan Languages, Archaeological Cultures, and Sinkiang: Where Did Proto-Iranian Come into Being and How Did It Spread?". In Mair. *The Bronze Age and Early Iron Age Peoples of Eastern and Central Asia*. Washington, D.C.: Institute for the Study of Man. ISBN 0-941694-63-1.
- Pereltsvaig, Asya; Lewis, Martin W. (2015), *The Indo-European Controversy*, Cambridge University Press

- Parpola, Asko (2015), *The Roots of Hinduism. The Early Aryans and the Indus Civilization*, Oxford University Press
- Pulleyblank, Edwin G. (1966). *Chinese and Indo-Europeans*[713]. University of British Columbia, Department of Asian Studies. Retrieved February 14, 2015.
- Renfrew, Colin (2003). "Time Depth, Convergence Theory, and Innovation in Proto-Indo-European: 'Old Europe' as a PIE Linguistic Area". In Bammesberger, Alfred; Vennemann, Theo. *Languages in Prehistoric Europe*[714]. Heidelberg: Universitätsverlag Winter GmBH. pp. 17–48. ISBN 978-3-82-531449-1.
- Ringe, Donald A. (2006). *From Proto-Indo-European to Proto-Germanic*. Linguistic history of English, v. 1. Oxford: Oxford University Press. ISBN 0-19-955229-0.
- Roisman, Joseph; Worthington, Ian, eds. (2010). *A Companion to Ancient Macedonia*[715]. John Wiley & Sons. ISBN 978-140517936-2. Retrieved 1 May 2016.
- Salmons, Joseph (2015), "Language shift and the Indo-Europanization of Europe", in Mailhammer, Robert; Vennemann, Theo; Olsen, Birgit Anette, *Origin and Development of European Languages*, Museum Tusculanum Press
- Samuel, Geoffrey (2010). *The Origins of Yoga and Tantra. Indic Religions to the Thirteenth Century*. Cambridge University Press.
- Treptow, Kurt W (1996). *A History of Romania*. Polygon. ISBN 978-0880333450.
- Underhill, Peter A. (2010), "Separating the post-Glacial coancestry of European and Asian Y chromosomes within haplogroup R1a", *Eur J Hum Genet*, **18** (4): 479–84, doi: 10.1038/ejhg.2009.194[716], PMC 2987245[717] ə, PMID 19888303[718]
- Underhill, Peter A. (2014), "The phylogenetic and geographic structure of Y-chromosome haplogroup R1a", *European Journal of Human Genetics*, **23**: 124–31, doi: 10.1038/ejhg.2014.50[719], PMC 4266736[720] ə, PMID 24667786[721]
- Wilkes, J. J. (1995), *The Illyrians*[722], Oxford, United Kingdom: Blackwell Publishing, ISBN 0-631-19807-5
- Witzel, Michael (1989). *Tracing the Vedic dialects. Dialectes dans les littératures Indo-Aryennes*. Paris,: Caillat. pp. 97–265.
- Witzel, Michael (1995), "Early Sanskritization: Origin and Development of the Kuru state"[723] (PDF), *EJVS*, **1** (4), archived from the original[724] (PDF) on June 11, 2007

Further reading

Books

- Bryce, Trevor (2006). *The Trojans and their Neighbours*. Taylor and Francis. ISBN 0-415-34955-9.
- Cadogan, Gerald; Langdon Caskey, John (1986). *The End of the Early Bronze Age in the Aegean*. Boston: Brill Academic Publishers. ISBN 90-04-07309-4.
- Chadwick, John (1976). *The Mycenaean World*[725]. Cambridge: Cambridge University Press. ISBN 0-521-29037-6.
- Drews, Robert (1994). *The Coming of the Greeks: Indo-European Conquests in the Aegean and the Near East*. Princeton, NJ: Princeton University Press. ISBN 0-691-02951-2.
- Gimbutas, Marija (1997). Dexter, Miriam Robbins; Jones-Bley, Karlene, eds. *The Kurgan Culture and the Indo-Europeanization of Europe: Selected Articles From 1952 to 1993*[688]. Journal of Indo-European Studies Monograph Series. **18**. Institute for the Study of Man. ISBN 978-094169456-8.
- Mallory, J.P. (1999), *In Search of the Indo-Europeans: Language, Archaeology, and Myth* (reprint ed.), London: Thames & Hudson, ISBN 0-500-27616-1
- Anthony, David W. (2007). *The Horse The Wheel And Language. How Bronze-Age Riders From the Eurasian Steppes Shaped The Modern World*. Princeton University Press.
- Parpola, Asko (2015), *The Roots of Hinduism. The Early Aryans and the Indus Civilization*, Oxford University Press
- Cunliffe, Barry (2015), *By Steppe, Desert, and Ocean: The Birth of Eurasia*[726], Oxford University Press

Journal articles

- Silva M, Oliveira M, Vieira D (23 March 2017), A genetic chronology for the Indian Subcontinent points to heavily sex-biased dispersals[727], BMC Evolutionary Biology

External links

Overview of steppe-theory

- The Human Journey, *The Indo-Europeans*[728]
- The Paleolithic Indo-Europeans[729]
- The Ukrainian Week, *The Cradle of Indo-Europeans. The dawn of Indo-Europeans on the Ukrainian steppes*[730]

- *Proto-Indo-European homelands – ancient genetic clues at last?*[731], Edward Pegler, *Armchair Prehistory* (blog)
- *The Indo-European homeland problem – part 1*[732], Mikkel Nørtoft

Genetics

- DNAeXplained – Genetic Genealogy, *Yamnaya, Light Skinned, Brown Eyed....Ancestors???*[733]
- *The Genomic Ancient DNA Revolution – Interview with David Reich*[734]
- Tony Joseph (2017), *How genetics is settling the Aryan migration debate*[735], The Hindu

Linguistics

- ScienceDaily, *New Insights into Origins of World's Languages*[736]
- Encyclopædia Britannica, *Indo-European languages*[737]

Alternative theories

- Indo-European.info[738] and indo-european.eu[739] (Carlos Quiles), relates the origins of Germanic to the Bell-Beaker culture
- Mario Alinei (2012), *The Paleolithic Continuity Paradigm for the Origins of Indo-European Languages*[740]

Maps

- Maps of Indo-European migrations[741] (serie of maps, from Paleolithic migrations to Medieval migrations)

Animated maps

- *Homeland time map*[742], University of Copenhagen
- The Spread of the Indo-Europeans[743]

Research centers

- *The Homeland*[744], University of Copenhagen

Proto-Uralic homeland hypotheses

Various **Proto-Uralic homeland hypotheses** on the origin of the Uralic languages and the location (Urheimat or homeland) and the period in which the Proto-Uralic language was spoken have been advocated over the years.

Europe versus Siberia

The Proto-Uralic homeland has always been located near the Ural Mountains, either on the European or the Siberian side. The main reason to suppose a Siberian homeland has been the traditional taxonomic model that sees the Samoyed branch splitting off first. Because the present border between the Samoyed and the Ugric branch is in Western Siberia, the original split was seen to have occurred there too.

However, because the Ugric languages are known to have been spoken earlier on the European side of the Urals, a European homeland would be equally possible. In recent years, it has also been argued that on the phonological basis the oldest split was not between the Samoyed and the Finno-Ugric but between the Finno-Permic and the Ugro-Samoyedic language groups.[745] The lexical level is argued to be less reliable, and lexical innovativeness (a small number of shared cognates) can be confused because of the great age of the division. For a long time, no new arguments for a Siberian homeland have been presented.

Both European and Siberian homeland proposals have been supported by palaeolinguistic evidence, but only such cases in which the semantic reconstructions are certain are valid. A Siberian homeland has been claimed on the basis of two coniferous tree names in Proto-Uralic, but the trees (*Abies sibirica* and *Pinus cembra*) have for a long time been present also in the far east of Europe. A European homeland is supported by words for 'bee', 'honey', 'elm' etc.[746] They can be reconstructed already in Proto-Uralic, when Samoyed is no more the first entity to split off.[747]

More recently also the loanword evidence has been used to support a European homeland. Proto-Uralic has been seen borrowing words from Proto-Indo-European,[748,749] and the Proto-Indo-European homeland has rarely been located east of the Urals. Proto-Uralic even seems to have developed in close contact with Proto-Aryan,[750] which is seen to have been born in the Poltavka culture of the Caspian steppes before its spread to Asia.[751]

Although Proto-Uralic is now located on the European side of the Urals, Pre-Proto-Uralic seems to have been spoken in Asia on the basis of early contacts with the Yukaghir languages[752] and typological similarity with the Altaic (in the typological meaning) language families.[753]

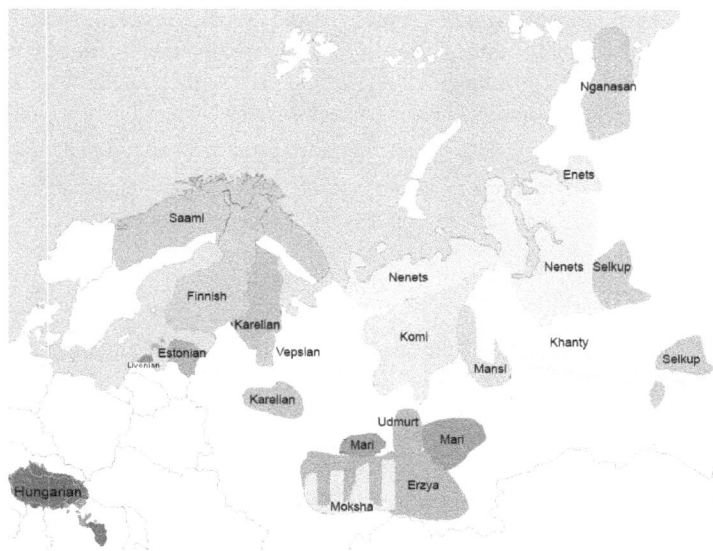

Figure 217: *Current distribution of the Uralic languages*

Continuity theories

Archaeological continuity has long been applied as an argument for linguistic continuity in Uralic studies since Estonians Paul Ariste and Harri Moora in 1956.[754] Just as long, this kind of argumentation has also been heavily criticised. The oldest version of the continuity theories can be called the moderate or shallow continuity theory. It claims that linguistic continuity in Estonia and Finland can be traced back to the arrival of Typical Combed Ware, about 6,000 years ago. This view became mainstream in the multidisciplinary Tvärminne symposium in 1980,[755] when there seemed to be no serious linguistic results to contradict that archaeological view.

The continuity argumentation in the Uralic studies gained greater visibility in the 1990s, when the next step was popularizlsed (even though this line of reasoning had been occasionally sported). In the radical or deep continuity theory, it is claimed that the linguistic continuity in Finland could be traced back to the Mesolithic initial colonization, beyond 10,000 years.[756,757]

However, in Indo-European studies, J. P. Mallory had already thoroughly scrutinized the methodological weakness of the continuity argumentation in 1989.[758] In Uralic studies, it was also soon noted that the one and the same argument (archaeological continuity) was used to support contradicting views, which revealed the method's unreliability.[759,760,761,762]

At the same time, new linguistic results appeared to contradictict the continuity theories: the datings of Proto-Saami[763,764] and Proto-Finnic[765] and of Proto-Uralic (Kallio 2006; Häkkinen 2009)[766] both are clearly younger than were thought in the framework of the continuity theories.

Now, linguists rarely believe in continuity theories because of their shown methodological flaws and their incompatibility with the new linguistic results, but some archaeologists and laymen may still claim such arguments.

Modern view

After the rejection of continuity theories, recent linguistic arguments have placed the Proto-Uralic homeland around the Kama River or, more generally, close to the Great Volga Bend and the Ural Mountains. The expansion of Proto-Uralic has been dated to about 2000 BC (4000 years ago), and its earlier stages go back at least one or two millennia earluer. Either way, that is considerably later than the earlier views of the continuity theories, which would place Proto-Uralic deep into Europe.

Evidence from population genetics

The characteristic genetic marker of Uralic-speaking peoples is haplogroup N1c-Tat (Y-DNA), also known as N-M46. 63% of Finns,[767] and 47% of Saami[768] and 41% of Estonians belong to this haplogroup. Samoyedic peoples mainly have more N1b-P43 than N1c.[769] Haplogroup N originated in the northern part of China in 20,000 -25,000 years BP[770] and spread to north Eurasia, through Siberia to Northern Europe. Subgroup N1c1 is frequently seen in Finno-Ugric people, N1c2 in Samoyedic peoples. In addition, haplogroup Z (mtDNA), found with low frequency in Saami, Finns, and Siberians, is related to the migration of Uralic peoples.

In recent genetic analysis of ancient human bones excavated from the remains of Liao civilization, haplogroup N1 (Y-DNA) is found with a high frequency, of 60-100%.[771] Therefore, a new possibility arises that the origin of Uralic languages (and perhaps also of the Yukaghir languages) may be Liao River region. The oldest Pit–Comb Ceramic, related to Finno-Ugric peoples, is also found in Liao civilization. That is also corroborated by the works of Vladimir Napolskikh, who studied the origins of the "earth-diver" creation myths and concluded that a certain variety of those myths, which is found in the folklore of Uralic peoples and other N1(Y-DNA) populations, originated in Northern Asia, possibly in the northeastern regions of today's China.[772]

Nilo-Saharan languages

Nilo-Saharan	
(undemonstrated)	
Geographic distribution	Central Africa, north-central Africa and East Africa
Linguistic classification	One of the world's primary language families
Subdivisions	• Berta • Fur • Gumuz • Koman • Kuliak • Kunama • Mabanl. be • Saharan • Songhay • Sudanic • Central Sudanic • Eastern Sudanic • Northern Eastern Sudanic • Nubian • Eastern Jebel • Nilotic • ? Kadu • ? Mimi-D • ? Shabo
ISO 639-2 / 5	<samp>ssa</samp>
Glottolog	*None*

Map showing the distribution of Nilo-Saharan languages

The **Nilo-Saharan languages** are a proposed family of African languages spoken by some 50–60 million people, mainly in the upper parts of the Chari and Nile rivers, including historic Nubia, north of where the two tributaries of the Nile meet. The languages extend through 17 nations in the northern half of Africa: from Algeria to Benin in the west; from Libya to the Democratic Republic of the Congo in the centre; and from Egypt to Tanzania in the east.

As indicated by its hyphenated name, Nilo-Saharan is a family of the African interior, including the greater Nile basin and the central Sahara desert. Eight of its proposed constituent divisions (excluding Kunama, Kuliak and Songhay) are found in the modern two nations of Sudan and South Sudan, through which the Nile River flows.

In his book *The Languages of Africa* (1963), Joseph Greenberg named the group and argued it was a genetic family. It contains the languages not included in the Niger–Congo, Afroasiatic or Khoisan groups. It has not been sufficiently demonstrated that the Nilo-Saharan languages constitute a valid genetic grouping, and some linguists have seen the phylum as "Greenberg's wastebasket", into which he placed all the otherwise unaffiliated non-click languages of Africa.[773,774] Its supporters accept that it is a challenging proposal to demonstrate but contend that it looks more promising the more work is done.[775,776,777]

Some of the constituent groups of Nilo-Saharan are estimated to predate the African neolithic. Thus, the unity of Eastern Sudanic is estimated to date to at least the 5th millennium BC.[778] Nilo-Saharan genetic unity would necessarily be much older still and date to the late Upper Paleolithic.

This larger classification system is not accepted by all linguists, however. *Glottolog* (2013), for example, a publication of the Max Planck Institute in Germany, does not recognise the unity of the Nilo-Saharan family or even of the Eastern Sudanic branch; Georgiy Starostin (2016) likewise does not accept a relationship between the branches of Nilo-Saharan, though he leaves open the possibility that some of them may prove to be related to each other once the necessary reconstructive work is done.

Characteristics

The constituent families of Nilo-Saharan are quite diverse. One characteristic feature is a tripartite singulative–collective–plurative number system, which Blench (2010) believes is a result of a noun-classifier system in the protolanguage. The distribution of the families may reflect ancient water courses in a green Sahara during the Neolithic Subpluvial, when the desert was more habitable than it is today.[779]

Major languages

Within the Nilo-Saharan languages are a number of languages with at least a million speakers (most data from SIL's *Ethnologue* 16 (2009)). In descending order:

- Luo (*Dholuo*, 4.4 million). *Dholuo* language of the Luo people of Kenya and Tanzania, Kenya's third largest ethnicity after the Niger–Congo-speaking Agĩkũyũ and Luhya). (The term "Luo" is also used for a wider group of languages which includes *Dholuo*.)
- Kanuri (4.0 million, all dialects; 4.7 million if Kanembu is included). The major ethnicity around Lake Chad.
- Songhay (3.2 million all dialects, mostly Zarma). Spread along the Niger River in Mali, Burkina Faso, and Niger, throughout the historic Songhai Empire, including its former capital Gao and the well-known city of Timbuktu.
- Teso (1.9 million). Related to Maasai.
- Nubian (1.7 million, all dialects). The language of Nubia, extending today from southern Egypt into northern Sudan. Many Nubians have also migrated northwards to Cairo since the building of the Aswan Dam.
- Lugbara (1.7 million, 2.2 if Aringa (Low Lugbara) is included). The major Central Sudanic language; Uganda and the Democratic Republic of the Congo.
- Nandi–Markweta languages (*Kalenjin*, 1.6 million). Kenyan Rift Valley.
- Lango (1.5 million). A Luo language, one of the major languages of Uganda.
- Dinka (1.4 million). The major ethnicity of South Sudan.
- Acholi (1.2 million). Another Luo language of Uganda.
- Nuer (1.1,million in 2011, significantly more today). The language of the Nuer, another numerous people from South Sudan and Ethiopia.
- Maasai (1.0 million). Spoken by the Maasai people of Kenya, one of the most well-known African peoples internationally.
- Ngambay (1.0 million with Laka). Central Sudanic, the principal language of southern Chad.

Some other important Nilo-Saharan languages under 1 million speakers:

- Fur (500,000 in 1983, significantly more today). The eponymous language of Darfur Province in western Sudan.
- Tubu (350,000 to 400,000) One of the northernmost Nilo-Saharan languages, extending from Nigeria, Niger, Chad into Libya. Most Tubu speakers live in northern Chad close to the Tibesti Mountains. Tubu has two main varieties: the Daza language and the Teda language.

The total for all speakers of Nilo-Saharan languages according to *Ethnologue* 16 is 38–39 million people. However, the data spans a range from ca. 1980 to 2005, with a weighted median at ca. 1990. Given population growth rates, the figure in 2010 might be half again higher, or about 60 million.

History of the proposal

The Saharan family (which includes Kanuri, Kanembu, the Tebu languages, and Zaghawa) was recognized by Heinrich Barth in 1853, the Nilotic languages by Karl Richard Lepsius in 1880, the various constituent branches of Central Sudanic (but not the connection between them) by Friedrich Müller in 1889, and the Maban family by Maurice Gaudefroy-Demombynes in 1907. The first inklings of a wider family came in 1912, when Diedrich Westermann included three of the (still independent) Central Sudanic families within Nilotic in a proposal he called *Niloto-Sudanic*;[780] this expanded Nilotic was in turn linked to Nubian, Kunama, and possibly Berta, essentially Greenberg's Macro-Sudanic (**Chari–Nile**) proposal of 1954. In 1920 G. W. Murray fleshed out the Eastern Sudanic languages when he grouped Nilotic, Nubian, Nera, Gaam, and Kunama. Carlo Conti Rossini made similar proposals in 1926, and in 1935 Westermann added Murle. In 1940 A. N. Tucker published evidence linking five of the six branches of Central Sudanic alongside his more explicit proposal for East Sudanic. In 1950 Greenberg retained Eastern Sudanic and Central Sudanic as separate families, but accepted Westermann's conclusions of four decades earlier in 1954 when he linked them together as *Macro-Sudanic* (later *Chari–Nile*, from the Chari and Nile watersheds). Greenberg's later contribution came in 1963, when he tied Chari–Nile to Songhai, Saharan, Maban, Fur, and Koman-Gumuz and coined the current name *Nilo-Saharan* for the resulting family. Lionel Bender noted that Chari–Nile was a historical artifact of the discovery of the family, and did not reflect an exclusive relationship between these languages, and the group has been abandoned, with its constituents becoming primary branches of Nilo-Saharan—or, equivalently, Chari–Nile and Nilo-Saharan have merged, with the name *Nilo-Saharan* retained. When it was realized that the Kadu languages were not Niger–Congo, they were commonly assumed to therefore be Nilo-Saharan, but evidence for this has not been presented.

Although progress has been made since Greenberg established the plausibility of the family, Nilo-Saharan has not been demonstrated. Koman and Gumuz remain poorly attested, and so are difficult to work with, while arguments continue over the inclusion of Songhai. Blench (2010) believes that the distribution of Nilo-Saharan reflects the waterways of the wet Sahara 12,000 years ago, and that the protolanguage had noun classifiers, which today are reflected in a diverse range of prefixes, suffixes, and number marking.

Internal relationships

Dimmendaal (2008) notes that Greenberg (1963) based his conclusion on sound evidence, and that the proposal as a whole has become more convincing in the decades since. Mikkola (1999) reviewed Greenberg's evidence and found it convincing. Roger Blench notes morphological similarities in all putative branches, which leads him to believe that the family is likely to be valid.

Koman and Gumuz, however, are poorly known, and have been difficult to evaluate until recently. Songhai is markedly divergent, probably due to massive influence from the Mande languages. Also problematic are the Kuliak languages, which are spoken by hunter-gatherers and appear to retain a non-Nilo-Saharan core; Blench believes they may have been similar to Hadza or Dahalo and shifted incompletely to Nilo-Saharan.

Dimmendaal (who had originally supported their inclusion) believes the Kadu languages form a small family of their own. Anbessa Tefera and Peter Unseth consider the poorly attested Shabo language to be Nilo-Saharan, though unclassified within the family due to lack of data; Dimmendaal considers it to be a language isolate on current evidence. Proposals have sometimes been made to add Mande (usually included in Niger–Congo), largely due to its many noteworthy similarities with Songhay rather than with Nilo-Saharan as a whole.

The extinct Meroitic language of ancient Kush has been accepted by linguists such as Rille, Dimmendaal, and Blench as Nilo-Saharan, though others argue for an Afroasiatic affiliation. It is poorly attested.

There is little doubt that the constituent families of Nilo-Saharan—of which only Eastern Sudanic and Central Sudanic show much internal diversity—are valid groups. However, there have been several conflicting classifications in grouping them together. Each of the proposed higher-order groups has been rejected by other researchers: Greenberg's Chari–Nile by Bender and Blench, and Bender's Core Nilo-Saharan by Dimmendaal and Blench. What remains are eight (Dimmendaal) to twelve (Bender) constituent families of no consensus arrangement.

Greenberg 1963

Joseph Greenberg, in *The Languages of Africa*, set up the family with the following branches. The Chari–Nile core are the connections that had been suggested by previous researchers.

<templatestyles src="Template:Clade/styles.css" />

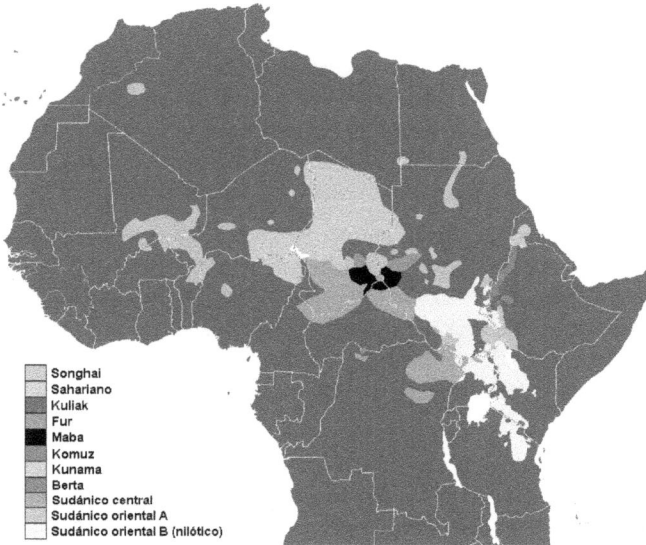

Figure 218: *The branches of the Nilo-Saharan languages.*

Nilo-
Saharan   <templatestyles src="Template:Clade/styles.css" />

                 Koman

                 Saharan

                 Songhay

                 Fur

                 Maban

        Chari–Nile   <templatestyles src="Template:Clade/styles.css" />

                      Central Sudanic

                      Kunama

                      Berta

                      Eastern Sudanic (including Kuliak, Nubian and Nilotic)

Gumuz was not recognized as distinct from neighboring Koman; it was separated out (forming "Komuz") by Bender (1989).

Bender 2000

By 2000 Bender had abandoned the Chari–Nile and Komuz branches, added Kadu, and removed Kuliak from Eastern Sudanic. He stated that Shabo could not yet be adequately classified, but might prove to be Nilo-Saharan.

<templatestyles src="Template:Clade/styles.css" />

Nilo-Saharan	<templatestyles src="Template:Clade/styles.css" />	
	Songhay	
	Saharan	
	Kuliak	
	Satellite–Core	<templatestyles src="Template:Clade/styles.css" />
		Maban
		Fur
		Central Sudanic
		Berta
		Kunama
	Core	<templatestyles src="Template:Clade/styles.css" />
		Eastern Sudanic
		Koman
		Gumuz
		Kadu

Blench 2010

With a better understanding of Nilo-Saharan classifiers, and the affixes or number marking they have developed into in various branches, Blench believes that all of the families postulated as Nilo-Saharan belong together. He proposes the following tentative internal classification, with Shabo possibly closest to Koman and Gumuz, and Songhai closest to Saharan, a relationship that had not previously been suggested:

<templatestyles src="Template:Clade/styles.css" />

Nilo-
Saharan

<templatestyles src="Template:Clade/styles.css" />

Kunama

Berta

<templatestyles src="Template:Clade/styles.css" />
<templatestyles src="Template:Clade/styles.css" />

Koman

Gumuz

Shabo

<templatestyles src="Template:Clade/styles.css" />
<templatestyles src="Template:Clade/styles.css" />

Saharan

Songhay

Kuliak

<templatestyles src="Template:Clade/styles.css" />

Maban

Fur

Kadu

Central Sudanic

Eastern Sudanic

? Mimi of Decorse

Blench 2015

By 2015,[781] and again in 2017,[782] Blench had refined the subclassification of this model, linking Maban with Fur, Kadu with Eastern Sudanic, and Kuliak with the node that contained them, for the following structure:

<templatestyles src="Template:Clade/styles.css" />

Nilo-   <templatestyles src="Template:Clade/styles.css" />
Saharan

          <templatestyles src="Template:Clade/styles.css" />
             Kunama

          <templatestyles src="Template:Clade/styles.css" />
                          <templatestyles src="Template:Clade/styles.css" />

                          Saharan

                          Songhay

          Central African   <templatestyles src="Template:Clade/styles.css" />
                             Kuliak

                          <templatestyles src="Template:Clade/styles.css" />
                             <templatestyles src="Template:Clade/styles.css" />

                             Maban

                             Fur

                          Central Sudanic

                          <templatestyles src="Template:Clade/styles.css" />
                             Kadu

                          Eastern Sudanic

          Berta

          <templatestyles src="Template:Clade/styles.css" />
             <templatestyles src="Template:Clade/styles.css" />

             Koman

             Gumuz

          Shabo (?)

Glottolog 2.7

In summarizing the literature to date, Hammarström et al. do not accept that
the following families are demonstrably related with current research:

- Berta
- Birri (putatively Central Sudanic)
- Central Sudanic (less Birri and Kresh–Aja)
- Daju (putatively East Sudanic)
- Eastern Jebel (putatively East Sudanic)
- Furan
- Gule

- Gumuz
- Kadugli–Krongo
- Koman (excluding Gule)
- Kresh–Aja (putatively Central Sudanic)
- Kuliak
- Kunama
- Maban (including Mimi-N)
- Mimi-Gaudefroy (Mimi-D)
- Nara (putatively East Sudanic)
- Nilotic (putatively East Sudanic)
- Nubian (putatively East Sudanic)
- Nyimang (putatively East Sudanic)
- Saharan
- Shabo
- Songhai (NS affiliation "thoroughly dismantled by Nicolaï")
- Surmic (putatively East Sudanic)
- Tama (putatively East Sudanic)
- Temein (putatively East Sudanic)

Starostin (2016)

Georgiy Starostin (2016),[783] using lexicostatistics based on Swadesh lists, is slightly more inclusive than Glottolog, and in addition finds probable and possible links between the families that will require reconstruction of the protolanguages for confirmation.

In addition to the families listed in *Glottolog* (previous section), Starostin considers the following to be established:

- Northern "K" Eastern Sudanic or "NNT" (Nubian, Nara, and Tama; see below for Nyima)
- Southern "N" Eastern Sudanic (Surmic, Temein, Jebel, Daju, Nilotic), though their exact relationships to each other remain obscure
- Central Sudanic (including Birri and Kresh–Aja, which may prove to be closest to each other)
- Koman (including Gule)

A relationship of Nyima with Nubian, Nara and Tama (NNT) is considered "highly likely" and close enough that proper comparative work should be able to demonstrate the connection if it's valid, though it would fall outside NNT proper (see Eastern Sudanic languages).

Other units that are "highly likely" to eventually prove to be valid families are:

- East Sudanic as a whole
- Central Sudanic – Kadu (Central Sudanic + Kadugli–Krongo)

- Maba–Kunama (Maban + Kunama)
- Komuz (Koman + Gumuz)

In summary, at this level of certainty, "Nilo-Saharan" constitutes ten distinct and separate language families: Eastern Sudanic, Central Sudanic – Kadu, Maba–Kunama, Komuz, Saharan, Songhai, Kuliak, Fur, Berta, and Shabo.

Possible further "deep" connections, which cannot be evaluated until the proper comparative work on the constituent branches has been completed, are:

- Eastern Sudanic + Fur + Berta
- Central Sudanic – Kadu + Maba–Kunama

There are faint suggestions that Eastern and Central Sudanic may be related (essentially the old Chari–Nile clade), though that possibility is "unexplorable under current conditions" and could be complicated if Niger–Congo were added to the comparison. Starostin finds no evidence that the Komuz, Kuliak, Saharan, Songhai or Shabo languages are related to any of the other Nilo-Saharan languages. Mimi-D and Meroitic were not considered, though Starostin had previously proposed that Mimi-D was also an isolate despite its slight similarity to Central Sudanic.

External relations

Proposals for the external relationships of Nilo-Saharan typically center on Niger–Congo: Gregersen (1972) grouped the two together as *Kongo–Saharan*. However, Blench (2011) proposed that the similarities between Niger–Congo and Nilo-Saharan (specifically Atlantic–Congo and Central Sudanic) are due to contact, with the noun-class system of Niger–Congo developed from, or elaborated on the model of, the noun classifiers of Central Sudanic.

Phonology

Nilo-Saharan languages present great differences being a highly diversified group. It has proven difficult to reconstruct many aspects of Proto-Nilo-Saharan language, and many authors remain skeptical about the validity of the family. Two very different reconstructions of the proto-language have been proposed, by the linguist Lionel Bender (linguist) and the historian Christopher Ehret.

Bender's reconstruction

The consonant system reconstructed by Bender for Proto-Nilo-Saharan is:

		Labial	Coronal	Palatal	Velar
plosive	voiceless		$*t, *t_2$		$*k, *k^h$
	voiced	$*b$	$*d, *d_2$	$*ɟ$	$*g$
fricative		$*f$	$*s$		
liquid			$*r, *l$	$*r_2$	
nasal		$*m$	$*n$		$*ŋ$
semivowel		$*w$		$*j$	

The phonemes /$*d_2$, $*t_2$/ correspond to coronal plosives, the phonetic details are difficult to specify, but clearly, they remain distinct from /$*d$, $*t$/ and supported by many phonetic correspondences (another author, C. Ehret, reconstructs for the coronal area the sound [ɖ], [d̪] and [ʈ], [t̪] which perhaps are closer to the phonetic detail of /$*d_2$, $*t_2$/, see infra)

Bender gave a list of about 350 cognates and discussed in deep the grouping and the phonological system proposed by Ch. Ehret. Blench (2000) "The classification of Nilo-Saharan", p. 299[784]Wikipedia:Link rot compares both systems (Bender's and Ehret's) and prefers the former because it is more secure and is based in more reliable data. For example, Bender points out that there is a set of phonemes including implosives /$*ɓ$, $*ɗ$, $*ʄ$, $*g$/, ejectives /$*p'$, $*t'$, ($*s'$), $*c'$, $*k'$/ and prenasal constants /$*mb$, $*nd$, ($*nt$), $*ñɟ$, $*ŋg$/, but it seems that they can be reconstructed only for core groups (E, I, J, L) and the collateral group (C, D, F, G, H), but not for Proto-Nilo-Saharan.

Ehret's reconstruction

Christopher Ehret used a less clear methodology and proposed a maximalist phonemic system:

		Labial	Dental	Alveol.	Retrof.	Palatal	Velar	Glottal
plosive	implosive	$*ɓ$		$*ɗ$	$*ᶑ$		$*g$	
	voiced	$*b$	$*d̪$	$*d$	$*ɖ$		$*g$	
	voiceless	$*p$	$*t̪$	$*t$	$*ʈ$		$*k$	
	aspirate	$*p^h$	$*t̪^h$	$*t^h$	$*ʈ^h$		$*k^h$	
	ejective	$*p'$	$*t̪'$	$*t'$	$*ʈ$		$*k'$	
fricative			$*θ$	$*s, *z$	$*ʂ$			

nasal	simple	*m		*n		*ɲ	*ŋ	
	prenasal	*ⁿb	*ⁿð	*ⁿd	*ⁿ d̪		*ⁿg	
liquid			*l̪	*r, *l				
approximant	plain	*w				*j		
	complex	*'w				*'j		*h

This maximalist system has been criticized by Bender and Blench. These authors state that the correspondences used by Ehret are not very clear, and because of this many of the sounds in the table may only be allophonic variations.Wikipedia:Citation needed

Further reading

- Lionel Bender, 1996. *The Nilo-Saharan languages: a comparative essay.* Munich: Lincom Europa.
- Lionel Bender, 2000. "Nilo-Saharan". In Bernd Heine and Derek Nurse, eds., *African Languages: An Introduction.* Cambridge University Press.
- Roger Blench and Colleen Ahland, 2010. "The Classification of Gumuz and Koman Languages",[785] presented at the *Language Isolates in Africa* workshop, Lyons, December 4
- Gerrit Dimmendaal, 2008. "Language Ecology and Linguistic Diversity on the African Continent", *Language and Linguistics Compass* 2/5:842.
- Joseph Greenberg, 1963. *The Languages of Africa* (International Journal of American Linguistics 29.1). Bloomington, IN: Indiana University Press.
- Pertti Mikkola, 1999. "Nilo-Saharan revisited: some observations concerning the best etymologies". *Nordic Journal of African Studies,* 8(2): 108–138.

External relationships

- Roger Blench, 2011. "Can Sino-Tibetan and Austroasiatic help us understand the evolution of Niger-Congo noun classes?",[786] CALL 41, Leiden
- Gregersen, Edgar (1972). "Kongo-Saharan". *Journal of African Languages.* **11** (1): 69–89.

External links

- Roger Blench: Nilo-Saharan[787]
  - Nilo-Saharan list[788] (Blench 2012)
- Nilo-Saharan Newsletter[789]
- Map of Nilo-Saharan[790]

Niger–Congo languages

Niger–Congo	
Niger–Kordofanian	
Geographic distribution	Africa
Linguistic classification	One of the world's primary language families
Subdivisions	• ? Dogon • ? Mande • Ijo (+ Defaka?) • Katla (Kordofanian) • Rashad (Kordofanian) • Atlantic–Congo languages (noun classes)
ISO 639-2 / 5	<samp>nic</samp>
Glottolog	*None*

Map showing the distribution of major Niger–Congo
languages. Pink-red is the Bantu subfamily.

The **Niger–Congo languages** constitute one of the world's major language
families and Africa's largest in terms of geographical area, number of speakers and number of distinct languages.[791] It is generally considered to be the
world's largest language family in terms of distinct languages, ahead of Austronesian, although this is complicated by the ambiguity about what constitutes
a distinct language; the number of named Niger–Congo languages listed by
Ethnologue is 1,540.[792] It is the third largest language family in the world by

number of native speakers, comprising around 700 million people as of 2015. Within Niger–Congo, the Bantu languages alone account for 350 million people (2015), or half the total Niger–Congo speaking population.

One of the characteristics common to most Niger–Congo languages (the Atlantic–Congo languages) is the use of a noun class system.[793] The most widely spoken Niger–Congo languages by number of native speakers are Yoruba, Igbo, Fula and Shona. The most widely spoken by number of speakers is Swahili.[794]

While the ultimate genetic unity of Niger–Congo is widely accepted (aside from Dogon, Mande and a few other languages), the internal cladistic structure of Niger–Congo is not well established. Its primary branches are Dogon, Mande, Ijo, Katla, Rashad and Atlantic–Congo.

Origin

The language family most likely originated in or near the area where these languages were spoken prior to Bantu expansion (i.e. West Africa or Central Africa). Its expansion may have been associated with the expansion of Sahel agriculture in the African Neolithic period, following the desiccation of the Sahara in c. 3500 BCE.[795,796]

According to Roger Blench (2004), all specialists in Niger–Congo languages believe the languages to have a common origin, rather than merely constituting a typological classification, for reasons including their shared noun-class system, shared verbal extensions and shared basic lexicon.[797] Similar classifications to Niger–Congo have been made ever since Diedrich Westermann in 1922.[798] Joseph Greenberg continued that tradition, making it the starting point for modern linguistic classification in Africa, with some of his most notable publications going to press starting in the 1960s.[799] However, there has been active debate for many decades over the appropriate subclassifications of the languages in this language family, which is a key tool used in localising a language's place of origin.[800] No definitive "Proto-Niger–Congo" lexicon or grammar has been developed for the language family as a whole.

An important unresolved issue in determining the time and place where the Niger–Congo languages originated and their range prior to recorded history is this language family's relationship to the Kordofanian languages, spoken now spoken in the Nuba mountains of Sudan, which is not contiguous with the remainder of the Niger–Congo-language-speaking region and is at the north-easternmost extent of the current Niger–Congo linguistic region. The current prevailing linguistic view is that Kordofanian languages are part of the Niger–Congo language family and that these may be the first of the many languages still spoken in that region to have been spoken in the region.[801] The evidence is insufficient to determine if this outlier group of Niger–Congo language speakers represent a prehistoric range of a Niger–Congo linguistic region that has since contracted as other languages have intruded, or if instead, this represents a group of Niger–Congo language speakers who migrated to the area at some point in prehistory where they were an isolated linguistic community from the beginning.

There is more agreement regarding the place of origin of Benue–Congo, the largest subfamily of the group. Within Benue–Congo, the place of origin of the Bantu languages as well as time at which it started to expand is known with great specificity. Blench (2004), relying particularly on prior work by Kay Williamson and P. De Wolf, argued that Benue–Congo probably originated at the confluence of the Benue and Niger Rivers in central Nigeria.[802,803,804,805,806] These estimates of the place of origin of the Benue-Congo language family do not fix a date for the start of that expansion, other than that it must have been sufficiently prior to the Bantu expansion to allow for the diversification of the languages within this language family that includes Bantu.

The classification of the relatively divergent family of the Ubangian languages, centred in the Central African Republic, as part of the Niger–Congo language family is disputed. Ubangian was grouped with Niger–Congo by Greenberg (1963), and later authorities concurred,[807] but it was questioned by Dimmendaal (2008).[808]

The Bantu expansion, beginning around 1000 BC, swept across much of Central and Southern Africa, leading to the extinction of most of the indigenous Pygmy and Bushmen (Khoisan) populations there.[809]

Major branches

The following is an overview of the language groups usually included in Niger–Congo. The genetic relationship of some branches is not universally accepted, and the cladistic connection between those who are accepted as related may also be unclear.

The core phylum of the Niger–Congo group are the Atlantic–Congo languages. The non-Atlantic–Congo languages within Niger–Congo are grouped as Dogon, Mande, Ijo (sometimes with Defaka as Ijoid), Katla and Rashad.

Atlantic–Congo

Atlantic–Congo combines the Atlantic languages, which do not form one branch, and Volta–Congo. It comprises more than 80% of the Niger–Congo speaking population, or close to 600 million people (2015).

The proposed Savannas group combines Adamawa, Ubangian and Gur. Outside of the Savannas group, Volta–Congo comprises Kru, Kwa (or "West Kwa"), Volta–Niger (also "East Kwa" or "West Benue–Congo") and Benue–Congo (or "East Benue–Congo"). Volta–Niger includes the two largest languages of Nigeria, Yoruba and Igbo. Benue–Congo includes the Southern Bantoid group, which is dominated by the Bantu languages, which account for 350 million people (2015), or half the total Niger–Congo speaking population.

The strict genetic unity of any of these subgroups may themselves be under dispute. For example, Roger Blench (2012) argued that Adamawa, Ubangian, Kwa, Bantoid, and Bantu are not coherent groups.

Glottolog (2013) does not accept that the Kordofanian branches (Lafofa, Talodi and Heiban) or the difficult-to-classify Laal language have been demonstrated to be Atlantic–Congo languages. It otherwise accepts the family but not its inclusion within a broader Niger–Congo.

The Atlantic–Congo group is characterised the noun class systems of its languages. Atlantic–Congo largely corresponds to Mukarovsky's "Western Nigritic" phylum.[810]

Atlantic

The polyphyletic Atlantic group accounts for about 35 million speakers as of 2016, mostly accounted for by Fula and Wolof speakers. Atlantic is not considered to constitute a valid group.

- Senegambian languages: includes Wolof, spoken in Senegal, and Fula, spoken across the Sahel.
- Bak languages, sometimes grouped with Senegambian
- Mel languages
- Limba language
- Gola language

Volta–Congo

- **North–Volta**
  - **Kru**: languages of the Kru people in West Africa; includes Bété, Nyabwa, and Dida.

  - Adamawa–Ubangi:
    - **Adamawa**: close to 100 languages and dialects scattered across the Adamawa Plateau, spoken by an estimated total of 1.6 million as of 1996; the largest is Mumuye, accounting for about a quarter of Adamawa speakers.
    - **Ubangian**: a group of minor languages spoken in the Central African Republic, grouped with Adamawa as "Adamawa–Ubangi".
  - **Gur**: about 70 languages spoken in the Sahel and Savanna regions of West Africa, accounting for some 20 million speakers (2010). The largest language of this group is Mossi (More, Mòoré), with about 8 million speakers as of 2010. Gur and Adamawa-Ubangi have also been grouped as Savannas languages.
  - **Senufo**: languages of the Senufo people (about 3 million speakers as of 2010), spoken in Ivory Coast and Mali, with a geographical outlier in Ghana; includes Senari and Supyire. Senufo has been placed traditionally within Gur but is now usually considered an early offshoot from Atlantic–Congo.

- **South–Volta**
  - **Kwa**: a divergent group of languages of uncertain genetic unity, spoken along the Ivory Coast, across southern Ghana and in central Togo, with a total of some 40 million speakers (2010s). The largest language in this group is Akan, spoken in Ghana, with about 22 million speakers as of 2014, followed by Twi (9 million in 2015).

  - **Volta–Niger** (also known as "West Benue–Congo" or "East Kwa"): a large group of West African languages, accounting for roughly 110–120 million speakers (late 2010s).
    - Gbe: spoken in Ghana, Togo, Benin and Nigeria, of which Ewe (7 million speakers in 2017) is the largest and best known.
    - "YEAI": a large group of languages centred on Nigeria, accounting for about 100 million speakers (late 2010s)
      - Yoruboid: 50 million speakers (2010s), including Yoruba (c. 40 million 2017)
      - Edoid: including Edo (5 million 2010s)
      - Akoko
      - Igboid: including Igbo (24 million 2011)
    - "NOI":
      - Nupoid: c. 3 million (c. 1990 estimates)

- Oko: a minor dialect continuum spoken in Kogi State
- Idomoid: group of languages of central Nigeria, including Idoma with 1 to 2 million speakers (2010s)
- Ayere–Ahan (moribund or extinct)

- **Benue–Congo** (East Benue–Congo)
  - Bantoid–Cross:
    - Cross River
    - "Bantoid":
      - Dakoid?
      - Fam?
      - Tikar?
      - Mambiloid
      - Bendi
      - Southern Bantoid or "Wide Bantu": includes the far-flung Bantu languages spread across Sub-Saharan Africa in the Bantu expansion from c. 1000 BCE to 500 CE.
        - Tivoid–Beboid: a large range of languages of southwestern Cameroon and southeastern Nigeria: Tivoid, Esimbi, East Beboid, West Beboid?, Momo?, Furu?, Buru?, Menchum?
        - Ekoid–Mbe
        - Mamfe
        - Grassfields
        - Jarawan–Mbam
        - **(Narrow) Bantu**: divided into Guthrie zones A–S, for a total of between 250 and 550 named languages.
  - Central Nigerian (Platoid): Jukunoid, Kainji, Plateau
  - other languages unclassified within Benue–Congo: Ukaan, Fali of Baissa, Tita.

Other

The Niger–Congo languages outside of the Atlantic–Congo supergroup are centred in the upper Senegal and Niger river basins, south and west of Timbuktu (Mande, Dogon), with a significant exclave at the Niger Delta (Ijoid). They account for a total population of about 100 million (2015), mostly Mandé and Ijaw.

- Mande: languages of the Mandé peoples, estimated at roughly 70 million as of 2016
- Dogon languages: languages of the Dogon people of Mali, estimated at 1.6 million as of 2013
- Ijoid languages: Ijaw, the language of the Ijaw people (14 million as of 2011), plus the moribund Defaka language (relationship disputed)

The Kordofanian languages of Sudan may or may not be grouped with Atlantic–Congo. They are spoken in south-central Sudan, around the Nuba
Mountains. "Kordofanian" is a geographic grouping, not a genetic one, named
for the Kordofan region. These are minor languages, spoken by a total of
about 100,000 people according to 1980s estimates. The genetic relationship
of this group of twenty or so languages with Niger–Congo is disputed. Some
linguists associate it with the Niger–Congo family, others consider them as
forming a separate *Niger–Kordofanian* language family and yet others do not
accept Niger–Kordofanian as a single group.

- Talodi–Heiban languages
- Lafofa languages
- Rashad languages
- Katla languages
- Kadu languages (now seen as Nilo-Saharan or independent)

The endangered or extinct Laal, Mpre and Jalaa languages are often assigned
to Niger–Congo.

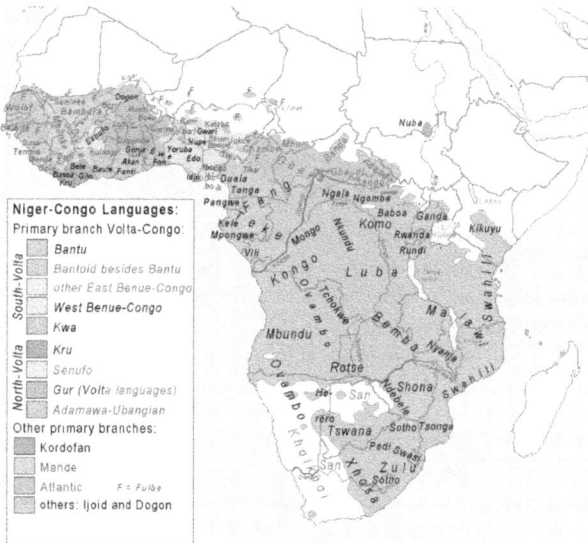

Figure 219: *Overview map*

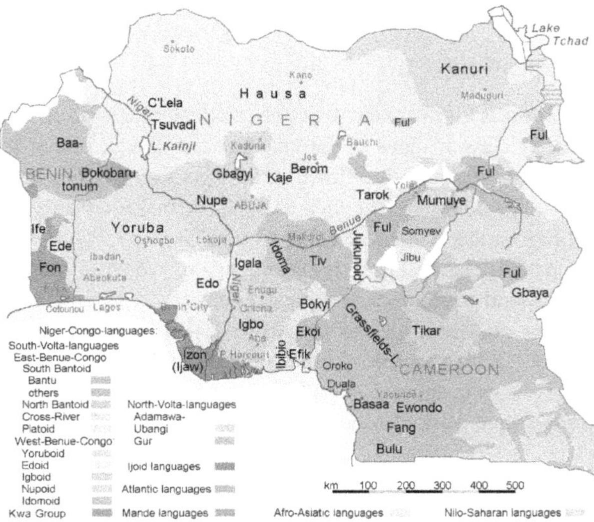

Figure 220: *Overview map of Nigeria and Cameroon*

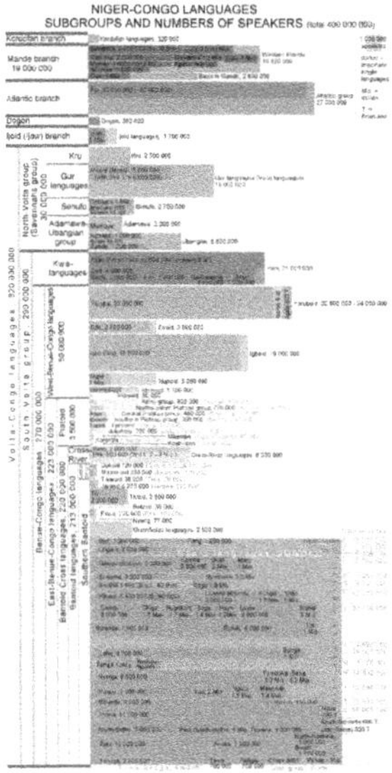

Figure 221: *Table of demographic estimates in the same color code as the maps (est. 400 million speakers as of 2007)*

Classification history

Early classifications

Niger–Congo as it is known today was only gradually recognized as a linguistic unit. In early classifications of the languages of Africa, one of the principal criteria used to distinguish different groupings was the languages' use of prefixes to classify nouns, or the lack thereof. A major advance came with the work of Sigismund Wilhelm Koelle, who in his 1854 *Polyglotta Africana* attempted a careful classification, the groupings of which in quite a number of cases correspond to modern groupings. An early sketch of the extent of Niger–Congo as one language family can be found in Koelle's observation, echoed in Bleek (1856), that the Atlantic languages used prefixes just like many Southern African languages. Subsequent work of Bleek, and some decades later the comparative work of Meinhof, solidly established Bantu as a linguistic unit.

In many cases, wider classifications employed a blend of typological and racial criteria. Thus, Friedrich Müller, in his ambitious classification (1876–88), separated the 'Negro' and Bantu languages. Likewise, the Africanist Karl Richard Lepsius considered Bantu to be of African origin, and many 'Mixed Negro languages' as products of an encounter between Bantu and intruding Asiatic languages.

In this period a relation between Bantu and languages with Bantu-like (but less complete) noun class systems began to emerge. Some authors saw the latter as languages which had not yet completely evolved to full Bantu status, whereas others regarded them as languages which had partly lost original features still found in Bantu. The Bantuist Meinhof made a major distinction between Bantu and a 'Semi-Bantu' group which according to him was originally of the unrelated Sudanic stock.

Westermann, Greenberg and beyond

Westermann, a pupil of Meinhof, set out to establish the internal classification of the then Sudanic languages. In a 1911 work he established a basic division between 'East' and 'West'. A historical reconstruction of West Sudanic was published in 1927, and in his 1935 'Charakter und Einteilung der Sudansprachen' he conclusively established the relationship between Bantu and West Sudanic.

Joseph Greenberg took Westermann's work as a starting-point for his own classification. In a series of articles published between 1949 and 1954, he argued that Westermann's 'West Sudanic' and Bantu formed a single genetic family, which he named Niger–Congo; that Bantu constituted a subgroup of the Be-nue–Congo branch; that Adamawa–Eastern, previously not considered to be related, was another member of this family; and that Fula belonged to the West Atlantic languages. Just before these articles were collected in final book form (*The Languages of Africa*) in 1963, he amended his classification by adding Kordofanian as a branch co-ordinate with Niger–Congo as a whole; conse-quently, he renamed the family *Congo–Kordofanian*, later *Niger–Kordofanian*. Greenberg's work on African languages, though initially greeted with scepti-cism, became the prevailing view among scholars.

Bennet and Sterk (1977) presented an internal reclassification based on lexico-statistics that laid the foundation for the regrouping in Bendor-Samuel (1989). Kordofanian was presented as one of several primary branches rather than being coordinate to the family as a whole, prompting re-introduction of the term *Niger–Congo*, which is in current use among linguists. Many classifi-cations continue to place Kordofanian as the most distant branch, but mainly due to negative evidence (fewer lexical correspondences), rather than posi-tive evidence that the other languages form a valid genealogical group. Like-wise, Mande is often assumed to be the second-most distant branch based on its lack of the noun-class system prototypical of the Niger–Congo family. Other branches lacking any trace of the noun-class system are Dogon and Ijaw, whereas the Talodi branch of Kordofanian does have cognate noun classes, suggesting that Kordofanian is also not a unitary group.

Glottolog (2013) accepts the core with noun-class systems, the Atlantic–Congo languages, apart from the recent inclusion of some of the Kordofanian groups, but not Niger–Congo as a whole. They list the following as separate families:

Atlantic–Congo, Mande, Dogon, Ijoid, Lafofa, Katla–Tima, Heiban, Talodi, Rashad.

Oxford Handbooks Online (2016) has indicated that the continuing reassess-ment of Niger-Congo's "internal structure is due largely to the preliminary nature of Greenberg's classification, explicitly based as it was on a method-ology that doesn't produce proofs for genetic affiliations between languages but rather aims at identifying "likely candidates.".....The ongoing descriptive and documentary work on individual languages and their varieties, greatly ex-panding our knowledge on formerly little-known linguistic regions, is helping to identify clusters and units that allow for the application of the historical-comparative method. Only the reconstruction of lower-level units, instead of "big picture" contributions based on mass comparison, can help to verify (or disprove) our present concept of Niger-Congo as a genetic grouping consist-ing of Benue-Congo plus Volta-Niger, Kwa, Adamawa plus Gur, Kru, the so-called Kordofanian languages, and probably the language groups traditionally classified as Atlantic."[811]

The coherence of Niger-Congo as a language phylum is supported by Grolle-mund, et al. (2016), using computational phylogenetic methods.[812]   The East/West Volta-Congo division, West/East Benue-Congo division, and North/South Bantoid division are not supported, whereas a Bantoid group consisting of Ekoid, Bendi, Dakoid, Jukunoid, Tivoid, Mambiloid, Beboid, Mamfe, Tikar, Grassfields, and Bantu is supported.

The Automated Similarity Judgment Program (ASJP) also groups many Niger-Congo branches together.

Niger–Congo and Nilo-Saharan

Over the years, several linguists have suggested a link between Niger–Congo and Nilo-Saharan, probably starting with Westermann's comparative work on the 'Sudanic' family in which 'Eastern Sudanic' (now classified as Nilo-Saharan) and 'Western Sudanic' (now classified as Niger–Congo) were united. Gregersen (1972) proposed that Niger–Congo and Nilo-Saharan be united into a larger phylum, which he termed *Kongo–Saharan*. His evidence was mainly based on the uncertainty in the classification of Songhay, morphological resemblances, and lexical similarities. A more recent proponent was Roger Blench (1995), who puts forward phonological, morphological and lexical evidence for uniting Niger–Congo and Nilo-Saharan in a *Niger–Saharan* phylum, with special affinity between Niger–Congo and Central Sudanic. However, fifteen years later his views had changed, with Blench (2011) proposing instead that the noun-classifier system of Central Sudanic, commonly reflected in a tripartite general–singulative–plurative number system, triggered the development or elaboration of the noun-class system of the Atlantic–Congo languages, with tripartite number marking surviving in the Plateau and Gur languages of Niger–Congo, and the lexical similarities being due to loans.

Common features

Phonology

Niger–Congo languages have a clear preference for open syllables of the type CV (Consonant Vowel). The typical word structure of Proto-Niger-Congo is thought to have been CVCV, a structure still attested in, for example, Bantu, Mande and Ijoid – in many other branches this structure has been reduced through phonological change. Verbs are composed of a root followed by one or more extensional suffixes. Nouns consist of a root originally preceded by a noun class prefix of (C)V- shape which is often eroded by phonological change.

Consonants

Reconstructions of the consonant set of several branches of Niger–Congo (Stewart for proto-Volta–Congo, Mukarovsky for his proto-West-Nigritic, roughly corresponding to Atlantic–Congo) have posited independently a regular phonological contrast between two classes of consonants. Pending more clarity as to the precise nature of this contrast it is commonly characterized as a contrast between fortis and lenis consonants. Five places of articulation are postulated for the consonant inventory of proto-Niger–Congo: labial, alveolar, palatal, velar, and labial-velar.

Vowels

Many Niger–Congo languages' vowel harmony is based on the [ATR] (advanced tongue root) feature. In this type of vowel harmony, the position of the root of the tongue in regards to backness is the phonetic basis for the distinction between two harmonizing sets of vowels. In its fullest form, this type involves two classes, each of five vowels:

[+ATR]	[−ATR]
[i]	[ɪ][813]
[e]	[ɛ]
[ə]	[a]
[o]	[ɔ]
[u]	[ʊ]

The roots are then divided into [+ATR] and [−ATR] categories. This feature is lexically assigned to the roots because there is no determiner within a normal root that causes the [ATR] value.[814]

There are two types of [ATR] vowel harmony controllers in Niger–Congo. The first controller is the root. When a root contains a [+ATR] or [−ATR] vowel, then that value is applied to the rest of the word, which involves crossing morpheme boundaries.[815] For example, suffixes in Wolof assimilate to the [ATR] value of the root to which they attach. Some examples of these suffixes that alternate depending on the root are:

[+ATR]	[–ATR]	Purpose
-le	-lɛ	'participant'
-o	-ɔ	'nominalizing'
-əl	-al	'benefactive'

Furthermore, the directionality of assimilation in [ATR] root-controlled vowel harmony need not be specified. The root features [+ATR] and [–ATR] spread left and/or right as needed, so that no vowel would lack a specification and be ill-formed.[816]

Unlike in the root-controlled harmony system, where the two [ATR] values behave symmetrically, a large number of Niger–Congo languages exhibit a pattern where the [+ATR] value is more active or dominant than the [–ATR] value.[817] This results in the second vowel harmony controller being the [+ATR] value. If there is even one vowel that is [+ATR] in the whole word, then the rest of the vowels harmonize with that feature. However, if there is no vowel that is [+ATR], the vowels appear in their underlying form. This form of vowel harmony control is best exhibited in West African languages. For example, in Nawuri, the diminutive suffix /-bi/ will cause the underlying [–ATR] vowels in a word to become phonetically [+ATR].

There are two types of vowels which affect the harmony process. These are known as neutral or opaque vowels. Neutral vowels do not harmonize to the [ATR] value of the word, and instead maintain their own [ATR] value. The vowels that follow them, however, will receive the [ATR] value of the root. Opaque vowels maintain their own [ATR] value as well, but they affect the harmony process behind them. All of the vowels following an opaque vowel will harmonize with the [ATR] value of the opaque vowel instead of the [ATR] vowel of the root.

The vowel inventory listed above is a ten-vowel language. This is a language in which all of the vowels of the language participate in the harmony system, producing five harmonic pairs. Vowel inventories of this type are still found in some branches of Niger-Congo, for example in the Ghana Togo Mountain languages.[818] However, this is the rarer inventory as oftentimes there are one or more vowels that are not part of a harmonic pair. This has resulted in seven-and nine-vowel systems being the more popular systems. The major-ity of languages with [ATR] controlled vowel harmony have either seven- or nine-vowel phonemes, with the most common non-participatory vowel being /a/. It has been asserted that this is because vowel quality differences in the mid-central region where /ə/, the counterpart of /a/, is found, are difficult to perceive. Another possible reason for the non-participatory status of /a/ is that there is articulatory difficulty in advancing the tongue root when the tongue body is low in order to produce a low [+ATR] vowel.[819] Therefore, the vowel inventory for nine-vowel languages is generally:

[+ATR]	[–ATR]
[i]	[ɪ]
[e]	[ɛ]
	[a]
[o]	[ɔ]
[u]	[ʊ]

And seven-vowel languages have one of two inventories:

[+ATR]	[–ATR]
[i]	[ɪ]
	[ɛ]
	[a]
	[ɔ]
[u]	[ʊ]

[+ATR]	[–ATR]
[i]	
[e]	[ɛ]
	[a]
[o]	[ɔ]
[u]	

Note that in the nine-vowel language, the missing vowel is, in fact, [ə], [a]'s counterpart, as would be expected.[820]

The fact that ten vowels have been reconstructed for proto-Atlantic, proto-Ijoid and possibly proto-Volta–Congo has led to the hypothesis that the original vowel inventory of Niger–Congo was a full ten-vowel system.[821] On the other hand, Stewart, in recent comparative work, reconstructs a seven-vowel system for his proto-Potou-Akanic-Bantu.[822]

Nasality

Several scholars have documented a contrast between oral and nasal vowels in Niger–Congo.[823] In his reconstruction of proto-Volta–Congo, Steward (1976) postulates that nasal consonants have originated under the influence of nasal vowels; this hypothesis is supported by the fact that there are several Niger–Congo languages that have been analysed as lacking nasal consonants altogether. Languages like this have nasal vowels accompanied with complementary distribution between oral and nasal consonants before oral and nasal vowels. Subsequent loss of the nasal/oral contrast in vowels may result in nasal consonants becoming part of the phoneme inventory. In all cases reported to date, the bilabial /m/ is the first nasal consonant to be phonologized. Niger–Congo thus invalidates two common assumptions about nasals:[824] that all languages have at least one primary nasal consonant, and that if a language has only one primary nasal consonant it is /n/.

Niger–Congo languages commonly show fewer nasalized than oral vowels. Kasem, a language with a ten-vowel system employing ATR vowel harmony, has seven nasalized vowels. Similarly, Yoruba has seven oral vowels and only five nasal ones. However, the recently discovered language of Zialo has nasal equivalent for each of its seven vowels.

Tone

The large majority of present-day Niger–Congo languages are tonal. A typical Niger–Congo tone system involves two or three contrastive level tones. Four level systems are less widespread, and five level systems are rare. Only a few Niger–Congo languages are non-tonal; Swahili is perhaps the best known, but within the Atlantic branch some others are found. Proto-Niger–Congo is thought to have been a tone language with two contrastive levels. Synchronic and comparative-historical studies of tone systems show that such a basic system can easily develop more tonal contrasts under the influence of depressor consonants or through the introduction of a downstep.Wikipedia:Citation needed Languages which have more tonal levels tend to use tone more for lexical and less for grammatical contrasts.

Contrastive levels of tone in some Niger–Congo languages

H, L	Dyula–Bambara, Maninka, Temne, Dogon, Dagbani, Gbaya, Efik, Lingala
H, M, L	Yakuba, Nafaanra, Kasem, Banda, Yoruba, Jukun, Dangme, Yukuben, Akan, Anyi, Ewe, Igbo
T, H, M, L	Gban, Wobe, Munzombo, Igede, Mambila, Fon
T, H, M, L, B	Ashuku (Benue–Congo), Dan-Santa (Mande)

PA/S	Mandinka (Senegambia), Fula, Wolof, Kimwani
none	Swahili

Abbreviations used: T top, H high, M mid, L low, B bottom, PA/S pitch-accent or stress
Adapted from Williamson 1989:27

Morphosyntax

Noun classification

Niger–Congo languages are known for their system of noun classification, traces of which can be found in every branch of the family but Mande, Ijoid, Dogon, and the Katla and Rashad branches of Kordofanian. These noun-classification systems are somewhat analogous to grammatical gender in other languages, but there are often a fairly large number of classes (often 10 or more), and the classes may be male human/female human/animate/inanimate, or even completely gender-unrelated categories such as places, plants, abstracts, and groups of objects. For example, in Bantu, the Swahili language is called *Kiswahili,* while the Swahili people are *Waswahili.* Likewise, in Ubangian, the Zande language is called *Pazande,* while the Zande people are called *Azande.*

In the Bantu languages, where noun classification is particularly elaborate, it typically appears as prefixes, with verbs and adjectives marked according to the class of the noun they refer to. For example, in Swahili, *watu wazuri wataenda* is 'good *(zuri)* people *(tu)* will go *(ta-enda)*'.

Verbal extensions

The same Atlantic–Congo languages which have noun classes also have a set of verb applicatives and other verbal extensions, such as the reciprocal suffix *-na* (Swahili *penda* 'to love', *pendana* 'to love each other'; also applicative *pendea* 'to love for' and causative *pendeza* 'to please').

Word order

A subject–verb–object word order is quite widespread among today's Niger–Congo languages, but SOV is found in branches as divergent as Mande, Ijoid and Dogon. As a result, there has been quite some debate as to the basic word order of Niger–Congo.

Whereas Claudi (1993) argues for SVO on the basis of existing SVO > SOV grammaticalization paths, Gensler (1997) points out that the notion of 'basic word order' is problematic as it excludes structures with, for example, auxiliaries. However, the structure SC-OC-VbStem (Subject concord, Object concord, Verb stem) found in the "verbal complex" of the SVO Bantu languages suggests an earlier SOV pattern (where the subject and object were at least represented by pronouns).

Noun phrases in most Niger–Congo languages are characteristically *noun-initial*, with adjectives, numerals, demonstratives and genitives all coming after the noun. The major exceptions are found in the western[825] areas where verb-final word order predominates and genitives precede nouns, though other modifiers still come afterwards. Degree words almost always follow adjectives, and except in verb-final languages adpositions are prepositional.

The verb-final languages of the Mende region have two quite unusual word order characteristics. Although verbs follow their direct objects, oblique adpositional phrases (like "in the house", "with timber") typically come after the verb, creating a **SOVX** word order. Also noteworthy in these languages is the prevalence of internally headed and correlative relative clauses, in both of which the head occurs *inside* the relative clause rather than the main clause.

Further reading

- Vic Webb (2001) *African Voices: An Introduction to the Languages and Linguistics of Africa*
- Bendor-Samuel, John & Rhonda L. Hartell (eds.) (1989) *The Niger–Congo Languages – A classification and description of Africa's largest language family*. Lanham, Maryland: University Press of America.
- Bennett, Patrick R. & Sterk, Jan P. (1977) 'South Central Niger–Congo: A reclassification'. *Studies in African Linguistics*, 8, 241–273.
- Blench, Roger (1995) 'Is Niger–Congo simply a branch of Nilo-Saharan?'[826] In *Proceedings: Fifth Nilo-Saharan Linguistics Colloquium, Nice, 1992*, ed. R. Nicolai and F. Rottland, 83–130. Köln: Rüdiger Köppe.
- —— (2011) "Can Sino-Tibetan and Austroasiatic help us understand the evolution of Niger–Congo noun classes?",[827] CALL 41, Leiden
- —— (2011) "Should Kordofanian be split up?"[828], Nuba Hills Conference, Leiden
- Capo, Hounkpati B.C. (1981) 'Nasality in Gbe: A Synchronic Interpretation' *Studies in African Linguistics*, 12, 1, 1–43.
- Casali, Roderic F. (1995) 'On the Reduction of Vowel Systems in Volta–Congo', *African Languages and Cultures*, 8, 2, December, 109–121.
- Dimmendaal, Gerrit (2008). "Language Ecology and Linguistic Diversity on the African Continent". *Language and Linguistics Compass*. **2** (5): 840–858. doi: 10.1111/j.1749-818X.2008.00085.x[829]

- Greenberg, Joseph H. (1963) *The Languages of Africa*. Indiana University Press.
- Gregersen, Edgar A. (1972) 'Kongo-Saharan'. *Journal of African Languages*, 4, 46–56.
- Nurse, D., Rose, S. & Hewson, J. (2016) Tense and Aspect in Niger-Congo[830], Documents on Social Sciences and Humanities, Royal Museum for Central Africa
- Olson, Kenneth S. (2006) 'On Niger–Congo classification'. In *The Bill question*, ed. H. Aronson, D. Dyer, V. Friedman, D. Hristova and J. Sadock, 153–190. Bloomington, IN: Slavica.
- Saout, J. le (1973) 'Languages sans consonnes nasales', *Annales de l Université d'Abidjan*, H, 6, 1, 179–205.
- Stewart, John M. (1976) *Towards Volta–Congo reconstruction: a comparative study of some languages of Black-Africa*. (Inaugural speech, Leiden University) Leiden: Universitaire Pers Leiden.
- Stewart, John M. (2002) 'The potential of Proto-Potou-Akanic-Bantu as a pilot Proto-Niger–Congo, and the reconstructions updated', in *Journal of African Languages and Linguistics*, 23, 197–224.
- Williamson, Kay (1989) 'Niger–Congo overview', in Bendor-Samuel & Hartell (eds.) *The Niger–Congo Languages*, 3–45.
- Williamson, Kay & Blench, Roger (2000) 'Niger–Congo', in Heine, Bernd and Nurse, Derek (eds) *African Languages – An Introduction*. Cambridge: Cambridge University Press, pp. 11–42.

External links

- An Evaluation of Niger–Congo Classification[831], Kenneth Olson
- Tense and Aspect in Niger-Congo[830], Derek Nurse, Sarah Rose & John Hewson

Circumpolar peoples

Circumpolar peoples and **Arctic peoples** are umbrella terms for the various indigenous peoples of the Arctic.

Prehistory

The earliest inhabitants of North America's central and eastern Arctic are referred to as the Arctic small tool tradition (AST) and existed c. 2500 BC. AST consisted of several Paleo-Eskimo cultures, including the Independence cultures and Pre-Dorset culture.[832] The Dorset culture (Inuktitut: *Tuniit* or *Tunit*) refers to the next inhabitants of central and eastern Arctic. The Dorset culture evolved because of technological and economic changes during the period of 1050–550 BC. With the exception of the Quebec/Labrador peninsula, the Dorset culture vanished around 1500 AD.[833]

Dorset/Thule culture transition dates around the 9th–10th centuries. Scientists theorize that there may have been cross-contact of the two cultures with sharing of technology, such as fashioning harpoon heads, or the Thule may have found Dorset remnants and adapted their ways with the predecessor culture.[834] Others believe the Thule displaced the Dorset.

Historical and contemporary peoples

By 1300, the Inuit, present-day Arctic inhabitants and descendants of Thule culture, had settled in west Greenland, and moved into east Greenland over the following century. Over time, the Inuit have migrated throughout the Arctic regions of Canada, Greenland, Russia and the United States.

Other Circumpolar North indigenous peoples include the Chukchi, Evenks, Inupiat, Khanty, Koryaks, Nenets, Sami, Yukaghir, and Yupik, who still refer to themselves as Eskimo which means "snowshoe netters", not "raw meat eaters" as it is sometimes mistakenly translated.

List of peoples by ethnolinguistic grouping

- Ancient Beringian - Siberia and Alaska
- Chukotko-Kamchatkan
  - Koryaks, Siberia (Kamchatka Krai), Russia
  - Chukchi, Siberia (Chukotka Autonomous Okrug), Russia
- Tungusic
  - Evenks, China (Inner Mongolia and Heilongjiang), Mongolia, Russia
  - Evens, Siberia (Magadan Oblast, Kamchatka Krai and Sakha), Russia

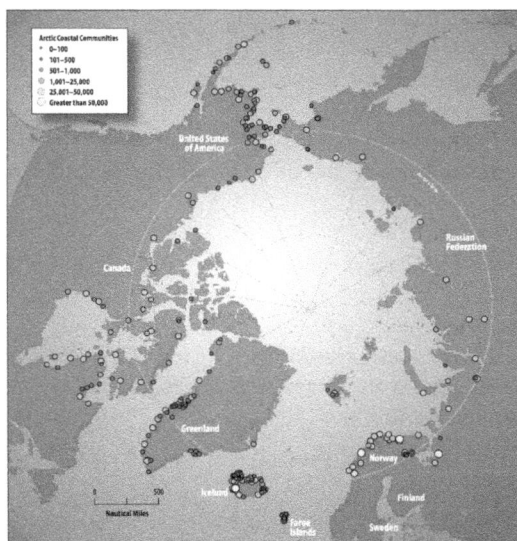

Figure 222: *Circumpolar coastal human population distribution ca. Hi 2009 (includes both indigenous and non-indigenous)*

- Turkic
  - Northeast Turkic
    - Dolgans, Siberia (Krasnoyarsk Krai), Russia
    - Yakuts, Siberia (Sakha), Russia
- Aleut
  - Yupik: Alaska and the Russian Far East (Chukotka Autonomous
    Okrug)
    - Alutiiq, Alaska
    - Central Alaskan Yup'ik, Alaska
      - Cupik, Alaska
    - Siberian Yupik, Siberia (Chukotka Autonomous Okrug), Russia
  - Inuit: Greenland, Northern Canada (Nunavut, Nunavik, Nunatsiavut,
    Northwest Territories (Inuvik Region) and Yukon), Alaska, United
    States
    - Kalaallit, Greenland
    - Iñupiat: Northwest Arctic and North Slope boroughs and the
      Bering Straits, Alaska, United States
  - Aleut: Aleutian Islands, Alaska, United States and Kamchatka Krai,
    Russia
- Uralic

- Ugric peoples, Yugra, Siberia, Russia
  - Khanty, Yugra, Siberia, Russia
  - Mansi, Yugra, Siberia, Russia
- Permian
  - Komi, Russia (Komi Republic and Perm Krai)
- Sami: Northern Norway, Sweden, Finland, Russia (Murmansk Oblast)
- Finnic
  - Finns, Finland
  - Karelians, Finland and Russia
- Samoyedic
  - Nenets, Russia
  - Enets, Siberia (Krasnoyarsk Krai), Russia
  - Nganasan, Siberia (Krasnoyarsk Krai), Russia
  - Selkup, Siberia, Russia
- Yukaghirs, East Siberia, Russia
- Indo-European
  - Germanic
    - North Germanic
      - Icelanders, Iceland
      - Norwegians, Norway
  - Slavic
    - East Slavic
      - Russians, Russia

References

- Takashi Irimoto, Takako Yamada (eds.) Circumpolar Religion and Ecology: An Anthropology of the North, University of Tokyo Press, 1994, ISBN 9780860085157.

Appendix

References

[1] The phrase *Out of Africa* used on its own generally refers to Out of Africa II, the expansion of anatomically modern humans into Eurasia.

[2] In a 2015 phylogenetic study, *H. floresiensis* was placed with *Australopithecus sediba*, *Homo habilis* and Dmanisi Man, raising the possibility that the ancestors of *Homo floresiensis* left Africa before the appearance of *Homo erectus*, possibly even becoming the first hominins to do so and evolved further in Asia.

[3] 1.85-1.78 Ma 95% CI.

[4] William H. Kimbel, Brian Villmoare, "From Australopithecus to Homo: the transition that wasn't" http://rstb.royalsocietypublishing.org/content/371/1698/20150248, *Philosophical Transactions of the Royal Society B*, 13 June 2016, DOI: 10.1098/rstb.2015.0248.

[5] Chauhan, P. R. (2009). "Early Homo Occupation Near the Gate of Tears: Examining the Paleoanthropological Records of Djibouti and Yemen", in: E. Hover and D.R. Braun (Eds.) *Interdisciplinary Approaches to the Oldowan*, Springer Netherlands, 49–59.

[6] Alimen, H. (1975). "Les 'Isthmes' hispano-marocain et Sicilo-Tunisien aux temps Acheuléens". *L'Anthropologie*, 79, 399–436.

[7] Bianchini, G. (1973). "Gli 'hacheraux' nei giacimenti paleolitici della Sicilia sud occidentale". *Proceedings of the XV Scientific Meeting of the Italian Institute of Prehistory and Protohistory*, 11–25 October 1972.

[8] Traill, L. (2010). Minimum viable population size. Retrieved from http://www.eoearth.org/view/article/154633

[9] Lewis, M. E., & Werdelin, L. (2007). "Patterns of change in the Plio-Pleistocene carnivorans of eastern Africa: Implications for hominin Evolution". In R. Bobe, Z. Alemseged, & A. K. Behrensmeyer (Eds.), *Hominin environments in the East African Pliocene: An assessment of the faunal evidence*. Springer, 77–106.

[10] Shipman, P. A. T. (1984). Hunting in Early Hominids: Theoretical Framework and Tests, 27–43.

[11] Lewis, M.E., Werdelin, L. (2010). "Carnivoran Dispersal Out of Africa During the Early Pleistocene: Relevance for Hominins?". In: A. Baden et al. (Eds.), *Out of Africa I: The First Hominin Colonization of Eurasia*. Springer Netherlands, pp. 13-26.

[12] Goodall, J., (1986). *The Chimpanzees of Gombe: Patterns of Behavior*. Belknap Press of Harvard University Press, Cambridge, MA.

[13] exhibit in LWL-Museum für Archäologie, Herne, Germany (2007 photograph). Reconstruction by W. Schnaubelt & N. Kieser (Atelier WILD LIFE ART); see *Westfalen in der Alt- und Mittelsteinzeit*, Landschaftsverband Westfalen-Lippe, Münster (2013), fig. 42.

[14] Klein, R. G. (1999). *The human career: Human biological and human origins*, (2nd ed.). Chicago: Chicago University Press. 249-250.

[15] Reconstruction by W. Schnaubelt & N. Kieser (Atelier WILD LIFE ART), 2006, Westfälisches Museum für Archäologie, Herne, Germany.

[16] Bruner, E. (2003). "Fossil traces of the human thought: paleoneurology and the evolution of the genus *Homo*". Rivista di Antropologia [*Journal of Anthropological Sciences*], 81, 29–56.

[17] Falk, D. (1988). "Enlarged occipital/marginal sinuses and emissary foramina: Their significance in hominid evolution". In: *The evolutionary history of the "robust" australopithecines* (eds. F. Grine. Aldine).

[18] Holloway, R. L., Sherwood, C. C., Hof, P. R., & Rilling, J. K. (2009). "Evolution of the Brain in Humans – Paleoneurology". In *Encyclopedia of Neuroscience*, 1326-1338.

[19] Aiello, L.C., Wheeler, P., 1995. "Expensive-tissue hypothesis: the brain and digestive system in human and primate evolution". *Current Anthropology* 36, 199}221.

[20] //doi.org/10.1146/annurev.anthro.33.070203.144024

[21] //doi.org/10.3998/jar.0521004.0064.202

[22] //www.jstor.org/stable/20371223

[23] //doi.org/10.1007/978-90-481-9036-2_8

[24] //doi.org/10.1007/978-90-481-9036-2_15

[25] https://books.google.com/books?id=coFA6_r4PTUC

[26] //doi.org/10.1007/978-90-481-9036-2_7

[27] based on numerous fossil remains of *H. erectus*. Museum of Prehistory Tautavel, France (2008 photograph)

[28] Reconstruction by John Gurche (2010), Smithsonian Museum of Natural History, based on KNM ER 3733 and 992. Abigail Tucker, " A Closer Look at Evolutionary Faces http://www.smithsonianmag.com/science-nature/A-Closer-Look-at-Evolutionary-Faces.html?c=y&page=2&navigation=next#IMAGES", Smithsonian.com, 25 February 2010.

[29] Reconstruction by W. Schnaubelt & N. Kieser (Atelier WILD LIFE ART), 2006, Westfälisches Museum für Archäologie, Herne, Germany.

[30] *H. erectus* may have appeared some 2 million years ago. Fossils dated to as much as 1.8 million years ago have been found both in Africa and in Southeast Asia, and the oldest fossils by a narrow margin (1.85 to 1.77 million years ago) were found in the Caucasus, so that it is unclear whether *H. erectus* emerged in Africa and migrated to Eurasia, or if, conversely, it evolved in Eurasia and migrated back to Africa.

[31] Klein, R. (1999). *The Human Career: Human Biological and Cultural Origins*. Chicago: University of Chicago Press, .

[32]

[33] Skull suggests three early human species were one : Nature News & Comment http://www.nature.com/news/skull-suggests-three-early-human-species-were-one-1.13972

[34] Swisher, Curtis & Lewin 2000, p. 70.

[35] from *sino*-, a combining form of the Greek Σίνα "China", and the Latinate *pekinensis*, "of Peking"

[36] "A partial maxilla assigned to H. habilis reliably demonstrates that this species survived until later than previously recognized, making an anagenetic relationship with H. erectus unlikely. [...] these two early taxa were living broadly sympatrically in the same lake basin for almost half a million years."

[37] "A partial maxilla assigned to H. habilis reliably demonstrates that this species survived until later than previously recognized, making an anagenetic relationship with H. erectus unlikely"

[38] (Servant 1983, pp. 462-464).

[39]

[40]

[41] Toth, Nicholas; Schick, Kathy (2007). In Henke, H.C. Winfried; Hardt, Thorolf; Tatersall, Ian. *Handbook of Paleoanthropology*. Volume 3. Berlin; Heidelberg; New York: Springer-Verlag. p. 1944. (PRINT: ONLINE:)

[42] The Earth Institute. (2011-09-01). Humans Shaped Stone Axes 1.8 Million Years Ago, Study Says http://www.earth.columbia.edu/articles/view/2839. Columbia University. Accessed 5 January 2012.

[43] Oldest stone tool ever found in Turkey discovered https://www.sciencedaily.com/releases/2014/12/141223084139.htm by the University of Royal Holloway London and published in ScienceDaily on December 23, 2014

[44] Everett, D. L. (2017). How Language Began: The Story of Humanity's Greatest Invention. Liveright Publishing.

[45] long assumed to have lived on Java at least as late as about 50,000 years ago but re-dated in 2011 to a much older age. Finding showing human ancestor older than previously thought offers new insights into evolution http://www.terradaily.com/reports/Finding_showing_human_ancestor_older_than_previously_thought_offers_new_insights_into_evolution_999.html, 5 July 2011.

[46] In 2017, it was suggested that *H. floresiensis* is a sister species to either *H. habilis* or to a minimally *habilis-erectus-ergaster-sapiens* clade, and its line much more ancient than Homo erectus itself.

[47] Kenneth A. R. Kennedy Arun Sonakia John Chiment K. K. Verma, "Is the Narmada hominid an Indian Homo erectus?", *American Journal of Physical Anthropology* 86.4 (December 1991), 475-496, doi:10.1002/ajpa.1330860404.

[48] //www.worldcat.org/issn/0027-9358

[49] //www.worldcat.org/oclc/643483454

[50] http://www.bradshawfoundation.com/origins/homo_erectus.php

[51] http://www.archaeologyinfo.com/homoerectus.htm

[52] http://humanorigins.si.edu/evidence/human-fossils/species/homo-erectus

[53] http://news.bbc.co.uk/1/hi/sci/tech/6937476.stm

[54] http://johnhawks.net/weblog/fossils/middle/kocabas/kappelman_2007_kocabas_tuberculosis.html

[55] http://www-personal.une.edu.au/~pbrown3/palaeo.html

[56] http://atlasofhumanevolution.com/HomoErectus.asp

[57] http://humanorigins.si.edu/evidence/human-evolution-timeline-interactive

[58] http://www.dartfordarchive.org.uk/early_history/magnified/clactonian_flake_tools.html

[59] http://news.bbc.co.uk/1/hi/england/kent/3821527.stm

[60] //en.wikipedia.org/w/index.php?title=Template:Paleolithic&action=edit

[61] //en.wikipedia.org/w/index.php?title=Template:Paleolithic&action=edit

[62] Hauser, O. (1906-1907), La Micoque (Dordogne), und ihre Resultate für die Kenntnis der paläolithischen Kultur.- 1. Teil; Basel.. Technologisch bilden die Werkzeuge des Micoquien einen Übergang vom Spät-Acheuléen zum Moustérien

[63] Hauser, O. (1916), La Micoque, die Kultur einer neuen Diluvialrasse. Leipzig.

[64] Hauser, O. (1916), Über eine neue Chronologie des mittleren Paläolithikums im Vézèretal. Dissertation Erlangen. Leipzig.

[65] Rolland, N. (1986), Recent Findings from La Micoque and other Sites in South-Western and Mediterranean France: Their Bearing on the "Tayacian" Problem and Middle Palaeolithic Emergence.- In: Bailey and Callow (Ed.): Stone Age Prehistory. Studies in Memory of Charles McBurney; Cambridge University Press; Cambridge; 121-151.

[66] Rosendahl, G. (1999), La Micoque und das Micoquien in den altsteinzeitlichen Sammlungen des Reiss-Museums Mannheim.- Mannh. Geschichtsblätter N. F. 6; Ubstadt-Weiher; 315-351

[67] Jöris, O. (2004), Zur chronostratigraphischen Stellung der spätmittelpaläolithischen Keilmessergruppen. Der Versuch einer kulturgeographischen Abgrenzung einer mittelpaläolithischen Formengruppe und ihr europäischer Kontext. 84. Ber. Röm.-German. Komm.

[68] http://blumammu.emhosting.de/infos/steinzeit.php

[69] https://web.archive.org/web/20110718230915/http://deposit.ddb.de/cgi-bin/dokserv?idn=973876069

[70] "The designation sub-Saharan Africa is commonly used to indicate all of Africa except northern Africa, with the Sudan included in sub-Saharan Africa."

[71] League of Arab States http://www.lasportal.org/ar/aboutlas/Pages/CountryData.aspx
Halim Barakat, *The Arab World: Society, Culture, and State*, (University of California Press: 1993), p. 80 https://books.google.com/books?id=kLCR9zGH774C&pg=PA80
Khair El-Din Haseeb et al., *The Future of the Arab Nation: Challenges and Options*, 1 edition (Routledge: 1991), p. 54
John Markakis, *Resource conflict in the Horn of Africa*, (Sage: 1998), p. 39
Hagai Erlikh, The struggle over Eritrea, 1962–1978: war and revolution in the Horn of Africa, (Hoover Institution Press: 1983), p. 59
Randall Fegley, *Eritrea*, (Clio Press: 1995), p. mxxxviii
Michael Frishkopf, *Music and Media in the Arab World*, (American University in Cairo Press: 2010), p. 61 https://books.google.com/books?id=KANOAYzkhA8C&

[72] "Sahara's Abrupt Desertification Started by Changes in Earth's Orbit, Accelerated by Atmospheric and Vegetation Feedbacks" https://www.sciencedaily.com/releases/1999/07/990712080500.htm, Science Daily.

[73] Nehemia Levtzion, Randall Lee Pouwels, The History of Islam in Africa, (Ohio University Press, 2000), p. 255.

[74] Sven Rubenson, The survival of Ethiopian independence, (Tsehai, 2003), p. 30.

[75] Jonah Blank, Mullahs on the mainframe: Islam and modernity among the Daudi Bohras, (University of Chicago Press, 2001), p. 163.

[76] F.R.C. Bagley et al., *The Last Great Muslim Empires*, (Brill: 1997), p. 174

[77] Bethwell A. Ogot, *Zamani: A Survey of East African History*, (East African Publishing House: 1974), p. 104

[78] James Hastings, *Encyclopedia of Religion and Ethics Part 12: V. 12*, (Kessinger Publishing, LLC: 2003), p. 490

[79] Shillington, Kevin(2005). History of Africa, Rev. 2nd Ed. New York: Palgrave Macmillan, p. 2, .

[80] Shillington, Kevin(2005). History of Africa, Rev. 2nd Ed. New York: Palgrave Macmillan, pp. 2–3, .

[81] Shillington, Kevin(2005). History of Africa, Rev. 2nd Ed. New York: Palgrave Macmillan, p. 3, .

[82] The genetic studies by Luca Cavalli-Sforza are considered pioneering in tracing the spread of modern humans from Africa.

[83] Stearns, Peter N. (2001) *The Encyclopedia of World History*, Houghton Mifflin Books. p. 16.

[84] Collins, Robert O. and Burns, James. M(2007). A History of Sub-saharan Africa. Cambridge: Cambridge University Press, p. 62,

[85] Davidson, Basil. Africa History, Themes and Outlines, revised and expanded edition. New York: Simon & Schuster, p. 54, .

[86] Shillington, Kevin(2005). History of Africa, Rev. 2nd Ed. New York: Palgrave Macmillan, p. 47, .

[87] McEvedy, Colin (1980) *Atlas of African History*, p. 44.

[88] , citing Magnavita 2004; Magnavita et al. 2004, 2006; Magnavita and Schleifer 2004.

[89] Peter Mitchell et al., The Oxford Handbook of African Archeology (2013), p. 855: "The relatively recent discovery of extensive walled settlements at the transition from the Neolithic to the Early Iron Age in the Chad Basin (Magnavita et al., 2006) indicates what enormous sites and processes may still await recognition."

[90] Appiah & Gates 2010, p. 254.

[91] Shillington, Kevin(2005). History of Africa, Rev. 2nd Ed. New York: Palgrave Macmillan, pp. 138–39, 142, .

[92] Oman in history By Peter Vine Page 324

[93] Shaping of Somali society Lee Cassanelli pg.92

[94] Futuh Al Habash Shibab ad Din

[95] Sudan Notes and Records – 147

[96] M. Martin, Phyllis and O'Meara, Patrick (1995). Africa 3rd edition, Bloomington and Indianapolis: Indiana University Press, p. 156, .

[97] Hua Liu, et al. A Geographically Explicit Genetic Model of Worldwide Human-Settlement History https://dx.doi.org/10.1086/505436. The American Journal of Human Genetics, volume 79 (2006), pp. 230–37,

[98] Daniel Don Nanjira, African Foreign Policy and Diplomacy: From Antiquity to the 21st Century, ABC-CLIO, 2010, p. 114

[99] Casson, Lionel (1989). The Periplus Maris Erythraei. Lionel Casson. (Translation by H. Frisk, 1927, with updates and improvements and detailed notes). Princeton, Princeton University Press.

[100] Chami, F. A. (1999). "The Early Iron Age on Mafia island and its relationship with the mainland." Azania Vol. XXXIV 1999, pp. 1–10.

[101] Chami, Felix A. 2002. "The Egypto-Graeco-Romans and Paanchea/Azania: sailing in the Erythraean Sea." From: Red Sea Trade and Travel. The British Museum. Sunday 6 October 2002. Organised by The Society for Arabian Studies

[102] Miller, J. Innes. 1969. Chapter 8: "The Cinnamon Route". In: The Spice Trade of the Roman Empire. Oxford: University Press.

[103] books.google.com/books?id=Ua_tAAAAMAAJ

[104] Hill, John E. 2004. Draft annotated English translation. See especially Section 15 on *Zesan* = Azania and notes.

[105] Roland Oliver, et al. "Africa South of the Equator," in Africa Since 1800. Cambridge, UK: Cambridge University Press, 2005, pp. 24–25.

[106] Mokhtar (editor), AnciGent Civilizations of Africa Vo. II, General History of Africa, UNESCO, 1990

[107] Davidson, Basil. Africa History, Themes and Outlines, revised and expanded edition. New York: Simon & Schuster, pp. 87–107, .

[108] According to the CIA Factbook http://www.umsl.edu/services/govdocs/wofact2008/index. html: Angola, Benin, Burundi, Burkina Faso, the Central African Republic, Cameroon, Chad, the Republic of Congo, the Democratic Republic of Congo, Djibouti, Equatorial Guinea, Eritrea, Ethiopia, Gabon, the Gambia, Ghana, Guinea, Guinea-Bissau, Kenya, Liberia, Madagascar, Malawi, Mali, Mauritania, Mozambique, Namibia, Nigeria, Rwanda, Senegal, Sierra Leone, Somalia, Sudan, Swaziland, Tanzania, Togo, Uganda, and Zambia

[109] (2009). Africa Development Indicators 2008/2009: From the World Bank Africa Database African Development Indicators. World Bank Publications, p. 28, .

[110] http://www.transparency.org/policy_research/surveys_indices/cpi/2009/cpi_2009_table

[111] http://www.doingbusiness.org/economyrankings/?direction=Asc&sort=2

[112] World Bank. Doing Business 2010, Economy Ranking http://www.doingbusiness.org/economyrankings/?direction=Asc&sort=2

[113] https://web.archive.org/web/20150930230930/http://en.rsf.org/press-freedom-index-2009%2C1001.html

[114] Bowden, Rob (2007). Africa South of the Sahara. Coughlan Publishing: p. 37, .

[115] Brown, Keith and Ogilvie, Sarah(2008). Concise encyclopedia of languages of the world Concise Encyclopedias of Language and Linguistics Series. Elsevier, p. 12, .

[116] African Languages at Michigan State University (ASC) | Michigan State University". Isp.msu.edu. 2010-10-08. Archived from the original on April 20, 2010. Retrieved 2013-04-30

[117] Peek, Philip M. and Yankah, Kwesi(2004). African folklore: an encyclopedia. London: (Rourledge)Taylor & Francis, p. 205, , 9780415939331

[118] Schneider, Edgar Werner and Kortmann, Bernd(2004). A handbook of varieties of English: a multimedia reference tool, Volume 1. Berlin: Walter de Gruyter, pp. 867–68, .

[119] Güldemann, Tom and Edward D. Elderkin (forthcoming) "On external genealogical relationships of the Khoe family". http://email.eva.mpg.de/~gueldema/pdf/Gueldemann_Elderkin.pdf In Brenzinger, Matthias and Christa König (eds.), Khoisan languages and linguistics: the Rieslern symposium 2003. Quellen zur Khoisan-Forschung 17. Köln: Rüdiger Köppe.

[120] Bellwood, Peter S.(2005). First farmers: the origins of agricultural societies. Wiley-Blackwell, p. 218, .

[121] "DRC" https://www.cia.gov/library/publications/the-world-factbook/geos/cg.html. CIA World Factbook. Retrieved 16 November 2014.

[122] "Rwanda" https://www.cia.gov/library/publications/the-world-factbook/geos/rw.html. CIA World Factbook. Retrieved 13 November 2014.

[123] "Angola" https://www.cia.gov/library/publications/the-world-factbook/geos/ao.html. CIA World Factbook. Retrieved 18 November 2014.

[124] "Republic of the Congo" https://www.cia.gov/library/publications/the-world-factbook/geos/cf. html. CIA World Factbook. Retrieved 18 November 2014.

[125] "Burundi" https://www.cia.gov/library/publications/the-world-factbook/geos/by.html. CIA World Factbook. Retrieved 13 November 2014.

[126] Darfur Relief and Documentation Centre (2010). 5th Population and Housing Census in Sudan – An Incomplete Exercise http://southsudaninfo.net/wp-content/uploads/reference_library/reports/5th_population_housing_census_sudan.pdf . Geneva: DRDC. Retrieved 16 November 2014.

[127] "The Zaghawa is one of the major divisions of the Beri peoples who live in western Sudan and eastern Chad, and their language, also called Zaghawa, belongs to the Saharan branch of the Nilo-Saharan language group."

[128] "Sudan" https://www.cia.gov/library/publications/the-world-factbook/geos/su.html. CIA World Factbook. Retrieved 20 November 2014.

[129] "Eritrea" https://www.cia.gov/library/publications/the-world-factbook/geos/er.html. CIA World Factbook. Retrieved 20 November 2014.

[130] "Somalia" https://www.cia.gov/library/publications/the-world-factbook/geos/so.html. CIA World Factbook. Retrieved 20 November 2014.

[131] Ethnologue http://www.ethnologue.com/show_language.asp?code=mlg, most of them are native speakers

[132] "Central African Republic" https://www.cia.gov/library/publications/the-world-factbook/geos/ct.html. CIA World Factbook. Retrieved 13 November 2014.

[133] "South Sudan" https://www.cia.gov/library/publications/the-world-factbook/geos/od.html. CIA World Factbook. Retrieved 13 November 2014.

[134] "Nigeria" https://www.cia.gov/library/publications/the-world-factbook/geos/ni.html. CIA World Factbook. Retrieved 13 November 2014.

[135] "Niger" https://www.cia.gov/library/publications/the-world-factbook/geos/ng.html. CIA World Factbook. Retrieved 13 November 2014.

[136] "Chad" https://www.cia.gov/library/publications/the-world-factbook/geos/cd.html . CIA World Factbook. Retrieved 16 November 2014.

[137]

[138]

[139] "South Africa" https://www.cia.gov/library/publications/the-world-factbook/geos/sf.html. CIA World Factbook. Retrieved 16 November 2014.

[140] "Botswana" https://www.cia.gov/library/publications/the-world-factbook/geos/bc.html. CIA World Factbook. 20 November 2014.

[141] "Malawi" https://www.cia.gov/library/publications/the-world-factbook/geos/mi.html. CIA World Factbook. Retrieved 16 November 2014.

[142] "Zambia" https://www.cia.gov/library/publications/the-world-factbook/geos/za.html. CIA World Factbook. 20 November 2014.

[143] "Mozambique" https://www.cia.gov/library/publications/the-world-factbook/geos/mz.html. CIA World Factbook. 20 November 2014.

[144] "Senegal" https://www.cia.gov/library/publications/the-world-factbook/geos/sg.html. CIA World Factbook. Retrieved 20 November 2014.

[145] "The Gambia" https://www.cia.gov/library/publications/the-world-factbook/geos/ga.html. CIA World Factbook. Retrieved 20 November 2014.

[146] "Cameroon" https://www.cia.gov/library/publications/the-world-factbook/geos/cm.html. CIA World Factbook. Retrieved 20 November 2014.

[147] "Mali" https://www.cia.gov/library/publications/the-world-factbook/geos/ml.html. CIA World Factbook. Retrieved 20 November 2014.

[148] P. Skoglund et al., "Reconstructing Prehistoric African Population Structure", PlumX Metrics, *Cell* Volume 171, Issue 1, p59–71.e21, 21 September 2017 doi:10.1016/j.cell.2017.08.049 https://doi.org/10.1016/j.cell.2017.08.049

[149] https://www.cia.gov/library/publications/the-world-factbook/rankorder/2173rank.html

[150] //en.wikipedia.org/w/index.php?title=Sub-Saharan_Africa&action=edit

[151] RedOrbit.com http://www.redorbit.com/news/science/441990/nuclear_vs_solar_energy_ which Redorbit

[152] Flatow, Ira. Could Africa Leapfrog The U.S. In Solar Power? http://www.sciencefriday.com/blog/index.php?/archives/306-Could-Africa-Leapfrog-The-U.S.-In-Solar-Power.html. Science Friday 6 June 2008.

[153] English, Cynthia. *Radio the Chief Medium for News in Sub-Saharan Africa* http://www.gallup.com/poll/108235/radio-chief-medium-news-subsaharan-africa.aspx. Gallup 23 June 2008.

[154] *Africa Calling: Cellphone usage sees record rise* http://www.mg.co.za/article/2009-10-23-africa-calling-cellphone-usage-sees-record-rise. Mail&Guardian: 23 October 2009.

[155] Aker, Jenny C.(2008). "Can You Hear Me Now?"How Cell Phones are Transforming Markets in Sub-Saharan Africa http://www.cgdev.org/files/894409_file_Aker_Cell_Phone_Niger.pdf, Center for Global Development.

[156] Pfanner, Eric. *Competition increases for pay TV in sub-Saharan Africa* https://www.nytimes.com/2007/08/06/technology/06iht-web-africa.6996947.html. New York Times 6 August 2007.

[157]

[158] John J. Saul and Colin Leys, Sub-Saharan Africa in Global Capitalism http://monthlyreview. org/1999/07/01/sub-saharan-africa-in-global-capitalism, *Monthly Review*, 1999, Volume 51, Issue 03 (July–August)

[159] Ken Gwilliam, Vivien Foster, Rodrigo Archondo-Callao, Cecilia Briceño-Garmendia, Alberto Nogales, and Kavita Sethi(2008). Africa infrastructure country diagnostic, Roads in Sub-Saharan Africa http://www.eu-africa-infrastructure-tf.net/attachments/library/aicd-background-paper-14-roads-sect-summary-en.pdf. World Bank and the SSATP: p. 4

[160] Ghazvinian, John (2008). Untapped: The Scramble for Africa's Oil. Houghton Mifflin Harcourt, pp. 1–16, .

[161] Christopher Ehret, (2002). The Civilization of Africa. University of Virginia Press: Charlottesville, p. 98, .

[162] Vandaveer, Chelsie(2006). What was the cotton of Kush? http://www.killerplants.com/plants-that-changed-history/20020226.asp KillerPlants.com, Plants That Change History Archive.

[163] National Research Council (U.S.). Board on Science and Technology for International Development (1996). Lost Crops of Africa: Grains. National Academy Press, .

[164] Business24-7.ae http://www.business24-7.ae/Articles/2009/11/Pages/10112009/11112009_0b22e598b6e14c18b1223669d7c778e7.aspx

[165] Agence Française de Développement, Agence universitaire de la Francophonie, Orange, & UNESCO. (2015). Digital Services for Education in Africa. *Savoirs communs, 17.* http://unesdoc.unesco.org/images/0023/002318/231867e.pdf

[166] UNESCO. (2012). *Education for All Global Monitoring Report 2012 – Youth and Skills: Putting Education to Work.* Luxembourg: UNESCO Publications. http://unesdoc.unesco. org/images/0021/002180/218003e.pdf

[167] UNESCO. (2012). *Education for All Global Monitoring Report 2012 – Youth and Skills: Putting Education to Work.* Luxembourg: UNESCO Publications. http://unesdoc.unesco. org/images/0021/002180/218003e.pdf

[168] Agence Française de Développement, Agence universitaire de la Francophonie, Orange, & UNESCO. (2015). Digital Services for Education in Africa. *Savoirs communs, 17.* http://unesdoc.unesco.org/images/0023/002318/231867e.pdf

[169] Emma Bonino, "A brutal custom: Join forces to banish the mutilation of women" https: //www.nytimes.com/2004/09/15/opinion/15iht-edbonino_ed3_.html, *The New York Times*, 15 September 2004; Charlotte Feldman-Jacobs, "Commemorating International Day of Zero Tolerance to Female Genital Mutilation" http://www.prb.org/Articles/2009/fgmc.aspx , Population Reference Bureau, February 2009.

[170] Encyclopædia Britannica. Britannica Book of the Year 2003. Encyclopædia Britannica, (2003) p. 306
However, Southern Africa is predominantly Christian. According to the Encyclopædia Britannica, as of mid-2002, there were 376,453,000 Christians, 329,869,000 Muslims and 98,734,000 people who practiced traditional religions in Africa. Ian S. Markham,(A World Religions Reader. Cambridge, MA: Blackwell Publishers, 1996.) http://www.greenwoodsvillage.com/gor/islam.htm is cited by Morehouse University as giving the mid-1990s figure of 278,250,800 Muslims in Africa, but still as 40.8% of the total. These numbers are estimates and remain a matter of conjecture. See Amadu Jacky Kaba. The spread of Christianity and Islam in Africa: a survey and analysis of the numbers and percentages of Christians, Muslims and those who practice indigenous religions. The Western Journal of Black Studies, Vol 29, Number 2, June 2005. Discusses the estimations of various almanacs and encyclopedium, placing Britannica's estimate as the most agreed figure. Notes the figure presented at the World Christian Encyclopedia, summarised here http://www.afrikaworld.net/afrel/Statistics.htm, as being an outlier. On rates of growth, Islam and Pentecostal Christianity are highest, see: The List: The World's Fastest-Growing Religions https://foreignpolicy.com/story/cms.php?story_id=3835, Foreign Policy, May 2007.

[171] Baldick, Julian (1997). Black God: the Afroasiatic roots of the Jewish, Christian, and Muslim religions https//books.google.com. Syracuse University Press:

[172] Christopher Ehret, (2002). The Civilizations of Africa. Charlottesville: University of Virginia, pp. 102–03, .

[173] Davidson, Basil (1969). The African Genius, An Introduction to African Social and Cultural History. Little Brown and Company: Boston, pp. 168–80.

[174] Eglash, Ron: "African Fractals: Modern computing and indigenous design." Rutgers 1999

[175] Bowden, Rob(2007). Africa South of the Sahara. Coughlan Publishing: p. 40, .

[176] Christopher Ehret, (2002). The Civilizations of Africa. Charlottesville: University of Virginia, p. 103, .

[177] http://www.metmuseum.org/toah/hd/aima/hd_aima.htm

[178] Alexandre, Marc(1998). World Bank Publication: DC.

[179] http://www.hamillgallery.com/SITE/Textiles.html

[180] Yoshida, Reiko. *Proclamation 2005: Barcloth making in Uganda* http://www.unesco.org/culture/ich/index.php?cp=UG&topic=mp Unesco: Intangible Cultural Heritage (Uganda) 13 May 2009

[181] http://www.metmuseum.org/toah/ho/11/sfc/ho_1999.522.15.htm

[182]

As can be seen: 800m is Kenya; 5000m is Ethiopia; 10000m is Ethiopia; marathon is Kenya. The two exceptions are the 1500m and 3000m steeplechase records, though the latter is held by Stephen Cherono, who was born and raised in Kenya.

[183] Tucker, Ross and Dugas, Jonathan. *Sport's great rivalries: Kenya vs. Ethiopia, and a one-sided battle (at least on the track)* http://www.sportsscientists.com/2008/07/kenya-vs-ethiopia.html, The Science of Sport, 14 July 2008.

[184] Towson.edu http://pages.towson.edu/thompson/Courses/Regional/Reference/SSA.Physical.pdf

[185] Transparency.org http://www.transparency.org/regional_pages/africa_middle_east/sub-saharan_africa

[186] https://creativecommons.org/licenses/by-sa/3.0/igo/

[187] http://unesdoc.unesco.org/images/0023/002318/231867e.pdf

[188] https://purl.fdlp.gov/GPO/gpo35755

[189] http://www.africanpeople.info

[190] http//web.worldbank.org

[191] http://www.bbc.co.uk/worldservice/africa/features/storyofafrica/index.shtml

[192] From 1984 to 2003, an alternative scientific hypothesis was the multiregional origin of modern humans, which envisioned a wave of *Homo sapiens* migrating earlier from Africa and interbreeding with local *Homo erectus* populations in varied regions of the globe.Robert Jurmain; Lynn Kilgore; Wenda Trevathan (20 March 2008). *Essentials of Physical Anthropology* https://books.google.com/books?id=TSaSPza9LMYC&pg=PA266. Cengage Learning. pp. 266–. ISBN 978-0-495-50939-4. Retrieved 14 June 2011.

[193] .

See also *Modern humans in China* ∼*80,000 years ago (?)* http://dienekes.blogspot.nl/2015/10/modern-humans-in-china-80000-years-ago.html, Dieneks' Anthropology Blog.

[194] McChesney: "...genetic evidence suggests that a small band with the marker M168 migrated out of Africa along the coasts of the Arabian Peninsula and India, through Indonesia, and reached Australia very early, between 60,000 and 50,000 years ago. This very early migration into Australia is also supported by Rasmussen et al. (2011).

[195] Young McChesney 2015.

[196] .

See also *mtDNA from 55 hunter-gatherers across 35,000 years in Europe* http://dienekes.blogspot.nl/2016/02/mtdna-from-55-hunter-gatherers-across.html, Dieneks' Anthroplogy Bog.

[197] Beyin (2011).

[198] ; see also .

[199] Appenzeller (2012).

[200] Kay Young McChesney: "Wells (2003) divided the descendants of men who left Africa into a genealogical tree with 11 lineages. Each genetic marker represents a single-point mutation (SNP) at a specific place in the genome. First, genetic evidence suggests that a small band with the marker M168 migrated out of Africa along the coasts of the Arabian Peninsula and India, through Indonesia, and reached Australia very early, between 60,000 and 50,000 years ago.

This very early migration into Australia is also supported by Rasmussen et al. (2011). Second, a group bearing the marker M89 moved out of northeastern Africa into the Middle East 45,000 years ago. From there, the M89 group split into two groups. One group that developed the marker M9 went into Asia about 40,000 years ago. The Asian (M9) group split three ways: into Central Asia (M45), 35,000 years ago; into India (M20), 30,000 years ago; and into China (M122), 10,000 years ago. The Central Asian (M45) group split into two groups: toward Europe (M173), 30,000 years ago and toward Siberia (M242), 20,000 years ago. Finally, the Siberian group (M242) went on to populate North and South America (M3), about 10,000 years ago.<ref name="FOOTNOTEYoung McChesney2015">Young McChesney 2015.

[201] The researchers used radiocarbon dating techniques on pollen grains trapped in lake-bottom mud to establish vegetation over the ages of the Malawi lake in Africa, taking samples at 300-year-intervals. Samples from the megadrought times had little pollen or charcoal, suggesting sparse vegetation with little to burn. The area around Lake Malawi, today heavily forested, was a desert approximately 135,000 to 90,000 years ago.<ref name="U of AZ">

[202] Finlayson (2009), p. 68.

[203] Liu, Prugnolle et al. (2006).

[204] .

See also *Ancestors of Eastern Neandertals admixed with modern humans 100 thousand years ago* http://dienekes.blogspot.nl/2016/02/ancestors-of-eastern-neandertals.html, Dienekes'Anthropology Blog.

[205]

See also 55,000-Year-Old Skull Fossil Sheds New Light on Human Migration out of Africa http://www.sci-news.com/othersciences/anthropology/science-55000-year-old-skull-fossil-manot-cave-israel-02443.html, Science News.

[206] Groucutt et al. (2015).

[207] ; summary in Kliman (ed.), *Encyclopedia of Evolutionary Biology* (2016), p. 451 https://books.google.com/books?id=_r4OCAAAQBAJ&pg=PA451#v=onepage&q&f=false

[208] Elizabeth Matisoo-Smith, K. Ann Horsburgh, *DNA for Archaeologists*, Routledge (2016).

[209] East Asians 2.3-2.6%, Western Eurasians 1.8-2.4% ()

[210]

Stringer, C. B. (1992). "Replacement, continuity and the origin of Homo sapiens". In: *Continuity or replacement? Controversies in Homo sapiens evolution.* F. H. Smith (ed). Rotterdam: Balkema. pp. 9–24.

Bräuer, G.; Stringer, C. (1997). "Models, polarization, and perspectives on modern human origins". In: *Conceptual issues in modern human origins research.* New York: Aldine de Gruyter. pp. 191–201.

[211] Liu Wu in Zhisheng, Weijian Zhou (eds.), *Quaternary Geology* VSP (1997), p. 24 https://books.google.com/books?id=QZym919tNigC&pg=PA24.

[212] "evidence that our species arose in Africa about 150 000 years before present (YBP), migrated out of Africa into Asia about 60 000 to 70 000 YBP and into Europe about 40 000 to 50 000 YBP, and migrated from Asia and possibly Europe to the Americas about 20 000 to 30 000 YBP."

[213] http://www.nature.com/news/human-migrations-eastern-odyssey-1.10560

[214] //doi.org/10.4061/2011/615094

[215] //www.ncbi.nlm.nih.gov/pmc/articles/PMC378623

[216] //doi.org/10.1086/345487

[217] //www.ncbi.nlm.nih.gov/pubmed/12478481

[218] https://books.google.com/books?id=EzBV3OPb5mAC&pg=PA68

[219] //doi.org/10.1002/evan.21455

[220] //www.ncbi.nlm.nih.gov/pmc/articles/PMC1288200

[221] //doi.org/10.1086/302863

[222] //www.ncbi.nlm.nih.gov/pubmed/10733465

[223] http://adsabs.harvard.edu/abs/2015Natur.520..216H

[224] //doi.org/10.1038/nature14134

[225] //www.ncbi.nlm.nih.gov/pubmed/25629628

[226] //www.ncbi.nlm.nih.gov/pmc/articles/PMC4933530

[227] http://adsabs.harvard.edu/abs/2016Natur.530..429K

[228] //doi.org/10.1038/nature16544

[229] //www.ncbi.nlm.nih.gov/pubmed/26886800

[230] //www.ncbi.nlm.nih.gov/pmc/articles/PMC1559480

[231] //doi.org/10.1086/505436

[232] //www.ncbi.nlm.nih.gov/pubmed/16826514

[233] http://www.nature.com/doifinder/10.1038/nature15696

[234] http://adsabs.harvard.edu/abs/2015Natur.526..696L

[235] //doi.org/10.1038/nature15696

[236] //www.ncbi.nlm.nih.gov/pubmed/26466566

[237] http://adsabs.harvard.edu/abs/2005Sci...308.1034M

[238] //doi.org/10.1126/science.1109792

[239] //www.ncbi.nlm.nih.gov/pubmed/15890885

[240] https://books.google.com/books?id=WrR9OShae2wC&pg=PT148

[241] http//www.cell.com

[242] //doi.org/10.1016/j.cub.2016.01.037

[243] //www.ncbi.nlm.nih.gov/pubmed/26853362

[244] //www.ncbi.nlm.nih.gov/pmc/articles/PMC1617318

[245] //doi.org/10.1128/JVI.00441-06

[246] //www.ncbi.nlm.nih.gov/pubmed/17005670

[247] //doi.org/10.1006/jhev.2002.0601

[248] //www.ncbi.nlm.nih.gov/pubmed/12473485

[249] http://sgo.sagepub.com/content/5/4/2158244015611712

[250] //doi.org/10.1177/2158244015611712

[251] http://www.britannica.com/EBchecked/topic/275670/human-evolution

[252] http://humanorigins.si.edu/evidence/human-evolution-timeline-interactive

[253] Metspalu et al 2006, Human Mitochondrial DNA and the Evolution of Homo sapiens. http://www.springerlink.com/content/h007402m82331750/

[254] Searching for traces of the Southern Dispersal http://www.human-evol.cam.ac.uk/Projects/sdispersal/sdispersal.htm , by Dr Marta Mirazón Lahr, et al.

[255] //en.wikipedia.org/w/index.php?title=Template:Paleolithic&action=edit

[256] Gilman, Antonio. 1996. Explaining the Upper Palaeolithic Revolution. pp. 220–39 (Chap. 8) in Contemporary Archaeology in Theory: A Reader. Cambridge, MA: Blackwell

[257] "'Modern' Behavior Began 40,000 Years Ago In Africa" https://www.sciencedaily.com/releases/1998/07/980707073901.htm, *Science Daily*, July 1998

[258] "In North America and Eurasia the species has long been an important resource—in many areas *the* most important resource—for peoples' inhabiting the northern boreal forest and tundra regions. Known human dependence on caribou/wild reindeer has a long history, beginning in the Middle Pleistocene (Banfield 1961:170; Kurtén 1968:170) and continuing to the present....The caribou/wild reindeer is thus an animal that has been a major resource for humans throughout a tremendous geographic area and across a time span of tens of thousands of years." Ernest S. Burch, Jr. "The Caribou/Wild Reindeer as a Human Resource" https://www.jstor.org/stable/278435, *American Antiquity*, Vol. 37, No. 3 (July 1972), pp. 339–368.

[259] "No Last Word on Language Origins" http://cas.bellarmine.edu/tietjen/images/anthropology(NoLastWordOnLanguageOrigins.htm , Bellarmine University

[260] Isabel Ellender and Peter Christiansen, *People of the Merri Merri. The Wurundjeri in Colonial Days*, Merri Creek Management Committee, 2001

[261] Gary Presland, *The First Residents of Melbourne's Western Region*, (revised edition), Harriland Press, 1997. Presland says on page 1: "There is some evidence to show that people were living in the Maribyrnong River valley, near present day Keilor, about 40,000 years ago."

[262] https://www.bbc.co.uk/news/science-environment-18449711

[263] https://doi.org/10.1126%2Fscience.1219957

[264] Prehistoric Archaeological Periods in Japan http://www.t-net.ne.jp/~keally/preh.html, Charles T. Keally

[265] "Prehistoric Japan, New perspectives on insular East Asia", Keiji Imamura, University of Hawaii Press, Honolulu,

[266]. Geoffrey Blainey; A Very Short History of the World; Penguin Books; 2004;

[267] Sea level data from *main article:* Cosquer cave

[268] Lloyd, J. & Mitchinson, J.: *The Book of General Ignorance*. Faber & Faber, 2006.

[269] M. Mirazón Lahr et al., "Inter-group violence among early Holocene hunter-gatherers of West Turkana, Kenya" https://www.nature.com/nature/journal/v529/n7586/full/nature16477.html, *Nature* 529, 394–398 (21 January 2016), doi:10.1038/nature16477. "Here we report on a case of inter-group violence towards a group of hunter-gatherers from Nataruk, west of Lake Turkana [...] Ten of the twelve articulated skeletons found at Nataruk show evidence of having died violently at the edge of a lagoon, into which some of the bodies fell. The remains [...] offer a rare glimpse into the life and death of past foraging people, and evidence that warfare was part of the repertoire of inter-group relations among prehistoric hunter-gatherers.". For early depiction of interpersonal violence in rock art see: .

[270] Mulvaney, D J and White, Peter, 1987, Australians to 1788, Fairfax, Syme & Weldon, Sydney

[271] Gary Presland, *Aboriginal Melbourne: The Lost Land of the Kulin People*, Harriland Press (1985), Second edition 1994, . This book describes in some detail the archaeological evidence regarding aboriginal life, culture, food gathering and land management, particularly the period from the flooding of Bass Strait and Port Phillip from about 7–10,000 years ago, up to the European colonisation in the nineteenth century.

[272] http://www.newarchaeology.com/articles/uprevolution.php

[273] http://www.anthropark.wz.cz/aagalery.htm

[274] based on Schlebusch et al., "Southern African ancient genomes estimate modern human divergence to 350,000 to 260,000 years ago" *Science*, 28 Sep 2017, DOI: 10.1126/science.aao6266 http://science.sciencemag.org/content/early/2017/09/27/science.aao6266.full, Fig. 3 https://d2ufo47lrtsv5s.cloudfront.net/content/sci/early/2017/09/27/science.aao6266/F3.large.jpg (*H. sapiens* divergence times) and (archaic admixture).

[275] https//books.google.pl

[276] Neanderthals: Bone technique redrafts prehistory : Nature News & Comment http://www.nature.com/news/neanderthals-bone-technique-redrafts-prehistory-1.15739

[277] //en.wikipedia.org/w/index.php?title=Template:Paleolithic&action=edit

[278] https//books.google.pl

[279] Shea, J. J., 2003: Neandertals [sic], competition and the origin of modern human behaviour in the Levant, *Evolutionary Anthropology*, 12:173-187.

[280] Andrew Lock, Charles R. Peters - Handbook of human symbolic evolution - 906 pages *Oxford science publications* Wiley-Blackwell, 1999 https://books.google.com/books?id=mVj4P8DCuqIC&pg=PA243&lpg=PA243 RETRIEVED 2012-01-06

[281] University of Oslo P.O. Box 1072 - Blindern-0316 Oslo-Norway email : fa-admin@admin.uio.no. / international@mn.uio.no - Universitetet i Oslo http://www3.hf.uio.no/sarc/iakh/lithic/MOUST/mousterian.html . Retrieved 2012-01-06

[282] http://www.nature.com/nature/journal/v512/n7514/full/nature13621.html

[283] Levy, T.(Ed.).(2001). *The Archaeology of Society in the Holy Land*. London : Leicester University Press.

[284] https://www.nytimes.com/2006/09/13/science/14neanderthal.html?ex=1315800000&en=ca90a9bfe57071f2&ei=5089

[285] The early presence from 45,000 years ago is informed by the dating of the Grotta del Cavallo fossil in 2011, earlier literature also cites 40,000 or 35,000 years. The upper limit of 15,000 marks the transition to the European Mesolithic, depending on the region also given in the range of 12,000 to 10,000 years ago.
Use of "Cro-Magnon" is mostly to times after the beginning of the Aurignacian proper, c. 37 to 35 ka () Genetically, EEMH form an isolated population between 37 and 14 ka, with significant Mesolithic admixture from the Near East and Caucasus beginning around 14 ka. (Fu et al. 2016:5)

[286] Q. Fu et al., "Genome sequence of a 45,000-year-old modern human from western Siberia" *Nature* 514, 445–449 (2014). Medline doi:10.1038/nature13810.

[287] The process leading to the development of smaller and more fine-boned humans seems to have begun at least 50,000–30,000 years ago. "Recent acceleration of human adaptive evolution" John Hawks, Eric T. Wang, Gregory M. Cochran, Henry C. Harpending, and Robert K. Moyzis PNAS vol. 104 no. 52 http://www.pnas.org/content/104/52/20753.abstract

[288] Posth, Cosimo; et al. (4 July 2017). "Deeply divergent archaic mitochondrial genome provides lower time boundary for African gene flow into Neanderthals". Nature Communications. 8: 16046. doi:10.1038/ncomms16046.

[289] P. Soares et al., "The Expansion of mtDNA Haplogroup L3 within and out of Africa", *Molecular Biology and Evolution*, Volume 29, Issue 3, 1 March 2012, 915–927, 10.1093/molbev/msr245 https://doi.org/10.1093/molbev/msr245.

[290] Kuhlwilm, M.; Gronau, I.; Hubisz, M.J.; de Filippo, C.; Prado-Martinez, J.; Kircher, M.; et al. (2016). "Ancient gene flow from early modern humans into Eastern Neanderthals". Nature. 530 (7591): 429–433. Bibcode:2016Natur.530..429K. doi:10.1038/nature16544. PMC 4933530.

[291] 42.7-41.5 ka (1σ CI). Katerina Douka et al., A new chronostratigraphic framework for the Upper Palaeolithic of Riparo Mochi (Italy), *Journal of Human Evolution* 62(2), 19 December 2011, 286-299, doi:10.1016/j.jhevol.2011.11.009.

[292] Jacobi, R.M.; Higham, T.F.G.; Haesaerts, P.; Jadin, I.; Basell, L.S. (2015). "Radiocarbon chronology for the Early Gravettian of northern Europe: New AMS determinations for Maisières-Canal, Belgium". Antiquity. 84 (323): 26–40. doi:10.1017/S0003598X00099749.

[293] S. Beleza et al., "The Timing of Pigmentation Lightening in Europeans", *Molecular Biology and Evolution*, Volume 30, Issue 1, 1 January 2013, Pages 24–35, doi:10.1093/molbev/mss207 https://doi.org/10.1093/molbev/mss207. see also: E. R. Jones, "Upper Palaeolithic genomes reveal deep roots of modern Eurasians", *Nature Communications* volume 6, Article number: 8912 (2015), https://www.nature.com/articles/ncomms9912 doi:10.1038/ncomms9912].

[294] Bar-Yosef, O & Zilhão, J (eds) 2002: Towards a definition of the Aurignacian. Proceedings of the Symposium held in Lisbon, Portugal, June 25–30. *Trabalhos de Arqueologia* no 45. 381 pages. PDF http://www.bris.ac.uk/archanth/staff/zilhao/ta452006.pdf

[295] Supporting Online Material http://worldtextile.aimoo.com/

[296] T. Higham et al., +Testing models for the beginnings of the Aurignacian and the advent of figurative art and music: The radiocarbon chronology of Geißenklösterle", *Journal of Human Evolution*, 8 May 2012, doi:10.1016/j.jhevol.2012.03.003

[297] A. Seguin-Orlando et al., "Genomic structure in Europeans dating back at least 36,200 years", *Science*, 6 November 2014, DOI: 10.1126/science.aaa0114.

[298] Museum of Natural History http://www.mnh.si.edu/anthro/humanorigins/ha/cromagnon.html

[299] Keith, A. (1911): Ancient Types of Man. Harper and Brothers Read book online, (Grimaldi man covered on pages 58–63) https://archive.org/stream/ancienttypesofma00keit#page/n11/mode/2up

[300] Bisson, M.S., Tisnerat, N., & Whit, R. (1996): Radiocarbon Dates From the Upper Paleolithic of the Barma Grande. *Current Anthropology* no 37(1), pages 156- 162.

[301] Bisson, M.S. & Bolduc, P. (1994): Previously Undescribed Figurines From the Grimaldi Caves. *Current Anthropology* no 35(4), pages 458-468.

[302] Lazaridis et al., "Ancient human genomes suggest three ancestral populations for present-day Europeans", *Nature*, 513(7518), 18 September 2014, 409–413, doi: 10.1038/nature13673. Supplemental Information 14; Extended Data Figure 6: "We observe a striking contrast between Europe west of the Caucasus and the Near East in degree of relatedness to WHG. In Europe, there is a much higher degree of allele sharing with Loschbour than with MA1, which we ascribe to the 60-80% WHG/(WHG+ANE) ratio in most Europeans that we report in SI14. In contrast, the Near East has no appreciable WHG ancestry but some ANE ancestry, especially in the northern Caucasus. (Jewish populations are marked with a square in this figure to assist in interpretation as their ancestry is often anomalous for their geographic regions.)"

[303] "beginning with the Villabruna Cluster at least ~14,000 years ago, all European individuals analysed show an affinity to the Near East. This correlates in time to the Bølling-Allerød interstadial, the first significant warming period after the Glacial Maximum. Archaeologically, it correlates with cultural transitions within the Epigravettian in southern Europe and the Magdalenian-to-Azilian transition in western Europe. Thus, the appearance of the Villabruna Cluster may reflect migrations or population shifts within Europe at the end of the Ice Age, an

observation that is also consistent with the evidence of mitochondrial DNA turnover" (Fu et al. 2016:5).

[304] Lipson et al., "Parallel palaeogenomic transects reveal complex genetic history of early European farmers", 'Nature *(2017), DOI: 10.1038/nature24476.*

[305] Kostenki-14 (Russia): C1b, Goyet Q116-1 (Belgium) C1a. Fu, Qiaomei; et al. (2016). "The genetic history of Ice Age Europe". Nature. doi:10.1038/nature17993.

[306] Seguin-Orlando et al.(2014) 「 structure in Europeans dating back at least 36,200 years http://science.sciencemag.org/content/346/6213/1113ⁿGenomic」

[307] Haplogroup N was found in two Gravettian-era fossils, Paglicci 52 Paglicci 12, see Caramelli et al. (2003).

[308] E.R. Jones et al., "Upper Palaeolithic genomes reveal deep roots of modern Eurasians", *Nature Communications* volume 6, Article number: 8912 (2015), doi:10.1038/ncomms9912 http://www.nature.com/ncomms/2015/151116/ncomms9912/full/ncomms9912.html.

[309] Bahn and Vertut, 88

[310] Bahn and Vertut, 90–91

[311] Portal, p. 25

[312] Portal, p. 26

[313]

[314] Lavallée, p. 88

[315] Lavallée, p. 94

[316] Lavallée, p. 115

[317] https//books.google.com

[318] //doi.org/10.1126/science.214.4516.64

[319] //www.ncbi.nlm.nih.gov/pubmed/17802575

[320] http://www.europreart.net/

[321] http://humanorigins.si.edu/evidence/human-evolution-timeline-interactive

[322] http://caveartproject.org/

[323] Oppenheimer, Stephen "Out of Eden: Peopling of the World" (Robinson; New Ed edition (March 1, 2012))

[324] Lazaridis et al., "Ancient human genomes suggest three ancestral populations for present-day Europeans", *Nature*, 513(7518), 18 September 2014, 409–413, doi: 10.1038/nature13673. "most present Europeans derive from at least three highly differentiated populations: West European Hunter-Gatherers (WHG), who contributed ancestry to all Europeans but not to Near Easterners; Ancient North Eurasians (ANE) related to Upper Paleolithic Siberians, who contributed to both Europeans and Near Easterners; and Early European Farmers (EEF), who were mainly of Near Eastern origin but also harbored WHG-related ancestry. We model these populations' deep relationships and show that EEF had ~44% ancestry from a "Basal Eurasian" population that split prior to the diversification of other non-African lineages."

[325] http://histories.cambridge.org/extract?id=chol9780521045056_CHOL9780521045056A002

[326] //en.wikipedia.org/w/index.php?title=Template:Paleolithic&action=edit

[327] Mann, Charles C. (Nov 2013), "The Clovis Point and the Discovery of America's First Culture," *Smithsonian Magazine*, http://www.smithsonianmag.com/history/the-clovis-point-and-the-discovery-of-americas-first-culture-3825828/

[328] https://web.archive.org/web/20060228200216/http://www.centerfirstamericans.com/mt.php?a=47

[329] http://www.bbc.co.uk/science/horizon/2002/columbus.shtml

[330] https://www.pbs.org/wgbh/nova/transcripts/3116_stoneage.html

[331] https://web.archive.org/web/20060114124835/http://www.primtech.net/Summer2003/Solutreanartifacts.htm

[332] https//www.washingtonpost.com

[333] http://www.anthropark.wz.cz/aagalery.htm

[334] Dates given vary somewhat: http://leseyzies-tourist.info/the-magdalenian, https//docs.google.com, Britannica.

[335] //en.wikipedia.org/w/index.php?title=Template:Paleolithic&action=edit

[336] (Sonneville-Bordes & Perrot, 1954–56)

[337] (Hemmingway 1980)

[338] (Housley et al. 1997)

[339] (Charles 1996)

[340] (Conkey 1980)

[341] https//docs.google.com

[342] https://web.archive.org/web/20090301000712/http://www.pole-prehistoire.com/page_site. php?site=20&base_arbo=187&arbo_id=187&page_id=304&lng=1

[343] http://www.anthropark.wz.cz/aagalery.htm

[344] Figure 4 of

[345] G.M. Santos, M.I. Bird, F. Parenti, L.K Fifield, N. Guidon, P.A Hausladen, "A revised chronology of the lowest occupation layer of Pedra Furada Rock Shelter, Piauí, Brazil: the Pleistocene peopling of the Americas", *Quaternary Science Reviews* Volume 22, Issues 21–22, November–December 2003, pp. 2303-2310, doi:0.1016/S0277-3791(03)00205-1 https://doi.org/10.1016/S0277-3791(03)00205-1.

[346] Gibbon, Guy E; Ames, Kenneth M (1998). Archaeology of Prehistoric Native America: An Encyclopedialwork=. By Guy E. Gibbon, Kenneth M. Ames (1998) .

[347] Michael R. Waters commented that "To demonstrate such early occupation of the Americas requires the presence of unequivocal stone artefacts. There are no unequivocal stone tools associated with the bones... this site is likely just an interesting paleontological locality." Chris Stringer said that "extraordinary claims require extraordinary evidence - each aspect requires the strongest scrutiny," adding that "High and concentrated forces must have been required to smash the thickest mastodon bones, and the low energy depositional environment seemingly provides no obvious alternative to humans using the heavy cobbles found with the bones.

[348] P. Skoglund, D. Reich, "A genomic view of the peopling of the Americas", *Curr Opin Genet Dev.* 2016 Dec; 41: 27–35, doi: 10.1016/j.gde.2016.06.016. "Recently, we carried out a stringent test of the null hypothesis of a single founding population of Central and South Americans using genome-wide data from diverse Native Americans. We detected a statistically clear signal linking Native Americans in the Amazonian region of Brazil to present-day Australo-Melanesians and Andaman Islanders ('Australasians'). Specifically, we found that Australasians share significantly more genetic variants with some Amazonian populations—including ones speaking Tupi languages—than they do with other Native Americans. We called this putative ancient Native American lineage "Population Y" after Ypykuéra, which means 'ancestor' in the Tupi language family."

[349] Humans may have taken different path into Americas than thought Arctic passage wouldn't have provided enough food for the earliest Americans' journey https://www.sciencenews.org/article/humans-may-have-taken-different-path-americas-thought?tgt=nr by Thomas Summer, published in "Science News" on August 10, 2016

[350] Van Tilburg, Jo Anne. 1994. *Easter Island: Archaeology, Ecology and Culture*. Washington D.C.: Smithsonian Institution Press

[351] Langdon, Robert. The Bamboo Raft as a Key to the Introduction of the Sweet Potato in Prehistoric Polynesia, *The Journal of Pacific History*, Vol. 36, No. 1, 2001

[352] "California islands give up evidence of early seafaring: Numerous artifacts found at late Pleistocene sites on the Channel Islands," ScienceDaily, March 4, 2011. https://www.sciencedaily.com/releases/2011/03/110303141540.htm

[353] //doi.org/10.1080/0043824042000303656

[354] //doi.org/10.1080/00438240601022001

[355] //www.jstor.org/stable/40024066

[356] //doi.org/10.1023/a%3A1013062712695

[357] //doi.org/10.1080/15564890701628612

[358] //doi.org/10.1002/evan.10048

[359] //doi.org/10.2307/2694209

[360] //doi.org/10.1086/200337

[361] //www.ncbi.nlm.nih.gov/pmc/articles/PMC1131883

[362] //doi.org/10.1371/journal.pbio.0030193

[363] //www.ncbi.nlm.nih.gov/pubmed/15898833

[364] https://books.google.com/books?id=RI32r548fUwC

[365] https://books.google.com/books?id=jWgZPz6oXSwC

[366] https://books.google.com/books?id=WAsKm-_zu5sC&pg=PP1

[367] https://www.nytimes.com/2008/04/04/science/04fossil.html?_r=1&scp=3&sq=&st=nyt&oref=slogin

[368] http://www.earthmagazine.org/article/first-americans-how-and-when-were-americas-populated

[369] http://www.smithsonianmag.com/science-nature/When-Did-Humans-Come-to-the-Americas-187951111.html?c=y&page=1

[370] http://www.uaf.edu/anlc/dy/

[371] https://www.youtube.com/watch?v=OV6A8oGtPc4

[372] https://www3.nationalgeographic.com/genographic/atlas.html

[373] http://www.bradshawfoundation.com/journey/

[374] http://www.nps.gov/history/seac/outline/02-paleoindian/index.htm

[375] https://web.archive.org/web/20100613070843/http://bama.ua.edu/~alaarch/prehistoricalabama/paleoindian.htm

[376] http://pidba.utk.edu/main.htm

[377] http://nationalhumanitiescenter.org/tserve/nattrans/ntecoindian/essays/pleistocene.htm

[378] Confidence intervals given in Moreno-Mayar et al. (2018): 26.1-23-9 kya for the separation of the East Asian lineage of ANA from modern East Asian populations; 25-20 kya for the admixture event of ANE and early East Asian lineages ancestral to ANA; 22.0-18.1 kya for the separation of Ancient Beringian from other Paleo-Indian lineages; 17.5-14.6 kya for the separation of Paleo Indian into North Native Americans (NNA) and South Native Americans (SNA). Supplementary Material https://media.nature.com/original/nature-assets/nature/journal/v553/n7687/extref/nature25173-s2.pdf p. 37. "the admixture event that gave rise to most Na-Dene-speakers, between NNA and a Siberian population occurred well after 11.5 kya and at least prior to ∼2.5 kya".

[379] (Detailed hierarchical chart) http://genome.cshlp.org/content/12/2/339/F1.large.jpg

[380] page 2 http://dsc.discovery.com/news/2008/02/13/beringia-native-american-02.html

[381] González-José, R. et al., "Craniometric evidence for Palaeoamerican survival in Baja California", *Nature* vol. 425 (2003), 62–65.

[382]

Neves W.A., Powell J.F., Ozolins E.G. 1999, "Extra-Continental Morphological Affinities of Palli Aike, Southern Chile", Interciencia, 24/4: 258- 263.

[383] P. Skoglund, D. Reich, "A genomic view of the peopling of the Americas", *Curr Opin Genet Dev.* 2016 Dec; 41: 27–35, doi: 10.1016/j.gde.2016.06.016. "Recently, we carried out a stringent test of the null hypothesis of a single founding population of Central and South Americans using genome-wide data from diverse Native Americans. We detected a statistically clear signal linking Native Americans in the Amazonian region of Brazil to present-day Australo-Melanesians and Andaman Islanders ('Australasians'). Specifically, we found that Australasians share significantly more genetic variants with some Amazonian populations—including ones speaking Tupi languages—than they do with other Native Americans. We called this putative ancient Native American lineage "Population Y" after Ypykuéra, which means 'ancestor' in the Tupi language family."

[384] Dillehay, Tom D.; Ocampo, Carlos (November 18, 2015). "New Archaeological Evidence for an Early Human Presence at Monte Verde, Chile". PLoS ONE. 10 (11): e0141923. doi: 10.1371/journal.pone.0141923.

[385] Chasteen (2004:4): "between the White elite and the mass of Amerindians and Negroes there existed by 1700 a thin stratum of population subject neither to Negro slavery nor Amerindian tutelage, consisting of the products of racial interbreeding among Whites, Amerindians, and Negroes and defined as mestizos, mulattoes and zambos (mixture of Indian and Negro) and their many combinations."

[386] . Principal Chief of the Cherokee Nation, Bill John Baker, reported as of "1/32 Cherokee" ancestry (which would amount to about 3%).

[387] //en.wikipedia.org/w/index.php?title=Genetic_history_of_indigenous_peoples_of_the_Americas&action=edit

[388] https://books.google.com/?id=FKmlyhxhw3sC&printsec=frontcover&dq=American+Indian++Genetic+Data#v=onepage&q&f=false

[389] https://books.google.com/books?id=Xwx6WQaoTJkC&pg=PP1
[390] https://books.google.com/books?id=aw-jLSUlUUcC&pg=PP1
[391] http://www.physorg.com/news169474130.html
[392] "four stages of the Bantu expansion: first, the initial push through the equatorial forest from the northern to the southern woodlands; second, the occupation of the southern woodland belt from coast to coast; third, the colonization of the Tanzania, Kenya and southern Somali coastline and of the northern sector of the lake region; fourth, the colonization south-wards, north-westwards and north-eastwards from this extended nucleus."
[393] Compare:
[394] "The Slow Birth of Agriculture" http://cas.bellarmine.edu/tietjen/images/neolithic_agriculture.htm , Heather Pringle
[395] Thissen, L. "Appendix I, The CANeW 14C databases, Anatolia 10,000-5000 cal. BC." in: F. Gérard and L. Thissen (eds.), The Neolithic of Central Anatolia. Internal developments and external relations during the 9th–6th millennia cal BC, Proc. Int. CANeW Round Table, Istanbul 23–24 November 2001, (2002)
[396] The Kuk Early Agricultural Site http://whc.unesco.org/en/list/887
[397] Scarre, Chris (2005). "The World Transformed: From Foragers and Farmers to States and Empires" in The Human Past: World Prehistory and the Development of Human Societies (Ed: Chris Scarre). London: Thames and Hudson. Page 188.
[398] Grinin L.E. Production Revolutions and Periodization of History: A Comparative and Theoretic-mathematical Approach. / Social Evolution & History. Volume 6, Number 2 / September 2007 http://www.socionauki.ru/journal/articles/129510/
[399] Hole, Frank., A Reassessment of the Neolithic Revolution, Paléorient, Volume 10, Issue 10-2, pp. 49-60, 1984. http://www.persee.fr/web/revues/home/prescript/article/paleo_0153-9345_1984_num_10_2_939
[400] Zohary, D., The mode of domestication of the founder crops of Southwest Asian agriculture. pp. 142-158 in D. R. Harris (ed.) The Origins and Spread of Agriculture and Pastoralism in Eurasia. UCL Press Ltd, London, 1996 https//books.google.com
[401] Zohary, D., Monophyletic vs. polyphyletic origin of the crops on which agriculture was founded in the Near East. Genetic Resources and Crop Evolution 46 (2) pp. 133-142 http://www.springerlink.com/content/jq7828u042t26716/
[402] Hillman, G. C. and M. S. Davies., Domestication rate in wild wheats and barley under primitive cultivation: preliminary results and archaeological implications of field measurements of selection coefficient, pp. 124-132 in P. Anderson-Gerfaud (ed.) Préhistoire de l'agriculture: nouvelles approches expérimentales et ethnographiques. Monographie du CRA 6, Éditions Centre Nationale Recherches Scientifiques: Paris, 1992
[403] Compiled largely with reference to: Weiss, E., Mordechai, E., Simchoni, O., Nadel, D., & Tschauner, H. (2008). Plant-food preparation area on an Upper Paleolithic brush hut floor at Ohalo II, Israel. Journal of Archaeological Science, 35 (8), 2400-2414.
[404] van Zeist, W. Bakker-Heeres, J.A.H., Archaeobotanical Studies in the Levant 1. Neolithic Sites in the Damascus Basin: Aswad, Ghoraifé, Ramad., Palaeohistoria, 24, 165-256, 1982.
[405] Hopf, Maria., "Jericho plant remains" in Kathleen M. Kenyon and T. A. Holland (eds.) Excavations at Jericho 5, pp. 576-621, British School of Archaeology at Jerusalem, London, 1983.
[406] Webber, Herbert John (1967–1989). Chapter I. History and Development of the Citrus Industry http://websites.lib.ucr.edu/agnic/webber/Vol1/Chapter1.htm in ORIGIN OF CITRUS, Vol. 1. University of California
[407] The Cambridge History of Africa https//books.google.com
[408] Smith, Philip E.L., Stone Age Man on the Nile, Scientific American Vol. 235 No. 2, August 1976: "With the benefit of hindsight we can now see that many Late Paleolithic peoples in the Old World were poised on the brink of plant cultivation and animal husbandry as an alternative to the hunter-gatherer's way of life".
[409] Denham, Tim et al. (received July 2005) "Early and mid Holocene tool-use and processing of taro (Colocasia esculenta), yam (Dioscorea sp.) and other plants at Kuk Swamp in the highlands of Papua New Guinea" (Journal of Archaeological Science, Volume 33, Issue 5, May 2006)

[410] Hoy, Thomas & Matthew Springs (1992), " Direct evidence for human use of plants 28,000 years ago: starch residues on stone artefacts from the northern Solomon Islands" (Antiquity Volume: 66 Number: 253 Page: 898–912)

[411] Fleisch, Henri., Notes de Préhistoire Libanaise : 1) Ard es Saoude. 2) La Bekaa Nord. 3) Un polissoir en plein air. BSPF, vol. 63.

[412] *Guns, Germs, and Steel: The Fates of Human Societies*. Jared Diamond (1997).

[413] James C. Scott,*Against the Grain: a Deep History of the Earliest States*, NJ:Yale UP, (2017), "The world's population in 10 000 BC, according to a careful estimate was roughly 4 million. A full five thousand years later it has risen only to 5 million...One likely explanation for this apparent human progress in subsistance techniques together with a long period of demographic stagnation is that epidemologically this was perhaps the most lethal period in human history".

[414] Sherratt 1981

[415] *Guns, Germs, and Steel: The Fates of Human Societies* - Jared Diamond, 1997

[416] http://www.pnas.org/content/early/2009/06/19/0812764106.full.pdf

[417] https://www.youtube.com/watch?v=Yocja_N5s1I

[418] Beckwith 2009, p. 30.

[419] //en.wikipedia.org/w/index.php?title=Template:Indo-European_topics&action=edit

[420] Anthony 2007.

[421] Beckwith 2009.

[422] Anthony 2007, p. 133.

[423] Anthony 2007, p. 262.

[424] Parpola 2015, pp. 37 f..

[425] Mallory & Adams 1997, p. 4.

[426] Mallory 1999, pp. 108 f..

[427] Anthony 2007, pp. 345, 361–367.

[428] Anthony 2007, pp. 368, 380.

[429] Mallory 1999, pp. 108, 244–250.

[430] Anthony 2007, p. 360.

[431] Haak 2015.

[432] Anthony 2007, p. 7.

[433] Jonathan Slocum, *What is Historical Linguistics? What are 'Indo-European' Languages?*, The University of Texas at Austin http://www.utexas.edu/cola/centers/lrc/general/histling.html

[434] Anthony & Ridge 2015.

[435] Kortlandt 2010.

[436] Kortlandt (2010) refers to Kortlandt, Frederik. 2007b. *C. C. Uhlenbeck on Indo-European, Uralic and Caucasian*. Several variants and elaborations of this theory exist: • The "Sogdiana hypothesis" of Johanna Nichols places the homeland in the fourth or fifth millennium BCE to the east of the Caspian Sea, in the area of ancient Bactria-Sogdiana.<ref name="FOOTNOTENichols1997">Nichols 1997.

[437] Nichols 1999.

[438] Allan Bomhard, *The Origins of Proto-Indo-European: The Caucasian Substrate Hypothesis (revised November 2016)* https://www.academia.edu/10261406/The_Origins_of_Proto-Indo-European_The_Caucasian_Substrate_Hypothesis_revised_November_2016_. Paper presented at "The Precursors of Proto-Indo-European: the Indo-Hittite and Indo-Uralic Hypotheses", a 2015 workshop at the Leiden University Centre for Linguistics, Leiden, The Netherlands, 9—11 July 2015.

[439] The Origins of Proto-Indo-European: The Caucasian Substrate Hypothesis http://eurogenes.blogspot.nl/2015/05/the-origins-of-proto-indo-european.html

[440] See Dzhebel http://encyclopedia2.thefreedictionary.com/Dzhebel, and V. A. Ranov and R. S. Davis (1979), *Toward a New Outline of the Soviet Central Asian Paleolithic http://repository.brynmawr.edu/cgi/viewcontent.cgi?article=1006&context=anth_pubs*

[441] Bernard Sergent (1995), *Les Indo-Européens – Histoire, langues, mythes*

[442] Anthony 2007, pp. 56–58.

[443] David Anthony: "Germanic shows a mixture of archaic and derived traits that make its place uncertain; it could have branched off at about the same time as the root of

Italic and Celtic [but] it also shared many traits with Pre-Baltic and Pre-Slavic."<ref name="FOOTNOTEAnthony200757">Anthony 2007, p. 57.

[444] Ringe 2006, p. 67.

[445] Anthony 2007, p. 100.

[446] Mallory 1999.

[447] Anthony 2007, p. 43.

[448] Anthony 2007, pp. 43–46.

[449] Parpola 2015, pp. 37–38.

[450] Mathieson, Reich et al. (2017), *The Genomic History of Southeastern Europe*.

[451] Anthony 2007, pp. 101, 264–265.

[452] Loewe & Shaughnessy 1999, pp. 83–88.

[453] Mallory & Adams 1997, p. 372.

[454] Ivanova 2012.

[455] Anthony 2007, p. 101.

[456] Anthony 2007, p. 408.

[457] Gimbutas 1997.

[458] Gimbutas 1997, p. 240.

[459] According to Gimbutas, these indigenous groups existed for nearly three millennia (c. 6500–3500 BCE, during the Neolithic, Chalcolithic and Copper ages), consisting notably of the Narva, Funnelbeaker, Linear Pottery, Cardium pottery, Vinča, early Helladic, Minoan cultures etc. As a "truncation" of these cultures Gimbutas perceived (1) the "abrupt absences" of certain traditions of urbanism, pottery and visual arts as well as in "symbols and script" as well as (2) the "equally abrupt appearance of thrusting weapons and horses infiltrating the Danubian Valley and other major grasslands of the Balkans and Central Europe", initiating "a dramatic shift in the prehistory of Europe, a change in social structure and in residence patterns, in art and in religion" which was to be "a decisive factor in the formation of Europe's last 5,000 years."

[460] Gimbutas 1997, p. 361.

[461] Gimbutas 1997, pp. 241, 316.

[462] *Old Europeans* were sedentary-horticulturalist, living in "large agglomerations" – probably part of theocratic monarchies presided over by a queen-priestess – and had an ideology which "focused on the eternal aspects of birth, death, and regeneration, symbolized by the feminine principle, a mother creatrix"; they buried their dead in communal megalith graves and were generally peaceful.

[463] Parpola 2015, p. 67.

[464] Mallory 2002.

[465] Witzel 2005, p. 347.

[466] Basu 2003, p. 2287.

[467] Anthony 2007, pp. 117–118.

[468] Pereltsvaig & Lewis 2015, pp. 208–215.

[469] Kroonen 2015.

[470] Karlene 1996.

[471] Pereltsvaig & Lewis 2015, p. 205.

[472] Anthony 2007, p. 117.

[473] David Anthony (1995): "Language shift can be understood best as a social strategy through which individuals and groups compete for positions of prestige, power, and domestic security [...] What is important, then, is not just dominance, but vertical social mobility and a linkage between language and access to positions of prestige and power [...] A relatively small immigrant elite population can encourage widespread language shift among numerically dominant indigenes in a non-state or pre-state context if the elite employs a specific combination of encouragements and punishments. Ethnohistorical cases [...] demonstrate that small elite groups have successfully imposed their languages in non-state situations."<ref name="FOOTNOTEWitzel200127">Witzel 2001, p. 27.

[474] Anthony 2007, p. 118.

[475] Parpola 2015, pp. 67–68.

[476] Parpola 2015, p. 68.

[477] Salmons 2015, p. 118.

478 Note the dislocation of the Indus Valley Civilisation prior to the start of the Indo-Aryan migrations into northern India, and the onset of Sanskritisation with the rise of the Kuru kingdom, as described by Michael Witzel.<ref name="FOOTNOTEWitzel1995">Witzel 1995.

479 Allentoft 2015.

480 Carlos Quiles, *Indo-European demic diffusion model*. Second edition, revised and updated. Badajoz 2017 (online text https://indo-european.info/indo-european-demic-diffusion-model-2.pdf, pdf).

481 Anthony 2007, p. 227.

482 Anthony 2007, pp. 300, 336.

483 Rajesh Kochhar (2017), "The Aryan chromosome" http://indianexpress.com/article/opinion/columns/aryans-dna-genetics-archaeology-4765740/, *The Indian Express*.

484 Demkina 2017.

485 Demkina et al. (2017): "In the second millennium BC, humidization of the climate led to the divergence of the soil cover with secondary formation of the complexes of chestnut soils and solonetzes. This paleoecological crisis had a significant effect on the economy of the tribes in the Late Catacomb and Post-Catacomb time stipulating their higher mobility and transition to the nomadic cattle breeding."<ref name="FOOTNOTEDemkina2017">Demkina 2017.

486 See also Eurogenes Blogspot, *The crisis* http://eurogenes.blogspot.nl/2017/07/the-crisis.html.

487 Bojtar 1999, p. 57.

488 Mallory 1997.

489 Mallory 2013.

490 Parpola 2015.

491 Anthony & Ringe 2015.

492 T. V. Gamkrelidze and V. V. Ivanov, Indo-European and the Indo-Europeans, 1995, Chapters Eleven and Twelve

493 Mallory 1989, p. 185.

494 Strazny 2000, p. 163.

495 Mallory: "The Kurgan solution is attractive and has been accepted by many archaeologists and linguists, in part or total. It is the solution one encounters in the *Encyclopædia Britannica* and the *Grand Dictionnaire Encyclopédique Larousse*."<ref name="FOOTNOTEMallory1989185">Mallory 1989, p. 185.

496 Gimbutas (1985) page 190.

497 Pereltsvaig & Lewis 2015.

498 Mallory & Adams 1997, 4 and 6 (Afanasevo), 13 and 16 (Anatolia), 243 (Greece), 127–128 (Corded Ware), and 653 (Yamna).

499 Haak 2015, p. 3.

500 Jones 2015.

501 Lazaridis 2016, p. 8.

502 Lazaridis et al. (2016), referring to Haak et al. (2015): "The spread of Near Eastern ancestry into the Eurasian steppe was previously inferred without access to ancient samples, by hypothesizing a population related to present-day Armenians as a source."<ref name="FOOTNOTELazaridis20168">Lazaridis 2016, p. 8.

503 Eurogenes.blogspot, *The genetic structure of the world's first farmers (Lazaridis et al. preprint)* http://eurogenes.blogspot.nl/2016/06/the-genetic-structure-of-worlds-first.html

504 https://hms.harvard.edu/news/new-branch-added-european-family-tree

505 http//www.dailymail.co.uk

506 http://dienekes.blogspot.nl/2015/11/westasian-in-flesh-hunter-gatherers.html

507 http://forwhattheywereweare.blogspot.nl/2016/01/caucasus-and-swiss-hunter-gatherer.html

508 Jones et al. (2015) further note that "Caucasus hunter-gatherers (CHG) belong to a distinct ancient clade that split from western hunter-gatherers ∼45 kya, shortly after the expansion of anatomically modern humans into Europe and from the ancestors of Neolithic farmers ∼25 kya, around the Last Glacial Maximum."<ref name="FOOTNOTEJones2015">Jones 2015.

509 See also: • eurogenes.blogspot, *The genetic structure of the world's first farmers (Lazaridis et al. preprint)* http://eurogenes.blogspot.nl/2016/06/the-genetic-structure-of-worlds-first. html • For what they were... we are (2016) *Ancient genomes from Neolithic West Asia http:*

*//forwhattheywereweare.blogspot.nl/2016/06/ancient-genomes-from-neolithic-west-asia.
html*

[510] Anthony 2007, p. 132.

[511] Anthony 2007, p. 135.

[512] Anthony 2007, p. 138.

[513] Anthony 2007, pp. 132, 145.

[514] Anthony 2007, pp. 145, 147.

[515] Anthony 2007, pp. 155–157.

[516] Anthony 2007, p. 164.

[517] Anthony 2007, p. 173.

[518] Anthony 2007, p. 175.

[519] Anthony 2007, p. 182.

[520] Anthony 2007, pp. 185, 190.

[521] Anthony 2007, p. 186.

[522] There are several datings available: • Gimbutas dated it to 5000 BCE. • According
to V.A.Dergachev (2007), *О скипетрах, о лошадях, о войне: Этюды в защиту
миграционной концепции М. Гимбутас*, ISBN 5-98187-173-3, dates Samara culture at cal.
C-14 5200–4500 BCE, with possible continuatation into first half of 5th millennium, while the
Khvalynsk culture is dated at ca. 4600–3900 BCE. These data are based on synchronisation, not
radicarbon dating or dendrochronology of Samara culture sites itself. • Mallory and Adams,
Encyclopedia of Indo-European Culture, gives the bare date "fifth millennium BC", while the
Khvalynsk culture, its reported successor, is dated at 4900–3500 BCE.

[523] Anthony 2007, p. 189.

[524] Anthony 2007, p. 244.

[525] Anthony 2007, pp. 244–245.

[526] Anthony 2007, p. 275.

[527] Anthony 2007, p. 300.

[528] Anthony 2007, pp. 274–277, 317–320.

[529] Anthony 2007, p. 321.

[530] Anthony 2007, pp. 301–302.

[531] Anthony 2007, p. 303.

[532] Anthony 2007, pp. 345, 361–362, 367.

[533] Anthony 2007, p. 367.

[534] Anthony 2007, pp. 360, 368.

[535] Anthony 2007, p. 229.

[536] Anthony 2007, pp. 47–48.

[537] Anthony 2007, p. 48.

[538] Anthony 2007, pp. 133, 262.

[539] Anthony 2007, pp. 264–265.

[540] D.W. Anthony, Two IE phylogenies, three PIE migrations, and four kinds of steppe pastoralism,
The Journal of Language Relationship, vol. 9 (2013), pp. 1–21

[541] . The dominant people in the western part of it, from the Altai of western Mongolia south
through the Kroraina area around the Lop Nor to the Ch'i-lien Mountains, the northern outliers of the Tibetan Plateau, were Caucasoid in race; those in the northern region seem to have
spoken North Iranian "Saka" languages or dialects, while those in the Kroraina area spoke
Tokharian languages or dialects.

[542] Beckwith 2009, p. 59.

[543] Mallory 1999, p. 155.

[544] Massive migration from the steppe is a source for Indo-European languages in Europe, Haak et
al, 2015 http://biorxiv.org/content/early/2015/02/10/013433

[545] Eight thousand years of natural selection in Europe, Mathieson et al, 2015 http://biorxiv.org/
content/early/2015/03/13/016477

[546] Anthony 2007, p. 344.

[547] Anthony 2007, p. 349.

[548] Anthony 2007, p. 359.

[549] Anthony 2007, pp. 359–360.

[550] Anthony 2007, pp. 361–362, 367.

[551] Anthony 2007, p. 362.

[552] Mallory & Adams 1997, p. 127.

[553] Anthony 2017, p. 54.

[554] Mallory 1999, p. 250.

[555] Mallory 1999, p. 108.

[556] Mallory & Adams 1997.

[557] Anthony 2017, p. 58.

[558] Anthony 2017, p. 54 f..

[559] Haak 2015, p. 1.

[560] Haak 2015, p. 11, figure 4c.

[561] Allentoft 2015, p. 108, topright map.

[562] Lazaridis & Haak 2015, p. 136.

[563] They further note: • "[...] the main argument in favor of the Anatolian hypothesis (that major language change requires major migration) can now also be applied to the Steppe hypothesis."<ref name="FOOTNOTELazaridisHaak2015136">Lazaridis & Haak 2015, p. 136.

[564] Yet, a major problem with this proposal is that those Yamna-migrants were R1b-carriers, which also appears in the Bell-Beaker people, while the Corded Ware people seem to have been R1a-carriers, which has not been found among Yamna-people. See: • Eurogenes Blog (18 December 2017), *Corded Ware as an offshoot of Hungarian Yamnaya (Anthony 2017)* http://eurogenes.blogspot.nl/2017/12/corded-ware-as-offshoot-of-hungarian.html; • Indo-European.eu (17 December 2017), *The new "Indo-European Corded Ware Theory" of David Anthony* https://indo-european.eu/2017/12/the-new-indo-european-corded-ware-theory-of-david-anthony/; • Indo-European.eu (26 December 2017), *The Great Hungarian Plain in a time of change in the Balkans – Neolithic, Chalcolithic, and Bronze Age* https://indo-european.eu/2017/12/the-great-hungarian-plain-in-a-time-of-change-in-the-balkans-neolithic-chalcolithic-and-bronze-age/.

[565] Heyd 2017, p. 350.

[566] Piggot 1965, p. 101.

[567] Bradley 2007, p. 144.

[568] See also Indo-European.eu (2017), *Heyd, Mallory, and Prescott were right about Bell Beakers* https://indo-european.eu/2017/06/heyd-mallory-prescott-were-right-about-bell-beakers/.

[569] Johannes Müller, Martin Hinz and Markus Ullrich, "Bell Beakers – chronology, innovation and memory: a multivariate approach", chapter 6 in *The Bell Beaker Transition in Europe: Mobility and local evolution during the 3rd millennium BC*, eds. Maria Pilar Prieto Martinez and Laure Salanova (2015).

[570] Curtis, Andy. *Color, Race, And English Language Teaching: Shades of Meaning*. 2006, page 192.

[571] SIL Ethnologue (2006). 95 million speakers of Standard German; 105 million including Middle and Upper German dialects; 120 million including Low Saxon and Yiddish.

[572] Dutch http://wayback.archive-it.org/all/20081219053002/http://www.ucl.ac.uk/prosp-students/prospectus/pdf/arts/ugp09_arts_dutch.pdf, University College London

[573] Holmberg, Anders and Christer Platzack (2005). "The Scandinavian languages". In *The Comparative Syntax Handbook*, eds Guglielmo Cinque and Richard S. Kayne. Oxford and New York: Oxford University Press. Excerpt at Durham University http://www.dur.ac.uk/anders.holmberg/resources/The%20Scandinavian%20Languages.pdf .

[574] Ethnologue: Germanic https://www.ethnologue.com/subgroups/germanic

[575] Cornell (1995) 44.

[576] *Encyclopædia Britannica*, s. v. "Latium".

[577] John M. Coles, *The Bronze Age in Europe: An Introduction to the Prehistory of Europe C. 2000–700 BC*, p. 422.

[578] Massimo Pallottino, *Etruscologia*, p. 40.

[579] David W. Anthony, *The Horse, the Wheel, and Language*, pp. 344, 367.

[580] K. Kristiansen, *Europe Before History*, p. 388.

[581] Uwe Pörksen, German Academy for Language and Literature's Jahrbuch [Yearbook] 2007 (Wallstein Verlag, Göttingen 2008, pp. 121–130)

582 See especially map 9.3 *The Ancient Celtic Languages c. 440/430 BCE* (third map in online text (PDF) http://www.wales.ac.uk/Resources/Documents/Research/ODonnell.pdf).

583 See especially map 9.2 *Celtic expansion from Hallstatt/La Tene central Europe* (second map in online text (PDF) http://www.wales.ac.uk/Resources/Documents/Research/ODonnell.pdf).

584 Cunliffe, Barry W. 2003. *The Celts: a very short introduction.* pg.48

585 "Language by State – Scottish Gaelic" http://www.mla.org/map_data_states&mode=lang_tops&lang_id=636 on *Modern Language Association* website. Retrieved 27 December 2007

586 "Languages Spoken At Home" http://www.omi.wa.gov.au/WAPeople%5CSect1%5CTable%201p04%20Aust.pdf from Australian Government *Office of Multicultural Interests* website. Retrieved 27 December 2007

587 Languages Spoken:Total Responses https//web.archive.org from Statistics New Zealand website. Retrieved 5 August 2008

588 G. Leitner, Australia's Many Voices: Australian English—The National Language, 2004, pg. 74

589 "Balto-Slavic languages" http://www.britannica.com/EBchecked/topic/51061/Balto-Slavic-languages. *Encyclopædia Britannica Online*. Retrieved 10 December 2012. <q>Those scholars who accept the Balto-Slavic hypothesis attribute the large number of close similarities in the vocabulary, grammar, and sound systems of the Baltic and Slavic languages to development from a common ancestral language after the breakup of Proto-Indo-European. Those scholars who reject the hypothesis believe that the similarities are the result of parallel development and of mutual influence during a long period of contact.</q>

590 Kortlandt, Frederik (2009), *Baltica & Balto-Slavica*, p. 5, <q>Though Prussian is undoubtedly closer to the East Baltic languages than to Slavic, the characteristic features of the Baltic languages seem to be either retentions or results of parallel development and cultural interaction. Thus I assume that Balto-Slavic split into three identifiable branches, each of which followed its own course of development.</q>

591 Derksen, Rick (2008), *Etymological Dictionary of the Slavic Inherited Lexicon*, p. 20, <q>"I am not convinced that it is justified to reconstruct a Proto-Baltic stage. The term Proto-Baltic is used for convenience's sake.</q>

592 Bojtár page 18.

593 Guests in the House; cultural transmission between Slavs and Scandinavians. Mats Roslund. 2008

594 The origin of Rus. O Pritsak; 1981; pp 14, 27–28. Pritsak argues that the eastern Vikings – the Rus – were a social group of seafaring nomads which consisted of not only Scandinavians, but also Frisians, Balts, Slavs and Finns.

595 Peter Somogyi. *New Remarks on the flow of Byzantine coins in wallachia and Avaria.*. In : The Other Europe in the Middle Ages: Avars, Bulgars, Khazars and Cumans; 2008

596 Fiona Hill, Russia — Coming In From the Cold? http://www.theglobalist.com/printStoryId.aspx?StoryId=3727, The Globalist, 23 February 2004

597 Robert Greenall, Russians left behind in Central Asia http://news.bbc.co.uk/2/hi/asia-pacific/4420922.stm, BBC News, 23 November 2005

598 Terry Kirby, 750,000 and rising: how Polish workers have built a home in Britain http://news.independent.co.uk/uk/this_britain/article344755.ece, The Independent, 11 February 2006.

599 Poles in the United States http://www.newadvent.org/cathen/12204c.htm, Catholic Encyclopedia

600 Barford, P. M. 2001. *The Early Slavs. Culture and Society in Early Medieval Europe.* Cornell University Press. 2001. , p 1

601 Bideleux, Robert. 1998. *History of Eastern Europe: Crisis and Change.* Routledge.

602 The catalogue of Kimbell Art Museum's 1998 exhibition *Ancient Gold: The Wealth of the Thracians* indicates a historical extent of Thracian settlement including most of the Ukraine, all of Hungary and parts of Slovakia. (Kimbell Art – Exhibitions http://www.kimbellart.org/exhibitions/past_gold.cfm)

603 Hoddinott, p. 27.

604 Casson, p. 3.

605 John Boardman, I.E.S. Edwards, E. Sollberger, and N.G.L. Hammond. *The Cambridge Ancient History, Volume 3, Part 1: The Prehistory of the Balkans, the Middle East and the Aegean World, Tenth to Eighth Centuries BC.* Cambridge University Press, 1982, p. 53. "Yet we cannot

identify the Thracians at that remote period, because we do not know for certain whether the Thracian and Illyrian tribes had separated by then. It is safer to speak of Proto-Thracians from whom there developed in the Iron Age..."

[606] Strabo & 20 AD, VII 3,12.

[607] Dionysius Periegetes, *Graece et Latine*, Volume 1 https://books.google.com/books?id=fGg_AQAAMAAJ&dq=, Libraria Weidannia, 1828, p. 145.

[608] Nandris 1976, p. 731.

[609] Husovská 1998, p. 187.

[610] Treptow 1996, p. 10.

[611] Ellis 1861, p. 70.

[612] Mountain 1998, p. 58.

[613] Dumitrescu et al. 1982, p. 53.

[614] Maggiulli, *Sull'origine dei Messapi*, 1934; D'Andria, *Messapi e Peuceti*, 1988; *I Messapi*, Taranto 1991

[615] : "The Balkan peninsula had three groups of Indo-Europeans prior to 2000 BCE. Those on the west were the Illyrians; those on the east were the Thracians; and advancing down the southern part of the Balkans, the Greeks."

[616] Eastern Michigan University Linguist List: The Illyrian Language http://linguistlist.org/forms/langs/LLDescription.cfm?code=xil: "An ancient language of the Balkans. Based upon geographical proximity, this is traditionally seen as the ancestor of Modern Albanian. It is more likely, however, that Thracian is Modern Albanian's ancestor, since both Albanian and Thracian belong to the satem group of Indo-European, while Illyrian belonged to the centum group. 2nd half of 1st Millennium BC – 1st half of 1st Millennium AD."

[617] Fol 2002, p. 225: "Romanisation was total and complete by the end of the 4th century A.D. In the case of the Illyrian elements a Romance intermediary is inevitable as long as Illyrian was probably extinct in the 2nd century A.D."

[618] : "The Illyrians certainly never collectively called themselves Illyrians, and it is unlikely that they had any collective name for themselves."

[619] Wilkes 1995, p. 92.

[620] http://www.albanianlanguage.net/

[621] Vahan Kurkjian, "History of Armenia", Michigan, 1968, History of Armenia by Vahan Kurkjian http://penelope.uchicago.edu/Thayer/E/Gazetteer/Places/Asia/Armenia/_Texts/KURARM/home.html; Armenian Soviet Encyclopedia, v. 12, Yerevan 1987; Artak Movsisyan, "Sacred Highland: Armenia in the spiritual conception of the Near East", Yerevan, 2000; Martiros Kavoukjian, "The Genesis of Armenian People", Montreal, 1982

[622] Thomas Gamkrelidze and Vyacheslav Ivanov, *The Early History of Indo-European Languages*, March 1990, p. 110.

[623] In other contexts, "Hellenic" and "Greek" are generally synonyms.

[624] Browning (1983), *Medieval and Modern Greek*, Cambridge: Cambridge University Press.

[625] Joseph, Brian D. and Irene Philippaki-Warburton (1987): *Modern Greek*. London: Routledge, p. 1.

[626] B. Joseph (2001): "Ancient Greek". In: J. Garry et al. (eds.) *Facts about the World's Major Languages: An Encyclopedia of the World's Major Languages, Past and Present*. (Online Paper http://www.ling.ohio-state.edu/~bjoseph/articles/gancient.htm)

[627] Dalby, David. *The Linguasphere Register of the World's Languages and Speech Communities* (1999/2000, Linguasphere Press), pp. 449f.

[628] "Sea Peoples: Large group of Indo-European peoples who attacked eastern Mediterranean lands shortly after 1200 B.C.E."

[629] Brixhe, Cl. "Le Phrygien". In Fr. Bader (ed.), *Langues indo-européennes*, pp. 165–178, Paris: CNRS Editions.

[630] Woodard, Roger D. *The Ancient Languages of Asia Minor*. Cambridge University Press, 2008, , p. 72. "Unquestionably, however, Phrygian is most closely linked with Greek."

[631] Beckwith 2009, p. 32.

[632] Burrow 1973.

[633] Parpola 1999.

[634] Beckwith 2009, p. 33 note 20, p. 35.

635 Beckwith 2009, p. 33.
636 Anthony 2007, p. 454.
637 Beckwith 2009, p. 33 note 20.
638 Beckwith 2009, pp. 376–7.
639 Malory 1989, pp. 42–43.
640 Anthony 2009, p. 390 (fig. 15.9), 405–411.
641 Anthony 2007, pp. 385–388.
642 Mallory 1997, pp. 20–21.
643 //tools.wmflabs.org/geohack/geohack.php?pagename=Indo-European_migrations&params=
55_53_N_55_42_E_
644 Diakonoff 1995, p. 473.
645 C.C. Lamberg-Karlovsky, "Archaeology and Language: The Indo-Iranians", *Current Anthropology*, vol. 43, no. 1 (Feb. 2002)
646 Kohl 2007, pp. 196–199.
647 Anthony 2007, p. 462.
648 Anthony 2007, pp. 454 f..
649 Bryant 2001.
650 Archaeological cultures identified with phases of Vedic culture include the Ochre Coloured Pottery culture, the Gandhara Grave culture, the Black and red ware culture and the Painted Grey Ware culture.<ref name="FOOTNOTEWitzel1989">Witzel 1989.
651 Witzel 1995, pp. 3–5.
652 Samuel 2010, pp. 49–52.
653 Flood 1996, p. 82.
654 Hiltebeitel 2002.
655 Beckwith 2009, pp. 376–377.
656 Beckwith 2009, pp. 29–38.
657 Beckwith 2009, pp. 84–85.
658 .. "domesticated horses were introduced to the western pre-Chinese area by the Indo-Europeans."
659 "It is now accepted that the chariot is an intrusive cultural artifact that entered Shang China from the north or northwest without any wheeled-vehicle precursors."
660 "The Chinese did not have wheeled vehicles before this period. They adopted the chariot from the foreigners who brought the fully formed artifact with them from the northwest."
661 .. "no earlier wheeled vehicles of any kind have ever been found in China proper."
662 .. "The wheel was introduced to China as a part of the chariot..."
663 Hollar 2011, pp. 62–63.
664 R.N Frye, "IRAN v. PEOPLE OF IRAN" in Encyclopedia Iranica. "In the following discussion of 'Iranian peoples', the term 'Iranian' may be understood in two ways. It is, first of all, a linguistic classification, intended to designate any society which inherited or adopted, and transmitted, an Iranian language. The set of Iranian-speaking peoples is thus considered a kind of unity, in spite of their distinct lineage identities plus all the factors which may have further differentiated any one group's sense of self."
665 Frye, Richard Nelson, *Greater Iran*, p.xi: "... Iran means all lands and people where Iranian languages were and are spoken, and where in the past, multi-faceted Iranian cultures existed. .."
666 Mario Alinei (with reference to Francisco Villar, *Los indoeuropeos y los orígenes de Europa. Lenguaje y historia*, Gredos, Madrid 1991): "The sharp, and now at last admitted even by traditionalists (Villar 1991) differentiation of farming terminology in the different IE languages, while absolutely unexplainable in the context of Renfrew's NDT, provides yet another fundamental proof that the differentiation of IE languages goes back to remote prehistory."
667 Bryant: "It must be stated immediately that there is an unavoidable corollary of an Indigenist position. If the Indo-Aryan languages did not come from outside South Asia, this necessarily entails that India was the original homeland of all the other Indo-European languages."<ref name="FOOTNOTEBryant20016">Bryant 2001, p. 6.
668 Bryant: "There is at least a series of archaeological cultures that can be traced approaching the Indian subcontinent, even if discontinuous, which does not seem to be the case for any

hypothetical east-to-west emigration."<ref name="FOOTNOTEBryant2001236">Bryant 2001, p. 236.

[669] http://www.nature.com/nature/journal/v522/n7555/full/nature14507.html
[670] http://adsabs.harvard.edu/abs/2015Natur.522..167A
[671] //doi.org/10.1038/nature14507
[672] //www.ncbi.nlm.nih.gov/pubmed/26062507
[673] //doi.org/10.1146/annurev-linguist-030514-124812
[674] https//www.academia.edu
[675] http://genome.cshlp.org/content/13/10/2277.full.pdf+html
[676] //doi.org/10.1101/gr.1413403
[677] //www.ncbi.nlm.nih.gov/pmc/articles/PMC403703
[678] //www.ncbi.nlm.nih.gov/pubmed/14525929
[679] https://books.google.com/books?id=-Ue8BxLEMt4C
[680] https://books.google.com/books?id=vXljf8JqmkoC
[681] https://books.google.com/books?id=0qAoqP4g1fEC
[682] https://www.academia.edu/4908240/
[683] http://adsabs.harvard.edu/abs/2017EurSS..50..791D
[684] //doi.org/10.1134/S1064229317070018
[685] https://books.google.com/books?id=bSxHgej4tKMC
[686] https://books.google.com/books?id=c_lN_q15ZiEC
[687] https://books.google.com/books?id=xmZiAAAAMAAJ
[688] https://books.google.com/books/about/The_Kurgan_Culture_and_the_Indo_European.html?id=hCZmAAAAMAAJ
[689] https://www.academia.edu/3742220/Ancient_Indo-Europeans._Chelyabinsk_Rifei_2002
[690] //arxiv.org/abs/1502.02783
[691] http://adsabs.harvard.edu/abs/2015Natur.522..207H
[692] //doi.org/10.1038/nature14317
[693] //www.ncbi.nlm.nih.gov/pmc/articles/PMC5048219
[694] //www.ncbi.nlm.nih.gov/pubmed/25731166
[695] http//unesdoc.unesco.org
[696] //doi.org/10.15184/aqy.2017.21
[697] https://books.google.com/books?id=kfyzAAAAQBAJ&printsec=frontcover&hl=nl#v=onepage&q&f=false
[698] https://books.google.com/books?id=oGH-RCW1fzsC
[699] https://books.google.com/books?id=SeOcAAAAQBAJ
[700] https://books.google.com/books?id=Zpp7AAAAMAAJ
[701] http://adsabs.harvard.edu/abs/2015NatCo...6E8912J
[702] //doi.org/10.1038/ncomms9912
[703] //www.ncbi.nlm.nih.gov/pmc/articles/PMC4660371
[704] //www.ncbi.nlm.nih.gov/pubmed/26567969
[705] https://books.google.com/books?id=HumKY7fn9cMC
[706] http://www.kortlandt.nl/publications/art269e.pdf
[707] https://books.google.com/books?id=GdIyAQAAQBAJ
[708] //doi.org/10.1101/059311
[709] https://books.google.com/books?id=cHA7Ey0-pbEC
[710] https://www.proto-indo-european.ru/ie-cradle/_pdf/clouds-over-ie-homelands-nallory.pdf
[711] https://books.google.com/books?id=C-TnAAAAMAAJ
[712] //www.worldcat.org/issn/0003-8008
[713] https://books.google.com/books?id=EOytGwAACAAJ
[714] https://books.google.com/books?ei=j6liVMvsJMbIsATfsYDoBA&id=_VxiAAAAMAAJ
[715] https//books.google.com
[716] //doi.org/10.1038/ejhg.2009.194
[717] //www.ncbi.nlm.nih.gov/pmc/articles/PMC2987245
[718] //www.ncbi.nlm.nih.gov/pubmed/19888303
[719] //doi.org/10.1038/ejhg.2014.50
[720] //www.ncbi.nlm.nih.gov/pmc/articles/PMC4266736

721 //www.ncbi.nlm.nih.gov/pubmed/24667786

722 https://books.google.com/books?id=4Nv6SPRKqs8C

723 https://web.archive.org/web/20070611142934/http://www.ejvs.laurasianacademy.com/
ejvs0104/ejvs0104article.pdf

724 http://www.ejvs.laurasianacademy.com/ejvs0104/ejvs0104article.pdf

725 https://books.google.com/books?id=RMj7M_tGaNMC&dq

726 https://www.world-archaeology.com/issues/by-steppe-desert-and-ocean.htm

727 https://bmcevolbiol.biomedcentral.com/articles/10.1186/s12862-017-0936-9

728 http://www.humanjourney.us/indoEurope.html

729 http://www.panshin.com/trogholm/wonder/indoeuropean/indoeuropean1.html

730 http://ukrainianweek.com/History/88577

731 http://armchairprehistory.com/2017/11/12/proto-indo-european-homelands-ancient-genetic-
clues-at-last/

732 https://homeland.sites.ku.dk/

733 http://dna-explained.com/2015/06/15/yamnaya-light-skinned-brown-eyed-ancestors/

734 https://www.edge.org/conversation/david_reich-the-genomic-ancient-dna-revolution

735 http://www.thehindu.com/sci-tech/science/how-genetics-is-settling-the-aryan-migration-
debate/article19090301.ece

736 https://www.sciencedaily.com/releases/2015/02/150218123429.htm

737 http://www.britannica.com/EBchecked/topic/286368/Indo-European-languages

738 https://indo-european.info/ie/Indo-European

739 https://indo-european.eu/

740 http://www.continuitas.org/intro.html

741 https://indo-european.eu/maps/

742 http://homeland.ku.dk/

743 https://www.youtube.com/watch?v=aQ283N_ZdKY

744 https://rootsofeurope.ku.dk/english/research/homeland/

745 Häkkinen, Jaakko 2007: Kantauralin murteutuminen vokaalivastaavuuksien valossak.

746 Sebestyén-Németh, Irene 1951–1952: Zur Frage des alten Wohngebietes der uralischen Völker.

747 Häkkinen, Jaakko 2009: Kantauralin ajoitus ja paikannus: perustelut puntarissa. – Suomalais-
Ugrilaisen Seuran Aikakauskirja 92, p. 9–56. http://www.sgr.fi/susa/92/hakkinen.pdf

748 Rédei, Károly 1986: Zu den indogermanisch-uralischen Sprachkontakten. (Toim. Manfred
Mayrhofer & Volfgang U. Dressler.) Veröffentlichungen der Kommission für Linguistik und
Kommunikationsforschung, Heft 16. Wien.

749 Koivulehto, Jorma 1991: Koivulehto, Jorma 1991: Uralische Evidenz für die Laryngaltheorie.
Österreichische Akademie der Wissenschaften. Philosophisch-Historische Klasse. Sitzungs-
berichte, 566. Band. Wien 1991.

750 Häkkinen, Jaakko 2012: Uralic evidence for the Indo-European homeland. http://www.elisanet.
fi/alkupera/UralicEvidence.pdf

751 Mallory, J. P. & Adams, D. Q. (editors) 1997: Encyclopedia of Indo-European Culture. London
and Chicago: Fitzroy Dearborn Publishers. p. 439

752 Häkkinen, Jaakko 2012: Early contacts between Uralic and Yukaghir. Tiina Hyytiäinen, Lotta
Jalava, Janne Saarikivi & Erika Sandman (editors): Per Urales ad Orientem Iter polyphon-
icum multilingue Festskrift tillägnad Juha Janhunen på hans sextioårsdag den 12 februari 2012.
Suomalais-Ugrilaisen Seuran Toimituksia 264, p. 91–101. Helsinki: Suomalais-Ugrilainen
Seura. http://www.sgr.fi/sust/sust264/sust264_hakkinenj.pdf

753 Janhunen, Juha 2001: Indo-Uralic and Ural-Altaic: On the diachronic implications of areal
typology. – Carpelan, Parpola & Koskikallio (editors): Early Contacts between Uralic and Indo-
European: Linguistic and Archaeological Considerations, p. 207–220. Suomalais-Ugrilaisen
Seuran Toimituksia 242.

754 Moora, Harri (editor) 1956: Eesti rahva etnilisest ajaloost. Tallinn.

755 Gallén, Jarl (editor) 1984: Suomen väestön esihistorialliset juuret. Tvärminnen symposiumi
17.–19.1.1980. Bidrag till kännedom av Finlands natur och folk, 131. Helsinki: Societas Scien-
tiarum Fennica.

756 Nuñez, Milton G. 1987: A Model for the Early Settlement of Finland. – Fennoscandia Archaeo-
logica 4.

396

[757] Wiik, Kalevi 2002: Eurooppalaisten juuret. Jyväskylä: Atena.

[758] Mallory, J. P. 1989: In Search of the Indo-Europeans. Language, Archaeology and Myth. London: Thames and Hudson.

[759] Mallory, J. P. 2001: Uralics and Indo-Europeans: Problems of time and space. Carpelan et al. (edited): Early Contacts between Uralic and Indo-European: Linguistic and Archaeological Considerations, p. 345–366. Suomalais-Ugrilaisen Seuran Toimituksia 242.

[760] Aikio, Ante & Aikio, Aslak 2001: Heimovaelluksista jatkuvuuteen. Suomalaisen väestöhistorian tutkimuksen pirstoutuminen. – Muinaistutkija 4/2001, p. 2–21. Helsinki: Suomen arkeologinen seura.

[761] Häkkinen, Jaakko 2006: Studying the Uralic proto-language. http://www.elisanet.fi/alkupera/Uralic.html [Translation from: Uralilaisen kantakielen tutkiminen. – Tieteessä tapahtuu 1 / 2006, p. 52–58.]

[762] Häkkinen, Jaakko 2010: Jatkuvuusperustelut ja saamelaisen kielen leviäminen (OSA 1). – Muinaistutkija 1 / 2010, p. 19–36. http://www.elisanet.fi/alkupera/Jatkuvuus1.pdf

[763] Aikio, Ante 2004: An essay on substrate studies and the origin of Saami. – Irma Hyvärinen, Petri Kallio & Jarmo Korhonen (toim.): Etymologie, Entlehnungen und Entwicklungen. Festschrift für Jorma Koivulehto zum 70. Geburtstag, s. 5–34. Mémoires de la Société Néophilologique de Helsinki, LXIII. Helsinki: Uusfilologinen yhdistys ry.

[764] Aikio, Ante 2006: On Germanic-Saami contacts and Saami prehistory. – Suomalais-Ugrilaisen Seuran Aikakauskirja 91, p. 9–55. Helsinki: Suomalais-Ugrilainen Seura. http://www.sgr.fi/susa/91/aikio.pdf

[765] Saarikivi, Janne & Grünthal, Riho 2005: Itämerensuomalaisten kielten uralilainen tausta. Muuttuva muoto. Kirjoituksia Tapani Lehtisen 60-vuotispäivän kunniaksi, s. 111–146. Kieli 16.

[766] Kallio, Petri 2006: Suomen kantakielten absoluuttista kronologiaa. – Virittäjä 1 / 2006, p. 2–25. http://www.kotikielenseura.fi/virittaja/hakemistot/jutut/2006_2.pdf

[767] Rosser ZH, Zerjal T, Hurles ME, Adojaan M, Alavantic D, Amorim A, Amos W, Armenteros M, Arroyo E, Barbujani G, Beckman G, Beckman L, Bertranpetit J, Bosch E, Bradley DG, Brede G, Cooper G, Côrte-Real H. B., De Knijff P, Decorte R, Dubrova YE, Evgrafov O, Gilissen A, Glisic S, Gölge M, Hill EW, Jeziorowska A, Kalaydjieva L, Kayser M et al. (2000). "Y-Chromosomal Diversity in Europe is Clinal and Influenced Primarily by Geography, Rather than by Language". The American Journal of Human Genetics 67 (6): 1526–1543. . Vancouver style error (help)

[768] Tambets K, Rootsi S, Kivisild T, Help H, Serk P, Loogväli EL et al. (2004). "The western and eastern roots of the Saami–the story of genetic "outliers" told by mitochondrial DNA and Y chromosomes". Am. J. Hum. Genet. 74 (4): 661–82. . Vancouver style error (help)

[769] Tambets, Kristiina et al. 2004, The Western and Eastern Roots of the Saami—the Story of Genetic "Outliers" Told by Mitochondrial DNA and Y Chromosomes

[770] Shi H, Qi X, Zhong H, Peng Y, Zhang X, et al. (2013) Genetic Evidence of an East Asian Origin and Paleolithic Northward Migration of Y-chromosome Haplogroup N. PLoS ONE 8(6): e66102.

[771] Cui, Hongjie Li, Chao Ning, Ye Zhang, Lu Chen, Xin Zhao, Erika Hagelberg and Hui Zhou (2013) "Y Chromosome analysis of prehistoric human populations in the West Liao River Valley, Northeast China. " BMC 13:216 http://www.biomedcentral.com/1471-2148/13/216 Yinqiu

[772] Napolskikh V. V. (Izhevsk, Russia). Earth-Diver Myth (A812) in northern Eurasia and North America: twenty years later https://www.academia.edu/4918926/Diving_Bird_Myth_after_20_years_2012.

[773] Lyle Campbell & Mauricio J. Mixco, A Glossary of Historical Linguistics (2007, University of Utah Press)

[774] P.H. Matthews, Oxford Concise Dictionary of Linguistics (2007, 2nd edition, Oxford)

[775] Gerrit J. Dimmendaal, "Nilo-Saharan Languages," International Encyclopedia of Linguistics (1992, Oxford), volume 3, pp. 100–104

[776] M. Lionel Bender, "Nilo-Saharan," African Languages, An Introduction (2000, Cambridge), pp. 43–73.

[777] Blench & Ahland (2010)

[778] John Desmond Clark, *From Hunters to Farmers: The Causes and Consequences of Food Production in Africa*, University of California Press, 1984, p. 31

[779] Drake NA, Blench RM, Armitage SJ, Bristow CS, White KH. 2011. "Ancient watercourses and biogeography of the Sahara explain the peopling of the desert." *Proceedings of the National Academy of Sciences*, 2011 Jan 11, 108(2):458–62.

[780] Diedrich Westermann, 1912. *The Shilluk people, their language and folklore* https://books.google.com/books?id=xtktAAAAMAAJ&pg=PA33&dq=%22niloto-sudanic%22&cd=1#v=onepage&q=%22niloto-sudanic%22&f=false

[781] Blench, Roger. 2015. Was there a now-vanished branch of Nilo-Saharan on the Dogon Plateau? Evidence from substrate vocabulary in Bangime and Dogon https//www.academia.edu.

[782] Africa over the last 12,000 years https://www.academia.edu/28768228/Africa_over_the_last_12000_years_how_we_can_interpret_the_interface_of_archaeology_linguistics_and_genetics

[783] George Starostin (2016) *The Nilo-Saharan hypothesis tested through lexicostatistics: current state of affairs* https://www.academia.edu/21582071/The_Nilo-Saharan_hypothesis_tested_through_lexicostatistics_current_state_of_affairs

[784] http://www.rogerblench.info/Archaeology%20data/Africa/Blench%20Chapter%203.pdf

[785] https://web.archive.org/web/20120316221945/http://25images.ish-lyon.cnrs.fr/player/player.php?id=72&id_sequence=433&quality=hd

[786] http://media.leidenuniv.nl/legacy/blench-call-leiden-2011.pdf

[787] http://rogerblench.info/Language/Nilo-Saharan/NS%20page.htm

[788] http://rogerblench.info/Language/Nilo-Saharan/General/NS%20language%20list.pdf

[789] http://sumale.vjf.cnrs.fr/nilsah/index.html

[790] http://starling.rinet.ru/maps/maps15.php?lan=en

[791] Irene Thompson, "Niger-Congo Language Family" http://aboutworldlanguages.com/niger-congo-language-family, "aboutworldlanguages", March 2015

[792] Simons, Gary F. and Charles D. Fennig (eds.). 2018. *Ethnologue: Languages of the World*, Twenty-first edition. Dallas, Texas: SIL International.

[793] "Niger-Congo Languages" http://languagesgulper.com/eng/Niger.html, "The Language Gulper", March 2015

[794] Irene Thompson, "Niger-Congo Language Family" http://aboutworldlanguages.com/niger-congo-language-family, "aboutworldlanguages", March 2015

[795] Katie Manning, *The demographic response to Holocene climate change in the Sahara* (2014), The demographic response to Holocene climate change in the Sahara https://www.sciencedirect.com/science/article/pii/S0277379114002728

[796] Igor Kopytoff, *The African Frontier: The Reproduction of Traditional African Societies* (1989), 9–10 (cited afer Igbo Language Roots and (Pre)-History http://amightytree.org/niger-congo-languages-and-history/, *A Mighty Tree*, 2011).

[797] Blench, Roger, THE BENUE-CONGO LANGUAGES: A PROPOSED INTERNAL CLASSIFICATION WORKING DOCUMENT: NOT A DRAFT PAPER NOT TO BE QUOTED WITHOUT PERMISSION this printout: Cambridge, 24 June, 2004 http://www.rogerblench.info/Language/Niger-Congo/BC/General/Benue-Congo%20classification%20latest.pdf. "No comprehensive reconstruction has yet been done for the phylum as a whole, and it is sometimes suggested (e.g. by Dixon 1997) that Niger-Congo is merely a typological and not a genetic unity. This view is not held by any specialists in the phylum, and reasons for thinking Niger-Congo is a true genetic unity will be given in this chapter. It is, however, true that the subclassification of the phylum has been continuously modified in recent years and cannot be presented as an agreed scheme. The factors which have delayed reconstruction are the large number of languages, the inaccessibility of much of the data, and the paucity of able researchers committed to this field. Emphasis will be placed on three characteristics of Niger-Congo; noun-class systems, verbal extensions, and basic lexicon." See also: Bendor-Samuel, J. ed. 1989. The Niger–Congo Languages. Lanham: University Press of America.

[798] Westermann, D. 1922a. Die Sprache der Guang. Berlin: Dietrich Reimer.

[799] Greenberg, J.H. 1964. Historical inferences from linguistic research in sub-Saharan Africa. Boston University Papers in African History, 1:1–15.

[800] Blench, Roger, Unpublished Working Draft http://www.rogerblench.info/Language/Niger-Congo/BC/General/Benue-Congo%20classification%20latest.pdf

[801] Herman Bell. 1995. The Nuba Mountains: Who Spoke What in 1976?. (The published results from a major project of the Institute of African and Asian Studies: the Language Survey of the Nuba Mountains.)

[802] Williamson, K. 1971. The Benue–Congo languages and Ijo. Current Trends in Linguistics, 7. ed. T. Sebeok 245–306. The Hague: Mouton.

[803] Williamson, K. 1988. Linguistic evidence for the prehistory of the Niger Delta. The early history of the Niger Delta, edited by E.J. Alagoa, F.N. Anozie and N. Nzewunwa. Hamburg: Helmut Buske Verlag.

[804] Williamson, K. 1989. Benue–Congo Overview. In The Niger–Congo Languages. J. Bendor-Samuel ed. Lanham: University Press of America.

[805] De Wolf, P. 1971. The noun class system of Proto-Benue–Congo. The Hague: Mouton.

[806] Blench, R.M. 1989. A proposed new classification of Benue–Congo languages. Afrikanische Arbeitspapiere, Köln, 17:115–147.

[807] Williamson, Kay & Blench, Roger (2000) 'Niger–Congo', in Heine, Bernd & Nurse, Derek (eds.) African languages: an introduction, Cambridge: Cambridge University Press.

[808] Gerrit Dimmendaal (2008) "Language Ecology and Linguistic Diversity on the African Continent", Language and Linguistics Compass 2/5:841.

[809] Martin H. Steinberg, *Disorders of Hemoglobin: Genetics, Pathophysiology, and Clinical Management*, Cambridge University Press, 2001, p. 717 https://books.google.co.uk/books?id=PM0zzm7wbvsC&pg=PA717.

[810] Hans G. Mukarovsky, *A Study of Western Nigritic*, 2 vols. (1976–1977). Blench (2004): "Almost simultaneously [with Greenberg (1963)], Mukarovsky (1976-7) published his analysis of 'Western Nigritic'. Mukarovsky's basic theme was the relationship between the reconstructions of Bantu of Guthrie and other writers and the languages of West Africa. Mukarovsky excluded Kordofanian, Mande, Ijo, Dogon, Adamawa-Ubangian and most Bantoid languages for unknown reasons, thus reconstructing an idiosyncratic grouping. Nonetheless, he buttressed his argument with an extremely valuable compilation of data, establishing the case for Bantu/Niger-Congo genetic link beyond reasonable doubt."

[811] http://www.oxfordhandbooks.com/view/10.1093/oxfordhb/9780199935345.001.0001/oxfordhb-9780199935345-e-3

[812] Rebecca Grollemund, Simon Branford, Jean-Marie Hombert & Mark Pagel. 2016. Genetic unity of the Niger-Congo family http://llacan.vjf.cnrs.fr/nigercongo2/abstracts/Grollemund_Hombert_Pagel-Genetic%20Unity%20of%20the%20Niger-Congo%20family.pdf. Towards Proto-Niger-Congo: comparison and reconstruction (2nd International Congress)

[813] Morton, Deborah. [ATR] Harmony in an Eleven Vowel Language http://www.lingref.com/cpp/acal/42/paper2759.pdf. Ohio State University, 2012:70–71.

[814] Unseth, Carla. Vowel Harmony in Wolof http://www.gial.edu/images/opal/No-7-Unseth-Wolof-Vowel-Harmony.pdf . Graduate Institute of Applied Linguistics, 2009:2–3.

[815] Bakovic, Eric. Harmony, Dominance and Control http://roa.rutgers.edu/files/360-1199/roa-360-bakovic-2.pdf. Diss. Rutgers, The State University of New Jersey, 2000:ii.

[816] "Clements, G. N. 1981. Akan vowel harmony: A non-linear analysis. Harvard Studies in Phonology 2.108–177."

[817] Casali, Roderic F. "Nawuri ATR Harmony in Typological Perspective." http://www.journalofwestafricanlanguages.org/Files/pdf/29-1/JWAL-29-1-Casali.pdf Summer Institute of Linguistics, 2002:29. Journal of West African Languages 29.1 (2002).

[818] "Anderson, C.G. 1999. ATR vowel harmony in Akposso. Studies in African Linguistics, 28(2): 185–214."

[819] "Archangeli, Diana, & Douglas Pulleyblank. 1994. Grounded Phonology (Current Studies in Linguistics, 25.) Cambridge: MIT Press."

[820] Casali, Roderic F. "ATR Harmony in African Languages." http://onlinelibrary.wiley.com/doi/10.1111/j.1749-818X.2008.00064.x/full Language and Linguistics Compass 2.3 (2008): 469–549.

[821] Doneux, Jean L. 1975. Hypothèses pour la comparative des langues atlantiques. Africana Linguistica 6.41–129. Tervuren: Musée Royal de l'Afrique Centrale. (Re: proto-Atlantic), Williamson, Kay. 2000. Towards reconstructing Proto-Niger-Congo. Proceedings of the 2nd World Congress of African Linguistics, Leipzig 1997, ed. H. E. Wolff and O. Gensler, 49–70.

Köln: Rüdiger Köppe. (Re: proto-Ijoid), Stewart, John M. Towards Volta-Congo Reconstruction: Rede. Leiden: Universitaire Pers Leiden, 1976., Casali, Roderic F. "On the Reduction of Vowel Systems in Volta-Congo." African Languages and Cultures 8.2 (1995: 109–121) (Re: proto-Volta-Conga)

[822] Stewart, John M., 2002. The potential of Proto-Potou-Akanic-Bantu as a pilot Proto-Niger-Congo, and the reconstructions updated. Journal of African Languages and Linguistics 23: 197–224.

[823] le Saout (1973) for an early overview, Stewart (1976) for a diachronic, Volta–Congo wide analysis, Capo (1981) for a synchronic analysis of nasality in Gbe (see Gbe languages: nasality), and Bole-Richard (1984, 1985) as cited in Williamson (1989) for similar reports on several Mande, Gur, Kru, Kwa, and Ubangi languages.)

[824] As noted by Williamson (1989:24). The assumptions are from Ferguson's (1963) 'Assumptions about nasals' in Greenberg (ed.) *Universals of Language*, pp 50–60 as cited in Williamson art.cit.

[825] Haspelmath, Martin; Dryer, Matthew S.; Gil, David and Comrie, Bernard (eds.) *The World Atlas of Language Structures*; pp 346–385. Oxford: Oxford University Press, 2005.

[826] https://www.academia.edu/2326473/Is_Niger-Congo_simply_a_branch_of_Nilo-Saharan

[827] http://media.leidenuniv.nl/legacy/blench-call-leiden-2011.pdf

[828] http://www.rogerblench.info/Language/Niger-Congo/Kordofanian/Nuba%20Hills%20conference%20paper%202011%20Kordofanian.pdf

[829] //doi.org/10.1111/j.1749-818X.2008.00085.x

[830] http://www.africamuseum.be/museum/research/publications/rmca/online/tense.pdf

[831] http://www.sil.org/silewp/2004/silewp2004-005.pdf

[832] Gibbon, pp. 28–31

[833] Gibbon, pp. 216–217

[834] Gibbon, p. 218

Article Sources and Contributors

The sources listed for each article provide more detailed licensing information including the copyright status, the copyright owner, and the license conditions.

Early expansions of hominins out of Africa *Source:* https://en.wikipedia.org/w/index.php?oldid=852826449 *License:* Creative Commons Attribution-Share Alike 3.0 *Contributors:* Amble, Bearcat, Bender235, CommonsDelinker, Dbachmann, Drbogdan, Espoo, Fraenir, Hairy Dude, Hmainsbot1, Jbeans, Jim1138, Joe Roe, Jonesey95, Kelapstick, Kober, Kortoso, Madalibi, Mogism, Mojoworker, Neils51, Nicolas Perrault III, OccultZone, Rcsprinter123, Rjwilmsi, The Transhumanist, Tompop888, Wavelength, Xaxafrad, 14 anonymous edits 1

Homo erectus *Source:* https://en.wikipedia.org/w/index.php?oldid=853350348 *License:* Creative Commons Attribution-Share Alike 3.0 *Contributors:* 120, 3primetime3, Abelmoschus Esculentus, Aboudaqn, Abyssal, Alfie Gandon, Anonywiki, Anso 4, Apokryltaros, Arminden, Audaciter, BD2412, Bender235, Bongwarrior, Bpod, CAPTAIN RAJU, Caftaric, CataracticPlanets, Chiswick Chap, ClueBot NG, Coreybchapman, Cynko, D Eaketts, DanielRigal, Dawnseeker2000, Dbachmann, Dbrodbeck, Dcirovic, Deli nk, Dgorsline, Dlohcierekim, Donner60, Dorsetonian, Drbogdan, EP111, Editor D.S, El cid, el campeador, Felicia777, FourLights, Garudamon11, Gerald wish, Gilliam, Goustien, GreenMeansGo, Greyjoy, Gulumeemee, Hddty., Heliotom, Henry Scott, HiLo48, Homoerotic, How23, Ian.thomson, IdreamofJeanie, Ihatetrump224, Ivgnyl, Jauerback, Jim1138, Jon Kolbert, Jonkerz, K6ka, Keith D, Kintaro, Kortoso, KylieTastic, L3X1, LW001, Laoris, LennartH21, LizardJr8, Lycurgus, MONGO, Maias, Mandruss, Marasama, Materialscientist, Maunus, Meganesia, MelbourneStar, Mellis, Metanoid, Milo21ww, Mitzi.humphrey, Moxy, Mrund, Mtpaley, Mukogodo, MusikAnimal, NamiJou123, Narrest, Natg 19, Nhannhan1, Nigelj, Nition, Nwbeeson, Oleg Alexandrov, Omid Ebrahimi Moghaddam, Oranjelo100, Oshwah, Ottgtbag, Patient Zero, Pauli133, Peter coxhead, PlantTrees, Plantdrew, PopSci, Qzd, Redhat101, Rich Farmbrough, Rjwilmsi, Samf4u, Septrillion, Serols, Shellwood, SimonAter, Smasongarrison, Stikkyy, SuperTah, TheDarkCurrent, TheTruithOfLife, Theinstantmatrix, Timawesomeness, TimidGuy, Tjdude19, Tom.Reding, TwoTwoHello, Wbm1058, Wikirictor, WolfmanSF, Xt3em3flip, Zppix, 大作曲家 , 178 anonymous edits 12

Clactonian *Source:* https://en.wikipedia.org/w/index.php?oldid=816305089 *License:* Creative Commons Attribution-Share Alike 3.0 *Contributors:* Adamsan, Alcuin, AlexR, Alfons Åberg, Anomalocaris, Bazonka, Bellroth, Bermicourt, CieloEstrellado, DavidAnstiss, Dbachmann, Dcirovic, Deville, Dimadick, Dudley Miles, Ezeu, Geos, Goustien, Hairy Dude, J04n, JMK, JayHenry, Jbeans, Jockrh, Johnsoniensis, Kelisi, Locutus Borg～enwiki, MIjy～enwiki, Markussep, Michaelwild, Micke-sv, Miranche, Nicolas Perrault III, Norbold, Omnipaedista, PatHadley, Paul H., Philip Trueman, Quisqualis, RJP, Sheynhertz-Unbayg, SomeGuyWhoRandomlyEdits, Speednat, Stevenmitchell, TomCerul, TritonFX, Vald, 18 anonymous edits 30

Micoquien *Source:* https://en.wikipedia.org/w/index.php?oldid=835895860 *License:* Creative Commons Attribution-Share Alike 3.0 *Contributors:* 1oblada, Archaeodontosaurus, Chronicler～enwiki, Dimadick, Dmitri Lytov, Dpleibovitz, Goustien, Jonkerz, Joostik, Kendrick7, Lottamiata, Omnipaedista, Rigadoun, Robin S, Solar-Wind, 3 anonymous edits 35

Sub-Saharan Africa *Source:* https://en.wikipedia.org/w/index.php?oldid=850586884 *License:* Creative Commons Attribution-Share Alike 3.0 *Contributors:* A Certain Lack of Grandeur, A.Savin, AcidSnow, Arado, BD2412, Bear-rings, Bearcat, Bender235, Borderlandor, BranStark, BrittneyWright, Buckshot06, Cacrats, Carlstak, Catasprone, ChristianCT95, Clevera, ClueBot NG, Comp.arch, Cresson hkv, Crystallizedcarbon, Cyberbot II, Damoon4all, DavidLeighEllis, Dawnseeker2000, Dbachmann, Dcirovic, Demmo, Derek R Bullamore, DisillusionedBitterAndKnackered, Doug Weller, El C, Entropy, Epson Salts, Etoukesteph, Faceless Enemy, Falcon Kirtaran, Fama Clamosa, Favonian, FrancessO, Frosty, Fyrael, Garrybracer, Gilo1969, Gob Lofa, Gog the Mild, GoodDay, Gyrofrog, Hertz1888, Hopehorne16, Inayity, Ira Leviton, J 1982, JJMC89, Jameel89ten, Jamie Tubers, JaysTV YT, Joe2719, Jonesey95, Julietdeltalima, Just a guy from the KP, Jynetti, Kifipe, Kifipepo, Kintetsubuffalo, Knife-in-the-drawer, Lapadite77, Largoplazo, LazMac, Liesonlinewik1, Lotje, Madhavanand, Mandruss, Marek69, Marubin2, Materialscientist, Medical2017, Melissacor, Midas02, Middayexpress, Mll mitch, Narky Blert, Natg 19, NeilN, Neill Patterson, Nemesis2473, NewEnglandYankee, Nfufu, Niceguyedc, Nikhil1234567, Octoberwoodland, Oganesson007, Oranjelo100, Oshwah, Paul2520, PericlesofAthens, Philip Trueman, RA0808, Rachmat04, Realityteller, ReformedPenal, Renamed user 156yagz5r48a5f1a1f, Richard0048, Rlewaldron, Rollingcontributor, Rupert loup, Russ3Z, Ryanoo, Ryon22, SUM1, Sangjinhwa, Shalor (Wiki Ed), Shmurak, Shoedgolgs, Skyblue100, Smashedmelon618, Soap, Soupforone, Srednuas Lenoroc, Srich32977, TAnthony, TYelliot, Timbuktu123, Trappist the monk, Troyoleg, Ubel, Vansockslayer, Vesperius, Vrac, Vsmith, WHYTFULIEING101, WOSlinker, Widr, XXGfHXx, Yamaguchi先生 , YeOldeGentleman, Zihepe, 王登輝 , 162 anonymous edits 39

Recent African origin of modern humans *Source:* https://en.wikipedia.org/w/index.php?oldid=852982611 *License:* Creative Commons Attribution-Share Alike 3.0 *Contributors:* 3primetime3, Adam9007, AfricaQuest, AldezD, Alex Bardill, Archaon, Bahudhara, BatteryIncluded, Ben MacDui, Beyond My Ken, BibleScholar, Boghog, Brett, Carlotm, CenfusRex, Cgx8253, Chakazul, Chhandama, ClueBot NG, Cuchullan, Dbachmann, Dcirovic, Drbogdan, Dudley Miles, Ebizur, Emowe1, Favonian, Fixer88, Flyer22 Reborn, FreeKnowledgeCreator, Frietjes, Gap9551, Geo1un, Goodtiming8871, Goustien, Groogle, Haeinous, Hairy Dude, Headbomb, IQ125, Javantea, Jdaloner, Jim1138, Joe Roe, Jonesey95, Jonkerz, Joshua Jonathan, Just a guy from the KP, Keith-264, Kgrad, Lampshade Maker, Magioladitis, Marek69, Maunus, Me, Myself, and I are Here, Mikalra, Monochrome Monitor, Moxy, Nihiltres, Omnipaedista, Onel5969, Oshwah, PLawrence99cx, Pavel Vozenilek, Phuzion, PlyrStar93, Precious Feelings, Quercus solaris, Rednblu, Rich Farmbrough, Richard Keatinge, Rjwilmsi, Scarpy, Scratplays, Smhanes, TAnthony, The Blade of the Northern Lights, TiMike, TimidGuy, Titus III, Tobus, TomS TDotO, Triggerhippie4, Twinsday, User000name, Utcursch, 69 anonymous edits 101

Southern Dispersal *Source:* https://en.wikipedia.org/w/index.php?oldid=848557502 *License:* Creative Commons Attribution-Share Alike 3.0 *Contributors:* Andrewjlockley, Annabaker21402, Bender235, Bhny, Billinghurst, Blaylockjam10, Bluezy, Chakazul, Citation bot 1, ClueBot NG, Dbachmann, Dcirovic, Delusion23, Dmitri Lytov, Doug Weller, Ebizur, Eio-cos, Espoo, Fences and windows, Florian Blaschke, Goustien, Headbomb, Hibernian, Hordaland, Hunnjazal, Inferno, Lord of Penguins, J.delanoy, J04n, JWB, Joe Roe, Materialscientist, Maulucioni, Moxy, Naviguessor, Noah Salzman, Optimusnauta, PLawrence99cx, PaleoNeonate, Piperh, Pjoef, PlyrStar93, Quebec99, RJFJR, Rich Farmbrough, Rjwilmsi, RttlesnkeWhiskey, Sietecolores, Squidkid233, Stemonitis, TerryAlex, Titus III, Tom.Reding, Tony Sidaway, Tony1, Trappist the monk, Travelmite, Wapondaponda, Wbm1058, Xover, Y-dna data file, YaG, Yamaguchi先生 , Yowanvista, 48 anonymous edits 117

Upper Paleolithic *Source:* https://en.wikipedia.org/w/index.php?oldid=853028364 *License:* Creative Commons Attribution-Share Alike 3.0 *Contributors:* 72, Abyssal, Alxndrdegrt, Anthonysenn, Asfreeas, Assasin Joe, BartlebytheScrivener, Bemis Ampleforth, Bender235, Bertport, Bismaydash, Botteville, Bped1985, Cbdorsett, Cefisher, Chuckiesdad, Classicwiki, ClueBot NG, Colonies Chris, CowboySpartan, Crash Underride, CubeSat4U, DVdm, Daß Wölf, Dbachmann, Deedee96, Deselliers, Discospinster, DocWatson42, Donama, Doug Weller, DragonCelery, Dutchy45, EagleFan, Eryk Norse, Eteethan, Facts707, Fama Clamosa, Florian Blaschke, Fortdj33, Fraenir, Funandtrvl, Gaynikka, Gob Lofa, GoingBatty, Grant65, HJJHolm, Hairhorn, Hairy Dude, Halcatalyst, Headbomb, Hibernian, Hugh16, Hughey, I20, ILoveCaracas, Immunize, Inwind, Iridescent, Iselilja, Jackfork, Jbeans, Jeandré du Toit, Jo-Jo Eumerus, Johnbod, Joshua Jonathan, K6ka, Lacrimosus, Ladytimide, Leoesb1032, Luciebalakova, Lumos3, MC10, MCTales, Mandruss, Maulucioni, Meganesia, Mr. bobby, Natg 19, Nicolas Perrault III, Ogress, Osamabinlatin, Paleolithic Man, Pariah24, Parkwells, Pasquale, Perkeleperkele, Phileklund, Phthinosuchusisanancestor, Physis, Poiuytre, PoizonMyst, Pol098, Q433, R'n'B, Randy Kryn, Richardlord50, Rjwilmsi, Roymarth, Rrotenbe, Seaphoto, SeoMac, Serendipodous, Sfan00 IMG, Shellwood, Skoglund, SpreadItOut, Srich32977, St. Caurgula, Stan J Klimas, Stroppolo, Sumanuil, SwisterTwister, SystemsAlliance, T H MITCHELL, Tapatio, Tassedethe, Thanos5150, TheWaffleH0use, Thestoneageman, Tuxedo junction, VanishedUser sdu9aya9fasdsopa, Veda784, Wangzilv1998, Weseo, White Shadows, Whitehex, Widr, Wikipelli, Wingedsubmariner, Wjfox2005, Zuchinni one, 140 anonymous edits 119

Mammoth steppe *Source:* https://en.wikipedia.org/w/index.php?oldid=850351373 *License:* Creative Commons Attribution-Share Alike 3.0 *Contributors:* Alfie Gandon, Alphathon, Altenmann, Ashphalt, Bender235, Bhudson, Bigdan201, Blaylockjam10, Bobo192, Botteville, ClueBot NG, CommonsDelinker, Concus Cretus, Crito10, Dawnseeker2000, Dbachmann, Dcattell, Dhartung, Diannaa, Florian Blaschke, FunkMonk, Gaius Cornelius, Ghirlandajo, GoingBatty, Hibernian, Hike395, Himbear, J 1982, Jarble, John, Jonkerz, Katefan0, Lappspira, Littie, Look2See1, Marcel Hendrik, Marcus Cyron, Materialscientist, Mattisse, Naviguessor, Nicolas Perrault III, Oshwah, Overagainst, Pearle, Pinethicket, PuffinSoc, Quinton Feldberg, Rcsprinter123, Renata3, Rjwilmsi, Ruzmutuz, Sigma 7, SuperTah, TBoaN, The way, the truth, and the light, TintoRetto, Topbanana, Widr, William Harris, WolfmanSF, Ylyandres, 24 anonymous edits 133

Interbreeding between archaic and modern humans *Source:* https://en.wikipedia.org/w/index.php?oldid=852869363 *License:* Creative Commons Attribution-Share Alike 3.0 *Contributors:* Agricolae, Aiurdin, Arthur Rubin, Auric, BD2412, BatteryIncluded, Bradeos Graphon, Chiswick Chap, Chris Capoccia, Chris the speller, Codrinb, Cold Season, Conquistador, Dbachmann, Dcirovic, Denisarona, Drbogdan, Drsphinx, Dudley Miles, Dusty relic, Epf, Eric Kvaalen, Erik.mohr, Esrogs, FreeKnowledgeCreator, Grifterlake, Hans Ekbrand, Headbomb, Heavenlyblue, Hergilei, Hibernian, Hmainsbot1, Howcheng, Igoldste, John of Reading, Joshua Jonathan, Kaldari, Ketiltrout, KingQueenPrince, Kohelet, KylieTastic, Lamedumal, Lappspira, M tartessos, Madalibi, Maxcip, Me, Myself, and I are Here, MegaSharkWiki, Moxy, Narssarssuaq, Nicolas Perrault III, Oranjelo100, Paleolithic Man, Prinsgezinde, Qwertyus, Rcsprinter123, Reenem, Rjwilmsi, Rodw, Rriegs, Satyadasa, Smeagol 17, Soupforone, Srich32977, Sunrise, Tamfang, The Quixotic Potato, The Rambling Man, Tobus, Tony1, Topbanana, Trappist the monk, Virion123, William Harris, WolfmanSF, Έλενα Λυκούση, 62 anonymous edits 143

Mousterian *Source:* https://en.wikipedia.org/w/index.php?oldid=853030556 *License:* Creative Commons Attribution-Share Alike 3.0 *Contributors:* Adagio Cantabile, Adamsan, Alphalphantor9, Altenmann, Ams80, Anomalocaris, Archaeodontosaurus, Archaeomoonwalker, Bastiche, Behaafarid, Bender235, Benw, Bhumiya, Böri, Chiswick Chap, Chris fardon, ChrisGualtieri, CieloEstrellado, CommonsDelinker, Comtebenoit, Crisco 1492, Cruccone, Cuchullain, Dbachmann, Dimadick, Dirrival, Domdeparis, Doug Weller, Dr. Norris, Dr.K., Drift chambers, Epastore, Fences and windows, Floris V, Fram, FunkMonk, Gilgamesh4, Glenn, Gob Lofa, Gongoozler123, Goustien, Gurch, Guérin Nicolas, Halveama, Hibernian, Hurmata, Hylobates, Icairns, Iselilja, J04n, JamesBWatson, JaxsSunflower14, Jcub, Jo3sampl, JoKing, Jonesey95, Joostik, Joy, KapitanCookie, Khamm, Manon Delamaison, Mattisse,

MeortNGHH, Meatsgains, Mervyn, Miaow Miaow, Mihosha, Mira3z, Moxy, Nascigl, NekoDaemon, Nicolas Perrault III, NobuTamura, Omnipaedista, Oranjelo100, PatHadley, Patrick MMA Bringmans, PaulWalter, Per Honor et Gloria, Permacultura, Quisqualis, RJP, Rainwarrior, Randy Kryn, Rich Farmbrough, Rjwilmsi, Roger de Lauria, Rudolf Pohl, Rye-96, Sheynhertz-Unbayg, Smithrod1, SomeGuyWhoRandomlyEdits, Soupforone, Speednat, St. Caurgula, Taromsky, Tktktk, Trappist the monk, Tubbienine, Unyoyega, Updatehelper, Vald, Wikirictor, Wingedsubmariner, Ziggurat, Zoeperkoe, Zyxwv99, 67 anonymous edits 157

European early modern humans *Source:* https://en.wikipedia.org/w/index.php?oldid=853477873 *License:* Creative Commons Attribution-Share Alike 3.0 *Contributors:* Alphalurion, Arjayay, Audaciter, Bender235, Blaylockjam10, Daiyusha, Dbachmann, Dcirovic, Doug Weller, Drbogdan, Fraenir, Gaia Octavia Agrippa, Ghirlandajo, Gogo Dodo, Grant65, Green daemon, Henry.smith1016, Jloris, Joe Roe, Joostik, Lamro, LilHelpa, Natg 19, Onel5969, Orenburg1, Petter Bøckman, RandomUser3510, Richard Keatinge, Rjwilmsi, Robert.paulson101019, Stikkyy, Sumanuil, Trappist the monk, Valerius Tygart, Wqrst, 8 anonymous edits 163

Art of the Upper Paleolithic *Source:* https://en.wikipedia.org/w/index.php?oldid=853125174 *License:* Creative Commons Attribution-Share Alike 3.0 *Contributors:* Aleister Wilson, Axl, Bender235, CaroleHenson, Citation bot 1, Colonies Chris, Cuchullain, Dbachmann, Dogwood123, Doug Weller, Drbogdan, Dudley Miles, Fafnir1, Florian Blaschke, Fraenir, Georgelazenby, Hillbillyholiday, Hmains, InverseHypercube, JMK, JMilty, Johnbod, LilHelpa, Lotje, Mac Dreamstate, Magioladitis, Me, Myself, and I are Here, Meganesia, Mogism, Mr. bobby, Nicolas Perrault III, Ost316, Parkwells, Pavel Fabian, Primateshumanos, Randy Kryn, Rjwilmsi, Ronhjones, Sankar1005, Sebastiangarth, Smasongarrison, Soupforone, Spicemix, Tassedethe, Trappist the monk, Unquiet pasts, Velella, Vexations, 17 anonymous edits 175

Hominid dispersals in Europe *Source:* https://en.wikipedia.org/w/index.php?oldid=847249249 *License:* Creative Commons Attribution-Share Alike 3.0 *Contributors:* 564dude, Ad Orientem, Agricolae, Alinor, BD2412, Bkonrad, ClueBot NG, Dbachmann, Ericaaaa, Goustien, Hugo999, J. Spencer, Joe Roe, Maxim11maxim, Mortee, NoLimitOnImagination, Phleg1, Rathfelder, Reddi, Rjwilmsi, Sarilho1, Tajotep, Tom.Reding, Woohookitty, 9 anonymous edits 182

Solutrean *Source:* https://en.wikipedia.org/w/index.php?oldid=853029370 *License:* Creative Commons Attribution-Share Alike 3.0 *Contributors:* 1oblada, ACPena, Adamsan, Adrian J. Hunter, Ahoerstemeier, Albertoarmstrong, Alphabet55, Andrew Dalby, Athaler, BOTarate, BobKostro, Bornintheguz, BotMultichill, Brycehughes, CJLL Wright, Chris 73, Chrissymad, ClueBot NG, Cogiati, Coldacid, Comtebenoit, Crpt2008, Curly Turkey, DASHBotAV, Daderot, David Trochos, Dbachmann, Ddddddddddkk, Dentren, DivermanAU, Doug Weller, ElinorD, Eric, Evans1982, Faizhaider, Florian Blaschke, Floris V, GB fan, George Bradford, Glenn, Gob Lofa, Goustien, Hammersoft, Hmains, IronGargoyle, J intela, J04n, Jabowery, Jandalhandler, Jeff G., Jheald, Johnbod, Jon-e-five, Jononmac46, Jramsay1927, Kanguole, Kintetsubuffalo, KrJnX, Lumos3, MPants at work, Magicmike, Miaow Miaow, Michael C Price, MisterFancyPants, Mrund, NYCJosh, Nagelfar, Ncip, Neddyseagoon, NekoDaemon, Nicolas Perrault III, NightMonkey, Nilfanion, Notmicro, Olivier, Ospalh, PaleoNeonate, Paleolithic Man, PatHadley, Penfold, Per Honor et Gloria, Piperh, RJP, RScheiber, Randy Kryn, RexNL, Richard Keatinge, Rjwilmsi, ShakespeareFan00, Shanmugamp7, Sheynhertz-Unbayg, Skybum, St. Caurgula, Sugaar, Taromsky, Tawkerbot4, The Editor 155, The Nth User, Trewornan, Trivialist, Twalls, Vald, Wiki13, Wikiwarrior07, WorldDownInFire, Xnn, Ymr68, Леонардо Кобеш, 108 anonymous edits .. 187

Magdalenian *Source:* https://en.wikipedia.org/w/index.php?oldid=853440937 *License:* Creative Commons Attribution-Share Alike 3.0 *Contributors:* 1297, 83d40m, Adamsan, Alphabet55, Anastrophe, AnonMoos, Aranel, Aspects, Bernorix, Bolivian Unicyclist, Böri, Cattus, Cavrdg, Cewvero, CieloEstrellado, ClueBot NG, Coldacid, Corinne, Csigabi, DavidCary, Dbachmann, Doug Weller, Dpleibovitz, Drallim, Drmies, Finn Bjørklid, Florian Blaschke, Floris V, Geog1, Glenn, Goethean, Goustien, Hadrianheugh, Hans Dunkelberg, Himbear, Hmains, Hutcher, Indymemerson1, Invertzoo, Inwind, IzzyFuzzy, J04n, Jargonash, Jeeber47, Jesper Willumsen, John Abbe, Johnbod, Jonkerz, Jorrit Delec, Julia Rossi, Kintetsubuffalo, Krano, Languagehat, Life of Riley, Luciebalakova, Lumos3, Marcocapelle, Martinl∼enwiki, Mattcolville, Melonkelon, Melsaran, Montgomery '39, NekoDaemon, Nicolas Perrault III, Non-dropframe, OCIDLE, OldCommentator, Omnipaedista, Peer Gynt, Per Honor et Gloria, Ptbotgourou, Qemist, RJP, Randy Kryn, Rathfelder, Reedy, Rickard Vogelberg, Rjwilmsi, Ronz, Rrobino, SMcCandlish, SethTisue, Sheynhertz-Unbayg, Spicemix, Sugaar, Suslindisambiguator, Sweepy, Taromsky, Tenbergen, TheNuszAbides, Tom87020, Ttotto∼enwiki, Uitlander, Unyoyega, Vald, Victuallers, Vsmith, WODUP, Walker Slake, William Harris, Xaxafrad, Yak, Yodin, Ziggurat, Znorz, Zoicon5, 76 anonymous edits 193

Settlement of the Americas *Source:* https://en.wikipedia.org/w/index.php?oldid=853837882 *License:* Creative Commons Attribution-Share Alike 3.0 *Contributors:* 23h112e, Abductive, Arthur Rubin, AtticusX, BD2412, Beland, Bender235, Beyond My Ken, Bgwhite, Bonadea, Buaidh, Castroyesid, Cdova, Chakazul, ClueBot NG, CommonsDelinker, Daniel Mietchen, Dawnseeker2000, Dbachmann, Dcirovic, Doug Weller, Dougmcdonell, Drbogdan, Eio-cos, Esperant, Facts707, Fixuture, Florian Blaschke, GenQuest, GeneralizationsAreBad, Gherald, Gilliam, Gladamas, Gog the Mild, Headbomb, Home Lander, Hypnosifl, ILoveCaracas, Idontknowwho, J 1982, JMilty, Jdaloner, Jerome Charles Potts, Joe Roe, Jonesey95, Justin15w, Kgrad, Kortoso, KylieTastic, Laurdecl, Malik Shabazz, Mandruss, Maragm, Maxl, Meters, Moncrief, Moxy, Mx. Granger, Myasuda, Nicolas Perrault III, Nightscream, North Shoreman, NottNott, ParadiseDesertOasis8888, Patty TROTTNER (KRADANGNGA), Paulmlieberman, Peacedance, Philip Trueman, Power∼enwiki, Pratyeka, Qzd, Raggz, Randy Kryn, Rantemario, Reinyday, Richard Keatinge, Rjwilmsi, Robert Brukner, Serols, Sfan00 IMG, Shellwood, Sietecolores, Simplexity22, Siroxo, Smallchief, Smd75jr, Smiley.toerist, StrayBolt, TAnthony, TGCP, The Quixotic Potato, Thomas Peardew, Titus III, Tom.Reding, Tonkawa68, Trappist the monk, Twinsday, Vorpzn, Vsmith, Widr, Wildcursive, William Harris, Wingedsubmariner, Xxxiv34, Y-dna data file, Yamaguchi先生, Yuchitown, Zarcademan123456, Zedshort, , 174 anonymous edits 199

Genetic history of indigenous peoples of the Americas *Source:* https://en.wikipedia.org/w/index.php?oldid=853205439 *License:* Creative Commons Attribution-Share Alike 3.0 *Contributors:* A2fnr, Albaalba, Alen1020, Amkilpatrick, AsteriskStarSplat, Aymatth2, BBooDoc, BD2412, Bender235, Betoine, Bgwhite, Bkalafut, Brout8, Cadenas2008, Carlotm, Chakazul, Chris the speller, Christian75, CommonsDelinker, Crovata, Darrend1967, Dbachmann, Dcirovic, Dcljr, Diannaa, Dicimah, Donner60, Double Clef, Doug Weller, Drbogdan, Ebizur, Eluchil404, Ephert, Fergananim, Fernirm, Fluous, FoxCE, Fraenir, Frietjes, Geekdiva, Giraffedata, GoingBatty, Goustien, Graham11, Grenzer22, Headbomb, Heironymous Rowe, Hmains, Hungarian Phrasebook, IceKarma, JWB, Jarble, KLRO6P, Kgrad, Khajidha, Khazar, Kintetsubuffalo, Leasnam, LoverOfArt, MadGuy7023, Magioladitis, Malik Shabazz, MaoGo, Marek69, Mark Ironie, Martarius, Maulucioni, Messir, Milemassi99, MistyMorn, Moxy, Mrwojo, Narwhaler, Nihiltres, Nihola, Node ue, Onel5969, Parkwells, Pierrewee, QLao, Quebec99, RebekahThorn, Rjwilmsi, Rua.lupa, ShelfSkewed, Sidoroff-B, Skyerise, Smarkham01, Squids and Chips, Stamptrader, Stevey7788, Student7, Tasedamp, TiMike, Trappist the monk, Uyvsdi, Waggie, WarriorsPride6565, Was a bee, Wildcursive, WolfmanSF, Woohookitty, Xb2u7Zjzc32, Y-dna data file, Δ, СЛУЖБА, 62 anonymous edits 218

Pre-modern human migration *Source:* https://en.wikipedia.org/w/index.php?oldid=849202073 *License:* Creative Commons Attribution-Share Alike 3.0 *Contributors:* 4pq1injbok, Ahmed 313-326, Alansohn, Altes, Andrew Lancaster, Auntof6, BD2412, Beetstra, Beland, Bgwhite, Blainster, Bws2002, CloudNine, ClueBot NG, CommonsDelinker, Cthuljew, Dbachmann, DivermanAU, Dlarmore, Doug Weller, Drbogdan, E-960, Eastcote, Eat me, I'm an azuki, Eddylyons, Elfalem, Elysium0820, Ephert, Fig wright, Fjpaffen, Florian Blaschke, Fraenir, FrederickE, Ftjrwrites, GFHandel, Gen Cow, Gjs238, Harizotoh9, Hmains, Hmainsbot1, Igodard, Iselilja, J 1982, J04n, Ja 62, Jeremy112233, Jmcw37, Jns4eva, JohnWhite1234, Jonah the Whale, Joshua Jonathan, K6ka, Ka Faraq Gatri, Kintetsubuffalo, Kozuch, Kwamikagami, La Pianista, Lanky, Laughingyet, LeadSongDog, LilHelpa, Mack2, Michael ohearn, Minna Sora no Shita, Mitch Ames, Mogism, Moxy, Mr Stephen, Muntuwandi, Naviguessor, Neelix, Neo-Jay, OccultZone, Onel5969, Petri Krohn, R'n'B, Radon210, Raz1el, Rich257, Richard Keatinge, Shanmugamp7, SilentWings, Skäpperöd, SnowFire, Snowolf, Sparkie82, Srednuas Lenoroc, Strongjam, Terjen, Tobby72, Uriber, Volunteer Marek, Waggers, Wikipelli, Wildspell, Wilston, Wurzeln und Flügel, Yanni576, 72 anonymous edits 233

Neolithic Revolution *Source:* https://en.wikipedia.org/w/index.php?oldid=851123801 *License:* Creative Commons Attribution-Share Alike 3.0 *Contributors:* Abductive, Activist, Alexander Davronov, Allthefoxes, Amal-Tallal, Andrew Lancaster, AndrewOne, Andrewcat58, Anyonamos, Articulant, Aspyer, Awesomegirlrules6, BallenaBlanca, Beko, Bender235, Berean Hunter, Bfinn, Bkonrad, Bryce Springfield, CAPTAIN RAJU, Candido, Charlotte Aryanne, Chickadee46 (alt), Chiswick Chap, ClueBot NG, CommonsDelinker, CoolieCoolster, Crystallizedcarbon, DVdm, Dan100, DatGuy, DavidLeighEllis, Dbachmann, Dcirovic, Dewritech, Donner60, Doug Weller, Doug4, Drewmutt, Ehrenkater, Elekes Andor, Escape Orbit, Fgnievinski, Flyer22 Reborn, Fmrauch, Foogoo2, Fraenir, Fuortu, Gamonetus, Gilliam, Gob Lofa, Gorthian, Grant65, Gulumeemee, HMSLavender, Hibernian, Holdencasey7, Hughesshots, Human3015, Isambard Kingdom, J 1982, Jandalhandler, JasperLawrence, Javert2113, Jessicaarroyo, Jim.henderson, Joe Roe, John of Reading, Johnbod, Josve05a, Just a guy from the KP, K6ka, Kerzhaw, KingUther, Kortoso, Luis Gandara30, MPS1992, Mais oui!, Marianna251, Marvellous Spider-Man, Materialscientist, Maxaxax, Maximajorian Viridio, Meganesia, MelanieN, Mistbreeze, Mizardellorsa, Mrconter1, Natg 19, Nationalmuseumofiran, North Shoreman, NottNott, Omid Ebrahimi Moghaddam, Omnipaedista, Onel5969, Oshwah, Palindromedairy, Pinkbeast, PlyrStar93, Pyrusca, QuackGuru, RA0808, Richard Keatinge, Richardlord50, Rjwilmsi, Ruyter, Satellizer, Scdavis527, Secondhand Work, Shadow 231, Siddiqsazzad001, SmallRepair, Smasongarrison, Snori, Spartan - 117, Stephenb, Stephenmckiernan, Sunny face, Sunrise, Surtsicna, Tajotep, TheBoyDuddes, TienShan0, Tjvmt, Tomalak geretkal, Trappist the monk, UnsungKing123, Vsmith, William Avery, Ypna, Zodess, শৌনক বন্দ্যোপাধ্যায়, 204 anonymous edits 244

Indo-European migrations *Source:* https://en.wikipedia.org/w/index.php?oldid=852761402 *License:* Creative Commons Attribution-Share Alike 3.0 *Contributors:* 0xF8E8, Adûnâi, Alexschmidt711, Apopp1219, Avoided, BD2412, Bgwhite, Blazearon21, CMEHalverson, Capitals00, Carlotm, Certes, Cgboeree, Clinamental, CommonsDelinker, Crawford88, Dbachmann, Deor, Deville, Dghmonwiskos, Dimadick, Future Perfect at Sunrise, Geebee100, Ghmyrtle, Headbomb, Hillbillyholiday, Hutchidyl, Jacob D, Joe Roe, John of Reading, Joshua Jonathan, Kautilya3, Kintetsubuffalo, Krakkos, Magioladitis, Malcolm77, Marek69, Maunus, Meganesia, Mojshahmiri, Neel.arunabh, Nitpicking polish, Nonsequitrist, Onel5969, Oranjelo100, Orenburg1, Pauli133, Quasar G., R'n'B, Redav, Rjwilmsi, Trappist the monk, WereSpielChequers, William Avery, 63 anonymous edits 260

Proto-Uralic homeland hypotheses *Source:* https://en.wikipedia.org/w/index.php?oldid=846856352 *License:* Creative Commons Attribution-Share Alike 3.0 *Contributors:* ABCEdit, Bearcat, Chiswick Chap, Cnwilliams, Finstergeist, Florian Blaschke, Headbomb, Hibernian, Jaakko Häkkinen, Jaakko Häkkinen∼enwiki, JorisvS, Kaiyr, Kanguole, Lisztrachmaninovfan, Magioladitis, Monegasque, Narky Blert, Newman2, Stevey7788, SwisterTwister, Tropylium, Urjanhai, Widr, СЛУЖБА, 9 anonymous edits 334

Nilo-Saharan languages *Source:* https://en.wikipedia.org/w/index.php?oldid=853418312 *License:* Creative Commons Attribution-Share Alike 3.0 *Contributors:* Abtinb, Aggelikiii, AlimanRuna, Andrew Dalby, Anubis2003, Aristophanes68, Artemka373, Ary29, Azalea pomp, BD2412, BaDyer, Bender235, Born Gay, Charles Matthews, Cit vësco, Citation bot 1, ClueBot NG, Dale Chock, DatGoodDude342, Davius, Dbachmann, Devahn58, Djduejdmdjd, Eric Kvaalen, Errantacademic, Erutuon, Ezeu, Florian Blaschke, FreeKnowledgeCreator, Goethean, Gorthian, Graham87, Hburton86, Headbomb, Hibernian, Hosenalwi, Howard McCay, Inayity, Inter&anthro, Iridescent, JWB, JaGa, Jarble, Jeffrey Mall, Jkrn111, JorisvS, Kborland, KennyHuang0513,

Image Sources, Licenses and Contributors

The sources listed for each image provide more detailed licensing information including the copyright status, the copyright owner, and the license conditions.

Image *Source:* https://en.wikipedia.org/w/index.php?title=File:Interactive_icon.svg *Contributors:* User:Evolution and evolvability 2
Image *Source:* https://en.wikipedia.org/w/index.php?title=File:Bab_el_Mandeb_NASA_with_description.jpg *License:* Public Domain *Contributors:* From WorldWind software 4
Image *Source:* https://en.wikipedia.org/w/index.php?title=File:STS059-238-074_Strait_of_Gibraltar.jpg *License:* Public Domain *Contributors:* NASA 5
Image *Source:* https://en.wikipedia.org/w/index.php?title=File:Strait_of_Sicily_map.png *License:* Creative Commons Attribution-Sharealike 3.0 *Contributors:* NormanEinstein 6
Figure 1 *Source:* https://en.wikipedia.org/w/index.php?title=File:Homo_habilis-2.JPG *License:* Creative Commons Attribution-ShareAlike 3.0 Unported *Contributors:* Reconstruction by W. Schnaubelt & N. Kieser (Atelier WILD LIFE ART) Homo_habilis.JPG: Photographed by User:Lillyundfrey 9
Figure 2 *Source:* https://en.wikipedia.org/w/index.php?title=File:Homo_erectus_new.JPG *License:* Creative Commons Attribution-ShareAlike 3.0 Unported *Contributors:* reconstruction by W. Schnaubelt & N. Kieser (Atelier WILD LIFE ART) Homo_erectus.JPG: photographed by User:Lillyundfreya 10
Image *Source:* https://en.wikipedia.org/w/index.php?title=File:Homme_de_Tautavel_01-08.jpg *License:* Creative Commons Attribution-Sharealike 3.0 *Contributors:* Gerbil 12
Image *Source:* https://en.wikipedia.org/w/index.php?title=File:Red_Pencil_Icon.png *License:* Creative Commons Zero *Contributors:* User:Peter coxhead 12
Figure 3 *Source:* https://en.wikipedia.org/w/index.php?title=File:Homo_erectus_adult_female_-_head_model_-_Smithsonian_Museum_of_Natural_History_-_2012-05-17.jpg *License:* Creative Commons Attribution-Sharealike 2.0 *Contributors:* reconstruction by John Gurche; photographed by Tim Evanson 14
Figure 4 *Source:* https://en.wikipedia.org/w/index.php?title=File:Homo_erectus_new.JPG *License:* Creative Commons Attribution-ShareAlike 3.0 Unported *Contributors:* reconstruction by W. Schnaubelt & N. Kieser (Atelier WILD LIFE ART) Homo_erectus.JPG: photographed by User:Lillyundfreya 14
Figure 5 *Source:* https://en.wikipedia.org/w/index.php?title=File:Homo_ergaster.jpg *License:* Creative Commons Attribution 2.5 *Contributors:* User:Luna04∼commonswiki 16
Figure 6 *Source:* https://en.wikipedia.org/w/index.php?title=File:Homo_Georgicus_IMG_2921.JPG *License:* Public Domain *Contributors:* Bogomolov.PL, Geekdiva, Kilom691, Nachosan, Rama, TMZ 111 17
Figure 7 *Source:* https://en.wikipedia.org/w/index.php?title=File:Dmanissi,_Georgia_;_Homo_georgicus_1999_discovery_map.png *License:* Public Domain *Contributors:* User:En rouge 18
Figure 8 *Source:* https://en.wikipedia.org/w/index.php?title=File:Homo-Stammbaum,_Version_Stringer-en.svg *License:* Creative Commons Attribution-Sharealike 3.0 Germany *Contributors:* Homo-Stammbaum, Version Stringer.jpg: Chris Stringer derivative work: Conquistador 20
Figure 9 *Source:* https://en.wikipedia.org/w/index.php?title=File:Human_evolution_chart-en.svg *License:* Creative Commons Attribution 2.5 *Contributors:* Reed DL, Smith VS, Hammond SL, Rogers AR derivative work: Conquistador 22
Figure 10 *Source:* https://en.wikipedia.org/w/index.php?title=File:Homo_erectus_tautavelensis.jpg *License:* Creative Commons Attribution 2.5 *Contributors:* User:Luna04∼commonswiki 26
Figure 11 *Source:* https://en.wikipedia.org/w/index.php?title=File:Tautavel_UK_2.JPG *License:* Creative Commons Attribution-ShareAlike 3.0 Unported *Contributors:* Gerbil 27
Figure 12 *Source:* https://en.wikipedia.org/w/index.php?title=File:Calvaria_Sangiran_II_(A).jpg *License:* Creative Commons Attribution-ShareAlike 3.0 Unported *Contributors:* Gerbil 27
Figure 13 *Source:* https://en.wikipedia.org/w/index.php?title=File:Homo_erectus_hand_axe_Daka_Ethiopia.jpg *License:* Creative Commons Attribution-Sharealike 3.0 *Contributors:* User:Commie cretan 28
Figure 14 *Source:* https://en.wikipedia.org/w/index.php?title=File:Pithecanthropus-erectus.jpg *License:* Public Domain *Contributors:* personal scan 120 28
Image *Source:* https://en.wikipedia.org/w/index.php?title=File:Commons-logo.svg *License:* logo *Contributors:* Anomie, Callanecc, CambridgeBayWeather, Jo-Jo Eumerus, RHaworth 29
Image *Source:* https://en.wikipedia.org/w/index.php?title=File:Hand-axe-Clactonian.JPG *License:* Public domain *Contributors:* File Upload Bot (Magnus Manske), Joostik, Liftarn, OgreBot 2, Cepheй 6662 30
Image *Source:* https://en.wikipedia.org/w/index.php?title=File:Biface_Micoquien_MHNT_PRE_.2009.0.193.1_(3).jpg *License:* Creative Commons Attribution-Sharealike 3.0 *Contributors:* User:Archaeodontosaurus 35
Figure 15 *Source:* https://en.wikipedia.org/w/index.php?title=File:Sub-Saharan_Africa_definition_UN.png *License:* Public Domain *Contributors:* Jcherlet: Jcherlet derivative work: Jcherlet (talk) 40
Figure 16 *Source:* https://en.wikipedia.org/w/index.php?title=File:Africa_map.png *License:* Creative Commons Zero *Contributors:* Soupforone 41
Figure 17 *Source:* https://en.wikipedia.org/w/index.php?title=File:East_and_southern_africa_early_iron_age.png *License:* Public Domain *Contributors:* User:Ulamm 42
Figure 18 *Source:* https://en.wikipedia.org/w/index.php?title=File:Meyers-L2.jpg *License:* Public Domain *Contributors:* Ain92, BrightRaven, Mapmarks, Soupforone 43
Figure 19 *Source:* https://en.wikipedia.org/w/index.php?title=File:Africa_map_of_Köppen_climate_classification.svg *License:* Public Domain *Contributors:* User:Ali Zifan 44
Figure 20 *Source:* https://en.wikipedia.org/w/index.php?title=File:Olduvai_stone_chopping_tool.jpg *License:* Creative Commons Attribution-Sharealike 3.0 *Contributors:* User:Alifazal 45
Figure 21 *Source:* https://en.wikipedia.org/w/index.php?title=File:Nzinga.jpg *License:* Public Domain *Contributors:* A.Savin, Hierakares, Joehawkins, Leyo, Roke∼commonswiki, SarahStierch, Zykasaa, 2 anonymous edits 46
Figure 22 *Source:* https://en.wikipedia.org/w/index.php?title=File:Gondereshe2008.jpg *License:* Creative Commons Attribution-Sharealike 3.0 *Contributors:* Warya 47
Figure 23 *Source:* https://en.wikipedia.org/w/index.php?title=File:ET_Gondar_asv2018-02_img03_Fasil_Ghebbi.jpg *Contributors:* A.Savin ..48
Figure 24 *Source:* https://en.wikipedia.org/w/index.php?title=File:Great-Zimbabwe-2.jpg *License:* Public Domain *Contributors:* Image taken by Jan Derk in 1997 in Zimbabwe. 49
Figure 25 *Source:* https://en.wikipedia.org/w/index.php?title=File:Tongoni_Ruins.jpg *License:* Creative Commons Attribution 2.0 *Contributors:* Airelle, Alifazal, FlickreviewR, Martin H. 50
Figure 26 *Source:* https://en.wikipedia.org/w/index.php?title=File:SphinxOfTaharqa.jpg *License:* Copyrighted free use *Contributors:* Captmondo, JMCC1, MGA73bot2, Neithsabes, Soerfm 51
Figure 27 *Source:* https://en.wikipedia.org/w/index.php?title=File:Nok_sculpture_Louvre_70-1998-11-1.jpg *License:* Public Domain *Contributors:* User:Jastrow 52
Figure 28 *Source:* https://en.wikipedia.org/w/index.php?title=File:Africa_population_density.PNG *License:* GNU Free Documentation License *Contributors:* BartekChom, Delusion23, Hoshie, Jmabel, MGA73bot2, Minzinho∼commonswiki, Roke∼commonswiki, Sven-steffen arndt, Timeshifter 54
Figure 29 *Source:* https://en.wikipedia.org/w/index.php?title=File:Fertility_Rates_and_Life_Expectancy_in_Sub-Saharan_Africa.png *Contributors:* User:Marobin2 54
Image *Source:* https://en.wikipedia.org/w/index.php?title=File:Flag_of_Angola.svg *License:* Public Domain *Contributors:* User:SKopp 55
Image *Source:* https://en.wikipedia.org/w/index.php?title=File:Flag_of_Burundi.svg *License:* Public Domain *Contributors:* User:Purnbaa80 ... 55
Image *Source:* https://en.wikipedia.org/w/index.php?title=File:Flag_of_the_Democratic_Republic_of_the_Congo.svg *Contributors:* User:Nightstallion 55
Image *Source:* https://en.wikipedia.org/w/index.php?title=File:Flag_of_Cameroon.svg *License:* Public Domain *Contributors:* User:SKopp ... 55
Image *Source:* https://en.wikipedia.org/w/index.php?title=File:Flag_of_the_Central_African_Republic.svg *License:* Public Domain *Contributors:* User:Nightstallion 55
Image *Source:* https://en.wikipedia.org/w/index.php?title=File:Flag_of_Chad.svg *License:* Public Domain *Contributors:* SKopp & others (see upload log) 55
Image *Source:* https://en.wikipedia.org/w/index.php?title=File:Flag_of_the_Republic_of_the_Congo.svg *License:* Public Domain *Contributors:* Andres gb.ldc, Anime Addict AA, Antemister, Benzoyl, Blackcat, Courcelles, Denelson83, Erlenmeyer, Estrilda, FischersFritz, Fry1989, HoheHoffnungen,

Homo lupus, Klemen Kocjancic, LA2, Madden, Mattes, Moyogo, Neq00, Nightstallion, Persiana, Pitke, Ratatosk, Reisio, Romaine, SiBr4, ThomasPusch, Thuresson, 6 anonymous edits ... 55

Image *Source:* https://en.wikipedia.org/w/index.php?title=File:Flag_of_Equatorial_Guinea.svg *License:* Public Domain *Contributors:* Allforrous, Andres gb.ldc, Anime Addict AA, Antonsusi, Benzoyl, Cathy Richards, Cycn, Duschgeldrache2, Emc2, Fastily, Fred the Oyster, Fry1989, Homo lupus, Klemen Kocjancic, Maks Stirlitz, Mattes, Neq00, NeverDoING, Nightstallion, OAlexander∼commonswiki, Permjak, Pitke, SiBr4, SouthSudan, ThomasPusch, 4 anonymous edits ... 55

Image *Source:* https://en.wikipedia.org/w/index.php?title=File:Flag_of_Gabon.svg *License:* Public Domain *Contributors:* User:Gabbe, User:SKopp 55

Image *Source:* https://en.wikipedia.org/w/index.php?title=File:Flag_of_Kenya.svg *License:* Public Domain *Contributors:* User:Pumbaa80 ... 55

Image *Source:* https://en.wikipedia.org/w/index.php?title=File:Flag_of_Nigeria.svg *License:* Public Domain *Contributors:* User:Jhs ... 55

Image *Source:* https://en.wikipedia.org/w/index.php?title=File:Flag_of_Rwanda.svg *License:* Public Domain *Contributors:* Achim1999, Albedo-ukr, Alkari, CemDemirkartal, Charlesjsharp, Erlenmeyer, EugeneZelenko, Fred J, Fry1989, Gmaxwell, GoldenRainbow, Homo lupus, Illegitimate Barrister, J Milburn, Klemen Kocjancic, Mattes, Perhelion, Persiana, Reisio, Rfc1394, Sangjinhwa, Sarang, SiBr4, Sixflashphoto, Smooth O, Steinsplitter, Sweeper tamonten, Theo10011, ThomasPusch, Vyacheslav Nasretdinov, Wester, Zscout370, Zzyzx11, 3 anonymous edits ... 55

Image *Source:* https://en.wikipedia.org/w/index.php?title=File:Flag_of_Sao_Tome_and_Principe.svg *License:* Public Domain *Contributors:* User:Gabbe ... 55

Image *Source:* https://en.wikipedia.org/w/index.php?title=File:Flag_of_Tanzania.svg *License:* Public Domain *Contributors:* User:Alkari, User:Madden, User:SKopp ... 55

Image *Source:* https://en.wikipedia.org/w/index.php?title=File:Flag_of_Uganda.svg *License:* Creative Commons Zero *Contributors:* tobias ... 55

Image *Source:* https://en.wikipedia.org/w/index.php?title=File:Flag_of_Sudan.svg *License:* Public Domain *Contributors:* Vzb83 ... 55

Image *Source:* https://en.wikipedia.org/w/index.php?title=File:Flag_of_South_Sudan.svg *License:* Public Domain *Contributors:* User:Achim1999 56

Image *Source:* https://en.wikipedia.org/w/index.php?title=File:Flag_of_Djibouti.svg *License:* Public Domain *Contributors:* Andres gb.ldc, EugeneZelenko, Fry1989, Homo lupus, Klemen Kocjancic, Martin H., Mattes, MyriamThyes, Neq00, Nightstallion, Nishkid64, Pymouss, Ratatosk, Sangjinhwa, Smaug the Golden, Str4nd, TFCforever, ThomasPusch, Tomasdd, Zaccarias, Zscout370, Ö, Şêr, Владимир турчанинов, 8 anonymous edits ... 56

Image *Source:* https://en.wikipedia.org/w/index.php?title=File:Flag_of_Eritrea.svg *License:* Public Domain *Contributors:* Alkari, Bukk, Cathy Richards, Counny, Crasstun, Fry1989, HJ Mitchell, HoheHoffnungen, Homo lupus, Klemen Kocjancic, Mattes, Michael seium, Moipaulochon, Neq00, Nightstallion, Ninane, Persiana, Ratatosk, Rodejong, SiBr4, TFerenczy, ThomasPusch, VulpesVulpes42, Vzb83∼commonswiki, WikipediaMaster, Zscout370, 8 anonymous edits ... 56

Image *Source:* https://en.wikipedia.org/w/index.php?title=File:Flag_of_Ethiopia.svg *Contributors:* Aaker, Anime Addict AA, Antemister, Benzoyl, BotMultichill, BotMultichillT, Cathy Richards, Cycn, Djampa, F l a n k e r, Fry1989, GoodMorningEthiopia, Happenstance, Homo lupus, Huhsunqu, INeverCry, Ixfd64, Klemen Kocjancic, Ludger1961, MartinThoma, Mattes, Mozzan, Neq00, OAlexander∼commonswiki, Pumbaa80, Rainforest tropicana, Reisio, Ricordisamoa, SKopp, SiBr4, Smooth O, Spiritia, ThomasPusch, Torstein, Wsiegmund, Xoristzatziki, Zscout370, 16 anonymous edits ... 56

Image *Source:* https://en.wikipedia.org/w/index.php?title=File:Flag_of_Somalia.svg *License:* Public Domain *Contributors:* see upload history . 56

Image *Source:* https://en.wikipedia.org/w/index.php?title=File:Flag_of_Botswana.svg *License:* Public Domain *Contributors:* User:SKopp, User:Gabbe, User:Madden ... 56

Image *Source:* https://en.wikipedia.org/w/index.php?title=File:Flag_of_the_Comoros.svg *License:* Public Domain *Contributors:* User:SKopp . 56

Image *Source:* https://en.wikipedia.org/w/index.php?title=File:Flag_of_Lesotho.svg *License:* Public Domain *Contributors:* Benzoyl, Cathy Richards, CommonsDelinker, Denelson83, Erlenmeyer, FSII, Fry1989, Homo lupus, JuTa, Klemen Kocjancic, Liftarn, Mattes, Nightstallion, OgreBot 2, Patricia.fidi, Pumbaa80, Rodejong, Sangjinhwa, Sarang, Shervinafshar, SiBr4, Sphilbrick, ThomasPusch, Typokorrektör, VulpesVulpes42, Zscout370, 6 anonymous edits ... 56

Image *Source:* https://en.wikipedia.org/w/index.php?title=File:Flag_of_Madagascar.svg *License:* Public Domain *Contributors:* User:SKopp ... 56

Image *Source:* https://en.wikipedia.org/w/index.php?title=File:Flag_of_Malawi.svg *License:* Public Domain *Contributors:* Achim1999, AnonMoos, Antonsusi, Awadewit, BartekChom, Cathy Richards, Erlenmeyer, Fred J, Fry1989, Gddea, GoldenRainbow, Homo lupus, IvanLanin, Klemen Kocjancic, Mattes, Phlegmatic, Rodejong, SKopp, Sangjinhwa, Sarang, Sebjarod, SiBr4, Sweeper tamonten, Theo10011, ThomasPusch, Zscout370, 6 anonymous edits 56

Image *Source:* https://en.wikipedia.org/w/index.php?title=File:Flag_of_Mauritius.svg *License:* Public Domain *Contributors:* User:Zscout370 .. 56

Image *Source:* https://en.wikipedia.org/w/index.php?title=File:Flag_of_Mozambique.svg *License:* Public Domain *Contributors:* User:Nightstallion 56

Image *Source:* https://en.wikipedia.org/w/index.php?title=File:Flag_of_Namibia.svg *License:* Public Domain *Contributors:* User:Vzb83 ... 56

Image *Source:* https://en.wikipedia.org/w/index.php?title=File:Flag_of_the_Seychelles.svg *Contributors:* - ... 56

Image *Source:* https://en.wikipedia.org/w/index.php?title=File:Flag_of_South_Africa.svg *Contributors:* Adriaan, Anime Addict AA, AnonMoos, BRUTE, Benzoyl, Cathy Richards, Charlesjsharp, Daemonic Kangaroo, Dnik, Duduziq, Dzordzm, Fry1989, Golden Bosnian Lily, Homo lupus, Illegitimate Barrister, Jappalang, Juliancolton, Kam Solusar, Klemen Kocjancic, Klymene, Lexxyy, MAXXX-309, Mahahahaneapneap, Manuelt15, Moviedefender, Mwtoews, NeverDoING, Nilli, Ninane, Pitke, Poznaniak, Przemub, Ricordisamoa, SKopp, Sarang, SiBr4, Stïnger, ThePCKid, ThomasPusch, Tvdm, Ultratomio, VulpesVulpes42, Vzb83∼commonswiki, Watchduck, Zscout370, 41 anonymous edits ... 56

Image *Source:* https://en.wikipedia.org/w/index.php?title=File:Flag_of_Swaziland.svg *License:* Public Domain *Contributors:* CemDemirkartal, Cycn, EugeneZelenko, Fry1989, Homo lupus, JMK, Klemen Kocjancic, Lojbanist, Mogelzahn, Nightstallion, OAlexander∼commonswiki, Ratatosk, Sangjinhwa, SiBr4, ThomasPusch, Wieralee, 1 anonymous edits ... 56

Image *Source:* https://en.wikipedia.org/w/index.php?title=File:Flag_of_Zambia.svg *License:* Public Domain *Contributors:* User:Zscout370 ... 56

Image *Source:* https://en.wikipedia.org/w/index.php?title=File:Flag_of_Zimbabwe.svg *License:* Public Domain *Contributors:* User:Madden ... 56

Image *Source:* https://en.wikipedia.org/w/index.php?title=File:Flag_of_Benin.svg *License:* Public Domain *Contributors:* Drawn by User:SKopp, rewritten by User:Gabbe ... 56

Image *Source:* https://en.wikipedia.org/w/index.php?title=File:Flag_of_Mali.svg *License:* Public Domain *Contributors:* User:SKopp ... 56

Image *Source:* https://en.wikipedia.org/w/index.php?title=File:Flag_of_Burkina_Faso.svg *License:* Public Domain *Contributors:* User:Gabbe, User:SKopp ... 57

Image *Source:* https://en.wikipedia.org/w/index.php?title=File:Flag_of_Cape_Verde.svg *License:* Public Domain *Contributors:* Drawn by User:SKopp ... 57

Image *Source:* https://en.wikipedia.org/w/index.php?title=File:Flag_of_Côte_d'Ivoire.svg *License:* Public Domain *Contributors:* User:Jon Harald Søby ... 57

Image *Source:* https://en.wikipedia.org/w/index.php?title=File:Flag_of_The_Gambia.svg *License:* Public Domain *Contributors:* Andres gb.ldc, Atamari, Avala, Cathy Richards, Courcelles, Denniss, Erlenmeyer, FischersFritz, Fry1989, HoheHoffnungen, INeverCry, Klemen Kocjancic, Materialscientist, Mattes, Neq00, Nightstallion, OAlexander∼commonswiki, Porao, Rkt2312, Rodejong, Sangjinhwa, Sarang, SiBr4, ThomasPusch, Vzb83∼commonswiki, WikipediaMaster, Xoristzatziki, Zscout370, 4 anonymous edits ... 57

Image *Source:* https://en.wikipedia.org/w/index.php?title=File:Flag_of_Ghana.svg *License:* Public Domain *Contributors:* AFBorchert, Benchill, Cathy Richards, Charlesjsharp, Cycn, Fry1989, Gunnex, Henswick, HoheHoffnungen, Homo lupus, Indolences, Jarekt, Kangseijoon, Klemen Kocjancic, Magasjukur2, MassiveEartha, Neq00, OAlexander∼commonswiki, Roberto Fiadone, SKopp, Sangjinhwa, SiBr4, ThomasPusch, Threecharlie, Torstein, Tulsi Bhagat, Vyacheslav Nasretdinov, Zscout370, 11 anonymous edits ... 57

Image *Source:* https://en.wikipedia.org/w/index.php?title=File:Flag_of_Guinea.svg *License:* Public Domain *Contributors:* User:SKopp ... 57

Image *Source:* https://en.wikipedia.org/w/index.php?title=File:Flag_of_Guinea-Bissau.svg *License:* Public Domain *Contributors:* User:SKopp 57

Image *Source:* https://en.wikipedia.org/w/index.php?title=File:Flag_of_Liberia.svg *License:* Public Domain *Contributors:* Government of Liberia 57

Image *Source:* https://en.wikipedia.org/w/index.php?title=File:Flag_of_Mauritania.svg *Contributors:* Ahmedsalem22, BrendonTheWizard, Cathy Richards, Fry1989, Guanaco, Gumruch, Hedwig in Washington, Herr chagall, Jcb, Jdx, JoaoPedro10029, Jon Harald Søby, Kimjiho2015, Sangjinhwa, Taivo, Todofai, Zscout370, 3 anonymous edits ... 57

Image *Source:* https://en.wikipedia.org/w/index.php?title=File:Flag_of_Niger.svg *License:* Public Domain *Contributors:* Made by: Philippe Verdy User:verdy_p, see also fr:Utilisateur:verdy_p. ... 57

Image *Source:* https://en.wikipedia.org/w/index.php?title=File:Flag_of_Senegal.svg *License:* Public Domain *Contributors:* Original upload by Nightstallion ... 57

Image *Source:* https://en.wikipedia.org/w/index.php?title=File:Flag_of_Sierra_Leone.svg *License:* Public Domain *Contributors:* Zscout370 ... 57

Image *Source:* https://en.wikipedia.org/w/index.php?title=File:Flag_of_Togo.svg *License:* Public Domain *Contributors:* Aaker, Ahsoous, Alkari, Benzoyl, Camervan, Cycn, Denniss, EugeneZelenko, File Upload Bot (Magnus Manske), Fry1989, Homo lupus, Klemen Kocjancic, Mattes, Mxn, Neq00, Nightstallion, Reisio, SiBr4, ThomasPusch, Vzb83∼commonswiki ... 57

Figure 30 *Source:* https://en.wikipedia.org/w/index.php?title=File:Languages_of_Africa_map.svg *License:* Creative Commons Attribution 3.0 *Contributors:* Seb az86556 ... 59

Figure 31 *Source:* https://en.wikipedia.org/w/index.php?title=File:San_tribesman.jpg *License:* Creative Commons Attribution-Sharealike 2.0 *Contributors:* Ian Beatty from Amherst, MA, USA ... 60

Figure 32 *Source:* https://en.wikipedia.org/w/index.php?title=File:Boerfamily1886.jpg *License:* Public Domain *Contributors:* Georgio ... 60

Figure 33 *Source:* https://en.wikipedia.org/w/index.php?title=File:Eritrean_Women.jpeg *License:* Creative Commons world66 *Contributors:* Dawit Rezenè ... 61

Figure 34 *Source:* https://en.wikipedia.org/w/index.php?title=File:Maasai_women_and_children.jpg *License:* Public domain *Contributors:* Bot-Multichill, Ephert, File Upload Bot (Magnus Manske), Mdd, OgreBot 2, Rodhullandemu, TomCatX ... 61

Figure 35 *Source:* https://en.wikipedia.org/w/index.php?title=File:Kwarastatedrummers.jpg *License:* Creative Commons Attribution 2.0 *Contributors:* Melvin "Buddy" Baker from St. Petersburg, Florida, United States ... 62

Figure 36 *Source:* https://en.wikipedia.org/w/index.php?title=File:Lagos_Island.jpg *License:* Creative Commons world66 *Contributors:* Photograph by Benji Robertson ... 66

Figure 37 *Source:* https://en.wikipedia.org/w/index.php?title=File:NBO5.jpg *License:* GNU Free Documentation License *Contributors:* Mkimemia 66

Figure 38 *Source:* https://en.wikipedia.org/w/index.php?title=File:Johannesburg_CBD.jpg *License:* Creative Commons Attribution 2.0 *Contributors:* FlickreviewR, Heather Elke, LX, M0tty, Xenonstain, 2 anonymous edits ... 67

Figure 39 *Source:* https://en.wikipedia.org/w/index.php?title=File:Greater_Cape_Town_12.02.2007_16-41-31.2007_16-41-33.JPG *License:* Creative Commons Attribution-Sharealike 3.0 *Contributors:* Simisa ... 68

Figure 40 *Source:* https://en.wikipedia.org/w/index.php?title=File:Front_de_mer.jpg *License:* Creative Commons Attribution-Sharealike 3.0 *Contributors:* User:Kennedy8kp ... 71

Figure 41 *Source:* https://en.wikipedia.org/w/index.php?title=File:Luanda_feb09_ost06.jpg *License:* Creative Commons Attribution-Sharealike 3.0 *Contributors:* Lars Rohwer ... 72

Figure 42 *Source:* https://en.wikipedia.org/w/index.php?title=File:Phenakite-262068.jpg *Contributors:* - ... 73

Figure 43 *Source:* https://en.wikipedia.org/w/index.php?title=File:Rwanda_GV5_lo_(4108942310).jpg *License:* Creative Commons Attribution-Sharealike 2.0 *Contributors:* CIAT ... 74

Figure 44 *Source:* https://en.wikipedia.org/w/index.php?title=File:2011-02-07_IMG_08.JPG *License:* Creative Commons Attribution 3.0 *Contributors:* Anagoria ... 75

Figure 45 *Source:* https://en.wikipedia.org/w/index.php?title=File:University_of_Botswana_Earth_Science.JPG *License:* Public domain *Contributors:* Apalsola, Aschroet, Ethansmith, OgreBot 2 ... 76

Figure 46 *Source:* https://en.wikipedia.org/w/index.php?title=File:University_of_Antananarivo_Madagascar.JPG *License:* Creative Commons Attribution-Sharealike 3.0 *Contributors:* User:Lemurbaby ... 77

Figure 47 *Source:* https://en.wikipedia.org/w/index.php?title=File:Komfo_Anokye_Teaching_Hospital,_Kumasi,_Ghana.jpg *License:* Creative Commons Attribution 2.0 *Contributors:* OER Africa ... 79

Figure 48 *Source:* https://en.wikipedia.org/w/index.php?title=File:AIDS_and_HIV_prevalence_2008.svg *License:* Public Domain *Contributors:* Escondites Permission= PD-self ... 79

Figure 49 *Source:* https://en.wikipedia.org/w/index.php?title=File:Bujumbura_Cathedral.JPG *License:* Public Domain *Contributors:* Croberto68, Denniss, Jeanot, KudzuVine, NeverDoING, Tequendamia, Threecharlie ... 81

Figure 50 *Source:* https://en.wikipedia.org/w/index.php?title=File:Saudi_mosque_in_Nouakchott.jpg *License:* Public Domain *Contributors:* Initsogan ... 81

Figure 51 *Source:* https://en.wikipedia.org/w/index.php?title=File:Ifedivination.JPG *License:* Creative Commons Attribution 3.0 *Contributors:* Kacembepower (talk) ... 82

Figure 52 *Source:* https://en.wikipedia.org/w/index.php?title=File:TrebleKalimba.jpg *License:* Creative Commons Attribution-Sharealike 2.5 *Contributors:* File Upload Bot (Magnus Manske), OgreBot 2, Peek park pure cussion, Rodhullandemu ... 84

Figure 53 *Source:* https://en.wikipedia.org/w/index.php?title=File:Chiwara_Chicago_sculpture.jpg *License:* Creative Commons Attribution-Sharealike 2.0 *Contributors:* Airelle, Maiella, T L Miles ... 85

Figure 54 *Source:* https://en.wikipedia.org/w/index.php?title=File:Fufu.jpg *License:* Creative Commons Attribution-Sharealike 3.0 *Contributors:* Londonsista ... 87

Figure 55 *Source:* https://en.wikipedia.org/w/index.php?title=File:Ugali_and_cabbage.jpg *License:* Creative Commons Attribution 2.0 *Contributors:* Mark Skipper ... 87

Figure 56 *Source:* https://en.wikipedia.org/w/index.php?title=File:Alicha_1.jpg *License:* Creative Commons Attribution-Sharealike 2.0 *Contributors:* Rama ... 88

Figure 57 *Source:* https://en.wikipedia.org/w/index.php?title=File:Kent_wove.jpg *License:* Creative Commons Attribution-Sharealike 3.0 *Contributors:* User:Bottracker ... 89

Figure 58 *Source:* https://en.wikipedia.org/w/index.php?title=File:Kangas_drying_in_Zanzibar.jpg *License:* Creative Commons Attribution 2.0 *Contributors:* Flickr user Lall ... 90

Figure 59 *Source:* https://en.wikipedia.org/w/index.php?title=File:AbidjanStade.JPG *License:* Creative Commons Attribution-Sharealike 3.0,2.5,2.0,1.0 *Contributors:* Zenman ... 91

Figure 60 *Source:* https://en.wikipedia.org/w/index.php?title=File:Namibia_Rugby_Team.jpg *License:* Creative Commons Attribution-Sharealike 2.0 *Contributors:* ozjimbob@flickr ... 92

Figure 61 *Source:* https://en.wikipedia.org/w/index.php?title=File:Afrika_MO.jpg *Contributors:* Einstein2, OgreBot 2, Redheylin, Skipjack ... 93

Figure 62 *Source:* https://en.wikipedia.org/w/index.php?title=File:LocationCentralMiddleAfrica.png *License:* Public Domain *Contributors:* User:E Pluribus Anthony∼commonswiki ... 94

Figure 63 *Source:* https://en.wikipedia.org/w/index.php?title=File:LocationEasternAfrica.png *License:* Public Domain *Contributors:* User:E Pluribus Anthony ... 95

Figure 64 *Source:* https://en.wikipedia.org/w/index.php?title=File:LocationSouthernAfrica.png *License:* Public Domain *Contributors:* User:E Pluribus Anthony∼commonswiki ... 97

Figure 65 *Source:* https://en.wikipedia.org/w/index.php?title=File:LocationWesternAfrica.png *License:* Public Domain *Contributors:* User:E Pluribus Anthony∼commonswiki ... 98

Image *Source:* https://en.wikipedia.org/w/index.php?title=File:Definition_of_Free_Cultural_Works_logo_notext.svg *License:* Public Domain *Contributors:* Marc Falzon ... 99

Figure 66 *Source:* https://en.wikipedia.org/w/index.php?title=File:Map-of-human-migrations.jpg *License:* GNU Free Documentation License *Contributors:* 84user, AnRe photography, ArachanoxReal, Atamari, Aude, Avsa, Chronus, Cwbm (commons), DEm, Dbachmann, DieBuche, Dudley Miles, Eleassar, Exsabuta, Fabartus, Glenn, Goustien, Ies, JMCC1, Jameslwoodward, Janbies, Joey-das-WBF, Joostik, Karlfk, Kintetsubuffalo, MGA73bot2, Noisy, Paulmallet, Phirosiberia, Ranveig, Rednblu, Themightyquill, VIGNERON, Verdy p, W!B:, Was a bee, Zemant, 16 anonymous edits ... 102

Figure 67 *Source:* https://en.wikipedia.org/w/index.php?title=File:Red_Sea2.png *License:* Creative Commons Attribution 2.0 *Contributors:* en:user:Muntuwandi ... 105

Figure 68 *Source:* https://en.wikipedia.org/w/index.php?title=File:African_Mitochondrial_descent.PNG *License:* Creative Commons Attribution 3.0 *Contributors:* Maulucioni ... 107

Figure 69 *Source:* https://en.wikipedia.org/w/index.php?title=File:Huxley_-_Mans_Place_in_Nature.jpg *License:* Public Domain *Contributors:* Benjamin Waterhouse Hawkins (1807–94) ... 110

Image *Source:* https://en.wikipedia.org/w/index.php?title=File:Lock-green.svg *License:* Creative Commons Zero *Contributors:* User:Trappist the monk ... 113

Figure 70 *Source:* https://en.wikipedia.org/w/index.php?title=File:Peopling_of_eurasia.jpg *License:* Creative Commons Attribution 2.0 *Contributors:* Metspalu et al. ... 118

Figure 71 *Source:* https://en.wikipedia.org/w/index.php?title=File:Rhinos_Chauvet_Cave.jpg *License:* anonymous-EU *Contributors:* AxelBoldt, OgreBot 2 ... 120

Figure 72 *Source:* https://en.wikipedia.org/w/index.php?title=File:Europe20000ya.png *License:* GNU Free Documentation License *Contributors:* User:Wobble ... 123

Figure 73 *Source:* https://en.wikipedia.org/w/index.php?title=File:Upper_Paleolihic_Art_in_Europe.gif *License:* Public Domain *Contributors:* Sugaar ... 124

Figure 74 *Source:* https://en.wikipedia.org/w/index.php?title=File:Venus_vom_Hohlen_Fels_Original_frontal.jpg *License:* Creative Commons Attribution 3.0 *Contributors:* Thilo Parg ... 125

Figure 75 *Source:* https://en.wikipedia.org/w/index.php?title=File:Venus-de-Laussel-vue-generale-noir.jpg *License:* Creative Commons Attribution 3.0 *Contributors:* photo 120, œuvre dont l'auteur est mort depuis environ 25 000 ans ... 126

Figure 76 *Source:* https://en.wikipedia.org/w/index.php?title=File:Venus_de_Brassempouy.jpg *License:* Public Domain *Contributors:* PHGCOM 127

Figure 77 *Source:* https://en.wikipedia.org/w/index.php?title=File:Lascaux_painting.jpg *License:* Creative Commons Attribution-ShareAlike 3.0 Unported *Contributors:* User:Prof saxx ... 129

Figure 78 *Source:* https://en.wikipedia.org/w/index.php?title=File:Sleeping_Reindeer_3_2918856445_7d66cc4796_o.jpg *License:* Creative Commons Attribution 2.0 *Contributors:* FlickreviewR, Victuallers ... 130

Figure 79 *Source:* https://en.wikipedia.org/w/index.php?title=File:Wells_Reindeer_Age_articles.png *License:* Public Domain *Contributors:* H. G. Wells ... 131

Figure 80 *Source:* https://en.wikipedia.org/w/index.php?title=File:Ukok_Plateau.jpg *License:* Creative Commons Attribution 2.5 *Contributors:* BotAdventures, Hardscarf, MGA73bot2, Maximaximax, Obakeneko, OgreBot 2, WhoNose ... 134

Figure 81 *Source:* https://en.wikipedia.org/w/index.php?title=File:Woolly_Mammoth_Climatic_Suitability_-_Nogués-Bravo_2008.png *License:* Creative Commons Attribution 2.5 *Contributors:* Dbachmann, FunkMonk, Karelj, William Harris, باسم ... 136

Figure 82 *Source:* https://en.wikipedia.org/w/index.php?title=File:Озеро_Дус-Холь_вечером._Тес-Хемский_кожуун.jpg *Contributors:* User:Александр Лещёнок ... 139

Figure 83 *Source:* https://en.wikipedia.org/w/index.php?title=File:ArtemisiaVulgaris.jpg *License:* GNU Free Documentation License *Contributors:* User:Fice ... 139

Figure 84 *Source:* https://en.wikipedia.org/w/index.php?title=File:Carex_halleriana.jpg *License:* GNU Free Documentation License *Contributors:* Ayacop, Chrizz~commonswiki, Jeantosti, MGA73bot2, Sadalmelik, Sir Antoni, WayneRay ... 140

Figure 85 *Source:* https://en.wikipedia.org/w/index.php?title=File:Grassflowers.jpg *License:* Public Domain *Contributors:* MILEPRI, Nomarcland, OgreBot 2, Thiotrix ... 140

Figure 86 *Source:* https://en.wikipedia.org/w/index.php?title=File:Salix-lanata-total.JPG *License:* Creative Commons Attribution-ShareAlike 3.0 Unported *Contributors:* Sten Porse ... 141

Figure 87 *Source:* https://en.wikipedia.org/w/index.php?title=File:Hjortron.jpg *License:* Public Domain *Contributors:* Philipum ... 141

Figure 88 *Source:* https://en.wikipedia.org/w/index.php?title=File:Potentilla_reptans_beauvais-carriere-bracheux_60_20062008_1.jpg *License:* Creative Commons Attribution-Sharealike 3.0 *Contributors:* Olivier Pichard ... 141

Figure 89 *Source:* https://en.wikipedia.org/w/index.php?title=File:Siberian-larch.jpg *License:* GNU Free Documentation License *Contributors:* Bggoldie~commonswiki, BotBln, BotMultichillT, Carnby, Clematis, MGA73bot2, MPF, Montrealais, WikipediaMaster ... 142

Figure 90 *Source:* https://en.wikipedia.org/w/index.php?title=File:Betukananabereza.jpg *Contributors:* User:Foledman ... 142

Figure 91 *Source:* https://en.wikipedia.org/w/index.php?title=File:Homo_sapiens_lineage.svg *Contributors:* User:Dbachmann ... 144

Figure 92 *Source:* https://en.wikipedia.org/w/index.php?title=File:Oase_2-Homo_Sapiens.jpg *License:* Creative Commons Attribution-Sharealike 2.0 *Contributors:* Ryan Somma ... 151

Figure 93 *Source:* https://en.wikipedia.org/w/index.php?title=File:Denisova_Phalanx_distalis.jpg *License:* Creative Commons Attribution-Sharealike 3.0 *Contributors:* Thilo Parg ... 153

Image *Source:* https://en.wikipedia.org/w/index.php?title=File:Pointe_Moustérienne_MHNT_PRE_2009.0.205.4_De_Maret.jpg *Contributors:* User:Archaeodontosaurus ... 157

Figure 94 *Source:* https://en.wikipedia.org/w/index.php?title=File:CurratExcoffierNeandethalmtDNA.png *License:* Creative Commons Attribution 2.5 *Contributors:* Mathias Currat, Laurent Excoffier ... 159

Figure 95 *Source:* https://en.wikipedia.org/w/index.php?title=File:Homo_neanderthalensis_adult_male_-_head_model_-_Smithsonian_Museum_of_Natural_History_-_2012-05-17.jpg *License:* Creative Commons Attribution-Sharealike 2.0 *Contributors:* Tim Evanson ... 160

Figure 96 *Source:* https://en.wikipedia.org/w/index.php?title=File:Range_of_Homo_neanderthalensis.png *License:* Creative Commons Attribution-ShareAlike 3.0 Unported *Contributors:* Nilenbert, Nicolas Perrault III ... 161

Figure 97 *Source:* https://en.wikipedia.org/w/index.php?title=File:Le_Moustier.jpg *License:* Public Domain *Contributors:* Abyssal, FunkMonk, Ixtzib, Judithcomm, Maky, Prioryman, Themightyquill, Thib Phil ... 161

Figure 98 *Source:* https://en.wikipedia.org/w/index.php?title=File:Pointe_levallois_Beuzeville_MHNT_PRE.2009.0.203.2.jpg *Contributors:* User:Archaeodontosaurus ... 161

Figure 99 *Source:* https://en.wikipedia.org/w/index.php?title=File:Cro-Magnon-male-skull.png *License:* Public Domain *Contributors:* Capmo, Guety, Hydro, Joostik, Nishkid64, Quadell, Un1c0s bot~commonswiki, 2 anonymous edits ... 164

Figure 100 *Source:* https://en.wikipedia.org/w/index.php?title=File:Silex_cromagnon_noir.jpg *Contributors:* User:Archaeodontosaurus ... 164

Figure 101 *Source:* https://en.wikipedia.org/w/index.php?title=File:Aurignacian_culture_map-fr.svg *License:* Creative Commons Attribution-Share Alike *Contributors:* Carte_Neandertaliens_classiques.svg: User:120 This map : Sémhur (talk) ... 165

Figure 102 *Source:* https://en.wikipedia.org/w/index.php?title=File:Homo_Sapiens_in_Europe_-_magdalenian_distribution_map-fr.svg *License:* Creative Commons Attribution-Share Alike *Contributors:* File:Blank_map_europe_no_borders.svg: This map : Sémhur ... 166

Figure 103 *Source:* https://en.wikipedia.org/w/index.php?title=File:Lions_painting,_Chauvet_Cave_(museum_replica).jpg *License:* Public Domain *Contributors:* HTO ... 168

Figure 104 *Source:* https://en.wikipedia.org/w/index.php?title=File:Flauta_paleolítica.jpg *License:* Creative Commons Attribution-Sharealike 2.5 *Contributors:* José-Manuel Benito ... 168

Figure 105 *Source:* https://en.wikipedia.org/w/index.php?title=File:Oase©Daniela_Hitzemann.JPG *Contributors:* Dbachmann, Fährtenleser . 170

Figure 106 *Source:* https://en.wikipedia.org/w/index.php?title=File:Cro-Magnon-female_Skull.png *License:* Public Domain *Contributors:* Guety, Joostik, Quadell, Un1c0s bot~commonswiki ... 171

Figure 107 *Source:* https://en.wikipedia.org/w/index.php?title=File:Abri_Pataud_-_Protomagdalenian_woman_skull_-_20090922.jpg *License:* Creative Commons Attribution-Share Alike *Contributors:* Sémhur ... 173

Figure 108 *Source:* https://en.wikipedia.org/w/index.php?title=File:Moulage_de_crâne,_Raymonden,_Chancelade,_Dordogne.jpg *License:* Creative Commons Attribution-Sharealike 3.0 *Contributors:* User:Symac ... 173

Figure 109 *Source:* https://en.wikipedia.org/w/index.php?title=File:Venus_vom_Hohlen_Fels_Original_frontal.jpg *License:* Creative Commons Attribution 3.0 *Contributors:* Thilo Parg ... 176

Figure 110 *Source:* https://en.wikipedia.org/w/index.php?title=File:Venus-de-Laussel-vue-generale-noir.jpg *License:* Creative Commons Attribution 3.0 *Contributors:* photo 120, œuvre dont l'auteur est mort depuis environ 25 000 ans ... 176

Figure 111 *Source:* https://en.wikipedia.org/w/index.php?title=File:VenusWillendorf.jpg *License:* GNU Free Documentation License *Contributors:* Photo taken by de:Benutzer:Plp at the Naturhistorisches Museum Wien ... 177

Figure 112 *Source:* https://en.wikipedia.org/w/index.php?title=File:Apollo-11_stone_slab.jpg *License:* Public Domain *Contributors:* José-Manuel Benito Álvarez —>Locutus BorgReference:*Bednarik, Robert G. (2003), The earliest evidence of Paleoart artíc ... 179

Figure 113 *Source:* https://en.wikipedia.org/w/index.php?title=File:Bradshaw_rock_paintings.jpg *License:* Creative Commons Attribution-Sharealike 2.0 *Contributors:* TimJN1 ... 180

Figure 114 *Source:* https://en.wikipedia.org/w/index.php?title=File:Ouranopithecus_macedoniensis.jpg *License:* Creative Commons Attribution 2.5 *Contributors:* 120 ... 183

Image *Source:* https://en.wikipedia.org/w/index.php?title=File:Homo_Sapiens_in_Europe_-_solutrean_distribution_map-en.svg *License:* Creative Commons Attribution-Share Alike *Contributors:* User:Sémhur & User:MPants at work ... 187

Figure 115 *Source:* https://en.wikipedia.org/w/index.php?title=File:Solutrean_tools_22000_17000_Crot_du_Charnier_Solutre_Pouilly_Saone_et_Loire_France.jpg *License:* Creative Commons Attribution-Sharealike 3.0 *Contributors:* World Imaging ... 191

Figure 116 *Source:* https://en.wikipedia.org/w/index.php?title=File:Aguja_y_anzuelo_Paleolitico.jpg *License:* Public Domain *Contributors:* José-Manuel Benito ... 191

Image *Source:* https://en.wikipedia.org/w/index.php?title=File:Homo_Sapiens_in_Europe_-_magdalenian_distribution_map-de.svg *License:* Creative Commons Attribution-ShareAlike 3.0 Unported *Contributors:* Homo_Sapiens_in_Europe_-_magdalenian_distribution_map-fr.svg: File:Blank_map_europe_no_borders.svg: This map : Sémhur (... 193

Figure 117 *Source:* https://en.wikipedia.org/w/index.php?title=File:Magdalenian_tools_17000_9000_BCE_Abri_de_la_Madeleine_Tursac_Dordogne_France.jpg *License:* Creative Commons Attribution-Sharealike 3.0 *Contributors:* World Imaging ... 196

Figure 118 *Source:* https://en.wikipedia.org/w/index.php?title=File:Pincevent_tent.gif *License:* Public Domain *Contributors:* José-Manuel Benito 196

Image *Source:* https://en.wikipedia.org/w/index.php?title=File:Wikisource-logo.svg *License:* Creative Commons Attribution-Sharealike 3.0 *Contributors:* ChrisiPK, Guillom, INeverCry, Jarekt, JuTa, Leyo, Lokal Profil, MichaelMaggs, NielsF, Rei-artur, Rocket000, Romaine, Steinsplitter ... 198

Figure 119 *Source:* https://en.wikipedia.org/w/index.php?title=File:Pre-clovis-sites-of-the-americas.svg *Contributors:* User:Pratyeka ... 200

Figure 120 *Source:* https://en.wikipedia.org/w/index.php?title=File:Beringia_land_bridge-noaagov.gif *License:* Public Domain *Contributors:* NOAA ... 201

Figure 121 *Source:* https://en.wikipedia.org/w/index.php?title=File:Map_of_gene_flow_in_and_out_of_Beringia.jpg *License:* Creative Commons Attribution 2.5 *Contributors:* Erika Tamm et al ... 204

Figure 122 *Source:* https://en.wikipedia.org/w/index.php?title=File:Journal.pone.0001596.g004.png *License:* Creative Commons Attribution-Sharealike 3.0 *Contributors:* Buzzzsherman ... 205

Figure 123 *Source:* https://en.wikipedia.org/w/index.php?title=File:Peopling_of_America_through_Beringia.png *License:* Creative Commons Attribution-Sharealike 3.0 *Contributors:* Ciaurlec, Dbachmann, Ephert ... 211

Figure 124 *Source:* https://en.wikipedia.org/w/index.php?title=File:World_Map_of_Y-DNA_Haplogroups.png *License:* Creative Commons Attribution-Sharealike 3.0 *Contributors:* Chakazul ... 213

Figure 125 *Source:* https://en.wikipedia.org/w/index.php?title=File:World_Map_of_Y-DNA_Haplogroups.png *License:* Creative Commons Attribution-Sharealike 3.0 *Contributors:* Chakazul ... 219

Figure 126 *Source:* https://en.wikipedia.org/w/index.php?title=File:Genetic_group_American_Native_American_DNA_subrace.png *License:* Creative Commons Attribution-Sharealike 3.0 *Contributors:* User:Ephert ... 220

Figure 127 *Source:* https://en.wikipedia.org/w/index.php?title=File:Haplogroup_Q_(Y-DNA).PNG *License:* Creative Commons Attribution 3.0 *Contributors:* Maulucioni ... 222

408

Figure 176 *Source:* https://en.wikipedia.org/w/index.php?title=File:Afanasevo_provisional.png *License:* GNU Free Documentation License *Contributors:* Angusmclellan, BotMultichill, Christophe cagé, Kilom691, MGA73bot2, OgreBot 2 284
Figure 177 *Source:* https://en.wikipedia.org/w/index.php?title=File:European_IE-migrations.jpeg *License:* GNU Free Documentation License *Contributors:* Joshua Jonathan () 20:46, 8 December 2017 (UTC) 288
Figure 178 *Source:* https://en.wikipedia.org/w/index.php?title=File:Dniester_map.png *License:* Creative Commons Attribution-Sharealike 3.0 *Contributors:* User:Kmusser 287
Figure 179 *Source:* https://en.wikipedia.org/w/index.php?title=File:Vistula_river_map.png *License:* Creative Commons Attribution-Sharealike 3.0 *Contributors:* User:Kmusser 287
Figure 180 *Source:* https://en.wikipedia.org/w/index.php?title=File:Dnipro_Basin_River_Town_International.png *License:* Creative Commons Attribution-ShareAlike 3.0 Unported *Contributors:* Francis McLloyd (reworked by Numerius Negidius) 287
Figure 181 *Source:* https://en.wikipedia.org/w/index.php?title=File:Danubemap.png *License:* Public Domain *Contributors:* Ciaurlec, Geologik, Shizhao, Superbfc, W!B:, Ymblanter, 8 anonymous edits 288
Figure 182 *Source:* https://en.wikipedia.org/w/index.php?title=File:TRB_culture_map.png *Contributors:* User:Xoil 290
Figure 183 *Source:* https://en.wikipedia.org/w/index.php?title=File:Map_Corded_Ware_culture-en.svg *License:* Creative Commons Attribution-Sharealike 3.0 *Contributors:* User:Alexrk2, User:Dbachmann, User:Sir Henry 290
Figure 184 *Source:* https://en.wikipedia.org/w/index.php?title=File:Bellbeaker_map_europe.jpg *License:* Public Domain *Contributors:* User:DieKraft 292
Figure 185 *Source:* https://en.wikipedia.org/w/index.php?title=File:Beaker_culture_diffusion.svg *License:* Creative Commons Attribution-Sharealike 3.0 *Contributors:* Diffusione_cultura_vaso_campaniforme.svg: *European_Union_topographic_map.svg: *European_Union_map_heightfield.svg: CIA 293
Figure 186 *Source:* https://en.wikipedia.org/w/index.php?title=File:Nordic_Bronze_Age.png *License:* Public Domain *Contributors:* User:Dbachmann 294
Figure 187 *Source:* https://en.wikipedia.org/w/index.php?title=File:Germanic_tribes_(750BC-1AD).png *License:* Creative Commons Attribution 2.5 *Contributors:* User:Berig 295
Figure 188 *Source:* https://en.wikipedia.org/w/index.php?title=File:Latin_Europe.png *License:* Creative Commons Attribution-Sharealike 3.0 *Contributors:* Aaker, Apocheir, Butko, Graphium, Hiddenhauser, Joan301009, Theutatis, 3 anonymous edits 296
Figure 189 *Source:* https://en.wikipedia.org/w/index.php?title=File:Celts_in_Europe.png *License:* Creative Commons Attribution-ShareAlike 3.0 Unported *Contributors:* AnonMoos, ArnoLagrange, Augusta 89, BotMultichill, Courcelles, David Kernow~commonswiki, Dbachmann, Dirk Hünniger, Dumdum~commonswiki, EisenHerz, Electionworld, Fideco, Fz22~commonswiki, George D. Bozovic, Henk B., Ilario111, Jafeluv, Jbribeiro1, Jianhui67, Joostik, Kopiersperre, Madrid647, Madrid747, Martin Kraft, Middle 8, Pava, QuartierLatin1968, Rocket000, Silar, Silverdamp, Spiridon Ion Cepleanu, The Ogre, Uhanu, Ulamm, Warburgout, Windsurf101, Winterkind, Zamprogna2, Zorion, 11 anonymous edits 297
Figure 190 *Source:* https://en.wikipedia.org/w/index.php?title=File:Balto-Slavic_lng.png *License:* Creative Commons Attribution 3.0 *Contributors:* Hxseek (Hxseek) Last edited by en:User:No such user 299
Figure 191 *Source:* https://en.wikipedia.org/w/index.php?title=File:East_europe_3-4cc.png *License:* Creative Commons Attribution-Sharealike 3.0 *Contributors:* Koryakov Yuri 300
Figure 192 *Source:* https://en.wikipedia.org/w/index.php?title=File:Slavic_peoples_6th_century_historical_map.jpg *License:* Creative Commons Attribution-ShareAlike 3.0 Unported *Contributors:* SeikoEn 301
Figure 193 *Source:* https://en.wikipedia.org/w/index.php?title=File:Slavic_tribes_in_the_7th_to_9th_century.jpg *Contributors:* User:Jirka.h23 301
Figure 194 *Source:* https://en.wikipedia.org/w/index.php?title=File:Dacia_82_BC.png *License:* Creative Commons Attribution-ShareAlike 3.0 Unported *Contributors:* Bogdan, BotMultichill, Codrinb, Electionworld, JuTa, Kopiersperre, LERK, Olahus, PANONIAN, Silenzio76, Spiridon Ion Cepleanu, 2 anonymous edits 302
Figure 195 *Source:* https://en.wikipedia.org/w/index.php?title=File:Dacia_around_60-44_BC_during_Burebista,_including_campaigns_-_French.png *License:* GNU Free Documentation License *Contributors:* User:Coldeel, User:Cristiano64 303
Figure 196 *Source:* https://en.wikipedia.org/w/index.php?title=File:Illyrians_Ethnogenesis_Theories_(English).jpg *License:* Creative Commons Attribution-ShareAlike 3.0 Unported *Contributors:* User:Megistias 304
Figure 197 *Source:* https://en.wikipedia.org/w/index.php?title=File:Illyrian_colonies_in_Italy_550_BCE.jpg *License:* Public Domain *Contributors:* Bratislav 305
Figure 198 *Source:* https://en.wikipedia.org/w/index.php?title=File:Proto_Greek_Area_reconstruction.png *License:* GNU Free Documentation License *Contributors:* self 307
Figure 199 *Source:* https://en.wikipedia.org/w/index.php?title=File:Map_Anatolia_ancient_regions-en.svg *License:* GNU Free Documentation License *Contributors:* Asia_Minor_Political_500BC.svg: *Mysia.svg: Emok derivative work: Mysia_map_ancient_community.jpg: User:Roke derivative 308
Figure 200 *Source:* https://en.wikipedia.org/w/index.php?title=File:Indo-Iranian_origins.png *License:* Creative Commons Attribution-ShareAlike 3.0 Unported *Contributors:* AnonMoos, Bender235, BotMultichill, Dbachmann, Karlfk, Verdy p, Дмитрий Кошелев 310
Figure 201 *Source:* https://en.wikipedia.org/w/index.php?title=File:From_Corded_Ware_to_Sintashta.jpg *Contributors:* User:Joshua Jonathan 311
Figure 202 *Source:* https://en.wikipedia.org/w/index.php?title=File:Andronovo_culture.png *License:* GNU Free Documentation License *Contributors:* Berillium, BotMultichill, Christophe cagé, Dbachmann, Firespeaker, Joostik, Karlfk, MGA73bot2, Maximaximax, TommyBee, 1 anonymous edits 312
Figure 203 *Source:* https://en.wikipedia.org/w/index.php?title=File:BMAC.png *License:* GNU Free Documentation License *Contributors:* Bontenbal, BrightRaven, Dbachmann, Look2See1, MGA73bot2, Sumerophile~commonswiki, Zaccarias, 1 anonymous edits 314
Figure 204 *Source:* https://en.wikipedia.org/w/index.php?title=File:Near_East_1400_BCE.png *License:* Creative Commons Attribution-Sharealike 3.0 *Contributors:* User:Javierfv1212 315
Figure 205 *Source:* https://en.wikipedia.org/w/index.php?title=File:South_Asian_Language_Families.jpg *License:* GNU Free Documentation License *Contributors:* Athaenara, File Upload Bot (Magnus Manske), JorisvS, Karlfk, Kwamikagami, MGA73bot2, OgreBot 2, Smjg, Sreejithk2000 318
Figure 206 *Source:* https://en.wikipedia.org/w/index.php?title=File:Early_Vedic_Culture_(1700-1100_BCE).png *License:* Creative Commons Attribution-Sharealike 3.0 *Contributors:* User:Avantiputra7 316
Figure 207 *Source:* https://en.wikipedia.org/w/index.php?title=File:Painted_Grey_Ware_Culture_(1200-600_BCE).png *License:* Creative Commons Attribution-Sharealike 3.0 *Contributors:* User:Avantiputra7 316
Figure 208 *Source:* https://en.wikipedia.org/w/index.php?title=File:Late_Vedic_Culture_(1100-500_BCE).png *License:* Creative Commons Attribution-Sharealike 3.0 *Contributors:* User:Avantiputra7 317
Figure 209 *Source:* https://en.wikipedia.org/w/index.php?title=File:Mahajanapadas_(c._500_BCE).png *License:* Creative Commons Attribution-Sharealike 3.0 *Contributors:* User:Avantiputra7 317
Figure 210 *Source:* https://en.wikipedia.org/w/index.php?title=File:Northern_Polished_Black_Ware_Culture_(700-200_BCE).png *License:* Creative Commons Attribution-Sharealike 3.0 *Contributors:* User:Avantiputra7 317
Figure 211 *Source:* https://en.wikipedia.org/w/index.php?title=File:Tarimrivermap.png *License:* Creative Commons Attribution-Sharealike 3.0 *Contributors:* Kmusser 319
Figure 212 *Source:* https://en.wikipedia.org/w/index.php?title=File:Wu-sun_Lage.png *License:* GNU Free Documentation License *Contributors:* Firespeaker, Flamarande~commonswiki, Karlfk, Krakkos, Leyo, MGA73bot2, Maksim, McPot, OgreBot 2, Sarang, Verdy p, Zaccarias, 2 anonymous edits 319
Figure 213 *Source:* https://en.wikipedia.org/w/index.php?title=File:Yueh-ChihMigrations.jpg *License:* Public Domain *Contributors:* BotMultichill, Draceane, Ismoon, It Is Me Here, Karlfk, Mogelzahn, Pieter Kuiper, Psychonaut, Verdy p, World Imaging, Zaccarias, 2 anonymous edits 320
Figure 214 *Source:* https://en.wikipedia.org/w/index.php?title=File:Scythia-Parthia_100_BC.png *License:* GNU Free Documentation License *Contributors:* Dbachmann 323
Figure 215 *Source:* https://en.wikipedia.org/w/index.php?title=File:ScythianGroups.png *License:* Creative Commons Attribution-Sharealike 3.0 *Contributors:* User:Slovenski Volk 324
Figure 216 *Source:* https://en.wikipedia.org/w/index.php?title=File:IndoScythianKingdom.svg *License:* Creative Commons Attribution-Sharealike 3.0 *Contributors:* User:DLommes 325
Figure 217 *Source:* https://en.wikipedia.org/w/index.php?title=File:Fenno-Ugrian_languages.png *License:* Creative Commons Attribution-Sharealike 3.0 *Contributors:* User:Free ottoman 335
Image *Source:* https://en.wikipedia.org/w/index.php?title=File:Nilo-Saharan.png *Contributors:* Ashashyou, Bender235, Huhsunqu, Karlfk, Mark Dingemanse, RHorning, Richie 337
Figure 218 *Source:* https://en.wikipedia.org/w/index.php?title=File:Lenguas_nilo-saharianas.PNG *License:* Creative Commons Attribution-Share Alike *Contributors:* Maulucioni 342
Image *Source:* https://en.wikipedia.org/w/index.php?title=File:Map_of_the_Niger–Congo_languages.svg *Contributors:* User:SUM1, User:Sting 350
Figure 219 *Source:* https://en.wikipedia.org/w/index.php?title=File:Niger-Congo_map.png *License:* Public Domain *Contributors:* Ulamm .. 356
Figure 220 *Source:* https://en.wikipedia.org/w/index.php?title=File:Nigeria_Benin_Cameroon_languages.png *License:* Creative Commons Attribution-Sharealike 3.0,2.5,2.0,1.0 *Contributors:* Ulamm 356
Figure 221 *Source:* https://en.wikipedia.org/w/index.php?title=File:Niger-Congo_speakers.png *License:* Creative Commons Attribution-Sharealike 3.0,2.5,2.0,1.0 *Contributors:* Ulamm 357

Figure 222 *Source:* https://en.wikipedia.org/w/index.php?title=File:Circumpolar_coastal_human_population_distribution_ca._2009.png   *License:* Public Domain *Contributors:* Al83tito, BMacZero 369

License

Index

Abashevo culture, 311
Abbreviations yr and ya, 33, 35, 36, 119, 144, 157, 158, 188, 193
Abdi-Heba, 322
Abedi Pele, 91
Abidjan, 67, 91, 98
Abies sibirica, 334
ABO blood group system, 219, 231
ABO (gene), 231
Aboriginal Australians, 109, 127
Abrahamic religion, 80
Abri de la Madeleine, 193
Abrigo do Lagar Velho, 173
Abri Pataud, 173
Abstinence, be faithful, use a condom, 78
Abstract art, 85
Abstraction, 10
Abuja, 98
Abyssinian–Adal War, 48
Accra, 98
Achaemenid, 323
Achaemenid Empire, 45, 309
Acheulean, 2, 4, 21, 22, 30, 31, 33, 35, 36, 44, 119, 157, 188, 193, 373
Acheulo-Yabrudian complex, 33, 36, 119, 157, 188, 193
Acholi dialect, 339
Achshaph, 322
Acre, Israel, 322
Adamawa–Ubangi languages, 354
Adamawa languages, 353, 354
Adamawa Plateau, 354
Adaptation, 10
Adaptive radiation, 182
Addis Ababa, 67, 96
Adjective, 366
Adobe, 52
Adorant from the Geißenklösterle cave, 169
Adposition, 366
Adriatic Sea, 124, 305
Advanced tongue root, 361
Aegean Sea, 124, 235, 275, 307
Aethiopia, 51
Afanasevo culture, 269, 275, 285, 312, 313

Afar Depression, 2
Afghanistan, 160
Afontova Gora, 34, 36, 120, 158, 189, 194, 225
Africa, 39, 65, 80, 255, 258, 350
Africa Cup of Nations, 91
African Cricket Association, 92
African Development Bank, 70
African Great Lakes, 40, 42
African immigration to the United States, 76
African languages, 337
African Languages and Cultures, 366
African Pygmies, 65
African rice, 74, 252
African Union, 80
Afrikaans, 63, 295
Afrikaner, 60
Afrikaners, 294
Afro-Arab, 50
Afro-Asiatic, 85
Afroasiatic languages, 41, 58, 59, 61, 65, 262, 338, 341
Afro-Asiatic languages, 63, 64, 80
Afroeurasia, 254
Afro-Eurasia, 30, 233
Age of Exploration, 233
Age of Migrations, 324
Age of the Reindeer, 195
Agricultural revolution in Africa, 236
Agriculture, 121, 234, 244
Agriculture in Africa, 338
Agriculture in Egypt, 252
Ahmad Hasan Dani, 329
Ahmarian, 33, 36, 119, 158, 188, 194
Ahmed Gurey, 48
Ahmed Yusuf (Gobroon), 48
Ahmose I, 322
Ahrensburg culture, 34, 36, 120, 132, 158, 189, 193, 194
AIDS, 78
Ain Hanech, 3
Ainu people, 167, 208
Ajuran Sultanate, 47
Akamba mythology, 83

Akan language, 64, 354
Akan languages, 364
Akan mythology, 82
Akan people, 90
Aka people, 65, 110, 155
Akkadian language, 58, 322
Akoko language, 354
Alamanni, 239
Al Andalus, 240
Alani, 324
Alan P. Merriam, 93
Alans, 319, 323
Alaska, 199, 214, 368, 369
Alaska Interior, 223
Alaska Natives, 215, 219, 220
Alaska North Slope, 369
Alaskan Peninsula, 201
Albania, 305, 306
Albanian, 306
Albanian language, 263
Alder, 135
Aleut, 227, 369
Aleutian Islands, 227, 369
Alexander Archipelago, 202
Alexander Häusler (archaeologist), 326
Alexander the Great, 309
Alf Hiltebeitel, 329
Alfred Hershey, 231
Alfred Nehring, 133
Algeria, 3, 93, 338
Algonquian peoples, 227
Al-Habash, 40
Alhambra Decree, 242
Alice Springs, 127, 132
Allan R. Bomhard, 265
Allan Wilson, 112
Allele, 231
Allele frequency, 150
Allerød oscillation, 123, 129
Alpine glaciers, 201
Altai Krai, 284
Altai Mountains, 125, 207, 226, 227, 285
Altai Republic, 138
Altai-Sayan region, 138
Altamira (cave), 178, 197
Alutiiq, 369
Alveolar consonant, 348, 361
Amarna letters, 322
Amazon Basin, 220
Amazon region, 222
American Journal of Human Genetics, 113
American Journal of Physical Anthropology, 210
American Museum of Natural History, 15
Americas, 121, 190, 199, 242
Amharic language, 63, 96

Amorite, 314
Amorites, 321
Amoudian, 132
Amur River, 208
Anagenetic, 16
Anatolia, 21, 234, 235, 249, 262, 275, 298, 303, 307, 309, 314, 325
Anatolian hypothesis, 274, 326, 394
Anatolian languages, 262, 280
Anatolians, 280, 308
Anatomically modern human, 101
Anatomically modern humans, 2, 101, 102, 121, 159, 163, 165, 184, 233
Ancient, 47
Ancient Beringian, 221, 368
Ancient Egypt, 256
Ancient Greece, 51
Ancient Greek, 264
Ancient Greek language, 303, 305
Ancient Greeks, 305
Ancient history, 310, 318
Ancient Iranian peoples, 235
Ancient Japan, 132
Ancient North Eurasian, 169, 184, 219, 221
Ancient North Eurasians, 165
Ancient Rome, 47, 283
Ancient warfare, 311
Andaman Islands, 108
Andes, 180, 221
Andrew M. T. Moore, 248
Andrew Sherratt, 256
Androgenic hair, 10
Andronovo culture, 270, 309, 310, 312
Angara, 132
Angiogenesis, 9
Angles, 239
Anglian Stage, 31
Anglo-Métis, 231
Anglo-Saxon invasion of Britain, 237
Anglo-Zulu War, 49
Angola, 55, 72, 85, 94, 96
Angolan kwanza, 94, 96
Angora goat, 257
Animal, 12
Animal domestication, 248
Animal husbandry, 279
Anoiapithecus, 182
Antananarivo, 77, 96
Antelian, 33, 36, 120, 158, 189, 194
Anthropological, 122
Anthropology, 260
Anthropology and genetics, 227
Anti-Lebanon, 251
Antimony, 72
Antler, 122, 190
Anuak language, 63

Anvil, 206
Anyi language, 364
Anzick-1, 213
Aoos, 305
Apapa, 65
Apes, 111
Apollo 11 Cave, 179
Appian, 304
Approximant, 349
Arab, 50
Arabia, 104, 108
Arabian Peninsula, 4, 117, 248
Arabic, 58
Arabic language, 50, 59, 96
Arabization, 241
Arab League, 39, 41, 93
Arabs, 240
Arab world, 39, 41, 93
Aranda people, 132
Archaeogenetics, 112, 234, 275
Archaeological culture, 194, 284, 311
Archaeological horizon, 312
Archaeological industry, 30, 122, 189
Archaeological record, 104
Archaeological site, 13, 160
Archaeological Site of Atapuerca, 160
Archaeologist, 30
Archaeology, 199, 260, 275
Archaeology of China, 126
Archaic human, 109, 183
Archaic human admixture with modern humans, 21, 101, 102, 104, 109, 112, 184
Archaic humans, 13, 25, 102, 117, 121, 163, 170, 182, 326
Architecture, 244
Architecture of Somalia, 47
Arctic, 221, 233, 368
Arctic Circle, 121
Arctic small tool tradition, 368
Arcy-sur-Cure, 157
Ardèche, 168
Argishti I, 306
Ariège (department), 128, 129
Aringa language, 339
Arkaim, 313
Arlington Springs Man, 130
Armenian Highland, 306
Armenian language, 263
Armenians, 239, 283
Armorica, 293
Aro confederacy, 53
Arrival, 117
Arrowhead, 190
Art, 175, 244
Artefact (archaeology), 121
Artemisia (genus), 139

Arthur Keith, 382
Artifact (archaeology), 30
Art of the Upper Paleolithic, 121, **175**
ArXiv, 329
Ashanti Empire, 52
Ashanti language, 90
Ashanti mythology, 82
Ashanti people, 89
Ashkelon, 322
A Short History of Progress, 247
Ashuku language, 364
Ashvins, 320
Asia, 13, 15, 19, 106, 121, 190, 250, 260, 263
Asia Minor, 274, 283, 298, 308
Asian people, 106
Asian Steppe, 312
Asioi, 285, 321
Asko Parpola, 330
Aspiration (phonetics), 348
Assyria, 58, 314, 323
Assyrian Empire, 282
Aswan Dam, 339
Atapuerca Mountains, 157, 183, 184
AtDNA, 220
Aterian, 33, 36, 119, 132, 157, 188, 193
Athabaskan languages, 220, 225
Athlone Power Station, 68
Atlantic–Congo, 351, 361
Atlantic–Congo languages, 350, 351, 359, 360
Atlantic languages, 353, 364
Atlantic slave trade, 230
Attalids, 309
AuDNA, 311
Aurignacian, 33, 36, 119, 126, 131, 132, 158, 163, 165–168, 175, 188, 194
Aurochs, 190, 195
Australasia, 109
Australia, 229, 242, 306
Australia (continent), 117
Australoid, 143, 205, 209
Australopithecina, 2, 15
Australopithecine, 19, 20
Australopithecines, 9
Australopithecus, 20, 23, 43
Australopithecus afarensis, 2, 9
Australopithecus garhi, 2
Australopithecus sediba, 371
Austrasia, 237
Austria, 306
Austrians, 294
Austronesia, 236
Austronesian language, 63
Austronesian languages, 59, 350
Austronesian peoples, 214
Austronesians, 236

Automated Similarity Judgment Program, 360
Autosomal, 220
Autosomal DNA, 190, 215
Autosome, 109, 147, 219
Auxiliary verb, 365
Avaris, 321
Avars (Carpathians), 240
Axumite Empire, 47
Ayere–Ahan languages, 355
Azania, 50
Azerbaijan, 126, 284, 322
Azilian, 166, 174, 193, 197
Azumah Nelson, 92

Bab al Mandab, 103
Bab-el-Mandeb, 4, 7
Bab-el-Mandeb straits, 105, 117
Babylonia, 58, 321
Bactria, 285, 320, 323, 387
Bactria–Margiana Archaeological Complex, 261, 270, 309, 314
Bactrian camel, 257
Bactrians, 323
Badarian, 252
Badegoulien, 187
Baden culture, 279, 290
Baden-Württemberg, 178
Bahrain, 322
Baikal, 207, 226
Bak languages, 353
Balkan–Danubian culture, 269
Balkans, 123, 166, 280, 298, 302, 305, 306, 309
Balochi language, 325
Baloch people, 323
Baltic Finnic people, 370
Baltic languages, 263, 269, 298, 299, 302
Baltic Sea, 269
Balve Cave, 35
Balver Höhle, 37
Balzi Rossi, 172
Bamako, 78, 99
Bamako Initiative, 78
Bambara language, 364
Bambara people, 85
Bambuti mythology, 83
Banana, 253
Bananas, 252
Banda languages, 63, 364
Band societies, 23
Bangui, 95
Banjul, 98
Bantoid languages, 353, 355, 360
Bantu expansion, 42, 50, 52, 58, 65, 233, 236, 253, 258, 351, 352, 355

Bantu languages, 48, 50, 59, 63, 350–353, 355, 358
Bantu Migration, 46
Bantu peoples, 46, 236
Banu Hilal, 241
Baradostian culture, 33, 36, 120, 158, 188, 194
Barbara (region), 40
Barley, 249
Barnfield Pit, 30, 32
Barnham, Suffolk, 30, 32
Bartolomeu Dias, 49
Basal ganglia, 149
Basic word order, 365
Basque language, 235, 270
Bâton de commandement, 178, 197
Baton fragment (Palart 310), 175
Battle axe, 322
Battle of Kadesh, 308
Battling Siki, 92
Bauxite, 72
Bavaria, 296
BBC News, 392
Beachcombing, 105
Bead, 189
Beans, 253
Bear, 172, 175, 190
Bedouin, 241
Before present, 121, 148, 150, 157, 159, 160, 189, 191, 195, 200, 244
Behavioral modernity, 121, 175
Beijing, 15, 128
Bekaa Valley, 254
Belarusians, 302
Bell Beaker, 289
Bemba people, 47
Bendi languages, 355
Bengali language, 262
Benin, 56, 98, 338, 354
Benue–Congo, 64, 352
Benue–Congo languages, 353, 355
Benue River, 236, 352
Berber languages, 58
Berber people, 40, 240
Berbers, 146
Beringia, 137, 190, 199, 200, 206, 219, 223
Bering land bridge, 121, 134, 190
Bering Strait, 223, 226, 228
Bering Straits, 369
Berlin conference, 48
Berta languages, 337, 342–345
Beshkent district, 313
Bété language, 354
Bethwell A. Ogot, 374
Betula nana, 143
Bibcode, 113, 114, 327–329
Bichon man, 174

Biface, 31, 37
Bill John Baker, 385
Biltong, 89
Binomial nomenclature, 12
Biological species concept, 19
Biologist, 219
Biome, 41, 133
Biomes, 39
BioRxiv, 330
Biped, 43
Bipedalism, 9
Birch, 135
Biridašwa, 322
Biridiya, 322
Birri language, 346
Bison, 133, 136
Bissau, 99
Bithynia, 302
Bithynians, 283
Black and red ware culture, 394
Black-eyed peas, 74
Blackfoot Confederacy, 232
Black Sea, 123, 234, 274, 298, 303, 324
Blackwater Draw, 211
Blade, 195
Blindness, 80
Bloemfontein, 97
Blombos Cave, 85, 121, 175, 179
Blood groups, 231
Blood proteins, 231
Blood types, 199
Blood vessel, 9
Blue eyes, 167
Bluefish Caves, 205
BMAC, 310, 312
Bnot Yaakov Bridge, 23
Bohemia, 298
Bohunician, 33, 36, 119, 158, 188, 194
Bois-Brûlés, 231
Bølling oscillation, 129
Bone, 189
Bone marrow, 8
Boreal forest, 380
Bornu Empire, 46, 52
Bororo (Brazil), 232
Bosnia and Herzegovina, 305
Bosniaks, 302
Botswana, 56, 76, 96
Botswana pula, 96
Boubou (clothing), 90
Bournemouth University, 19
Bow and arrow, 167
Boxgrove, 31
Bradshaw rock paintings, 180
Bradshaws, 179
Brain drain, 76

Brassempouy, 128
Brazil, 205, 306
Brazzaville, 95
BRIC, 67
Brill Publishers, 329
British colonization of the Americas, 231
British Columbia, 214
British Empire, 53
British Isles, 240
Brittany, 293, 298
Brno, 128
Brocas area, 23
Bronze, 311
Bronze Age, 244, 262, 275, 279, 282, 283, 306, 307, 311, 312
Bronze Age Collapse, 283, 307
Broomcorn millet, 251
Brow ridge, 195
Bruce Grobbelaar, 91
Bryges, 309
Buddhism, 318
Buganda, 51
Bug-Dniester culture, 277
Buhl Woman, 209, 228
Bujumbura, 81, 94, 96
Bulb of percussion, 30
Bulgarians, 302
Bulgars, 240
Bunurong, 132
Burebista, 302
Burgundian language (Germanic), 295
Burgundians, 239
Burin (lithic flake), 122
Burkina Faso, 57, 98, 339
Buru language (Nigeria), 355
Burundi, 47, 55, 81, 94, 96
Burundian franc, 94, 96
Bushmen, 352
Bushongo mythology, 83
Bushveld, 42

C14 dating, 17
Cabbage, 87
CAF Champions League, 91
CAF Confederation Cup, 91
Cairo, 65, 339
Calibrated years, 289
Calibration of radiocarbon dates, 201
California Academy of Sciences, 217
Calvaria (skull), 15, 27, 152
Cambrian, 12
Cambridge Reference Sequence, 112
Cambridge University Press, 217, 330, 367
Camel, 45
Cameroon, 55, 59, 85, 95
Campsite, 121

Canaan, 307
Canada, 133, 306
Canberra, 128
Candomblé, 80
Cannibalism, 172
Cap Blanc rock shelter, 173
Cape Breton Island, 298
Cape Colony, 49
Cape Guardafui, 47
Cape of Good Hope, 49
Cape Town, 49, 67, 68, 93, 97
Cape Verde, 57
Capsian, 132
Carboniferous, 12
Cardium pottery, 388
Caribbean, 258
Carinate, 197
Carleton S. Coon, 111, 152
Carl Meinhof, 358
Carlo Conti Rossini, 340
Carl O. Sauer, 253
Carl Sauer, 247
Carnivore, 197
Carnivorous, 185
Carpathian Mountains, 303, 324
Carrion, 170
Carrying capacity, 7
Carthage, 45
Cartography, 39
Caspian Sea, 265, 274, 387
Cassava, 86
Casta, 230
Castlereagh, New South Wales, 125
Castor beans, 74
Catalan language, 296
Cataracts of the Nile, 39
Category:Indo-European, 260
Catherine the Great, 242
Catholic Encyclopedia, 392
Cattle, 248
Caucasian languages, 235
Caucasian race, 285, 310, 318
Caucasoid race, 152
Caucasus, 145, 235, 279, 280, 283, 322, 323
Caucasus (geographic region), 227
Caucasus Mountains, 274
Causative, 365
Cave, 189
Cave art, 126, 197
Cave bear, 167, 170
Cave of Altamira, 129, 193
Cave of Dzhebel, 265
Cave painting, 122, 167, 175, 178
Caves and Ice Age Art in the Swabian Jura, 169
Caves of Nerja, 126
Celt, 239

Celtiberians, 298
Celtic diaspora (disambiguation), 298
Celtici, 298
Celtic invasion of the Balkans, 304
Celtic languages, 263, 269, 297
Celtic nations, 297
Celts, 237, 294
Cemetery H culture, 310
Cengage Learning, 329
Central Africa, 40, 43, 59, 337, 351
Central African CFA franc, 95
Central African Federation, 94
Central African Republic, 55, 95, 352, 354
Central Alaskan Yupik, 369
Central and Eastern Europe, 300
Central Asia, 234, 260, 268, 300, 311, 323, 324
Central Australia, 132
Central Europe, 37, 270, 300
Central Iran, 160
Central Sudanic languages, 337, 341–346, 360
Centum, 262
Cephalic index, 209
Cereal, 249
Cerebellum, 149
Cerebral blood flow, 9
Certificate of Degree of Indian Blood, 231
Cerutti Mastodon site, 206
Cervical cancer, 156
Chad, 41, 55, 95, 339
Chadic languages, 58, 64
Chalcolithic, 184, 272, 326
Chancelade, 173
Chancelade man, 173
Channel Islands of California, 215
Charcoal, 22, 127
Charente, 160, 198
Chariot, 270, 311, 312, 321, 322
Chariots, 282
Chari River, 60, 337, 340
Charles Darwin, 13, 111
Charles R. Knight, 161
Chatelperronian, 122
Châtelperronian, 33, 36, 119, 131, 157, 158, 160, 162, 188, 194
Chauvet Cave, 126, 168, 178
Chek Lap Kok, 126
Chelyabinsk Oblast, 313
Cherokee, 225, 231
Chesowanja, 22
Chewa language, 63
Chibcha, 221
Chibchan languages, 220
Chickpea, 249
Chile, 130, 180, 214, 215
Chimpanzee, 23, 43, 111

China, 15, 106, 133, 261, 285, 286, 320, 321, 336
Chinese language, 104, 318, 320
Chiwara, 85
Chopper (archaeology), 30
Chopping tool, 30
Chordate, 12
Chris Stringer, 20, 384
Christianity, 80
Christopher Ehret, 347, 348, 377, 378
Christopher I. Beckwith, 310, 318, 327
Chromium, 72
Chronological items, 16, 70
Chukchi people, 222, 368
Chukotka Autonomous Okrug, 368, 369
Chukotko-Kamchatkan peoples, 368
Church of Saint George, Lalibela, 47
CIA World Factbook, 376
Cimmerians, 239, 309, 323, 324
Ciomadul, 127
Circumpolar North, 368
Circumpolar peoples, 237, **368**
Cisalpine Gaul, 298
Cis-regulatory element, 149
CITEREFAllentoft2015, 389, 391
CITEREFAnthony2007, 387–391, 394
CITEREFAnthony2009, 394
CITEREFAnthony2017, 391
CITEREFAnthonyRidge2015, 387
CITEREFAnthonyRinge2015, 389
CITEREFAppenzeller2012, 378
CITEREFAppiahGates2010, 374
CITEREFBasu2003, 388
CITEREFBeckwith2009, 387, 390, 393, 394
CITEREFBeyin2011, 378
CITEREFBojtar1999, 389
CITEREFBradley2007, 391
CITEREFBryant2001, 394, 395
CITEREFBurrow1973, 393
CITEREFDemkina2017, 389
CITEREFDiakonoff1995, 394
CITEREFDumitrescuBoardmanHammond-Sollberger1982, 393
CITEREFEllis1861, 393
CITEREFEndicott et al.2003, 109
CITEREFFinlayson2009, 379
CITEREFFlood1996, 394
CITEREFGimbutas1997, 388
CITEREFGroucutt et al.2015, 106, 379
CITEREFHaak2015, 387, 389, 391
CITEREFHeyd2017, 391
CITEREFHiltebeitel2002, 394
CITEREFHollar2011, 394
CITEREFHusovská1998, 393
CITEREFIvanova2012, 388
CITEREFJones2015, 389

CITEREFKarlene1996, 388
CITEREFKohl2007, 394
CITEREFKortlandt2010, 387
CITEREFKroonen2015, 388
CITEREFLazaridis2016, 389
CITEREFLazaridisHaak2015, 391
CITEREFLiu, Harding et al.2000, 109
CITEREFLiu, Martinón-Torres et al.2015, 104
CITEREFLiu, Prugnolle et al.2006, 379
CITEREFLoeweShaughnessy1999, 388
CITEREFMacaulay et al.2005, 103, 106
CITEREFMallory1989, 389
CITEREFMallory1997, 389, 394
CITEREFMallory1999, 387, 388, 390, 391
CITEREFMallory2002, 388
CITEREFMallory2013, 389
CITEREFMalloryAdams1997, 387–389, 391
CITEREFMalory1989, 394
CITEREFMountain1998, 393
CITEREFNandris1976, 393
CITEREFNichols1997, 387
CITEREFNichols1999, 387
CITEREFParpola1999, 393
CITEREFParpola2015, 387–389
CITEREFPereltsvaigLewis2015, 388, 389
CITEREFPiggot1965, 391
CITEREFPosth et al.2016, 103, 106
CITEREFRinge2006, 388
CITEREFSalmons2015, 388
CITEREFSamuel2010, 394
CITEREFShackelton et al.2006, 109
CITEREFStrabo20 AD, 393
CITEREFStrazny2000, 389
CITEREFSwisherCurtisLewin2000, 372
CITEREFTreptow1996, 393
CITEREFWells2003, 103, 104
CITEREFWilkes1995, 393
CITEREFWitzel1989, 394
CITEREFWitzel1995, 389, 394
CITEREFWitzel2001, 388
CITEREFWitzel2005, 388
CITEREFYoung McChesney2015, 378, 379
Cities of the ancient Near East, 314
Civilization, 244
Clactonian, **30**, 33, 36, 119, 157, 188, 193
Clacton-on-Sea, 30, 32
Clade, 372
Cladogenesis, 16
Classical antiquity, 239, 294, 305, 308
Classifier (linguistics), 338
Cleaver (tool), 2
Click languages, 338
Climate zone, 41, 44
Clovis culture, 199
Clovis, New Mexico, 210
Clovis Point, 211

Club (weapon), 190
Coalescent theory, 148
Coastal migration, 184
Coastal migration (Americas), 117, 205
Coffee, 74, 252
Cognate, 348
Colette Caillat, 331
Colin Renfrew, 234, 274, 326
Collective, 338
Colocasia esculenta, 253
Colonial empire, 48
Colonial empires, 233
Colonialism, 39, 242
Colonies, 242
Colonisation (biology), 182
Coltan, 72
Common Era, 323
Common name, 163
Commons:Category:Homo erectus, 29
Commons:Category:Indigenous nations of the
    Americas, 218
Commons:Category:Magdalenian, 199
Commons:Category:Micoquien, 38
Commons:Category:Mousterian, 162
Commons:Category:Solutrean, 192
Commonwealth Scientific and Industrial Re-
    search Organisation, 253
Comorian franc, 96
Comorian language, 96
Comoros, 39, 56, 96
Company rule in India, 49
Comparative method, 264, 265, 299
Complementary distribution, 364
Composite bow, 322
Computational phylogenetic, 360
Conakry, 98
Condyloid process, 150
Confederation of African Rugby, 92
Congolese franc, 94
Conquest of Canaan, 237
Consciousness, 10
Consonant, 294
Constitutional Court of South Africa, 67
Continental Divide of the Americas, 211
Conurbation, 65
Convergent evolution, 109
Copper, 72, 311
Copper Age, 274
Copper Hoard Culture, 310
Corded Ware, 271, 311
Corded Ware culture, 234, 260, 261, 269, 289,
    311
Cordilleran Ice Sheet, 201, 211
Cornwall, 298
Coronal consonant, 348
Coronoid process of the mandible, 150

Corpus mandibulae, 151
Cosmology, 82
Cosquer cave, 129, 178, 381
Cotton, 74
Couscous, 86
Cranial capacity, 167
Crash Course (YouTube), 259
Cratylus (dialogue), 309
Cremation, 313
Creswell Crags, 157, 178, 190
Creswellian culture, 130
Cretaceous, 12
Cricket World Cup, 92
Croatia, 305
Croats, 302
Crohns disease, 148
Cro-Magnon, 122, 182, 184
Cro-Magnon 1, 164, 166, 172
Cro-Magnon rock shelter, 163, 171
Crop yield, 249
Cross River languages, 355
Cross River (Nigeria), 236
Crown of Castile, 242
Cucuteni-Tripolye culture, 277
Cucuteni-Trypillian culture, 260, 269
Cueva de las Manos, 130
Cuneiform (script), 282
Cupik, 369
Current Anthropology, 382
Cushitic languages, 58, 63
Cyperaceae, 140
Cyprus, 307
Cyrus the Great, 309
Czechs, 302

Dacia, 302, 303
Dacian language, 302, 304
Dacians, 303
Dagbani language, 364
Dahalo language, 341
Dahomey mythology, 82
Dakar, 77, 99
Daka skull, 26, 28
Dakoid languages, 355
Damascus, 322
Dam Dam Chesme II, 265
Danes, 294
Dangme language, 364
Daniel Everett, 23
Daniel Zohary, 249
Danish language, 295
Dan-Santa language, 364
Danube, 269, 288, 298, 303
Danubian corridor, 166
Dard people, 309
Dar es Salaam, 65

Darfur, 94, 339
Dart (missile), 122
Darug, 132
Dashiki, 90
Dates and numbers, 226
David Lewis-Williams, 175
David Lordkipanidze, 17
David Reich (geneticist), 244
David Rindos, 247
Davidson Black, 15
Dayuan, 285
Daza language, 339
Dean Falk, 9
Declension, 264
Defaka language, 350, 352, 355
Defining race, 230
Deforestation, 244
Dehydration, 8
Demic diffusion, 326
Democratic Republic of Congo, 85
Democratic Republic of the Congo, 41, 42, 55, 94, 338, 339
Demographics of Nigeria, 53
Demonstrative, 366
Denisova Cave, 145, 160
Denisova hominin, 109, 125
Denisovan, 25, 153
Denisovans, 143
Denizli Province, 26
Denmark, 291
Dennis Stanford, 190
Dental consonant, 348
Denticulate tool, 197
Derbyshire, 178
Derbyshire, England, 190
Dervish state, 48
Descent of Man, 111
Desmond Tutu HIV Foundation, 78
Developing countries, 71
Development aid, 72
Devils Tower (Gibraltar), 157
Devonian, 12
Diabetes mellitus type 2, 148
Diadochi, 309
Dialect or language, 350
Diamonds, 73
Diaspora, 306
Dick Tiger, 92
Dida language, 354
Didier Drogba, 91
Diedrich Hermann Westermann, 358
Diedrich Westermann, 340, 351
Diet (nutrition), 10
Digital object identifier, 11, 113, 114, 181, 216, 217, 327–329, 331, 366
Dinka language, 63, 339

Dinka mythology, 83
Dionysius Periegetes, 393
Dioscorea, 253
Disease, 172
Disputed statement, 105, 195, 213
Division of labour, 244
Djenné-Djenno, 52
Djibouti, 39, 56, 70, 80, 96
Djiboutian franc, 96
Dmanisi, 2, 3, 17–19
Dmanisi Man, 371
Dmanisi skull, 18
Dmanisi skull 3, 17
Dmanisi skull 4, 18
Dmanisi skull 5, 13
DNA, 199
DNA analysis, 199
Dnieper, 274
Dnieper-Donets culture, 277, 278
Dniepr, 269, 279, 289
Dniestr, 279, 289
Dodoma, 96
Doggerland, 124
Dogon languages, 350–352, 355, 364, 365
Dogon people, 355
Dogrib people, 225
Dolgans, 369
Dolichocephalic, 195
Domba, 241
Domesticate, 254
Domesticated horse, 321
Domestication, 129, 244, 245, 258
Domestication of animals, 244
Domestication of the horse, 274
Domingo García, Segovia, 178
Donkey, 74
Don River (Russia), 127
Dordogne, 128, 129, 159, 172, 194, 196, 198
Dordogne (département), 37
Dorian invasion, 239
Dorset culture, 237, 368
Downstep, 364
Drava, 305
Drawing, 177
Dromedary, 254, 257
Dryopithecus, 111, 182
Dubrovnik, 306
Dur-Kurigalzu, 321
Dutch East India Company, 49
Dutch East Indies, 13
Dutch Empire, 49
Dutch language, 295, 297
Dutch people, 294
Dutch Republic, 242
Dyula language, 364

E1b1a, 258
E1b1b, 258
Early Bronze Age, 303, 304
Early European Farmers, 165, 169, 174, 184
Early expansions of hominins out of Africa, **1**
Early Helladic, 388
Early hominin expansions out of Africa, 102
Early Homo, 23
Early human migrations, 101, 117, 121, 233
Early modern humans, 145
Early Modern period, 233, 297
Early Pleistocene, 2, 3, 12
Early Slavs, 233
Earth-diver, 336
Earth (magazine), 218
East Africa, 15, 43, 104, 337
East African Community, 95
East Asia, 104, 156, 225, 254
East Asians, 145, 218, 221
East Beboid languages, 355
Eastern Asia, 260
Eastern Cape, 48
Eastern Europe, 37, 274, 275, 300, 311
Eastern Jebel languages, 337
Eastern Lunda, 47
Eastern Mediterranean, 4, 307
Eastern miombo woodlands, 42
Eastern Province, Rwanda, 74
Eastern Sudanic, 338
Eastern Sudanic languages, 337, 341–346, 360
East Germanic, 295
East Java, 13
East Kazakhstan Province, 284
East Slavs, 300, 302, 370
East Sudanese savanna, 41
East Sudanic languages, 346
Eblaite language, 58
Eburran industry, 34, 36, 120, 158, 189, 194
Economic and Monetary Community of Central Africa, 95
Economic Community of Central African States, 94
Economic Community of West African States, 98
Economic growth, 71
Ecuador, 180
Eddoe, 86
Edgar Charles Polomé, 271
Edoid, 354
Edo language, 354

Édouard Lartet, 195

Education For All, 77
Edward Lhuyd, 298
Edward L. Shaughnessy, 330

Edwin Bryant (author), 328
Edwin G. Pulleyblank, 285, 331
Eem, 35
Eemian, 37
Efficient energy use, 8
Efik language, 364
Efik mythology, 82
Egypt, 45, 51, 65, 93, 146, 282, 307, 321, 338, 339
Eighteenth Dynasty of Egypt, 314, 322
Einkorn, 249
Ejective consonant, 348
Ekoid languages, 355
Ekwesh, 308
Elaeis guineensis, 74
Electricity, 71
Emiran, 33, 36, 119, 157, 158, 188, 194
Emireh culture, 132
Emmanuel Adebayor, 91
Emmer, 249, 251
Empire, 309
Encephalisation, 9
Encephalization, 185
Encyclopædia Britannica (company), 329
Encyclopædia Britannica Eleventh Edition, 198
Encyclopædia Britannica Online, 392
Encyclopedia of Indo-European Culture, 280, 290, 310, 314, 390
Endaruta, 322
Endocast, 9
Endurance, 8
Eneolithic, 284
Enets people, 370
Engineering, 47
England, 30, 32, 160, 240
English, 285, 297, 298, 303, 308
English Channel, 124
English language, 262, 295, 297
English people, 294
Engraving, 177
Enset, 74, 88
Ensete, 252
Eora people, 132
EPAS1, 155
Epigravettian, 34, 36, 120, 132, 158, 189, 194, 197
Epi-Gravettian, 166
Epipaleolithic, 248, 254
Epoch (geology), 195, 244
Equatorial Africa, 42
Equatorial Guinea, 55, 59, 95
Eric P. Hamp, 309
Eritrea, 40, 47, 56, 70, 80, 88, 96, 105
Eritrean nakfa, 96
Ernst Haeckel, 111
Ernst Mayr, 12, 15, 19

Esimbi language, 355
Eskimo, 232, 368
Eskimo–Aleut languages, 219
Essex, 30
Estonia, 335
Estonian people, 235
Estonians, 336
Ethiopia, 22, 40, 41, 47, 48, 56, 70, 80, 88, 92, 96, 339
Ethiopian birr, 96
Ethiopian Empire, 48
Ethiopian Highlands, 252
Ethnic group, 309
Ethnic groups in Europe, 165
Ethnic groups of Europe, 167
Ethnicity, 121
Ethnic option, 231
Ethnocultural subdivisions, 302
Ethnogenesis, 304
Ethnolinguistics, 293, 297, 299, 300, 322
Ethnologue, 262, 295, 350
Ethnonym, 302
Etruscans, 308
Eugène Dubois, 12, 13
Euphrates, 248
Eurasia, 134, 182, 222, 258, 275, 336
Eurasian nomads, 274
Eurasian steppe, 282, 309, 311, 320
Europe, 35, 121, 168, 182, 183, 188, 190, 195, 234, 239, 260, 270, 298, 300, 307
European colonization of the Americas, 218, 229
European early modern humans, **163**, 182, 184
European Hippopotamus, 30
European Mesolithic, 166, 381
European Neolithic, 174
Eustatic sea level, 200
Evaporation, 10
Evaporite, 5
Evenks, 368
Evens, 368
Evidence as to Mans Place in Nature, 110
Ewe language, 354, 364
Expulsion of the Moriscos, 242
Extinction event, 182
Extinction vortex, 7
Extinct language, 296

Fali of Baissa, 355
Faliscan language, 296
Fam language, 355
Faroese language, 295
Farsi, 59
Fasil Ghebbi, 48
Fauna, 17
Fauresmith, 132

Federation of Rhodesia and Nyasaland, 95
Federmesser culture, 34, 36, 120, 158, 189, 194, 198
Female genital mutilation, 80
Fertile Crescent, 234, 245, 249, 250, 252, 255
Fertility goddess, 251
Ficus, 249
FIFA World Cup, 91
Fifteenth Dynasty of Egypt, 321
Figurines, 197
File:Egypt adm location map.svg, 32
File:England location map.svg, 32
File:Europe blank laea location map.svg, 35, 188
Financial centre, 65
Finger millet, 252
Finland, 335
Finnish people, 235
Finno-Permic, 334
Finno-Ugric, 334
Finno-Ugric people, 336
Finno-Ugric peoples, 336
Finns, 336, 370
Firearm, 258
Fire worship, 313
First Babylonian Dynasty, 314
First Nations, 232
Fish hook, 122
Flax, 168, 249
Flemish people, 294
Flint, 158, 190, 254
Flintknapper, 190
Flint tool, 122
Floristic province, 39
Folsom Site, 211
Fon language, 364
Forest-savanna mosaic, 39
Forest steppe, 311
Fornols-Haut, 178
Fortis and lenis, 361
Founder effect, 108, 109, 206, 219
Founding myth, 237
Foxtail millet, 251
Fractal, 83
Fractals, 86
France, 27, 37, 172, 194, 196, 231, 242, 293, 294
Francesco Benozzo, 326
Franco-Cantabrian region, 131
Frank Hole, 248
Franks, 237
Franz Weidenreich, 15
Frederik Kortlandt, 392
Free content, 99
Free license, 99
Freetown, 98

French colonization of the Americas, 231
French language, 96, 194, 264, 296
Fricative, 348
Fricative consonant, 348
Friedrich Müller (linguist), 340, 358
Frisians, 294
Frontal bone, 20
Frontal lobe, 9
Fuegians, 209, 229
Fufu, 86, 87
Fula language, 64, 351, 353, 365
Fulani language, 59
Funnelbeaker, 388
Funnelbeaker culture, 271, 291
Fur, 60
Fur language, 63, 339
Fur languages, 337, 342–345
Furu languages, 355
Fusional language, 264

Gaam language, 340
Gabarnmung, 179
Gabon, 55, 59, 70, 71, 95
Gaborone, 76, 96
Gabriel de Mortillet, 195
Gadeb, 22
Gaels, 237
Galatia, 298
Galatians (People), 283
Galindians, 300
Gallaeci, 298
Gallic invasion of the Balkans, 298
Gambia, 85
Gambian dalasi, 98
Game (food), 43
Ganda language, 63
Gandhara Grave culture, 310, 394
Ganges, 318
Gangetic plain, 286, 321
Gansu, 285
Gao, 339
Garri, 86
Gâtinais, 293
Gauls, 294, 298
Gaut, 293
Gauteng, 65
Gban language, 364
Gbaya language, 364
Gbaya languages, 63
Gbe languages, 354
Geissenklösterle, 166, 168, 169
Geledi Sultanate, 48
Gender inequality, 256
Gene, 231, 249
Gene flow, 144
General number, 360

Genetic admixture, 104
Genetic code, 199
Genetic diversity, 220
Genetic drift, 108
Genetic history, 218
Genetic history of indigenous peoples of the
    Americas, 206, **218**
Genetic (linguistics), 338
Genetic marker, 112, 336
Genetic relationship (linguistics), 351
Genetics, 260
Genitive, 366
Genographic Project, 218
Genome, 152
Genotype, 220
Geologic time scale, 2, 24, 177, 244
Geologist, 189
Geology, 199
George Soros, 75
George Taubman Goldie, 53
George Weah, 91
Georgia (country), 2, 13, 17, 19
Georgiy Starostin, 338, 346
German dialects, 391
Germanic languages, 63, 263, 269, 286, 293
Germanic peoples, 325, 370
Germanic tribes, 239
German language, 264, 295, 297
Germans, 241, 294
Germany, 37, 306
Gerrie Coetzee, 92
Getae, 303
Ghana, 57, 79, 80, 85, 98, 354
Ghana Empire, 52
Ghana Health Services, 80
Ghanaian cedi, 98
Ghana Togo Mountain languages, 362
Ghost population, 156
Gikuyu language, 63
Gilgal I, 249
Gjuha shqipe, 306
Glacial period, 5, 133, 247
Glenoid cavity, 150
Globular Amphora culture, 279, 290, 291
Glottal consonant, 348
Glottochronology, 272
Glottolog, 337, 338, 350, 353, 359
Goat, 248
Gola language, 353
Golasecca culture, 298
Gold, 72
Gombe Stream National Park, 8
Gondershe, 47
Gönnersdorf, 177
Goosefoot, 253
Gorani people, 302

Gordium, 308, 309
Gordon Hillman, 249
Gorhams Cave, 157, 160
Gorilla, 43, 111
Gorillini, 3
Gothic language, 295
Gourd, 74
Goyet Caves, 383
Gracile australopithecines, 2
Gracility, 172
Graeco-Phrygian, 309
Graecopithecus, 3
Graecopithecus freybergi, 183
Gramineae, 140
Grammatical conjugation, 264
Grammatical gender, 365
Granary, 249
Gran Chaco, 220
Gran Dolina, 184
Grasses, 140
Grassfields languages, 355
Grassland, 274
Gravel, 125
Gravettian, 33, 36, 120, 131, 151, 158, 163,
    166, 174, 187, 189, 194
Gray matter, 149
Great ape, 43
Great Britain, 231
Great Coastal Migration, 108
Greater Iran, 260, 323
Great Fish River, 48
Great Morava, 305
Great Mosque of Djenne, 52
Great Rift Valley, Kenya, 339
Great Serbian Migrations, 242
Great Zimbabwe, 49
Greco-Roman, 47
Greece, 306
Greek Dark Ages, 239
Greek language, 263, 307–309
Greek people, 305
Greeks, 40, 283, 308
Greenland, 215, 219, 369
Grimaldi Man, 172
Grimms law, 294
Griphopithecus, 182
Gross national product, 77
Grotta del Cavallo, 163, 169, 381
Grotte du Bichon, 174
Ground stone, 127
Guinea, 57, 80, 98
Guinea-Bissau, 57, 99
Guinea fowl, 74
Guinean forest-savanna mosaic, 41
Guinean franc, 98
Gulf of Lion, 293

Gumuz language, 63, 343–345
Gumuz languages, 337, 340, 341
Guns, Germs, and Steel, 216, 258, 259, 387
Gur languages, 64, 353, 354, 360
Gustav Heinrich Ralph von Koenigswald, 27
Guthrie classification of Bantu languages, 355
Gyrification, 149

Habesha people, 40
Habiru, 322
Habsburg, 242
Hadza language, 341
Hadza people, 58, 110, 156
Hafting, 167, 168
Haibak, 160
Haida Gwaii, 202
Haida people, 214
Haile Gebrselassie, 93
Hair, 108
Halfan culture, 33, 36, 120, 158, 189, 194
Half-breed, 231
Hallstatt, 298
Hallstatt culture, 297, 298
Hamburg culture, 34, 36, 120, 158, 189, 194
Hamites, 41
Hamitic, 265
Hammerstone, 30, 206
Han Chinese, 208, 238
Handaxe, 31, 159
Han Dynasty, 321
Hans Henrich Hock, 329
Haplogroup, 206
Haplogroup A (mtDNA), 227
Haplogroup B (mtDNA), 227
Haplogroup C3 (Y-DNA), 222
Haplogroup C-F3393, 174
Haplogroup C-M130 (Y-DNA), 225
Haplogroup C-M217, 213
Haplogroup C (mtDNA), 227
Haplogroup C (Y-DNA), 117
Haplogroup D (mtDNA), 227
Haplogroup D (Y-DNA), 117
Haplogroup E-M96, 147
Haplogroup H (mtDNA), 170
Haplogroup IJ, 174
Haplogroup IJK, 165
Haplogroup I-M170, 174
Haplogroup I-M438, 174
Haplogroup J (Y-DNA), 258
Haplogroup K2a (Y-DNA), 174
Haplogroup L0 (mtDNA), 107
Haplogroup L1 (mtDNA), 107
Haplogroup L2 (mtDNA), 107
Haplogroup L3 (mtDNA), 104, 107, 117, 147,
    165
Haplogroup M1, 107

Haplogroup M (mtDNA), 107, 108, 117
Haplogroup N-M231, 336
Haplogroup N (mtDNA), 107, 117, 165, 174
Haplogroup Q1a3a (Y-DNA), 207, 223
Haplogroup Q-L54 (Y-DNA), 224
Haplogroup Q-M242, 219
Haplogroup Q-M3, 223
Haplogroup Q-M346 (Y-DNA), 224
Haplogroup Q-MEH2 (Y-DNA), 224
Haplogroup Q-NWT01 (Y-DNA), 224
Haplogroup Q-P89.1 (Y-DNA), 224
Haplogroup Q-SA01 (Y-DNA), 224
Haplogroup Q (Y-DNA), 215, 222
Haplogroup Q-Z780 (Y-DNA), 224
Haplogroup R1b (Y-DNA), 224
Haplogroup R1 (Y-DNA), 224
Haplogroup R-M207, 225
Haplogroup R (mtDNA), 174
Haplogroup U (mtDNA), 174
Haplogroup X (mtDNA), 224, 226, 227
Haplogroup Z, 336
Haplorhini, 12
Haplotype, 218
Harappa, 313
Harare, 97
Hardwood, 190
Hare, 172
Harpoon, 122, 195
Hattians, 282
Hattusa, 308
Haua Fteah, 157, 160
Hausa language, 58, 64
Hayasa-Azzi, 306
Healthcare reform, 78
Heather Pringle, 386
Heavy Neolithic, 251
Hebrew Bible, 237
Hebrews, 322
Hebron, 322
Heffingen, 174
Heiban languages, 353
Heilongjiang, 368
Heinrich Barth, 340
Helladic period, 307
Hellenic languages, 263
Hellespont, 309
Hemoglobin, 155
Hengistbury Head, 130
Henotheism, 80
Henriette Alimen, 6
Henri Fleisch, 254
Henry Christy, 195
Henry Harpending, 326
Henry Testot-Ferry, 189
Herbivore, 133
HERC2, 167

Herd, 122
H. ergaster, 19
Herodotus, 309
Hexian, 26
H. georgicus, 44
H. habilis, 19
H. heidelbergensis, 21
Hide (skin), 122
Highlife, 85
High Speed 1, 31
Hillfort, 279
Hilly Flanks, 247
Hindi, 262
Hindu, 80
Hispanopithecus, 182
Historical linguistics, 262, 264
Historical Vedic religion, 317, 318
History, 23
History of Australia (1788–1850), 49
History of hide materials, 257
History of human migration, 233
History of Iran, 323
History of Oman, 104
History of writing, 244
Hittite cuneiform, 314
Hittite Empire, 235, 306, 308
Hittite language, 280
Hittites, 269, 275, 280, 282, 307, 314, 321
HLA type, 154
Hoabinhian, 132
Hogan Bassey, 92
Hohlenstein-Stadel, 126
Hokkaido, 208
Holocene, 108, 121, 137, 175, 205, 244, 247
Holocene climatic optimum, 174, 233
Holocene extinction, 130
Holotype, 26, 170
Holstein interglacial, 30
Holy Roman Empire, 241
Hominid, 43, 121
Hominidae, 12, 182
Hominid dispersals in Europe, **182**
Hominin, 23, 183
Hominina, 18, 33, 35, 119, 157, 188, 193
Homininae, 2, 3, 12
Hominini, 1, 12, 24, 175, 182
Hominins, 2
Homo, 2, 12, 15, 182
Homo antecessor, 13, 25
Homo cepranensis, 25
Homo Denisova, 13
Homo erectus, 2, 3, 10, **12**, 44, 112, 183, 378
Homo erectus erectus, 25
Homo erectus georgicus, 23, 25, 26
Homo erectus lantianensis, 25
Homo erectus nankinensis, 25

Homo erectus palaeojavanicus, 25
Homo erectus pekinensis, 25
Homo erectus soloensis, 25
Homo erectus tautavelensis, 25, 26
Homo erectus yuanmouensis, 25
Homo ergaster, 3, 13, 19, 21, 25, 44, 185
Homo floresiensis, 3, 25, 44
Homo gautengensis, 19
Homo georgicus, 13
Homo habilis, 2, 9, 13, 15, 18, 19, 44, 371
Homo heidelbergensis, 13, 21, 25, 30, 109, 143, 183
Homo naledi, 25
Homo neanderthalensis, 13, 15, 159–161
Homo rhodesiensis, 25
Homo rudolfensis, 3, 13, 15, 19
Homo sapiens, 13, 25, 44, 101, 102, 126, 159, 184
Homo sapiens idaltu, 25
Hong Kong International Airport, 126
Hoover Institution Press, 373
Horn of Africa, 40, 42, 48, 88, 101, 108
Horse, 133, 136, 167, 190, 322
Horse burial, 321, 322
Horse worship, 321
Hot desert climate, 42, 44
Hot semi-arid climate, 41, 42, 44
Hovenweep National Monument, 129
Hoxnian Stage, 30
Hoya Negro skeleton, 209
HTLV-1, 209
Huguenots, 242
Human, 131
Human cranium, 19
Human culture, 244
Human evolution, 15
Human fossil bones from the Muierii Cave and the Cioclovina Cave, Romania, 171
Human genetic clustering, 65
Human history, 21, 244
Human migration, 233, 298
Human mitochondrial DNA haplogroup, 118, 219, 226
Human mitochondrial DNA haplogroups, 206
Human remains, 25
Human settlement, 121
Human subspecies, 25, 163
Human Y-chromosome DNA haplogroup, 112, 117, 219
Human Y-chromosome DNA haplogroups, 206
Hungarian conquest of the Carpathian Basin, 233
Hungarian landtaking, 237
Hungary, 296, 303, 306, 392
Huns, 239, 240

Hunter-gatherer, 23, 126, 222, 244, 245
Hurrian, 314
Hurrian language, 314, 322
Hurrians, 309, 322
Hydraulic, 47
Hydropower, 69
Hyksos, 321
Hylobates, 111
Hyperthermia, 10
Hypothesis, 190, 326

Iazyges, 324
Iberian Peninsula, 123, 230, 298
Iberomaurusian, 34, 36, 120, 158, 189, 194
Ibero-Maurusian, 132
Ibibio language, 64
Ice age, 6, 122, 177, 195
Icelanders, 294, 370
Icelandic language, 295
Ice sheet, 133
Ice-sheet, 123
Ideology, 244
Idoma language, 355
Idomoid, 355
Ifá, 82
Ife, 53
Igboid, 354
Igbo language, 59, 64, 351, 353, 354, 364
Igbo mythology, 82
Igbo people, 52
Igede language, 364
Ijaw languages, 351, 352, 355
Ijaw people, 355
Ijoid languages, 352, 355, 365
Ijo languages, 350
Ili River, 285, 320
Illyria, 305
Image gallery, 135
Image:World 820.png, 239
Imperial cult, 46
Imperialism, 48
Implosive consonant, 348
Inbreeding, 7
Inca Empire, 220, 258
Independence I culture, 368
India, 47
Indiana University Press, 367, 374
Indian subcontinent, 117, 260, 318
Indigenous Australians, 108, 121
Indigenous languages of the Americas, 199, 219, 226
Indigenous peoples, 220
Indigenous peoples in Peru, 232
Indigenous peoples of Siberia, 222
Indigenous peoples of the Americas, 106, 203, 218

Indo-Aryan languages, 262, 322
Indo-Aryan migration, 237, 310
Indo-Aryan peoples, 314, 318, 321, 322
Indo-Aryans, 235, 270, 309, 317, 323
Indo-European ablaut, 264
Indo-European expansion, 184, 233
Indo-European family, 285
Indo-European language family, 280, 307
Indo-European languages, 59, 60, 63, 263, 264, 280, 289, 296, 298–300, 305, 306, 309, 321, 325
Indo-European migrations, **260**
Indo-European origins, 306
Indo-European people, 303
Indo-European studies, 260, 280
Indo-Hittite, 265
Indo-Iranian language, 261
Indo-Iranian languages, 263, 270, 309, 313
Indo-Iranian migration, 310
Indo-Iranians, 312
Indonesia, 13, 253
Indo-Scythians, 324
Indo-Uralic, 265
Indra, 314
Indus River, 323
Industry (archaeology), 37
Indus Valley Civilisation, 389
Indus Valley Civilization, 313
Infectious diseases, 258
Influenza, 258
Information and communication technologies, 72
Ingala Valley, 313
Injera, 88
Inner Asia, 310, 318
Inner Mongolia, 368
Institute of Vertebrate Paleontology and Paleoanthropology, 15
Insular Celts, 298
Intensive gathering, 249
Interbreeding between archaic and modern humans, **143**
Interglacial, 30
Interleukin 18, 148
Internal reconstruction, 264, 265
International Standard Book Number, 11, 99, 113–115, 181, 216, 217, 233, 244, 259, 327–332, 370, 378, 390
International Standard Serial Number, 29, 330
Interorbital region, 150
Interracial marriage in the United States, 231
Interstadial, 123, 135
Intraparietal sulcus, 149
Introgression, 145, 148
Inuit, 215, 219, 226, 227, 232, 237, 368, 369
Inuit expansion, 237

Inuit languages, 221
Inuktitut, 368
Inupiat, 226
Iñupiat, 369
Inupiat people, 368
Inuvik Region, 369
Iran, 234, 261, 322
Iranian languages, 261, 285, 322, 323, 325
Iranian people, 309
Iranian peoples, 320
Iranian plateau, 235, 262, 313, 322, 323
Iraq, 322
Iraq ed-Dubb, 251
Ireland, 231, 237, 240, 298
Irish Sea, 124
Iron, 48
Iron Age, 42, 47, 235, 283, 297, 303, 321
Iron Gates, 170
Iron (material), 283
Iron ore, 72
Irrigation, 72, 244
Islam, 80
Islands of the Pacific, 236
Isle of Man, 298
ISO 639-2, 337, 350
ISO639-3:nic, 350
ISO639-3:ssa, 337
ISO 639-5, 337, 350
Isostasy, 202
Israel, 23
Isturitz, 166
Italian language, 264, 296
Italian Peninsula, 296, 305
Italic languages, 263, 269
Italic peoples, 296, 308
Italo-Celtic, 309
Italy, 239, 293, 306
Ivory, 122, 197
Ivory Coast, 57, 85, 91, 98, 354

Jabroudian, 132
Jacques Cauvin, 251
Jadeite, 293
Jainism, 318
Jake Matlala, 92
Jalaa language, 356
James C. Scott, 387
Jan Czerski, 133
János Harmatta, 329
Jan van Riebeeck, 49
Japan, 106, 121, 126
Japanese Paleolithic, 132
Jarawan languages, 355
Jared Diamond, 216, 255, 256, 258, 259, 387
Java, 3, 13, 28
Java Man, 12, 13, 15, 16, 25

Javanthropus soloensis, 12
Javelin, 167
Jaxartes, 313
Jay-Jay Okocha, 91
Jazz, 84
JC virus, 109
Jebel Faya, 103
Jeju island, 178
Jerf el Ahmar, 249
Jericho, 234, 251
Jerusalem, 322
Jewelry, 175
Jie people, 285
Jim G. Shaffer, 326
Johan Gunnar Andersson, 15
Johanna Nichols, 330, 387
Johannesburg, 65, 67
John Bendor-Samuel, 359, 366, 367
John Chadwick, 332
John Cheruiyot Korir, 93
John D. Hawks, 29
John Gurche, 372
John Lloyd (writer), 381
John Mitchinson (researcher), 381
John Robinson (sculptor), 218
John T. Robinson, 16
John Wiley & Sons, 328
Jōmon, 132, 208
Jōmon period, 132
Jomtien Beach, 77
Jon Erlandson, 214, 215
Jordan, 251
Jordan Rift Valley, 251
Jordan Valley (Middle East), 249
Joseph Greenberg, 338, 341, 349, 351, 358
Jos Plateau, 73
Journal of African Languages and Linguistics, 367
Journal of Human Evolution, 114
J. P. Mallory, 280
J.P. Mallory, 330
JSTOR, 11, 216
Juba, 94
Judaism, 80
Jukunoid languages, 355
Jukun Takum language, 364
Jurassic, 12
Jutes, 240
Jutland, 299

Kadu languages, 337, 340, 341, 343–346, 356
Kaftan, 90
Kainji languages, 355
Kalaallit, 369
Kalahari Basin, 42
Kalahari Desert, 42, 59

Kalenjin language, 63
Kalimba, 84
Kama River, 336
Kambojas, 323
Kamchatka Krai, 368, 369
Kamoya Kimeu, 20
Kampala, 96
Kanembu language, 339, 340
Kanem Empire, 46, 52
Kanesh, 282
Kanga (African garment), 89, 90
Kangju, 285
Kanuri language, 63, 64, 339, 340
Kanuri people, 61
Karagwe, 51
Karasahr, 285
Karelians, 370
Karl Landsteiner, 231
Karl Richard Lepsius, 340, 358
Karoo, 42
Kasem language, 364
Kassite language, 321
Kassites, 321
Katla languages, 350–352, 356
Kay Williamson, 352
Kazakhs, 225
Kazakhstan, 274, 313
Kebaran, 34, 36, 120, 158, 189, 194
Kebarian, 132, 265
Keetmanshoop, 75
Keilor, 380
Kelp, 214
Kendricks Cave Decorated Horse Jaw, 175, 178
Kenenisa Bekele, 93
Kenkey, 86
Kennewick Man, 209
Kent, 30
Kente, 89
Kente cloth, 90
Kent Flannery, 247
Kents Cavern, 163, 169, 193, 198
Kents Cavern 4 (KC4) Maxilla, 169
Kenya, 2, 16, 19, 20, 22, 42, 50, 55, 67, 80, 89, 92, 96, 130, 339
Kenyan shilling, 96
Kenyapithecus, 182
Keratin, 148
Kerch Strait, 283
Ket people, 222
Khabur (Euphrates), 315
Khandivili, 132
Khanty people, 368, 370
Khartoum, 97
Khar-Us Lake, 138
Khat, 252

Khiamian, 34, 36, 120, 158, 189, 194
Khoikhoi, 58, 60
Khoi languages, 58
Khoisan, 41, 65, 352
Khoi-San, 58
Khoisan languages, 41, 48, 59, 60, 65, 236, 338
Khoisan religion, 83
Khormusan, 33, 36, 120, 158, 188, 194
Khvalynsk culture, 278, 390
Kigali, 94, 96
Kikuyu people, 339
Kimbell Art Museum, 392
Kimberley region of Western Australia, 180
Kimwani, 365
Kingdom of Baguirmi, 46
Kingdom of Benin, 53
Kingdom of Great Britain, 49
Kingdom of Hungary, 242
Kingdom of Kongo, 47
Kingdom of Kush, 341
Kingdom of Matamba, 46
Kingdom of Ndongo, 46, 47
Kingdom of Nri, 52
Kingdom of Urartu, 306
King Ezanas Stele, 47
Kinshasa, 67, 94
Kinyarwanda, 63, 94, 96
Kirundi, 63, 96
Kizomba, 85
Knap of Howar, 246
KNM ER 3733, 26, 372
KNM-ER 3733, 3, 16
KNM ER 3883, 26
KNM ER 992, 372
Kogi State, 355
Kola nut, 74, 252
Kolo Touré, 91
Koman languages, 337, 340–346
Komi peoples, 370
Komi Republic, 370
Komuz languages, 347
Kongo language, 63
Koobi Fora, 16, 22
Koppet Dag, 313
Kordofan, 94, 356
Kordofanian, 359
Kordofanian languages, 63, 350, 351, 353, 356
Körös culture, 277
Koryaks, 222, 368
Kosovo, 306
Kostenki-12, 170
Kostenki-14, 163, 169, 383
Kostyonki (palaeolithic site), 127
Kostyonki, Voronezh Oblast, 170
Krasnoyarsk Krai, 369, 370

Kresh languages, 346
Kristian Kristiansen (archaeologist), 296
Kroraina, 390
Kru languages, 353, 354
Kru people, 354
Ksar Akil, 125
Kuba Kingdom, 47
Kuban River, 284
Kufi, 90
Kuk Swamp, 245, 253
Kuliak, 338
Kuliak languages, 337, 341–345
Kültepe, 274
Kumasi, 79
Kunama language, 63
Kunama languages, 337, 342–345, 347
Kunama people, 338
KUR, 314
Kura (Caspian Sea), 283
Kurdish language, 325
Kurds, 323
Kurgan, 274
Kurgan culture, 234, 265
Kurgan hypothesis, 234, 235, 261, 264, 268, 272–274, 280, 286, 325
Kurgan stelae, 279
Kurile Islands, 214
Kuru kingdom, 389
Kushan Empire, 285, 321
Kwa languages, 64, 353, 354
KwaZulu-Natal, 48, 49
Kyrgyzstan, 313
Kyushu, 209
Kyzylkum desert, 313

Laal language, 353, 356
Labial consonant, 348, 361
Labial-velar consonant, 361
Labrador, 368
Lafofa languages, 353, 356
Lagoa Santa, Minas Gerais, 209
Lagos, 53, 65, 66
Lagos State, 65
Lake Baringo, 22
Lake Chad, 339
Lake Malawi, 379
Lake Toba, 105
Lake Turkana, 2, 20, 130
La Madeleine (prehistoric site), 194
Lamba (garment), 90
Lamu, 48
Land bridge, 4, 182, 199
Landes (department), 128
Lango dialect, 339
Language, 23
Language change, 260

Language families, 337
Language family, 233, 262, 298, 337, 350
Language isolate, 58
Language revitalization, 298
Languages of Africa, 350, 358
Languages of Europe, 262
Languages of Nigeria, 353
Languages of South Asia, 262
Lantian Man, 25
Lapedo child, 150, 173
Lapita, 236
Larch, 135, 142
Laryngeal theory, 264
Lascaux, 128, 129, 178, 193, 197
Last Common Ancestor, 183
Last Glacial Maximum, 123, 128, 133, 135, 163, 174, 197, 199, 200, 203, 212, 218, 221, 233
Last Glacial Maximum refugia, 123, 174
Last glacial period, 122, 123, 133, 175, 195
Late Bronze Age, 235
Late Glacial Maximum, 197
Late Harappan, 317
La Tène culture, 298
Late Pleistocene, 12, 170, 195
Later Zhao, 285
Latgalians (modern), 300
Latin, 296, 297
Latin language, 264, 303, 305
Latvian language, 299
Latvians, 300
Laugerie-Basse, 173, 198
Laugerie Haute, 190
Laurentide Ice Sheet, 199, 201, 211
Lavallee, 383
Lebanon, 125, 254
Le Mas-dAzil, 128
Le Moustier, 157, 159, 161
Lentil, 249
Leo Klejn, 303
Leonid Grinin, 248
Lepontii, 298
Les Eyzies, 172, 190, 198
Les Eyzies-de-Tayac-Sireuil, 35, 37
Lesotho, 56, 96
Lesotho loti, 96
Levallois technique, 103, 159
Levant, 8, 65, 159, 175, 245, 248, 283, 315, 321, 322
Levantine corridor, 4, 249, 251
Lewis Binford, 247
Lexicon, 271
Leyla-Tepe culture, 284
LGM refugia, 166
Liao civilization, 336
Liao dynasty, 321

Liao River, 336
Liberia, 57, 98
Liberian dollar, 98
Libreville, 71, 95
Libya, 93, 338, 339
Light skin, 167
Ligures, 298
Liguria, 172
Lilongwe, 96
Limba language, 353
Limpopo River, 48, 49
Lincombian-Ranisian-Jerzmanowician, 33, 36, 119, 158, 188, 194
Lineage (anthropology), 44
Linear Pottery, 388
Linear Pottery culture, 234
Lingala, 63
Lingala language, 364
Lingua franca, 58, 59
Linguistic reconstruction, 264, 275, 338
Linguistics, 260
Linguists, 219
Linkage disequilibrium, 150
Lionel Bender (linguist), 340, 347, 349
Lion-human, 126
Lion-man, 169
Liquid consonant, 348, 349
List of ancient tribes in Illyria, 305
List of countries and outlying territories by total area, 55
List of countries and territories by fertility rate, 53
List of countries by Human Development Index, 55
List of countries by population, 55
List of hominina fossils, 111
List of human evolution fossils, 15
List of Indo-European languages, 262
List of islands in the Arctic Ocean, 133
List of languages by number of native speakers, 262
List of Nigerian cities by population, 65
List of sovereign states and dependent territories in Africa, 39
List of tropical and subtropical moist broadleaf forests ecoregions, 42
Lithic analysis, 7
Lithic flake, 30, 122
Lithic reduction, 190
Lithic technology, 43, 44, 158
Lithuanian language, 299
Lithuanians, 300
Littoral, 203
Liujiang man, 104, 106
Llama, 258
Loanword, 334

Loan word, 59
Loan-words, 50
Loire, 293
Lombards, 239
Lombok Strait, 7
Lomé, 99
Lomekwi, 2
London Zoo, 111
Lonetal, 37
Lotuko mythology, 83
Louis Lartet, 163, 164, 167
Louis Laurent Gabriel de Mortillet, 189
Louvre, 52
Lower Paleolithic, 30, 33, 35, 119, 157, 188, 193
Lower Pleistocene, 18
Low German, 391
Lozi mythology, 83
Luanda, 67, 72, 94, 96
Luba Kingdom, 46
Luca Cavalli-Sforza, 374
Ludwik and Hanka Herschfeld, 231
Lugbara language, 339
Lugbara mythology, 83
Luhya languages, 63
Luhya people, 339
Lunda Empire, 46
Luo dialect, 339
Luo language, 63
Luo languages, 339
Luo people of Kenya and Tanzania, 339
Lupembian, 132
Lurs, 323
Lusaka, 97
Lusitanians, 297
Luxembourg, 174
Luzia Woman, 205, 209, 229
Lycia, 308
Lycians, 308
Lydia, 309
Lynford Quarry, 157, 160

Maasai language, 63, 67, 339
Maasai people, 61, 147, 339
Maban languages, 337, 342–345, 347
Macaque, 19
Macedonians (ethnic group), 302
Macedonia (Roman province), 302
Mâcon, 189
Macro-haplogroup L (mtDNA), 107
Madagascar, 56, 77, 96
Madelenian, 198
Madhya Pradesh, 25
Madjedbebe, 106
Madrasian Culture, 33, 35, 119, 157, 188, 193
Magadan Oblast, 368

Magdalenian, 34, 36, 120, 131, 158, 163, 166, 173, 178, 187, 189, 190, **193**, 194
Magdalenian Girl, 173
Maghreb, 98, 241
Magosian, 132
Magyars, 240
Mahajanapada, 318
Mahajanapadas, 317
Maize, 253
Makossa, 85
Makua language, 63
Malabo, 95
Malagasy ariary, 96
Malagasy language, 63, 96
Malakunanja II, 180
Malao (ancient), 47
Malaria, 80
Malawi, 42, 56, 65, 90, 96, 379
Malawian kwacha, 96
Mali, 41, 56, 78, 80, 99, 179, 339, 354, 355
Mali Empire, 52
Malta, 191, 221
Malta boy, 169
Malta-Buret culture, 225, 227
Malta–Buret culture, 33, 36, 120, 158, 189, 194
Mambila language, 364
Mambiloid languages, 355
Mamfe languages, 355
Mammal, 12
Mammals, 111, 195, 258
Mammoth, 128, 167, 172, 190, 195
Mammoth spear thrower, 175
Mammoth steppe, **133**, 199
Mammut americanum, 206
Mande languages, 341, 350–352, 355, 365
Mandé peoples, 355
Mandibular foramen, 151
Mandibular notch, 150
Mandinka language, 365
Mandinka people, 155
Manganese, 72, 168
Maninka language, 364
Manioc, 253
Manot 1, 106
Manot Cave, 106
Mansi people, 370
Manure, 257
Maputo, 96
Maputo Protocol, 80
Marathi language, 264
Marathon, 93
Marcel Otte, 234, 326
Marcomanni, 239
Maribyrnong River, 380
Marija Gimbutas, 234, 270, 271, 274, 286, 296

Marine archaeology, 124
Marine Isotope Stage, 8
Marine Isotope Stage 5, 104
Mario Alinei, 326, 333
Mark Stoneking, 112
Marta Mirazón Lahr, 380
Martha Chase, 231
Martin Meredith, 114
Maryannu, 322
Masai mythology, 83
Masalit language, 63
Masalit people, 60, 94
Maseru, 96
Massagetae, 323, 324
Material culture, 303, 304, 311
Maternal mortality, 80
Matrimonial, 271
Maurice Gaudefroy-Demombynes, 340
Mauritania, 39, 41, 57, 81, 94, 98
Mauritanian ouguiya, 98
Mauritian rupee, 96
Mauritius, 56, 80, 96
Maxilla, 169
Max Muller, 317
Max Planck Institute, 338
Maya peoples, 220, 232
Maykop culture, 269, 279, 284
Maykop kurgan, 284
Mazouco, 178
Mbabane, 97
Mbalax, 85
Mbam languages, 355
Mbanza-Kongo, 47
Mbaqanga, 85
Mbe language, 355
Mbuti, 107
Mbuti people, 65
MC1R, 109
Meadowcroft Rockshelter, 206
Meadowcroft Rock Shelter, 205
Measles, 80, 258
Mechian, 252
Medes, 261, 270, 283, 323
Medieval period, 40
Mediterranean climate, 42
Mediterranean Europe, 227
Megaannum, 12
Megacity, 65
Megadiverse countries, 41
Megadrought, 103
Megafauna, 126
Megalith, 388
Meganthropus, 25
Meganthropus paleojavanicus, 12
Melanesia, 229, 245
Melanesians, 109, 143, 152

Melanocortin 1 receptor, 109
Melbourne, 126
Mel languages, 353
Member states of the Arab League, 39
Menchum language, 355
Mende people, 110, 156
Menouthias, 50
Meroitic language, 341, 347
Mesoamerica, 253
Mesoamerican, 221
Mesolithic, 34, 37, 121, 124, 158, 163, 175,
    189, 194, 254, 265, 335
Mesolithic Europe, 174
Mesopotamia, 58, 244, 321
Messapii, 305
Metallurgy, 311
Métis people (Canada), 231
Mexica, 220
Mezhirich, 167
Mezhyrich, 128
Mezmaiskaya cave, 145
Michael Essien, 91
Michael Loewe, 330
Michael R. Waters, 384
Micoquien, 33, **35**, 36, 119, 157, 162, 188, 193
Microcephalin, 148
Microlith, 110
Microliths, 197
Micronesia, 236
Microsatellite, 219
Microsatellite (genetics), 215
Middens, 105
Middle Ages, 239, 283, 286, 297
Middle Assyrian Empire, 315
Middle Awash, 22
Middle-Danube Urnfield culture, 296
Middle East, 245, 282, 321
Middle Paleolithic, 33, 35–37, 119, 121, 143,
    157, 159, 188, 193
Middle Pleistocene, 4, 183, 184, 380
Migration period, 233, 237, 295
Migrations Period, 239
Milford Wolpoff, 112
Milk, 257
Millennium Development Goals, 71, 77
Millet, 74
Mimi-D, 337, 347
Mimi of Decorse, 344
Minatogawa Man, 106
Mindel glaciation, 30
Minimum viable population, 7
Ministry of Health, Ghana, 80
Minoan civilization, 388
Minusinsk, 313
Minusinsk Hollow, 284
Miocene, 182

Misliya cave, 103
Missing link (human evolution), 15
Mitanni, 261, 270, 306, 310
Mitochondrial DNA, 102, 107, 112, 147, 167
Mitochondrial Eve, 107, 112
Mittani, 309
Mixed-blood, 231
Mixed-race, 230
Mladeč caves, 171
Moesia, 302
Mogadishu, 67, 96
Mohammed Abdullah Hassan, 48
Moldova, 303
Molecule, 199
Momo languages, 355
Mongol invasions, 233
Mongoloid race, 285
Mongols, 225
Monomotapa, 49
Monrovia, 98
Montastruc decorated stone (Palart 518), 175
Montenegrins (ethnic group), 302
Montenegro, 305, 306
Monte Verde, 206, 212, 215, 229
Monthly Review, 377
Moors, 240
Moravia, 171, 172, 296
Moravian Banovina, 303
More language, 64
Morocco, 93, 146
Moroni, Comoros, 96
Morphology (biology), 106, 184
Morphology (linguistics), 264
Moscow River, 299
Mossi language, 354
Mount Ararat, 306
Mousterian, 30, 33, 35, 36, 119, 122, 131, 157, **157**, 188, 189, 193, 373
Mousterian Pluvial, 123, 125, 128
Mozambican metical, 96
Mozambique, 42, 49, 56, 96
Mpre language, 356
MtDNA, 117
Mt-DNA haplogroup, 174
Mt-MRCA, 112
Mucin 7, 156
Mullerthal, Luxembourg, 174
Multi-cordoned ware culture, 303
Multilingualism, 263
Multiregional origin of modern humans, 112, 378
Mumuye language, 354
Mundford, 160
Mungo Lake remains, 106
Mungo Man, 112
Munzombo language, 364

Murle language, 340
Murmansk Oblast, 370
Mursili II, 281
Musée dArchéologie Nationale, 127
Mushki, 239
Musk ox, 136
Muslim, 50, 240
Mycenaean Greece, 275
Mycenaean Greek, 262, 307
Mycenean Greece, 307
Mysia, 302
Mythological Cycle, 237

Na-dene, 221
Na Dene, 219
Na-Dené, 215, 219
Na-Dene languages, 225
Nafaanra language, 364
Nairi people, 306
Nairobi, 66, 67, 96
Nairobi River, 67
Naledi Pandor, 76
Namazga, 313
Namibia, 56, 75, 90, 96, 179
Namibia national rugby union team, 92
Namibian dollar, 96
Nandi–Markweta languages, 339
Nanjing Man, 25
Napoleonic Wars, 53
Nara language, 63, 340
Narva culture, 388
Nasal consonant, 348, 349
Nasality in Gbe, 400
Nasal stop, 364
Nasal vowel, 364
National Geographic Channel, 218
National Geographic (magazine), 29
National Geographic Society, 218
National Humanities Center, 218
National Museum of Natural History, 29, 115, 181
National Park Service, 218
Native American ancestry, 231
Native American identity, 231
Native American reservation politics, 231
Native Americans in the United States, 232
Native Hawaiians, 232
Natufian culture, 34, 36, 120, 158, 189, 194
Natural environment, 244
Natural History Museum, Vienna, 128
Natural selection, 109, 258
Nature (journal), 227, 327
Naute Dam, 75
Navajo, 232
Navajo people, 227
NDjamena, 95

Neanderthal, 25, 104, 112, 131, 143, 160, 170, 173, 182, 184
Neanderthal admixture, 165
Neanderthal admixture theory, 21
Neanderthal extinction, 121, 165
Neanderthals, 109, 126, 158, 159, 163, 167, 184
Neanderthals in Southwest Asia, 165
Near East, 104, 159, 227, 265, 323
Near Oceania, 117
Needles in archaeology, 191
Negritos, 109
Negro, 41
Nenets people, 368, 370
Neo-Babylonian Empire, 321
Neogene, 12
Neo-Hittite, 283
Neolithic, 234, 244, 254, 265, 275, 325, 326
Neolithic Europe, 184, 279, 286, 303, 304, 307, 326
Neolithic founder crops, 249
Neolithic Revolution, 184, 233, **244**, 274, 325
Neolithic Subpluvial, 338
Netherlands, 306
Netiv Hagdud, 249, 251
New Caledonia, 236
New Guinea, 117
New Kingdom of Egypt, 307, 322
New Partnership for Africas Development, 70
New World, 219
New York City, 15
New York Times, 162
New Zealand, 236, 306
Ngambay language, 339
Nganasan people, 370
Ngandong, 132
Niamey, 99
Niger, 41, 57, 80, 94, 99, 339
Niger-Congo, 236
Niger-Congo languages, 41, 59, 62, 63, 65
Niger Delta, 355
Niger–Congo, 84
Niger–Congo languages, 59, 63, 64, 80, 338, 339, 341, 347, **350**
Nigeria, 55, 65, 73, 98, 339, 352, 354
Nigeria at the 1996 Summer Olympics, 91
Nigerian naira, 98
Niger River, 352, 355
Nile, 4, 30, 32, 39, 60, 337, 340
Nile River, 31
Nile Valley, 179
Nilo-Saharan, 84, 85
Nilo-Saharan languages, 41, 59–61, 63–65, 80, **337**, 356, 360
Nilotic, 50, 59, 60
Nilotic languages, 337, 342

Nok culture, 52
Nomad, 244, 254
Nomadic, 245
Nomadic pastoralism, 257
Noog, 88, 252
Noongar, 132
Norbert Jokl, 306
Nordic Bronze Age, 294
Norfolk, 160
Normandy, 240
North Africa, 39, 98, 108, 159
North America, 199, 219
North American fur trade, 231
North Asia, 300
North Atlantic Current, 135
Northern Africa, 93
Northern Asia, 336
Northern Black Polished Ware, 317
Northern Bulgaria, 303
Northern Congolian forest-savanna mosaic, 41
Northern Eastern Sudanic languages, 337, 346
Northern Europe, 30, 260, 293, 294, 336
Northern India, 261
Northern Low Saxon, 295
Northern Sotho language, 63
Northern Territory, 127
North Germanic languages, 295
North Sea, 124, 298
Northwest Arctic Borough, Alaska, 369
Northwestern Iran, 265
Northwest Territories, 369
Norwegian language, 295
Norwegians, 294, 370
Nouakchott, 81, 98
Noun class, 351, 353, 365
Noun-class, 360
Noun classifier, 340
Noun-classifier, 360
Noun phrase, 366
Nuba, 63, 94
Nuba Mountains, 356
Nubia, 51, 337, 339
Nubian language, 63
Nubian languages, 337, 339, 342
Nubian people, 60, 94
Nuer language, 63, 339
Nuer people, 339
Numeral (linguistics), 366
Nunatsiavut, 369
Nunavik, 369
Nunavut, 369
Nupoid, 354
Nuristani people, 309
Nuu-chah-nulth people, 227
Nwankwo Kanu, 91
Nyabwa language, 354

Nyima languages, 346
Nzinga Mbande, 46

Oase 1, 170
Oase 2, 151
Oases, 247
Oasis, 45
Occipital bone, 149
Occipital bun, 150
Occitan language, 296
Ochre, 170
Ochre Coloured Pottery culture, 394
OCLC, 29
OECD, 75, 76
Ofer Bar-Yosef, 8, 259
Oghuz Turks, 283
Ohalo II, 250
Oil lamp, 122
Oil palm, 252
Ojibwa, 220
Ojibwe, 225
Oka River, 299
Okinawa, 106
Oko language, 355
Okra, 74
Old Chinese, 318
Old Crow Flats, 205
Older Dryas, 129
Oldest Dryas, 128
Old European culture, 235
Old Europe (archaeology), 269, 272, 280
Old Indic, 318
Old Nubian language, 61
Oldowan, 3, 21, 30, 33, 35, 43, 119, 157, 188,
    193
Old Prussians, 300
Olduvai Gorge, 45
Old World, 44, 311
Olorgesailie, 22
Oman, 48, 322
Onagers, 257
Onchocerciasis, 80
One dimension, 2, 24, 177
Ontology, 82
Open syllable, 360
Open terrain, 7
Opone, 47
Optic disk, 148
Orang Asli, 108
Orange (fruit), 251
Orangutan, 25
Orbit (anatomy), 167
Orbitofrontal cortex, 149
Orce, 3
Ordovician, 12
Oreopithecus, 183

Origin of the Romani people, 241
Orok people, 208
Oromo language, 63
Oscan language, 296
Ossetia, 323
Ossetians, 323
Ostrava, 128
Ostrogoths, 239
Ostsiedlung, 241
Otto Hauser, 37
Ottoman Empire, 242
Ouagadougou, 98
Ouranopithecus, 3, 183
Out of Africa I, 102, 111
Out of Africa II, 371
Out of Asia theory, 111
Overseas Development Institute, 71
Oxide, 168
Oxus, 313
Oxygen isotope, 200
Oyo Empire, 53

Pacific Islands, 233, 258
Pacific Northwest, 214
Packaging and labeling, 130
Painted Grey Ware culture, 310, 316, 394
Pakistan, 108, 322, 323
Palaeochannel, 30
Palatal consonant, 348, 361
Paleoanthropologist, 13, 19
Paleoanthropology, 101
Paleo-Eskimo, 227, 368
Paleogene, 12
Paleo-Indian, 229
Paleo-Indians, 129, 199, 223
Paleolithic, 21, 33, 35, 119, 121, 157, 188,
    193, 234, 250, 254, 265
Paleolithic art, 169
Paleolithic Continuity Theory, 234
Paleolithic Europe, 163
Paleolithic flute, 169
Paleolithic flutes, 126, 168, 175
Paleolithic warfare, 130
Paleontological, 104
Paleontologist, 189
Paleontology, 17, 43
Paleo-Siberian, 221
Palestine (region), 308, 322
Palgrave Macmillan, 374
Pamir Mountains, 313, 321
Pannonia, 302
Pannonian Avars, 301
Pannonian plain, 240
Pantheon Books, 244
Panthera leo fossilis, 190
Panthera spelaea, 168

Pap (food), 89
Papillomavirus, 156
Papua New Guinea, 108, 252, 253
Parallel evolution, 101
Paranthropus aethiopicus, 2
Paranthropus boisei, 9
Paranthropus robustus, 9
Parc archéologique et botanique de Solutré, 187–189
Parietal bone, 149
Parietal region, 149
Parramatta, 127
Parsimonious, 150
Parthia, 47
Parthian Empire, 323
Parthians, 261, 270, 323
Pashto language, 325
Pashtun people, 323
Pashtuns, 323
Pastoralism, 236, 260, 311, 318
Patagonian, 220
Pataliputra, 285, 321
Pathology, 172
Patriarchal, 270
Patrilinear, 270
Paul Tergat, 93
Pavlovian culture, 132
PBS, 218
Pea, 249
Peach, 251
Peanut soup, 87
Pearl millet, 252
Pech Merle, 128, 178
Pedra Furada, 205
Peking Man, 15, 16, 19, 25, 26
Peleset, 308
Pendant, 172
Peñon woman, 209
Pergamon, 309
Pericúes, 209
Périgordian, 33, 36, 120, 131, 158, 188, 194
Perim, 4
Periplus of Pseudo-Scylax, 305
Permafrost, 135
Permian, 12
Permians, 370
Perm Krai, 370
Persia, 104, 108, 323
Persian empire, 322
Persian Gulf, 313, 323
Persian language, 325
Persian people, 50, 283, 323
Persian plateau, 117
Persians, 261, 270
Perth, 125
Peru, 180, 215

Peştera cu Oase, 151, 163, 170, 174
Peştera Muierilor, 150, 171
Peter Richerson, 247
Petroglyph, 121, 178
Petrovka settlement, 313
Phalanx bone, 153
Pharaohs, 322
Phenakite, 73
Phenotype, 149, 209
Philistines, 308
Phoenicia, 238
Phonology, 360
Photovoltaic, 70
Phrygia, 309
Phrygian language, 309
Phrygians, 283, 308
Physical anthropology, 199
Piauí, 205
Pierolapithecus, 182
Pierre-Emerick Aubameyang, 91
Pigs, 248
Pikimachay, 214
Pin, 189
Pine, 135
Pinhole Cave Man, 175
Pinniped, 202
Pinus cembra, 334
Pirro Nord, 3
Pit-Comb Ware culture, 335
Pit–Comb Ceramic, 336
Plantain (cooking), 252
Plantations of Ireland, 242
Plateau languages, 355, 360
Plateau State, 73
Plate tectonics, 6
Platinum, 72
Plato, 309
Pleistocene, 13, 18, 21, 31, 112, 133, 199
Pliocene, 2, 4, 33, 35, 119, 157, 183, 188, 193
Plosive, 348
Plosive consonant, 348
Plurative, 338, 360
Pluvial, 39
Poland, 303
Poles, 302
Politics and government, 67
Pollen, 202
Poltavka culture, 279, 311, 334
Polyglotta Africana, 358
Polynesia, 236
Polynesians, 232
Polyomavirus, 109
Polyphyletic, 353
Polytheism, 321
Pontic-Caspian steppe, 274, 275
Pontic–Caspian steppe, 260, 264

Pontic steppe, 272, 274
Pontic steppes, 268
Population bottleneck, 108, 109, 150
Population density, 54, 244
Population genetics, 102, 107, 203
Population history of American indigenous peoples, 258
Population history of indigenous peoples of the Americas, 218
Populations, 19
Portable art, 178, 197
Portal, 383
Port Louis, 96
Porto-Novo, 98
Portugal, 230
Portuguese colonization of the Americas, 230
Portuguese language, 63, 262, 296
Potatoes, 253
Potentilla, 142
Pottery, 130, 244, 254, 388
Po valley, 293
Preadaptation, 10
Preboreal, 124
Precambrian, 12
Pre-Columbian trans-oceanic contact theories, 216
Předmostí u Přerova (archeology), 172
Pre-Dorset, 368
Prefrontal cortex, 9
Prehistoric art, 175, 189
Prehistoric Australia, 101
Prehistoric Europe, 175
Prehistoric Georgia, 168
Prehistoric migration and settlement of the Americas from Asia, 218, 223
Prehistoric music, 175
Prehistoric Rock-Art Site of the Côa Valley, 178
Prehistory, 182, 275
Prehistory and antiquity, 227
Pre-modern human migration, **233**
Prepared-core technique, 159
Pre-Pottery Neolithic, 65, 254
Pre-Roman Iron Age, 293, 294
Přerov, 172
Presevo Valley, 306
Pretoria, 97
Prevalence, 79
Primary biliary cirrhosis, 148
Primary language, 61
Primary visual cortex, 149
Primate, 12
Prince of Wales Island (Alaska), 202
Princeton University Press, 327
Principal Chief of the Cherokee Nation, 385
Prismatic blade, 122

Prognathism, 167
Projectile point, 159
Pronunciation of Celtic, 297, 298
Property, 244
Proto-Anatolian, 268
Proto-Armenian, 268
Proto-Aryan, 334
Proto-Balto-Slavic, 261, 268
Proto-Balto-Slavic language, 299
Proto-Celtic, 261, 268, 298
Proto-Celtic language, 239, 298
Proto-Germanic, 261, 264, 268, 271, 293
Proto-Germanic language, 294
Proto-Greek language, 268
Proto-Indo-European, 334
Proto-Indo-European culture, 268
Proto-Indo-European homeland, 260, 286
Proto-Indo-European language, 234, 260, 268, 272, 274, 275, 299, 325, 326
Proto-Indo-European origins, 326
Proto-Indo-Europeans, 264, 268, 280, 293, 299, 300, 303, 304, 308, 310, 318, 321, 322, 325
Proto-Indo-European society, 260, 279
Proto-Indo-European Urheimat hypotheses, 261, 268, 274, 275, 326
Proto-Indo-Iranian, 268
Proto-Indo-Iranians, 235
Proto-Italic, 261, 268
Protolanguage, 338
Proto-language, 264
Proto-Mongoloid, 163, 167
Proto-Niger-Congo, 360
Proto-Samic language, 336
Proto-Samoyed language, 334
Proto-Slavic, 299
Proto-Tocharian, 268
Proto-Uralic homeland hypotheses, 184, **334**
Proto-Uralic language, 334
Proto-Villanovan culture, 296
Protrusive, 20
Provenance, 31
Province, 65
Przewalskis Horse, 172
Public domain, 198
PubMed Central, 113, 114, 217, 327, 329, 331
PubMed Identifier, 113, 114, 181, 217, 327, 329, 331
Puget Sound region, 201
Punjabi language, 264
Punjab region, 235
Purifying selection, 146
Pygmy, 59, 352
Pygmy peoples, 110, 156

Qadan culture, 34, 36, 120, 158, 189, 194

Qafzeh, 103
Qaraoun culture, 251
Quaternary, 189
Quaternary extinction event, 138, 247
Quaternary glaciation, 133
Quebec, 368
Queen Charlotte Islands, 214
Quern-stone, 248

R1a, 286
R1b, 271, 286
Racial admixture, 229
Racial purity, 231
Racloir, 122, 159
Radiator theory, 9
Radio carbon dating, 212
Radiocarbon dating, 46, 127, 163, 171, 172, 197, 200, 201, 284
Raffia palm, 74
Ralph Holloway, 10
Ran Min, 285
Rap, 84
Raphael Pumpelly, 247
Rashad languages, 350–352, 356
Rebecca L. Cann, 112
Recent African origin, 165
Recent African origin of modern humans, 39, 50, **101**, 117, 227
Reciprocal (grammar), 365
Recorded history, 262
Red fox, 172
Red Lady of Paviland, 127, 170
Red Sea, 4, 40, 47, 103, 105, 117
Refugium (population biology), 183
Reggae, 84
Reindeer, 122, 129, 136, 138, 167, 172, 190
Relative clause, 366
Reproductively isolated, 16
Republic of Dagestan, 283
Republic of Macedonia, 306
Republic of the Congo, 55, 95
Retouch (lithics), 30
Retroflex consonant, 348
Rhapta, 50
Rhine, 293, 294, 298
Rhinoceros, 190
Rhythm and Blues, 84
Rice, 251
Richard G. Klein, 121
Richard Leakey, 20, 23
Richard Nelson Frye, 394
Rick Derksen, 392
Rigveda, 235, 237
Rig Veda, 317
Rigvedic deities, 318
Ripari Villabruna, 174

Riparo Mochi, 166
Riss glaciation, 30, 37
Ritual, 172
River Jordan, 251
Robert Bettinger, 247
Robert Boyd (anthropologist), 247
Robert Braidwood, 247
Robert Broom, 16
Robert Drews, 332
Robin Hood Cave Horse, 178
Robustness (morphology), 184
Rock art, 128
Rock of Solutré, 189, 191
Rock & Roll, 84
Rock shelter, 128
Roger Blench, 341, 349, 351, 353, 360
Roger Milla, 91
Romance languages, 63, 263, 296, 297
Roman Empire, 239, 309
Romania, 127, 170, 171, 303
Romanian language, 296
Roman Republic, 305
Ronald Wright, 247
Roots of Hinduism, 318
Rope, 122
Rouran Khaganate, 321
Roxolani, 324
Royal Niger Company, 53
Rubus chamaemorus, 141
Rudapithecus, 182
Rugby union, 92
Rugby World Cup, 92
Rus people, 392
Russia, 223, 234, 274, 324
Russian Far East, 226
Russian language, 262
Russians, 302, 370
Rwanda, 47, 55, 74, 94, 96
Rwandan franc, 94, 96
Rye, 249

Saami people, 336
Sabaeans, 47
Sadio Mané, 91
Sahara, 39, 123, 338
Saharan languages, 64, 337, 342–345
Sahara pump theory, 39
Sahel, 39, 41, 42, 252, 351, 353
Saho people, 61
Sahul Shelf, 154
Saiga antelope, 138
Saint-Germain-en-Laye, 127–129
Saka, 320
Sakas, 285, 320
Sakhalin, 208
Sakha Republic, 368, 369

Salishan languages, 220
Salix, 141
Salsa music, 84
Samara culture, 235, 261, 274, 278
Samba, 84
Sami languages, 235
Sami people, 235, 336, 368, 370
Samoyedic languages, 334
Samoyedic peoples, 336, 370
Samuel Etoo, 91
Samuel Peter, 92
Samu (Homo erectus), 26
Sandawe people, 58, 107, 110, 156
Sangiran, 3, 26, 27
Sango, 95
Sangoan, 33, 36, 119, 157, 188, 193
Sanitation, 72
San people, 58–60, 85, 107, 110, 155
San religion, 82
Sanskrit, 264
Sanskritisation, 389
Santería, 80
Sao civilization, 46
Saône-et-Loire, 191
São Tomé, 94
São Tomé and Príncipe, 55, 94
São Tomé and Príncipe dobra, 94
Sara languages, 63
Sardinian language, 296
Sardinians, 308
Sarmatia, 302, 323
Sarmatians, 239, 323, 324
Sassanid Persia, 241
Satatna, 322
Satem, 262
Savanna, 41, 43
Savannah, 135
Savannas languages, 353, 354
Saw, 190
Saxons, 239
Scandinavia, 240, 306
Schist, 195
Schwäbische Alb, 178
Science (journal), 19, 144
Scotland, 240, 298
Scottish colonization of the Americas, 231
Sculpture, 86
Scythia, 323
Scythia Minor, 302
Scythian language, 285
Scythians, 285, 304, 320, 323, 324
Scyths, 261, 270
Sea level, 128, 199
Sea levels, 5
Sea of Galilee, 250
Sea Peoples, 235, 283, 307, 308

Sebilian, 34, 36, 120, 158, 189, 194, 252
Secondary products revolution, 257
Second Greek colonisation, 238
Sections and groups of the three Alpine divisions, 151
Sedentism, 244
Sedges, 140
Seine, 293
Selection (biology), 148
Selective breeding, 249
Seljuk Turks, 240
Selkup people, 222, 370
Seminole, 225
Semitic languages, 58, 63, 322
Semitic people, 41, 265
Semi-tropical, 44
Semivowel, 348
Senari language, 354
Senckenberg Museum, 27
Sen-Doki, 132
Senegal, 57, 77, 80, 85, 99, 353
Senegal River, 355
Senegambian languages, 64, 353
Sensu lato, 13, 19
Sensu stricto, 13
Senufo languages, 354
Senufo people, 354
Serbia, 305, 306
Serbs, 242, 302
Serengeti, 42
Serer creation myth, 82
Serer religion, 82
Seroglazovo culture, 274
Sers, Charente, 188
Sesotho, 96
Seth (mythology), 322
Settlement of Iceland, 237
Settlement of the Americas, **199**, 233
Settler, 245
Seven Years War, 243
Seward Peninsula, 223
Sewing needle, 122
Sexual dimorphism, 20
Seychelles, 53, 56, 70, 96
Seychellois Creole, 96
Seychellois rupee, 96
Shabo language, 337, 341, 343–345
Shakha, 317
Shamanism, 170
Shangchen, 2
Shanidar 1, 160
Shanidar Cave, 160
Sheep, 248
Shekelesh, 308
Shepherd, 254
Shepherd Neolithic, 254

Sherden, 308
Shilluk Kingdom, 46
Shilluk language, 63
Shona language, 63, 351
Siberia, 121, 145, 160, 199, 218, 219, 222,
    275, 284, 300, 312, 336, 368
Siberian Yupik, 227, 369
Sicily, 240, 306
Sickle, 245
Siculi, 308
Sidrón Cave, 145
Siega Verde, 178
Sierra Leone, 57, 80, 98
Sierra Leonean leone, 98
Sigismund Wilhelm Koelle, 358
SIL International, 295
Silk Road, 286, 321
Silk Road transmission of Buddhism, 286, 321
Silurian, 12
Sima del Elefante (1996-), 5
Simian, 12
Simon & Schuster, 374
Sinai, 106
Sinai Peninsula, 4
Sinanthropus pekinensis, 12, 15
Singapore, 306
Single origin hypothesis, 204
Single-origin hypothesis, 44
Singulative, 360
Singulative number, 338
Sinology, 285
Sintashta, 313
Sintashta culture, 261, 270, 279, 309, 312
Sioux, 225, 227
SiSwati, 97
Skeleton, 172
Skhul and Qafzeh hominids, 159
Skin color, 109
Skull D2700, 18
Slaves, 242
Slavic languages, 263, 269, 298, 300
Slavic migrations, 237
Slavic people, 370
Slavic peoples, 239
Slavs, 240, 325
SLC24A5, 109, 167
SLC45A2, 167
Slovakia, 303, 392
Slovaks, 302
Slovenes, 302
Slovenia, 305
Smallpox, 258
Smithsonian Institution, 29, 115, 181, 190
Smithsonian Museum of Natural History, 372
Soanian, 33, 35, 119, 157, 188, 193
Social complexity, 10

Social evolution, 245
Society, 121, 244
Sogdia, 285, 320, 323
Sogdiana, 387
Solo Man, 25, 26
Solomon Islands (archipelago), 253
Solo River, 13
Solutré, 189
Solutrean, 33, 36, 120, 123, 131, 158, 163,
    166, 174, **187**, 189, 193, 194
Solutrean hypothesis, 207, 221, 228
Solutré-Pouilly, 191
Solutrian epoch, 195
Soma (drink), 314
Somalia, 39, 47, 56, 70, 80, 96
Somaliland Campaign, 48
Somali language, 63, 96
Somali people, 40, 48
Somali shilling, 96
Songhai Empire, 52, 339
Songhai language, 64
Songhai people, 61, 338
Songhay languages, 337, 339, 342–345, 360
Sorbs, 302
Sorde-lAbbaye, 173
Sorghum, 74, 252
Sotho language, 63
Soukous, 85
Sound law, 299
South Africa, 16, 41, 53, 56, 65, 68, 70, 85,
    97, 255
South African rand, 97
South America, 219, 221, 223, 228, 253
South American Indigenous people, 224
South Asia, 76, 234, 242, 260, 262, 268, 285,
    321
South Caucasus, 3
Southeast Africa, 40
Southeast Asia, 117, 214, 225, 252
Southeast Asians, 143
Southeastern Europe, 269, 302
Southeast Europe, 300, 302
Southern Africa, 41–43, 49, 58
Southern African, 236
Southern African Development Community,
    97
Southern Bantoid languages, 353, 355
Southern Bug, 303
Southern Dispersal, 101, 103, **117**, 143
Southern Eastern Sudanic languages, 346
Southern Europe, 307
Southern Highlands Province, 253
South-German Urnfield culture, 296
South Korea, 178
South Picene language, 296
South Semitic languages, 58

South Slavs, 302
South Sudan, 41, 56, 76, 89, 94, 338, 339
Soybean, 251
Soyuqbulaq, Agstafa, 284
Spain, 3, 133, 190, 230, 293
Spanish colonization, 230
Spanish language, 262, 296
Spanish Netherlands, 242
Spear, 167, 190
Spear thrower, 178
Spear-thrower, 128, 167
Species, 13
Species barrier, 112
Speech communication, 23
Spencer Wells, 114, 217, 218
Sphinx, 51
Spitsyn culture, 127
Spoke, 312
Spruce, 135
Squash (plant), 253
Sramana, 318
Sredny Stog culture, 235, 261, 278
Sri Lanka, 262
Srubna culture, 312, 313
Stade Félix Houphouët-Boigny, 91
Stadial, 128, 129
Standard German, 391
Starčevo culture, 234
States of Nigeria, 65
Stele, 47
Stem cell factor, 109
Stephen Cherono, 378
Steven Mithen, 175
St.-Germain-en-Laye, 129
Stillbayan, 132
Stone Age, 34, 37, 104, 121, 158, 159, 189, 194
Stone tool, 21, 122
Storm god, 322
St. Paul Island, Alaska, 136
Strait of Gibraltar, 5, 7
Strait of Sicily, 6, 7
Straits of Juan de Fuca, 201
Strategic Studies Institute, 99
Stratigraphy, 17, 202
Subarctic climate, 124
Subclade, 223
Subject–object–verb, 365
Subject–verb–object, 365
Subregion, 94, 95, 97, 98
Sub-Saharan Africa, **39**, 143, 236, 242
Sub-Saharan Africans, 109
Subtropical climate, 182
Sudan, 40, 41, 51, 53, 55, 93, 97, 98, 104, 338, 339, 351
Sudanese pound, 94, 97

Sudanic languages, 337, 358
Sudan (region), 39, 40
Suebi, 239, 293
Suffolk, 30
Sugarcane, 253
Suggested macrofamilies, 264
Sultanate of Adal, 48
Sumer, 244, 245
Sumerian language, 58
Sumpweed, 253
Sundadont, 229
Sundaland, 117
Sunflower, 253
Sungbos Eredo, 53
Superciliary arches, 150
Suppiluliuma I, 281, 283
Supyire language, 354
Sussex, 31

Šuwardata, 322

Swabia, 168, 169
Swabian Alb, 169
Swabian Alps, 126
Swahili Coast, 50, 65
Swahili culture, 50, 89, 96
Swahili language, 50, 59, 63, 351, 365
Swahili people, 50, 86
Swanscombe, 30
Swanscombe Heritage Park, 30
Swartkrans, 16
Swaziland, 56, 97
Swazi lilangeni, 97
Sweden, 291
Swedes, 294
Swedish language, 295
Swiderian culture, 34, 37, 120, 158, 189, 194
Swimming Reindeer, 130, 175, 178
Swiss Jura, 174
Switzerland, 306
Sword, 258
Sydney, 127
Sympatric, 16
Synonym (taxonomy), 12
Syria, 58, 160, 307, 314, 322
Systemic lupus erythematosus, 148
Szeletian, 131

Taforalt, 85
Tagus Estuary Natural Reserve, 293
Taharqa, 51
Taiga, 313
Taima-Taima, 212
Taimyr Peninsula, 136
Tajikistan, 313, 322
Tajik people, 323

Talodi–Heiban languages, 356
Talodi languages, 353
Taman Peninsula, 283
Tamaz V. Gamkrelidze, 389
Tanga, Tanzania, 50
Tanzania, 42, 50, 51, 55, 58, 65, 80, 89, 96, 338
Tanzanian shilling, 96
Tarim Basin, 269, 285, 320, 321
Tarim mummies, 269, 285
Taro, 252, 253
Tasian, 252
Taurus Mountains, 247
Tautavel, 27
Tautavel Man, 12, 16, 25
Taxon, 249
Taxonomy (biology), 12
Tchadanthropus uxoris, 17
Tebu languages, 339, 340
Techno-complex, 158
Technology, 122
Teda language, 339
Teff, 74, 88, 252
Telanthropus capensis, 13
Telecommunications, 71
Tell Aswad, 251
Tell Ramad, 248
Tel Megiddo, 322
Temne language, 364
Temperate climate, 44
Temperature, 122
Template:Indo-European topics, 260
Template:Is this date calibrated?, 193–196
Template:Life timeline, 2, 24, 177
Template:Nature timeline, 2, 24, 177
Template:Paleolithic, 34, 37, 121, 158, 189, 194
Template talk:Indo-European topics, 260
Template talk:Paleolithic, 34, 37, 121, 158, 189, 194
Temporal bone, 149
Terms of use, 99
Terracotta, 52
Teshik-Tash, 160
Teso language, 339
Thailand, 77, 108
The American Journal of Human Genetics, 114
Thebes, Egypt, 322
The Book of General Ignorance, 381
The Gambia, 57, 80, 98
The Globalist, 392
The Horse, the Wheel, and Language, 327, 332, 391
The Independent, 392
The Journey of Man, 114
The Languages of Africa, 338, 341, 359

The Low Countries, 298
The Mind in the Cave, 175
Theodiscus, 293
The Quest for the Origins of Vedic Culture, 328
Thermoregulation, 8, 185
The Seven Daughters of Eve, 115
The World Until Yesterday, 256
Thomas Gamkrelidze, 393
Thomas Huxley, 111, 152
Thrace, 302
Thracian language, 304, 323
Thracians, 303, 393
Thraco-Cimmerian, 239
Thule culture, 237
Thule people, 227, 368
Tian Shan, 309, 313
Tianyuan man, 106, 148, 154
Tibesti Mountains, 339
Tibetan Plateau, 134, 285
Tichit, 52
Ticuna people, 223
Tigrinya language, 63, 96
Tikar language, 355
Timber, 122
Timber grave culture, 303
Timbuktu, 339, 355
Timor, 253
Tita language, 355
Tivoid languages, 355
Toba catastrophe theory, 103
Tocharian languages, 264, 285
Tocharians, 269, 282, 285, 320
Togo, 57, 99, 354
Tohono Oodham, 225
Tonal language, 59
Tone (linguistics), 364
Tongoni Ruins, 50
Tool, 121, 189
Toquepala Caves, 180
Total fertility rate, 53
Tourism, 93
Trachilos footprints, 3
Trade, 244, 257
Trans-Atlantic slave trade, 230
Transcaucasus, 17
Trans-cultural diffusion, 298
Trans–New Guinea languages, 253
Transitional fossil, 15
Trans-Saharan trade, 45, 52
Trevor R. Bryce, 332
Trialetian, 34, 36, 120, 158, 189, 194
Triassic, 12
Tribal chief, 127
Tribal disenrollment, 231
Tribal DNA, 220
Tribe, 294, 297

Trifunctional hypothesis, 270
Trinil, 13
Trinil 2, 26
Tripartite language, 338
Tripolye culture, 289
Tropical Africa, 39, 41, 42
Tropical and subtropical grasslands, savannas, and shrublands, 42
Tropical climate, 44
Tropical rainforest, 42
Tropical savanna, 39, 42
Tshiluba language, 63
Tswana language, 63, 96
Tumbuka mythology, 83
Tumulus, 274
Tundra, 380
Tungusic peoples, 368
Tunisia, 93
Turfan, 285, 321
Turin King List, 322
Turkana boy, 19, 20, 23
Turkey, 21, 274, 306, 322
Turkic expansion, 233, 240, 325
Turkic languages, 274, 285, 325
Turkic people, 239
Turkic peoples, 369
Turkmenistan, 160, 313
Tursac, 194, 196
Twi, 90, 354
Type site, 30, 35, 157, 159, 187, 193, 194, 211
Type-site, 189
TYRP1, 167
Tyrrhenians, 308
Tyrsenian languages, 270
Tyumen Oblast, 313

Ubangian languages, 63, 352–354
UBC Department of Asian Studies, 331
Ubeidiya, 4, 8
Ubsunur Hollow, 138
Ubsunur Hollow Biosphere Reserve, 139
Ugali, 86–88
Uganda, 55, 89, 96, 339
Ugandan shilling, 96
Ugric languages, 334
Ugric peoples, 370
Ukaan language, 355
Ukok Plateau, 134, 138
Ukraine, 128, 167, 234, 265, 274, 303, 306, 392
Ukrainians, 302
Ulch people, 208
Ulm, 126
Umbrian language, 296
Umbundu language, 63
Unclassified language, 321

UNESCO, 41, 298, 329
UNESCO Institute for Statistics, 78
UNESCO World Heritage Site, 129
United Arab Emirates, 104
United Kingdom, 306
United Nations, 39, 40
United States, 231, 306
United States 2010 census, 231
Universal Primary Education, 77
Université de Liège, 326
University College London, 391
University of Alabama, 218
University of Antananarivo, 77
University of Bologna, 326
University of Botswana, 76
University of California Press, 373
University of Exeter, 190
University of Oregon, 215
University of Oslo, 381
University of Tennessee, 218
University of Utah, 326
University of Valencia, 326
University Press of America, 366
UN subregion, 93
Unsupported attributions, 16, 257
Upper Austria, 296
Upper Mesopotamia, 283
Upper Miocene, 111
Upper Palaeolithic, 189
Upper Paleolithic, 33, 36, 119, **119**, 143, 158, 175, 178, 187, 188, 193, 194, 199, 326, 338
Uralic languages, 235, 265, 313, 334
Uralic peoples, 369
Ural Mountains, 313, 334, 336
Ural region, 265
Ural River, 309, 313
Urals, 313
Uranium, 72
Urartians, 239
Urartu, 309
Urban agglomeration, 65
Urbanism, 388
Urban Revolution, 257
Urdu, 264
Urheimat, 235, 272, 334
Urnfield, 298
Urnfield culture, 289, 296
Usatovo culture, 289
Ust-Ishim man, 163, 174
Uyghur people, 285
Uzbekistan, 160, 322

Vakhsh, Tajikistan, 313
Vallesian crisis, 182
Vallon-Pont-dArc, 126

Vanadium, 72
Vancouver Island, 201
Vandalic language, 295
Varangian, 240
Varna (Hinduism), 318
Vedic culture, 260
Vedic people, 261, 270
Vedic period, 317
Velar consonant, 348, 361
Venezuela, 212
Venus figurine, 178
Venus figurines, 122, 167, 175
Venus figurines of Balzi Rossi, 172
Venus of Brassempouy, 127, 128
Venus of Dolní Věstonice, 127, 175
Venus of Hohle Fels, 126, 169, 176, 178
Venus of Laussel, 126, 176
Venus of Petřkovice, 128
Venus of Willendorf, 128, 177, 178
Verb applicative, 365
Vertebra, 23
Vertebrae, 172
V. Gordon Childe, 245, 247
Vicia ervilia, 249
Victoria, Seychelles, 96
Victualler, 49
Vienna, 306
Vietnam, 241
Viking Age, 233, 237
Vikings, 240
Villabruna 1, 174
Villanovan culture, 289
Vinča culture, 388
Vindija Cave, 145, 157
Visigoths, 239
Vistula, 279, 289
Visual arts, 388
Visual cortex, 149
Vladimir I. Georgiev, 307
Vladimir Napolskikh, 336
Vojvodina, 242
Volga, 242, 274, 299, 313, 336
Volga Delta, 265
Volga Germans, 242
Volga River, 197
Volgograd, 313
Volta–Congo, 354, 361
Volta–Congo languages, 353
Volta–Niger, 64
Volta–Niger languages, 353, 354
Vowel harmony, 361
Vyacheslav Ivanov (philologist), 389, 393

Wadai Empire, 46
Wadi, 248
Wadi Faynan 16, 251

Wales, 298
Wallace Line, 153
Walls of Benin, 53
Walter de Gruyter, 329, 375
Washukanni, 314
Wastebasket taxon, 338
Watermelon, 74
Water supply, 72
Wathaurong, 132
Wayuu people, 224
Wei–Jie war, 285
Welded tuff, 22
Welsh language, 298
Wends, 302
W:Epigravettian, 123
West Africa, 40, 236, 252, 351, 354
West African CFA franc, 98, 99
West African Economic and Monetary Union, 98
West African Vodun, 80
West Asia, 76
West Beboid languages, 355
Western Australia, 179
Western Eurasians, 145, 163
Western Europe, 187, 193, 194, 260, 268, 275
Western Highlands Province, 253
Western Hunter-Gatherers, 184
Western Sahara, 93
Western Sudan, 40
Western Sudanic languages, 360
Western Sydney, 127
West Eurasians, 165
West European Hunter-Gatherer, 166, 174
West Germanic languages, 295, 297
West Slavs, 302
Wet Sahara, 39, 340
Whadjuk, 132
Wheat, 251
Wheel, 321
White matter, 149
Whole genome sequencing, 65
Whole-genome sequencing, 144
Who We Are and How We Got Here, 244
Wikipedia:Adding open license text to Wikipedia, 99
Wikipedia:Citation needed, 4, 5, 8, 19, 21, 26, 76, 108, 124, 127, 179, 190, 212, 215, 235, 253, 257, 268, 279, 349, 364
Wikipedia:Citing sources, 83
Wikipedia:Identifying reliable sources, 230
Wikipedia:Link rot, 348
Wikipedia:No original research, 253
Wikipedia:Please clarify, 129, 169, 222, 249, 327
Wikipedia:Reusing Wikipedia content, 99
Wikt:erectus, 13

Wikt:Landnahme, 237
Wilhelm Bleek, 358
William Buller Fagg, 86
William Jones (philologist), 264
Willow, 135
Wiltonian, 132
Windhoek, 96
Wisconsin glaciation, 134, 200, 224
Witwatersrand, 67
W. K. Gregory, 163
Wobe language, 364
Wolf, 172
Wolof language, 59, 64, 353, 361, 365
Wolverine, 172
Wonderwerk Cave, 23
Wool, 257
Woolly mammoth, 133, 136
Woolly rhinoceros, 136
Working animal, 257
World Archaeology, 216
World Bank, 99
World Education Forum, 77
World Health Organization, 78
World War I, 231
World War II, 15, 172
WP:NOTRS, 328
Wrangel Island, 136, 138
W:Solutrean, 123
Würm glaciation, 37
Wurundjeri, 132
Wushan Man, 25
Wusun, 261, 270, 285, 310, 318, 320

Xanthus (historian), 309
Xaverio Ballester, 326
X chromosome, 147
Xhosa language, 63
Xhosa people, 48
Xinjiang, 285
Xiongnu, 285, 320

Yakama, 227
Yakuba language, 364
Yakutia, 135, 137
Yakuts, 369
Yamna culture, 234, 261, 270, 271, 274, 275,
    279, 296, 311
Yamnaya, 260
Yamnaya culture, 278
Yamoussoukro, 98
Yam (vegetable), 74, 86, 252, 253
Yana River, 206
Yaoundé, 95
Yaya Touré, 91
Yaz culture, 310
YBP, 133

Y-DNA haplogroup, 174
YEAI, 354
Yedoma, 135
Yenisei River, 138, 207
Yerevan, 306
Yiddish, 391
Yidya, 322
Yoruba language, 59, 64, 351, 353, 354, 364
Yoruba mythology, 82
Yoruba people, 53, 62, 110, 156
Yoruboid, 354
Yotvingians, 300
Younger Dryas, 124, 130, 135
Younger Dryas event, 247
YouTube, 218, 259
Yuanmou County, 3
Yuanmou Man, 25
Yuezhi, 285, 320
Yukaghir languages, 334, 336
Yukaghir people, 368
Yukaghirs, 370
Yukon, 134, 369
Yukuben language, 364
Yupik peoples, 226, 368, 369
Yves Coppens, 17

Zafarraya, 157
Zaghawa language, 63, 340
Zaghawa people, 60, 94
Zagros, 160
Zagros mountains, 247
Zagwe dynasty, 47
Zambezi, 49
Zambia, 56, 90, 97
Zambian kwacha, 97
Zande language, 63
Zanj, 40
Zanzibar, 50
Zar Cave, 126
Zarma language, 64, 339
Zarma people, 61
Zarzian culture, 34, 36, 120, 158, 189, 194,
    265
Zebu, 255
Zeravshan River, 313
Zhirendong, 103
Zhoukoudian, 15, 26, 154
Zialo language, 364
Zigula language, 63
Zimbabwe, 49, 56, 76, 97, 178
Zimbabwean dollar, 97
Zoblazo, 85
Zoomorphic, 179
Zoonosis, 8
Zulu Kingdom, 49
Zulu language, 63

Zulu mythology, 83
Zygoma, 20
Zygosity, 218